Table of Contents

Acknowledgments

I began this book far too late to interview so many whom I would have liked to have spoken with, including, of course, Cummings. Consequently, this effort was largely the result of archival research. Indeed, without the cooperation and assistance of Ms. Leslie Morris, Thomas Ford, and the staff of the Cummings Collection at Harvard University's Houghton Library, this book would not have been possible. Similarly, I am grateful for the help I received from the librarians in the Berg Collection of American Literature at the New York Public Library, and at the Beinecke Library at Yale.

I have also relied on the two previous biographies of Cummings for information. The late Charles Norman's memoir *E. E. Cummings: The Magic Maker* was helpful in a general way. Of greater substance and value was the late Richard S. Kennedy's *Dreams in the Mirror*.

I also need to thank the following who did share their memories of Cummings and his circle: Robert Cabot, Joanne Koch Potee, Edward Foster, the late Paul Bowles, the late Virgil Thomson, the late Allen Ginsberg, and the late Edouard Roditi. Others, too, on the Cummings periphery leant their support. Poet and magus Gerrit Lansing brought composer Stephen Scotti to my house one memorable winter afternoon, where Stephen belted out tunes, to his own accompaniment on the piano, from his marvelous musical *Viva Cummings*.

Friends also leant their support, in particular Michael and Isabel Franco, William Corbett, Ellen Cooney, Stephen Alter, Anita Desai, and Ben and Judy Watkins. To Judy Watkins must go additional thanks for her able assistance with the notes. I am also grateful to my family: my mother, Anne Garcia, a fan of Cummings from the 1940s on; my wife, Patricia Pruitt, who put up with my absence from a great deal of daily life while I toiled on this book; and my daughters and sons-in-law, Sarah Pruitt-Dahl and Carsten Dahl, Jessica Pruitt-Gonzalez and Felipe Gonzalez Perez. My grandchildren, Imogene Grace Pruitt-Spence and Eva and Felix Pruitt-Dahl continually helped return me to earth. And thanks to Salty and the late Argos, my dogs, who were constant habitués of my study, who patiently waited for walks while I wrote just one more sentence.

Thanks, too, to my agent extraordinaire, Roslyn Targ, and her British agent, Mary Clemmey. Hillel Black at Sourcebooks in New York worked with me from day one on shaping, refining, and rethinking this book. His keen eye, his acute ear, and his brilliant editorial sense made this biography a much better one than it would have been without his extraordinary skills. Sarah Tucker, his assistant, also provided excellent assistance as did Kelly Barrales-Saylor, who carefully copyedited the manuscript. Thanks to Jenna Jakubowski, who meticulously formatted all of the poetry. At MIT, Nick Altenbernd, Maya Jhangiani, and Susanne Martin provided both logistical support and good cheer for this undertaking.

I am also extremely grateful to George J. Firmage and Victor Schmalzer, agents for the E. E. Cummings Trust, who facilitated permission to quote from the unpublished Cummings material. To George Firmage, I also owe a second debt. His Cummings bibliography was invaluable, as were his conscientious and meticulous editions of Cummings's work.

Thank you all.

A Note on the Capitalization of E. E. Cummings's Name

"I am a small eye poet," Cummings wrote his mother as a way of explaining his well-known practice of not capitalizing in his poetry the first person pronoun. The key word here is "poet" not person: note that he capitalizes the "I" at the beginning of the sentence. Indeed, in most of his personal correspondence, he signed his name in capitals. To publishers, too, he asked that his name be capitalized on the title page. And in his journal entries, more often than not, he capitalizes "I." In capitalizing Cummings's name, therefore, I am simply following his convention.

Preface

It was an unusually hot afternoon for early September in New Hampshire. However, Edward Estlin Cummings, aware of what a New England winter could be, was splitting wood to ensure that the old farmhouse would be warm. Since his childhood, the farm had provided a retreat from city life. The day before, he had spent time in the flower garden, noting in his journal that the "new delphiniums…have long since lost their blue-glorious blossoms and gone to seed. But yesterday I noticed a lovely light-blue (& far smaller) blossomer who'd come to her beauty all alone." After splitting a fair number of logs and neatly stacking them, he sharpened the axe, returned it, as always, to its place in the barn, and went into the house. He had just reached the top of the stairs that led to the second floor bedroom when he crashed to the floor. His partner for thirty years, photographer Marion Morehouse, hearing the fall, rushed upstairs to find Cummings unconscious but still breathing. Unable to rouse him, she called an ambulance. At 1:15 the following morning, September 3, 1962, in the hospital at North Conway, New Hampshire, Cummings died, victim of a cerebral hemorrhage. He was sixty-seven years old.

Cummings's death was front-page news around the world. A September 4, 1962, front-page headline in the *New York Times* read: "E. E. Cummings Dies of Stroke; Poet Stood for Stylistic Liberty." The copy elaborated on his life, noting that he had received an AB degree in Classics from Harvard in 1915, and an AM the following year. The obituary also reported that he had been the recipient of numerous prizes and awards and was the author of more than a dozen books of prose and poetry. But most of all, the article stressed his unconventionality, in his verse and life. Not a bad summation, but hardly sufficient either.

E. E. Cummings was an American original. Throughout his forty-five years of professional writing life, he consistently celebrated the ordinary, reviled pretentiousness, scourged conformity, ardently championed the individual (and nature) against the machine, experimented boldly with words and syntax and punctuation, and wrote some of the most erotic and tender love poetry in the English language. Dubbed by Ezra Pound "Whitman's one living descendant," Cummings sang of himself and of America in a unique voice, as resonant now as it was a half-century ago.

As a poet, Cummings defies neat classification and cannot easily be grouped with any "ism." While a master of formal verse—his sonnets are among the most exquisite in twentieth-century poetry—he was also a major linguistic innovator, authoring a substantial amount of verse that pushed language to its limits. His work also resists strict evolutionary analysis. He was as experimental (or formal) in his later years as in his youth. Yet there are common threads from his earliest efforts to the poetry of his old age: an insistence on lyricism, a profound appreciation of the mystery that is life, and an unflagging anarchist spirit.

No one else wrote prose quite like Cummings, either. *The Enormous Room* (1922), the autobiographical account of his brief imprisonment in France in La Ferté-Macé detention camp, is dazzling. Allegorical in structure, experimental in its expression, darkly comic in intent, the book is also a major social commentary on injustice, repression, and confinement. *Eimi*, a satiric account of his 1931 visit to the Soviet Union, is idiosyncratic, engaging, even at times highly amusing. A triumph of narrative form, even more challenging (and richer) linguistically than *The Enormous Room*, it is an important statement on the role and rights of the individual in society.

Cummings also wrote unique plays and a children's book that have all the hallmarks of his distinctive style: attention to language, concern with saying something that had not before been said, as well as generous helpings of whimsy and outrageousness. In addition to his literary accomplishments, Cummings was a painter of some note. Indeed, sketching, drawing, and painting occupied him nearly as much as writing. But because his gift for words overshadowed his accomplishments as a painter, his visual art is less well known.

Famous among the famous, Cummings always seemed to be in the right places at the right time, and was a major presence wherever he resided—whether in Cambridge, Europe, New York, or on the family farm in New Hampshire. Among his friends he counted some of the most important artists of his time: Ezra Pound, John Dos Passos, William Carlos Williams, Archibald MacLeish, Hart Crane, Edmund Wilson, Marianne Moore, Kenneth Burke, Malcolm Cowley, Louis Aragon, Gaston Lachaise, Kenneth Patchen, David Diamond, Lincoln Kirstein,

Dylan Thomas, Allen Tate, and the list goes on. Nevertheless, he was also as comfortable in conversation with waitresses and handymen and farmers as he was with his more renowned friends.

His life was rich, fascinating, complex, and unconventional. Accounts by those who knew him well often mention his brilliant conversation, charm, energy, courtesy, wit, mischievousness, generosity, and sharp eye for the beauty of small things. When Cummings entered a room, the dynamic abruptly changed, the electricity markedly increased. As John Dos Passos noted in his memoir, *The Best Times*, "Cummings was the hub." He drew people toward him and drew people out of themselves. He could, in Dos Passos's words, "deliver himself of geysers of talk comical ironical learned brilliantlycolored intricatelycadenced damnably poetic and sometimes just naughty. It was as if he were spouting pages of prose and verse from an unwritten volume." But he not only held forth; he was also a responsive and sensitive listener. He could, as well, be truculent, wrong-headed, emotional, and egotistical. Though outwardly confident, inwardly he was often tormented by self-doubt. He was erotic and erratic, and remained playful and young in heart and mind well into his last years. He described himself as "somebody who can love and who shall be continually reborn, a human being."

I was fourteen and it was spring when I read my first poems of E. E. Cummings. The discovery of Cummings occurred at the tiny school library in Durango, Mexico. I do not remember why I took the dusty, aging volume of *Collected Poems* off the shelf, but probably it was because it was in English, and there were few books in my native language in the library. I was not a total stranger to poetry. I was already in love with Lorca and Alberti and Alfonso Reyes; I had translated some Verlaine and Baudelaire from French into Spanish. But I had never heard of Cummings. For me, poetry in English was Kipling or Longfellow and Cummings was not, by any stretch of the imagination, either of these.

I opened the collection at random. "may i feel said he" grabbed my attention immediately. This was a thrillingly "dirty" poem. And in a library book! My eyes searched for more stimulation. I found it in "she being Brand / -new" and "i like my body when it is with your / body." This poet, I decided, was speaking directly to me. I made a mental note to memorize these verses in case I might be able to use them on my own behalf. But then I came upon "r-p-o-p-h-e-s-s-a-g-r." I could not make out at first what appeared to be sheer nonsense—syllables or partial phrases or something—but definitely not words as I understood words. Then at the end the clue: "grasshopper." I must have smiled because I can still remember my joy at deciphering that this poem was about a grasshopper, the words hopping out of themselves over the page. I had never read anything even remotely this strange but I instantly approved. Language, even stodgy English, could be interesting, even fun.

I do not recall exactly what poems I read next but I know that within a few days I had memorized a fair number of the more ribald verses, and adopted Cummings's famed conscientious objector, Olaf, as a new hero. His bold lines, slightly censored in that edition, "I will not kiss your f.ing flag," and "there is some s. I will not eat," thundered unbowdlerized in my head, and around the house when no one was at home. I did some rough translations into Spanish of some of the naughtier poems to share with my friends but they did not share my enthusiasm. (Perhaps it was the translations.)

Though I do not think I ever used any of Cummings's poems for the purposes of seduction, I did recite a great many of his anti-war poems to crowds mobilized against the Vietnam War in the fall of 1969. At one of the early California Moratoriums against the war I whipped up a crowd with "my sweet old etcetera," "plato told / him," and "the bigness of cannon / is skilful." When I got to "i sing of Olaf glad and big" a number of young men at the gathering set their draft cards on fire. Poetry, as Cummings knew, is powerful.

From those moments in Durango, through the Vietnam War era, and up to the present, Cummings has remained part of my poetic consciousness. A great many others have confessed that for them Cummings was also their first major poet. During the research and writing of this book, whenever I told people that I was working on a Cummings biography, the effort was nearly universally applauded. A neighbor gave me a T-shirt passed out at her daughter's wedding on which was lettered a Cummings love poem. Others would respond by reciting a verse or two. A few talked, with great joy, of hearing him read. Another friend told me that the first thing he did upon arriving in New York in the early 1960s was to go to Cummings's home at Patchin Place and wait until Cummings emerged from his apartment so that he could catch a glimpse of the great poet.

One question that kept recurring, even among the enthusiasts, was why Cummings had seemingly fallen out of fashion. The answer is complex; indeed, a variety of factors seem to have contributed to his decline, at least in the eyes of critics and anthologists, as one of the great modernist poets. One reason is that Cummings was a popular poet, indeed far more popular in his time than Pound or Williams or Stevens. And popularity, at least in the academic mind (and academic critics play a large role in shaping reputations), is a curse, often equated with simplicity of expression or lack of rigor. Accordingly, a writer with broad appeal can be dismissed. But Cummings, despite his large following throughout a good deal of the last century, was hardly a simple poet—which is not the same thing as saying he wrote poems that were often simple, or lyrical, or direct. It is these poems—such as "if there are any heavens my mother will(all by herself)have" or "my father moved through dooms of love" or "i thank You God for most this amazing"—that contributed both to his popular acceptance and to charges from critics that he was lacking in real substance. And yet these poems are representative of only one (and at that a minor) side of Cummings's art.

It is exactly this recognition that prompted Richard Kostelanetz to edit his own wonderful anthology, *AnOther E.E. Cummings*, which regroups the poet's work into stylistic categories to demonstrate Cummings's truly inventive and original gifts. The result is rather extraordinary: Cummings emerges as one of the foremost innovators in modernism, as a granddaddy of L=A=N=G=U=A=G=E poets, as a consummate experimenter with what a writer can do with language. This would not have been news to Cummings's contemporaries such as Ezra Pound, Marianne Moore, or William Carlos Williams, who recognized early on that Cummings's voice was unique and his art indubitably able and complex.

Cummings's disinterest in writing a long poem perhaps also helped to dethrone him from prominence. The fashion in American poetry from the 1940s onward has been to write a book-length poem or a poetic sequence. Pound's *Cantos*, Williams's *Paterson*, Olson's *Maximus*, Ashbery's *Flow Chart*, and Graham's *Swarm* are all fully remarkable, have won wide favor, and became models for subsequent and present generations. But Cummings never wrote a long poem, never felt the need to write, in Pound's words, "a poem, including history." When he wanted to do this, he wrote prose.

His politics in his old age might also have contributed to his disregard by certain critics. Certainly the publication of his prose masterpiece, *Eimi*, in the 1930s, in which he served up a raw critique of the Soviet Union, lost him a good many supporters among the left-leaning critics, a trend that was picked up again with even greater force in the 1960s and 1970s. And yet the right could not fully embrace him either because he was ultimately less a right winger than an anti-authoritarian individualist who steadfastly refused to wave the flag.

Despite the lack of serious critical attention in recent years, Cummings has hardly disappeared from the map of American letters. He continues to sell and continues to be read. Websites, many by college students who do not need professors to tell them how to feel a poem, post a verse or two. More than once I have noticed a subway rider engrossed in *The Enormous Room* or in one of his volumes of poetry. He endures. He is more than undead: he is alive. He still manages to seem rebellious and individual and totally human. Always human: Cummings never wrote a word that was not felt, that was not earned from experience.

My aim in this biography is to link the words he wrote with the life he led. By presenting this American original in full, my ultimate goal is to send readers back to his extraordinary work so that they can experience the thrill—as I did nearly forty years ago—of entering into the world and words of one of the modernist movement's most important and accomplished writers. Or as Marianne Moore described him, a "concentrate of titanic significances."

one

Their Son

His birth at home, on October 14, 1894, was not easy, as his mother's meticulous journal entries testify:

> Held on to Edward and tugged—About 5 towels were arranged and I tugged as hard as possible—Later part of P.M. took lots of gruel—Miss McMahon saw child's hair at 4—Tug of war till 6 then very reluctantly took ether as Dr. Hildreth said it would be bad for the child to wait longer—Dr. Taylor gave the ether (20 minutes). Then Dr. Hildreth delivered the child with forceps—Boy born at 7—weighed 8 ¾ + pounds… I was torn and so Dr. Hildreth sewed me up—not more than 8 stitches—no ether.

For ten days, "the boy was fed on milk and water—Persistent efforts of Miss McMahon to put boy on breast & with help of Phoenix nipple shield finally succeeded." While his mother described in detail her delivery ordeal and attendant's difficulties, she devoted only one line in her record (on December 8) to another important event: "Edward christened the boy at 5:00." Even this milestone did not elicit a formal recording of the child's name; his mother simply began to use her son's middle name, Estlin, in her subsequent diary notes. Apparently, neither she nor her husband ever called their son Edward, his actual first name. No, Edward was clearly Edward the father, Harvard instructor in sociology, eminent man of learning and accomplishment. The child, Edward Estlin

Cummings, should never be confused with his father, despite their shared first names.

Indeed, Edward Cummings was a formidable figure. At the time of his son's birth he was, at thirty-three, a largely self-made man, descended from a long line of New England farmers, tradesman, and shopkeepers—people who valued skill with one's hands over formal education. His earliest American ancestors were Isaac Cummings from Ipswich, Massachusetts, who in 1638 purchased land in Topsfield, Massachusetts, and on his mother's side, Nathaniel Merrill, who settled in Newbury, Massachusetts, in 1634. Through various peregrinations, descendants of the Cummingses and Merrills eventually made their way to Colebrook, New Hampshire. In the late 1840s, Sherburn Rowell Merrill became the owner of grist and starch mills. In the late 1850s, he went into the general store business with Edward Norris Cummings, the young son of an enterprising local tavern-keeper. Not long after forming their partnership, Merrill's oldest daughter, Lucretia Frances Merrill, married Edward Norris Cummings. In 1861, in Colebrook, their son Edward Cummings was born.

Estlin's grandfather, Edward Norris Cummings, was a stern Congregationalist of the "hellfire variety" who ruled over his household with an iron fist. He took much less interest in his son's education beyond that of learning how to use tools. As a consequence, Edward did not attend school until he was eight, and then only at Lucretia's insistence.

Around 1870 Edward Norris Cummings moved his family to Woburn, Massachusetts. Though Edward was allowed to attend school, he was also expected to work. After classes and during summer vacations, he apprenticed as a carpenter, and throughout his years at Woburn High School held down a variety of carpentry jobs. But all that changed when, in 1879, he was admitted to Harvard, becoming the first in his family to pursue higher education. He excelled in his undergraduate studies in economics, philosophy, and political science, graduating *magna cum laude* in 1883.

After graduation he enrolled in Harvard Law School, but changed direction after one term and entered Harvard Divinity School, where he hoped to combine his interest in social work with the ministry. He received his AM in Divinity in 1885. By this point, however, he was somewhat disillusioned with his course of study, for he found that his interest in ministering to the poor and oppressed did not fit particularly well with the school's program that emphasized theology and pulpit studies over social issues. And while he could have obtained a position in one of the local Boston or Cambridge churches, his attraction to learning led him to continue his studies of the social sciences at Harvard Graduate School. While a graduate student, he was also employed as a graduate assistant in the English department, and from 1887–88 served as Instructor in English.

Perceived by his professors as a rising star, he was awarded, in 1888, the first six hundred dollar Robert Treat Paine Fellowship "to study ethical problems of society and the efforts…to ameliorate the lot of the masses of mankind." He chose to study in Europe. This was not the only honor he received that year. One of his teachers, William James, thought so highly of the young bachelor that he took it upon himself to introduce him to a young Bostonian named Rebecca Haswell Clarke, the rather shy twenty-nine-year-old granddaughter of a family friend, John Jones Clarke, former mayor of Roxbury, Massachusetts, and at that time a member of the Massachusetts State Legislature. Miss Clarke made quite an impression on Edward Cummings. Though he went on to Europe, they exchanged numerous letters during his three years abroad.

During Edward's residency in Europe, he conducted a comparative study of the economic and social conditions of workers in England, France, Germany, and Italy. In London, he worked under Reverend Samuel Barnett at the Toynbee Hall settlement house, and at Oxford, studied under Professor J. Estlin Carpenter. Carpenter, a professor of social work and religion, was a pioneering thinker in the new field of sociology, and quickly became a mentor so important that Edward would not only later give his child the middle name of Estlin, but also ask Professor Carpenter to be the child's godfather.

After studies at the University of Berlin and the University of Paris, he returned to Cambridge, Massachusetts, (and Rebecca) in 1891. After securing an appointment at Harvard as Instructor in Political Economy, he felt worthy to ask Rebecca Clarke to marry him. She happily agreed, and on June 25, 1891, they were married in Boston. That fall he began teaching the college's first course in sociology. The following year, with the establishment of sociology as an area of study, his faculty title was altered to Instructor in Sociology. By the time his son was born in 1894, he was well on his way to becoming an eminent Harvard professor.

In Cummings's eyes, his father was, of course, not just the sum of his resumé or ancestry. His own description focuses on other aspects of the man:

> He was a New Hampshire man, 6 foot 2, a crack shot & a famous fly-fisherman & a first rate sailor…& a woodsman who could find his way through forests primeval without a compass & a canoeist who'd stillpaddle you up to a deer without ruffling the surface of the pond & an ornithologist & taxidermist & (when he gave up hunting) an expert photographer (the best I've ever seen) & an actor who portrayed Julius Caesar in Sanders Theatre & a painter (both in oils and watercolours) & a better carpenter than any professional & an architect who designed his own houses before building them & (when he liked) a plumber who just for the fun of it installed all his own waterworks.

Rebecca Clarke was well suited to become the wife of such an important man. Descended on her mother's side from a long line of distinguished forebears, she was quite at home in the cultural and social milieu of upper-class Cambridge. Among her more illustrious ancestors she could count her great-great-great aunt, the English-born Susanna Haswell Rowson, author of one of the first American novels, *Charlotte Temple*, published in 1794. Anthony Haswell, a cousin of Susanna, was a political balladeer during the Revolutionary War and the editor and printer of *Haswell's Massachusetts Spy or American Oracle of Liberty*. Her great-grandfather, Reverend Pitt Clarke, was an early leader of the Unitarian Church, and pastor in Norton, Massachusetts. His son, John Jones Clarke, was not only a major political figure, but also a noted lawyer.

The impressive lineage, however, ended with her grandfather. Her own father, John A. Hanson, forged his father-in-law's name to a check, and J. J. Clarke, so aggrieved by what he perceived as his son-in-law's treachery, not only sent him to jail but also "obliterated his name from the family archives." Disgraced by the incident, Rebecca's mother, Mary Clarke Hanson, sought and received an annulment to the fifteen-year marriage; reclaimed her maiden name for herself and her children, George and Rebecca; and moved back to her parents' house. The effect of this family disaster on fourteen-year-old Rebecca is hard to gauge as she was fairly reticent about the matter. She did later confide to her son that "during her childhood she supposed that her father had been hanged." (He had not, but after his release from jail, he disappeared.) Also, according to her son, "she grew up a shy—or (as we now say) neurotic—girl; who had to be plucked from under sofas whenever friends came to call."

She also wrote poetry, read widely, and though she did not attend college, was a well-educated young woman, fluent in French and knowledgeable about classical languages and literature. Unitarianism had, as well, left its stamp on her. In her son's words, "it was an integral part of herself, she expressed it as she breathed and as she smiled." He also reflected that "never have I encountered anyone more joyous, anyone healthier in body and mind, anyone so quite incapable of remembering a wrong, or anyone so completely and humanly and unaffectedly generous."

According to Cummings, he could not have been born into a better family: "I was welcomed as no son of any king or queen was ever welcomed. Here was my joyous fate and my supreme fortune." The record bears this out. His mother's journal charts with enormous affection and pride baby Estlin's development on an almost daily basis. Among the more interesting aspects of these entries, in which nearly every movement, gesture, or incident seemed worthy of chronicling, is the involvement of Edward Cummings, who, unlike many fathers of that era, was an obvious and important presence in his son's life. Or as Cummings recalled: "My father is the principal figure of my earliest remembered life; when he cradled me in his arms, i reposed in the bosom of God Himself; & when i rode on God's shoulder i was king of the world. His illimitable love was the axis of my being."

Rebecca Cummings's diary detailed every event, large and small, in her son's first months of life. Among the entries are notations such as "Boy shed his first real tear;" "Boy's first real smile—Boy circumcised by Dr. Hildreth—Bore it very well—Cried lustily till Edward spoke to him telling him to bear it bravely. [T]hen the boy actually stopped crying;" and "Shows great tenacity in holding things and puts things in his mouth with no hesitation and with excellent aim—watches moving objects in the street from his window." By early 1895, she described with great pleasure that "the boy" "Articulates 'ah' very clearly and in a deep voice," and "Converses at length." By April she could say, "April 14th [1895]…He talks very vehemently in his own language." And there is, of course, physical description. On June 17, 1895, she made this entry: "14 ¼ lbs.…hair long and silky, a light yellow color—His eyes are still the most beautiful dark blue they were when he was born—and he has a dimple in his right cheek." The journal continues throughout Estlin's infancy. Duly recorded are daily rides on his father's shoulders, his delight in smelling the roses in his father's garden, the date at which he was fully weaned (April 17, 1895), his love of animals, his first word ("hurrah," uttered in response to his father's singing him "Marching through Georgia"), and his first steps at fifteen months. Estlin's acquisition of language was a matter of great interest to his parents for his mother devoted a number of entries to this topic. Not long after his first birthday, for instance, she noted that her son "understands almost everything that is said to him and makes himself perfectly understood." By his second birthday Estlin "sings 'Yankee Doodle,' 'Lohengrin Wedding March,' 'Daisy bell,' 'Marching through Georgia,' 'Only One Girl,' 'John Brown's Body' but makes up words, keeps tune." On February 16, 1897, Rebecca Cummings wrote, "for more than two months Estlin has known all his letters."

In the eyes of his parents, Estlin was clearly destined for great things. Such a notion was not kept from their son, either. As a baby, Estlin sported a white sweater on which his mother had embroidered a crimson "H" for Harvard. His father frequently took him for strolls across the Harvard campus. An entry for October 14, 1897 (Estlin's third birthday) reads: "He is very fond of John Harvard [the statue then in front of Memorial Hall] and says 'when I get a 'ittle bigger Mullah, I'm going to be a big college boy and go to college with Fader.'" The "decidedly left-handed" Estlin was also encouraged to develop his motor skills, as an entry for April 14, 1896 testifies: "Father lets him saw wood in mitre saw."

His artistic talents were in evidence at an early age. Rebecca preserved scores of drawings, which she dutifully dated, from his early childhood on. Most are of animals—dogs, cats, elephants, and giraffes seem to have been his favorite subjects—that for a child of three or four are rendered rather remarkably. Each figure is recognizable as what it is intended to be, and there is already a hint of perspective. The putting together of words into "poetic" form came early, too. When Estlin was three and a half, Rebecca, acting as scribe, recorded "Estlin's Original Poems:"

Oh, my little birdie oh,
with his little toe, toe, toe!

Next comes:

There was a little Fader
and he made his Moder harder.

And, of course, there were books, beginning with a picture book his parents gave Estlin two months before his first birthday, and followed rapidly by volumes ranging from poetry to children's stories to classics and adventure tales. As Cummings later recalled, "I read or was read, at an early age, the most immemorial myths, the wildest animal stories, lots of Scott and quantities of Dickens (including the immortal *Pickwick Papers*), *Robinson Crusoe* and *The Swiss Family Robinson*, *Gulliver's Travels*, *Twenty Thousand Leagues Under the Sea*, poetry galore, *The Holy Bible*, and *The Arabian Nights*."

By the time Estlin was four he was reading, and writing his name on his sketches. When he was five his mother gave him a diary, instructing him on how to keep it. Initially, Estlin dictated the entries to her. The first, in Rebecca's hand, is dated May 19, 1900: "In bed with cold. Played with my music box. Cold rain. Read *Robinson Crusoe*. Looked at picture cards. Had a good night. Eat a little breakfast, two dropped eggs, two pieces of toast one orange." On May 22 he went to the circus: "Saw jaguars, hyena, bear, elephants, baby lions and a father lion, baby monkeys climbing a tree." This entry is illustrated with animal sketches. By the March after his sixth birthday he is entering his own accounts of his day's activities. Most of these are short and to the point: "A good day." "Snowing." "I was going to swing." "I was in bed."

Occasionally, the entries are longer, such as this poem written in a child's neat printing on December 18, 1900, when Estlin was six:

Sunny in the morning,
Beautiful & Fair
Maple trees are happy
In the frosty air.

Or this one, from December 20, 1900:

On the chair is sitting
Daddy with his book.
Took it from the bookcase
Beaming in his look.

During these early years of Estlin's life, his house was the center of the universe. "One of the many wonderful things about a home is that it can be as lively as you please without ever becoming public," he later wrote. "The big Cambridge home was in this respect, as in all other respects, a true home. Although I could be entirely alone when I wished, a varied social life awaited me whenever aloneness palled." This house, at 104 Irving Street in Cambridge, Massachusetts, in the long shadow of Harvard University, was an imposing three-story Colonial Revival structure, with fifteen rooms and thirteen fireplaces. The construction, to Edward Cummings's specifications, was begun late in the fall of 1893, and completed in the summer of 1894. The dwelling was ready for occupancy by mid-July. On August 1, 1894, Edward and Rebecca Cummings moved from a rented house on nearby Brattle Street into their new residence. Though definitely grand, the home was not overly ostentatious, reflecting a style in keeping with the rather conservative characters of its first owners. It was one of many, recently built, that were all situated on substantial landscaped lots with green lawns shaded by oaks, maples, and elms, and with an abundance of shrubs and flowers. Across the street, and erected in 1889, was the home of Harvard philosophy professor William James and his family.

Cummings remembered that his home "faced the Cambridge world as a finely and solidly constructed mansion, preceded by a large oval lawn and ringed with an imposing white-pine hedge. Just in front of the house itself stood two huge appletrees; and faithfully, every spring, these giants lifted their worlds of fragrance toward the room where I breathed and dreamed. Under one window of this room flourished (in early summer) a garden of magnificent roses."

By the age of five he began exploring his upscale neighborhood, a realm dominated by Harvard professors and their families. "Our nearest neighbor, dwelling (at a decent distance) behind us, was Roland Thaxter; primarily the father of my loveliest playmate and ultimately the professor of cryptogamic botany. To our right, on Irving Street, occurred professors [William] James and [Josiah] Royce and [H. Langford] Warren; to our left, on Scott Street, transpired professor of economics [Frank] Taussig. Somewhat back of the Taussig House happened professor [Charles] Lanman...the celebrated Sanskrit scholar."

With many of their children as his playmates, Estlin was welcomed into the homes of all these esteemed Harvard academics. Among them were Betty Thaxter, Francis and Alec James, Catherine and Helen Taussig, and Jack and Esther Lanman. Together they played games—tag, cops and robbers, fox and geese—and roamed the thirty-five-acre woods of the estate of Harvard's former president, Charles Eliot Norton, which Cummings remembered as "a mythical domain of semi-wilderness," "only a butterfly's glide" from his home. "Here, as a very little child, I first encountered that mystery who is Nature; here my enormous smallness entered Her illimitable being; and here someone actually or infinitely or impossibly alive—someone who might almost (but not quite) have been myself—wonderingly wandered the mortally immortal complexities of her beyond imagining imagination."

Nature was not entirely confined to Estlin's exploration of Norton Woods, or "Shady Hill" as the Norton Estate was actually named. During the first five years of his life, the family would journey to nearby Lynn, Massachusetts, where his father's parents and his sister Jane lived at 135 Nahant Street. Edward kept his boat, the *Actress*, in the harbor there and a good many summer days were spent on the water, exploring the waters off Cape Ann, or simply wandering along the beach. Some fifty years after these excursions, Cummings recollected them in a journal note: "A little boy's excitement at low tide running down the huge newly revealed expanse of glittering hardpacked sand, with a feeling of mystery all around me in dense clouded air through which I glimpsed marvellous things reeking treasures shells seaweed stones pebbles. something moves in a rackpool."

There were also trips into Nahant. Ficket's Blacksmith Shop, "a mere shack," was a particularly fascinating place: "[It] was filled with the mystery of the ferocious reek of charcoal—as intense in its way as the stink of the Lynn mudflats (with all the boats leaning-over in various positions...only to (gradually right themselves, as the tide came in."

Despite his delight in the sea and the beach and the blacksmith house, and the strong affection he held for his doting grandmother and aunt

Jane; his grandfather, Edward Norris Cummings, seemed to have cast a pall over the five year old's visits, as a journal entry written more than a half-century later reveals:

> Hated (FEARED) him; & his dog (setter-Bark)
> Harsh to his wife — my Nana Cummings
> " " " son " father
> " " " daughter-in-law " mother
> ("do you realise you are going to Hell?
> And I said cheerfully—I'm afraid very rudely (pertly) "I'll see you there, Sir!")

In the fall of 1898, Edward sold the *Actress*. In its place he purchased a farm near Silver Lake, New Hampshire. According to the "official" family version, the change was made because Rebecca did not like the sea and became immediately seasick when on the boat. But it is also likely that at least part of the motivation was to escape the mean-spirited gloominess of Edward Norris Cummings.

Rebecca recorded the New Hampshire purchase in the first of several leather-bound volumes with "Joy Farm" stamped in gold on their covers: "Edward and Rebecca Cummings first saw Joy Farm Sept. 26th, 1898. Mrs. Ella F. Young of Chicago, sold us Joy Farm, the house and barn and all they contained; '100 acres more or less,' November 15th, 1898." While it is unlikely that either Rebecca or Edward realized it at the time, Joy Farm would become their son's most cherished place, a refuge throughout his life.

With the purchase settled, Edward Cummings immediately began renovating the one-hundred-year-old house, with its hand-sawed floorboards and joists and twin brick fireplaces. He added second-story dormers and a fifty-foot-long porch that faced the mountains. The interior plaster was repaired, and the rooms refurbished. On June 30, 1899, when Estlin, a few months shy of his fifth birthday, caught his first glimpse of Joy Farm, work was still underway, but the main house with its spacious living or "reception" room, dining room, two double bedrooms, and six smaller rooms was in good shape for the family's arrival. The plumbing was not yet installed—that was a year or two away—but a well with a hand pump provided ample water for drinking and washing. Oil and kerosene lamps provided illumination at night.

Though the farm's name derived from a previous owner, Ephriam Joy, the other meaning of "joy" was also apt. Indeed, for the Cummings family Joy Farm was an enchanted and enchanting place, especially for young Estlin. More fascinating even than the house was the barn, with its "savagely hand-hewn timbers" and its assortment of animals—pigs, hens, and a goat named Nan who allowed herself from time to time to be hitched to a cart. The family soon added other creatures: Buttercup-Daisy, a milk cow named by Estlin; a horse who was given the name Thomas à Kempis; and a donkey, more simply called Jack.

Surrounding the barn were pastures and hayfields punctuated by large granite boulders and forested woodlands, home to deer and rabbits and foxes and even the occasional moose. A good-sized stream flowed through the property as well. In the early 1900s, Edward had a dam built to create a pond for swimming and canoeing, one of his many projects to enhance life at the farm. In the distance rose the Sandwich Range of the White Mountains, dominated by Mount Chocorua.

That first summer at the farm was devoted to settling in. Lists of acquisitions or items that needed to be bought take up a great many of the entries in Rebecca's diary. Weather reports are also a common feature, as is the frequent notation, "Read to Estlin."

In some respects Edward Cummings was a typical young academic. He took his teaching seriously and published numerous articles on a variety of topics such as penal reform, trade union strike arbitration, social strife as a consequence of the Industrial Revolution, and the role of philanthropic institutions. But, unlike many of his colleagues, he was also a man of action, not afraid to encounter first hand the subjects he wrote about. As an active board member of the Boston Associated Charities, he diligently parceled out funds to worthy causes. Most important, however, was his work at the Hale Settlement House, the social arm of the South Congregational (Unitarian) Church, situated at the corner of Newbury and Exeter Streets in Boston. Through Hale House he became close to the esteemed minister of the South Congregational Church, Edward Everett Hale, fiery speaker, social reformer, abolitionist crusader, and noted author of fiction, poetry, essays, and stories. His best-known story is probably "The Man Without a Country," a tale of a man who foreswears allegiance to the United States and is condemned to spend his days wandering the world.

Edward Cummings had tremendous respect for Hale's philosophy of social action, which included the founding of numerous organizations for "improving mankind's lot," most notably the Lend-a-Hand Societies and the Harry Wadsworth Clubs, both which involved young people in helping those "less fortunate than themselves." Additionally, he admired Hale's reflective writings, and found his sermons inspiring. By that time, they were already being collected in several volumes. Likewise, Hale and his congregation found the energetic Harvard instructor exactly the sort of man suitable for carrying on the important community role the Second Congregational Church had carved out for itself over nearly half a century. It was hardly a surprise then, when in the spring of 1900, the members of the church, and Hale, who at seventy-eight was planning his retirement, asked Edward Cummings to become associate minister.

Edward Cummings accepted the post immediately, feeling that he had succeeded in finally finding the exact opportunity he had hoped would come his way years earlier through the Divinity School. Indeed, the job fit Edward's highest hopes and expectations. The position not only drew on his strengths as a teacher, intellectual, and public speaker, but also matched his strong dedication to improving the lot of the lower and working classes. In addition to giving a rousing and inspirational Sunday sermon, he was expected to devote at least 50 percent of his time to social issues, in keeping with the Church's motto "That They May Have Life More Abundantly." On October 1, 1900, just two weeks before Estlin's sixth birthday, the unordained Edward Cummings took over the leadership of the South Congregational Church.

This was not the only change in store for the Cummings family. That same fall Rebecca announced to Edward that she was pregnant again, with the baby due sometime in the spring. In Rebecca's diaries from the period during her pregnancy, she recorded, as usual, the day's little activities, and commented on her physical state, particularly her weight gain. However, she makes no mention of when or how her "precious boy" was informed that soon he was going to have a sibling. There does not seem to be any concern over his potential jealousy, or any attempt made to explain what the future for him would be like. Presumably, Edward and Rebecca felt that in an age where large families were commonplace, a sibling's imminent arrival did not require special preparations. A note

Cummings wrote years later does shed a little light on the moment of his sister's birth: "When my Sister arrived: my F[ather] & i are standing by the chest in the (upstairs) hall just outside my M[other]'s room (where she is) he takes me into his room & tells me how my sister has come out of my mother—out of her body."

Rebecca Cummings's rather perfunctory entry for April 29, 1901, concentrated on the ease (in contrast to Estlin's difficult birth) with which her second child was born: "First 'labor pain' brought the dear baby's head into the world and another (both automatic) brought her feet and she cried lustily."

A month or so after her birth, the "dear baby" was christened Elizabeth Frances Cummings in a small family ceremony held in the living room at the Irving Street house.

two

In Just- Spring

Elizabeth's birth expanded the members of the Cummings household to eight. Aside from the immediate family, the inhabitants included Rebecca's mother, Mary "Nana" Clarke; Rebecca's brother, George Lemist Clarke; and at least two live-in maids, the most permanent being a young Irishwoman, Mary McKenna. Not long after Elizabeth's birth, Edward's father died, and his mother Lucretia (Nana Cummings) and Edward's sister Jane moved in as well. An African American handyman, Sandy Hardy, though not a lodger, was also a daily presence. He often stayed long into the evening to help Edward with his various building projects. Among the family pets were a dog, cat, goldfish, and rabbits.

Fortunately, the residence could easily accommodate this extended family. The house's interior matched the stately presence of its exterior, though from Cummings's descriptions, in fine Victorian fashion, just about every available space was filled with furniture, including a piano and gramophone. Books reposed in mahogany bookcases and a variety of paintings graced the walls. They included large oils of Rebecca and Edward painted by the distinguished Boston artist Charles Hopkinson, and Edward's own landscape of a Norwegian fjord. Decorative objects abounded, most notably Edward's trophies: a mounted seven-pound trout, a giant set of antlers, and a large number of stuffed birds. The kitchen was equipped with a combination coal and wood stove, a table and chairs for informal dining, and a hot water tank from which water could be dipped for washing dishes. Sometime in the early 1900s, Edward built a telephone closet into one corner of the kitchen in order to accommodate the acquisition of a hand-cranked telephone, the first one to be installed in a residence in Cambridge.

On the second floor were two master bedrooms and two somewhat smaller bedrooms, all with fireplaces, and in the hall a dumbwaiter that Edward had fashioned into a lift for hauling firewood. Three small rooms were devoted to cleanliness: a toilet room, a shower room, and a bathing room, with its claw-footed bathtub, ideal for sailing toy boats. At the top of the skylight-illuminated stairs, on the third floor, were five more rooms, of which two or three were used by the servants. One special room, also with a skylight, situated off the landing was a combination woodworking shop and darkroom. Edward had partitioned off one section of the space and installed a sink, shades impermeable to light, and his photographic baths and enlarger so that he could develop and print photographs. In her memoir, Cummings's sister, Elizabeth Cummings Qualey, described the other half of the room: "There was a long tool bench with a vise and a rack full of tools and, of course, wood to make things of, and all sorts of nails and screws. I couldn't use the tools, but I loved to help my father and brother."

In another large room, under the roof, the children could play games, draw, read, and talk without adult interference. Its most exciting feature consisted of a set of stairs that led to the roof. As Elizabeth recalled, "we could go up onto the flat roof if we were careful and walked softly. It was made of copper and had a railing all around it.... My brother made a box kite and a windlass for it, and used to take it up on the flat roof and fly it there. He let me help him turn the windlass."

The large yard, with flowerbeds and ample grassy areas, also became a place of enchantment. The lawn was outfitted with a swing, a bar, and hanging rings. "My father liked to have us play in our yard, and used to say he was raising children and not grass," Elizabeth wrote. "We could call and shout, but we were forbidden to scream unless we were hurt."

In one of the several "good climbing trees," Edward, with Estlin's help, built a tree house. "It was a sturdy little house, and cozy too," Elizabeth remembered. "You climbed up to the door by a strong ladder with wide rungs. There was a little stove with a real stove pipe, and a bunk big enough for my brother to sleep on, and a real window with a wooden shutter. There was room for at least six people inside the house, and there was a small porch, with a railing around it, facing the street. We spent a lot of time in the tree house in all kinds of weather. The stove kept it warm in cold weather and, though it was a heating stove and not a cook stove, we could make toast, and cocoa, and pop corn on it. My brother used to go to the tree house to be alone, and sometimes spent the night there."

Because children were so welcome, the Cummings's house and yard served as a popular destination for their neighborhood playmates. Esther Lanman, who lived nearby, mentioned in her diary for 1908 (when she was ten) of going to "Estlin's house" on twenty-two separate occasions. "After school went up to Estlin's tree house. We made toast and cooked some apples and had a few peanuts then we popped corn."

Not all of Estlin's play with the neighborhood girls was quite so innocent. In his private notes, written in the 1950s, he recalled several incidents from when he and Betty Thaxter, his friend who lived next door, explored one another's anatomy. He was six or seven at the time the first encounter occurred in the privacy of the lilac bushes at Norton Woods, where Estlin, Betty, and Betty's friend Gertrude Thurber, stripped in front of one another. The thrill was short-lived as they were quickly chased out by the estate's caretaker, Bernard McGrath. Despite their fright at almost being discovered, Betty and Estlin were undeterred in their explorations. Subsequently, however, they opted for a safer venue: "Betty and i go into bathroom of her house (we have been playing there) and she(?) locks door. We undress, standing, facing each other, approach: (without knowing our parts) touch each other—she me on john,i her on bellybutton(as I remember). The door is tried—I almost faint—Professor Thaxter's...voice: 'Bet-tie?' 'Yes, papa.' 'What are you doing?' Answer. He goes away. We dress(hurriedly.)"

Such was Estlin's moral upbringing that he couldn't contain his guilt. "This doing haunted me,my conscience wouldn't let me sleep for several nights: then I broke down,one night, as my Mother was sitting on the edge of the bed about to repeat with me the Lord's Prayer,and told her,sobbing terribly. She asked merely(tho sternly);'Did you touch anything in particular?' My conscience was sufficiently salved by the amount which I had confessed,so that I Lied saying No, I don't think so."

Estlin also found pleasure in solitude: drawing, reading, writing, inventing elaborate fantasy worlds, listening at night to the sounds of the trains rolling over the nearby railroad tracks, "weeeeeeeeeee (steam running down) chuttling, pumpingheartlike." "The idea of home is the idea of privacy," he noted in his lectures at Harvard. "But again—what is privacy? You probably never heard of it.... The notion of a house, as one single definite particular and unique place to come into, from the anywherish and everywherish world outside—that notion must strike you as fantastic." For the young Estlin, it was far from being a fantastic notion. Indeed, his home was a refuge, a house "as lively as you please without ever becoming public," a place where Estlin could indulge himself, and be indulged, a place where he could thrive.

From the numerous examples of his early creative output (carefully saved by his mother), a picture emerges of a highly precocious and talented boy whose every imaginative impulse was nurtured by those around him. Among the hundreds of drawings is an alphabet book from when Estlin was six, with each letter illustrated with the concept described:

> O is for OSTLICH
> I is for Indians Running a Mile
> D is for Duck
> S is for stars and stars
> A stag was running about in the Field when suddenly he was caught in a trap. He called for his Farmers and Cowboys.

Indeed, from a very early age animals held a special place in Estlin's imagination. One collection of sketchbook drawings from 1901, titled *Animals at the Zoo* contains a variety of well-executed sketches of various beasts including a seal, bird, giraffe, horse, camel, and a number of elephants. Elephants were an especially favorite subject, and would remain so for his entire life, becoming, as he put it, his "totem."

It was not only at the zoo or in picture books that elephants became part of his childhood. The circus was a particularly excellent source for observing his beloved pachyderms. Indeed, circus-going was a fairly regular event from the time Estlin had turned six, and like his love for elephants, would remain a lifelong passion. Among the many circuses Estlin took in during his childhood were Forepaugh and Sells Brothers Circus; Barnum and Bailey, where he saw his first sideshow; Ringling Brothers; and Bostock's Animal Show with Captain Bonavita and his Matchless group of twenty-seven forest-bred African lions. Elephants are featured in his play, as well. Inspired by his trips to the circus, he sought in some fashion to reenact at home the feats he had seen performed under the Big Top. Under the six-year-old's well-rendered drawing of an elephant, he affixed the following legend:

Edward Estlin Cummings
The animal ruler and
his matchless group of
32 elephants little and big

And then there is a "season ticket" for the "circus" presented to "Mrs. Edward Cummings" for an "entertainment."

Season Ticket
Estlin's Great Animal Arena
POSITIVELY NOT TRANSFERABLE IF PRESENTED
BY OTHER PERSON THAN PARTY HEREIN NAMED
Ticket will be taken up and not renewed.

Elephants also functioned in a game he often played with his father. At first, Edward played the role of elephant, porting Estlin about on his back. But once Estlin encountered Rudyard Kipling's *The Jungle Book*, the play was elaborated, and Estlin became Kala Nag, the elephant, and Edward, Little Toomai, the boy caretaker. Nearly a half century after this role-playing, Cummings wondered if the game had a deeper meaning: "My F[ather] makes ME the huge enormous elephant...& himself the loving-but-tiny (and therefore helpless black (Indian,native) boy who rode him & NOTA BeNE runs,controls him."

Cummings's note—to be sure, a *post-hoc* analysis—nonetheless reveals something about the complexity of the relationship he had with his father. For all of Estlin's respect, admiration, and love for his father, he also felt from time to time overpowered, even constrained by Edward, who continually expected his son to measure up to his standards of strength, resilience, and courage. In another note written in middle age, Cummings remembered an incident from his childhood involving a sledding mishap: "One day I was given a new sled, and went out with my nurse to coast—the sled, going fast, hit something and threw me off, and I cried: I begged the nurse not to tell my father—and when we came in, and he asked how I'd enjoyed the sled, she said, 'O he had a wonderful time.' I was always afraid of my father."

It is clear from a number of other statements scattered throughout his journals and notes that this "fear" did not derive from Edward being heavy-handed, or even terribly strict. Indeed, everything in Cummings's private notes indicate that Edward ruled his son not through force but through example. However, it was a powerful example, and a difficult one for Estlin to follow at times. "My father was a walking Platonic triad—the good,the true,the beautiful," Cummings noted.

An incident that involved removing large rocks from a field at Joy Farm in order to construct a tennis court shows how Estlin continually attempted to prove his worthiness to his father: "My F[ather]: 'please don't Chub [Edward's nickname for Estlin]—you'll strain yourself,' apropos stones, which I lifted from the ground & carried with all my strength, anxious to show my F[ather] how strong I (his only son) was, IN SPITE OF MY SLIM ARMS AND UNDERSIZEDNESS."

Estlin *was* small, even delicate. One June 24, 1904, when Estlin was nine, Rebecca recorded his measurements "in house clothes" as weighing fifty-nine pounds and standing four feet, five inches tall. (In contrast, Elizabeth, six and a half years younger, weighed thirty-nine pounds and was three feet, four inches tall.) For Estlin, his physical strength and stature were always negative factors in the ongoing comparison with his father who was rugged; six feet, two inches in height; and very strong. As a child, these perceived virtues were the most tangible evidence of his father's "superiority;" and while he would never become the tall, broad-shouldered man his father was, his preoccupation with measuring up to Edward would take a different form in adolescence, and even adulthood, when Estlin would find his father's inherent morality and "sheer goodness" far more difficult challenges to overcome.

If Edward was a "walking Platonic triad," his mother was "a lesser triad: healthy & honest & brave." Indeed, from the moment of his birth Estlin enjoyed a very special relationship with his doting mother. A constant presence who bolstered him in every endeavor, she was also largely responsible for his early education, since Estlin did not attend school until he was almost eight.

Of the other family members in residence, Cummings recalled that "after myself and my father and mother, I loved most dearly my mother's brother George. He was by profession a lawyer, by inclination a bon vivant, and by nature a joyous human being. When this joyous human being wasn't toiling in his office, or hobnobbing with socalled swells at the Brookline country club, he was always my playfellow."

In September of 1902, a month before Estlin's eighth birthday, Rebecca enrolled her son in Miss Webster's School, a private primary school near

Harvard Square. Among his classmates were his neighbors Betty Thaxter and Gertrude Thurber. Already quite advanced, Estlin could read and write well, was a good speller, had an extensive vocabulary, some knowledge of history and geography, and even knew the Greek alphabet. But his mother had apparently not tutored him much in math. "I was sent to the board with an arithmetic example & couldn't do it and CRIED Every Single Day." To compound Estlin's unease, "fuzz-redish-cheeked" Miss Webster assigned Steven Holman, "a spindlelegged jibbity boy…a whiz at arithmetic," to share his double desk. If Miss Webster thought that Steven would encourage Estlin in math, the strategy backfired for the boy with the predilection for words and images quickly came to the conclusion that his mathematically inclined deskmate was wasting his time doing calculations.

Recitation of the Lord's Prayer was also a daily ritual, but the version recited at Miss Webster's was that of the King James Bible with "debts" and "debtors" used in lieu of "trespassers" and "those who trespass against us." It was the latter translation that young Estlin had learned from his father. Consequently he not only decided that this "substitution" was wrong—since it contradicted the text that Edward had taught him—it was also "ugly." A nosebleed suffered one day at the end of the recitation only solidified his sense of outrage. Words, even then, mattered a great deal to Estlin; as did, of course, the absolute belief in his father's authority on religious subjects.

Despite his father's profession, religion was not dominant within the Cummings household; it was simply one more strand in the complex fabric of life. On Sunday, naturally, the family attended services at the South Congregational Church where Rebecca would greet the congregation at the door, and where a black-robed Edward would preach. His actor's booming voice and the liveliness of his topics, complete with puns, wordplay, and memorable slogans, made churchgoing an easier obligation for Estlin and Elizabeth.

Indeed, Edward's sermons were distinctly non-liturgical. A sampling of his titles include: "Mud Pies," "Spiritual Perennials," and "Invisible Barriers or the Bird in the Window." "The Elevator or the Ups and Downs of Life" was a philosophical discourse on the illusion of motion while standing still; in "The Parable of the Sugar Place," the Reverend Cummings transformed the art of making maple syrup into a morality tale in which man, like maple sugar, is boiled down to his essence in the face of adversity.

After the service, Estlin and Elizabeth would be given a few cents to go around the corner to the drugstore and buy candy. When Estlin was ten or eleven, they were even permitted to take the streetcar home by themselves while Edward and Rebecca lingered to meet with the South Congregational Citizenship Committee, the civic and social group within the church. Inevitably, a few members of the congregation were invited home for Sunday dinner.

In September 1904, when Estlin was a month shy of his tenth birthday, his parents enrolled him in Agassiz School (a Cambridge public school), mainly, it seems, because of the reputation of its African American principal, Maria Baldwin. In his lectures at Harvard, Cummings profiled her: "Miss Baldwin...(...a lady, if ever a lady existed) was blessed with a delicious voice, charming manners, and a deep understanding of children. Never did any demidivine dictator more gracefully and easily rule a more unruly and less graceful populace. Her very presence emanated an honour and a glory: the honour of spiritual freedom—no mere freedom from—and the glory of being, not (like most extant morals) really undead, but actually alive. From her I marvellingly learned that the truest power is gentleness."

Whether because of his two years at Miss Webster's, or, more likely, due to his extensive "home schooling," Estlin was placed in seventh grade. The placement was apparently correct, for on October 28, 1904, Maria Baldwin reported that "in all work, except arithmetic, he is quite the equal in attainment of the seventh grade pupils."

While he continued to have difficulty with math, Estlin distinguished himself in other areas. Of particular delight was the required memorization of scores of poems, mostly by nineteenth-century New England poets such as Whittier, Longfellow, and Emerson.

In eighth grade, Maria Baldwin herself became his teacher, and under her tutelage Estlin thrived, particularly in English and social studies. Scott's *Ivanhoe* and *Lady of the Lake*, Macaulay's *Lays of Ancient Rome* and Towle's *Pizarro: His Adventures and Conquests* were among the books assigned that year. Scott so inspired him that he took it upon himself to illustrate, with numerous detailed drawings, episodes from these tales of knighthood. Tales of adventure also inspired him to write stories based on historical fiction. Among these prose sequels are the forty-page "In Cromwell's Time," in which Edward Longwood joins up with Cromwell's forces, becoming a colonel at the tender age of eighteen. Another story,

"For Henry and England" follows the sojourn to London from the rural countryside of two friends who along the way meet Robin Hood.

It was not only his reading at school that provoked Estlin's literary and visual output. His Uncle George also aided in kindling Estlin's imagination. Cummings later recalled that his uncle owned "a gruesome history of the Tower Of London." "Every Night after dinner, if George were on deck, he would rub his hands and wink magnificently in my direction and call to my maiden aunt 'Jane, let's have some ruddy gore!' whereupon Jane would protestingly join us in the parlour; and George would stealthily produce the opus; and she would blushfully read; and I would cling to the sofa in exquisite terror. We also read—for sheer relaxation—Lorna Doone (with whom I fell sublimely in love) and Treasure Island." *Treasure Island* made such an impression on him that twenty years after having first encountered the book, Cummings could write out from memory a complete synopsis, accurate in detail and names of characters.

While historical romances were prominent in his imaginative output, Estlin did not divorce himself entirely from the world around him. The death of Rebecca's mother, "Nana Clarke," in 1904, when Estlin was nine, led him to compose two memorials:

1.

DEDICATED TO DEAR NANA CLARKE
When looking at that picture, all the past
Life of the sweet one cometh back to me;
And with emotions deep, I think when last
I saw her, in this world of vanity.

2.

As rooms are separated by a curtain,
So are our lives; yes, like those rooms; the first
One is our present life; the second is
Our life to come,—our better life in Heaven;
The separating curtain,—it is death.

Always encouraged in his pursuit of the arts, Estlin early on developed a reputation within the family and among his friends for his precociousness as a writer and artist. His sister, Elizabeth, recalled that her brother "was great fun to be with. He could draw pictures, and tell stories, and imitate people and animals, and invent games, and could make you laugh, even when you thought you felt miserable.... When we had whooping cough we were sick for weeks and weeks.... About half the children in the neighborhood had the whooping cough, or had been exposed to it. My brother formed a club called the 'Whooper Club.' Anyone could belong who had whooping cough or who expected to come down with it. My brother was president, and editor of the "Whooper Club' paper, which he typed on mother's old Hammond typewriter. Every member of the 'Whooper Club' had to write or dictate a story for the paper.... My brother used to make different kinds of drawings, too, sometimes little ones (a little like the ones in the funny papers) that he mounted on strips of cardboard. They told stories about us, our animals, and all sorts of things."

While Estlin's world centered largely around family, school, and the imagination, by the time he was at Agassiz School his environs began to play a more important role in his life. Turn of the century Cambridge was a small city in transition. Although the area around Harvard Square, and on the nearby streets to the west and south, such as Boylston, Brattle, Church, and Garden were decidedly upscale and genteel, the streets and byways near the Cummings house were largely unpaved. Kirkland Street, for instance, just a few blocks from Irving, was a noisy thoroughfare connecting the light manufacturing areas of East Cambridge and Somerville to West Cambridge (and over the bridge across the Charles River) to Brighton and Boston. It was probably along Kirkland Street that Estlin first got a glimpse of what he would term in later years, "manunkind:"

> As a child I see ragged worried dirty-looking cows being driven through the street by a couple of louts with sticks.... And gradually I realize they're going 'to the slaughterhouse,' are being driven to their deaths: and I stand hushed, almost unbreathing, feeling the helplessness of a pity which is for some whole world.... The drivers suddenly become animals themselves; ferocious animals; hideously which smite the crotted rumps and scarred bony sides of the rearplunging, murderously laying-into the helpless feminine-foolish beings in their care—O this sickens me. The men brutes...I wish I could kill them both foreverandever—look at the soft wild eyes of the kine! Who but a monster would hate easycoming strokable creatures?"

Not far from Estlin's realm of the well-bred, dwelled youngsters who were not so polite. Termed "muckers" by the denizens of Irving and Scott streets, these children lived on the "wrong side of the track" in adjacent Somerville. They "possessed fists which hit below the belt and arms which threw snowballs containing small rocks." Estlin, apparently, did not engage in fisticuffs with these toughs: "As a boy I was afraid of fighting: if anyone challenged me, I took refuge in playing up to him; and pretended he hadn't insulted me, really. I never dared lose my temper because I was afraid of being beaten."

But the immediate neighborhood was not so sinister. On the triangular corner where Irving, Scott, and Farrar Streets intersected, every year the spring thaw created a "mud-luscious" giant puddle in a pothole in the street. It was there that an annual event took place. Or as Cummings's sister recalled, "The first and most exciting sign that spring had really come was the balloon man. First you heard his whistle in the distance; then he would come walking down the street, carrying a basket full of balloons of all colors tugging at their strings." Some ten years later, when Cummings was just twenty-one, he memorialized both spring and the advent of the balloon man in one of his most famous poems:

in Just-
spring   when the world is mud-
luscious the little
lame balloonman

whistles   far   and wee

and eddieandbill come
running from marbles and
piracies and it's
spring

when the world is puddle-wonderful

the queer
old balloonman whistles
far   and   wee
and bettyandisbel come dancing

from hop-scotch and jump-rope and

it's
spring
and
      the

            goat-footed

balloonMan   whistles
far
and
wee

three

Poet of Simplicity

Agassiz only enrolled students through the eighth grade, so in the fall of 1906, Estlin, then almost twelve, and his classmates transferred to Peabody School on the corner of Linnaean and Avon Streets, a short hike from his house. The traditional New England education he had begun receiving under Maria Baldwin's guidance continued at Peabody, where Estlin added to his repertoire of reading and memorization of verse. Again, he floundered in math, but was at the top of his class in American history and English. Charlotte Ewell, to whom Estlin took an instant liking, taught both these classes. Shakespeare's *Julius Caesar* and *As You Like It* were on the curriculum in her English class, as was Andrew Lang's *Tales of Troy and Greece*. Apparently one of Miss Ewell's assignments was to summarize in detail the *Iliad* and the *Odyssey*—as gleaned from Lang—for among the surviving papers from this year is a synopsis and outline of each book of Homer's epics. For history, Estlin wrote compositions on Lincoln, Daniel Webster, and a fairly sophisticated essay on "Free Trade and Protective Tariff."

Memorizing poems was also high on Miss Ewell's list, a task in which Estlin delighted. Among the works he committed to memory that year were Lincoln's Gettysburg Address, Longfellow's "O Ship of State," Gray's "Elegy Written in a Country Churchyard," and Holmes's "The Chambered Nautilus" and "Old Ironsides." Miss Ewell insisted that her students not just memorize the verses, but deliver them in unison in a high rhetorical fashion with accompanying gestures.

Estlin, meanwhile, inspired by the poetry he was reading and memorizing, compiled his first book of poems containing a selection of work he had written from the time he was nine to twelve. Copied neatly in his own hand into a small notebook, his "collected verse" consists of five poems, including the two previously quoted that reflected on the death of Nana Clarke. In contrast to the stories he wrote at the time, he did not illustrate his poetry with drawings. But then the poetic themes he chose do not lend themselves terribly well to illustration. God, the hereafter, and patriotism are the major subjects—one poem even being titled "God" and another "Our Flag." "Our Flag" begins "O flag of our nation! O Red,White and Blue! / O symbol of liberty,waving anew!" The final piece in the collection, a meditation on the Charles River titled "The River of Mist," is actually in prose. It is also the most interesting in that Estlin's language—for at least the first half—actually manages to convey the scene with a certain poetic intensity and vividness:

> Stretching away to westward the great river lies quiet beneath me. So still it lies, that it seems as if it had not yet awakened from the delicious sleep brought on by the silence of the night. A little distance from the shore a boat is moored on the glossy surface,—perfect to every detail the reflection glimmers below it. All is still and sombre and wonderful, as dawn gives way to daylight and night to morning.

Estlin was twelve when he wrote "The River of Mist."

Despite his difficulty in geometry, Estlin managed to learn enough math to pass, and thereby graduate with his class. At the ceremony, Edward Cummings delivered the commencement address. His son recited Henry Holcomb Bennett's "The Flag Goes By," and the entire class declaimed Theodore Roosevelt's speech, "A Task for Each Generation," as well as Longfellow's "Build Me Straight," a part of his longer poem "Building of the Ship."

It was probably about the time that he graduated from Peabody that the onset of puberty began to awaken a strong curiosity about sex. Despite the liberal atmosphere within the Cummings household, sex was not a topic that Estlin felt he could openly discuss with either of his parents. Or as he remembered, "being precocious sexually, and playing with little girls when other boys played with boys, I was always getting sexual pleasure in secret and lived in terror of being found out." "Getting sexual pleasure in secret" took a couple of forms: masturbation and spying on their maid, Mary McKenna, and her lover, who was perhaps a Cambridge policeman.

"My first memory of GOING OFF," recalled Cummings, "is in Uncle George's...room reading *L'Homme Qui Rit* of Victor Hugo." Though excited by the experience, he immediately felt himself flooded with guilt. When he twice came down with chicken pox, he decided it was God's way of punishing him for masturbating and that he was surely going to die. For a time he abstained, but resumed the practice once recovered. Guilt still accompanied the act, however, and he frequently prayed for God to forgive his transgression. In many respects he was very much a minister's son.

In late middle age, he reflected on this conflict in his early life:

> The immense mistake which my New England downbringing tried its best to make of me equals that "virtue" and volupté are opposites; I say mistake, for(my nature having immediately invited me to volupté)I was left to conclude that my nature was wrong(sinful,wicked);whereupon I became pathetically striving towards a negation of my nature—which I supposed would equal virtue. No wonder this "virtue" was transparent and unattainable! I was trying to lift myself by my own bootstraps. I thought I was doing a devilish thing every time I tried to do a devilish thing,deny myself. In those days—and nights!—I kept cursing myself as a foul traitor to "virtue"...and the more I cursed, the more masturbation assumed an overpowering importance.

Because he did not feel he could inquire about sex, nor suppress his interest in it, he learned about procreation from schoolmates, and from the handyman, Sandy Hardy, who was apparently the first to inform him of how babies were born. Once at Joy Farm, Hardy took it upon himself to instruct Estlin about sex by informing him that men and women produced babies in the same way as rabbits did. Eventually his father talked with his son about sex, but as Cummings noted, the information came "too late." From his notes on Edward's lecture it does not seem to have been terribly useful either: "Told me a young man and young girl get (lie) under a tree, and first thing they know it's happened."

In his attempt to learn more about love, he took to observing on the sly the maid who would smooch with her lover in the kitchen. Cummings recalled one incident:

a. i crept down back stairs, spying on Mary McKenna & a man
b. i fled into the telephone closet
c. she caught me
"I'll give him a box on the ear"

The box on the ear "stunned me: made my head ring," noted Cummings. Estlin's fear must have been palpable, or perhaps the maid was simply concerned about losing her job, for as he remembered it, Mary immediately apologized: "'There dear, did I hurt you, did Mary hurt you;' never mind 'it'll be all right' (Mary's sorry she hurt you.)"

Another, even more dramatic incident, left him perplexed. One night, while in his bed, he heard his mother call out "Edward." "What happened a) to make her cry out in room betw. rooms b) afterwards?—the room (=doors locked) did I get out of bed & listen at the door-jamb—or even open the door silently—and hear…& did I thereupon, white, trembling with terror, decide I'd never take any more of my F[ather]'s hypocrisy [?]"

Estlin also began to discover other forbidden pleasures when he was about twelve. With his neighbor Jack Lanman, he began to smoke homemade fern tobacco in clay pipes in the dumbwaiter shaft that ascended to Edward's tool room, and smoked leaves rolled into "cigars" in his tree house. On the way home from school, as they passed through Harvard Yard, he and his classmates would throw snowballs at the Harvard students, then run. Estlin admitted that he wasn't terribly skilled at snowballing as he "couldn't throw hard or accurately at the same time." Nonetheless, he found the sport amusing and thrilling.

Because Estlin was small for his age, and also the youngest in his class, he frequently felt puny in relation to his peers who could run faster, jump higher, throw snowballs farther, and even fight. His uncle George, obviously aware of Estlin's concern about his physical strength, decided to give him boxing lessons. Estlin welcomed the instruction, and learned the rudiments of thrusting and jabbing and blocking, but recoiled in horror, "consciousstricken," when in one sparring match he hit his uncle in the stomach, causing him to double up in pain.

Estlin was less worried about slight harm coming to his five-year-old sister, for he began to harbor some resentment toward Elizabeth. Estlin felt that his father, who demonstrably doted on his daughter, preferred her over him. It is fairly evident that Edward also held his son in high regard, but was far less effusive in showing his affections. Estlin's negative feelings toward Elizabeth were hardly constant, but made themselves known from time to time. Cummings recalled that on one occasion he was swinging his sister in a hammock: "She fell and bawled & I terrified of my father feigned sympathy—while really hating her."

In the fall of 1907, a month before his thirteenth birthday, Estlin entered prestigious Cambridge Latin School, just a few short blocks from his house. In 1907, the school was one of a handful of public preparatory schools from which Harvard picked its entering class. Accordingly, the curriculum was designed with an eye to its graduates passing the Harvard entrance exam. At the time of his admission, Estlin expected to study there for five years since Harvard required the extra year of its potential matriculants.

Cambridge Latin placed a heavy emphasis on the study of language and literature. Latin was a required four-year subject, Greek was mandated for at least two years, a modern language for three. Students also had to enroll in an English class each year, and take three years of ancient history. Though the study of math—algebra and geometry—was also routine, science was generally offered only to fifth-year students. Estlin actually graduated without ever having taken a science class.

Estlin's first year at Cambridge Latin was neither particularly rewarding nor inspiring. Latin class, which met every day, in contrast to the other subjects that were held on alternate days, consisted mainly of grammar drills and paradigm memorization. Estlin suffered through it, knowing that Latin literature lay ahead. Ancient history proved to be more fun and interesting, despite the emphasis on memorizing dates and battles. As usual, he stumbled in math but managed to pull off a passing grade by year's end. Even English did not hold his interest as much as he had hoped since most of the reading—based on the Harvard reading list—was far less intriguing than the books he could encounter at home. In addition, he was teased because of his small size (he was just over five feet tall). His chief tormentors were the Dearing brothers, who would consistently and loudly taunt him with the phrase "Cummings my little lambkin, god forgive our SHORT comings." Estlin could hardly wait for the summer to escape to Joy Farm, particularly now that his father had purchased a touring car.

Joy Farm, in fact, held an increasingly greater place in his affections. There, in the bosom of his family, he could wander with his bull terrier, Rex, over the fields and in the woodlands, help his father with his constant renovations, read and be read to (for Rebecca still made it a practice of reading aloud to the family every evening), and play a variety of games. "I dressed as a Red Indian," noted Cummings, "slept in a teepee, and almost punctured our best Jersey cow with a random arrow; in emulation of the rightful inhabitants of my wronged native land." Estlin could also be by himself, writing, imagining, or drawing.

Among Edward's building projects were studies for himself and Estlin. Elizabeth recalled that her father "built a study at the edge of the woods. It was a very unusual one because it had so many sides that it was almost round. It had a big fireplace with a sunken hearth, and on each side of the fireplace were cement steps leading to a little room upstairs. Outside the upstairs window was a wide walk that went all the way around the study and was like a sort of balcony. There were beds there, and downstairs my father built himself a desk."

Estlin's study was constructed under a tree about halfway between the house and his father's study. Though less grand, it was eminently serviceable. Again, the design was unique, boasting a hinged roof that could be raised at an angle to provide shade, air and light. The roof was kept lowered when it rained or snowed. According to his sister, "There was a long plank the right height for a desk and about long enough for three people to sit at it at once. There was another long plank the right height for a bench. There was a wall at the back with a window in it, and walls at each end with cupboards and cubbyholes for books and things."

Estlin's second year at Cambridge Latin went much better than his first. In Latin he progressed to Caesar and Ovid and Nepos; the reading in English was more interesting, too: *Silas Marner*, *David Copperfield*, selections from Tennyson's *The Idylls of the King*, Irving's *The Sketch Book*. But a new class, French, proved especially appealing, and he quickly progressed (with help from both his parents) through conjugations and grammar drills to conversation and short readings. That fall, fourteen-year-old Estlin also began writing for the school magazine, the *Cambridge Review*, which contained a mix of fiction, poetry, essays, jokes, gossip, and student news. All of Estlin's first contributions to the *Cambridge Review* consisted of prose, and none of it was very good. Cummings would later refer to these juvenile tales as "sentimental stories," and they are, with a fair amount of melodrama thrown in for good measure. These fledgling forays into prose, however, did help to bolster Estlin's confidence about himself as a writer.

He apparently did not contribute poetry during the first year he associated himself with the *Review*. It is possible, of course, that he did, and that it was rejected. But no notice of it being turned down exists in the archive, in contrast to rejection slips from the same period from the *Atlantic Monthly*, *Outlook*, and *Youth's Companion*. He apparently chose to submit only works of prose, and his prose at that juncture was in the main inferior to his verse. One poem composed in the early spring of 1909, when he was fourteen, has interesting rhymes and slant rhymes, and though the octaves do not adhere to conventional models in their meter and rhyme scheme, the language (archaism's excepted), as well as many of the images, are quite sophisticated. In addition, a hallmark of what would later become Cummings's style makes its first appearance here: the lack of a space after a comma. The untitled poem begins this way:

A chilly,murky night;
The street lamps flicker low,
A hail-like,whispering rain
Beats 'gainst the streaked,bleak pane;
The sickly,ghostly glow
Of the blurred,blinking,wavering,flickering light
Shines on the muddy streets in sombre gleams
Like a weird lamp post on a road of dreams.

As usual, Estlin spent the summer of 1909 largely at Joy Farm, where he used part of his time to compile his "second collection" of poems, written over the previous year or so. There are thirty-seven of them, grouped under headings in the Table of Contents as "Songs of the Seasons," "Songs of the Great Outdoors," "Songs of the Past," "Songs of the Immortal Soul," etc. There are also a number of narrative poems, in the worst manner of Tennyson or Longfellow, that retell historical events such as the Battle of Waterloo or Alexander's conquests. The best is "The Legend of Mt. Chocorua," which details Chief Chocorua's struggle for his native land against the puritan forces led by Cornelius Campbell:

The second Charles had mounted the English throne, and his round-head-hate
Had driven some 'cross seas,
While others on their knees
Groveled round the royal feet
At the blood-stained mercy-seat

The shorter lyrics in the collection are better than the narratives. While mature in language and theme, most are still fairly uneven: good starts are followed by melodramatic and didactic trailings off, often with religious undertones. But even the lesser pieces are fairly remarkable when it is remembered that the poet was only thirteen or fourteen at the time he wrote them.

Cummings later referred to these poems (and to those that had formed his "first collection") as having been composed during his "second poetic period," in which "the one and only thing which mattered about any poem...was what the poem said; it's so called meaning. A good poem was a poem which did good, and a bad poem was a poem which didn't: Julia Ward Howe's Battle Hymn of the Republic being a good poem because it helped free slaves. Armed with this ethical immutability, I composed canticles of comfort on behalf of griefstricken relatives of persons recently deceased; I implored healthy Christians to assist poor-whites afflicted with The Curse of the Worm (short for hookworm); and I exhorted right-minded patriots to abstain from dangerous fireworks on the fourth of July."

By Estlin's third year at Latin, he had hit his stride. He had done so well in French I that he enrolled in both French II and III, where he read Mérimée and Hugo and la Fontaine. In Latin he had finally progressed to the *Aeneid*, which he found far more stimulating than Caesar. History of Rome was also of interest, since it dovetailed nicely with his reading in Latin. But the class that most excited him was Greek I, taught under Cecil Derry, an enthusiastic and inspiring teacher who had recently obtained a Harvard AM in classics. In his lectures at Harvard, Cummings singled him out, along with Maria Baldwin, as one of the most influential figures in his early education. "Concerning Mr Derry, let me say that he was (and for me will always remain) one of those blessing and blessed spirits who deserve the name of teacher: predicates who are utterly in love with their subject; and who, because they would gladly die for it, are living for it gladly. From him I learned (and am still learning) that gladness is next to goodliness."

On October 14, 1909, Estlin turned fifteen. Among the presents he received was a book from his uncle George that would become a prized possession. The book was *Thomas Hood Jr.'s The Rhymester or The Rules of Rime*, a prosody text that contained a variety of poetic models and styles, along with a wealth of information about scansion, feet, meter, and rhyme. "The Rhymester diverted my eager energies from what to how: from substance to structure," noted Cummings. "I learned that there are all kinds of intriguing verse-forms, chiefly French; and that each of these forms can and does exist in and of itself, apart from the use to which you or I may not or may put to it." Thus dawned Estlin's "third poetic period." Within weeks, he was experimenting with new forms. By December, he had written a better than decent rondeau. Sonnets, ballades, triolets, and villanelles would soon follow.

Among the products of this experimentation with form was a sonnet that would become his first published poem. It appeared in the January 1910 issue of the *Cambridge Review*, and was written to commemorate the retirement of Latin's principal, William F. Bradbury, who had also been his math teacher. Though Estlin was not all that fond of Mr. Bradbury, and certainly detested the subject he taught, he rose to the occasion. The second stanza ended like this:

> **Now when we find ourselves about to lose**
> **Your leadership, whose strength will ever dwell**
> **In us and by us to the very end.**
> **We know no better title we can use**
> **In wishing you a final fond farewell,**
> **Than that which fits you best,—our faithful friend.**

Estlin's delight in seeing a poem in print quickly diminished, however, when he read the published piece, for the printer had omitted "you" from the sestet's last line. Although a small error, it cemented an everlasting distrust in Estlin of typesetters. Later in his life he would become the bane of printers, insisting on galley after galley that he would examine with extreme care, correcting the most minute mistakes.

That same issue of the magazine also contained a Cummings short story, his best to date. "This Little Quarter" tells the tale of a small but extraordinarily gifted quarterback for the high school football team who is forced to quit the squad in order to hold a job to help out his widowed mother. However, he answers the call to return for the season's last and crucial game, and manages to throw the winning touchdown just as he is tackled and injured. So serious are the little quarterback's injuries, however, that he ends up permanently paralyzed. While "This Little Quarter" is very typical of the "boy hero" stories Estlin read at the time, it also reflects the young writer's fantasy of triumphing over his own lack of athletic ability, while also revealing the possible consequences of engaging in a sport for which he was really too small. A year later, Estlin wrote another story, "Blind," which won second prize in the school fiction contest. Here the hero is a poet who goes blind but nonetheless manages to woo a beautiful girl away from his rival, the star athlete. Apparently, by this point Estlin had decided that art could ultimately triumph over athletics.

Cummings's notes on his adolescence, though written many years afterward, shed some light on the private personality behind the public doings. What emerges from these journal entries is a portrait of a precocious boy who, while inwardly beginning to feel the stirrings of rebellion, is outwardly still very much obedient to the dictates of his family. He dutifully served as an usher at church and passed the collection basket, engaged his parents in conversation and was engaged by them, and quite obviously enjoyed sharing in the life of his extended family. He sought his parents' approval for his fledgling literary efforts—and got it.

At the same time he was, as he put it, "breaking away, on the sly." This breaking away consisted mainly of smoking and masturbating, hardly major acts of rebellion, but in Estlin's mind they loomed rather large. He even wrote a poem, "Never any more, My God," which though now lost, was apparently in the form of a prayer to recite to himself when the temptation to masturbate arose. Judging from his journal entries, he apparently felt fairly free to disregard his own admonition, but this hardly freed him from guilt. "FEAR & SEX go together in my life," he wrote. "With sex I associate, also, GUILTINESS."

There is no evidence that Estlin drank while still in high school. This would have been a true revolt against his father, a staunch teetotaler, who had even served for many years as the secretary of Boston Mayor's Advisory Committee on Penal Aspects of Drunkenness, and was an ardent supporter of the Watch and Ward Society dedicated to suppressing vice, chiefly prostitution and drunkenness. But his father's piety began to weigh on him in other ways. One of Edward's pet enunciations, "Face the music," he found particularly grating. "How I hate that phrase,"

Estlin noted in his journal. His negative comparison with his father continued to plague him, as well. Estlin's relatively small physical size was still a major issue for him, as was his poor ability at sports. Acne, particularly on his back and chest, further intensified his sense of somehow being less than his father, who, as a grown male, quite naturally did not have to contend with the same problem. Estlin also compared his own genitals to those of his father, and came up lacking against Edward's "long black snake." More important than any physical comparison, though, was what he perceived as a serious character flaw: "lack of aggressiveness" or "lack of courage: not daring to ask for something."

He had other issues with his father, as well. Chief among them was Edward's controlling behavior. A small incident that involved a stamp trade Estlin made with his neighbor Edward Thaxter reveals the way his father asserted his authority. The deal involved Estlin's swap of a rare Tasmanian stamp from his collection (given to him by his father) for a Barbados stamp imprinted with a "sea horse rearing on it—pinkish faded" that Estlin found far more interesting. But when he returned home and boasted about his great trade, his father became enraged. He duly informed his son that he had been cheated, and that he needed to get the precious stamp returned. As a result, a sheepish Estlin was forced to ask Edward Thaxter to return his Tasmanian rarity, which apparently his friend did. But the affair left Estlin feeling thoroughly humiliated and miserable.

Edward's domineering demeanor also extended over his wife, and this, too, was cause for further schism between father and son. As an adolescent, Estlin was paying careful attention to the relationship between his parents, and began increasingly to resent what he considered Edward's unfair criticism of Rebecca, toward whom he felt very protective. He reacted angrily to his father's snide remarks about his mother being fat (Rebecca at the time weighed in at about 160 pounds and stood five feet four inches), and found his comments about her mishandling of his "hard earned money" mean and unwarranted. "All this overheard by me whom am(supposed to be)doing my lessons in library. I REVOLT ag[ainst] my F[ather]: would like to KILL HIM," Cummings recalled.

As for Estlin's social life, it still largely centered around his extended family and neighborhood friends. From his doting grandmother and aunt he learned the fundamentals of playing the piano, and delighted in family sing-alongs. His uncle George provided a fun-filled alternative to his father. With his uncle he shared books, little confidences, and excursions to the circus, theatre, and on occasion the Brookline Country Club, where George spent a great deal of time. A writer of vers de société, he recited his witty poems to Estlin, and, in exchange, heaped encouragement upon his nephew for his own fledgling literary efforts.

Though Estlin made some new friends at school, his main companions were still Jack Lanman, Edward Thaxter, and Francis and Alec James, whom he had known from his earliest childhood. With them he shared games and adventures, explored the neighborhood and the city beyond, at times even venturing into Somerville and Boston. But he was also quite happy in adult company, enjoying a number of his father's friends, in particular, Josiah Royce.

Royce's Harvard colleague, philosopher George Santayana, described him this way: "His great head seemed too heavy for his small body, and his portentous brow, crowned with thick red hair, seemed to crush the lower part of his face. 'Royce,' said William James of him, 'has an indecent exposure of forehead.' There was a suggestion about him of the benevolent ogre or the old child, in whom a preternatural sharpness of insight lurked beneath a grotesque mask. If you gave him any cue, or even without one, he could discourse broadly on any subject; you never caught him napping."

Estlin would have definitely concurred with Santayana's description. With fondness and awe he recalled Royce once picked up a book of Horace in Latin off the table in the Cummings parlor, and opening it at random, proceeded to translate flawlessly Horace's words into English. Cummings also remembered with similar delight the annual excursion to the Royce home at Christmas to see the tree and eat Mrs. Royce's cakes and cookies.

The summer of 1910 was an eventful one in New Hampshire. Having acquired a piece of land directly on the shore of Silver Lake, Edward decided to build a new house for the family. With the assistance of Sandy Hardy and some local carpenters, the large wooden house, with a flat-topped roof that could double as a deck, went up rapidly. From the Joy Farm log entries, it seems as if Estlin did not participate a great deal in the project. Instead, he spent most of his time at the farm, a few miles away, where along with fishing and boating, he dedicated himself to writing a poem each day. In this task he obviously succeeded, for a wealth of poems are still extant from this summer. In one poem, written that summer, when he was fifteen, he made an attempt to capture his philosophy of poetics:

MY PRAYER

God make me the poet of simplicity,
Force,and clearness. Help me to live
Ever up to ever higher standards. Teach me to lay
A strong,simple,big-rocked wall
Firmly,the first of all,
And to fill in the fissures with the finer stones and clay
Of alliteration,simile,metaphor. Give
Power to point out error in sorrow and in felicity.
Make me a truthful poet,ever true to the voice of my
Call,
Groping about in blackest night
For ever clearer,dearer light,
Sturdily standing firm and undismayed on a Pillar of
Right,
Working with heart,and soul,and a willing might,
Writing my highest Ideal large in whatsoever I write,
Truthfully,loftily,chivalrously,and cheerfully ever,
Fearfully,never.

While Cummings would, within a few years, no longer find such virtue in simplicity or clearness, he would adhere to much of the posture enunciated in this credo. He would become a poet of force, would use alliteration, simile, and metaphor to fine effect, would always be a truthful poet who sought to stand firm on a pillar of Right. And above all, fearfully, never.

When Estlin returned to Latin High in the fall of 1910 for his fourth year, he arrived more confident in his poetic ability and stronger—perhaps as a consequence—in spirit. Over the summer he painted a number of landscapes and animal pictures, and kept his vow to write a poem a day. He worked on a number of prose pieces, as well. A Wild West tale, "The Story of a Man and a Pack of Cards," tells of a rancher named Kingston

Clarke who has a series of adventures with outlaws and gamblers. (Interestingly, the protagonist's name is the same as that Estlin gave an imaginary friend with whom he "played" when he was five or six.) As a result of all this writing, he felt himself fully able to take on the important responsibility of being literary editor of the *Cambridge Review*, in charge of soliciting, accepting, and editing manuscripts for publication in the magazine. He naturally also felt free to publish his own work, including poems, prose, and sketches.

His studies, now at a fairly advanced level, particularly in the languages and literatures—French, Latin, Greek, and English—were also more satisfying. In French, he read Racine, Corneille, and Molière, and wrote *explications de textes*. In Latin, he worked through the last four books of the *Aeneid*, and toiled over composing precise Latin prose. English brought him Pope's translation of the *Iliad*, some more Washington Irving, and novels by Thackeray and Dickens.

Greek, under the guidance of Cecil Derry, remained his favorite subject. He read all of Xenophon's great battle narrative, *Anabasis*, portions of his historical work *Hellenica*, and attempted independent verse translations of a few Greek lyrics and some passages from Homer. The flavor and relaxed style of Derry's teaching is evident from the homework assignments Estlin submitted. In the margins of many of these papers, in which he ably rendered Greek sentences into English and English sentences into Greek, he also felt free to draw cartoons and caricatures. By the end of the year, he had decided to major in Greek in college.

College would soon be on Estlin's mind, for in the fall of 1910, Harvard changed its admissions policy for the entering class of 1911. Rather than require five years of study at Cambridge Latin, the college ruled that any Latin High student who could pass the rigorous entrance examination at the end of four years would be admitted. Although Estlin had not been an outstanding pupil—his final term grades were consistently in the eighties, with seventies in math—he was sure he could succeed in gaining early admission. Grades were one thing; brains, another, he reasoned. After consulting his parents, and persuading his teachers, he was allowed to sit for the arduous all-day exam in the spring of 1911. No tally was kept on how many actually took the test, but out of the more than one hundred students eligible to make the attempt to enter Harvard a year early, only two of the fourth-year students were admitted: Robert Cowley and Edward Estlin Cummings.

The graduation ceremonies from Cambridge High and Latin School (the two divisions having merged in 1910) were held on June 14, 1911, in Sanders Theater at Harvard. Two hundred and two students received diplomas in a fairly perfunctory ceremony. Estlin, just sixteen, was among the younger graduates. Despite his age, he was well-prepared academically to go on to Harvard. He was fairly fluent in French and had a sound knowledge of Latin, Greek, and ancient history. He had read widely and could write better than most. While secure in his knowledge, he was less sure of himself as an individual than he might have been. The relatively coddled and sheltered life he had led thus far allowed him to lag behind in emotional maturity. But an incident a month or so after graduation would help convince him that he also possessed more than a modicum of self-reliance.

On a sparkling summer afternoon in New Hampshire, sixteen-year-old Estlin; Elizabeth, just ten; and their beloved dog, Rex, went out in a small canvas canoe on Silver Lake. They had paddled fairly far from shore where the water was about forty feet deep, when Rex, in pursuit of a hornet, suddenly leaped to one side, causing the boat to capsize and precipitously sink. Fortunately, two boxes that were used as seats floated in the water, and Elizabeth and Estlin quickly caught hold of them. The bull terrier, meanwhile, began swimming for the distant shore. But at some point, Rex decided to swim back to his owners. "He was thrashing around in a frightened way," recalled Elizabeth, "He must have felt himself at the end of his strength and, hearing our familiar voices, turned back to us for help. My brother raised himself out of the water enough to shout loudly to Rex to go back. But Rex did not understand, and swam all the more frantically toward the voice he knew he could trust."

By the time the dog neared the children he was in a panic, and jumped onto Elizabeth's shoulders in an attempt to cling to something solid. She lost hold of the box and plunged under water. Elizabeth had just resurfaced when Rex again jumped onto her. For a second time, Elizabeth lost her grip and was pushed underwater by the weight of the frightened terrier. By this point Estlin was swimming toward them, shouting all the while at the dog who was floundering, still seeking someone or something to which he could cling.

"I came up spluttering," Elizabeth remembered, "and got hold of the box again.... The next thing I knew, Rex and my brother were struggling in the water; then I didn't see Rex any more. I could only guess how my brother must feel. I knew he would have done anything to save Rex, but he could not let Rex keep forcing me under water."

For some time the two drifted in the chilly water without making much progress toward shore. Finally, in the distance they heard a motorboat. Its occupants—Edward, Rebecca, Aunt Jane, and Nana Cummings—were out for a pleasure ride to catch the sun that was just beginning to set. It was Edward who first noticed the heads bobbing in the water and decided to advise the swimmers that it was dangerous to be out this far from the shore. "When the boat came close…the family could hardly believe their eyes," Elizabeth wrote. "My brother's voice, telling them to pick me up first, sounded natural, but actually he was chilled and almost exhausted."

The next day Estlin found the body of the dog he had been forced to drown to save his sister washed up on the shore, and carried it home for burial. Edward presided over the solemn service, then later crafted a cement grave marker incised with the bull terrier's name to mark the spot of the dog's internment. Estlin wrote Rex's epitaph:

Rex, you and I have loved each other
As dog and man
Only can,
And you have given your silent best,
With silent cheerfulness to me,
And now that our great mother
Holds your poor body to her breast
I come to give you my best, you see
Dear dog, to that pure Rex whom we,
We two, know lies not here at rest.

Estlin never had another dog. Edward enshrined the boxes in the lake house to remind him "whenever things seem to be bad."

four

A Smattering of Languages, a First Taste of Independence, and the Truest Friends

Unlike most of the 739 freshmen who entered Harvard College in the fall of 1911, Cummings lived at home. The arrangement made practical sense as it saved his father two hundred dollars in fees for room and board, fifty dollars more than the tuition. But Edward's main reason for keeping his son ensconced on Irving Street was that he felt that Cummings, who had not yet turned seventeen, could benefit from a few years more in the family nest. Cummings did not protest the decision, as he too felt he was somewhat unready for complete independence. At the same time, living at home deprived him of college life in its totality and made going to Harvard not so terribly different from being in high school.

His courses for his freshmen year included German, History of Ancient and Modern Philosophy, Physiology I, English A, and Greek I. With the exception of German, which was a new language for Cummings, the other classes were very much a continuation of his high school studies. While he did very well in English and Greek, and passably in German, he struggled, much to his father's chagrin, in Philosophy. The class simply did not interest him; nor could he apply himself to think in a traditionally philosophical manner. He did manage to earn a gentlemanly "C" for the year, and was quite content with the mark. Physiology I seemed to have been more of a health or sex education class, in which the students were given precise details of the horrors of venereal disease.

Perhaps because he was not so integrated into the larger aspects of Harvard, Cummings spent most of his first year there largely apart from his classmates, who for the most part came from far wealthier and influential families than did he. Many, in fact, could (and would) proudly trace their ancestry back to the Mayflower. There were also a fair number who came from more recent wealth, acquired mainly through business and manufacturing. Though he did have a white Anglo-Saxon protestant heritage in common with the majority, he found most of his peers overly privileged, pseudo-sophisticated, conservative, and quite self-indulgent. During his freshman year he would no doubt have agreed with George Santayana's assessment of the Harvard students he taught at that time:

> The students were intelligent, ambitious, remarkably able 'to do things'; they were keen about the matters that had already entered into their lives, and invincibly happy in their ignorance of everything else. A gentle contempt for the past permeated their judgements.... The fluent and fervid enthusiasms so common among European students, prophesying about politics, philosophy, and art, were entirely unknown among them.

But Cummings, that first year, did not seek out new friends among his fellow students either, or try to find exceptions to the general run. He joined no clubs, did not attend many social functions, nor did he take part in athletics. Instead, he spent a fair amount of time in the library where he read widely and often outside the established curriculum. Marlowe was a major discovery for him that year. Not only did Cummings respond to his "mighty line" and fine craftsmanship, he also found captivating his themes of love and lovers, particularly in *Hero and Leander* and in his exuberant translation of Ovid's *Amores*. So engaged was he by Marlowe that it was not uncommon for him to remain reading in the library until closing. An admiring librarian, noting the young "scholar" immersed in Marlowe, eventually commented positively to him on his choice of reading. Cummings later remarked that he was pleased with the attention, but was sure the librarian would have been quite surprised had Cummings informed him that it was not just Marlowe's literary merits that so engrossed him, but the work's eroticism.

One course he took his freshman year did hold his keen interest: the year-long class in first-year Greek, taught by a graduate assistant, Theodore "Dory" Miller, just seven years older than Cummings. Selections from Homer's *Odyssey* were the focus of study the first term;

the second semester was devoted to a close reading of Euripides's plays *Hippolytus* and *Medea*, and *The Frogs* by Aristophanes. Cummings was thrilled by both the subject and teacher. Miller encouraged his student to attempt verse translations of Homer and Euripides, which Cummings eagerly did. His versions, particularly of passages from *Medea*, reveal that the young poet was determined to render Euripides into English that was fresh and unencumbered by the locutions employed by nineteenth-century translators. Indeed, Cummings was as interested in making the poetry of Euripides come alive as in providing a literal translation. Medea's words as she is about to kill her children, for example, display her stark and dark conviction:

My sons, my little sons! ye go to dwell
In a city of many homes, a city vast,
But mother at the gates must say farewell

Into another country am I cast
Afar off, never to be reached by ye,
Hot-foot with joy from portals unsurpassed

Despite Cummings's less than exact literalness, Miller, who, unlike many of his own professors, was as attuned to poetry as much as to Greek, wholeheartedly approved the experiments, and encouraged him to do more. He also introduced his student to Catullus, Horace, and Sappho, as well as to Shelley, Keats, and Swinburne, and exhorted him to eschew Longfellow as any sort of poetic model. Within weeks of discovering Keats, the British poet had supplanted Longfellow as a model for Cummings. His notebooks reveal that not only did Cummings begin to change poetic styles (the didacticism, for instance, of many of the Longfellow-inspired poems largely disappears), but that the young poet studied Keats's craft with extreme care. Pages are devoted to an examination of visual and verbal images in Keats's long poem *Lamia*. One detailed entry, replete with examples, is entitled "Impressions Which Various Vowels Give the Ear."

The culmination of all this study was a poem filled with Keatsian phrasing that he wrote the summer between freshman and sophomore years. "Fame Speaks" opens like this:

Stand Forth,John Keats! On earth thou knews't me not;
Steadfast through all the storms of passion,thou,
True to thy muse,and virgin to thy vow;
Resigned,if name with ashes were forgot,
So thou one arrow in the gold had'st shot!

Miller approved of Cummings's effort, objecting only to the phrase "virgin to thy vow." He did not have such a favorable response to other poems, and exhorted his prize student to cut back on the sentimental locutions, and not to force or over-elaborate the imagery. Among Cummings's responses to Miller's criticisms was the leaner, tighter "Semi-Spring" that begins:

A thin, foul scattering of grim, grey snow,
Reaching out scrawny limbs, deep digs its nails
Into the bleeding face of suppliant earth,
And grins with all its broken, yellow teeth. . . .

While Cummings's paean to nature is quite in keeping with his embrace of Keats, it does have a far more modern cast to it than much of the verse he had been writing just a short time before. Though overburdened by metaphor, the description is nonetheless far more direct. Absent, too, is the Victorian phrasing with its poetic apostrophes and the line endings with forced rhymes. Cummings is clearly learning how to find his own way into a subject; as such, "Semi-Spring" marks a definite step forward in his ability to manipulate the English language in a fresh, original manner.

Toward the end of Cummings's freshman year, the student-teacher relationship turned into a deep friendship. Along with lengthy discussions over coffee in Cambridge, they took in the titillating Boston production of *Kismet*, in which a wide-eyed Cummings watched scantily-attired harem girls dive into an onstage pool. Miller also introduced Cummings to his favorite Boston restaurants, the Athenia and Parthenon. The food left Cummings with a lifelong taste for Greek and Middle-Eastern cuisine, while the exotic atmosphere would, a few years later, make its way into several poems:

… chased two flights of squirrel-stairs into
a mid-victorian attic which is known as
Ο ΠΑΡΘΣΝΩΝ
                                        and having ordered
yaoorti from
Nicho'
settled my feet on the

ceiling inhaling six divine inches
of Haremina   in
the thick of the snick-
er of cards and smack of back-

gammon boards i was aware of an entirely
dirty circle of habitués their
faces like cigarettebutts, chewed
with disdain,   led by a Jumpy

Tramp who played each
card as if it were a thunderbolt red-
hot   peeling
off huge slabs of a fuzzy

language with the aid of an exclamatory
tooth-pick…

As their friendship continued to flourish, Miller began bestowing books on Cummings, complete with flowery verse inscriptions. "But if I think on thee, dear friend, // All losses are restored and sorrows end," Miller wrote in a copy of the *Greek Anthology* he gave Cummings as a birthday gift. Cummings, too, was more than a little taken with Miller. "One friend have I of whom I speak out lovingly from my heart at all times," Cummings noted in his journal. "I love him as I love no other friend; I worship him for good, imitate him for worthiness. His life also has grown into mine. The honour of his friendship he has placed with perfect confidence in my trembling hands; if I do wrong, I commit an unfaithfulness to him who I admire most of my friends. If I do right, his the glory equally with the deeds."

Although Cummings noted in journal entries from the 1950s that Miller was gay, or as he put it, "queer," there is absolutely no evidence that the relationship between Miller and Cummings was anything but a friendship, despite the declarations of love on both sides. Indeed, Cummings seems to have seen Miller as an ideal older brother who was eager to teach his younger "sibling" all that experience and learning had taught him. Gauging Miller's sense of his friend is a bit more difficult; his letters to Cummings from the period are decidedly romantic in tone, though never overtly suggestive. If Miller was trying to woo his student into something more than a platonic relationship, Cummings appears blissfully unaware of it. Despite his interest in sex, his actual naïveté at that time regarding sex in any form, in combination with a staunch heterosexual bent, no doubt protected him at this age—he was a young seventeen—from even perceiving any attempt at sexual seduction on Miller's part.

During July, between freshman and sophomore years, Miller came up to the Cummings house at Silver Lake. Together they hiked in the mountains, sketched Mount Chocorua, swam in the lake, even helped Edward with his various building projects. But mostly they talked about literature, with Miller urging Cummings on in his own work and to further explorations of classical, medieval, and romantic literature.

Among the medieval works Miller urged on the apprentice poet was the twelfth-century French tale *Aucassin et Nicolete*. The *chantefable*, with its theme of love prevailing over family, war, lengthy separation, and imprisonment definitely appealed to Cummings. So did the unique style, in which prose narratives alternate with poetic flights. By August, Cummings had worked out a poem inspired by the medieval work, particularly descriptions of the fair Nicolete. His version is not a translation—even a free one—but an imitation of style and subject, a re-creation and elaboration of scenes in his own fashion, with a diction derived as much from the English Romantics as from Medieval French.

On the other hand, his translations of Horace, begun the following year while enrolled in Latin B, more closely parallel the Latin originals. To be sure, Cummings takes a fair amount of liberty with his versions, particularly with his rendering of "Ode 5" from Book IV (mistakenly identified in *Complete Poems* as "Book IV, Ode 6") in which he condenses stanzas, omits a fair amount of imagery and detail, and even alters, on occasion, the actual sense of the poem. Despite his lack of literalness, even in "Ode 5," the spirit of Horace comes through largely intact. But most important, he has created fine poems in English. His translations of "Ode 4" from Book I and "Ode 7" from Book IV, for instance, are triumphs of not only translation, but of art. His version of Horace's justly famous "Ode 7" begins like this:

Farewell,runaway snows! For the meadow is green,and the tree stands
Clad in her beautiful hair.
New life leavens the land! The river,once where the lea stands,
Hideth and huggeth his lair.
Beauty with shining limbs 'mid the Graces comes forth,and in glee stands,
Ringed with the rhythmical fair….

A reader familiar with the original will immediately see that Cummings has freely adapted Horace's lines. "Farewell,runaway snows" is more poetic than the straightforward "Diffugere nives" [The snow has dispersed]; the simple declaration "redeunt iam gramina camis / arboribusque comae" [already the grass returns to the fields / the leaf-hair to the trees] becomes in Cummings a slightly more elaborated image: "For the meadow is green,and the tree stands / Clad in her beautiful hair." And yet the young poet has also got it right: Horace sings.

Despite his enthusiasm for Horace, Cummings found much of Latin B, which he took his sophomore year, less than stimulating. With the notable exception of Horace, most of the course was taken up with Livy's prose and a play by Terence, neither of which particularly interested him. Perhaps as a consequence, Cummings did not take another course in Latin. Although the German class Cummings enrolled in as a freshman had not greatly inspired him either, he did sign up his second year for History of German Literature in Outline. While some of the reading appealed to him, Cummings did not take to the professor, the arrogant Kaiser-supporting (also distinguished historian) Kuno Francke, founder of Harvard's Germanic museum.

Much more to his liking were Bliss Perry's fall term course Lyric Poetry, and the year-long Greek II, taught by C. P. Parker. Under Perry, Cummings was introduced to Herrick, Campion, Waller, and Lovelace, and also greatly expanded his knowledge of verse form, accentuation, rhythm, and rhyme. Indeed, he was so taken by the class and the professor that he enrolled the following term in Perry's course on Tennyson. In Greek, he read Thucydides's *History of the Pelopenesian War*,

Aristophanes's *The Birds*, Aeschylus's *Prometheus Bound*, and *Oedipus Rex* by Sophocles. Like Miller, Parker encouraged his students to translate. Cummings happily rose to the challenge, producing a strong version of Sophocles's "Choral Ode" from Act One.

The focus on translation did not mean that Cummings was neglecting his own creative endeavors. Indeed, the young poet was learning craft from his work with other writers, and using it for good measure in the poems he was writing at the time. From Horace, he learned how to use metaphor more effectively; from the Greeks, directness of expression and economy of style. From his reading of English lyric poets, he was gaining a sense of stanzaic and metrical variety, and a greater subtlety over his themes. "Mist," written early in 1913, when Cummings was just eighteen, embodies a fair amount of these newly acquired characteristics. The extended metaphor is borrowed from Horace, the metric from Greek via the Elizabethans. The stunning last line, however, comes from no one but Cummings. The poem concludes like this:

> **As a great miser, morbid with gain,**
> **Pricked by unhealthy frettings, drowns dismay**
> **In gorging on his plunders, one by one,—**
> **Sudden—out of the vault of Heaven—the Sun**
> **Unlocks the rainbow's glory, and the day.**
> **The air is strange with rare birds after rain.**

Another major poetic discovery that year was Dante Gabriel Rossetti, to whom Cummings was introduced by his neighbor, philosopher Josiah Royce. According to Cummings, he came upon Royce as the professor was walking home from a lecture. "'Estlin' his courteous and gentle voice hazarded 'I understand that you write poetry.' I blushed. 'Are you perhaps' he inquired, regarding a particular leaf of a particular tree 'acquainted with the sonnets of Dante Gabriel Rossetti?' I blushed a different blush and shook an ignorant head. 'Have you a moment?' he shyly suggested, less than half looking at me; and just perceptibly appended 'I rather imagine you might enjoy them.' Shortly thereafter, sage and ignoramus were sitting opposite each other in a diminutive study (marvellously smelling of tobacco and cluttered with student notebooks of an ominous bluish shade)—the ignoramus listening, enthralled; the sage intoning, lovingly and beautifully, his favorite poems. And very possibly (although I don't, as usual know) that is the reason—or more likely the unreason—I've been writing sonnets ever since."

The effect of Rossetti on Cummings's verse was nearly immediate. Here's the opening of Rossetti's "Mid-Rapture" from his sonnet sequence *The House of Life*:

> Thou lovely and beloved, thou my love;
> Whose kiss seems still the first; whose summoning eyes
> Even now, as for our love-world's new sunrise,
> Shed very dawn; whose voice, attuned above
> All modulation of the deep-bowered dove,
> Is like a hand laid softly on the soul;
> Whose hand is like a sweet voice to control
> Those worn tired brows it hath the keeping of…

And here the opening of an untitled Cummings sonnet from around 1912:

> Thy face is a still white house of holy things,
> Graced with the quiet glory of thy hair.
> Upon thy perfect forehead the sweet air
> Hath laid her beauty where girlhood clings.
> Thine eyes are quivering celestial springs
> Of naked immortality, and there
> God hath Hope, where those twin angels stare,
> That sometimes sleep beneath their sheltering wings….

The intense Rossetti phase would last through the next year or so, until he was buffeted by newer forces that began to influence his style and sense of what was poetic. Love poems and sonnets, of course, would endure throughout his career, but would find radically different expression as he evolved and became more secure in himself as a poet. But from Rossetti he learned a great deal about form, metaphor, and rhythmic control.

Rossetti was not the only one who made an impact on Cummings that year. Having become far more acclimated to Harvard, he began making a few friends among his classmates, most importantly a young man, nearly two years older but in the class of 1914 (a year ahead of Cummings): S. Foster Damon. They met in Francke's German literature course, where the alphabetical seating placed the first of the Ds (Damon) behind the last of the Cs (Cummings). Unlike Cummings, Damon had already taken Harvard by storm. Talented as a musician, composer, and writer, he would shortly become president of the Harvard Music Society and was already an editor of the *Harvard Music Review*. He was also on the editorial board of the *Harvard Monthly*, the rival literary magazine to the older *Harvard Advocate*. But these distinctions were not what impressed Cummings most about Damon. What he most admired was Damon's profound enthusiasm and knowledge of all things new. In his *i six nonlectures*, Cummings credited Damon for opening his eyes and ears "not merely to Domenico Theotocopuli and William Blake, but all ultra (at that moment) modern music and poetry and painting."

It was Damon who introduced Cummings to Debussy, Stravinsky, and Satie; who traded him piano and composition lessons for Greek; who held forth about El Greco, Cézanne, and Matisse, leading Cummings to share his enthusiasm for these painters; who took him to the Armory Show when it traveled to Boston in 1913, where Cummings fell in love with Brancusi's sculptures; who loaned him Gertrude Stein's *Tender Buttons* and Ezra Pound's *Ripostes*, and later Pound's *Cathay* and his anthology *Des Imagistes* that featured poems in a totally different vein by poets such as H. D., Richard Aldington, James Joyce, Amy Lowell, and William Carlos Williams.

It was also Damon who encouraged Cummings to send his work to the *Harvard Monthly* rather than the *Advocate*. Cummings had, in fact, already published a rather undistinguished poem, "Vision," whose subject was Harvard, in the *Harvard Monthly* during his first year, but had not sent any other work before meeting Damon. Instead, in the late fall of 1912, he had submitted to the rival publication several poems, including "Of Nicolette," inspired by his reading the summer before of the medieval love tale, as well as "Summer Silence" and "Sunset." All had been eagerly accepted, and were published in the March 21, 1913 issue.

Indeed, the *Advocate* was very much courting Cummings, pressing him for new work, even inviting him to join the editorial board. Cummings happily complied with their request for poetry, sending them one more poem, "Ballade," but perhaps because Damon was urging him to join the *Monthly*, he did not readily accept their invitation to become an editor.

Meanwhile, the *Monthly* had printed some of Cummings's best work to date, including "Mist," "Water-Lilies," and "Music." Since the publication of three contributions entitled a student to be elected to the board, Cummings was now faced with the pleasant decision of deciding between the two publications, the *Monthly* having also invited Cummings to join their editorial ranks.

The difference between the two magazines was not just one of substance, but of style. In the words of Malcolm Cowley, "the *Monthly* and the *Advocate*…looked down on each other—or to be accurate, they nodded to each other coldly from the facing doors of their respective sanctums on the dusty third floor of the Harvard Union. The Monthlies thought that the board of the *Advocate*, which then appeared fortnightly, was composed of journalists, clubmen, athletes and disciples of Teddy Roosevelt, a former editor, and not a man of letters among them. The Advocates suspected that the Monthlies were aesthetes (as indeed most of them came to be called), scruffy poets, socialists, pacifists or worse."

Given these distinctions, it is not surprising that even without Damon's encouragement, Cummings opted for the *Monthly*, and with his friend's sponsorship, was made an editor later that spring. As a consequence, the *Advocate* never received another poem from Cummings.

As an editor at the *Monthly*, Cummings had an equal say in deciding what did or did not get printed in the magazine. "It was the custom for the editors to write comments on the material submitted, signing their initials, and the piece was accepted or rejected according to consensus," remembered Robert Hillyer, formalist poet and literary scholar. "Some aspirant handed in a poem that began with the line: 'Thou hast faun eyes.' Cummings's comment took graphic form—a small horned deer with large and soulful eyes. On another poem he wrote, 'Good but poor.' That has always seemed to me an excellent phrase, accurately descriptive of much that is published."

At the time Cummings joined the *Monthly*, he had no sense that the decision would be one that would profoundly affect the rest of his life. He was simply gravitating toward a magazine that was eager to publish him, with an editorial openness that he found quite compatible with his own tastes. But what he discovered, as he began to frequent the cramped offices, was more than a group of fellow students united around a common literary endeavor; he found "the truest friends any man will ever enjoy," who would remain friends (as well as his ardent champions), almost without exception, for the rest of his life.

To begin with, aristocratic and urbane philosophy and literature student Scofield Thayer, was the secretary of the *Monthly* who wrote the official letter on May 13, 1913, inviting him to join the board. Then there was the slightly stuttering, almost self-effacing John Dos Passos, who astutely looked out at the world through thick-lensed spectacles, who painted and wrote poems and studied languages, and whom he got to know much better during his junior and senior years. Gilbert Seldes was also an editorial board member. Raffish, with a dry sense of humor, Seldes was already on his way to becoming a writer and critic. Within a decade he would take up the cudgels for popular culture, which he deemed as important as any established (or establishment) art. Next was Stewart Mitchell, sophisticated, scholarly, and dapper, who would become the magazine's editor in chief two years later. There was also Arthur "Tex" Wilson, from Junction, Texas, painter and writer, explorer of Boston nightlife, who wrote Cummings upon his election to the board that he deeply regretted that the *Monthly* had not had the opportunity to publish "Of Nicolette."

Within a year, Cummings would amplify these initial associations to include Robert Hillyer, who would win the 1934 Pulitzer Prize for poetry, and Edward Nagle, the only close Harvard friend of Cummings who was not a member of the *Monthly*. But Nagle, the stepson of French sculptor Gaston Lachaise, like most of Cummings's other compatriots, was a confirmed modernist. Through Nagle, Cummings expanded his knowledge of modern art and began to develop a keen appreciation for European painting and sculpture. But most important of those he met that following year was the shy, pensive J. Sibley Watson, confirmed avant-gardist, who would become Cummings's closest friend for his entire life.

What they had in common, aside from coming from privileged backgrounds—the norm at Harvard in those years—was the *Monthly* and each other's friendship. There was no group mentality, no badges of identification that screamed like-mindedness, no secret handshakes or even codes of conduct. Thayer, for instance, was quite unlike most of his friends at the *Monthly*. The scion of an extremely wealthy family from Worcester,

Massachusetts, he had attended Milton Academy where T. S. Eliot was among his classmates, then traveled in Europe with a tutor before enrolling at Harvard. Tall, thin, handsome, with oiled coal-black hair, deep brown eyes, and a cultivated sardonic smile, he was the true aesthete of the group.

Though he personally emulated in his style and philosophical attitudes the English decadents—Beardsley, Wilde, and Burne-Jones—he was intensely interested in all that was modern in art, literature, or music. He was continually on a quest for the new—Picasso, Braque, and Kandinsky in painting; Brancusi and Lachaise in sculpture; Pound, Yeats, the Imagists, and the French Symbolists in poetry; Debussy, Ravel, and Stravinsky in music. He and Cummings did not become fast friends immediately, in large part because by the time they met, Thayer was on his way to Magdalen College at Oxford where he would remain for two years. It was only on his return to Harvard for further graduate studies in 1915 that they would form their deep and lasting friendship.

In contrast to the well-dressed and refined Thayer was the scruffier Dos Passos, who was more interested in life, experience, politics, and modern literature than in being a Harvard man (though, like Cummings, he too excelled in his studies). In the first volume of his *USA Trilogy*, *The 42nd Parallel*, he vividly recalled his dissatisfaction:

> ...get A's in some courses but don't be a grind be interested in literature but remain a gentleman don't be seen with jews or socialists
>
> and all the pleasant contacts will be useful in Later Life say hello pleasantly to everybody crossing the yard
>
> sit looking out into the twilight of the pleasantest four years of your life
>
> grow cold with culture like a cup of tea forgotten between an incense-burner and a volume of Oscar Wilde cold and not strong like a claret lemonade drunk at a Pop Concert in Symphony Hall...
>
> ....
>
> it was like the Magdeburg spheres the pressure outside sustained the vacuum within
>
> and I hadn't the nerve
>
> to jump up and walk out of doors and tell
> them all to go take a flying
> Rimbaud
> at the moon

Dos Passos's attitude had some bearing on Cummings, who launched his own rebellion against Harvard conformity, but even more than Dos Passos, he embraced, good Cambridge boy that he was, what Harvard had to offer.

Dory Miller still remained a close friend, but now that Cummings had peers with which to share the arts and good times, his influence and importance began to decline. At the end of Cummings's junior year, Miller left to become a professor at Princeton. Though they continued to exchange letters for a time, with Miller continually urging his friend to come visit (which Cummings never did), Miller became less and less a model, even a friend. With Damon, Dos Passos, Wilson, Watson, or Thayer, he could share more than literature, could allow more of his youthful enthusiasm for life (in all its forms) to emerge.

A further consequence of Cummings's socializing more with his new friends was that Irving Street became less of a haven. The friction between father and son that had already been developing during the years of Cummings's puberty became more pronounced. The young man chafed at his father's continual attempts to impose his authority. Arguments between Edward and Estlin, usually over small matters such as Cummings's unkempt appearance or infrequent attendance at church, began to occasionally shake the household.

But the rebellion was usually far from overt. "I led a double life," noted Cummings about this period, "getting drunk and feeling up girls but lying about this to my Father and taking his money all the time." With Damon he began to frequent Jacob Wirth's, a working-class bar and restaurant in Boston's Theatre District, famous for its seidels of dark German beer. On his first outing, probably in the spring of 1913, which was also perhaps the first time he had consumed much liquor, he ended up hanging over the Longfellow Bridge that spans the Charles River between Boston and Cambridge, vomiting into the river. The rather sordid experience did not deter him, however, from further drinking escapades. Healey's Palace was another, somewhat rougher, destination to which Cummings and company also made pilgrimages:

In Healey's Palace I was sitting—
Joe at the ivories, Irene spitting
Rag into the stinking dizzy
Misbegotten Hall, while Lizzie,

Like a she-demon in a rift
Of Hell-smoke, toured the booths, half-piffed....

The pursuit of women also began to occupy the nineteen-year-old Cummings's attention about this time. On a rather innocent level were the dances at Brattle Hall attended by the politer society of Cambridge, Boston, and Brookline. Among his dancing partners was Dorothy Chester, a young woman he knew from church, who could more than match Cummings's flair for the tango, turkey trot, and bunny hop. They danced so well together, in fact, that they even entered a contest in Boston, but did not win. Despite his appreciation for Chester as a dancer, he apparently was not sufficiently attracted to her to ask her out.

Instead, he set his sights on Amy de Gozzaldi, the daughter of a Cambridge language teacher. He knew de Gozzaldi through the theatre, having first met her in his last year of high school when he acted opposite her in a production of J. M. Barrie's *The Little Minister* at the Cambridge Social Dramatic Club. In 1913, they renewed their acquaintance when Cummings got a part in the club's play, *The New Lady Bancroft or Fanny and the Servant Problem* by Jerome K. Jerome, in which de Gozzaldi played the leading role of Lady Bancroft.

One scene in the play required the second footman, acted by Cummings, to kiss Lady Bancroft. Though Cummings very much wanted to play his part to the hilt, having developed a serious crush on de Gozzaldi, during rehearsals his shyness kept his "acting" quite timid. He was also well aware that de Gozzaldi seemed interested in the rather intense Harvard graduate student in philosophy who played Lord Bancroft, a fellow by the name of Tom Eliot. But when the play opened to the public, Cummings manfully rose to the occasion, planting a long kiss on Lady Bancroft. Such was his passion that neither he nor she would soon forget his "performance." It is unclear as to whether Tom—later and better known as T. S. Eliot—reciprocated de Gozzaldi's interest, or even recognized that Cummings was perhaps somewhat more ardent in his acting than he needed to have been, but on closing night Eliot did present her with a huge bouquet of flowers. Not to be outdone, Cummings gave her a poem that began:

Do you remember when the fluttering dusk,
Beating the west with faint wild wings, through space
Sank, with Night's arrow in her heart? The face

> **Of heaven clouded with the Day's red doom**
> **Was veiled in silent darkness, and the musk**
> **Of summer's glorious rose breathed in the gloom....**

Not quite a love poem, but not exactly tepid either in its declaration (or hope) of togetherness. De Gozzaldi obviously read it that way. Whatever designs she earlier had on Eliot had waned, and by June Cummings was borrowing Edward's Ford to take her on outings to Revere Beach, to the circus, and to the Copley Plaza to drink gin fizzes and dance to a live band. Cummings's perceived victory over Eliot was doubly sweet, for not only had he wooed de Gozzaldi away, he had also triumphed over an older, more sophisticated man, and a rival not just in love but in matters poetic: the young Eliot was a member of the *Advocate's* staff and well regarded at Harvard as a poet with some promise.

Cummings's courtship of de Gozzaldi continued over the summer, and while the two enjoyed each other's company, their relationship was more platonic than passionate, although he did note that "she grabbed me—first time a girl ever had." He also recalled one instance of "feeling her up" at Old Orchard Beach in Maine. From his notes, however, it is fairly clear that Cummings was more often than not very much the gentleman, fully respecting his friend's chastity, never attempting "undue liberties." A peck on the cheek or a warm embrace was about as far as either of them would venture. Which is not to say that Cummings was necessarily satisfied with behaving so chivalrously; he was simply very much a believer in a double standard regarding women. When he wanted a bit more "action," he and his friends would try to pick up young women they deemed "less respectable," which meant young women of a somewhat lower class.

Even when successful on these escapades, Cummings remained somewhat restrained. "I masturbated incessantly (secretly)," he wrote in a note that looked back on this time. "This taking refuge in my imagination (masturbation, self abuse) instead of seeking reality (women) is the essential characteristic of my life (ideas versus facts). It was accentuated by the fear of DISEASE which had been instilled in me by my family (danger of catching syphilis eliminated by masturbating).... During college I never once screwed a girl.... Thus my own sexual satisfaction was always a compromise. I never dared take a chance, or go the whole hog."

Life, of course, was a balancing act, in which writing poems, chasing women, getting drunk, or discussing modernism with his friends was squeezed in around Cummings's major task: classroom learning. And learn he did, selecting classes that not only interested him, but that challenged him and expanded his knowledge in the humanities. Even a partial list of the courses in which Cummings enrolled his last two years (1913–15) is fairly impressive. His comprehension of Latin and French, he decided, was enough to allow him to read other romance languages, so he signed up for a class in Dante in Italian, under the renowned scholar C. H. Grandgent. With George Lyman Kittredge, as famous as Grandgent in their respective fields, he undertook a year's worth of Shakespeare. With William Neilson he studied Chaucer, and under one of the founders of the relatively new discipline of comparative literature, William Schofield, he took Literary History of England and Its Relation to that of the Continent. There was also Greek VI—a study of selected plays of the major Greek dramatists—with polymath Chandler Post; and Leo Weiner's History of Russian Literature. Finally, there was Advanced Composition, taught by Le Baron Russell Briggs, the new Dean of Harvard College and President of Radcliffe.

The course selection is interesting given that Cummings's declared major was Classics. Among the subjects he chose there is not one Latin class, and only one course in Greek. Instead, his program of study reads very much like a curriculum in comparative literature. Harvard must have thought so too, for in his junior year he learned that unless he took more Latin, he would not be able to graduate in Classics. If, however, he attended more literature classes, as well as the year-long Greek 6, and agreed to submit to written and oral examinations in Greek language and literature, the college would grant him an AB in Literature with concentrations in Greek and English. And if he did well enough, he could even gain honors in his major. Cummings thought this was a fine solution since the prescribed Latin curriculum was long on prose, which did not much interest him, and light on poetry, which did. Greek, too, favored philosophy and history over literature, subjects that he did not find terribly compelling. The literature curriculum, on the other hand, was wide ranging. Accordingly, he switched his major to Literature, and in his senior year dutifully took the two-part Greek exam.

"Honours in Greek are at stake," wrote Cummings in a journal entry. "A written examination is over; this is the oral.… Professor Gulick…suddenly asks me to say something about Greek choruses. To my great surprise and mild pleasure, I reply that Greek choruses are like free verse. Free verse has just made its appearance in American letters through Ezra Pound, an expatriate, & Miss Amy Lowell who smokes cigars.... The Professor, hearing my answer, staggers slightly; (slowly turning) he strolls to the nearest window: Stands. Smoking."

What he did take is more important than what he did not. His selection of classes was far from random. He chose Dante because of his passion for Rossetti; Chaucer and the year-long Literary History of England and Its Relation to that of the Continent complimented his interest in medieval poetry that had begun with his reading of *Aucassin et Nicolete*. The Greek course, while mandated, also furthered his considerable enthusiasm for the ancient dramatists and for translation. Finally, the class in English Composition, long suggested by Dory Miller, allowed him to concentrate on developing his talents as a writer. But Cummings, unlike many of his fellow students, did not pursue these subjects only to gain scholarly knowledge; instead, he used what he learned in the classroom to abet his own literary ends. Out of the class in Dante, for instance, came his poetic portrait of Dante that concludes with these lines:

> Terrible, beautiful face, from whose pale lip
> Anathema hurtled upon the world,
> Stern mask, we read thee as an open scroll:
> What if this mouth Hate's bitter smile has curled?
> These eyes have known Love's starry fellowship;
> Behind which trembles the tremendous soul.

Almost twenty years later, Dante would still be a force; in his narrative of his travels in the Soviet Union, *Eimi*, Cummings returned to *The Divine Comedy* for the allegorical grid upon which to overlay his quite worldly adventures.

His study of Chaucer also elicited a portrait in verse, but his real tribute to Chaucer (and the medieval poets, in general) was his ballad "All in green went my love riding," which begins:

> All in green went my love riding
> on a great horse of gold
> into the silver dawn.

four lean hounds crouched low and smiling
the merry deer ran before.

Fleeter be they than dappled dreams
the swift sweet deer
the red rare deer.

Four red roebuck at white water
the cruel bugle sang before. . . .

Like Dante, Chaucer, because of his acute sense of language and rhythm, lingered in his consciousness. In the late 1940s, he would write a magnificent sonnet "honour, corruption, villainy, holiness," a true homage to the Middle English master.

But it was Dean Briggs's two-term course in composition that perhaps had the greatest impact on Cummings as a writer. Dos Passos, who also enrolled in English 5, affectionately remembered that "no one could help being moved by [Briggs's] lovely candor, his tenderhearted irony, and the salty small town way he had of putting things." Briggs scrutinized each essay that his students wrote every week, offering a sound and helpful commentary on style and content. Little seems to have escaped his keen eye. His model was clarity and precision, and with extreme care he cleaned up Cummings's essays, pruning overwrought language, dead phrases, mixed metaphors, personification, and empty assertions. His comments, while on the mark, were not always kind: "You write as if you put down combinations of such words as you associate with poetry and hoped they would mean enough to pass muster. Sometimes they have poetry that burns through the fog; sometimes they seem ill advised, not quite normal, as if caught from writers who lack a man's strength."

Cummings apparently took Briggs's admonitions seriously; by the end of the year, his prose style was considerably sharper, the language vivid, the "poetic" elaborations minimized. Briggs thought his final paper in the class, "The New Art," Cummings's first attempt to write about the contemporary movements in art, literature, and music, "an interesting and able essay, showing a good sense of style, good power of analysis, love of the subject, and a courage and persuasiveness of treatment."

For his senior year at Harvard, Cummings, who turned twenty that fall, was finally permitted to live on campus, where he took a room costing $155 for the year in Thayer Hall, a residence reserved for seniors. He was thrilled by the opportunity since he could come and go as he pleased, stay out late socializing with his friends, lead less of the "double life" that living at home seemed to require. Or, as Cummings put it, "now I could roam that surrounding world sans peur, if not sans reproche: and I lost no time in doing so. A town called Boston, thus observed, impressed my unsophisticated spirit as the mecca of all human endeavors—and be it added that, in this remote era, Boston had her points."

He frequently went to concerts with friends, took in traveling art exhibitions at the Museum of Fine Arts, and attended the ballet, where he was greatly moved by Anna Pavlova "who danced a ditty called Nix On the Glowworm into the most absolute piece of aristocracy since Ming." At the theater he saw plays and musicals, even a performance by Sarah Bernhardt, "whose each intonation propitiated demons and angels." There was also a fair amount of carousing and dancing and drinking and late nights on the town. "Nothing could exceed the artistry of Washington Street bartenders, who positively enjoyed impeccable Pousse-Cafés in the midst of Ward Eights and Hop Toads," wrote Cummings. "Nor could anything approach the courtesy of Woodcock waiters, who never obeyed any ring but your own and always knocked twice before entering."

Malcolm Cowley remembered that Cummings "became a gossiped-about figure in the groups that surrounded the *Monthly*. It was the only time in his life that he formed part of a group, but even then he stood apart from most of the others and preferred to keep his relations one to one. He was intensely shy and private in the Cambridge fashion."

Despite the greater freedom that he enjoyed by living on campus, Edward Cummings was never too distant. Robert Hillyer recalled that after a party thrown by Dos Passos, he and four or five others, including Cummings, fell asleep on chairs and couches in Dos Passos's room: "Early the next morning (or it seemed early) there was a knock at the door. Cummings rightly guessed that it was his father, the Reverend Dr. Cummings, the most famous Unitarian minister in Boston. The room was a shambles. What a to-do there was to whisk bottles and glasses into hiding places and bring some sort of order to the room before admitting the paternal divine! It went off all right; Dr. Cummings was either very unobservant or very wise."

On June 24, 1915, Harvard held its commencement ceremony. The June 30, 1915, Harvard *Alumni Bulletin* noted that among the speeches delivered at graduation was one by Edward Estlin Cummings, class of 1915, who spoke on "The New Art." That Cummings was invited to speak at commencement had virtually nothing to do with his academic record at Harvard, though he did distinguish himself academically. He graduated *magna cum laude* with honors in Literature, especially Greek and English, the only member of his class to achieve this distinction. But the speech at commencement was not tied to his scholarly accomplishments. Rather, at the urging of his friends, he simply submitted to the class marshals, who judged the open competition for a "Commencement Part," a revised version of the paper he had written in Briggs's composition class.

"The New Art" was not the result of his learning in Harvard classrooms; instead, it was very much the product of his own reading, listening, and looking. Its subject was "the parallel developments of the New Art in painting, sculpture, music and literature," a topic not at that time embraced by the rather traditional, even conservative, curriculum. Among the artists he singles out for their "courageous and genuine exploration of untrodden ways" are Matisse, Cézanne, Brancusi, Duchamp, Franck, Debussy, Ravel, Satie, Stravinsky, Schönberg, Scriabin, Amy Lowell, Donald Evans, and Gertrude Stein.

On an unseasonably cool June 24, a somewhat nervous Cummings rose to the podium to deliver his speech. Since entering Harvard, he had grown physically, intellectually, and creatively. He now stood at his full height of five feet, eight inches; his shoulders had broadened; he was much more a young man than an adolescent, though there was something still rather boyish about his face. The acne that had plagued him throughout high school and in his early undergraduate years had largely disappeared. His straw-blond hair, cut for the occasion, was barely visible around the edges of his mortar board. He wore his learning lightly, despite his intimacy with Sappho, Homer, Aeschylus, Sophocles, Euripides, Horace, Catullus, Dante, and a score of French and English poets. A *bon mot*, a pun, or a joke was more likely to slide from his lips than an intellectual pronouncement. His own work had progressed significantly in four years as well. The

Longfellow imitations that had come with him to Harvard had long been replaced with other models: Rossetti, Chaucer, Dante, Shakespeare, Horace. But his own uniqueness as a writer was also nascent; his poems were beginning more and more to resemble those of no one else.

The beginning of Cummings's talk, delivered with expression and enthusiasm in his somewhat high-pitched voice, went well enough, though the audience, consisting mainly of parents and relatives of the graduates along with a few local dignitaries, was perhaps a bit shocked by his championing of Duchamp's "Nude descending the Staircase," or his description of Schönberg's work as resembling "bristling forests contorted by irresistible winds," to which he appended the comment: "His work is always the expression of something mysteriously terrible—which is probably why Boston laughed."

The last part of the speech, however, which embraced the "new poetry," raised more than a few eyebrows. His first example of verses that "illustrate different phrases and different degrees of the literary parallel to sound painting," was "Grotesque" by Amy Lowell, who also happened to be the sister of Harvard's president, A. Lawrence Lowell. After introducing the poem by noting that "'Grotesque' affords a clear illustration of development from the ordinary to the abnormal," he went on to read it. Foster Damon recalled that "Sanders Theatre shuddered in sibilant horror as he recited: 'Why do the lillies goggle their tongues at me'.... One aged lady (peace be to her bones!) was heard to remark aloud: 'Is that our president's sister's poetry he is quoting? Well, *I* think it is an *insult* to our president!' Meanwhile the president's face, on which all eyes were fixed, was absolutely unperturbed."

If Cummings's quotations from Amy Lowell caused the audience to murmur, his last selection of verse from Gertrude Stein's *Tender Buttons* "brought down the house." "Gertrude Stein subordinates the meaning of words to the beauty of the words themselves," intoned a righteous Cummings. "Her art is the logic of literary sound painting carried to its extreme." He then went on to read lines from Stein such as these:

> A sound.
> Elephant beaten with candy and little pops and chews all
> bolts
> and reckless, reckless rats, this is this.

And:

> Salad Dressing and an artichoke.
> Please pale hot, please cover rose, please acre in the red
> stranger, please butter all the beef-steak with regular
> feel faces.

Amidst the gasps and titters from the audience, he concluded his remarks on Stein by noting that "the book from which these selections are drawn is unquestionably a proof of great imagination on the part of the authoress, as anyone who tries to imitate her work will discover for himself."

In his Norton Lectures, delivered at his alma mater in the 1952–53 academic year, Cummings wrote: "Officially, Harvard presented me with a smattering of languages and sciences; with a glimpse of Homer, a more than glimpse of Aeschylus Sophocles Euripides and Aristophanes, and a deep glance at Dante and Shakespeare. Unofficially, she gave me my first taste of independence: and the truest friends any man will ever enjoy."

five

The Graduate Student as Poet

It was not easy for Cummings to leave Harvard. By his senior year, he was truly thriving and so enjoying both learning and friendships that he decided to stay on for another year to earn a master's in English Literature. The course, as Cummings well knew, was not arduous; since there were no qualifying exams nor thesis to write, and the choices of classes were quite liberal, he did not feel himself in danger of becoming a stuffy scholar. Indeed, graduate study at the AM level, in contrast to the doctoral program, was essentially a continuation of the undergraduate curriculum that had already greatly nurtured his aim of becoming a man of letters. But the major reason he decided to remain at Harvard was that he had benefited enormously from his rich associations with fellow classmates, particularly S. Foster Damon, John Dos Passos, Sibley Watson, Tex Wilson, Scofield Thayer, and Stewart Mitchell—men whom he regarded as kindred souls, as equally dedicated as was he to pursuing the "new art," for whom experience of the world (and books and music and painting) beyond the brick walls of Harvard held even more meaning than classroom learning.

There was also Doris, a blonde debutante from Brookline, Massachusetts, a few years younger than Cummings, on whom he had developed a rather serious crush during the last months of his senior year. During the summer between graduation and the beginning of his graduate studies, they spent a great deal of time together. He visited her at her family's seaside summer home where they sailed, swam, and walked the beach under the moon:

there is a
moon sole
in the blue
night

amorous of waters
tremulous,
blinded with silence the
undulous heaven yearns where

in tense starlessness
anoint with ardor
the yellow lover...

Like Cummings, she was fond of parties, dancing, concerts, tennis, and long, intense conversations; unlike Cummings, she was a member of the country club set and was thoroughly at ease in high society. She owned her own car, a red Scripps-Booth roadster, and would frequently chauffeur her admirer on outings in the country where they would unfold a picnic basket and dine beside a stream.

Her letters to "Billiken," her pet name for Cummings, reveal that while she was quite enamored of her Harvard suitor, and encouraged his affections, she was not about to surrender her virginity to him before marriage. She also worried that men were only interested in her sexually: "Some people seem to consider a girl or a woman as being merely a 'toy'.... Don't any men love a girl for anything besides physical attraction?"

Cummings's answer is lost, but his subsequent actions seem to indicate his response. By the spring of 1916, he ended his courtship of Doris, deciding instead to obtain more instant gratification through women he could pick up on the streets or at bars.

With Tex Wilson or S. Foster Damon, Cummings would from time to time make forays into the seamier side of Boston. A journal entry records an escapade with three South Boston "shop girls" in great detail, including reproduction of dialogue: "oo, just a minute, a button's killing me, dear;honest i'll let you put it right back." This careful reconstruction of the spoken language would become a hallmark of Cummings's verse in later years, in which poem after poem would attempt to capture natural speech.

There was also an incident at about that time that involved Cummings, Tex Wilson, a prostitute, and, indirectly, Edward Cummings. According to detailed notes Cummings kept, after a night of serious drinking, he and Wilson drove Edward's Ford to the apartment of a seamstress named Marie Hayes, or, as Cummings described her, "a good-natured whore." Whatever expectations the two young men had, they were quickly dashed when it was apparent that Wilson was in such a drunken stupor he could barely stand. Cummings, always the good friend, decided to fetch some oranges to help Wilson sober up. While on his errand of mercy, the Boston police arrived, and seeing the illegally parked Ford "with a green cross on back licenseplate—meaning 'doctor' or 'clergyman'—hauled [it] away." When Cummings returned with oranges, he not only found that his father's car was gone, but that Edward had been duly informed of the towing by none other than the tipsy Miss Hayes, who, thinking she was doing a good deed, had rung the Reverend at three in the morning to tell him his car had been seized by the Boston Police.

Somehow Cummings got Wilson home, then arrived at 104 Irving Street as dawn was breaking. His father was waiting for him on the steps. Before Cummings could even offer an explanation, his father, staunch supporter of the Watch and Ward Society, launched into a tirade, accusing his son of having disgraced the family, particularly his mother. Cummings countered by noting that Jesus had also associated with prostitutes. The argument grew more intense and heated, culminating in his father threatening to evict his son from the house. "Go ahead," replied Cummings. At that his father began sobbing. Through his tears he cried out, perhaps to God or Estlin or Rebecca, who had by now joined the scene, or maybe just to himself: "I thought I had given birth to a god."

The effect of this statement on Cummings was profound. In autobiographical notes written thirty, even forty years after the event, Cummings occasionally mulled over the phrase, pondering his father's terrible moment of realization that his son was, in fact, a mere mortal. It was for Cummings an indication of how highly his father truly regarded him; it also served to show Cummings how out of touch Edward had been with the man his son had become for Cummings in no way regarded himself as a god or even approaching godliness. Indeed, he felt himself, at twenty-one, quite profane, a man of the world whose interests, aside from art, revolved largely around the flesh. He drank, he caroused, frequented burlesque shows at the Old Howard, fantasized about sex, and masturbated almost daily. How then to put together the schism between his own image of himself, of who he knew himself to be, and his father's naïve and lofty perceptions of him?

He realized that he was in no small way responsible for allowing his father to perceive him in such an exalted fashion. He had long withheld his true inner being from his father, preferring to practice deception, or as he put it "lead a double life." He had never engaged his father in a true conversation about what he was thinking or feeling and had never dared or even wanted to puncture the image he knew his father had of him. And yet, that image was a skewed one, if not a lie. But now the lie was at least partially exposed. Perhaps, Cummings thought, it was not such a bad thing. Perhaps it would lead to father and son entering into a more real relationship.

And yet, at the time, that did not really seem possible, either. Reverend Cummings was a man of such upright character, so utterly grounded in morality and virtue, so accustomed to sermonizing, that honest dialogue seemed doomed. The forces that were acting on Cummings had never seemed to attract, or even remotely interest, his father. "He is a man who never allowed the faintest suggestions of temptation to grip him, and expects the high and pure of his son," Cummings noted in his journal. How then, he wondered, could he possibly appreciate his son's all-too-human self? In the end, Cummings decided not to risk exposing himself for fear of being rebuffed. Instead, he simply retrieved the car, apologized, and was forgiven for the "unfortunate episode." It would take him a few more years to realize the true mettle of his father, to fully appreciate that he could share more of his own being with the Right Reverend Cummings.

Despite Cummings's sense that his father could not truly comprehend the complexity of his character, he nonetheless continued to seek approval for pursuits he knew his father could endorse. Although he had largely stopped attending church services, he nearly always showed up for Sunday dinner, often with friends in tow. Among the news he brought the family during the year of his graduate study was his part in helping to found the Harvard Poetry Society, whose faculty sponsor was Dean Briggs. The Society, whose membership was primarily that of contributors and staff members of the *Harvard Monthly*—Damon, Dos Passos, Stewart Mitchell (now editor in chief of the *Monthly*), Dudley Poore, John Brooks Wheelwright, Robert Hillyer, Scofield Thayer (back at Harvard after two years of graduate study at Oxford), and a few others—held regular meetings every few weeks in the *Monthly* offices, reading new poems to one another, and occasionally inviting a more recognized poet to give a reading.

In principle, the Society was open to anyone at Harvard, but in practice, membership was restricted to the select few who shared the founders' vision of the avant-garde. The gatherings, too, were exclusive affairs, with only members invited, though invitations were extended to the larger community when a guest poet, such as Robert Frost or Vachel Lindsay, appeared. Consequently, gossip began to circulate rather quickly about the Society. In addition to the general charge that the Society was a clique, a cruder characterization alleged that the group was populated by "pansies," owing perhaps to the inclusion of Mitchell and Wheelwright, who were both gay. The rumors reached such a point, in fact, that the *Monthly's* rival the *Advocate*, to which Wheelwright frequently contributed, printed a stern editorial denouncing the calumny:

> There has been gossip abroad concerning just what sort of an organization the Harvard Poetry Society is. There have been hints of effeminacy, of desires on the part of its members to grasp the flickering halo of aestheticism that hovers about the long locks of pseudo-geniuses. The falsehood of such gossip is something that is not to be discussed. But the seeming malice of what has been the current libel is something to be deplored and to be stopped at once. The Harvard Poetry Society is doing its small best to gain more intellectual and artistic benefit, by their meetings and the privilege of listening to well-known poets than is required to enter 'the brotherhood of educated men' by reason of English A and sixteen other courses. If those who disapprove of such endeavor do not care to join the society, or who, by lack of ability, are unable to secure admission, let them by all means remain absent. And let the howling, that is seemingly so much in vogue, cease. It ill-befits students with any claim to seriousness. Let those who scoff ape gentlemen, or let them at least swallow their sour grape scorn in silence.

The *Advocate*'s involvement in the fray does say something about the importance of poetry in campus life in 1915–16. What Cummings and company were spearheading through the Society was a radically new direction in poetry, very much in keeping with the international war against traditional verse being waged by poets such as Pound, Eliot, H. D., Stein, Amy Lowell, Williams, and the European post-Symbolists and Dadaists. It was a battle against staidness and rigidity, against "beauty" and clichéd poetic diction, against loftiness and metrical constriction in favor of spontaneity of expression and rhythm, free (or at least freer) verse, and fresh, even startling, images. No restrictions were to be placed on the subject matter for a poem; meter was to mirror the naturally occurring rhythm in actual speech.

Ezra Pound, torchbearer and major propagandist for making it new, admired, studied, and emulated by members of the fledgling Society, noted in 1915 that "poetry to be good poetry should be at least as well written as good prose." He further wrote that "emotion is an organiser of form, not merely of visible forms and colours, but also of audible forms.... Poetry is a composition or an 'organisation' of words set to 'music.' By 'music' here we can scarcely mean much more than rhythm and timbre. The rhythm form is false unless it belongs to the particular creative emotion or energy which it purports to represent.... There are certain emotions or energies which are not to be represented by the over-familiar devices or patterns; just as there are certain 'arrangements of form' that cannot be worked into dados."

More important for Cummings than any of Pound's pronouncements, however, was his creative work. That fall Damon showed Cummings Pound's poem "The Return" (1912) and as a result, a whole new way of writing verse suddenly appeared to Cummings. As he noted, "EP['s "The Return"] gave me (the rudiments) of my writing style." Because of its importance for Cummings, it is worth quoting in full:

THE RETURN

See, they return; ah, see the tentative
Movements, and the slow feet,
The trouble in the pace and the uncertain
Wavering!

See, they return, one, and by one,
With fear, as half-awakened;
As if the snow should hesitate
And murmur in the wind,
                    and half turn back;
These were the "Wing'd-with-Awe,"
                    Inviolable.

Gods of the wingèd shoe!
With them the silver hounds,
                    sniffing the trace of air!
Haie!   Haie!
          These were the swift to harry;
These the keen-scented;
These were the souls of blood.

Slow on the leash,
                    pallid the leash-men!

What did Cummings see? To begin with, the metric, in which no two lines are exactly equivalent, yet each is marked by a strong rhythm. He also quickly took in the liberty, even importance of spacing. No longer did a poem's lines always have to start on the extreme left-hand side of the page. Rhythm was about breath, about space. By starting a phrase in the middle of a line, a subtle effect could be achieved, namely that of changing the metrical balance, throwing both the eye and ear off-kilter. Such spacing also forced a reader to regard that line differently, feel its weight, take in its position visually. "The inaudible poem—the visual poem, the poem not for ears but eye—moved me," Cummings later noted in connection with Pound's bombshell. But most important, what the young poet recognized was that meter and the visual element of spacing could actually define meaning, for "The Return," as much as anything is about itself, about the way in which poetry is returning in new rhythms, new forms. Pound's influence would change the way Cummings wrote poems, not just for the next year or so, but for the rest of his life.

What Cummings learned from the work of Pound and others was nothing less than a profound revolution in poetics. It began in Europe in the later part of the nineteenth century with the French Symbolists, who in reaction to the floridness of Romanticism began writing poetry, chiefly short lyrics, rhymed and metered, in which an explicit meaning is subordinate to expression. In other words, a poem could no longer be said to have an explicit meaning; instead, it was the task of the reader to decipher what a meaning could be. More important than meaning, though, was the vehicle that expressed meaning: the language, which the Symbolists recognized was itself a symbolic system.

It did not take long for the Symbolist aesthetic to find sympathies outside of France. In Ireland, Yeats began to write his own versions of what he took to be Symbolist poetry, in which the mysterious and the miraculous are conveyed through a rich symbolic tapestry. Pound, who had gone to England in 1908, and who became friendly with Yeats, began to appropriate the new French tradition in his own manner in which the quest for a purity of expression, a goal of the Symbolists, was welded to the notion of precision. The result was Imagism, Pound's moniker for a movement that included (at least initially) poets such as H. D., Amy Lowell, and Richard Aldington. It was a reaction to the "softness" and "abstraction" Pound found in Symbolism. In their place was hardness, clarity, and intensity. Abstraction was out, concreteness was in, but "meaning" was still elusive. Of greater significance than "meaning" was "direct treatment" of the "thing," conveyed with a minimum of words, and with a metric that followed a musical phrase, rather than a metronomic evenness or strict accentuation. Form, in other words, followed function. Rhyme and meter were not superimposed on poetical expression but, as in Pound's "The Return," grew out of the subject itself. Free verse, as a consequence, was born.

Imagism itself was largely defunct as a movement by the time Cummings was beginning to write his post-graduate verses, but its legacy of placing such emphasis on language itself, on precise expression, of instantaneous presentation, and of free verse had worked its way solidly into the work of younger poets. The young T. S. Eliot, who began reading the Symbolists while a doctoral student at Harvard, and who had come under Pound's wing in England, perhaps best exemplified both the Symbolist and Imagist movements in his 1916 collection, *Prufrock and Other Observations*. Eliot was not yet on the map, however, but Pound was.

This is in part because not only was he an able practitioner of these new tendencies, he was also the chief "barker" for modernism. In his numerous essays, widely circulated at Harvard and elsewhere, he was seen as inviting a whole generation of poet wannabes to take in the three-ring poetical circus that was becoming the modernist movement. As a result, it was Pound who caught the attention of the young Harvard undergraduates.

Indeed, the Harvard Poetry Society would have liked nothing better than to have brought Pound to Harvard, but since he had long been living in Europe, it was deemed impossible. A more local practitioner of the new art, who lived across the river in Brookline, was Amy Lowell, sister of Harvard's president, who had been championed by Cummings in his commencement speech. As a result, Lowell was invited to address the group (which they also opened up to the larger Harvard community). On February 28, 1916, the flamboyant Miss Lowell, puffing almost constantly on her manila cigars, sat in front of a packed hall. For forty-five minutes she expounded on *vers libre*, then read some examples from her own work.

Though the talk and reading were well received, the discussion that followed revealed that the Society members still retained a fair amount of youthful bravado and disdain for authority, even an authority they held in respect. After a few polite questions, John Wheelwright, who would himself later become a distinguished Boston poet, rose and asked Lowell, "What do you do when you want to write a poem and haven't anything to write about?" Lowell, flustered, sat silently, glaring at her interlocutor, refusing to answer, then decided to exit. But before she could scurry out, Cummings caught her attention, and with a grin solicited her opinion of Gertrude Stein. "Do *you* like her work?" she retorted. "Why—yes—." responded Cummings. "I don't!" she yelled back, and made a run for the stairs.

Other poets brought to campus that year included Robert Frost, whose books *A Boy's Will* (1913) and *North of Boston* (1914) had been lauded by Pound for their naturalness of speech upon their publication in England, where Frost had been living. Not long after Frost's return to his homeland in 1915, he was summoned to read at Harvard. Though Cummings did not leave any personal record of the event, that spring he wrote a whimsical parody of Frost, perhaps indicating that he was less than overwhelmed at the time by his work.

It was not just the Harvard Poetry Society that was fostering poetic experimentation. Dean Briggs unwittingly found himself more involved than he would probably have liked in aiding the emerging shift in poetics. His class, English Versification, offered in the spring of 1916, drew not only Cummings but other members of the Society including Foster Damon, now also a graduate student, as well as Hillyer, Mitchell, and Dudley Poore. While Briggs viewed poetry through a conservative lens, he allowed students to experiment rather freely so long as they followed in some fashion the assignments that largely consisted of imitating established verse forms. In neat handwriting, Cummings filled up composition books with poems employing a wide variety of forms: heroic couplets, hexameters, iambic pentameters, Sapphic Odes, blank verse, and sonnets. A good many of these verses are rather hilarious (though somewhat sophomoric) parodies not only of conventional prosody, but of the poets themselves. In one tour-de-force titled "Others," he mimicked the style and affectations of William Dean Howells, Amy Lowell, Vachel Lindsay, John Masefield, and Robert Frost, finishing off with E. Estlin Cummings. Each poet individually was given his due; but Cummings did even more than that. The parodies of Lindsay, Masefield, Frost, and himself, while each distinct, also together formed a sonnet:

Vachel Lindsay
Time was, I cursed the newer charioteers
Who drive the wain of Art at break-neck pace;
Time was, I thought th' entire human race
Had been absorbing much too many beers;

John Masefield
Time was, I felt assured that this round earth
Was really going straight, straight, straight to H-ll;
Time was I thought of leaving home and hearth
For gaudy climes of gelded culture... Well,

Robert Frost
I was quite wrong, and I will tell you why,
And you will be surprised,—I'll wager that.
You see it was like this. Yesterday I,
Opening the kitchen door, saw our old fat

E. Estlin Cummings   Phlegmatically feministic cook
Weeping great buckets over Rupert Brooke!

Cummings was also writing more substantial verse for Briggs. A fourteen-line poem, metrically irregular, though simply rhymed in couplets, recalls the lyrics of Campion and Wyatt, with a mix of American folk song and traditional hymn:

When God lets my body be
From each brave eye shall sprout a tree;
Fruit which dangles therefrom
The purple world will dance upon.
From my lips that did sing
A flower shall bring forth the spring,
Which maidens whom passion wastes
Will lay between their little breasts.
My strong fingers beneath the snow
Into strenuous birds shall go;
My love walking in the grass
Their wings will touch, e'er they pass.
And all the while shall my heart be
With the bulge and nuzzle of the sea.

Briggs was less than impressed. "Almost too much variety,—or rather, too many licences of doubtful worth." In response to the rhyme of "wastes" and "breasts" he noted, "This will do for a rhyme if need be," but objected to the gratuitousness of the image of the flower being laid between little breasts. As for the last line "With the bulge and nuzzle of the sea," his teacher wrote that it was "bold rather than happy." What Briggs failed to perceive, or at least failed to remark upon, was the poem's originality, lyrical exuberance, tight imagistic control, and with a few exceptions, the natural diction. Cummings was apparently not too crushed by his professor's comments. Unlike many of his previous efforts, Cummings selected the poem for inclusion in his first volume *Tulips and Chimneys*, but with a few changes in word choice, and in a rearranged form that rendered the use of couplets less obvious. He also replaced the one "poetic" line, "Their wings will touch, e'er they pass," with slant rhymed, more natural phrasing: "their wings will touch with her face."

He also continued to press on Briggs a number of verses even more radically experimental. Among them is his remarkable poem celebrating Boston nightlife that begins "In Healey's Palace I was sitting" (quoted in the last chapter), as well as others—"stinging / gold swarms / upon the spires," "writhe and / gape of tortured / perspective"—that would also make their way into print. But undoubtedly the finest and most enduring poem he wrote that year was his celebration of childhood: "In Just- / spring when the world is mud- / luscious the little / lame balloonman / whistles far and wee."

Given the amount of effort Cummings was putting into writing, it is not surprising that he felt it necessary to slack off some in his other classes. During the fall, he enrolled in Bliss Perry's Types of Fiction where he read a dozen or so novels ranging from eighteenth-century classics by Richardson, Fielding, and Defoe to nineteenth-century books by Scott, Hugo, Eliot, Flaubert, and Tolstoy. Unable to deduce any real design in Perry's reading list, or make much sense out of Perry's classroom observations, he wrote for his term paper a rambling essay in which he recounted his impressions of seemingly randomly selected titles: Defoe's *Captain Singleton*, Le Sage's *Gil Blas*, Bernadin de Saint-Pierre's *Paul et Virginie*, Richardson's *Pamela*, Fielding's *Joseph Andrews*, and Goethe's *The Sorrows of Young Werther*. Perry remarked: "Very clever but don't do it again."

The following term he took another class with Perry, the English Critical Essay. Again, he failed to appreciate either the letter or spirit of the class. The notion of criticism just did not interest him, and in characteristic fashion he rebelled. Instead of producing the required paper for the class—a long critical essay—he chose to write a satire titled "MS found in a Bottle." In keeping with the parodies he was composing for Briggs, he created a literary salon in which William Dean Howells, acting as master of ceremonies, introduces George Eliot, who is to give a disquisition on "My Favorite Insect and Why" to a distinguished assembly of author/respondents—Melville, Hawthorne, Dreiser, Poe, Henry James, Tolstoy, Balzac, Flaubert, and Amy Lowell. Although Cummings quite adeptly mimicked the styles of each of those assembled, Perry could not deduce any merit in the work. He refused even to grade it, feeling that Cummings was not taking either him or the class seriously. Cummings apparently submitted a more sober paper because he passed the class, but only with a C.

He fared better in William Neilson's Nature and History of Allegory. The course had a theme, and the reading—from the Bible to Bunyan—resonated with him. Indeed, Bunyan's *Pilgrim's Progress* would later form the frame against which he would build his own allegory of his internment during the first World War, *The Enormous Room*. Along with Dos Passos, he also enrolled in Art and Culture of Spain, taught by his former Greek professor, Chandler Post. This class did not disappoint either Cummings or Dos Passos, though they took from it different inspiration. It cemented for Dos Passos his burgeoning love affair with Spain; for Cummings, Post's insightful observations on painting taught him more about art than anyone else ever had.

Cummings, in fact, was as interested in painting as he was in poetry. He continued to sketch and paint at every opportunity, frequented the museums, and made sure to take in any traveling exhibitions that came to Boston or Cambridge. From Post, whose interests and expertise were historically oriented, he began to get a sense of how art had developed over the centuries. But his guide to what was modern, even contemporary, was primarily Scofield Thayer. He had met Thayer during his sophomore year through the *Monthly*, and had spent a fair amount of time with him during the spring and summer of 1913, even visiting him at his family's summer home on Martha's Vineyard. The friendship had been interrupted for two years, however, since Thayer had been at Oxford from the fall of 1913 until the summer of 1915. Now, though, with Thayer back at Harvard, the two became close.

Had it not been for their shared passion for all that was modern, it seems unlikely that the two would have become such fast friends. Thayer, in many ways, was very much the opposite of Cummings. If a great night on the town for Cummings consisted of getting sloshed in one of the dives on Washington Street, then navigating Scollay Square with its prostitutes, then maybe taking in the raunchy burlesque show at the Old Howard; for Thayer a fabulous evening was to have his chauffeur drive him and select company to the Ritz, to the opera, to a recital at Symphony Hall, or perhaps give a dress party in his elegant lodgings.

But even the refined Thayer could, from time to time, be persuaded to accompany Cummings on his prowls for tawdrier entertainment. In one of his notes, Cummings recalled that one evening he and Thayer picked up a couple of young women on the streets: "ST & I—2 gals, 1 healthy & attractive, other wicked and sicklooking take us to Hotel 'Richmond.'" While Thayer knew what to do, Cummings "afraid of disease, only went to a certain point, being satisfied with only what would make [him] go off." While Cummings yearned to be worldly, Thayer truly was. Occasional slumming aside, he much preferred more genteel pursuits and company. He had his own box at Carnegie Hall and at the Met, was as at home in London, Paris, or New York as in Cambridge, or at his family's estate in Worcester, Massachusetts.

Hildegarde Lasell Watson, who was courted by Thayer while he was still an undergraduate at Harvard, recalled that Thayer was an extraordinary presence, one of those individuals "with magnificent looks and personality who, upon entering a room, will turn all heads in their direction." Remembering his attendance at a party at her home, she wrote: "Scofield appeared magnificently apparelled in, as he explained, an authentic Louis XVI costume. He bowed to my mother, at the same time remarking: 'Mrs. Lasell, I apologize for my shoes, unable as I was to find vermilion heels of the period.'"

She also recalled visiting Thayer in his own family home with its "high front parlor, lighted here and there by heavy-shaded lamps, its atmosphere as thick as night. On a table was a reproduction of a drawing of William Butler Yeats as a young man by John Singer Sargent, oddly out of place in that Victorian atmosphere.... I had admired it so because of the arresting likeness to [Thayer]. the similar flashing eyes and full expressive mouth.... During the meal, his fine resonant voice continued in what seemed nothing less than discourse; indeed all other conversation had stopped. I was later to learn this happened almost invariably wherever Scofield was present."

While Cummings was most certainly drawn by Thayer's magnetism and deep intelligence, his affectations and snobbery occasionally put him off. There was a genuine class divide between them—Cummings came from the bourgeoisie, Thayer from old money made in manufacturing—but these differences were largely put aside because of their absolute engagement in the arts. In 1915, Thayer presented Cummings with a copy of Willard Huntington Wright's *Modern Painting*, which Cummings devoured. For months they discussed Wright's ideas about modernism that attempted to bridge the impressionists to the cubists. Thayer was so enamored of Wright that Cummings began affectionately to refer to his friend as Willard Huntington Wright, Jr. A sonnet Cummings wrote that year, celebrating their friendship, is titled "W.H.W., Jr.," and bears the dedication "In Memory of 'A House of Pomegranates,'" a reference to Wilde's prose poem that Thayer had shared with Cummings. Cummings's poem begins:

> Speak to me, friend! Or is the world so wide
> That souls may easily forget their speech,
> And the strong love that binds us each to each
> Who have stood together watching God's white tide
> Pouring, and those bright shapes of dreams which ride
> Through darkness; we who have walked the silent beach
> Strown with strange wonders out of ocean's reach
> Which the next flood in her great heart shall hide?...

During that year, his friendship also deepened with James Sibley Watson, then a senior but the same age as Cummings. Aside from Wilson and Nagle, Watson was the only member of Cummings's inner circle who did not fancy himself a poet. He wrote short stories, however, and a good deal of criticism that he published in the *Monthly*. He was also a proficient translator of the French Symbolists and Post-Symbolists. It was probably Watson who introduced Cummings to Rimbaud, Verlaine, Mallarmé, and Corbière, poets who would remain important for Cummings.

Like Thayer, who was also Watson's close friend, Watson came from considerable wealth; unlike Thayer, he did not flaunt it. Tall, with fair hair and dark eyes, he was well-mannered, cordial but rather shy, even somewhat self-effacing. "Anonymous," "monosyllabic," "mysterious," was the way Cummings described him. Marianne Moore observed that Watson "simulates part of the landscape as if he wasn't implicated in it and yet he's all alert in there and responsible—so wary you hardly dare breathe, for fear you might be threatening his technique. Have to be as harmless as you know how to be, and try to imitate him for fear he'll go away, he's so natural." Hildegarde Lasell Watson, who would marry Watson in the fall of 1916, was initially drawn to Watson because of his looks: "Of striking appearance, he looked like someone from another era." To which she added, "I had never seen such a handsome person."

Cummings greatly appreciated Watson's quiet, critical intelligence, his depth, and his enthrallment with the arts. He was also perhaps drawn to his physical appearance as well. In a cryptic note written many years after an all-night drive from Boston to New York with the infamous Marie Hayes (of towed car fame), Cummings recalled his own physical attraction to his friend:

> Homosexual feelings toward Watson: (big, my F[ather])
> time we drove fr. Boston-NY all night
> with Marie (french seamstress)
> @ w. cuddled up — i woke him up ab[out] a sign
> sleeping—which way?
> @ arriving at the [Hotel] Breevort
> "No —you stay in the car"
> (about getting rooms) immorality
> he went to bed next day

While Cummings never acted upon his impulses, probably never even let Watson know of his attraction, the note reveals their association was perhaps a bit more charged than most of his other friendships. It's also not terribly surprising that Cummings would have felt some sort of homosexual stirring. He lived in a largely male society, in which his primary and deepest relationships were with other young men. His friends were his confidantes, constant companions, even inspiration. Although he did write a couple of poems to Doris, he also wrote poems for Damon, Watson, and Thayer that celebrated their devotion to one another.

It was not just art, good times, and the boons of friendships that were preoccupying Cummings and his pals. Though slow in coming, concern over the war in Europe that had begun in August 1914 gradually penetrated the complacency of the Harvard campus, eventually even disturbing the aesthetes. In 1915, Harvard urged its students to enroll in summer officer training at Plattsburg, and established military science as a course in the spring of 1916. The move was polarizing. A total of 864 Harvard men eagerly signed up for ROTC, while others began launching protests. The student newspaper, the *Harvard Crimson*, denounced the decision to turn scholars into soldiers, urging instead that students join the Collegiate Anti-Militarism League. None other than distinguished alumnus Theodore Roosevelt responded in a blistering editorial in the *Advocate*, in which he thundered against "the absurd and mischievous professional-pacifist or peace-at-any-price movements which have so thoroughly discredited our country." Though not mentioned by name, a major target of Roosevelt's criticism was an organization called The World Peace Foundation, of whom one of its trustees (and by 1916 its executive secretary) was another well-regarded Harvard graduate, Reverend Edward Cummings, Class of 1883.

Cummings does not record in his notes from the time any specific conversations with his father about the war, but given Edward's tendency to hold forth at the dining room table on subjects near and dear to him, it is fairly obvious that his son was being barraged with a fair amount of anti-war rhetoric. Edward's sermons during that period, always preached to a packed church, were often dedicated to pacifist subjects. Even if Cummings, by then an irregular churchgoer, had not actually heard his father's sermons, Reverend Cummings would have made sure his son knew his views. Fittingly, the calendar for the South Congregational (Unitarian) Church designated 1915 as the "Year of the Peacemaker."

Edward's isolationist position regarding the United States' involvement in the war was one belief held by his father against which Cummings did not rebel. At the same time, he was hardly as ardent a pacifist as his father. His position is probably best summed up in a verse he wrote in 1916 whose middle section contains these lines:

> The gloom
> is flat,
> as a poor pancake is
> flat;"My dear, our church sent
> three thousand bandages only last week
> to those poor soldiers"—Whew!
> how they reel
> those sweet people. But I'm
> going into the Parthenon [restaurant]
> to lap yaoorti with my eyes shut
> tight.

Other poems addressed the conflict with greater intensity. "From a Newspaper August 1914" (later retitled "Casualty List") is a rather sentimental commentary on the outbreak of war. "Belgium," written on the occasion of the fall of Belgium to the Kaiser in 1915, laments rhapsodically the suffering of the people, containing more sentiment than real feeling. The second stanza reads:

Oh thou that mournest thy heroic dead
Fallen in youth and promise gloriously,
In the deep meadows of their motherland
Turning the silver blossoms into gold,
The valor of thy children comfort thee.

Despite its rather formulaic treatment of war and death, it was Cummings's first poem to reach an audience outside student publications. It was published in the *New York Post* on May 20, 1916.

Here is a much better and far more biting poem on the same theme, which he also wrote that year and never published:

All is over,—a shrug from the world's broad shoulders,
    What more?
There is earth to bury a corpse. Is a nation's sword-
    edge dull
The world will whet it again, and a skull is only
    a skull;
And what cares the priest for a little stain on the
    altar floor?
'Twill wash; it is only War.

Cummings's father was not the only person urging his views on his son. His friends, too, most notably Dos Passos and Watson, were decidedly anti-war. Even the *Monthly*, with which Cummings was closely associated, and that had heretofore been largely concerned with art and literature, found itself drawn into the fray. A galvanized editorial board—with Mitchell, Watson, and Dos Passos on the side of the pacifists, while the other members aligned themselves with the "patriots"—began printing articles for and against the United States entering the conflict. (By the time war was officially declared by the United States in 1917, the disputes had become so fractious that the magazine ceased publication.)

Among the many pieces the *Monthly* printed was Dos Passos's story "Malbrouk," which details a Parisian woman's anguish over the fate of her husband, who is at the front. Watson's contribution was an article titled "Fair Play," which laid a large part of the blame on "Pan-Slavist" Russia for starting the war. Other articles, such as Norman Hapgood's "Germany's Disease," were a virulent assault on Germans and German-Americans.

That the magazine became so politicized reflected the considerable controversy brewing on campus, particularly after the sinking of the *Lusitania* on May 7, 1915. Professor Hugo Münsterberg publicly defended Germany, as did Cummings's former German literature teacher, Kuno Francke. Some of Harvard's prestigious alumni called for their dismissal, a sentiment that would have met with the approval of former Harvard president Eliot, who was urging for the United States' intervention. President Lowell, however, defended his faculty's right to dissent. More fuel was added to the blaze when John Reed, a 1910 graduate who had already made a considerable name for himself in leftist circles with the publication of *Insurgent Mexico* in 1914, returned to his alma mater in 1915 to speak out against the involvement of the United States in the war. Both Dos Passos and Cummings were in attendance.

Despite his increased interest in politics, art and love and friendship were still far more important to Cummings than any political cause (and always would be). Most of his poems and notes from the period reflect far more on these aspects of life than on his concern about the war in Europe, or even alarm that he might end up drafted. Indeed, he seemed to have no real awareness that the war could suddenly affect him personally. More important in his mind as the spring of 1916 came to an end, with another graduation again imminent, was the crafting of a poem for Thayer's wedding to Elaine Orr, a young woman from Troy, New York.

Thayer had met Orr in England in the summer of 1915. She was on a summer holiday; he was finishing up his two years of graduate study at Oxford. At the time she was just nineteen, while he was twenty-five. They fell in love immediately, and in the fall of 1915, Thayer made numerous visits to Orr. When he proposed that winter, Orr, with her uncle's blessing, readily and happily accepted. During the school year, Cummings had heard a great deal about her from Thayer. Among the information imparted by his friend was that Elaine was soft-spoken, refined, and gorgeous, or, in Thayer's words, a "lovely creature" with chestnut hair, pale skin, and large brown eyes. Cummings also learned something about her background. Tragedy had struck early when her father, a wealthy paper manufacturer, died when she was just eight. Two years later her mother died also, and she and her two sisters—one older, one younger—were put into the care of their uncle. He promptly shipped them off to boarding schools, first in Connecticut, and then to Miss Bennett's School in Millbrook, New York. At Miss Bennett's, a sumptuous "finishing school" for the wealthy, she studied the classics, French, art and music; wrote a one-act play; and garnered a number of prizes for her skill in equestrian sports.

In the spring of 1916, Thayer brought Orr to Cambridge to introduce her to his Harvard friends. Cummings first met her on May 20, at a theater party given by Thayer after a performance of Galsworthy's *Justice*. "My homosexual friend Mitchell and I were present, in addition to *les fiances*," Cummings later noted. "I considered EO [Elaine Orr] as a princess, something wonderful, unearthly, ethereal, the like of which I had never seen. She was well and expensively dressed, perfumed, delicate—the exact opposite of my mother (healthy, frank, stout, lively, plain, caring nothing for dress, no association with money)." It was not only Cummings who was awestruck. "I never saw anyone prettier than Elaine," remarked Hildegarde Watson. Dos Passos compared her to Rossetti's celebrated maiden. For him she was "the Blessed Damozel, the fair, the lovable, the lily maid of Astolot." "Not only men but women turned in the street, she was so beautiful," recalled Mitchell.

It was probably on that visit that Thayer asked Cummings to write an epithalamion for the occasion. Cummings was deeply honored by the request and set to work at once. Over the next month he produced in the best classical fashion (with more than a nod to Spenser, as well) a long rhymed poem in varying pentameters consisting of twenty-one stanzas of eight lines each. The first of three sections, with its extensive references to Greek mythology and literature, reveals better than any examination of the classes how much Cummings had actually learned as an undergraduate. The second section conventionally unites spring and love, and characteristically extols the loveliness of the bride:

O still miraculous May!O shining girl
of time untarnished!O small intimate
gently primeval hands,frivolous feet
divine!O singular and breathless pearl!
O indefinable frail ultimate pose!
O visible beatitude sweet sweet
intolerable!silence immaculate
of god's evasive audible great rose!

The last section of the poem begins with a Catullus-like evocation:

Lover,lead forth thy love unto that bed
prepared by whitest hands of waiting years,
curtained with wordless worship absolute,
unto the certain altar at whose head
stands that clear candle whose expecting breath
exalts upon the tongue of flame half-mute,
(haste ere some thrush with silver several tears
complete the perfumed paraphrase of death)....

and ends with a request from the gods for a blessing:

...O thou to whom belong
the hearts of lovers!—I beseech thee bless
thy suppliant singer and his wandering word.

Effusive, excessive, exuberant, Cummings's "Epithalamion" was exactly what a wedding song should be, at least according to the classical notion that it be a poem that extolled the bride and groom. It also marked a return on the poet's part to his earlier training, reading, and even composition style. There is little wordplay here, minimal irregular spacing, few syntactical departures. There is also a decided lack of personal allusions to the actual couple getting married. The groom, in fact, is hardly evoked at all, even abstractly, which is somewhat surprising given the close friendship between Thayer and Cummings. Indeed, because of the conspicuous absence of specific detail, the poem could serve as well for any wedding as for the one for which it was written. While this was also in keeping with the tradition, it was a real departure for Cummings, whose practice at the time was that of injecting reality, even in-jokes into his poems. The last lines of the poem do stretch the form a bit, though. Rather than beseeching the gods to bless the couple, he asks that he, the "suppliant singer and his wandering word" receive the blessing.

The closure may reflect more than just a certain devilishness. It is likely that Thayer had informed Cummings in advance that he intended to pay him for the poem. The ending could, therefore, be read as a wry commentary in which Cummings is beseeching Thayer to bless him with cash. It would hardly have been beyond Cummings to indulge himself in this kind of mischievous double meaning.

A week before the wedding, Cummings presented the poem to Thayer. In his notes, he recorded his feelings about the wedding, as well as the scene when he handed over the poem:

> I never for a second felt jealous of my friend ST [Scofield Thayer]. He was a king and she would be his queen, naturally. On the other hand, I felt no inferiority, rather pride at being his friend, at helping him attain his wish.... When my epithalamion was finished, ST invited me to lunch at the [Hotel] Touraine, asking me to bring the poem...After the meal, ST, to my embarrassment read the poem aloud. My misery was increased by the fact that everyone else had long since left the dining room and the waiters were hanging around, restless. He was very enthusiastic, which delighted me; although a remark he made at one line, "Lead forth, lover thy love unto that bed" [sic] ("Now we come to the interesting part!") I thought coarse. It hurt me, or rather my idea of him.

The wedding took place on June 21, 1916, in Troy, New York. It was a gala celebration, attended by the wealthy and their offspring. Although apparently invited, Cummings was not among the celebrants. Instead, he was in New York, hoping to get a job in publishing. He had come armed with letters of introduction from both Bliss Perry and Amy Lowell to various editors in New York. Perry's letters have disappeared, but Lowell's were less than enthusiastic: "Although I have very little hope that you will have anything to give him, perhaps you would be so kind as to see him for a few minutes and give him some excellent advice."

The editors apparently followed Lowell's recommendation. Cummings wrote to his parents of his travails:

> After keeping me on edge for three days, [Frank] Crowninshield [the editor of *Vanity Fair*] showed me in an hour and a half that my humour was not of the "Vanity Fair" variety, etc.—which I knew all the time.... A healthy humiliation, Estlin—as Sco [Scofield Thayer] might say. Afterward in the open air I was thankful as I was doubtful all along whether I could do ha has and poems at the same time.... I am now on the trail of a livelihood thru Mrs. Roberts of "the Craftsman." Her husband edits the "Digest." If he has not work for me, she has promised "a strong letter" to every editor in N.Y. individually—most generous lady. Of course I have seen nearly all. But I shall get two or three letters to great unknowns from her, and stick to it for a while longer.

In a postscript, he added, "I feel like the 'questing Beast' of Malory." The allusion, though probably intended as playful, was actually right on the mark. Like Malory's mythic beast, who was never brought to heel on earth, Cummings's unsuccessful job search allowed him to remain outside the world of work.

While it does not seem as though he was terribly bothered by not coming up with employment, whatever sting of rejection he might have felt was quickly mitigated when, upon his return to Cambridge, he received a one thousand-dollar check from Thayer, who indeed remembered to bless the "suppliant singer" of the wedding ode. Cummings was ecstatic. He saw the cash—the equivalent of about fifteen thousand twenty-first-century dollars—as the means by which he could make his way in the world as an artist. His father, on the other hand, was outraged, or as Cummings recalled, "furious at me for accepting it [the check]. He had always worked hard all his life and considered the money 'unearned.'"

Although Cummings very much wanted to leave Cambridge and what he saw as the rather stultifying atmosphere of 104 Irving Street, he also noted in the letter he sent to his family from New York that a job might interfere with his work as a poet. As a result, he decided to bide his time and devote himself to his art. His decision to remain in Cambridge, at least for a few months, would turn out to be a wise move. Over that summer and early fall he would polish his craft as a poet and explore how he could make himself into an artist.

six

Poetic Excursions

The summer and early fall of 1916 was, for the twenty-one-year-old Cummings, a period of intense artistic experimentation. After receiving his master's, he decided to remain in Cambridge in order to take full advantage of the free room and board so that he could dedicate himself to writing and painting without having to worry about supporting himself. Whatever desires he had for greater freedom were mitigated by the arrangement. As he wrote Thayer, "Up at 10, bed at 2:00 AM. I am king—by the which,would say,writing when I should, & loafing when I should/not." The work foremost in his mind was gathering together a batch of poems for publication in an anthology that his friend Stewart Mitchell was proposing.

The idea had come to Mitchell in the spring of 1916 during the end of his tenure as editor in chief of the *Monthly*. Spurred by the realization that he and most of his friends were graduating, or had graduated, and would therefore not have the Harvard publications in which to place their work, he began to explore possibilities for their continued appearances in print. By the summer, he was moving ahead on the project, tentatively titled *Seven Harvard Poets*. The seven were Cummings, Damon, Dos Passos, Hillyer, Dudley Poore, and Cuthbert Wright. By the fall, a friend of Hillyer's, William Norris, was added and the volume became *Eight Harvard Poets*.

Cummings selected eight of his poems for the book: four sonnets and four free-verse experiments. The four sonnets were "Thou in whose swordgreat story shine the deeds;" "when thou hast taken thy last applause,and when;" "this is the garden:colours come and go;" and "it may not always be so;and i say." The four others were "i will wade out" (which he titled "Crepuscule" in the collection); "Finis;" "you little voice;" and "Tumbling-hair" (titled "Epitaph" in the collection). All but "Finis" were later republished by Cummings in his first books, but with the titles dropped. Unlike most of the contributors who submitted poems previously published in the *Monthly* or the *Advocate*, only one of Cummings's verses had appeared earlier: "it may not always be so;and i say." The other poems were mostly written during that summer, perhaps with the anthology in mind.

Of the sonnets, two are quite remarkable. "Thou in whose swordgreat story shine the deeds," while ostensibly a eulogy honoring Jean Froissart, the fourteenth-century Flemish chronicler of war, the poem is also a commentary on the war being waged in Europe. Written in the intricately rhymed and metered Italian variant sonnet style of Rossetti, with skillful use of enjambment to propel the lines forward, the poem is highly sophisticated in its craft.

The second sonnet of distinction is "this is the garden." This poem, later frequently anthologized, was written, as many of Cummings's best poems were, as a response to nature. In this case, the garden described was that of the Watson estate in Rochester, New York, which Cummings visited with his friend J. Sibley Watson during either the summer of 1915 or 1916. The original, probably composed on location, was given to Watson's mother, who preserved it in her guest book. The published version, though containing the same words, is punctuated quite differently, and with most of the capital letters lowercased. Instead of four stanzas, it has only two, with Cummings's trademark parentheses enclosing the seventh line, "(of harps celestial to the quivering string)."

In the original version, the first two stanzas (combined into one in later versions) looked like this:

This is the garden. Colors come and go:
Frail azures fluttering from night's outer wing,
Strong silent greens serenely lingering,

Absolute lights like baths of golden snow.
This is the garden. Purséd lips do blow
Upon cool flutes within wide glooms, and sing—
Of harps celestial to the quivering string—
Invisible faces, hauntingly and slow.

It is not surprising that Cummings altered the poem, for over that summer and early fall he truly began to free his poetry from convention—even when written in conventional forms. In October, just after his twenty-second birthday, he wrote to Thayer that "about the end of Sept., I definitely denied myself all punctuation.... When I'm strong enough maybe I'll come back to the cute little commas and silly colons."

His notebooks testify to the amount of labor he expended in his effort to create radically new directions in writing. For instance, "Crepuscule," went through a number of changes. At one point he even considered running every other line backwards so that instead of the poem's opening looking like this:

I will wade out
                                        till my thighs are steeped in burn-
ing flowers.

it looked like this:

                                                                        I will wade out

                                        srewolf gninrub ni depeets era shgiht ym llit

In the end, he opted for running all the lines left to right but with great liberties in spacing, in the style of Pound's "The Return." He also later dropped the title, a wise decision since the poem has little to do with twilight. Here's the poem as it appeared in *Eight Harvard Poets*:

I will wade out
                                        till my thighs are steeped in burning flowers.
i will take the sun in my mouth
and leap into the ripe air
                                        Alive
                                                with closed eyes
to dash against darkness
                                        in the sleeping curves of my body
Shall enter fingers of smooth mastery
with chasteness of sea-girls
                                        Will I complete the mystery
                                        of my flesh

I will rise
After a thousand years
lipping
flowers
And set my teeth in the silver of the moon

The ultimate effect, as Cummings had hoped, was that the poem's form presents itself to the eye, thereby focusing attention on the actual shape. In doing so it becomes quickly apparent that the reader is drawn not just aurally or intellectually, but visually as well, into the movement described in the poem. There is nothing arbitrary about the spacing; Cummings saw these phrases as units that in addition to what they say, have an individual existence as visual entities. Likewise, the setting off of single words like "lipping," "flowers," and the capitalized "Alive," gives these words more weight, causes the reader to pause, linger for a while, take in their meaning.

Pound, of course, had first awakened in Cummings the notion that a poem could have a pictorial presence. But Pound was not the only influence. At the same time Cummings was beginning his poetic explorations with spacing and rhythms, he was also painting a series of semi-abstract canvases in a style quite his own but indebted to the cubists. As he described it, "organizations of colour and line." The experimentation with the two art forms overlapped, one reinforcing the other. Just as he observed that in painting the whole was larger than the sum of its parts, yet each part contributed to the whole, so too was the arrangement of words on a page. He likened word-craft to that of a crazy quilt, "made so that every inch of it seems good to me. And so that if you put your hand over one inch,the other inches loose in force. And so that in every inch there is a binding rhythm which integrates the whole thing and makes it a single moving ThingInItself."

The writer William Slater Brown, a lifelong friend of Cummings, perceptively noted the relationship between the poet's paintings and his poems:

> His knowledge of word value is as profound as his knowledge of color, and it is largely for this reason, because he has carried over the eye and method of art into the field of poetry, that the fresh, living, glamorous forms he has

> created seem so intangible....The spatial organization of color has become the durational organization of words, the technical problem that of tempo. Words, like planes in abstract painting, function not as units in a logical structure, but as units functioning in a vital and organic structure of time. Logic and all its attributes of grammar, spelling and punctuation, become subservient to the imperial demands of form. The words must come at the *moment juste*, the spark perfectly timed must ignite them at their fullest incipient power.

That summer and fall, Cummings continued to work on poems that would provide, in Dos Passos's phrase, "excitement for the eye." Among his bolder experiments was a poem (or "fait" as he referred to these verses) that integrates sound into shape. The subject matter is a rather ordinary drunken conversation, but the arrangement of vowel sounds into columns is anything but ordinary: Cummings wrote a note to himself at the bottom of the page that shows what he was trying to achieve:

> In Music there are (12) units which differ in pitch, corresponding to the (19) vowel sounds; BUT the representation of the occurrence of any and all these units by a common symbol, whose form (or picture) changes only to portray prolongation, confers a suitability to horizontal progression which does not exist in the case of a fait where the sound (units) are presented by visible equivalents (generally speaking) calling for vertical progression.

In other words, Cummings was attempting to combine the temporal (horizontal) qualities of sound with a visual (vertical) presentation.

It is quite evident, both from the untitled poem and the poet's note, that he was working quite hard at breaking the mold, was attempting to create poetry that could appeal equally to the eye, ear, and mind. Also, here is the first instance of a poetic practice that would later become a hallmark of his style: running words together to mimic speech as it was heard.

                       two   brass   buttonsoff
                       your   scar   let   coatlo
                                        ret   taone   old   dint
                                        ed   and
                a   new   one
                       you   don't   re
                                        mem
                               ber
                       you   were   drunk
                                        when
        i   askedret   ta   for   the
                                                                rose in
                               her
                hair
                       you   can't   havethatshe
        smiled   lar
                riehe
                                                                        give
                methe
                       bloom
                ain't   itpretty
                                                but   kid
                       you   gut
                a
        knife   yes   op'   nit   thanks
        my
                teeth
                aint   strong   it's   the
                       booze   gets 'm   and   she
                                                                                hands
                methe
                       two   brass   buttons
                                                nev
                       er   drink
dear

"The day of the spoken lyric is past," he noted in his journal. "The poem which has taken its place does not sing itself;it builds itself,three dimensionally, gradually,subtly,in the consciousness of the experience." This wasn't just posturing. He labored to turn these ideas into practice. Among his papers from this period are charts based on the color wheel, as well as long lists on consonant and consonant-vowel combinations. He filled pages with notations on syllable qualities, and divided consonants into combinational categories: primal, intermediate, and final. To these he added vowels to create word lists. The word lists occasionally were arranged into poems:

of bunged mug
blousy gob
glued lipped
muddle lidded

ole liz
goggle glimmed
bag bodied
pimple bummed

slow slob-
bers down
babble belly
blubber boobied

Cummings was so involved with words and sounds, so attuned to the nuances of pitch and tone residing in common phrases, that even his letters during this period reveal his preoccupation. On October 14, Cummings's twenty-second birthday, James Sibley Watson married Hildegarde Lasell in a "sumptuously arranged wedding" at Lasell's home in Whitinsville, Massachusetts. In a letter written to Watson the day after the event, he rendered a remark by Watson's uncle this way:

```
                                        sf
                                      g  o              !
                 in  lin            n    r
              sure       g           i     a
         plea                       m       s
     take                           m        peec       !
  I           cal  on         u                h
                              C
                         Mr.                             !
```

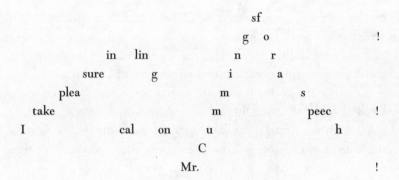

(I take pleasure in calling on Mr. Cummings for a speech!)

Cummings never published any of these "faits," nor (like many of these early radical experiments in language) were they included in the so-called *Complete Poems 1904–1962*. He did not send them to Mitchell, either, opting instead for the somewhat tamer mix of verse noted earlier.

Mitchell, in fact, had moved ahead with the anthology. After having it rejected by Houghton-Mifflin, in the fall of 1916, he presented the manuscript to an acquaintance of his aunt's, a New York publisher named Laurence Gomme. Publishing was actually Gomme's sideline, his main business being bookselling at his store The Little Book Shop Around the Corner, located at 2 East 29th Street. Nonetheless, he had already published some handsome volumes by authors such as Hilaire Belloc, Joyce Kilmer, John Jay Chapman, and Clement Wood. His predecessor in the business, Mitchell Kennerly, had had the distinction of bringing out Edna St. Vincent Millay's first book, *Renascence and Other Poems*, written while an undergraduate at Vassar. Once he had received *Eight Harvard Poets*, he sent it out to his reader, the critic and traditional poet Clement Wood. On October 19, 1916, Wood responded noting that "it contains…enough good poetry to warrant its publication." He did remark, though, that the collection also contained "crudities…that wider experience would eradicate." This comment was aimed directly at Cummings. He went on to elucidate his criticism:

> The first poet, Cummings, I might use as an example of this. Even his grammar is sometimes bad (as in line 2 of the opening poem, which should be "soundest," shouldn't it); the line

> before he has used "history her heroes" which is a silly archaism, to me; and in his third sonnet, the 7th line is a dreadful inversion. To the contrary, the second sonnet's last line is quite more effective; and his *vers libre*, while affected, is pleasing. I feel more maturity would rub these artificial excresences from his work, and let him say in a thoroughly understandable manner what he is getting at. Take him all in all, he is only fair.

Of the other poets in the anthology, he approved of all but Damon's work, which he found "more like Cummings, inclined to be too much only a fair distiller of overused poetic material."

Probably because of Wood's enthusiasm for the majority of poets in the collection, Gomme decided to publish the book. But because he feared that sales would be slim, he wrote to Mitchell that he could only undertake publication if each of the authors agreed to buy thirty copies at sixty-six cents each (two-thirds of the dollar retail price). All agreed to the arrangement, expecting that soon the book would see the light of print. More wrangling was to come, however.

The first issue was Cummings's typography. While preparing the manuscript for the printer, Gomme decided to take exception to the use of small "i"s in Cummings's poem "Crepuscule." Whether he communicated with Cummings or not about the matter is unclear, since no letters between Cummings and Gomme have survived. But Dos Passos weighed in on the matter at the end of the year, writing to Gomme that he could be "as high handed" as he liked. In January of 1917, another contributor, Cuthbert Wright, suggested to Gomme that if Cummings made any difficulty about the poem it could be omitted. In the end, the uncapitalized pronoun was capitalized, with or without Cummings's approval.

This was not the only matter holding up publication. Gomme was struggling as a bookseller. Even with the money he knew he would receive from the eight authors to help pay the printer's bill, he did not feel he could go forward with the anthology. Finally, John Dos Passos, now in Europe but still very much involved in the process, persuaded his father, a wealthy Washington lawyer, to put up $750 to pay the printer. This act of largesse, however, did not end the matter, for at the end of January, Dos Passos Sr. died of complications from pneumonia. The estate, however, had plenty of cash to subvent the publication, as John Dos Passos assured Gomme.

Still, a book did not emerge. In May 1917, Gomme closed up the bookshop, and the collection was left in limbo. After a great deal of further negotiation and a few threats, including one from Edward Cummings, *Eight Harvard Poets* was finally published in August of 1917 in an edition of two thousand copies. According to Gomme, each author received one hundred copies, but letters from the contributors to Gomme indicate that most of the poets (or their families, as in the case of Cummings) purchased only thirty copies at a price of twenty dollars.

Cummings had not been simply sitting in Cambridge awaiting his first appearance in book form. In the late fall of 1916, the young poet ran into his former professor William Neilson. In the course of their conversation, Neilson mentioned to Cummings that he knew of a job available in New York at P. F. Collier. Cummings, imagining himself working for the weekly magazine, jumped at the offer and immediately got in touch with the office. As it turned out, the job available was not on the magazine, but in the office of the publishing firm, which sold books by mail. The position required someone to answer correspondence about orders from book buyers. Though his hope of being on the staff of the magazine was dashed, he accepted the offer anyway.

In late December, he realized his dream of moving to New York. After a brief search, he took a studio with his college friend, Tex Wilson, at 21 East 15th Street, on the periphery of Greenwich Village. Cummings called the apartment "an enormous room, twenty by twenty" but deemed it more than adequate. Along with a kitchenette, it also had a working fireplace and a piano. On January 2, he started work at Collier's. He immediately found employment less than stimulating, but because business was slack, he had plenty of time on his hands. In between answering correspondence and arranging for the shipping of orders, he found space to both read and write. Among the books he reported reading were the Scandinavian *Eddas*, *Crime and Punishment*, and Pound's memoir of the sculptor Gaudier-Brzeska.

New York overwhelmed him. Writing much later of his first impressions, he described the city as "a telemicroscopic chimera, born of the satanic rape of the mind; a phallic female phantasm, clothed in thunderous anonymity and adorned with collosally floating spiderwebs of traffic;

a stark irresistibly stupendous newness, mercifully harboring among its pitilessly premeditated spontaneities immemorial races and nations." After work and on Sundays he wandered the streets, acquainting himself with his new home, marveling at the buildings, the shops, the rush of humanity. On January 2, 1917, he wrote to his mother that he had already met "several aggressively intellectual people of the literary world," and had "dined several times divinely upon foods of diverging nationalities."

While working, painting, and writing took up a fair amount of Cummings's time, he still found ample opportunities for socializing. He met up frequently with his Harvard friend Edward Nagle, now also living in New York. Through Nagle, he met others, chief among them Dillwyn Parrish, who had just returned from France after a tour of duty with the Norton-Harjes Ambulance Corps. Dos Passos was also in New York, having had to return from Europe to help his half-brother, Louis, settle their father's estate. (Dos Passos's mother, his father's second wife, had died while Dos Passos was at Harvard.) Together with friends, or alone, Cummings took in museums and concerts, became acquainted with a number of rather shabby bars, and discovered that the burlesque show at the National Winter Garden outstripped that of Boston's Old Howard. To rousing tunes pounded on the piano by Cummings or others, a fair amount of alcohol was known to flow on select winter evenings in the Cummings/Wilson apartment.

Letters and journal entries from the time reveal that Cummings clearly reveled in his independence. He even returned a generous check his father had sent him. "We are all right and not in need of a single thing (in fact, the trouble is to find a reputable burglar to remove our superfluous stuff)," he noted. He then added a further explanation: "In short (as Mr. Micawber would say) I am 'earning my own living,' and as I find it excessively banal, I had rather not mix it up with any more pleasant methods, such as accepting, borrowing (etc.) that which is popularly known as 'mazuma' from source or sources other than this dear, beloved sweet, beneficent, spunky 'office,' or 'firm' as some prefer to name it."

Cummings hardly confined himself to sending out book orders at the "spunky firm." On January 11—less than two weeks after he had started the job—he read an obituary in the *New York Evening Sun* of one of his childhood heroes, William F. "Buffalo Bill" Cody. On P. F. Collier stationery, alongside book order information, he wrote "Buffalo Bill is dead," then above the word "dead," penned "defunct." A second sheet of clean stationery has these words:

Buffalo Bill is defunct
who used to ride a white horse and shoot pidgeons
with his long hair like reindeer moss on the old stone of his face.

The next version, more evocative in its language, adds dimension and action. Buffalo Bill now rides a "smooth silver stallion," his hair "streaming," and "breaks one two three four five pidgeons before one fell." It concludes with these lines:

how d'you like him, death
he had you always in his eye.

At the bottom of the page he has scrawled two phrases: "brave old boy," and "blue eyed boy."

What began as a kind of eulogy has begun to turn into a sardonic comment on life and death. The final version (intermediate drafts, if any, are lost) pushes both form and substance:

Buffalo Bill 's
defunct
          who used to
          ride a watersmooth-silver
                                        stallion
and break onetwothreefourfive pigeonsjustlikethat
                                                            Jesus
he was a handsome man
                                   and what I want to know is
how do you like your blueeyed boy
Mister Death

It would become one of Cummings's best-known poems.

Given Cummings's predilection for carrying on his own business as opposed to the work he was assigned, it is no surprise that he did not last long in the position. On February 25, 1917, less than two months after beginning the job, he resigned. In a letter to his boss, F. J. Reynolds, he explained the reasons for his decision: "I am thoroughly and definitely convinced [resignation] is best for my own welfare, not to mention that of the department in which I have had the honour to be employed. My ability, if I have any, certainly does not lie in the direction indicated by a career in the publishing business."

He did not look back for a moment. He had not spent much (if any) of the money he had received from his godfather and Thayer and, therefore, could afford to live quite comfortably for some time without working. Indeed, it appears that he used the job largely as an acceptable cover for leaving home. Or as he noted, "ST [Scofield Thayer] was the person who removed me from my family. I owed him my independence." Now freed from employment, he decided to "honor Thayer" by dipping into his nest egg in order to devote himself, when not wandering the city, to painting and writing. He bought an easel, oils, and canvas and began painting in earnest. He also sent home for Wright's *Modern Painting* and Eddy's *Cubism and Post Impressionism.* Writing seemed to occupy him less, but in a letter to his family he asked them to mail him all his manuscripts and a few books of poetry, an indication, as well as his rental of a typewriter, that he was still actively engaged in writing.

But painting was in the foreground of his activity. His letters to family and friends written during this period are largely devoted to his paintings: "2 new pictures have seen the light; and I am beginning to feel happier, inasmuch as I now invariably desire to throw away the-thing-before-last as soon as it is done." In another letter he remarked that his gainful unemployment was allowing him to "work." He told his mother his artistic pursuits amounted to the "mental concentration equivalent to 80 weeks in 'Colliers.' I can't express to you, even, how excellent it is to be my own master (instead of the alarm clock's servant)." Also, in a letter to his mother, he described one of his canvases as "3 figures heaving on a lever. Find the three figures and get a nickel cigar."

Cummings's idyll was not to last long. On April 6, 1917, President Wilson, noting famously that "the world must be made safe for democracy" prevailed upon Congress to declare war. The next day Tex Wilson walked into the army recruiting office and signed up to be an aviator. Cummings, fearing he would be drafted—he was twenty-two—wrote a letter to the Norton-Harjes Ambulance Corps, a division of the Red Cross, volunteering for service in France. Curiously, though, he did not inform his family of his decision. Instead, on the same day, he wrote his mother a rather nonchalant letter: "I shan't go to a war unless I go in a real one—or in the aeroplane squad…I don't know why I talk of this pseudo 'war' as I have no interest in it—and am painting and scribbling as ever…I read but one paragraph of [Woodrow] Wilson's speech, being taken with a dangerous fit of laughter." Despite his words, he was deeply concerned about being drafted into service: "Thank god, the room is in [Tex] Wilson's name—I wouldn't be a "resident of NY" for a good deal, as (you may know) any such is automatically conscripted." On April 23, he wrote to Thayer that "pricked by the drafty pitchfork, tweaked by my divinity, and escorted by my irremediable discontent, i set toward France my eyes."

Cummings's decision to volunteer for the ambulance service had little to do with patriotism, nor did it mark a change in his anti-war feelings. Like most young men at the time, he was simply facing a difficult choice. He could either apply for service as a conscientious objector, enlist in the armed forces, or volunteer for ambulance duty. Although it is likely, due to his father's influence, that he would have been granted conscientious objector status, he did not relish the idea of alternative service that would have probably kept him stateside. And yet he was enough of a pacifist that he could not see bearing arms, either. The third option, therefore, was the logical one for him to pursue. It involved him in the war in a noncombatant capacity, while allowing him a deferment from military duty.

On April 17, having received a positive response from the Norton-Harjes Ambulance Corps, he went over to their headquarters at 2 Rector Street in Manhattan and officially enrolled. He wrote his mother about his decision: "After lengthy consideration, far exceeding that of some Greek (Socrates?) who often remained rapt for a day at a time, I signed up with Eliot Norton to go over (with several others) on the 28th of this month (i.e. week from this Saturday) to drive old Fords, Packards, Motorblocs, Renaults (in fact anything on wheels) 'without animus' as your friend the President would say. Hope the war isn't over before I get there." In a separate letter to his pacifist father he explained that he was led to sign up for two reasons: the prospect of adventure and a desire to avoid the draft. "It will mean everything to me as an experience to do something I want to in a wholly new environment, versus being forced to do something I don't want to & unchanging scene."

His family was naturally concerned. Though relieved that their son had not gone into the regular army, they were still worried for his safety, as the ambulance service was hardly risk free. A number of Corps members had died or had been wounded. Anticipating objections (which were not, in reality, forthcoming), Cummings let it be known that his decision was firm: "You can hurl questions, shake fingers (and milliondollarbanknotes) all the evening and morning at me.... Once more, O Family: be calm and sit still if you love me. Don't forget that I am NOT a little lost woodchuck."

The Norton-Harjes American Ambulance Corps was founded in 1915 by Richard and Eliot Norton, sons of former Harvard president Charles Eliot Norton (a neighbor and friend of the Cummings family), and Henry Harjes, whose investment firm Morgan, Harjes & Co. was Paris-based. Since both Richard Norton and Harjes were directing operations in France, Eliot Norton handled the recruiting on the American side from the Rector Street office. By April 1917, Richard Norton and Henry Harjes had already been awarded the French War Cross for their distinguished service in saving lives at the front. Since its inception, the Ambulance Corps had seen a steady stream of volunteers who signed up for six-month tours of duty. In January of 1917, with the war heating up, it expanded its operation to include a third section. By the time Cummings volunteered, the Corps, attached to the French Army, consisted of seventy-five cars and one hundred and twenty men.

Cummings spent the next week running around New York obtaining references in order to complete the requirements for service. He asked Wilson to ship his clothes and odds and ends home. He wrote to Thayer that "there are three or four paintings,a few faits,some verses,some indecipherable music: these I am putting together in manuscript,for your unutterable keeping."

On April 27, with his references obtained, and his gear, paintings, and manuscripts disposed of, he informed his mother that "after waiting 1 ½ hours" he succeeded in seeing Eliot Norton, who gave him a list of what volunteers needed to have. He also informed her that his friend Dillwyn Parrish, a former Norton-Harjes driver who had greatly influenced his decision to volunteer, had taken him around to the French Consul and French Line so that he could obtain a visa and passage. "I have a fine cabin—and pay only $78 and something—owing to reduction given Volunteers, I got $50 in French notes today—wonderful! I want to kiss them!!!"

On April 28, Rebecca Cummings came to New York to see her son off. His father sent a telegram of support:

As I said in advance
I envy your chance
of breaking a lance
for Freedom in France
by driving and mending
an ambulance
best love and luck a soldier ever had,
From Betsy, Mother, Jane, Nana and Dad

Wilson, Nagle, Parrish, and his mother assembled to see him off on April 28. After his mother's tearful good-bye, and a succession of manly hugs from his friends, he boarded the *Touraine*. He stood a long while on the railing, taking in the harbor, peering at the receding skyline of "the real that was New York, a leonine uproar of rose in the unpunctual stupidity of heavenless heaven." Once on the open ocean, he went down to his cabin and took out a notebook. Rather than reflect on farewell or the future about to unfold on the other side of the Atlantic, the young writer was firmly fixed in the moment. And that moment could not pass unnoted:

the   saintly
sweetness   of
sea
blowings from the   unimaginable
gulls
lift   ing   in
curviness

seven

La Guerre

The first part of the Atlantic crossing was far from pleasant. A fierce storm that lasted five days sent the *Touraine* pitching and rolling, and Cummings's stomach "grinning from the mast-head." A week into the voyage, with the northeaster gone, he wrote his family lengthy and lively details of the ordeal. He also noted that he had made some friends among his fellow passengers: "(1) a Mick from Cambridge, Mass. (2) a gentle thuglike person named 'Edgar Guy Lemon' (3) a wholly possible boy from Worcester, the home of the Bartletts, whom I met on the strength of my brothership to Lucy's playmate, 'Elizabeth Cummings.' His name is W. S. Brown. He suffered 'neath Talcott Williams at Columbia, incidentally."

In the months to come, the Cummings family would learn a great deal more about "the wholly possible boy," William Slater Brown, who was also a Norton-Harjes volunteer, for subsequent letters home are peppered with mentions of him. Indeed, by the time the *Touraine* docked at Bordeaux, the two had become fast friends.

At the time Cummings and Brown met, the twenty-year-old Brown was two years younger than Cummings, and had just graduated from Columbia with degrees in English and French. As they sat in the ship's bar getting to know one another, they both realized they had met long before, when the Brown family had rented the Thaxter's house on Irving Street for a year, hence the reference in Cummings's letter to "Lucy's playmate." Originally from Webster, Massachusetts—a town his great-great-grandfather, Samuel Slater, had founded—Brown was a doctor's son. Brown and Cummings quickly discovered that they had a lot in common. Both came from illustrious families, a legacy that made them both feel constrained. Like Cummings, Brown was smart and irreverent, with a keen sense of humor. He too was interested in the arts and quite knowledgeable about literature. Also like Cummings, Brown was thoroughly anti-war. Indeed, in early April, he and Edgar Guy Lemon had traveled to Washington to participate in a demonstration against the war. His motivation in joining the Ambulance Corps was also similar to that of Cummings: to stay out of the army, yet see France.

On arrival on *terra firma*, Cummings and Brown boarded the train for Paris. But when they arrived in Paris on the evening of May 10, they got off at the Gare d'Orleans instead of the Gare d'Austerlitz where the rest of the volunteers and their leader had exited. Cummings wrote his mother the details: "Emerging on the quai from the tomb-like station void of cable office, we lost ½ hr. waiting for some means of conveyance, and then a pieds started for 7 Rue François Premier [headquarters of Norton-Harjes].... It was ¾ hr. before we reached 7, and there a magnificent scrub-lady (may she live for ever!!!) escorted us jokingly around the corner on the Cours la Reine to the Hôtel du Palais."

As a result of the mix-up, Brown and Cummings, unlike the other volunteers who were shipped off much sooner to the front, would end up "stranded" in Paris for the next five weeks awaiting their uniforms and orders. Nothing could have suited them more: "We never get up for Petit Déjeuner, but stroll down the Avenue d'Antin to the Rond Point des Champs Elysées, on whose N. W. corner is the Alexander III Hotel. Under an awning we sit and drink our cafés, with Le Matin & Figaro to keep us company. Generally we eat away at noon, and sometimes again at supper."

As the weeks went by, Cummings and Brown explored seemingly every inch of Paris. They marveled at the masterpieces in the Louvre and were thrilled when they stumbled onto the Caillebotte Collection of Impressionist paintings at the Luxembourg Museum. They poked their heads into galleries where they caught glimpses of the cubist revolution in art. They sought out books by French writers Rémy de Gourmont, Paul Fort, and Henri de Régnier—poets Amy Lowell had singled out for praise in her *Six French Poets* that Brown had read before leaving New York. And though he did rework a couple of poems written on board the ship, "a connotation of infinity," and "come nothing to my comparable soul," Cummings was far more preoccupied with seeing the sights and recording them visually rather than in words. With his sketchbook in hand, he wandered the streets, pausing now and then to sketch scenes of both the ordinary (passersby, children jumping rope) and the monumental (portions of the Notre Dame façade).

They saw the Ballet Russe, and took in multiple performances of Stravinsky's *Petrouchka* and *Les Sylphides*, which were being performed as a benefit for the War Fund. Cummings was now experiencing first hand "the new art," about which he had declaimed so forthrightly in his commencement speech at Harvard. But he was about to witness even newer art. On the evening of May 18, owing to their mutual enthusiasm for Satie and Picasso, they attended the premiere of a new ballet at the Théâtre du Châtelet. *Parade*, as the piece was called, was a collaboration of Jean Cocteau (libretto), Diaghilev and Léonide Massine (choreography), Picasso (cubist-inspired sets and costumes), and Satie (score). The program notes were by Apollinaire, who coined a new phrase when he enthusiastically recommended that the audience take in the "sur-realism" of the spectacle.

Whatever expectations Cummings and Brown may have had, they could not have in any way matched the actual performance. Nor surely did they realize that they were to be present at the creation of one of the great moments in the history of the avant-garde. The unique music featured not just a full orchestra but additional percussive sounds created by a variety of non-instruments including typewriters, sirens, telegraph tickers, and lottery wheels. Critic Roger Shattuck described the scene: "On stage [the audience] saw not a ballet but a road show. According to plan, the incidental racket and the manager's costumes (built ten feet high into 'moving scenery') seemed to overwhelm the essentially modest music and dance movements.... Whistling and clapping intermingled in the auditorium, and a few fists were raised."

Cummings and Brown were among those who applauded. At one point Cummings even rose in his chair to shout insults at the naysayers. Ten years later, the memory of the performance would no doubt come again to Cummings's mind when his own play *Him* would meet with comparable derision when it opened in New York. Shock was still possible in art in that era.

But Cummings did not require extraordinary entertainment to be enthralled with his days in Paris. "I spent $12 already on Cézanne and Matisse photogravures, and threaten daily to buy a painting outfit, which will cost as much again," he reported to his parents. "Also Brown and I never walk less than 10 miles a day here, and never return without a small library between us. I'm getting used to eating vegetables as a separate course after the entrées, and of being waited on by one-eyed-pop-eyed, wise-in-their-own-conceit garçons. Everyone who isn't at war is a cripple of some variety—with blatant exceptions."

While he delighted in the French, he had less kind words for his countrymen: "The Englishmen...are a bunch of bums, only worsened by the Americans—who are the most abhorrent human tripe ever spilled from the swill-can, tout et seul. Willie's exception. How we dread meeting them! How we flee them!"

Though he did tell his mother that Paris had "the finest girls god ever allowed to pasture in the air of this fresh earth," he did not write his parents about his nightly excursions into another side of Paris. On more than one occasion, he and Brown gazed at the dancers on stage at the Folies Bergère and mingled with them during intermission. "The whores are very beautiful with their diseased greenness, slobbering on the tight Americans and Englishmen between the acts of the Folies Bergère—with the smell of their many deaths about them," he wrote his friend Dillwyn Parrish.

Since prostitution was legal in France, it was not just at the Folies that Cummings and Brown encountered an assortment of "ladies of the night." Indeed, they seemed ubiquitous, strolling any number of streets, lounging in doorways, hanging on street corners. Cummings was enchanted with the open display of sexuality, with what he took to be a natural expression of a basic human drive. Not long after his arrival, he got much better acquainted with prostitution in the form of Marie-Louise Lallemand, whom he met while she was plying her trade with her partner, Mimi, at the Place de l'Opéra. Cummings was struck by her youth, beauty, and open sensuality; Brown had the same feelings for Mimi. A romance began.

But it was a rather old-fashioned romance, in which Cummings and Brown behaved themselves like the gentlemen they were. They took their dates to the Concert Mayol, lunched with them in some of the small Paris restaurants they had begun to frequent, walked the city, arm in arm, under the moonlight, went on a picnic to Nogent-sur-Marne. They even paid them for the time they spent together when normally the women would have been "working." Marie-Louise called Cummings "Edouard" since Estlin was difficult for her to pronounce correctly. Brown was "Bel." Cummings sketched them both, with a pencil in his sketchbook, and in words:

> **Mimi à**
> **la voix fragile**
> **qui chatouille Des**
> **Italiens**
>
> **the putain with the ivory throat**
> **Marie Louise Lallemand**
> **n'est-ce pas que je suis belle**
> **chéri? les anglais m'aiment**
> **tous, les américains**
> **aussi…"bon dos,bon cul de Paris?" (Marie**
> **Vierge**
> **Priez**
> **Pour**
> **Nous)**

While it was more than obvious to Cummings that Marie-Louise would willingly have consented to have sex with him, he did not choose to lose his virginity, though he did spend a night fondling her in bed. Cummings's reticence was largely due to his upbringing in which sex, if mentioned at all, was viewed distastefully. And though he was trying to reverse his attitudes, see sex in positive, even joyful terms, he was still a victim of his household's straitlaced views. The specter of picking up a venereal disease—this was before penicillin—also haunted him. And so while he took advantage of her easiness, becoming for the first time truly intimate with a woman's body, delighting in it, he did not ultimately surrender to his desire (and likely hers) to, as he put it, "go whole hog." (Brown, apparently, was not so restrained.)

On June 12, 1917, the inevitable happened. Brown and Cummings were summoned to headquarters by none other than Henry Harjes, the head of the Ambulance Corps. After admonishing them for not keeping in touch on a regular basis, they were told they would be shipped out the next day. According to Brown, Harjes decided to send Cummings to a "de luxe Harvard section," but Cummings refused, insisting he and Brown be sent together. Harjes backed down. That evening they bid adieu to Marie-Louise and Mimi, packed up, and got ready to head to the front.

Cummings wrote a farewell to Marie-Louise in the form of a sonnet. Unless he had translated it into French, she would probably not have even been aware that he had written the poem.

> goodby Betty,don't remember me
> pencil your eyes dear and have a good time
> with the tall tight boys at Tabari'
> s,keep your teeth snowy,stick to beer and lime,
> wear dark,and where your meeting breasts are round
> have roses darling,it's all I ask of you—
> but that when light fails and this sweet profound
> Paris moves with lovers,two and two
> bound for themselves,when passionately dusk
> brings softly down the perfume of the world
> (and just as smaller stars begin to husk
> heaven)you,you exactly paled and curled
>
> with mystic lips take twilight where i know:
> proving to Death that Love is so and so.

The *Section Sanitaire XXI*, based in the village of Ham, near St. Quentin, consisted of a unit of about fifty men. Attached to the French Army, the *Section* had twenty ambulances at its disposal. Drivers were assigned in pairs and made daily excursions to the front, where their job was to evacuate the wounded. Although the fighting had been fierce the spring before, by the time Cummings and Brown arrived, the Germans had largely retreated, leaving only a small force to carry out sporadic attacks.

"No excitements whatever so far—I have been technically 'under fire' twice—very dull," Cummings wrote to his mother on July 2, 1917, a little more than two weeks after his official induction into the Corps. "Not one air-duel. Every day a dozen or so planes shot at by anti-aircraft bosch guns without results." Indeed, there was not much action where Cummings and Brown were stationed. He described the routine in a letter home: "Once every 3 days the cars of a section leave this place and go 'in post' —this meaning simply that the conducteur and aide of each take their bedding and canned cold food and leave at 10 A M, then go a few miles, park the car, and fall asleep waiting for malades, of whom none exist at present in our sector. At 11, 12 or 1 on the next day they are 'relieved' by their 'comrades,' and go 'home.'"

After the freedom and thrills of Paris, Cummings and Brown both found the routine quite grinding. Because of their subordinate status, they were not even allowed to drive. Instead, they worked as part of the maintenance crew. Their chief tasks seemed to be cleaning mud from the fleet of Ford and Fiat ambulances, then oiling and greasing them. Neither found their fellow Americans much to their liking. "My conducteur is the most despicable, perhaps, 'fellow' in the 'camp,'" Cummings wrote. "He's a tight-fisted, pull-for-special-privilege, turd, about 5 feet high with a voice in b natural upper.... Much worse, still 'perhaps,' is the 'chef' of the section, 'Mister Phillips'.... His 'assistant' Mister 'Andy' who keeps doing nothing to the cars, which consequently run well, has the benefit of a <u>complete</u> lack of education plus a <u>perfect</u> absence of inherent intelligence.... The men are, as you would expect, 'average' Americans, sans taste, imagination, etc."

The situation did not improve. Their section chief, John T. Phillips, denied both Cummings and Brown leave, telling Cummings that his conduct was "lacking in sticktuitiveness and enthusiasm." Cummings's response was to blow cigarette smoke in his "chef's" face. Cummings did get relieved of his duties as aide to his "conducteur," a man named Donaldson, but not because of his own grousing, rather because the driver asked that Cummings be replaced. In late July, the former assistant chief, Harry Anderson, took over from Phillips. Cummings summed him up as "autre cloche, même son," [another bell, same sound], noting that he was "un homme stupide, sans éducation, et qui se fache toujours, comme son prédécesseur méchant, de mon ami et particulièrement de moi" [a stupid, uneducated man, and who is always angry, like his mean predecessor, at my friend and particularly at me].

He did not have kind words for Richard Norton either, who, sporting a monocle, came to inspect the camp: "Dans un mot, un âne agréable et sans raison d'être" [In a word, an agreeable ass, and without reason for being]. Part of Cummings's distaste probably had something to do with Norton informing him that he and his lot were nothing more than spoiled brats without hope unless they mended their ways, who were responsible for driving their former chief, the "noble" Phillips, to join the army.

Although the *Section Sanitaire* was continually shifting from town to town in the region to keep up with the front lines, there was still little fighting in the sector. "PLEASE don't get the idea that I am ever in danger of my life, or that I ever carry wounded soldiers, or that I am ever anything but grateful for the little incidents which serve to puncture the desperate situation of being quartered in Divine Country with a bunch of _____s. incapable of escape, action or anything else."

Camp life began to get somewhat better when Brown and Cummings, fluent in French—in contrast to the majority of Americans in their group—gave up socializing with their American "comrades" and began spending more and more time with French soldiers, both those assigned to the Corps as mechanics and cooks and men engaged at the front. With the French they exchanged jokes, songs, and dirty stories, drank as much wine as they could get their hands on, gossiped, and, naturally, bitched about their superiors and the war. While the two Americans occasionally dined with the French officers, they preferred the common soldier—or *poilus*—over the company of captains and lieutenants, feeling that the enlisted men shared more of their attitudes toward the war.

In an August letter to his mother written in French in an attempt to outwit the American censors who could not read the language, Cummings reported on the views of the *poilus*: "La guerre—c'est pour eux, les français, une chimère abominable, qui a mangé leur amis et leur amies, tout ce qu'ils aiment et pour lequel ils vivaient. Par exemple: un méchanique qui s'est associé avec la section sanitaire, me disait qu'au cour de quinze jours de la guerre il a perdu son père et ses deux frères. Sa mère est morte. 'Je suis patriot,' me disait-il, 'mais pas comme ça. La guerre—non, non.'" [The war—is for them, the French, an abominable chimera, that has eaten their male and female friends, whom they love and for whom they live. For example: a mechanic who is himself associated with the section sanitaire, told me that in the course of fifteen days of the war he lost his father and his two brothers. His mother is dead. 'I am a patriot,' he told me, 'but not like that. The war—no, no.']

Brown was even more specific: "Everyone is sick of war here and I look forward to a revolution in France soon. The French soldiers are all despondent and none of them believe that Germany will ever be defeated. They maintain the war just as they hold on to the Church or marriage or a sensescent institution."

While their friendships with the French proved quite rewarding, the association did not sit well with the other Americans in their unit, particularly with the chief, Harry Anderson. Or as Cummings described the situation: "B[rown] and I and Mr. A[nderson] didn't get on well. We were in fundamental disagreement as to the attitude which we, Americans, should uphold toward the poilus in whose behalf we had volunteered assistance,Mr. A. maintaining 'You boys want to keep away from those dirty Frenchmen' or 'We're here to show those bastards how they do things in America',to which we answered by seizing every opportunity for fraternization."

Anderson had other issues with his two volunteers, as well, not the least of which was their general dishevelment, which he took as further sign of their insipid insubordination. Anderson was, of course, quite right in his judgment. The youthful rebellions that both Cummings and Brown had staged while at their respective universities had continued unabated. They were as sure as ever that they possessed a much keener understanding and appreciation of what life had to offer. They were also certain that the war was fundamentally stupid, and a great waster of the lives of countless human beings. It was a conclusion both had come to before volunteering, but between what they personally witnessed and what they learned from the French soldiers, they were even more steadfast in their opinions.

Anderson's authoritarian antics only helped reinforce their position, providing them with fodder for their resistance to being controlled, particularly by someone whom they deemed unintelligent, woefully ignorant, and uncouth. Anderson, an ex-garage mechanic from the Bronx—bullheaded, arrogant, and mean—was an easy target, helping to assure them that their perceptions were absolutely correct. As a result, they perceived no reason to change their views of the war, or those in charge.

A war zone is not a university, nor is it a democracy. While Cummings and Brown had much more leeway in breaking rules than they would have had in the army, they were still subject to regulations strictly enforced in war. Perhaps the most sacred of these regulations had to do with not betraying loyalty to the country for which one was fighting. Treason was not a slight infraction of the rules. While it was permissible to gripe about one's conditions, expressing any sort of solidarity with the enemy was quite a different matter. And so when Brown wrote to friends in the United States that he wondered how "any one can hate the Germans," or expressed the view that the "war will [not] end with victory for either side," or reported that the French (and perhaps English) were shooting their own officers, or noted that the French "admire the Germans very much," his words caught the eyes of the censors, who passed them on to the French authorities.

Other letters also seemed questionable. The first was a letter jointly signed by Cummings, Brown, and another American in their unit who was sent to the undersecretary of the French Air Corps in which they volunteered for training as aviators. The second was a joint request by Cummings and Brown to Norton inquiring about the possibility of their joining a new ambulance section being formed for service in Russia. Both communications were inspired by their desire to get out of the *Section Sanitaire*. Both were intercepted.

These letters would perhaps not have caused suspicion had it not been for Brown's earlier statements in the letters already impounded. Though the first letter is lost, according to a report later filed by Norton, the trio also stated in their request to become flyers that they did not want to kill Germans. Cummings, however, does not mention this. Indeed, when asked later by his French interrogators whether he would have any hesitation in dropping bombs on Germans, he replied that he would not. He also wrote his mother that he and Brown had applied to the aviation service in good faith.

∞

At 11:00 AM, on Sunday, September 23, 1917, Cummings noted the arrival in the camp at Ollezy of a "spic not to say span gentleman in a suspiciously quiet French uniform." A few minutes later, when Cummings moseyed over to the tent to investigate who the newcomer might be, he found Brown "dragging all his belongings into a central pile of frightening proportions." When Cummings inquired as to what was going on, he was informed by one of the men surrounding his friend that Brown was going to Paris, to which another added, "prison you mean." Brown said nothing. Cummings decided that the French "potentate" had arrived to give Anderson his comeuppance by whisking out from under him the two men whom he had most abused and insulted. Cummings rushed to headquarters to confirm his supposition, which seemed to be right when he was also ordered to gather his belongings and pile them into a car. A few minutes later, Cummings found his way, under guard, rattling along the rutted road away to somewhere. Brown had preceded him, he assumed, since by the time he had himself left the camp, his friend and the first car had vanished.

It took a while, apparently, for Cummings to realize that he was actually being arrested. Even after learning that the distinguished officer was Monsieur le Ministre de Sûreté de Noyon, he did not fully comprehend what was happening to him and Brown. It was only after the driver began asking him what was going on that it dawned on Cummings that he and Brown were under arrest. Even then he was not concerned: "As a matter of fact I was never so excited and proud. I was,to be sure,a criminal! Well,well,thank God that settled one question for good and all—no more section sanitaire for me! No more Mr. A.and his daily lectures in cleanliness,deportment,etc. In spite of myself I started to sing."

On arrival in Noyon, some twenty miles away, he was fed. Then, after catching a glimpse of Brown, who called out that it looked as if they were indeed going to prison, Cummings was brought into a room for interrogation before a committee of judges. The Minister of Security acted as prosecutor. After answering questions regarding his close association with Brown, and their mutual difficulties with Anderson, the Minister then asked, "You are aware that your friend has written to friends in America and to his family very bad letters." Noted Cummings:

> In a flash I understood the motivation of Monsieur's visit to Vingt-et-Un [*Section Sanitaire XXI*]: the French censor had intercepted some of B's letters, and had notified Mr. A. and Mr. A.'s translator,both of whom had thankfully testified to the bad character of B and (wishing very naturally to get rid of both of us at once) had further averred that we were always together and that consequently I might properly be regarded as a suspicious character.

The questioning continued. Cummings was asked about why he wanted to join French aviation. He replied, quite simply, because "the French are after all the finest people in the world." A bit taken aback, the

Minister pressed his prisoner on Brown's loyalty, to which Cummings responded: "Write this down in the testimony—that I,here present,refuse utterly to believe that my friend is not as sincere a lover of France and the French people as any man living!" Again, the Minister seemed somewhat uncomfortable. Finally, Cummings was asked whether he hated the Germans:

> I had won my own case. The question was purely perfunctory. To walk out of the room a free man I had merely to say yes. My examiners were sure of my answer.... And Noyon had given up all hope of making me out a criminal. I might be rash, but I was innocent;the dupe of a superior and malign intelligence. I would probably be admonished to choose my friends more carefully next time and that would be all.
>
> Deliberately I framed my answer:
>
> 'Non. J'aime beaucoup les français.'
>
> Agile as a weasel,Monsieur le Ministre was on top of me. 'It is impossible to love Frenchmen and not hate Germans.'
>
> ...And my case was lost,forever lost. I breathed freely once more. All my nervousness was gone. The attempt of the three gentlemen sitting before me to endow my friend and myself with different fates had irrevocably failed.

Cummings's refusal to betray Brown, or his own principles, was one of his finest moments as a young man. While he had long resisted authority as much for the sake of resistance as out of any highly held beliefs, it is hard to see him here as anything but heroic, courageous, and admirable. Even though he faced an uncertain fate, he followed the dictates of his own conscience rather than seek an easy exit. Or in the words of another man, "more brave than me, more blond than you," who also steadfastly refused to bow to authority: "'there is some shit I will not eat.'"

Two days later, after one night spent in a cell in another town, and after an overnight train ride to Paris where he and his guards changed trains, Cummings arrived in the evening in the "unlovely town of Briouze," in

Normandy. Cummings was confused. When he had asked where they were going, his captors had told him Macé, which he heard as Marseilles, "where one has new colours and strange customs." But Briouze was clearly not Marseilles, nor was it, as he learned, his final destination. To get there they would have to walk twelve kilometers. Since the town was hardly inviting, Cummings was delighted at the prospect of a promenade. Around midnight, several hours after they set out, they reached a village. A "long dull dirty mass" rose up to meet them. "Toward this we turned," wrote Cummings. "All too soon I made out its entirely dismal exterior. Grey long stone walls,surrounded on the side by a fence of ample proportions and uniformly dull colour.... No living soul seemed to inhabit this desolation."

After another brief interrogation, Cummings was escorted to a large room that had once been a chapel. He still did not know where he had really arrived, but decided for the present just to take in the scene: "The shrinking light which my guide held had become suddenly minute; it was beating,senseless and futile,with shrill fists upon a thick enormous moisture of gloom. To the left and right through lean oblongs of stained glass burst tiny burglars of moonlight.... My nostrils fought against the monstrous atmospheric slime which hugged a sweet unpleasant odour." He staggered in with a straw mattress, found a place to lay it down, then exhausted, fell upon it, fully dressed, noting as he quickly drifted off to sleep that he was surrounded by a cacophony of voices all speaking different languages.

The next morning he was roused by a fellow inmate offering him coffee, who in the process of filling a tin cup from a pail of dark liquid informed him that his friend was sleeping a few cots away. A joyful reunion quickly followed. Within a few minutes Cummings learned that he was not in Marseilles, but being held at La Ferté-Macé, a detention center for "undesirables" and "spies." Cummings reacted, asking whether he and Brown were spies, too. "'Of course,' B said enthusiastically. 'Thank God! And in to stay. Every time I think of the section sanitaire, and A. and his thugs, and the whole rotten red-taped Croix Rouge,I have to laugh. Cummings,I tell you this is the finest place on earth.'" After some reflection on Anderson and life at the *Section Sanitaire*, Cummings "laughed for sheer joy."

By the end of his first full day in confinement, Cummings had a sense of what Brown was really talking about. The living conditions were fairly appalling, with buckets for toilets, little ventilation and light since the windows on three sides were boarded up, and the meals barely adequate (thin potato soup and stale bread). Even so, he found his fellow high-spirited inmates to be quite engaging. They hailed from a dozen countries and were generally imprisoned because they seemed to have been aliens in the wrong place at the wrong time. Or, as Cummings wrote, "Who was eligible to La Ferté? Anyone whom the police could find in the lovely country of France(a)who was not guilty of treason(b)who could not prove that he was not guilty of treason." Like Brown and Cummings, they felt themselves unjustly imprisoned, and were intent on circumventing the rules at every turn. In the exercise yard, for instance, under the eyes of a disinterested guard, they managed to break every rule within a matter of minutes.

Among the forty-some odd prisoners (about the same number as in the *Section Sanitaire*) housed in the enormous room was an aristocratic English painter, Count Charles Bragard, who had known Cézanne; a kind diminutive Russian, M. Auguste; a handsome bearded gypsy dubbed "The Wanderer;" a Norwegian ship's stoker, Fritz; Pompon, from Belgium and Harree, a Dutchman, the clowns of the unit; and "the Bear," a large, good-natured Pole.

Le Dépôt de Triage de La Ferté-Macé had originally been a seminary. Closed in 1906, the complex consisted of two large buildings, each three stories high, plus the converted chapel where Cummings was housed. A high stone wall encircled the makeshift internment center. Women resided on the first floor. Some were prostitutes who had been picked up for plying their trade in war zones; others were, like the men, "enemy aliens;" others were wives of the male prisoners, who voluntarily chose to live in confinement in order to be closer to their husbands.

Strictly speaking, La Ferté-Macé was not a prison, though the prisoners were guarded, even punished for infractions by solitary confinement. But there was no prison uniform. The inmates were allowed to have their own belongings—Cummings, for instance, had his bags with clothes, as well as all his books, sketchbooks, notebooks, pencils, and pens. They could also send and receive mail. Cummings and Brown ordered a set of Shakespeare from Brentano's in Paris. Cummings wrote his family and a few friends regularly, and received replies from his family (along with socks knitted by his grandmother). Thayer wrote him that he was going to collect his poems from Wilson and try to get them published. Cecil Derry, his Greek teacher at Boston Latin, also sent him a letter of cheer.

Money also bought privileges: inmates with cash could purchase items like tobacco, chocolate, and extra food from the canteen; private rooms within the complex were available for a price; and a few of the interned were even allowed to take lodgings in town. Though Cummings and Brown did have francs at their disposal, out of a sense of solidarity they chose to use their money sparingly, mainly to buy items now and then from the canteen. They did splurge on a birthday celebration in October—Cummings turned twenty-three, Brown twenty-one—by making hot chocolate, which they shared with their friends.

On October 1, 1917, Cummings wrote his mother that he had been interned, then went on to reassure her that his life at La Ferté-Macé was far from awful: "The following program is ours now till 15th October, when a commission comes up to examine us for pacifism or something of the sort: 6-up. Coffee. 7 down to yard. 9:30 up. 10 down to salle à manger. 4:30-7 yard. 7 up. 9-lights out. I am having the time of my life." At the time Cummings wrote this letter, his family had no idea that he had been arrested. Nor did they learn the news from him directly. Instead, on October 17, more than three weeks after he had been imprisoned, they received a blunt telegram from the head of the Ambulance Corps, Richard Norton:

> EDWARD E. CUMMINGS HAS BEEN PUT IN A CONCENTRATION CAMP AS RESULT OF LETTERS HE HAD WRITTEN STOP AM TAKING UP THE MATTER THROUGH EMBASSY TO SEE WHAT CAN BE DONE

That Norton took so long to inform the family (with whom he was well acquainted, as he had grown up at Norton Woods, just up the road from Irving Street) reflects both his own ineptness as well as the incompetence of the Ambulance Corps of which he was in charge. He was obviously aware much sooner than mid-October of 1917 of what had taken place in his own unit on September 23. In a letter to Edward Cummings, written on October 29, he apologized for not communicating with him earlier, saying that he "could not get sufficient information to be able to write intelligently." At the same time, he laid the blame on "an amazing lack of perception on the part of the Red Cross authorities" whom he could not induce "to do anything in any efficient and vigorous manner for a long time."

Edward Cummings, of course, did not know on receipt of the cable that his son had already been in custody since September. In the hope of getting him released quickly, he immediately cabled Norton, asking him to "do everything," and even said that he would come to France "if needed." Rebecca, in turn, sent a telegram to her son in care of Norton advising him to "take greatest care for my sake." Although his family was ignorant of what their son had actually done, they were unequivocally in his corner. Edward stated this quite clearly in a compassionate, heartfelt letter he wrote his son on the day he received the news of his detention:

> You and I have a longstanding debit and credit account running through many years; and there is still a big balance in your favor. Once by your own courage and address you saved from drowning two lives that were dearer to me than my own—and they still are. I told you then that if you ever make a fool of yourself—and who of [us] does not soon or late?—You could remind me of that debt, and draw on that account, and I would honor the draft. And I will.... I know the real stuff you are made of. No child of your mother could ever lack courage or patriotism. You have plenty of both.

In response to this letter and his mother's telegram, Cummings wrote to his family that he had attained "perfection at last," then went on to insist that he would "see the thing thru, alone, without any monocled Richards, American ambassadors, or anything else. Nothing under H. can change my resolve, and everybody but me, i.e., Gods, men women & children had best keep butted out!!!!"

Cummings's parents, naturally, were not about to butt out. Reverend Cummings, dissatisfied with the lack of immediate progress, was even preparing to take the matter up in Washington, as he informed Norton on October 21. Norton advised him to wait, telling him that he would approach the embassy in Paris to see if they could intervene. Norton replied on the twenty-fifth, saying that "everything going slowly but well." The cable was clearly meant to appease the elder Cummings, for the record shows that Norton had not yet even contacted the embassy. Finally, obviously prodded by the Cummings family, on October 29, Norton did ask the Ambassador to look into the matter. The First Secretary replied the next day that while they had made inquiries, they had not been able to do anything.

What the Americans did not seem to know was that on the same day Norton sent the first cable to Cambridge, Cummings and Brown were coincidentally appearing before the French Commission that would decide their fate. Cummings wrote to his family about the "interview:"

> After a long wait I entered the chamber. One of 3 people asked me lots of questions, proving from collected translations of passages censored in letters of my friend that the latter was not a hater of Germans or a lover of war. I assured them I hated ("détesté" was their delicious word) nobody in the world, laying this breadth of view to my father's weekly occupation. Whether this made a hit or not I don't know, nor care a white ostrich plume, inasmuch as it happens to be true of me. My friend demanded an interpreter, yet I decided to sick the great in their own way, and launched thunders of American-French eloquence over the terrified trio.

Meanwhile, despite frequent cables between Paris and Cambridge, and Cambridge and Paris, the anxious family failed to learn much more about the actual state of affairs. On November 6, Norton sent a telegram to Reverend Cummings that hardly helped to boost his or his family's spirits:

> HAVE BEEN RELIEVED OF ALL WORK WITH RED CROSS STOP IMPOSSIBLE FOR ME TO DO MORE FOR YOU STOP ADVISE USING ALL INFLUENCE TO STIR AUTHORITIES TO MORE VIGOROUS ACTION.

Edward responded by telling Norton he was "asking help from Washington."

Help from Washington came in the form of George W. Anderson, a friend of Dr. Cummings. Formerly the attorney general of Massachusetts, he was now head of the Interstate Commerce Commission, as well as a trustee of the World Peace Foundation that the elder Cummings directed. Within twenty-four hours, Anderson talked to the secretary of state who had apparently already been contacted by Massachusetts Senator Henry Cabot Lodge on behalf of Brown's family. Curiously, there seems to have been no communication between the Brown family and the Cummings family; each seemed to be independently pursuing the case of their respective son.

Secretary of State Robert Lansing did not waste time in taking up the young men's case. When Anderson arrived in Cambridge for a meeting of the World Peace Foundation, two days after he had first learned the news from Edward Cummings, he was able to tell his friend that Lansing had personally cabled Ambassador William Sharp to take charge of the matter. Despite this high-level intervention, no real results were forthcoming.

Finally, on November 18, Anderson wrote Reverend Cummings that "on October 17th the Examining Board decided that Cummings be released and Brown be interned. The final decision will be made by the Ministry of the Interior and will be cabled as soon as received." On November 21, a telegram came from Richard Norton who, through the ambassador, had become reinvolved in trying to secure the release of Cummings and Brown:

> HAVE FINALLY SEEN ALL PAPERS IN CASE ABSOLUTELY NOTHING AGAINST YOUR BOY WHO I UNDERSTAND AFTER CERTAIN FORMALITIES WILL BE IN FEW DAYS HIS OWN MASTER.

The jubilation was quickly dashed, however, by another telegram that came to Anderson, who was again in Boston, from the Assistant Secretary of State, William Phillips:

> FOLLOWING TELEGRAM JUST RECEIVED FROM PARIS QUOTE HAVE LEARNED FROM AMERICAN NAVAL AUTHORITIES THAT EDWARD ESTLIN CUMMINGS EMBARKED FOR UNITED STATES ON THE ANTILLES AND THAT HE IS REPORTED AMONG THOSE LOST END QUOTE.

Anderson broke the news to Edward, who having just received the telegram from Norton stating that his son was still imprisoned, was unsure of what he should make of the naval authorities' report. At the same time, given all the confusion that had consistently accompanied information about the internment, he feared the worst. He shot off a cable to Norton asking for a clarification; Anderson sent one to Phillips requesting that he try to clear up the confusion. When Edward returned to Irving Street that evening, he did not inform Rebecca of the cable; instead, he called her attention to newspaper reports of mid-October reporting that the *Antilles* had gone down on October 17, and that among the passengers was an H. H. Cummings. In a letter from Rebecca to Cummings written on November 23, she informed her son that his father had been fretting about an H. H. Cummings who had died when a German submarine torpedoed his passenger ship. "I never saw a man change as he has done in these two days of anxiety," Rebecca wrote her son.

While Edward secretly anguished over the possibility that his son was on board the *Antilles*, and Rebecca continued to feel upbeat, Cummings was completely oblivious to the report of his drowning, or even that he was scheduled for release. "Our life here is A1," he wrote his father. "Never have I so appreciated leisure. I continually write notes on painting, poetry, and sculpture, as well as music. My days, spent in delightful discussions with my good friend, whose tastes so happily coincide with my own, remind me of the mental peregrinations of your favorite Socrates, insofar as they have illumined many dark crannies in the greatest of all sciences—Art." His notebooks from the period reveal that he was not just putting on a good front for the folks at home. His sketchbooks are filled with drawings of the enormous room and its inhabitants.

Numerous entries in the notebooks recount his experiences and observations, mostly of his fellow inmates and records of conversations. The complaints are largely about the unvarying routine: rising at 6:30, breakfast (bread and coffee) three floors below at 7:00, exercise in the yard afterward, lunch (thin soup and bread, meat three times a week), cleaning of the room, a light dinner, bed at 9:00. In between, and in the evening, though, there were ample opportunities for conversation, and even sketching and writing.

Of the several poems he wrote during his imprisonment, none overtly comments on his confinement. Only one of the poems he wrote while interned, "Doll's boy's asleep," can be seen as perhaps related to his captivity. It recounts a dream fantasy of women, an obvious subject for a young man deprived of all but a glimpse, now and then of a female among those also confined at La Ferté-Macé. One poem, though not included in the drafts in his notebooks, and therefore probably written after his release, does describe a scene at Le Dépôt de Triage:

> The moon falls thru the autumn   Behind prisons she grins,
> where people by huge whistles scooped from sleep land breathless
> on their two feet, and look at her between bars.   She stands
> greenly over the flat pasteboard hill with a little pink road
> like a stand of spilled saw-dust.   The sentinel who walks asle
> ep under apple-trees yawns.   The moon regards little whores
> running down the prison yard into the dawn to shit, and she is
> tickled too.   (Trees in morning are like strengths of young
> men poised to sprint.)   There's another sentinel wanders al
> ong besides a wall perhaps as old as he.   The little moon
> pinks into insignificance:a grouch of sun gobbles the east—
> She is a white shadow asleep in the reddishness of
> Day.

Three days after the receipt of the spurious telegram, Reverend Cummings finally learned that his son had not perished at sea. After learning the news, Edward wrote his boy to tell him how welcome the announcement had been. He also confessed the extent of his anguish: "So down I went into the depths of Hell, and suffered as [I] did not suppose I was capable of suffering,—until my tortured soul had nothing worse to dread. These were days that seemed like years of agony, when I would have given all I had or hope for in exchange for the right to believe you were safe."

But Cummings, of course, still languished in La Ferté-Macé, and though he had been recommended for release, no discharge seemed forthcoming. Finally, on December 8, 1917, two-and-a-half months after his arrest, the authorities at Le Dépôt de Triage received word from the commission that though Cummings was not found guilty of criminal intent, he remained a "suspect." As a result, he would be sprung from detention at La Ferté-Macé, but not allowed to leave France. Brown, on the other hand, was to be transferred to the French prison of Précigné for the remainder of the war. The judgment, Cummings wrote, "knocked me for a loop. I spent the days intervening between the separation from 'votre camarade' and my somewhat supernatural departure for freedom in attempting to particularly straighten myself."

On December 14, Brown was removed from La Ferté-Macé and sent to Précigné. Brown's transfer was extremely difficult for Cummings. He fell into a depression that was quickly noticed by the superintendent of the facility. In an attempt to cheer him up, the superintendent reminded Cummings that he should be happy as he would soon be set free. Cummings could only reply, "I should rather have gone to prison with my friend."

His fellow inmates tried their best to bolster their comrade. They urged to see that he must accept that Brown's fate was not his, and make plans as to where he wanted to go in France upon his release. One of his companions told him he should choose Cannes; another, a diminutive Belgian dubbed "The Machine Fixer," advised him to ask to be sent to a town in the Pyrenees, Oloron-Sainte-Marie: "You will have a very fine time,and you can paint: such scenery to paint! My God—not like what you see from these windows." A distressed Cummings decided that when release came, he would ask to go to Oloron. On December 17, he told the officials at La Ferté-Macé of his decision.

Although the French had informed the embassy that Cummings would be given his freedom, they had not specified a timetable for his release. By early December, the family on Irving Street had grown extremely frustrated. Edward, hitting the limit of his patience, finally decided on December 8 to write directly to President Wilson. It was a strong, eloquent letter in which Dr. Cummings exhorted the president to intervene. It concluded with this paragraph:

> Pardon me, Mr. President, but if I were president and your son were suffering such prolonged injustice at the hands of France; and your son's mother had been needlessly kept in Hell as many weeks as my boy's mother has,—I would do something to make American citizenship in the eyes of Frenchmen as Roman citizenship was in the eyes of the ancient world. Then it was enough to ask the question, "Is it lawful to scourge a Roman, and uncondemned?" Now, in France, it seems lawful to treat like a condemned criminal a man that is an American, uncondemned and admittedly innocent!

The office of Interstate Commerce Commissioner Anderson hand-delivered the letter on December 10. There was no direct response, but on December 15 Secretary of State Lansing dispatched a testy cable to the Ambassador in Paris that concluded by saying "Reason for failure of Embassy to follow up matter cannot be understood Cable reply promptly." In response to Lansing, Ambassador Sharp, who had by now gotten personally involved, renewed his "energetic representations to Foreign Office and Ministry of Interior." While this last round of efforts probably did not get Cummings out of detention any sooner, it did provoke the French to decide to release Cummings to the American Embassy, rather than sending him to Oloron.

On the morning of December 19, a week short of three months of internment, Cummings was summoned to the director's office. He was told that he would shortly be leaving for Paris. Cummings recorded his amazement:

> "I? Am? Going? To? Paris?" somebody who certainly wasn't myself remarked in a kind of whisper.
>
> "Parfaitement...." But how changed. Who the devil is myself? Where in Hell am I? What is Paris—a place,a somewhere,a city, life,to live:infinitive. Present first singular I live. Thou livest...."Edward E. Cummings will report immediately." Edward E. Cummings....A piece of yellow paper....Paris. Life. Liberté La liberté. "La Liberté"—I almost shouted in agony.

After heartfelt good-byes, Cummings, a free man, boarded the train for the French capital. He arrived that evening and treated himself to a ride in a *fiacre* to the elegant Hôtel Des Saints-Péres. He took a much-needed bath, ate a much-needed meal, and went to bed. The next morning he was appalled that his bed and body were still inundated with fleas, despite the bath. After breakfast, he went over to the American Embassy. Though jaunty, he had lost almost twenty pounds due to the meager rations at La Ferté-Macé, had developed a skin infection on his face, three fingers on his hand were infected, and an ulcerous sore had erupted on his leg. Given the poor sanitary conditions at the facility, he was fortunate that these were the only ills that plagued him. Brown, in fact, had come down with scurvy, which as Cummings noted, made his own "mutilations look like thirty cents or even less."

Cummings's home (circa 1900) at 104 Irving Street, Cambridge, Massachusetts, that "faced the Cambridge world as a solidly constructed mansion."

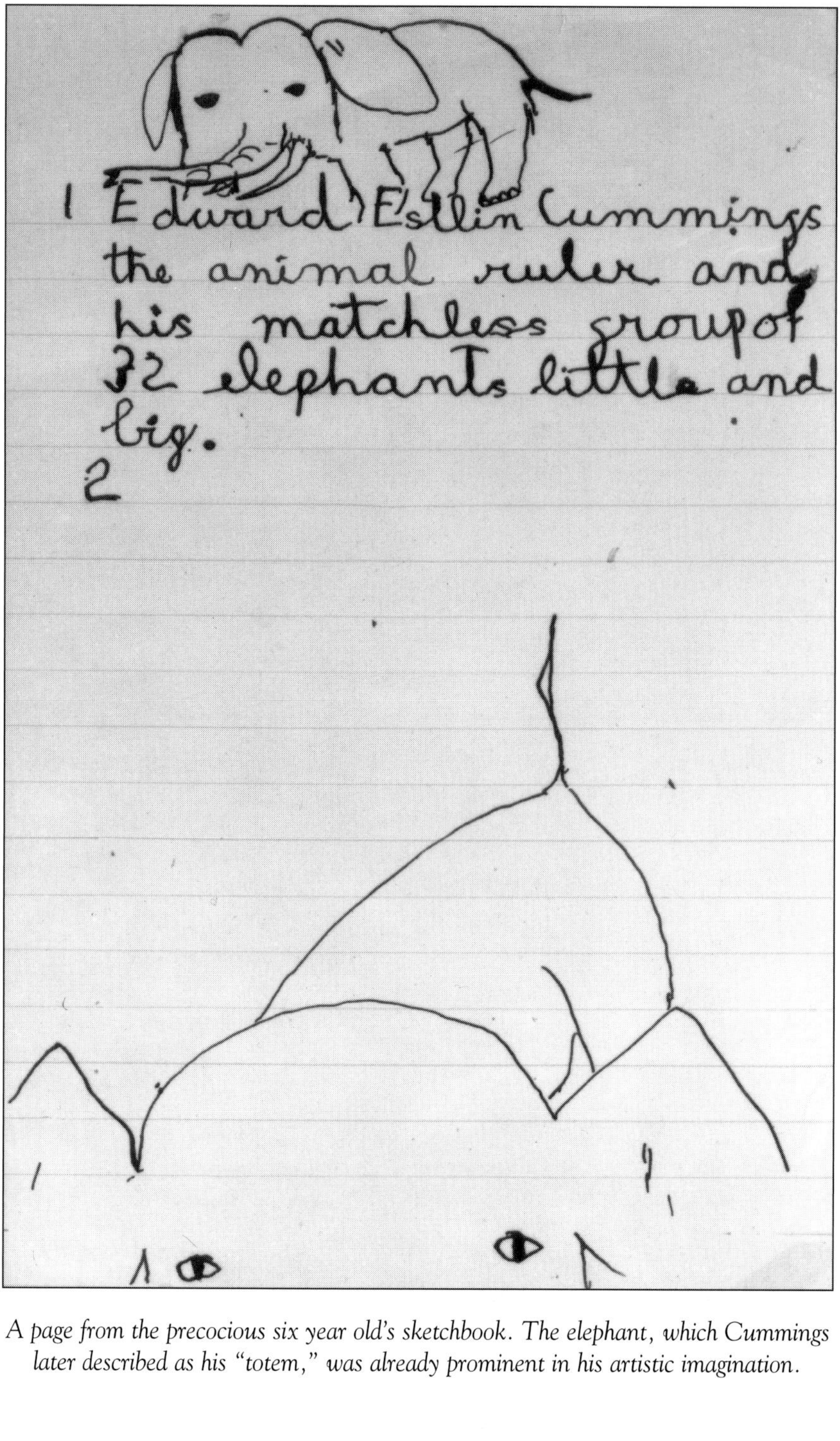
1 Edward Estlin Cummings
the animal ruler and
his matchless group of
32 elephants little and
big.
2

A page from the precocious six year old's sketchbook. The elephant, which Cummings later described as his "totem," was already prominent in his artistic imagination.

The house at Joy Farm around 1905, with Estlin's tepee in the foreground.

In front of the barn at Joy Farm, the Cummings family's summer house in Silver Lake, New Hampshire, in about 1904. Handyman Sandy Hardy is at the left; Rebecca Cummings, the poet's mother, in her flowing white dress holds forth at left center; Estlin sits atop the horse; his sister Elizabeth clings to the donkey; while one of their maids holds the family bull terrier, Rex.

Young Estlin (in sombrero) with his younger sister, Elizabeth, mounted on their donkey, Jack, in a photo from 1905.

Estlin strikes a Huck Finn pose in this photo from about 1906.

The very youthful-appearing champion of "the new art,"
Edward Estlin Cummings, as seen in his 1915 Harvard graduation photo.

Elizabeth Cummings, the poet's sister, in a photo from around 1917.

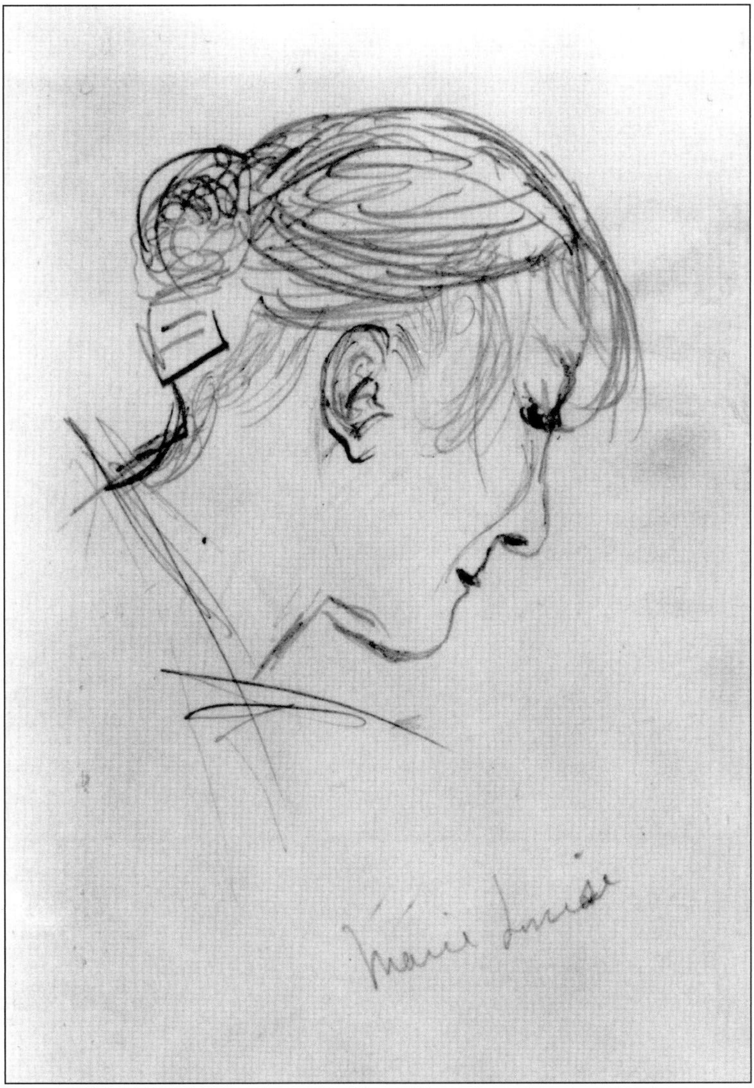

Sketch of Marie Louise Lallemand, "the putain with the ivory throat." She was Cummings's "girlfriend" in Paris in the days before he entered the Ambulance Corps during World War I.

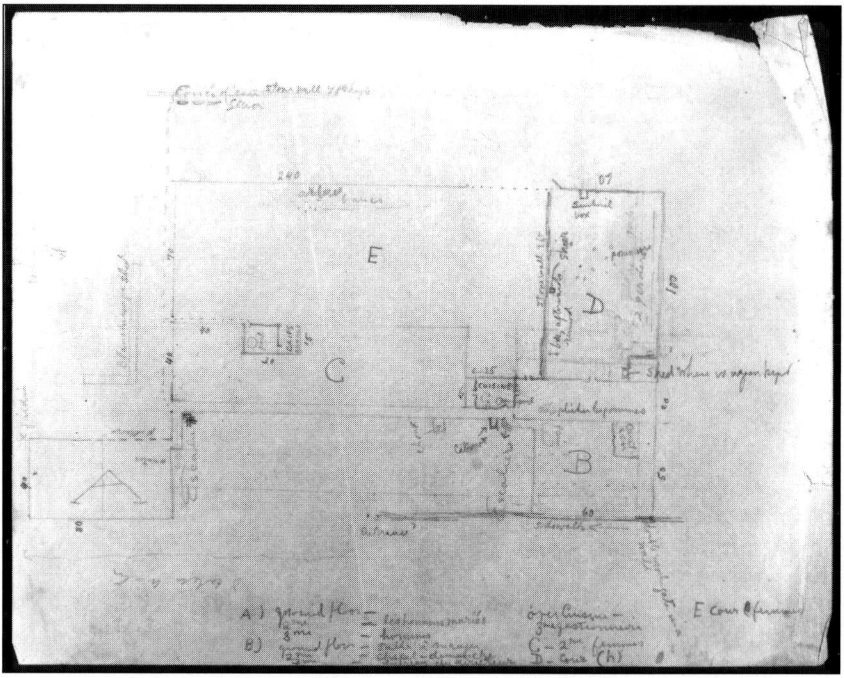

Plan of La Ferté-Macé, the prison where Cummings was interned during World War I, that inspired his first book, The Enormous Room.

Fellow inmates in "The Enormous Room" as sketched by Cummings in 1917. Clockwise from left: the young skipper's mate, Judas, the young skipper's mate from another angle, Bath-house John, and one of "The Delectable Mountains" Jean-Le-Nègre.

The pacifist Private Cummings at Fort Devens, Massachusetts, in 1918, at about the time he met Olaf, "more brave than me:more blond than you."

The dashing young Cummings in Paris, at the time his first book of poems, Tulips and Chimneys *(1923), was being published in New York.*

Scofield Thayer, Cummings's friend and patron, in a photo from around 1919.

A 1919 photo of Cummings's "puella mea," Elaine Orr, the poet's first wife, at the summer home of her first husband, Scofield Thayer.

Sketch of Scofield Thayer, drawn at the time Cummings was having an affair with Elaine, Thayer's wife.

At the moment he arrived for his interview at the embassy, Ambassador Sharp was in the process of dictating a telegram for transmission to the secretary of state informing him that Cummings had been released. He had just finished stating that Cummings was, "in accordance with [his] request," going to be allowed to return to the United States when an aide announced that Cummings was downstairs. A very welcoming ambassador greeted him and plied him with questions. Cummings answered them politely, but pressed firmly for continued action on Brown's case. The official agreed to do what he could.

Toward the end of their meeting, Ambassador Sharp told Cummings he had two choices: "To enter the american [*sic*] army de suite or depart." The decision was easy, remembered Cummings: "I consented to a severance." The ambassador informed him that a ship would sail to New York in two days, and that it was highly advisable that he should book passage. The prodigal happily agreed; within hours he purchased a ticket for December 22 to sail on the *Espagne*.

In the two days before sailing, he celebrated his freedom by wandering around the city: "The streets. Les rues de Paris. I walked past Notre-Dame. I bought tobacco.... Jesus it is cold. Dirty snow. Huddling people. La guerre. Always la guerre. And chill.... Everyone hurried. Everyone hard. Everyone cold. Everyone huddling. Everyone alive;alive:alive."

He was not just idly strolling, though. He had a fixed destination: the apartment of Marie-Louise Lallemand. He had not heard from her except once, while still in the Ambulance Corps. She had informed him that she was ill and had to go to the hospital. His own letters to her after that point had not received replies. When he reached her apartment there was no response to his knock. He left her a note: "Si tu penses que j'ai oublié les jours et nuits que nous avons passé ensembles, tu te trompes, Marie Louise.... Jusqu' à mon retour, acceptes ces baisers!" [If you think that I have forgotten the days and nights we spent together, you are wrong, Marie Louise. Until my return accept these kisses.] In hope that he might find her in one of her usual haunts between the Place de la République and Place de l'Opéra, he plied the boulevards and side streets in search of her, but could find no trace of her presence. Nor could he find Mimi. Both seemed to have vanished; no one seemed to know where they had gone, nor did anyone seem to care.

On the evening of December 21, 1917, he went to a restaurant he and Brown had frequented during their stay in Paris, La Sultana Cherqui.

Over a dinner of couscous, he began flirting with the young waitress, Berthe, whom he had gotten to know slightly on his previous visits. After she finished work he invited her out. The snow was falling as they walked arm in arm to her apartment off the Faubourg Montmartre where they drank champagne and "talked gradually of the war / France death my prison,all pleasant things." But this time Cummings did not confine himself just to talk, but gave himself fully to her, losing, as he put it, his "pucelage" [virginity]. He recorded the event in two prose poems. The first ends like this:

To Undress—laughably mechanical   how my great ludicrous silent boots thrown off Eye each other,really
As she lay:the body a flapping rag of life;I see pale whim of suppressed face framed in the indignant hair,a jiggling rope of smile hung between painted cheeks. and the furry rug of tongue where her Few teeth dance slowly like bad women
My thumb smashes the world—
frot of furied eyes on brain!heart knotted with A suddenly nakedness—.

The second poem, less concrete than the first, is written on a pad of paper bearing the official insignia of the American Embassy in Paris:

The moon-lit snow is falling like strange candy into the big eyes of the
little people with smiling bodies and wooden feet

hard thick feet full of toes

left-handed kiss

I think Berthe is the snow,and comes down into all corners of the city with a smelling sound.   The moon shines all green in the snow.

then saw I 1 star cold in the nearness of sunset. the face of this star was a woman's and had worked hard.   the cheeks were high and hard,it powdered them in a little mirror before everybody saying always nothing at all.   The lips were small and warped,it redenned them.   The one cried to it & it cried Je viens and went on looking at itself in the little mirror saying always nothing —Then I ask the crowding orange—how is that star called? she answers Berthe,

changing into a violet very stealthily
O with whom I lay
Whose flesh is stallions
Then I knew my youth trampled with thy hooves of nakedness

23years lying in the bed in the little street off the Faubourg Mon
martre

tongue's cold wad knocks

On New Year's Day, 1918, the *Espagne* sailed into New York harbor. At the pier to welcome him home were his mother and his friend from Harvard, Sibley Watson.

eight

Singing of Olaf and Elaine

On the morning of January 1, 1918, the rather grim, gaunt twenty-three-year-old Cummings, wrapped in his fur coat and sporting his Harvard hat, from which protruded his straw-blond hair, strode down the *Espagne*'s gangplank to greet Watson and Rebecca. Over lunch at the Watson's house, Cummings, "silent, unsmiling," sat opposite his mother, who, ignoring her son's taciturn manner, filled him in on recent events in the Cummings family. Only two items of information—the death in November of his beloved uncle George, and the receipt of the publication of *Eight Harvard Poets*—seemed to catch his interest.

Watson reported on his own activities and those of their mutual friends. Now enrolled at New York University Medical School, Watson had spent the summer of 1917 working in a hospital outside Paris. Dos Passos was in Italy with the Red Cross. He too had volunteered (a bit later than Cummings) for the Norton-Harjes Ambulance Corps, but had been assigned to *Section Sanitaire LX*, and sent to a different locale from Cummings and Brown. That fall, when Norton-Harjes was subsumed under the command of the American Army, he had enlisted as a "gentleman volunteer" with the Red Cross in Italy. While in Paris awaiting his orders, he had learned of his friend's detention, but despite all his efforts, could not contact him. Thayer, who had fallen arches, had been classified 4F. He and his wife, Elaine, were now living in New York, after spending fifteen months in Chicago. He was an associate editor at *Dial* magazine, a journal dedicated to the arts. Wilson was in the South, receiving military training, Damon was in officer school in Barre, Massachusetts. Others, such as Hillyer and Dudley Poore, were in France.

Later that day, Edward arrived. Though joyous that his son had been returned to him safely, he was still angry and upset at the abuse "his boy" had suffered. Cummings tried to shrug off his father's fuming indignation; his concern was now only for Brown, whom he already knew was suffering from scurvy and malnutrition, and was worried that his physical condition would only worsen.

The Cummings family returned to Cambridge the next day. Cummings was less than pleased to be back in the nest, but realized that he needed a good, plentiful diet and some medical attention. Both would be easier to receive with the help of his family. Recovery was not all that speedy. On the 22 of January, he wrote to Dos Passos of his recuperation, noting that he was somewhat better. He also asked his friend to send Brown some cigarettes or at least a postcard. Brown was, in fact, much on his mind. On his return, he had contacted Brown's family, and both Cummings and his father had pressed his case. So had Senator Henry Cabot Lodge, who was a friend of Paul Bartlett, Brown's uncle. Finally, on January 23, the embassy in Paris notified the secretary of state that Brown would shortly be released and allowed to return to the United States. Washington cabled the happy news to the Cummings family. A subsequent telegram of mid-February confirmed Brown's departure from Bordeaux.

Life at home during these early months of 1918 was not going that well for Cummings, who was chafing at the nurturing confinement. He was particularly at odds with his father, who, still outraged at his son's imprisonment, wanted to go public with the information so that Americans would know the "humiliating truth." His ordeal behind him, Cummings was reluctant to do so. Argument followed argument. Eventually, father and son came to a compromise: Cummings would write the tale of his imprisonment; his father would not press the issue further. In addition, Reverend Cummings would give his son a one thousand dollar liberty bond as compensation for his work.

They could not come to agreement, however, on what Cummings should do about the draft. Edward was urging him to volunteer for officer's training. Cummings wanted no part of being an officer or even a soldier, but thought it better, if worse came to worse, to be thrown in with common soldiers than become an officer. As he put it, he would "take a chance with the guys-born-in-mangers rather than with ginks born in silk shirts." The discussions and arguments eventually ended in a shouting match. To regain some modicum of freedom, Cummings left for New York in late February to visit his friends Watson, Nagle, and Parrish. As it turned out, Parrish, who was leaving town, wanted to sublet his small Christopher Street apartment. Cummings jumped at the opportunity. On March 2 he moved out of the Brevoort Hotel, where he had been staying, and took up residence at 11 Christopher Street, in the West Village. "The studio is made of 3 rooms, sleeping, living and cooking; small and cozy," he wrote his mother on March 12, 1918.

Cummings was delighted to be on his own again in New York. He set up an easel, bought art supplies, and began painting. In early April, Brown joined him as a roommate. Though not completely recovered from scurvy, he, like Cummings, preferred the freedom of being independent of the ministrations of his doctor father and what he saw as the stultifying atmosphere of the family home in Webster, Massachusetts. Cummings immediately introduced Brown to his friends, including Nagle, the Watsons, and the Thayers. Thayer had persuaded the management of the *Dial* to relocate its office to New York. As an associate editor of the magazine, Thayer had already tried to place some of Cummings's poems in the review, but had not met with success. When the magazine's editor, Martyn Johnson, came to New York that spring, Thayer arranged for him to meet Cummings. "I've dined twice with J. [Martyn Johnson] of the Dial,to whom Scofield introduced me.... He will take some stuff,he says,tho' what stuff troubles him,or rather his Georgian anatomy. Another man dead—if not from the neck upward,at least downward," he wrote to his father.

Thayer was not just interested in Cummings's poetry; he was also enthusiastic about his painting, even commissioning four cubist works at $150 each. One of the paintings, "Traffic," Cummings described as "a fairly large organization of spinning, jerking, and generally petulant chromatic planes, the effect of whose mating upon the gentle spectator might be said to produce a sensation analogous to that obtained by peeking into a dynamo-room of a large electric station." Edward Cummings also commissioned a painting from his son, which Cummings rendered somewhat less abstractly than most of the other works he labored on during this period.

Cummings's career as a painter got another boost that spring when he met Nagle's stepfather, the French sculptor Gaston Lachaise, who had immigrated to the United States some years before. Though twelve years older than Cummings, Lachaise and Cummings quickly became friends. Cummings greatly admired Lachaise's work, which he would often view in progress at his studio on 14th Street. Lachaise also liked what his young friend was doing. The fledgling painter was thrilled when Lachaise pronounced a painting of Brooklyn Bridge that he was working on as "beoot'fool," praised the painting for his father as "poetic," and called "Traffic" "healthy." "He honoured me by seeing a fitness of form-to-color," he wrote to his father.

As is evident from the amount of time and attention he devoted to painting, Cummings was at this point as committed (or even more committed) to being an artist as he was a poet. His efforts were not without merit. While certainly influenced by the cubists and futurists, he was developing his own style, which in 1918 was evolving in three linked directions. These stylistic tendencies he categorized as "presentative, semi-abstract, and abstract. Figures often taken in design, more often machinerish elements." Though few of these early paintings have survived, from the canvases that are in existence, a definite technique emerges. Colors and lines define planes, that because of the tension created by their juxtaposition, seem at war with each other. The use of multiple perspectives, and/or figures embedded within the color fields, lends an extra dimension to the work, creating depth on the flat surface. The consequence of all this activity is that the viewer is forced to enter the work at a number of points, but once inside, the point itself vanishes, leaving the observer in a tangle of lines and shapes. Nothing in the field is quite as it seemed at first glance; the illusion of dimensionality, created largely by the alternation of warm and cool colors, is actually a nonlinear geometry in which the collision of color elements continually transforms perception.

While Cummings devoted himself primarily to painting, he did not entirely neglect his writing. However, the account of his imprisonment that he had promised his father did not engage him. Instead, he wrote verse. In tandem with his painterly explorations, his poems of this interlude in New York reflected his continued experimentation with form, or as he wrote on the cover of a binder into which he inserted the typed sheets: "Most significant poems Everything is in arrangement Sounds not words Purity for the first time." That he worked hard at these "arrangements" is evident from looking at the progress between drafts and final product. An early draft reads like this:

Want to spend seven dollars kid?
Seven dollars.
Two for the room and five for the girl.
Give me time to think it over.
Sure.

—Did you hook the bo?
No.

Comin?
Well. I guess not.
I'm sorry.
—Didn't have the seven!

Additional jottings include this note:

I) dark,perfect olive complexion, slight,14-15. Voice sweet
(Irish?

Here's the final version:

wanta
spendsix

dollars Kid
2 for the room
and
four for the girl
thewoman wasnot

quite Fourteen till she smiled
then

Centuries **she**
soft ly
repeated
well **whadyas ay**
dear
wan
taspend

six

Dollars

Cummings hardly spent all of his time painting or writing. With Brown, and often Nagle and Lachaise, he wandered the streets, marveling at the continually engaging sights and sounds of Manhattan. He was, in fact, so taken by listening to the Yiddish spoken on the Lower East Side that he decided to learn the language that, due to his knowledge of German, he could at times penetrate. As before, he delighted in the burlesque shows at Minsky's National Winter Garden Theater, at Second and Houston, and enjoyed introducing his friends to the spectacle. Because of the fondness he and Brown had for Middle Eastern food, they sought out small eating establishments, like Khoury's at 95 Washington Street, that served Cummings's favorite dishes such as eggplant and shish kebab. (A menu is preserved among his papers.)

There were also gatherings at Elaine Thayer's apartment, at 3 Washington Square North, usually in the early evenings, where the charming Elaine hosted her husband's friends. Thayer himself lived in his former apartment in the Benedict, at 80 Washington Square East, though he was occasionally present during these soirées at Elaine's. When Thayer was out of town, as he often was that spring during the time of the *Dial*'s transition from Chicago to New York, Elaine happily presided over the assembled group. Though Thayer explained that the separate living arrangements were necessary for him to be able to get more writing done, Hildegarde Watson, who had known Thayer longer than anyone, felt that the marriage was "full of unrest." The others, including Cummings, appeared to have been content, at least initially, with Thayer's explanation, preferring, perhaps, to enjoy unquestioningly the lavish hospitality Elaine quickly became noted for in their circle. In June he reported that one evening, to his great delight, he "danced with Elaine."

Cummings, aware that Elaine was alone a great deal of the time, also took it upon himself to take her out. As Elaine recalled in a letter to Cummings: "I remember how you used to come to 3 [Washington Square] insisting that I go dancing or on parties with you and B[rown] & you would stay until you had persuaded me to join you. Always I was the one who did not want to walk in the evenings or go to a restaurant but preferred to stay at 3 alone. If you couldn't get me out you had everybody at 3 & raised cain till all hours." That Cummings was paying so much attention to Elaine was well known to her husband. He not only approved but was so grateful that on May 21 he sent a check to Cummings "for the time, energy and other things you have expended upon Elaine."

Cummings apparently cashed the check. But he did so with mixed emotions for over the months during which he had kept Elaine company, he had also begun to fall in love with her, and she in love with him. She had confided to him that Thayer, despite his willingness to lavish money and gifts on her, had become increasingly cold, remote, and uninterested in her sexually. She felt confused, rejected. Thayer dismissed her pain; indeed, he seemed to delight in torturing her with a variety of scornful remarks and put-downs, often made in public. Cummings was sympathetic, seeing her as "someone wronged—suffering, rudely treated—abused," but remained loyal to his friend.

His regard for Thayer—friend, patron, and supporter—was soon to be sorely tested when one night Cummings felt that Elaine had attempted to seduce him: "She 1st looked at me (her bedroom) I felt physical fascination I doubt—no,She couldn't mean me! that I would Desire her—<u>Because she is Another's</u> She Belongs to <u>Another Person</u>. She was somebody's wife. Not only that—but my friend's." Cummings remembered that he "did not touch her" just "looked deservingly, and left the room." But the emotional wrangling with himself continued. "I was ASTONISHED & PLEASED (my vanity immensely flattered)," he noted in his private journal, in which he wrote obsessively about the situation: "I see E[laine] not as she is—a dissatisfied girl who needs a fuck…nor do i want to fuck her, much —no, no, I want to love, <u>PROTECT</u> deserve her.... "I HAVE AN IDEE FIXE OF RIGHT & WRONG."

He saw himself initially not as her lover but as a "chivalrous rescuer" and she as "an angel, a superhuman person." He blamed his upbringing for his ambivalence, recalling his father's often repeated dictum "'a gentleman is always chivalrous to a lady.'" He thought his "sexual ignorance" also contributed to his being "afraid of reality," of himself. At the same time, he could not overcome his attraction or desire for her. During the course of an evening out on the town with Thayer and Elaine, Thayer had belittled Elaine on several occasions. On the way back home, in a taxi Cummings shared with them, Cummings put his arm around Elaine, feeling her breast. "I felt no sex attraction but merely resented Thayer's vulgarity or roughness." Thayer did not react.

By early summer, the relationship had progressed to a stage of greater intimacy, "lying together, naked, without Screwing—mutual self denial." Cummings thought of himself as "being led." Or as he reflected later, "I pushed the responsibility (adultery) on to HER, I refused any responsibility myself.... She had to make every move. I was purely passive." Even when they finally did have intercourse, it was Elaine who took the lead. "You had to tell me to go in:'go in, oh please go in'.!.... You took me & put me inside with your hand.... I go off TOO SOON."

It is not clear when or how Thayer found out about the affair, or who informed him, but he was apparently neither surprised nor upset. He told Cummings that sometime before he had even "come on the scene" he had had "a neurotic turning away from Elaine but it was not conscious." In retrospect, it appears what was actually going on with Thayer was that he was in the throes of a sexual identity crisis in which he found himself increasingly attracted to adolescent boys. There is no evidence that he initially shared his internal struggle or impulses with either Cummings or Elaine, or if he did, he chose to subsume it under the general doctrine of his firm belief in sexual liberty. In essence, both Cummings and Elaine felt that Thayer had given them permission to pursue their relationship, which they ardently did. In exchange, Thayer reserved the right to seek out others, a compromise that seemed more than fair to the new couple. The friendship between the two men continued as closely as it had before.

On May 6, 1918, Cummings's idyll in New York had an ominous shadow cast over it in the form of a notice from the Cambridge Draft Board that he was "subject to call for service." Not long after receiving the news, he learned that he had to report by July 1 to his local draft board to explain why he was either not in the army or working in a vital industry. The war, in fact, was raging in Europe, and recruits were desperately needed. The Somme, where Cummings had been stationed, was now engulfed in battle. Had Cummings not been arrested, he would have been in the thick of fighting by this point, and rather than idling, would have been frantically evacuating scores of wounded soldiers.

Reverend Cummings, aware of the conflict's intensity and high casualty rates, informed his son that he could secure him an "essential job" in Boston. But Cummings, madly in love with both Elaine and with his life in New York, would have none of it. "I would rather die than leave New York at this moment.... My presence here on this spot and moment is requisite to my absolute and individual success in existence," he defiantly wrote his father.

But he did not die when he, in fact, was summoned for induction in July and was shipped off to Camp Devens in Massachusetts on July 24. On July 29, he wrote his mother of his first few days in the army: "Have signed my preference to be interpreter. Occupation artist.... The Yid who took down all this data was a medical discipulo, & addenda'd (après 'Artist,' 'Specialist in Cubism.' This occupied all-yesterday; later the grand Looker-Over-of-17,0000000 papers said 'I wonder what they'll do with an artist in the army.'"

The grand Looker-Over's question was shortly answered. Cummings's preference to serve as an interpreter was ignored; instead, he was assigned to the infantry. On August 14, 1918, he wrote his mother of "the greatest misfortune:" "A number of privates were pulled out of the ranks to 'go to school' for non-commissioned officers, drill squads,etc. I was unhappily 1. After 10 minutes argument with the captain,I was told to continue 'schooling' and if necessary,drop out when the time for promotion came. I told the captain about my temperment,my occupation,my equivocal behaviour under fire,etc.—no impression whatever,as I expected." To his further chagrin, his plea was not only ignored by the captain, but he was promoted "acting corporal on basis of 'very high psychological examination.'" By the end of August, he reported to his mother that he was "out of 'school.'" Then added, "no officer's job for this weevil dodger."

Despite his gripes, Cummings endured his training without landing himself in the stockade. He was by no means a model soldier; he simply figured out how much in step he had to be, and whenever he could, he marched to his own drummer. To his chagrin, however, he had not had the good fortune to find a soulmate, like Brown, among the ranks: "Out of 250 more or less male bipeds with whom I cohabited night and day, our unhero could only find a pair of human beings," Cummings later recalled. The "pair of human beings" he did somewhat find to his liking—a bakery delivery man named Coty and a semi-illiterate butcher named Perry—were friends only in the context that they unwillingly shared the same fates. The other 248 "male bipeds" he found either too uncouth, or, worse, too accepting of their roles. Their acquiescence to military discipline, their blind belief that they were in fact fighting "to save the world for democracy," grated on him. At least at La Ferté-Macé he had found kindred spirits, all in rebellion. He could not understand how his fellow soldiers could be so content with "a complete separation from all I hold to be life."

Cummings was not an all-out snob, for he truly did not judge others by their education or upbringing, or by how much money they (or their fathers) had in the bank. He did, however, highly value intelligence and individualism. Interest in the arts certainly helped, too, but most of all he was drawn to those who could think for themselves. He found few at Camp Devens. Even fewer seemed appalled at the pro-American, anti-German sentiments that accompanied military training, and so repulsed Cummings: "2 lieutenants, antiphonally;—'Don't forget you men want to have guts at <u>both</u> ends of your guns'. 'Yes, we don't want any helmets as souvenirs, we want <u>guts</u>,we prefer 'em,we can use 'em for <u>fertilizer</u>.'" Bayonet practice was as much indoctrination as gaining prowess in the art of death: "'<u>Stick it in the bellies,And Don't Stick it In Deep,stick it in A Little Way. There's nothing better than to see a Bosch die</u>.... <u>Let them die slowly</u>.... <u>We don't take German Prisoners. We only have to feed 'em if we do. So we stick 'em</u>'"

There was one soldier who believed even more than Cummings that obedience to one's own consciousness was vastly more important than allegiance to authority. The man was "a big blond perfect stranger" whom Cummings met in the barracks. The day Cummings first made his acquaintance, the soldier was lying on his bunk reading *Religio Medici* by Sir Thomas Browne. He was waiting for an interview with the commanding officer, who wanted an explanation for the man's refusal to pick up a gun. Cummings was immediately drawn to this principled pacifist, and they struck up a conversation in which they shared their views on the army. Cummings liked his sense of humor, yet sensed that he was stronger than steel in his convictions. Upon his return from the meeting with the commander, the blond man reported that the officer had tried to break his resolve by asking him what he would do if a German came through the window and raped his sister. The man reported his answer to Cummings: "I told the truth. Sir, I have no sister."

The next day, the man disappeared. The rumor was that he had been transferred to an army prison. This meant, as Cummings soon learned, that a brutal fate awaited the conscientious objector. In a letter to his father, Cummings wrote of what he had heard from a lieutenant: "You men ought to take a look at what they do to a man at the military prisons,Jay,New York;Leavenworth,Kansas;Fort Angel(?)California.... When a man comes to Fort Jay,the first thing they do is give him a g.d. fine beating. They black his eyes for him. They do that on principle down there."

Cummings did not know or at least record the man's name. But neither he nor his principles nor his probable punishment were forgotten. For generations of readers, the man has been known as Olaf, and the responses to his torturers enshrined in the great literature of rebellion:

> i sing of Olaf glad and big
> whose warmest heart recoiled at war:
> a conscientious object-or
>
> his well beloved colonel(trig
> westpointer most succinctly bred)
> took erring Olaf soon in hand;
> but—though an host of overjoyed
> noncoms(first knocking on the head
> him)do through icy waters roll
> that helplessness which others stroke
> and brushes recently employed
> anent this muddy toiletbowl,
> while kindred intellects evoke
> allegiance per blunt instruments—
> Olaf(being to all intents
> a corpse and wanting any rag
> upon which God unto him gave)
> responds,without getting annoyed
> "I will not kiss your fucking flag"
>
> ....

Christ(of his mercy infinite)
i pray to see;and Olaf,too

preponderatingly because
unless statistics lie he was
more brave than me:more blond than you.

Cummings's own sense of dissatisfaction with the army was augmented by his acute sense of deprivation from what and whom he most loved: freedom, art, and Elaine. As a soldier he was constantly herded from one task to another, with little opportunity to engage his own being freely. In the evenings and on Sundays, he did manage to write letters, sketch, work on a poem or two, but he felt extremely curtailed, confined. Given how little time he actually had for writing, the amount of work he produced is remarkable. At least a dozen fine poems, and a great many more lesser efforts, were given voice during this period. But he was lonely, often on the verge of depression, and bored.

A visitor occasionally arrived to break the monotony. Cummings wrote to Hildegarde Watson of a visit he received from her mother: "One day Mrs. Lasell drove up to camp in a great black Cadillac laden with baskets of food and long bottles of wine. She'd had an invitation by a Colonel friend to visit him in a very swank officers' club nearby. Followed by myself, Mrs. Lasell swept in the door. No mere private like myself had ever stepped in there before. Breaking all rules, we wined and dined together magnificently." Hildegarde Watson added that Cummings told her that "in the midst of the depressing camp life," it was "one of the happiest experiences he ever had. He described the Colonel's speechless quiescence before my handsome mother's introduction of her escort, the lively, young albeit 'Private' poet."

But the one person he most wanted to see—Elaine—did not come. In August, Cummings put in for a weekend furlough in the hope of being able to see his beloved. The weeks of waiting were fraught with anxiety as it was unclear whether he would actually be given leave, and if he did, whether he would be able to see Elaine. The one surviving letter Elaine wrote to Cummings during this period reveals her own unease: "I heard W[atson] & Sco[field] talking over the telephone & it was about you & as

I was on W's end I heard almost nothing except that it was about you & I thought maybe they had heard you weren't going to get fur low or something. But I couldn't ask W & I may not see Sco till hours and hours."

A rather sardonic note from Thayer to Cummings probably did little to raise the lover's spirits: "That we may understand each other more adequately, can you make your appointment with E.E. [Elaine Eliot] for New York instead of Boston? Should you do so I shall study well my exits and entrances. I have written E.E. of the possibility. Wire her if you can and when you can. If you can get to Boston but not N. Y., entrust all to her ear. She can (on occasion) be faithful." In late September, Cummings did get his leave. He met Elaine in Boston, seeing no one else but her.

His preoccupation with Elaine is evident from the poetry he wrote while at Camp Devens. Among notebook pages interspersed with erotic drawings are drafts and versions of love lyrics that alternate between seeing the woman as an idealized object of desire and a degraded and degrading whore. This dichotomy can be seen as a reflection of Cummings's own ambivalence as to whether sex was, as he had been taught throughout his childhood and adolescence, "dirty" and forbidden, or was an act natural and spontaneous, ecstatic and celebratory. He wondered how he could reconcile his love for "BEAUTIFUL ELAINE DEAR SWEET GIRL MY IDEAL, MY INCOMPARABLE, MY TO BE WORSHIPED" with his consistent "attraction to whores" and a notion that would not unloose itself from his brain that "sex was sinful."

Examples of his feelings are contained in poems with lines such as these:

the bed is not very big

a sufficient pillow shoveling
her small manure-shaped head...

or:

...my

god—a patter of kisses,the chewed stump

of a mouth,huge dropping of a flesh from
hinging thighs...

or:

the dirty colours of her kiss have just
throttled
my seeing blood…

or:

O It's Nice To Get Up In,the slipshod mucous kiss
of her riant belly's fooling bore

These are all indicative of Cummings's more negative attitudes toward the sexual act in which the woman is viewed, in his words, as an "amiable putrescence." While these poems are not without merit, the portrayal of sex and women is hardly commendable. Man is seen as a victim of his animal sex drive—"huge passion like a business"—that forces him to overcome his revulsion at the actuality of a woman's far-from-perfect flesh for the purposes of self-gratification.

In contrast to these verses are love poems of a very different sort that reveal a more refined sensibility. All written for Elaine, they mirror his regard for her as an exquisite being, "delicate,craving gentleness." One of his more tender lyrics is this one, written after his rendezvous in Boston:

my little heart is so wonderfully sorry
lady,to have seen you on its threshold
smiling,to have experienced the glory

of your slender and bright going, and it is so cold
(nothing being able to comfort its grief)
without you,that it would like i guess to die.
Also my lady do i feel as if
perhaps the newly darkening texture of my
upon nothing a little clumsily closing
mind keep always something who has

fallen,who being beautiful is gone
and suddenly. As if you will point at the evening

"in this particular place,my lover,the moon
unspeakably slender and bright was"

In both types of poems, death and damnation make several appearances. Despite his struggle to see sexuality in something other than pejorative terms, he never fully abolishes the idea that "the wages of sin are death," thus we get lines like these:

...breathings stopped
to

hear,indarkness,water the lips of death

or:

—and Love 's a coach with gilt hopeless wheels mired
where sits rigidly her body's doll
gay exactly perishing sexual,

Even one of his best poems from the period casts him and Elaine in the role of Paulo and Francesca, Dante's adulterous lovers doomed to spend eternity with each other in Hell's Second Circle where, as Cummings writes, "fiends with pitchforkthings / will catch and toss me lovingly to and fro." In another he speaks of "my deathly body's deadly lady."

Cummings is clearly perplexed by his inability to have a more natural view of sex. One entry in his journal concludes that Elaine must love him for his mind for the rest of him is "coarse, vulgar (sexual) ugly poor strong, healthy coarse but INTELLIGENT." Other notes indicate that he feels part of his problem has to do with his "complete sexual ignorance" that gets in the way of him being himself, and that leads to his being unable to see women in a less diametrically opposed fashion: lady and whore. It would take him a good many years to resolve the issue.

On November 11, 1918, less than four months after Cummings had been inducted into the army, the war ended. Private Cummings, now more than ever, wanted to resume his former life in New York, but a discharge did not seem to be forthcoming in the forseeable future. He angled for interviews with the commander, hoping that he might be able to win his freedom. His attempts apparently only prolonged his distress. On January 2, 1919, he wrote to his mother that "the entire Société de Droits Humains of which i am an ex-officio officer, has been stuck in the kitchen with threats as to the permanence of their new position as KP." Finally, on January 13, 1919, he was able to inform his father that the "recommended-for-discharge" list had his name on it.

In the interview with the captain, which entailed "much mental fisticuffs," he reported that he had abruptly told the officer that he "was probably the most ill-fitted man to be here, and most un-at-home." The captain was unfazed, but seemed more slightly moved by Cummings's account of having volunteered for the Ambulance Corps. "Perhaps my best card was the contract with Mr. Thayer of New York for 4 pictures,$600 to be paid me on completion of the 4th and how the call-to-arms left me with only 3 completed."

The next day, January 14, he was given a final physical exam. On the seventeenth, the twenty-four-year-old Cummings walked out of Camp Devens his own man.

nine

Poet, Painter, and Papa in New York

Cummings headed for New York within days of his discharge. He was eager to resume his former life after six months of having his "destiny diverted," as had Brown, with whom he met up in the city. After a few days spent together at a hotel, Brown and Cummings rented a studio at 9 West 14th Street for twenty dollars a month. On February 9, 1919, Cummings wrote to his mother that they had "no gas-jets,a skylight,an open fire,2 closets." After suffering one night of bitter cold, Cummings acquired some coal from Elaine to heat the apartment.

Aside from the lights on Broadway blazing again—the wartime "lightless" edict having been rescinded—the city had not outwardly changed much in the six months Cummings had been at Camp Devens. However, the mood was quite different. When Cummings had departed for the army, the metropolis, along with the entire country, was tense, anxious about the war and the American soldiers dying by the thousands in French trenches. But with the armistice of November 11, 1918, euphoria had descended, and the population began once again look to what the future would hold. As the new year began, there was talk of prosperity and peace.

The only dark cloud on the political horizon appeared to be the rising threat of Bolshevism, but the authorities were doing their best to ensure that the zeal in some quarters for the victory of the Reds in the Russian Revolution would not take root on American soil. Mayor Hylan of New

York, in response to pro-Bolshevist meetings and demonstrations, banned the display of red flags in the streets and vowed to "disperse all unlawful assemblies." Nonetheless, crowds still gathered at a mass Socialist meeting at Madison Square Garden, where after a confrontation between the Socialists and the Anti-Socialists, the police were called in to restore order. Cummings's sympathies were with the Socialists, but his main interest was in another form of revolt: art.

The revolution in literature that had already gathered momentum in Europe was far less evident in New York. The "big" American books of 1918–19 were *The Education of Henry Adams*, Willa Cather's *My Antonia*, and Booth Tarkington's *The Magnificent Ambersons*. Stateside Experimentalism was largely confined to the pages of Margaret Anderson's avant-garde literary magazine the *Little Review*, which had just moved from Chicago to New York. But even then, most of the more radical work published in the magazine was that of Europeans, most notably James Joyce, whose *Ulysses* began running in serial form in the *Little Review* in 1918.

"I'm to pieces pleased," Cummings wrote to Hildegarde Watson over the *Ulysses* installments. He also took note of a little book Thayer had sent him at Camp Devens called *Prufrock and other Observations*, published in England, but written by a Harvard-educated American named T. S. Eliot. There is no indication that Cummings connected the author with the Tom Eliot who had acted opposite him a few years before in the Cambridge production of *Fanny and the Servant Problem*.

While the literature of the new was extremely important for Cummings, he was not just looking at literature as a measure of modernism. In what appears to be a draft for an essay written while he was in the army, he attempted a survey of "the actual and significant dancings of the few" in which he tried to "distinguish in the vivid plastic tumult certain vital musical gestures." He then went on to say:

> I may as well avoid misunderstanding by giving these vital musical gestures their proper names. They are:
>
> Brancusi (especially the polished brass Mlle. at the last Independent)
> Ezra Pound (δωρια)

Gleizes (skyscraper motifs)
The best of Matisse (before he imitated Matisse)

———

T.S. Eliot (Preludes and Rhapsody on a Windy Night)
Schoenberg (Five Orchestral Pieces)
The Woolworth Building
The Russian Ballet (Parade, Till, L'Après Midi,and Petroushka)

To this list of genuine phenomena the months have latterly added James Joyce (Ulysses).

Cummings's awareness that modernism was interconnected, that vitality lurked as much in a building or in painting or in music as in a poem, was in many ways a continuation of the ideas he had espoused in his commencement part, "The New Art." But the intervening years had also led him to experiment actively in his own work—both plastic and poetic—in translating these ideas into practice. His "faits" are clear examples of synesthesia, in which visual and verbal elements combine to create an overall effect. In his painting, too, he attempted to portray a verbal concept (the title) in a pictorial fashion. This nascent principle of uniting the arts would endure in his own work for the rest of his life.

Within days of moving into the studio, Cummings had set up his easel and was painting again. He completed the promised fourth painting for Thayer, as well as three drawings of nudes that he also gave his friend. Thayer was enthusiastic; he framed them all, displaying them in the "black room" of his apartment. He also tried to interest collectors, including Gertrude Stein's brother, Leo Stein, in purchasing further Cummings paintings. There is no record, though, of any sales at this time to anyone but Thayer.

Cummings was not entirely relying on Thayer to push his work. At the urging of Nagle and Lachaise, he submitted two paintings, *Sound* [number one] and *Noise* [number one] for the March 1919 exhibition of the Society of Independent Artists in New York. He described *Sound* as "a lot of circles going on a bat;" *Noise* as "more swimmingish." In more prosaic terms, the paintings are a synthesis of cubism and futurism. From cubism, Cummings appropriated the emphasis on intersecting planes defined by bold colors; from futurism he invigorated the geometry with motion. The result is whirls, swirls, and faceting imposed on a planar structure.

At the Independent Artists' Show, amidst a sea of landscapes, Cummings's work stood out. A critic for the *New York Sun* noted that "the brilliant sally in color by Mr. Cummings will greatly impress those who have arrived at an appreciation of the abstract in art." Even more important to Cummings was the praise he received from painters:

> [Albert] Gleizes(the "first cubist"—probably the most individual,though somewhat cold abstract painter in America,and after Picasso—best known among painters of a type was(to use Lachaise's phrase)"TAKEN OUT OF HIS FEET" by the two things of mine at the Independent. According to Nagle,he said later on that they were the "best things in oil" he had seen "in America". Mr. [Walter] Pach, the director [of the Independent Show],was(as you may imagine)highly pleased;and said very pleasant things.... (Pach,you may be amused to know,came within an ace of selling "Sound.")

Cummings also reported that Mrs. Lachaise was highly enthusiastic, asking him "How does it feel to be the Sensation of the Independent?" He received encouragement from his father, as well: "My paternal pride is gratified by the appreciation which your work is receiving." He also put his money where his mouth was, offering to purchase a painting "at the regular exhibition price." Cummings could not sell *Noise* [number one] to his father, as it had already been taken by Thayer who had the painting "hung in the 'black room' (or rather screwed; at great cost, to a wall)." It is unclear what painting, if any, he did furnish his father for his letters in response to Edward's offers of money are all met with rebuffs. Cummings was determined and delighted that he was able to make his own living.

Cummings was not totally self-serving, however. To Thayer he wrote that "It would please me far more...should you like Lachaise's head...enough to buy it;than should you buy either of my things." Thayer complied with Cummings's request, but also, of course, came through on purchasing a Cummings, as well.

Cummings's success at the Independent Artists' Show was followed by his placing *Noise Number 2*, in The Penguin Gallery, on Washington Square, run by a friend of Lachaise, Horace Brodsky. Cummings reported that while Brodsky willingly accepted the canvas, he had to ask the artist which side of the painting was up. Though the painting was well displayed, Brodsky did not manage to sell it and eventually returned it to the artist.

Though the paintings of this time bear the influence of Cummings's acquaintance with the work of Joseph Stella, Albert Gleizes, Picasso, and the early John Marin, they are not derivative. Just as with his work in words, Cummings "made it new." Indeed, painting, for Cummings, was never separate from language, as this note on his own work clearly shows:

> This is not the painting of forces. It is Force the painter Himself. Or—not painting but Forcing,if the verb be felt as intransitive. It is the Selfing of things. You have doubtless had the common experience of sitting in a dusk-nibbled room,say Elaine's,the probable room-full-of-furniture is not disintegrating;there is integrating delicately a cubist pulp. The nouns are gone,the adjectives have fainted,an adverbial stress seizes(i am still talking about the room). There is what we mistakenly call a moment,a point Now,a Verb=Is. Distinctness. or: this cubic pulp SELFS.

While the note approaches the abstractness of his paintings, it, like his canvasses, can be deciphered with a little work. In effect, Cummings is saying that the artist, not the paint nor some intellectual concept, makes the product. That product becomes meaningless if the viewer attempts to break it down into constituent units, since all the components contribute invisibly to the support of the structure as a whole. In essence, it becomes an "IS," which Cummings defined in another note:

> IS = the cold 3rd singular of the intense live verb, to feel.
> Not to completely feel = thinking, the warm principle.
> incomplete thinking = Belief, the box in which god and all other nouns are kept.

In *The Enormous Room* he elaborated further on "IS:"

> There are certain things in which one is unable to believe for the simple reason that he never ceases to feel them. Things of this sort—things which are always inside of us and in fact are us and which consequently will not be pushed off or away where we can begin thinking about them—are no longer things;they,and the us which they are,equals A Verb;an IS.

The notion of "IS" is crucial in understanding Cummings's approach to both his work and his life. Feeling, for Cummings, is always superior to thinking; thinking is superior to belief. To act out of feeling is the highest good; to act out of a blind belief that one should do *x* or *y* is folly. To paint a picture or write a poem out of thinking or belief can only result in an inferior product. The artist must feel his feelings, and those feelings must be first. They must always be the force that creates and drives the work. Living, too, is about being an "IS." For Cummings there was no distinction between creating a work and creating life. The same "ISness" had to be present if one were to live fully engaged with oneself and with others.

Feeling was very much what guided Cummings in his relationship with Elaine that he also ardently resumed upon his return to New York. Unlike Thayer, who continued to see the affair in philosophical terms—a person should be free of convention—Cummings did not attempt to intellectualize his emotions:

> the spring has been exquisite and the
> summer may be beautiful.   But,
> tell me with eyes quiteshut
> did you love me,will you love me
>
> and perfectly so forth;i see,
> kissing you—only kissing
> you(it is still spring
> and summer may be beautiful)...

In May the dynamic of the romance was altered considerably when Elaine told her lover that she was pregnant. There was no doubt that Cummings was the father. Thayer, informed of the news, suggested Elaine have an abortion. Cummings noted that he "wanted E[laine] as a mistress." He then added, "I was not interested in her having a child—in fact, I advised her, like Thayer (following his suggestion) to PREVENT the child, with an operation." Elaine balked at the idea. Watson suggested pills to bring on a miscarriage. If Elaine took them, they did not have any effect.

Curiously, there are few mentions in Cummings's surviving notes or journals to indicate his state of mind or the state of the relationship at that time. Cummings apparently did not express his feelings to his closest friends either, not even informing Brown, who was well aware of the affair, that he was the father of the child Elaine was carrying. What is clear from the fragments preserved from this time is that Cummings was totally unprepared to accept the responsibilities of paternity. "I was not really interested in her but in my work," Cummings wrote. Another note throws some light on his way of acting: "The artist, if something goes wrong, escapes from something by way of (via) IDEAS, imagines that it isn't wrong."

Cummings's statement was not simply philosophic; it was exactly what he did, throwing himself alternately into work (mainly painting) and carousing with Brown and friends. He did not entirely ignore Elaine, but was hardly as ardent in his pursuit as he had been before. Indeed, it seems as if Cummings did all he could to purge from his mind the reality of Elaine's pregnancy. He noted, "Art happens if—&—when you're forgetting everything—&—everyone (and first of all Herself!) in La Vie, in Mystère; in MoreThanYou." Cummings's desire for oblivion was given a boost by Thayer, who, some time that spring or in early summer, magnanimously informed both his friend and Elaine that he would assume responsibility for fatherhood. Elaine agreed to the pretense.

Officially relieved of any claims of paternity, Cummings happily spent most of the summer painting and writing, seemingly no longer concerned that Elaine was carrying his baby. He remained preoccupied with both visual and verbal work. Over that summer he completed another in his series of *Noise* paintings, and sketched prodigiously. He also began working with words again, attempting to begin writing the book he had promised his father he would render—the account of his imprisonment at La

Ferté-Macé. But he seems to have made little progress. As for poetry, he devoted himself less to writing new work than to rewriting and revising, in order to put together a manuscript of poems that he hoped he might get published. He probably had Thayer in mind as a potential publisher. As early as July of 1917, he had suggested to his patron and friend that he might want to bring out a book of his poems. While Thayer had not embraced the idea at the time, he had not rejected it either. And he had continually been supportive of Cummings as both painter and poet.

In July, Cummings interrupted his work to visit Thayer and Elaine, who were staying with Thayer's mother at her house in Edgartown on Martha's Vineyard. Though the air was undoubtedly charged with undercurrents—perhaps because of the presence of Thayer's mother and Elaine's sister, Constance—Cummings, Thayer, and Elaine generally opted for pretense over reality. (Cummings even stayed in a house separate from the Thayers.) Indeed, Thayer and Elaine seemed very much the couple. It was not a total charade on Elaine's part. Cummings quotes Elaine as saying that she still loved Thayer. But Thayer, acknowledging what he termed his own "neurotic" attitude, confessed to Cummings that he could not reciprocate her love; instead, he felt only detachment.

Despite the occasional dark cloud punctuating the atmosphere, the holiday proceeded with a high degree of gentility and politeness. Cummings wrote his mother, "Daily,Elaine,generally her sister,and myself row,or paddle (in Scofield's canoe) to the bathing beach,—an infection of the hand keeping Scofield away temporarily. . . . We drove a great deal in Elaine's car,and play tennis occasionally." Poetry, naturally, was also an ingredient in their time together. Cummings had brought the manuscript of his new book with him, and read or recited some of the poems to Thayer and Elaine and others. Thayer was particularly taken with Cummings's recitation of "the Cambridge Ladies who live in furnished souls," and asked to see the finished manuscript. Cummings happily agreed to let Thayer see the book, probably sending it to him in early or mid-September.

After his somewhat charged visit to Thayer and Elaine, Cummings went up to Silver Lake to work further on his manuscript, and do some sketching and painting in the quiet of the New Hampshire mountains. But the memory of Edgartown stayed with him. On August 16, 1919, he wrote to Thayer thanking him for his hospitality. The letter closes with a salutation to Elaine: "with love to deliciae meae puellae [my darling girl]."

He then appends, in Latin and in full, Catullus's poem "Lugete, o Veneres Cupidinesque [Mourn, oh Venuses, Cupids]." It was not a haphazard choice. Catullus's verse is addressed to his lover, his "deliciae meae puellae," and laments the death of his girl's beloved sparrow whom she loved more than her eyes. The sparrow now travels in shadows, never to return, and his girl's eyes are red and swollen with tears.

It is unlikely that Cummings wrote out Catullus's poem simply as a way of explaining his phrase "deliciae meae puellae." Perhaps he intended for Thayer and Elaine to recognize that he was projecting himself into the sparrow. But given what he had learned from Thayer about his "neurotic turning away from Elaine," it seems more the case that he saw Thayer, with whom Elaine was still in love, in the role of the sparrow, now "dead" to her.

If Thayer responded, the letter is lost. What was not lost was Cummings's newly rediscovered obsession with Elaine. A month later he wrote to Thayer that "i have been like Hel working, like sissyphus of stone fame, upon the greatest Chanson d'Amour of the Centuries. it is called PUELLA MEA." Cummings's claim was not entirely unfounded; "Puella Mea," the longest poem he ever wrote, is one of the more remarkable sustained love poems in English in the twentieth century.

Unabashed, excessive, exuberant, tender, and florid, the irregularly rhymed poem celebrates his "darling girl" or "puella mea" in both a conventional and unconventional manner. As in "Epithalamion," he employs a good deal of allusion to the classical tradition, comparing Elaine to, among others, Helen, Iseult, Grania, Salomé, and Guenevere, but adds that "lovely as those ladies were / mine is a little lovelier." Unlike the wedding poem, though, the form and formula of "Puella Mea" are frequently overwhelmed by lush, fresh images unique to Cummings:

my fragile lady wandering
in whose perishable poise
is the mystery of Spring
(with her beauty more than snow
dexterous and fugitive
my very frail lady drifting
distinctly,moving like a myth
in the uncertain morning,with
April feet like sudden flowers
and all her body filled with May)...

And:

the immanent subliminal
fern of her delicious voice
(of her voice which always dwells
beside the vivid magical
impetuous and utter ponds
of dream;and very secret food
its leaves inimitable find
beyond the white authentic springs,
beyond the sweet instinctive wells,
which make to flourish the minute
spontaneous meadow of her mind)...

Cummings does not neglect to extol any part of Elaine's being. He duly describes and rapturously praises her feet, head, eyes, face, voice, mind, wrists, hands, fingers, hair, breasts, waist, belly, thighs, sex, lips, mouth, and smell. And, naturally, no other of legend or myth or actuality can compare: "Harun Omar and Master Hafiz / keep your dead beautiful ladies."

By the end of the poem, though, the fantastical celebration is returned to reality with the recognition that beauty is ultimately doomed: "Eater of all things lovely—Time!" This awareness, therefore, makes the moment even more precious and does not diminish what is:

in life's very fragile hour
(when the world was like a tale
made of laughter and of dew,
was a flight,a flower,a flame,
was a tendril fleetly curled
upon frailness)...

Although Cummings probably sent a copy of the poem to Elaine, there is no record of her receiving it. To Thayer, though, he wrote that he intended to include "Puella Mea" in the manuscript, apparently already in his friend's possession, along with three unnamed new sonnets for the "Realities" section and two sonnets destined to be placed in the section he titled "Actualities." The book, by now, had a title: *Tulips &*

Chimneys. Cummings had arrived at the title through an amusement frequently indulged in by him and Brown, that of placing disjunctive words together. But as Cummings also reflected, the title had another significance: "Tulips = Two Lips Chimneys = Penises."

When Cummings returned to New York from Silver Lake in late September or early October, a few weeks before his twenty-fifth birthday, he re-immersed himself in his work, and in what New York could give him: an ever-changing panorama of people viewed on numerous rambles through the city, the "exotic" fare to be had at ethnic restaurants, the fun of burlesque shows, and frequent late nights drinking with friends at bars or at their respective apartments. If he saw much of Elaine during this time, he did not bother to mention it in his journals or notes. This may have been due to the arrival of her sister, Constance, who had come down from upstate New York to be with her during her final months of pregnancy. Again, the urgency of pretense outstripped the importance of reality. His *puella* had become more of a figure in a poem than a living, breathing presence in his life.

He did see Thayer quite often; but, like Cummings, Thayer was far more preoccupied with matters other than his wife's pregnancy. His main focus that fall was bringing forth another sort of baby into the world, a literary one: the *Dial*. Since 1918, when Thayer had first associated himself with the magazine, he had provided financial support. In September of 1918, he gave the magazine twenty thousand dollars. In exchange, he took back ten thousand dollars in stock and ten thousand dollars in notes. By January of 1919, his contributions totaled thirty thousand dollars.

Thayer naturally believed that his financial stake in the fortnightly journal entitled him to a fair amount of editorial control. The publisher, Martyn Johnson, believed otherwise. This set the stage for considerable wrangling between the two men, with Thayer trying to push the magazine in a more literary direction, while Johnson was attempting to turn the *Dial* into a politically oriented organ. Thayer did not object to Johnson's left-leaning politics. Thayer, in fact, prided himself in voting the Socialist ticket. The problem was simply that his conception of the magazine was that it should be devoted to promoting the new in art. By the end of 1918, the skirmish had turned into a war. The last straw for

Thayer was the publication on December 14, 1918, of an issue that ignored the arts in favor of politics—the promotion of the new Soviet Union. Though Thayer supported the Bolsheviks, he was infuriated that Johnson was spending his money in this way. He resigned as editor and secretary-treasurer but did not immediately call in his notes.

By the fall of 1919, Johnson was in dire straits financially. When in October he could not meet the agreement he had signed with Thayer the year before for repayment of ten thousand dollars, Thayer, through his lawyer, sought control over the magazine. Johnson attempted to negotiate. By November, he and Thayer had worked out an agreement by which Thayer, and his new partner in publishing, Sibley Watson, would buy out Johnson.

The *Dial*'s masthead for November 28, 1919, listed J. S. Watson, Jr. as president and Scofield Thayer as secretary-treasurer of the reborn publication. Cummings announced the news to his mother on November 25, to which he added that the *Dial* "will change its format,drop political and take on literary characteristics." He also noted that at Thayer's suggestion he had acquired a photograph of a Lachaise relief for publication in the first real issue they would edit, that of January 1920: "It's great fun to be purveyor of such tidings to a man whom I like so much as Lachaise. Also to act as agent not to mention publisher for someone who,like Lachaise,is a good deal my senior! As always,I am peculiarly lucky to have such friends." In another letter to his mother a few weeks later he wrote, with obvious delight, that "The Dial,unless something happens,should contain Four of Five pieces of verse and four-full-pages of drawings by me."

While he had given Thayer his choice of poems to print from the poetry manuscript, he was insistent, remembering how his work had been changed in *Eight Harvard Poets*, that his style not be altered. He told Thayer, "In case any taken, prière de ne pas changer spacing or punctuation in any particular,e.g. if something begins with a small-letter,or a parenthesis,or has an uncapitalized personal pronoun,or if one line only in each stanza should be capitalized au commencement,or if small letter should follow a period."

In late December, the January first issue of the *Dial*, solely edited by Thayer and Watson, with Stewart Mitchell as managing editor, went on sale. Along with the frontispiece photo of the Lachaise bas-relief were four Cummings drawings of the National Winter Garden Burlesque Show (comedian, tap dancer, and ladies), as well as seven Cummings poems selected by Thayer from the *Tulips & Chimneys* manuscript: "little tree," "the bigness of cannon," "Buffalo Bill 's," "when god lets my body be," "why did you go," "when life is quite through with," and "O Distinct." Thayer had been rather conservative in his selection. He did not choose some of the more ostentatious poems about prostitutes, which he liked quite well, nor the more radically experimental ones.

Cummings was not displeased in the least with Thayer's choices. It marked, aside from his poem "Belgium" that had appeared in the *New York Evening Post* in May of 1916, his first magazine publication outside of Harvard. These were also the first poems Cummings, now twenty-five, had published in a periodical since leaving university. Or as his "contributor note" stated: "E.E. Cummings, now living in New York, has not previously published in any of the regular periodicals." *Eight Harvard Poets* had not brought him public attention. But his appearance in this much-anticipated first issue of the new *Dial* would, he knew, give him national, even international exposure.

The other event of major importance for Cummings near year's end was the birth, on December 20, 1919, of his unacknowledged child. The birth certificate listed Elaine Eliot Thayer as mother, Scofield Thayer as father, and the baby girl's name as Nancy. The only surviving entry about the birth among Cummings's vast quantity of papers is one cryptic note: "She is estranged from me Thayer takes care of her—hospital." Brown remembered years later how Cummings learned the news: "As we were going out to dinner, or perhaps returning, Cummings made a phone call and returned to say that Elaine had given birth to a girl and that 'Thayer was very pleased.' I had more than a strong suspicion that Cummings knew he was the father but from his remark I gathered that I was to refer to the girl as Thayer's."

Cummings's unresponsiveness, even callousness, was largely due to his extreme self-centeredness. He had consistently made himself and his work the focus of his attention, and could see only that fatherhood would likely interfere with his own drive. As a consequence, he seems to have been more than willing to let Elaine slip away from him during this time. As the months went on, the division only grew, and she found herself relying more and more on Thayer who rose, in some fashion, to the occasion. It seems that Cummings's only response that fall to the separation from Elaine was to ask Thayer in a postscript to a letter concerning his poems, "And by the way is Elaine angry,or merely dead?"

Although the gulf between them had far more to do with Cummings than with Elaine, Cummings managed to convince himself that it was Elaine who had turned him away. What he failed to realize was that his refusal to accept any responsibility for his actions could only have felt to her as an extreme form of rejection. And when she saw that Cummings was obstinately unwilling even to acknowledge his role, she must have felt even further scorned. The reality was that only his work fully engaged him; indeed, during her pregnancy he threw himself more and more into writing and painting. From his notes, this does appear to have been a way to sublimate his feelings; he simply was genuinely dedicated to pursuing his goal of becoming an artist. Even accepting fatherhood, let alone acting in any way as a father, was simply not going to be of concern.

Once Elaine returned home, Cummings did tear himself away from his other pursuits to stop by to see her and the baby. But he did not go immediately. He saw Elaine's pregnancy as having come between them, and as curious as he was to see the daughter he had helped produce, he also noted that he "bitterly resented" Nancy. "Now Nancy becomes my rival," he wrote. "I supress my real hatred I cannot love E as a prostitute but as a mother E. has less sexual appeal but because she is the mother of my child I refuse to admit it." His resentment of Nancy was alleviated once he actually saw her, but his feelings of conflict continued, as one of his reflective notes, written a few years later, reveals:

> After Mopsy's [Nancy's] birth—Idealization
> extended:includes,Motherhood
> so mysterious to me that Elaine,so slender,so young,could be
> a mother
> she does everything for Mopsy—my child. I don't feel her
> efforts appreciate
> i sit back,do nothing to help—never ask her
> to marry me
> <u>i don't really</u>, <u>want</u> to participate in my own child!
> assume responsibility of menage!
> be husband,with Elaine as my wife!

I prefer the lover-mistress arrangement:more freedommy
work
Puella Mea .... sexual: at its strongest
(idealization:strongest at same time)

In another jotting he took himself to task for his "callousness: not understanding Elaine suffers.... i have no thought of Mopsy—except as Elaine's." But he also reflected that he was "socially barred from acting as husband or father. Thayer here shines." If Thayer was seen to "shine" it was, in Cummings's mind, at least, because he had the financial means to do so. Indeed, Cummings continually saw his lack of money as an excuse not to step forward: "I-inferior, playing up to him [Thayer] i:poor he: [Thayer] rich AGGRESSIVE i:passive." In another rumination on the situation, he noted his gratitude to Thayer for assuming the father role, but added that "ST [Scofield Thayer] could do it:wealth i: nothing, only my art."

Although Cummings was obviously bewildered and in turmoil, and more than aware of the consequences of his actions (or inactions), he seems to have kept any internal anguish very much to himself. As when Elaine announced she was pregnant, Cummings retreated: "i withdrew from reality.... & sought refuge in unreality,ideas,my little circle,art." Having decided on this course of conduct, the public persona carried on very much as it had before. His letters to others, for instance, are replete with reports on his own artistic doings or with long commentaries on politics. He rarely mentions Elaine or Nancy.

The few times he does, there is no hint of any emotion. On February 3, 1920, for instance, he wrote his sister that "Elaine Thayer's daughter looks just like a doll—she has ever so much very long hair which Mrs. Thayer has Dutch-cut and the result is extremely becoming." Where previously in his letters home he had referred to Elaine by her first name, any references now are to Mrs. Thayer. In March, for instance, he reported to his mother that he had seen "Mrs. Thayer and her daughter." On May 22, he noted in passing in a letter to his mother that "Mrs. Thayer" had decided not to baptize "little Elaine," though she had been invited to do so in tandem with Sibley and Hildegarde Watson on the occasion of the christening of their first son, Michael, whose godfather was Cummings.

Elaine must have felt at this time quite abandoned by both her men. Despite Cummings's sense that Thayer was acting quite responsibly toward her, he was hardly attentive. Nor was Cummings. The *Dial* was of far greater interest to Thayer than Elaine or her baby. Cummings, too, was quite preoccupied with his role as a primary contributor to the magazine. As a follow-up to his securing a photograph of Lachaise's work for the January first issue, Cummings was asked to write a review of the sculptor's second one-man show at the Stephan Bourgeois Galleries in New York. He readily agreed, producing a strident but sound appreciation of his friend. It was just the second essay ever written on Lachaise, who was still relatively unknown as an artist. Indeed, he had to make his living working in the sculpture studio of the public artist Paul Manship.

For Cummings, Lachaise was to sculpture what Cézanne was to painting: "new and fundamental." "Both men are intrinsically great geniuses," Cummings wrote. "The significance of their production lies in the fact that it goes not beyond but under conventional art." The essay is interesting not only for Cummings's solid and insightful commentary on what Lachaise was really about, but also for Cummings's expressions of ideas about art and artists. He used the opportunity to hold forth on his own views on art, complete with notions important for his own creative impulses. "No art which depends for its recognition upon the casting of a spell on the intelligence can, except in the case of an undeveloped mind, endure beyond a few moments or a few hours at best." Instead, art that is truly successful for both artist and viewer requires "an intelligent process of the highest order, namely the negation on our part, by thinking, of thinking...." Here, also, for the first time in print, Cummings enunciated his cherished concept of "IS:" "We are compelled to undress one by one the soggy nouns whose agglomeration constitutes the mechanism of Normality, and finally to liberate the actual crisp organic squirm—the IS."

The essay went through several drafts before Cummings was pleased with it. "I did a good deal of distinctively difficult labor,mostly between the hours of 10 PM and seven A.M....I happened to notice that once it took two hours and three quarters to write exactly three sentences—not that I wanted three in particular." His efforts were not in vain. When he sent the essay to Lachaise for his approval, the sculptor responded with this note: "Couming. That great very great—may I just that now I will say as I can fully when I see you—We all say the same at home."

Cummings's next essay for the *Dial*, which he began on the heels of finishing the Lachaise piece, was a review of T. S. Eliot's second book, titled simply *Poems*. Eliot, Thayer's long-time friend, and former classmate at Milton Academy, Harvard, and Oxford, had already been recruited by Thayer to contribute a monthly "London Letter" to the *Dial*. He had also assigned emerging poet Marianne Moore to review Eliot's first collection of essays, *The Sacred Wood*. But Thayer, who was even more enthusiastic about Eliot's verse than about his prose, wanted to ensure that his friend's new book of poetry, just published in the United States by Knopf, got the attention he felt it deserved.

While his choice of Moore for the essays was brilliant, his decision to ask Cummings to review the poems was a bit odd. To be sure, Cummings was well aware of Eliot's work, having read *Prufrock and Other Observations* at Camp Devens, but he had little experience writing critically about literature. His feelings about Eliot were also ambivalent; he generally approved of Eliot's verse but disliked his essays on literature, feeling that he intellectualized the intellectual. Or as he wrote Thayer in January 1919, "Why can't TS gather fuel in vacant lots instead of x raying the bust of Marcus Aurelius? For Christ's sake. amen." Eliot, for his part, would have preferred Aldous Huxley or John Middleton Murry as a reviewer, and had written to Thayer that he knew Cummings "only as a contributor to the two numbers of the *Dial* that I have seen." (He had apparently forgotten that he and Cummings had acted opposite one another while both were at Harvard.)

Cummings struggled with the Eliot piece. After nine drafts he finally turned it in, then got it back from Thayer for one further revision before it was printed in the June issue. In spite of his labors, it was not a brilliant review. He began with the assertion that *Poems* "is an accurate and uncorpulent collection of instupidities." He then went on to blast Ezra Pound for his attempt to "lasso" Eliot into the Vorticist camp, the artistic movement championed by painter and writer Wyndham Lewis: "[Pound] deserves to be drawn and quartered by the incomparably trite brush of the great and the only and the Wyndham and the Lewis."

His few remarks on Eliot's actual accomplishments were accurate. He noted, for instance, that the merits of Eliot's verse included "a vocabulary almost brutally tuned to attain distinctness; an extraordinarily tight orchestration of the shapes of sound; the delicate and careful murderings…of established tempos by oral rhythms." But beyond these statements, there was no further examination of what made Eliot special or unique. He simply quoted selected passages, and concluded by saying that "at the risk of being jeered for an 'uncritical' remark we mention that this is one of the huge fragilities before which comment is disgusting."

Eliot did not acknowledge Cummings's review. Given that Eliot was quite gentlemanly about offering thanks, his lack of any response was probably a sign that he was less than overwhelmed with Cummings's critique. He had, for instance, written directly to Marianne Moore to congratulate and thank her for her substantive review of his essays that had run in the March number of the *Dial*.

Pound, Paris editor of the *Dial*, did respond, writing to Thayer that "Cummings has put several backs up, among the which mine is not; for I think he is perfectly just in his remarks.... However, Cummings is stupid to sneer at W.L.'s [Wyndham Lewis's] writing.... When Cummings has really seen the mass of W.L.'s work he will be in a better position to criticize and decide what sort of intelligence resides in said Wyndham." Cummings was apparently not bothered by Eliot's silence, but he must have sensed that literary criticism was not his métier. He never again reviewed another literary work, though he did throughout his life occasionally write on art and artists.

If Cummings did not particularly shine as a literary critic, as a poet he was well on his way to distinguishing himself. Five of his poems appeared in the May 1920 issue of the *Dial*: "into the strenuous briefness," "O sweet spontaneous," "but the other," "in Just- / spring" and "spring omnipotent goddess thou dost." Thayer's selection this time was far riskier than the first set he had chosen. These poems truly broke the standard verse mold, surpassing in their inventiveness and liberties with style, language, and even verse that at the time was considered "experimental." Not all the poems were new. "but the other" was probably written either in Cambridge in 1916 or when he was in New York later that year; "in Just- / spring" dates from when Cummings was still at Harvard.

But both these poems had been reworked in light of his more recent discoveries about the impact of spacing and punctuation. The attention Cummings had devoted over the years to wordcraft, in an effort to express himself uniquely and forcefully, had paid off. He had truly found his voice, a voice that would be distinctly his for the rest of his career. Indeed, "in Just- / spring" and "O sweet spontaneous" would become two of Cummings's better known poems.

The poem he liked the best was his most recent, "into the strenuous briefness." One of many of Cummings's poems that fall into the category of "carpe diem" verse, "into the strenuous briefness" is simple but not simplistic: a distillation of his credo of how to live:

into the strenuous briefness
Life:
handorgans and April
darkness,friends

i charge laughing.
Into the hair-thin tints
of yellow dawn,
into the women coloured twilight

i smilingly
glide.   I
into the big vermillion departure
swim,sayingly;

(Do you think?)the
i do,world
is probably made
of roses & hello:

(of solongs and,ashes)

What is identifiably Cummings style is all here: the uncapitalized "i;" the use of parentheses and the ampersand; the spacing for visual and aural purposes; the punctuation for effect; the running of words together to create a wholeness out of separateness; the unique imagery ("hair-thin tints," "women coloured twilight"); the syntactical interruptions; and the creation of an adverb—"sayingly" out of another part of speech. And yet these are not just tricks for the sake of a unique semantic; the saying is integral to the meaning. One's journey through life is often oddly punctuated, filled with unusual pairings, juxtapositions, and intervals between words and actions, contains parenthetical moments and the melding of the individual into the collective. But, if we are fortunate, we also have startling newnesses and roses and laughter even if we keep in mind the inevitableness of the "big vermillion departure" and "solongs and,ashes."

For Cummings, the space between words (or the lack of such space) was by no means arbitrary. In his mind the "silent" interstices between uttered words also had enormous value. In one of his many notes on his own poetic theory, he stated the relation between sound and silence:

> "sound" = what begins when silence ends
> is caused by the termination of Silence
> altho we call a sound an audible sensation and say we "hear" it,&
> say we cannot "hear" silence —nonetheless,our consciousness
> is of silence equally with sound.
> Sound emerges from & retreats with silence.
> Every sound has its own peculiar silence!

As for his idiosyncratic punctuation, he wrote to Thayer, "Note punctuation exemplifying a theory in my soul that every 'word' purely considered implies its own punctuation."

Edward Cummings was among the first to offer his praise for the new work. In response, Cummings wrote that "it is a supreme pleasure to have done something FIRST—and 'roses & hello' also the comma after 'and' ('and,ashes') are Firsts. I need not say that I am extraordinarily that is as usual lucky in having what amounts to my own printing press in Thayer and Watson—by which I refer to the attention which such minutiae as commas and small i's,in which minutiae my Firstness thrives,get at the hands of these unique gentlemen."

As long as Edward and his son communicated about literature, they were generally in agreement. But the arts were not Cummings's only concern at the time. Politics was also a major focus for Cummings, and on this topic he and his father held rather divergent views. Cummings was an ardent supporter of the Bolshevik revolution in Russia; his father was not. Similarly, Cummings was appalled at the government crackdown on socialists and trade unionists, while his father worried about a Communist takeover either at home or abroad. His letters home from the time he got out of the army until the early 1920s are filled with accounts of strikes and protests in New York and news about the Russian revolution. As heated as he could get about "the kaki(khaki?)clad hoodlums of our well-known Uncle" who ran amok attacking protesters, his involvement in politics was not as a participant but as a spectator and sympathizer. Or as he wrote his mother, "don't think we [Brown and Cummings] are wholly political in our lives—au contraire, the main and only interest is(as always)painting,poetry,etc."

One other source of contention between father and son was Cummings's lack of tangible progress on the manuscript about his internment in France. In response to yet another of his father's inquiries, he replied with the following explanation:

> As for the Story of the Great War Seen From The Windows of Nowhere, please don't expect a speedy conclusion or rather completion of this narrative;for this reason:that in consenting(it almost amounted to that)to "do the thing up" I did not forego my prerogative as artist,to wit—the making of every paragraph a thing which seemed good to me,in the same way that a "crazy-quilt" is made so that every inch of it seems good to me....Not that I am held up in my story,but simply progress is slow. I am sure the result will say(eventually that is)that no other method was possible or to be considered. It is not a question of cold facts per se. That is merely a fabric:to put this fabric at the mercy of an Everlasting Rhythm is somethingelse.

Apparently satisfied with his son's response, Edward ceased, at least for a while, to press Cummings about the book. Cummings, in fact, was not particularly working on the manuscript. Instead, he was devoting most of his time to poetry and painting, and was having success in both art forms.

Indeed, Cummings's painting, like his verse, was not only progressing but attracting attention. Four separate reviewers of the March-April 1920 Society of Independent Artists Exhibition, to which Cummings had submitted two large paintings, *Noise Number 5* and *Sound Number 5*, singled out the artist (among several hundred) for praise. S. Jay Kaufman, in the *New York Globe and Advertiser* called for a show of abstract art, noting that "In any such exhibition paintings by E.E. Cummings should be included." The critic for *New York World* referred to the paintings as "a striking bit of post-impressionism." The critic for the *Evening Post* said that while he preferred *Noise*, "both of them are interesting. Of course, these irregular patterns of sharp positive color are banners of a small army of theorists, and the theories will either entrance you or set your teeth on edge.... But if the paintings can be looked at with the eye, if they can be seen as frankly as one sees the pattern of a roll of linoleum, they are bound to be admired."

What had attracted the critics were two of Cummings's best paintings. Though only one painting was entirely abstract—a seated nude is discernible in *Sound Number 5*—the overall impression of both was, to use his term, a "crazy-quilt" of colorful planes. That a submerged figure lingered in *Sound Number 5* was due to Cummings's composition method that often began with realistic representation. Or as he explained, "The 'helps' or 'raw material' are occasionally 'bodies,' 'scenes,' 'faces,''naturae mortae.' Other incidentals crop out I dare say or go under."

The method was not unlike that which he used for his poems in which actual observations are skewed or submerged under a dazzling array of stylistic devices. Also, as with some of his poetry, the paintings attempted to represent the audible in a visual manner. Auditory signals, though, are by no means equal; hence the difference in representation within each painting, and between each series that attempted to guide the viewer to the distinction between sound and noise. The *Sound* paintings, for instance, are less chaotic, less dynamic than the *Noise* series. The notion that sound should not be confused with noise (or silence) was probably worked out by Cummings while at Harvard. In one of his college notebooks he commented on the difference between the regularity of sound and the irregularity of noise, a premise he seemed to have applied to his painting.

Changes were afoot. In June of 1920, Brown and Cummings were forced to leave the building in which they lived when it was slated for demolition. They moved temporarily into an apartment at 109 Waverly Place, but neither liked the place much. He and Brown were also increasingly bothered by domestic politics; the passage of the Volstead Act, over President Wilson's veto, that ushered in prohibition, had been in effect since January. While liquor was still in plentiful supply, it was now illegal to purchase or drink it.

In addition to politics, Cummings's personal life was still in turmoil. He and Elaine had become estranged, and no breakthrough seemed imminent, or even possible. Cummings, of course, had his poetry and painting, but he also had developed a fairly acute case of wanderlust, fueled partly by letters from Dos Passos who had remained in Europe after the war. Cummings and Brown began to make plans for summer travel.

They first thought they might venture to Asia, then decided to work their way to South America as seamen. Edward Cummings was appalled at the idea. Cummings was not moved by his father's entreaties:

> There is nothing like <u>Now</u>—there is also nothing like trying!....
>
> There are several ways to end this letter—but the way I prefer is this:I wish respectfully to state
>
> (1)that I do <u>not</u> need money!!
>
> (2) " " " " " sympathy!—because being a good(if innocuous)Lenninite or Trotskyite or what-you-like-it I should be very considerably hampered in my aims by a superfluity of the former(whereof I have plenty)and being a person of tolerable taste and intelligence I really cannot conscientiously accept or find a place for the latter.

He concludes his letter by stating that "you will let me go my own way in my flannel shirt and my ideas."

Edward was non-plussed. He renewed his call for Cummings to come up to Silver Lake for the summer and work on his "French Notes," offering to finance the trip he and Brown had planned if he would spend the summer working on his manuscript. In the end, that is exactly what Cummings did. The desire to work unencumbered by the hustle and bustle of New York ultimately won out over his desire to travel. It would turn out to be a victory for both Reverend Cummings and his son.

ten

The Enormous Room

In July, 1920, Cummings left New York for Cambridge, then went with his family to Silver Lake in New Hampshire. He quickly set up his writing headquarters in a large tent at Hurricane Point (which he reached by canoe) and established a work routine. During the day he labored on his manuscript about his internment. In the late afternoon he would canoe back to the cottage on the lake shore. In the evening he dined with the family, then canoed back to his tent. For Cummings, it was an unusually rigid way of working, but as he explained to his father, he found it "impossible to determine anything,in prose at least,which I cannot mouth to myself—hence need for solitariness."

Aside from the vividness of his experiences, Cummings did have some material to work from, as well as a fairly clear notion of the aesthetics he wished to employ. Shortly after his return from France he had started writing but did not get far before he got caught up in other pursuits. He did take the opportunity to compare notes with Brown after they had joined up in New York. He wrote to his father that it was "very amusing noting down the thousand et one incidents of ex-convictdom in the course of let us say a two hour conversation." At Camp Devens, he also worked on the book, but mostly he seemed to have elaborated theories of art that he could and would make use of when he actually was able to write without interruption on what he called his "French Notes." At that time he developed a notion of "organic sensation," in which all senses must come into being for a work of art to succeed.

Though he had sketched prodigiously while at La Ferté-Macé, he had written little. Most often his written accounts were jotted down, to use his description, in "telegraphic technique:"

> Card table: 4 stares play banque with 2 cigarettes(i dead)&
> A pipe the clashing faces tanked by a leanness if one candle
> bottle-stuck (Birth of X)where sits The Clever Man who
> pyramids,sings(mornings)"Meet Me…"

Cummings's memory was acute, however, and the ordeal so remarkable, that he had little trouble recalling incidents, impressions, coloration, even speech. The task involved rendering what he knew so well in a prose that was as alive as his experiences. For Cummings, this meant creating a "binding rhythm which integrates the whole thing and makes it a single moving ThingInItself."

In August, Brown came up to New Hampshire to "help" Cummings with his manuscript about their internment. Brown's role seems to have been largely that of a discussant who assisted Cummings in recalling specific details about characters and events, and who was able to corroborate or dispute Cummings's impressions of their shared travails. How much actual aid Brown provided his friend is questionable, since Cummings continued his routine of "solitariness," and did not show any pages to Brown while he was in the process of writing.

What is clear is that Cummings was working diligently, not allowing himself to be distracted by anyone or anything. He even turned down a fall invitation to visit Thayer, Elaine, and Nancy in Edgartown, on Martha's Vineyard, though he did note that he "should like to see [Elaine's] kid." To Stewart Mitchell he wrote, "Here I've been working(as worked the sons of Egypt to build the pyramids,you understand—in other words,like H.)upon a little historical treatise of vast import to my Family and Nobody in General—comprising my experiences in France,or more accurately en prison. Honestly to say,I haven't done nawthing else."

In mid-September, when the family returned to Cambridge, Cummings presented his father with four chapters of the manuscript. On October 2, Edward wrote his son that he had just finished reading the chapters and found them "superlative stuff," adding, "I am sure now that you are a great writer." Edward reinforced his praise with a generous birthday gift that Cummings described in a letter to Mitchell, written on October 14 (his twenty-sixth birthday), as: "two hundred and sixty from an enthusiastic father;also a fur coat;also a charge account at 'The Continental Clothing House' also(sequitur)a pair or two of shoes and maybe a hat,also(it is on the way)a pair of corduroy trousers—!"

Cummings had nearly finished the book. He was pleased with it, but was also aware that his achievement might not amount to anything. Indeed, on his birthday he found himself "without a book published, without a meticulous molecule of worship or confidence outside of…friends." It was a realistic, not negative assessment, and did not dissuade him from pressing on with the manuscript.

On October 18, Cummings happily wrote his father that he had "completed the final chapter of my French Notes. Not that it, as well as others, will not have to be worked over. Nor that certain insertions will not have to happen here and there." On October 21, he and Brown left Silver Lake for New York from where he mailed other chapters to his father. These chapters, as with the preceding ones, were dutifully typed by Edward's secretary at the World Peace Foundation, Mary MacDonald.

On November 18, 1920, Edward wrote Cummings that Miss MacDonald was "about through with your French Notes." At Christmas, in Cambridge, Cummings read through the entire "fair copy" of the manuscript, and made a few more revisions, corrections, and additions. By the end of January, two copies of the manuscript had been completely retyped in final form. Cummings had meanwhile forwarded a set of drawings that he selected from the many he had executed at La Ferté-Macé for inclusion with the manuscript. The book was ready to be sent to publishers.

The initial editors to which the manuscript was sent—at Ginn, Harper's, Houghton-Mifflin, Scribner's, Atlantic Monthly Press—were all confounded by the book that crossed their desks. The narrative was not linear, the style or styles hardly conventional, French phrases and sentences sat astride English, and the rather fierce anti-war, anti-authoritarian sentiments were more than a bit off-putting. It was hard even to classify. Was it a novel? Autobiography? Or something in-between? In other words, it was, and still is, a unique presentation of experience, told in a manner that alternates from the lyrical to the surreal—often within the same paragraph.

The book that eventually came to bear the title *The Enormous Room*, is, on the surface, an account of Cummings's ordeal as a prisoner at La Ferté-Macé. It begins with details about his arrest, removal from *Section Sanitaire XXI*, and subsequent detention in "the enormous room." The linearity breaks down after these opening chapters, and is replaced by a series of portraits of fellow inmates and captors. The last chapters return to linear narrative as the author recounts his release and final days as a detainee. But this summary hardly explains why or how the book works, or why or how it succeeds. Nor does it account for its complexity or grand design. To do that, it is necessary to examine how Cummings told his tale.

To begin with, *The Enormous Room* is imbued with allegory. Its model—no surprise for the son of Reverend Cummings and for the able student of William Neilson at Harvard—was John Bunyan's *The Pilgrim's Progress*. Cummings made every effort to inform his readers of this through frequent allusions to Bunyan's book. His first chapter, for instance, is entitled "I Begin a Pilgrimage," and the third "A Pilgrim's Progress," even though the subject matter of these chapters is actually his arrest and transportation to La Ferté-Macé. Subsequently, like Bunyan, he invents names for his characters that reflect their attributes as beings. When he felt it useful, he even appropriated designations lifted from Bunyan. Four inspiring inmates are called "Delectable Mountains," a reference to the sublime peaks that surround the Celestial City by which "Pilgrims are steady kept by faith and fear;" the director of the prison is given the name of Apollyon, Bunyan's "monster…hideous to behold." He and B (his designation for Brown) are said to be in the "Slough of Despond" when they are stuck in the Section Sanitaire.

References themselves do not make the book allegorical; rather its structure is indebted to allegory. *The Enormous Room*, like *The Pilgrim's Progress*, is a record of a journey, but, unlike Bunyan's book, the hero does not achieve a more profound understanding of the divine scheme of things. Instead, his sojourn is an earthly one, in which C (Cummings's name for himself), acquires worldly enlightenment. Cummings saw his time at La Ferté-Macé in mythical terms, and wrote about it in this way. His book is as much about his internal "progress" as a human being as it is about incident, though each incident is related with the idea of advancing what C comes to learn about himself and humanity. Unlike Christian (Bunyan's protagonist), C is not aided by biblical higher powers, nor does he come to a greater appreciation of these divine forces;

rather, he is the master of his own realizations about life, and the knowledge he gains is distinctly earthly.

This is not to imply that he does not have help in his discoveries. From "The Delectable Mountains"—four individuals resolute in their individuality—he learns, for example, the virtues of innocence, the saving grace of laughter in the face of despair, and the absolute and invaluable importance of not yielding one's self to any authority but one's own. Through their (admittedly peculiar and iconoclastic) examples he gains his own courage to be courageous.

Courage is not intellectual; indeed, for Cummings, the ability to reason and rationalize one's own lot in life is antithetical to being an "IS." And the doctrine of "ISness," that he developed and expounded upon in the course of writing *The Enormous Room* is the fundamental "unknowledge" C gains as he "progresses" on his journey. It is "unknowledge" because it is not wisdom learned through thinking. One feels this sort of thing, and while it may ultimately inform the intelligence, it is not intellectual knowledge. The distinction is simply this: intelligence is not to be confused with intellectualizing. Intelligence (or the lack of it) is innate, and it is impossible to negate (at least wholly) what one is simply born with. Intellectualizing one's intelligence, on the other hand, is acquired.

To quote from *The Enormous Room*: "There is and can be no such thing as authentic art until the bon trucs(whereby we are taught to see and imitate on canvas and in stone and by words this so-called world)are entirely and thoroughly and perfectly annihilated by that vast and painful process of Unthinking which may result in a minute bit of personal Feeling. Which minute bit is art." This important notion of "unthinking" as the basis for authentic art is a cornerstone of Cummings's philosophy, and the basic belief that he would rely on and continually refine for the rest of his life.

Although *The Enormous Room* is not an intellectual work, it is nonetheless a highly intelligent one. Cummings did not arrive at such a style or structure without a great deal of intelligence, generously applied, nor without a fairly large amount of sheer labor over his words. While he had genuinely interesting material upon which to base his account, how he told the story is what has made the book endure and endear.

Cummings quite remarkably understood that a book is not just a series of elaborated episodes; it is a structural entity, or to use Buckminster Fuller's term, a patterned integrity. Since Cummings only used the chronological method to describe his arrival and departure from La Ferté-Macé—"because the diary or time method is a technique that cannot possibly do justice to timelessness"—he had to find another way of shaping his account of the period he actually spent in confinement. The method he chose was to create synergy within and between chapters, thereby achieving an orchestration akin to that in music.

As a result, *The Enormous Room* is composed like a three-part symphony, with each "movement" having its own swells, crescendos, climaxes, and falls. In each chapter the narrative gradually builds—through the propelling accumulation of detail, description, asides, reported speech, and other devices—to some sort of a climax, then quietly descends only to be repeated in a similar pattern (but obviously with different narrative building blocks). In addition, the book as a whole has a parallel structure, with a climax for each distinct section.

The climax for the first part of the book occurs when C realizes that despite his precarious situation he can rejoice in the experience:

> "By God" I said, "this is the finest place I've ever been in my life."
>
> "It's the finest place in the world" said B's voice.

For the portraits, which become more complex and more compelling with each character sketch, the crescendo crests with Cummings's vivid and indignant description of the brutal, racist attack on one of the Delectable Mountains, the childlike Jean le Nègre. The "fall," in the form of a eulogy, after this poignant scene, is one of the most beautiful passages in the book:

> And I think of Jean le Nègre.... You are something to dream over,Jean;summer and winter(birds and darkness)you go walking into my head;you are a sudden and chocolate-coloured thing,in which you have a habit of holding six or eight plantons (which you are about to throw away)and the flesh of your body is like the flesh of a very deep cigar. Which I am still and always quietly smoking;always and still I am inhaling its very fragrant and remarkable muscles....
>
> —[T]ake me up into your mind once or twice before I die(you know why:just because the eyes of me and you will be full of dirt some day). Quickly take me into the bright

> child of your mind,before we both go suddenly all loose and silly(you know how it will feel). Take me up (carefully;as if I were a toy)and play carefully with me,once or twice, before I and you go suddenly all limp and foolish. Once or twice before you go into great Jack roses and ivory—(once or twice Boy before we together go wonderfully down into the Big Dirt laughing,bumped with the last darkness).

The last climax in *The Enormous Room* is not followed by a "fall;" fittingly, it is the concluding paragraph of the book in which Cummings describes his view of New York from sea:

> The tall,impossibly tall,incomparably tall, city shouldering upward into hard sunlight leaned a little through the octaves of its parallel edges,leaningly strode upward into firm hard snowy sunlight;the noises of America nearingly throbbed with smokes and hurrying dots which are men and which are women and which are things new and curious and hard and strange and vibrant and immense,lifting with a great undulous stride firmly into immortal sunlight.

Cummings's prose is the prose of both a poet and a painter. The poet's ear, always on the lookout for unusual metaphors and word combinations, and continually attuned to the rhythms of language and nuances of speech, is united with the painter's eye that is always searching his surrounds for visually arresting detail. Instances abound of this fortuitous combination, as in this passage:

> The road was absolutely deserted;the night hung loosely around it,here and there tattered by attempting moonbeams. I was somewhat sorry to find the way hilly,and in places bad underfoot;yet the unknown adventure lying before me,and the delicious silence of the night(in which our words rattled queerly like tin soldiers in a plush-lined box)boosted me into a condition of mysterious happiness.

It is a simple description, yet a rich one. The cadence, with its pauses and stops, mirrors that of walking on an uneven surface. The commonplace observation of night and landscape is made vivid and vital through the unique choice of words: "night hung loosely," "tattered by attempting moonbeams," and the sounds of words that "rattled queerly like tin soldiers in a plush-lined box." In short, Cummings employs the senses (feeling filtered through intelligence) to show us the scene, pushes us to enter his experience, and turns the ordinary into the extraordinary.

He, of course, had models. From the Romantics he appropriated the notion that external observation can be described most powerfully, maybe even most accurately, by rendering it in terms of inner response. It was not enough just to name the attributes of what was seen; instead, it was necessary to state how the perception was perceived: "on my right,grey sameness of stone,the ennui of the regular and the perpendicular,the ponderous ferocity of silence." Cummings here is not just telling us what he saw, but how it felt to see it.

The heirs of the Romantics, the Symbolists, were also important for Cummings. Their aesthetic of "precise nuance," in which realism is married to sensation, fit well with Cummings's own desire for unusual combinations of words:

> [R]ight over my head, the grey stone curdled with a female darkness;the hard and angular softening in a putrescent explosion of thick wriggling laughter. I started, looked up, and encountered a window stuffed with four savage fragments of crowding Face: dour livid shaggy disks focussing hungrily;four pair of uncouth eyes rapidly smouldering;eight lips shaking in a toothless and viscious titter.

The French Symbolist poet Paul Verlaine, whose "Parsifal" Cummings had committed to memory while at Harvard, would have nodded with approval at this melding of exact description with qualities that evoke something else entirely: "the grey stone curdled with a female darkness;" "putrescent explosion of thick wriggling laughter;" "savage fragments of crowding Face;" "shaggy disks focussing hungrily."

There was also Joyce. At Camp Devens, Cummings had avidly read *A Portrait of the Artist As a Young Man* and *Dubliners*. Also while in the army he began reading the installments of *Ulysses* that were appearing in the *Little Review*, beginning in March of 1918, and continued to do so after his return to New York. He was so enthusiastic about Joyce's work that he had even written an essay on Joyce that the *Dial* under Johnson had turned down. The essay is lost, but what he gleaned from Joyce about the use of interior monologue is manifest in the pages of *The Enormous Room*, as this passage describing his voyage home amply demonstrates:

> Snow falling. Almost slid through the railing that time. Snow. The snow is falling into the sea;which quietly receives it:into which it utterly and peacefully disappears. Man with a college degree returning from Spain,not disagreeable sort,talks Spanish with that fat man who's an Argentinian. -Tinian? -Tinish,perhaps. All the same. In other words Tin. Nobody at the table knows I speak English or am American. Hell,that's a good one on nobody. That's a pretty fat kind of joke on nobody.

Models, yes. But *The Enormous Room* is modeled on nothing except Cummings's own perceptions of his experiences, and on his own conception of how those perceived experiences must be set down. It is totally original: a war book without a gun or gunshot; an account of a pilgrimage to nowhere; an allegory devoid of requisite uplift or overt moral lesson. Or as Gertrude Stein remarked, "Cummings did not copy, he was the natural heir of the New England tradition with its aridity and its sterility, but also with its individuality."

Individuality, in the best New England sense, is indeed the hallmark of *The Enormous Room*. Not only does it celebrate in its theme the individual over the "mob," it also bears the mark of a specific individual, with his quirks and attitudes and even postures, all mirrored in a unique style and structure. It is ultimately intensely human, intensely felt, intensely created. Whether a novel, as Cummings occasionally claimed, or autobiography, as he more often suggested, it is a triumph. Or as Ernest Hemingway pronounced, without wasting words, "it is one of the great books."

eleven

Abroad

On his return to New York at the end of October 1920, Cummings stayed initially at Mitchell's on 71st Street, then with Dos Passos, now back from a lengthy sojourn in Europe, at 213 E. 15th Street. Finally, in December, he and Brown moved into a studio apartment at 107 Bedford Street. He resumed his painting, but the effort he had expended on *The Enormous Room* seemed to have temporarily drained him of enthusiasm for words. Though Cummings could never entirely suppress the impulse to write, he was not feeling terribly inspired. Part of the reason, undoubtedly, had to do with the negative responses by publishers to *The Enormous Room*. His manuscript of *Tulips & Chimneys* that Mitchell, acting on his friend's behalf, had tried to place with several editors, had fared no better.

On a more positive side, he and Elaine were seeing each other once again regularly and Cummings was starting to become more involved in his daughter's life. He would accompany Elaine on strolls with Nancy through the park, bounce his daughter on his knee, and play with her at Elaine's apartment. There is no account in Cummings's private writings that explains why he and Elaine suddenly drew so much closer, but since Thayer had ceased all pretense of involvement with Elaine, it is likely that both Cummings and Elaine felt that they could once again pursue their relationship.

Indeed, Thayer, by this time, had totally stepped aside. He was becoming involved in a relationship with writer Alyse Gregory, whom he had hired as an editorial assistant at the *Dial*, and was also pursuing his secretary, Sophia Wittenberg. Since both he and Elaine had settled into new liaisons, they had over that year frequently discussed divorce; they were now prepared to act on it. Perhaps as a way of publicly demonstrating how far removed he was from Elaine, he published a version of Cummings's "Puella Mea" in the January 1921 *Dial*.

While Cummings was seeing Elaine almost daily, he was spending even more time with Dos Passos, who, like Cummings, was master over his day. Or as Dos Passos recalled:

> Cummings and I would occasionally lunch together at a Syrian restaurant [Khoury's] he frequented down on Washington Street. We would eat a special clabber known as leben and a marvelous dish of raw eggplant mashed to a paste with sesame oil.... Afterward we'd roam around the vegetable and flower stalls of the old Washington Market or go to see the fish in the Aquarium down at the Battery. Cummings never tired of drawing sealions. As he walked he would be noting down groups of words or little scribbly sketches on bits of paper. Both of us lived as much for the sights we saw as for the sound of words.

In mid-afternoon, the two would split up and go home to work. Dos Passos was faring better than his friend with publishers. His first novel, *One Man's Initiation: 1917*, was hot off the press of Allen & Unwin in London; he had an agent, Carl Brandt of Brandt and Kirkpatrick; and his new novel, *Three Soldiers*, had been accepted by Doran in New York. Work, for Cummings, largely consisted of painting, though he did write a fair number of love poems for Elaine.

His major artistic focus that winter was a new canvas for the 1921 Independent Artists' Show. The work that engaged him was a forty-by-forty-inch painting, the tenth in his *Noise* series. As with the previous paintings in this group, it was an abstraction: spiralling ovals in vivid, not necessarily complementary, colors. In February 1921, Cummings had finished *Noise Number 10* and submitted it to the Independent's exhibition. Again he received notice, but this time the review was noncommital, at best. "E.E. Cummings displays a theme of eccentric ovates. He calls it a noise and numbers it." Still, among hundreds of painting on exhibit, he did get noticed.

When Cummings found time to work is something of a mystery for he seemed to have spent most of his time in pursuit of other pleasures. But as Dos Passos noted, "though we seemed to be spending an awful lot of time eating and drinking we managed to get work done." For Cummings, though, work was not a major focus. Most evenings would find him at Elaine's apartment, once again a gathering place for his and her circle of friends. Dos Passos remembered that Edward Nagle, Slater Brown, Stewart Mitchell, and the Lachaises were often present at her "teas." "After an hour or so of talk—though [Elaine] was silent as a mouse nobody ever dared show off too much at Elaine's—we would go to our Italian speakeasy…for supper."

At these dinners, according to Dos Passos, "Cummings had a way of looking like a chimp at times. As we poured down the dago red he would become mischievous as a monkey. Nagel [sic] was already a bit neurotic. Cummings would tease poor Nagel until the top of his head was ready to fly off. Elaine hardly said anything, but a word from her would heal all sores."

As the evening wore on, and the consumption of wine increased, Cummings would become more and more expressive. "His mind was essentially extemporaneous," recalled Dos Passos. "His fits of poetic fury were like the maenadic seizures described in the Greek lyrics." Alternating with these "geysers of talk," was a cryptic form of communication that he frequently employed with Dos Passos. "'Dos d. your w.' he would say severely when he thought I wasn't drinking fast enough. When Lachaise and Nagel's mother, who looked like one of Lachaise's nudes with clothes on, were of the party, they'd leave about this time. They didn't like to see young people drink too much."

Both Cummings and Dos Passos were restless. Or as Dos Passos recalled, they were "fed up with New York and the marts of trade. When I found a Portuguese freighter that would take a few passengers out of New Bedford for Lisbon at a very low rate, Cummings decided to go along. He was pining for Paris and I was hell-bent for Persia." Cummings's desire to get to France was also fueled by a decision Thayer and Elaine had reached: to get a divorce in Paris during the summer of 1921. Elaine was already making plans for herself and Nancy to be in Paris by early summer; Thayer was also readying himself to leave. Cummings could think of nothing better than to be in the city he most loved with the woman he most loved. He had managed to save one thousand dollars, accumulated through the sale of his paintings to Thayer, his contributions to the *Dial*, the payment from his father for *The Enormous Room*, along with additional generous gifts of cash Edward had bestowed on his son. Dos Passos had his advance for *Three Soldiers* from Doran.

On March 15, 1921, Cummings and Dos Passos set sail for Lisbon on board the *Mormugão*. The voyage took three weeks, as the ship called at several ports in the Azores and in Madeira. They made friends with the crew, whiling away a fair number of hours in conversations with the sailors. They read to each other Henry and Brooks Adams' *Degradation of the Democratic Dogma*. "We hated the book, each for a separate reason," recalled Dos Passos. "Cummings because it offended some Emersonian streak in his early training...and I, because it went against the Walt Whitman-narodnik optimism about people." They also worked. In the tiny shipboard *fumador* [smoking room], Cummings sketched, scribbled notes about language and art, worked on a few poems; Dos Passos occupied himself with translating poems from *The Greek Anthology* and Camöens' *Lusiads*.

Portugal did not impress Cummings. Dos Passos remembered that "New Englander to the core he was repelled by the rankness of the Manueline style [architecture]. When I tried to rub his nose in the great panels of Nuno Gonçalves' São Vicente he said he'd rather look at Rembrandt. At Coimbra some ancestral phobia against popery came to the surface. The students all looked to him like plainclothes Jesuits." In Porto, instead of sampling wines, Dos Passos spent most of his time finding Cummings a dentist to treat his ulcerated tooth.

Spain, where they arrived in mid-April, proved to be much more to Cummings's liking. They journeyed south from Salamanca to Palencia, Cacares, and Sevilla. In Sevilla, Cummings witnessed bullfights, which he wrote about in great detail in a letter to his mother. Both drawn to the spectacle and appalled by it, he nonetheless had to conclude that it was an "extraordinary experience." His tooth was still bothering him. Dos Passos again found him a dentist who "opened or lanced or cut [his] abcess,and thereby rendered Sevilla possible...Dos as interpreter for dentists has acted in an extremely valuable capacity."

From Sevilla, they headed north to Toledo, where Cummings sketched the cathedral and marveled at the "aesthetic intensity" of El Greco's *Burial of Count Orgaz*. The next stop was Madrid, which did not particularly appeal to either of them. By early May they were in the Basque country, which totally enthralled Cummings. He sketched everything that came into his sights: buildings, plazas, old men in berets, donkeys, goats, and ox-carts.

By May 10, he and Dos Passos had crossed the Pyrenees into France. A week later, they were in Saint-Jean de Luz, "whereupon i seize a train and suddenly i am in Paris toward night,inMai." On arrival, Cummings received some welcome news from his mother. Shortly after his departure, Horace Liveright, head of the New York publishing firm of Boni & Liveright, and champion of a number of new writers, had indicated that he was interested in reading the manuscript about Cummings's internment "with a view of publishing it." The book had come to Liveright's attention through the writer Mary Heaton Vorse, a Greenwich Village acquaintance of Cummings and Liveright author herself, who had read the manuscript and enthused about it to the publisher. Cummings was delighted: "[Liveright would] be likely to publish M.S. undeleted—much more than Scribners."

As expectant as he was about his book, Cummings did not sit in his hotel awaiting news. Paris enthralled anew:

> **Along the river trees are letting go scarcely and silently wisps,parcels of incense,which drop floatingly through a vista of talking moving people; timidly which caress hats & shoulders,wrists and dresses;which unspeakingly alight upon the laughter of men and children,girls and soldiers.**
>
> . . . .
>
> **. . .I am alive,I go along too,I slowly go up the vista among the hats and soldiers,among the smiles and neckties,the kisses and old men,wrists and laughter. . . .**

By day he and Dos Passos wandered the city. His sketchbooks reveal the scenes: the Flower Market, Luxembourg Gardens, war veterans leaning on crutches, children playing in the park, barges tied up at the quais along the Seine, even a funeral procession that he also recorded in the form of a prose poem that he entitled "AFTER SEEING FRENCH FUNERAL." It opens like this:

> **in front of the cathedral hovered a mumbling nobody:its greenish fumbling flesh swathed with crumbling alive rags,its trunk topped abruptly by a**

> **slouch hat under which carefully existed the deep filthy face and out of which sprouted wisely a decayed yellowish width of beard....**

Like Gershwin, he was attuned to the sounds of Paris:

> **taxis toot whirl people movingly perhaps laugh into the slowly**
> **millions and finally O it is spring since at all windows**
> **microscopic birds sing fiercely...**

In the evening, he and Dos Passos would dine at their favorite restaurants, including La Sultana Cherqui where Cummings had picked up Berthe, with whom he had his first sexual experience. They took in the show at the Folies and gawked at the prostitutes in Pigalle; they did not, however, succumb to their charms. Cummings was being true to Elaine; Dos Passos was simply not attracted.

Indeed, Cummings and Dos Passos, though they had much in common and enjoyed each other tremendously, differed in their interest in sex. Edmund Wilson recalled that this was a source of bemused frustration for Cummings. In his notebook, he recorded Cummings's impressions of his friend's sexual naïveté:

> One day [Cummings] said to him: "Dos, don't you ever think about women?" No. "Don't you ever dream about sex?" No. What I went through with that man! He'd wake me up in the night groaning and throwing himself around in his sleep. I'd say, "What's the matter, Dos?" He'd say, "Why I thought there were some beautiful wild swans flying overhead."

Dos Passos was, nonetheless, a good sport, quite willing to accompany his friend on his nocturnal ramblings.

Their carefree life was suddenly interrupted on June second when Cummings received a telegram informing him that his friend, the painter Edward Nagle, who was in the Netherlands, had been detained by the authorities because he was acting "insane." He and Dos Passos could not get immediately to Rotterdam because they did not have Dutch visas, but they did arrange through the American consul to get Nagle sent home. Dos Passos and Cummings, along with Elaine, who was about to leave New York for Paris, put up five hundred dollars for Nagle's passage. On Nagle's return, Thayer arranged for his own psychiatrist, Dr. L. Pierce Clarke, to examine Nagle. The doctor wrote Thayer that Nagle "suffered from a psycogenic delirium due in all probability to Oedipus, and in this delirium there was a certain paranoid trend." For a time Nagle was institutionalized but was released by autumn; Thayer apparently picked up the bill.

Not long after the Nagle incident, Dos Passos left for the Middle East. But Cummings was not alone for long. Stewart Mitchell came through for a brief visit with his aunt, the concert pianist Mrs. G. H. Thomas. But the one he most wanted to see—Elaine—arrived with Nancy in mid-June. They stayed at the fashionable Hôtel d'Iéna near Etoile, an establishment in marked contrast to his Spartan hotel on the left bank. With Elaine's arrival, the allure of Paris was heightened even further. She was there to secure her divorce from Thayer, who was coming over in July on his way to Vienna where Sigmund Freud had accepted him as a patient. From New York, she had already contacted lawyers in Paris, who had begun to amass a dossier of papers that would prove she was entitled to a divorce on the grounds that Thayer had deserted her. Thayer amicably was helping her to assemble her case, even assisting her with changing lawyers when Elaine became dissatisfied with the attorney she had chosen.

Cummings's reunion with Elaine was all he had hoped it would be: passionate, free, and freeing. They were both madly in love with each other again. The attraction was not just physical, although to be sure this did play a part. In addition, other qualities in their respective beings drew them together. For Elaine, Cummings's liveliness, adventurousness, and unconventionality played a major role in her affections for him. To be with Cummings was also to be in rebellion against her high-society upbringing that was staid, conservative, wealthy, and to her way of thinking, rather boring. She, of course, still had the best of both worlds, as her trust fund from her deceased parents ensured that rebellion would not leave her materially uncomfortable.

Cummings's ardency for Elaine appears to have been based on a combination of physical attraction—Elaine truly was beautiful in a very classic way—and on her understanding of his need for freedom. At this time, he did not regard her as a true partner in his life, rather as his mistress who made herself available to him on his terms. He could get from

Elaine what he needed—affection and respect for his primal need to make art—without having to participate too fully in a day-to-day relationship with her. She seems to have been ever-welcoming, ever-indulgent of Cummings when he decided to see her, and does not appear to have pressed him to change his way of interacting with her. Cummings felt that this equated with mutual freedom, a value he held dearly: he would not attempt to change her; she would not impose demands on him.

While Elaine could believe herself in revolt against her class by pursuing Cummings, he could be seen to be psychically replicating the relationship he had with his mother. Like Elaine, Rebecca adored him for who he was yet did not seem to ask much in return. She indulged his desire for freedom; delighted in his wit, charm, and cleverness; praised his artistic efforts; and took care of the practical. She was quick to forget slights, was more than content to settle for affectionate words now and then, and did not seem to expect her son to be terribly responsible for anything other than his own art. As a result, Cummings had little understanding or appreciation of what it meant to be a true reciprocal partner in a relationship. Raised to be a taker, he saw nothing out of place with this mode of being. In fact, it was who he was, and in Elaine he had found a woman who, at least initially, saw herself as a giver.

For Cummings, Elaine also represented a kind of muse. He could idealize, even immortalize her in poems, pay homage to his feelings and to her beauty in poetic form. To his way of thinking, that was sufficient proof of his devotion; that he lived apart from her, did not share much of his life with her, or allow her to share her life with him was of little consequence. She was, after all, his *puella*, as he had told her and the public. What more need be said? What practical action was required?

At the same time, with divorce from Thayer imminent, Cummings and Elaine began to make plans for some sort of future together. But if Elaine had hoped that her "legal availability" would significantly alter their relationship, Cummings did not see it that way. He was perfectly content to carry on as he had. One major change, however, was that he began acting more like a father to Nancy, taking her to the park, drawing her pictures, playing silly games with her. While he clearly had allowed himself to become far more affectionate toward his daughter, he was not at all prepared to accept much more than occasional responsibility for her. After a few hours of visiting with her, he was more than ready to go off on his own singular pursuits.

Brown, who was now working as Thayer's secretary, arrived with his "boss" at the Gare St. Lazare in mid-July. Cummings met them at the train that had brought them from Cherbourg. After escorting Thayer to the Hôtel Inter-Continental, he and Brown made their way across the river to the left bank Hôtel Marignan, at 13 rue du Sommerard. On July 23, just a few days after their arrival, Cummings wrote his mother that he had been "four times to the theatre with S.T. [Thayer], which is to say the least a novelty,since the vie chère in Paris had kept me outside the doors of all save two shows there-before. And have dined(whisper)at Voisin,etc."

But of more significance than fine meals and evenings at the theater was a chance encounter he and Thayer had on the street:

> The other night,as we were walking back from Rip revue "Ca Va" Pound disengaged himself from a pillar and bowed. Thayer had previously threatened to allow me to meet the great one,I demurred. "Sooner than might have been expected" was P's remark:leaving the editor at that person's hotel; I began an evening with the poet. Which lasted until the croissement of the Boulevard S Germain with the rue des Saints Pères,where I tentatively promised to visit the great one and disappeared. If it would amuse you:MR. Ezra Pound is a man of my own height,reddish goatee and ear whiskers,heavier built,moves nicely,temperment very similar to J. Sibley Watson,Jr.(as remarked by Thayer)—same timidity and subtlety,not nearly so inhibited. Altogether,for me,a gymnastic personality. Or in other words somebody,and intricate.

Cummings was not unknown to Pound. As Paris Editor of the *Dial*, Pound had read his work and seen his drawings in the magazine, and approved of both. He had not even taken umbrage at Cummings's swipe at him in his essay on Eliot ("[Pound] deserves to be drawn and quartered by the incomparably trite brush of… Lewis"), though Pound did write Watson that "Cummings is stupid to sneer at W.L. [Wyndham Lewis]." He had also suggested Cummings as a translator for poems by French poet and novelist Paul Morand and for a story by the French writer Louis Aragon (neither of which Cummings did). As for Cummings, Pound was still a literary hero, as is evident from his remarks in the letter. Even so, Cummings did not immediately rush to visit "the great one," despite his promise. It would be nearly two years, in fact, before he would again seek out Pound in Paris.

On July 28, 1921, the French Civil Court issued its divorce decree. The accusation read, in part, that Thayer "s'est detaché de l'exposante et a manifesté à son égard la froideur las plus absolue…. M. Thayer, sans motif, quitté le domicile conjugal, abandonnant sa femme et son enfant." [detached himself from the petitioner and has manifested toward her the greatest possible indifference…. Mr. Thayer, without cause, left the conjugal domicile, abandoning his wife and his child.] As part of the agreement, Thayer agreed to provide for Nancy. On November 1, 1921, a few weeks after the divorce became final, Thayer created a trust fund composed of stocks and bonds for "the support, maintenance and education of Nancy Thayer;" the recorded value was one hundred thousand dollars, the equivalent of more than ten times that amount in current U.S. dollars. No money was awarded to Elaine; her own sizable trust fund, both she and Thayer agreed in advance, was sufficient to ensure that her lavish lifestyle would not be encumbered.

That Thayer was generous is a given, but to suggest that he was so munificent because money meant nothing to him is neither sufficient as an explanation nor true. While it was legally required, since he was officially Nancy's father, that he provide for her, it was not Elaine who proposed the large sum; it was Thayer. His letters to Elaine make it clear that he did feel something for Nancy, did feel an obligation to make sure she had everything she could need or want. But these feelings alone do not explain why he felt the need to settle on her such a large trust. Guilt likely played some part. Despite his frequent declarations that one should be free to love freely, he struggled with his bisexual nature and, at times, felt unable to be a proper lover to Elaine. This, in tandem with his numerous infidelities, not to mention public displays of cruelty toward Elaine during the early years of their marriage, made him feel somewhat responsible for driving Elaine into Cummings's arms.

Friendship, though, played an even larger part in compelling him to act so generously toward the child who was not his actual daughter. This sense of loyalty to one's friend emerges implicitly, if not explicitly, in his letters to both Cummings and Elaine in which he comments on his belief in their continued friendship. In retrospect, it seems that Thayer was probably in love with Cummings, but there is no evidence that he ever acted physically upon it. However, he continually revealed how much he cared for his friend, how much he wanted Cummings's approval, respect, and even admiration.

Indeed, Thayer valued his friendship with Cummings more than with any other. At every turn he sought to show Cummings this affection. Not only did he consistently express praise for his friend's achievements, unlike others he showed his appreciation in the most tangible manner possible: buying his work. In addition, his concern for Cummings's opinion was paramount. He listened to what Cummings had to say, seeking out what Cummings told him was worth discovering. On a practical level, he helped out Lachaise and Nagle financially—purchasing work from Lachaise, paying Nagle's doctor's bills—because Cummings asked him to do so. In the end, providing for Nancy was just one more way of showing Cummings—woefully unprepared and unwilling to accept the responsibilities of fatherhood—how true a friend he was, and would continue to be.

Cummings gladly and graciously accepted whatever Thayer wanted to give him, yet at times felt that unwarranted largesse put him in an "inferior" position, one in which he was "taken up by Thayer." "Money buys," he wrote in his journal, then noted that Thayer, because he had money, "can command…is the boss—controls things." In another jotting he reflected that Thayer used his money "to make people without money feel poor—i.e., myself as writer." If Cummings ever expressed these feeling to Thayer, as he frequently did to his father in response to his gifts or offers or money, no evidence exists. Clearly Cummings felt entitled to receive money from Thayer for any work he produced; he only became squeamish when he felt Thayer was simply "trying to buy him."

Cummings never allowed himself to feel indebted to his friend for any assistance received. He wrote Thayer rather frankly, even acerbically, "Let me assure you that there is only one accidental & therefore momentous indebtedness on my part which the debtor has not forgotten nor is likely to forget:I refer,oddly enough,to my having,through yourself,made the acquaintance of someone for whose esteem I increasingly care daily,not to mention nightly;someone whom I should as perfectly like to understand me as I should like to understand her."

Thayer left Paris in August 1921 to go first to Cologne, then to Vienna, where he had arranged to begin psychoanalysis with Freud. He had invited Cummings to meet him in Austria, but as Cummings wrote Nagle, "My teeth have killed me with immeasurable cubic agony and I am headed not to Vienna,therefore." Instead, Cummings, Brown, Elaine, and Nancy went to England to visit Elaine's sister, Alexis, who was in Dover, arriving August 15. Brown and Cummings quickly left Elaine with her sister, then headed up to London to take in the sights. The National Gallery particularly appealed to him—he made three separate visits to it within a week—but otherwise London does not seem to have won him over. By the beginning of September, after a brief tour of Belgium, they were all once again in Paris.

Since first learning in June that Liveright was interested in *The Enormous Room*, Cummings had been eagerly awaiting news of his verdict. On July 23, he inquired about it in a letter to his parents: "I anticipate hearing from one of you about all of you and S.Lake—also concerning the famous Prison Tales Or Eleven Nights Without a Bar-Room." His mention of the book probably prompted his mother to prod Liveright. Finally on August 26, 1921, Liveright wrote to Cummings's mother—Edward was in Geneva attending a World Peace Foundation meeting—that he wanted to publish the book. The news was sent on to Dr. Cummings who brought the happy announcement to his son in mid-September when he met up with him in Paris.

Cummings could not have been happier that his book had not only been accepted, but that it was Liveright who had taken it. Best known initially for starting the Modern Library, at Liveright's urging the press had increasingly become more daring about what it published. In existence at that time for just six years, the house could already count among its authors such mavericks as John Reed, Eugene O'Neill, Sherwood Anderson, Ezra Pound, and Theodore Dreiser.

Quite naturally, a great deal of the brief time Edward spent with his son was taken up with discussions about the imminent book. Cummings had entrusted his father to act as his agent, but wanted to ensure that his father understood exactly what the young author expected. Among the topics they talked about was Cummings's wish that the sketches he had drawn in confinement be sent on to Liveright for inclusion in the printed book. They also agreed that Edward Cummings would supply an "introduction" for the book consisting of his letters to President Wilson and others. On Edward's departure for Boston, Cummings again reminded him that Boni & Liveright were not to tamper with his style or words.

It was a jubilant Cummings who, with Brown, pedaled out of Paris on September 28 on a biking trip to Italy. Their route took them through southwest France, then over the Alps to Turin. By October 11, less than two weeks after their departure, they were in Genoa. By the end of the month they were in Rome and in early November in Naples. Cummings recorded the whirlwind trip—they never seemed to stay anywhere more than a day or two—more in pictures than in words. His sketchbooks are filled with landscapes of views along the road, of people in villages, of cathedrals, and building façades. In Naples they left their bicycles and returned to Paris by train.

Among the mail awaiting him in Paris was a copy of the contract from Boni & Liveright, signed by his father on his behalf. The terms stipulated that Cummings would receive an advance of three hundred dollars. Cummings acknowledged receipt to his mother, informing her that his name be listed as "E.E. Cummings (not E. Estlin,not Edward E.,not Edward Estlin)." He also asked her to make sure that if obscenities needed to be stricken from the book, dashes, rather than substitutions, should be used: "In cutting use dash———e.g.'———-it,' said etc.(not 'chuck it,' said etc." On November 12, Cummings forwarded on to his father a two-paragraph addition to the "Jean le Nègre" chapter that he wished to include. His father, meanwhile, had sent on the sketches, per his son's request, to Liveright who responded to Edward that he thought "it would help the book very much if we use the sketches your son did."

The book still did not have a title. Liveright, who was hoping to get the book out by spring, was getting anxious. He suggested "Hospitality." Dr. Cummings found it "attractive," but knew that only his son could decide. On November 15, he sent his son twenty-six suggestions for possible titles. Among them was his father's favorite, "Lost and Found."

Others included "Held on Suspicion," "Unwilling Guest," "Caught in the French Net," and "The Enormous Room." On November 25, Cummings cabled his father: "Title of book The Enormous Room."

Elaine was leaving Paris for New York in December 1921. Since her arrival in June, Cummings had been paying her more attention than ever, the trips to England and Italy being the only times he was not in her company most days. He was warming to Nancy, now always called Mopsy, taking newfound and genuine delight in her. She was now nearly two years old, had begun to talk, but even without words was quite able to express herself through gestures. Around this period he described in a poem his wonderment at his own affection for Mopsy as filtered through Elaine:

look
my fingers,which
touched you
and your warmth and crisp
littleness
—see?do not resemble my
fingers.   My wrists hands
which held carefully the soft silence
of you(and your body
smile eyes feet hands)
are different
from what they were.   My arms
in which all of you lay folded
quietly,like a
leaf or some flower
newly made by Spring
Herself,are not my
arms.   I do not recognise
as myself this which i find before
me in a mirror.   i do
not believe
i have even seen these things;
someone whom you love

and who is slenderer
taller than
myself has entered and become such
lips as i use to talk with,
a new person is alive and
gestures with my
or it is perhaps you who
with my voice
are
playing.

He had still not divulged to his parents that Nancy was his daughter, though in letters home he frequently mentioned her: "B. and I have fine parties with Elaine and Mopsy(who runs extraordinarily fast,and is now learning English,having long since created a new language and being cognizant of French in addition.) We take her to the Merry go round,the little one in the Champs-Elysées—or give her tea in state at Fouquet's,or simply all 4 promenade together in a lofty manner and to the amazement of each other and the gendarmes."

What his actual feelings were for Elaine at the time are a bit hard to determine. His poems from the period (mostly not published in his lifetime) almost uniformly celebrate his union with her:

when of your eyes one smile entirely brings down
the night in rain over the shy town of my mind
when upon my heart lives the loud alive darkness
and in my blood beating and beating with love
the chuckling big night puzzles asquirm with sound
when all my reaching towers and roofs are drenched with love
my streets whispering bulge my trembling houses yearn
my walls throb and writhe my spires curl with darkness…

But his private jottings, mostly recorded after his time in Paris, contain a mixture of lofty expressions of love and desire "MY BEAUTIFUL ELAINE, MY INCOMPARABLE," along with more bitter reflections:

> After N[ancy]—whom I bitterly resented until I saw her
> I was repelled,disappointed physically

nipples brown & wrinkled vs pink
cunt—bigger
I pocketed the disgust
pretended to E that was crazy about her because
I didn't want to hurt her feelings
i.e.I began to idealize her
(a)the fact not there (beauty)
(b)I substitute,for the fact,an idea—mother
I feel that I owed her something
To owe=to not desire an avoidance of saying to
myself that I didn't want E

Both sentiments were probably true. It is hard to believe, given the large number of love poems he wrote at the time, that he was not fully in love with Elaine, even passionate about her. It is also likely that from time to time he questioned his ardor, attempted to distance himself from it. Cummings was quite capable of holding contradictory emotions in his head simultaneously. In the case of his father, for instance, he both cherished and resented him. The same may very well have been the case with Elaine. What is clear is that after she left Paris, he missed her and Nancy terribly:

along the brittle treacherous bright streets
of memory comes my heart,singing like
an idiot,whispering like a drunken man...

Cummings found himself new lodgings, this time at the Hôtel Le Havane at 42 St. Andre des Arts on the left bank. He had hoped to obtain a studio in which he could live and paint, but found them too expensive. As a result, he settled for a large room, the best in the hotel. He set up his easel and began painting again, but did not continue with the large abstractions in the *Sound* and *Noise* series that he had dedicated his talents to in New York. Instead he produced small canvases, often in watercolors, as well as scores of ink drawings. His sketchbooks reveal that he was still intent on working out theories of abstraction, but he did not neglect representation either. His rather meager amount of money probably played a major role in determining at least the size of canvases. Canvas and oils were not cheap. Even if he did spring for them, he needed more space than a hotel room—even a large one—could provide; the cost of shipping home large paintings was also expensive.

Despite Elaine's absence, Cummings was still glad to be in Paris:

Paris,thou art not
merely these streets trees silence
twilight,nor even this single star jotting
nothing busily upon the green edges of evening;
nor the faces which sit and drink on the boulevards,laughing
which converse smoke smile,thou art
not only a million little ladies fluttering merely upon darkness—

these things thou art and thou art all which is alert perishable
alive:thou art the sublimation of our
lives eyes voices
thou art the gesture by which we express to one another all
which we hold more dear and fragile than death,...

On New Year's Eve, Brown and Cummings got so drunk that he broke the vow he had made to himself about not making love with anyone but Elaine. It was a chance and quick encounter with a prostitute in a seedy Pigalle hotel room, but the next day Cummings was remorseful. He gave up drinking and smoking for eighteen days, partly as penance, partly because he somehow thought it was a way of warding off a sexually transmitted disease of which he was horribly afraid. But he also had to admit to himself that "all the time he loved [Elaine] he was attracted to whores."

He was probably even more unsettled by the experience because he knew that his mother had just lunched in New York with Elaine (who had toted back Christmas presents for the family). On January 13, 1922, in response to a letter from his mother in which she expressed her enjoyment at seeing Elaine and the baby, he wrote to his mother that "Nothing has given me greater pleasure than the thought of you lunching with Elaine! I hope you'll let me know how she is. I'm glad you liked Mopsy—I agree with Nagle: 'I wish I might find a suitable phrase to tell you how rare a person Mopsy appears to me.'"

In early February, his social life improved with the arrival of Dos Passos from the Middle East and Stewart Mitchell, with aunt in tow, from Montpelier in Southern France. "Fortunately for all concerned,the a. [aunt] fell ill,enabling her charge to disport himself a goodly deal with myself,Dos,and Brown. We had several really remarkable parties—and Dos(who paid left and right)borrowed 800 fr. from me to get home with."

In the same letter he informed his mother that Dos Passos "is seeing publishers to Hell in my behalf anent some poems." "Some poems" were those he had collected in *Tulips & Chimneys*, his book-length manuscript that Mitchell had tried but failed to place with publishers the year before. While in Paris, Cummings had further revised the manuscript, adding new poems, subtracting others. The result was far from "a slim volume." It consisted of 152 poems roughly divided into two major sections: "Tulips" and "Chimneys."

Cummings was quite reluctant to submit his own work for publication. He always preferred to rely on "the kindness of friends" to do this for him; or, at the very least, only sent work to those whom he knew he could count on, such as Thayer or Watson. Fortunately he had friends who were quite willing to act as agents. Mitchell had done all the initial work on getting *Eight Harvard Poets* into print, and had tried to interest publishers in *Tulips & Chimneys*. His father, and a Greenwich Village acquaintance, had been responsible for finding a publisher for *The Enormous Room*. Even as a painter, he did little to promote his own work. Had it not been for Lachaise, he would probably not have bothered to place his canvasses in the Independent Artists' Shows. Cummings now fully expected that Dos Passos, who had previously helped Cummings get a few poems accepted by the leftist New York magazine, the *Liberator*, would be able to interest someone in taking his first verse collection.

That Cummings rarely submitted his own artistic efforts for publication had less to do with shyness or fear of rejection than with his distaste for business of any sort. He also had a definite sense of entitlement. He felt his task was simply the lofty one of creating the work; he should not have to "sully" himself by engaging in "the commerce of art." It was a stance inculcated in him from childhood on. As a child he drew the pictures; his mother framed them. As a young man he studied; his father paid the bills.

As an adult the pattern was still present. When he painted now, Thayer (or Edward) bought the canvas. When he wrote a poem, Thayer most often published it. In part, *The Enormous Room* got written because his father paid him to write it. Edward continued to send frequent checks to help sustain him as a poet-painter in Paris. Why should he not feel entitled? Why should he exert efforts or lose time as a creator to get his work into print when others were so willing (and so able) to do it for him?

Accidents occasionally happened. Early in 1922, he had sent some poems to the Paris-based literary magazine *Broom*. It was not a "blind submission;" he had met the editor, American poet Alfred Kreymbourg, who had asked for work. But when he received the acceptance of "seven out of twelve" poems, it came not from Kreymbourg but from Harold Loeb, *Broom*'s new editor, Kreymbourg having given up the post. Cummings was surprised that Loeb, whom he had not yet met, had taken them. Loeb was, in fact, a rather brilliant editor with an eye for the unique. Though not known to Cummings, he was familiar to the Montparnasse crowd. A few years later, a young American writer named Ernest Hemingway, who had recently arrived in Paris, would use him as the model for Robert Cohn in his first novel, *The Sun Also Rises*.

The Enormous Room was now in proofs. Edward cabled his son to come home and correct them himself but Cummings decided to assign the task to the returning Dos Passos, "it having been agreed…that his published-prestige should go to the general cause of uncensored MS." He explained further that he "pondered the situation with great solemnity,and decided that it would be extremely foolish to leave just then,for the pays des libres et le chez-eux des braves." As it turned out, because of time constraints, Edward read the proofs himself. It would be a decision both would end up regretting.

In early May, Elaine and Mopsy, along with Elaine's personal maid, Eva Prior, and Nancy's nanny, Winifred Rudy, returned to Paris. They stayed at the Hôtel Wagram, on the Rue de Rivoli. Elaine brought with her four copies of *The Enormous Room*, hot off the press. He was delighted with their return; he was dismayed with the book. On May 13, 1922, he vented his spleen at his parents:

> Appalling is no word.... Greatest burlesque achievement of the ages—I refer to my book's publication with misplaced commas,"ands" for "hads", "moir" for "noir" etc.... Didn't {Dos and} you read proof on this? Or who did? And how could you have written me that Boni hadn't changed anything except in the case of certain French phrases,translated? Change anything!—where is Jan's portrait,and the Young Skipper's portrait;and the description of the surveillant dropping a letter,which description brings in the Belgium Farmer and several others? Why are all these left out utterly,if I may ask? If the dropouts occurred between you or somebody's proof reading and the final printing,—if (that is) it's Boni's doing,someone ought to kill Boni and kill him good and hard.... I shall give the book to noone I like.

Unable to wait for a response from his family, the next day he sent an excoriating letter to Boni & Liveright:

> I desire that one of two things happen to "The Enormous Room":either
>
> A)it be immediately surpressed,thrown in a shitoir
>
> B)each and all of the below-noted errors be immediately and completely rectified without loss of time,fear of money,or any-thing-damned-else

The letter continued with a long list of omissions that Cummings demanded be replaced along with explanations of why they were essential for the narrative flow. He concluded his tirade by noting that "the appeal of the book is largely documentary;as a document let it appear complete or for Christ's Sweet Sake NOT AT ALL. As a piece of writing,I do not argue—I know how it should be,and if anyone thinks he knows better than I,let him F him-or her-self.... AS IT STANDS the book is not merely an eye-sore but an insult."

An additional grievance, later commented on by Cummings but not mentioned in these initial fulminations, is that only one of Cummings's drawings was used, though he had to concede, at least appropriately: for the jacket.

Dr. Cummings replied quickly, taking blame for the errors and omissions. The proofs had come to him as in the final version, but because he did not want to delay publication, he had accepted the deletions and changes, feeling that the omitted passages "seemed…less of a sacrifice than any others which could have been chosen." He also reminded his son that he had to take a fair share of the blame: Edward had cabled him to come home to look over the galleys himself but he had refused. Since the book had been approved the way it was printed, neither Edward nor Boni & Liveright felt that any of Cummings's demands needed to be met. And they were not. The English edition of 1928 and that of The Modern Library of 1934 did restore the omitted passages and corrected the typographical errors. But it was not until 1978, with the publication of the "typescript edition," meticulously edited by George Firmage, that *The Enormous Room* finally appeared in the form Cummings intended, complete with his drawings and with every word, spelling, capitalization, and punctuation mark exactly as its author had wanted.

twelve

An American in Paris

Within two weeks of the publication of *The Enormous Room*, on April 27, 1922, reviews began to appear. It is clear from the ink spilled in newspapers and magazines that the book that detailed Cummings's experiences as an inmate of La Ferté-Macé caused considerable stir, both because of its unique style and contents. Even its classification—whether it was an autobiographical novel or simply autobiography—was a subject of controversy. (Cummings, himself, never called it a novel, though Liveright did.)

"Mr. Cummings is honest. He is also sensitive, so sensitive that the lightest tremors of life make his tongue, like some cubistic seismograph, record them in a cryptic, half insane dance of words." Robert Littell's comment came from the first review of *The Enormous Room* that appeared in the *New Republic* on May 10, 1922. While generally positive, Littell noted that he had to dig for the gold: "I feel as if I had been rooting long, desperate hours in a junk heap, irritably but thoroughly pawing over all sorts or queer, nameless garbage." After a long inventory detailing his "excavation," he concludes, "I had come away at last with some lumps of curious, discolored but none the less precious metal."

Four days later the theme of gold appeared again, this time in a review by Louis Kantor, a friend of Brown's, who wrote in the *New York Tribune* that he could find "the veins of pure gold in Cummings's composition with an unhasty eye; show me another young American prose artist in whose composition gold can be mined without a patient pickaxe."

The positive trend did not continue. A week later Thomas L. Masson, writing in the *New York Times*, attacked Cummings for both his lack of patriotism and obscure style. Initially bothered that *The Enormous Room* was a product of "the Harvard school of writers," and clearly a "Bolshevist book," he did finally grudgingly admit that "apart from its crudities, its mistaken, disgruntled attitude and its bad writing, the book is quite worthwhile."

Not content with the bashing Masson had delivered, the next day the *New York Times* again took on Cummings, this time in editorial form: "It is a pity that men of peculiar sensitiveness and irritability so frankly confessed by Mr. Cummings ever entered any form of military service, and a greater pity that they will insist on writing books like this one and [Dos Passos's] *Three Soldiers*.... Books that are utterly false because they are only a part, and a very small part, of the truth."

Cummings had clearly succeeded in stirring up a tempest. Not only was his book iconoclastic in its style, its anti-authoritarian views raised considerable hackles. Indeed, judging from a good number of the early reviews, his book was read more as a political commentary than as an artistic achievement whose subject, almost indirectly, is society, and even more indirectly, war. (The same fate had met Dos Passos when his *Three Soldiers* had been published the year before.)

That Cummings's artistry was less prominent for reviewers than his politics should have come as no surprise given the political climate in the United States in the years following the war. In 1922, the "Big Red Scare" was in full bloom and "super-patriots," to use historian Frederick Lewis Allen's term, were setting the national agenda. Anyone who disagreed with the established view that the war had been fought to save democracy, and/or that the United States was the greatest country on earth, was immediately branded a "Bolshevist." Or as Katharine Fullerton Gerould wrote in *Harper's Magazine* in 1922, "America is no longer a free country in the old sense; and liberty is, increasingly, a mere rhetorical figure.... No thinking citizen, I venture to say, can express in freedom more than a part of his honest convictions." The response to her piece was overwhelming. Several thousand letters, many of them laced with threats, poured into *Harper's* accusing her of subversion and Bolshevism.

Not everyone, of course, shared the majority view. Ben Ray Redman, reviewing *The Enormous Room* for the left-leaning *Nation* courageously declared that "this book is not an indictment of war, or of prisons, or of the French Government, as has been variously suggested. It is at once an indictment and glorification of the incredible animal Man." Redman got it right. All the same, his attention is far more directed toward what Cummings said, than on how he said it. With the exception of Kantor, who made some observations on Cummings's style, it was not until the summer—when reviews began to appear in literary magazines—that *The Enormous Room* began to receive attention for its innovative artistic merits.

Dos Passos led the charge with his review in the July *Dial*. He linked Cummings's prose with his poetry, praising the book as "a distinct conscious creation separate from anything else under heaven." Gilbert Seldes, who had known Cummings at Harvard and who, with the resignation of Mitchell was now serving as managing editor of the *Dial*, persuaded the *Double-Dealer* to accept his highly positive evaluation of Cummings's "aesthetic qualities" that to him, seemed of "first importance." John Peale Bishop, writing in *Vanity Fair*, focused on *The Enormous Room* as "a presentation of emotions," noting that the book in this regard met what Ezra Pound claimed was "the supreme test" for art.

But the most masterful critique of the work came the following year with Gorham Munson's piece, "Syrinx," in his magazine *Secession*. This article is far more than just laudatory; it is a brilliant display of understanding of what Cummings was really about as both a prose writer and poet. Munson begins by noting that any study of Cummings needs to take into account his painting and drawing, then shows that his work as a painter has affected his writing: "he sees freshly. Cummings sees words."

Munson then goes on to show that "*Cummings makes punctuation and typography active instruments for literary expression*." [italics, Munson] He follows this statement up with a number of well-chosen examples from the small body of Cummings's verse printed in literary magazines, mainly the *Dial*. Next, he dissects with precision *The Enormous Room*, concluding with this remark: "Each page of this book is a rewarding study in mechanics; overwhelming as Cummings's subject matter was, it has all been crystallized in a way to give the last jerk and whirret that inhered within. Cummings has jabbed his pen into life, but he has also twisted it in the wound, and it is this twist of the pen that makes literature."

The fact that those who appreciated *The Enormous Room* for its artistry happened to be Cummings's friends (Dos Passos and Seldes) and acquaintances (Bishop and Munson) says as much about the rather small circle that comprised the avant-garde as it does about mutual "back scratching." To be sure, the practice of friends reviewing friends almost ensured that a positive critique would result; at the same time, none of the reviews can be construed as "puff pieces." The articles written by Cummings's associates all contributed substantially to an understanding of what Cummings had truly achieved.

Cummings was pleased that *The Enormous Room* had been well received, even admired, by those in his circle. To his father, however, who wrote to congratulate him on the book, he replied that his "drawings, poems, essais" were worth "30 (triente) Enormous Rooms." The statement, on one hand, reflects Cummings's genuine desire to move on with his work; on the other, it is indicative of his ongoing struggle to free himself from his father. The matter was complicated. Cummings still relied, at least in part, on financial support from Edward. Consequently, his father felt entitled to offer advice on what his son should do with his life. One of Edward's suggestions—reiterated in a number of letters—was that he felt it was time that his son, now twenty-seven, return to the United States and get a job at a magazine or in publishing. Cummings defiantly refused even to consider the proposition:

> While fully realizing the ignominy attaching to one who,unlike yourself,cannot enjoy the satisfaction of asking his son to not forget that he has been working for half a century,and earning his own living most of the time,and the living of a lot of other people to boot(end of quotes)—a satisfaction impossible for the twain more or less simple reasons (a)I am not,have never been,and do not anticipate being self-supporting (b)I have, to my knowledge,no son just at present—the present writer has always been,is,and in all human and supernatural probability will remain,so everlastingly sure of and stuck on himself.

To his sister, Elizabeth, about to graduate from Radcliffe, and feeling equally stifled in her ambition to escape the over-protectiveness of their father, he wrote a long letter in which he set forth his philosophy of following his own vision as a model for her to follow: "Insofar as I am alive,I will be a son of a b. if anyone shall tell me 'what life is' or 'how to live.' For,if anyone can tell me those items,then pray,what use is there in my living?.... NOTHING IS SO DIFFICULT AS TO BE ALIVE!!!!!!!! which is the ONLY THING WHICH YOU CANNOT LEARN ever,from anyone,anywhere."

Cummings was not just uttering words; he was ardently attempting "to be alive," that is, live according to his own plan for himself. It was easy to do so in Paris where he was very much in control of his own life and his own affairs. He had his work; he had Elaine and Mopsy; and he had friends among the French and in the American expatriate community. Americans, in fact, were flocking to Paris. Among those present in the City of Light in the early 1920s were Hemingway, Fitzgerald, Djuna Barnes, Ezra Pound, H. D., Edna St. Vincent Millay, Malcolm Cowley, Archibald MacLeish, Kay Boyle, Glenway Wescott, Gertrude Stein, John Peale Bishop, Matthew Josephson, Samuel Putnam, Robert McAlmon, Alfred Kreymbourg, Elliot Paul, and (on and off) Dos Passos and Gilbert Seldes. In other words, Paris was home to a great number of writers, many of whom would become luminaries—Cummings, of course, included.

In part because of the large influx of Americans, as well as other English language writers—chief among them James Joyce and Ford Madox Ford—literary journals and presses began to spring up seemingly every season. The first of the Paris-based English language magazines was *Broom*, edited by Harold Loeb and Alfred Kreymbourg, which began in 1921. In 1923, Margaret Anderson, editor of the *Little Review*, moved herself and the magazine to Paris from New York following a lengthy court battle (that she lost) over alleged obscenity in one of the works she had been running in serial form in the review. The "obscene" book she fought for was none other than one of the great masterpieces of twentieth-century literature: Joyce's *Ulysses*. Because of the obvious inability to publish the finished book in the United States, another American, Sylvia Beach—owner of the English language bookstore Shakespeare and Company—turned publisher and issued *Ulysses* in 1922.

Other literary magazines quickly followed, among them *This Quarter*, *transition*, and the *transatlantic review*. Presses too began turning out the work of Americans resident in Paris: Contact Editions, founded by Robert McAlmon in 1921, published Mina Loy, Gertrude Stein, William Carlos Williams, and Hemingway's first book, *Three Stories and Ten Poems*. William Bird's Three Mountains Press brought out elegant editions of writing by the expatriates, including Hemingway's second book, *In Our Time*. By 1927, Harry and Caresse

Crosby had started up the legendary Black Sun Press that would issue works by a number of notables including Hart Crane, Archibald MacLeish, Kay Boyle, and Ezra Pound.

Cummings would never have a book published by one of the Paris presses, but his poems did appear in *Broom*, the *Little Review*, the *transatlantic review*, and *This Quarter*. Unlike a number of his American contemporaries, Cummings did not court editors or publishers; for the most part, they came to him. Nor did he spend most of his time "being seen" in the places where Americans congregated. As Malcolm Cowley observed, "I can picture Cummings writing...lines at a café table with a drink in front of him—and no fear of having it snatched away by a Prohibition agent—but it would not be in the Dôme or the Rotonde or the Select, for he seldom or never appeared in them.... Nevertheless those three cafés in Montparnasse, and the Dôme in particular, were...the heart and nervous system of the American literary colony."

Cowley was right; Cummings's "café" was La Reine Blanche on the Boulevard Saint-Germain, "opposite cluny's gladly miraculous / most vierge et l'enfant." While Cummings may not have patronized the favorite haunts of the Lost Generation, he did socialize with his fellow American writers. At the same time, he never strongly identified (nor was identified with) the expatriate community. He preferred to spend his free time with Elaine and Mopsy, though occasionally he did get swept up into the larger group scene by folks like Cowley, John Peale Bishop, Archibald MacLeish, or others.

While now and then he certainly enjoyed a wild night out on the town with writer friends, he also reveled in the simple pleasures he shared with Elaine and Mopsy: "Elaine and I(when the heat is most)dine outdoors on the top of Paris—at the place du tertre(montmartre);Mopsie enjoys the heat." There were strolls through the Tuileries Gardens where they would stop to "drink beer at little green tables under the trees." Elaine and Mopsy were, in fact, becoming more and more important to him. His love affair, too, was blooming, particularly after Elaine decided to remain in Paris for a longer period than she had originally intended. Her decision seems reflected in one of his poems of the period:

this fear is no longer dear.   You are not going to America and
i but that doesn't in the least matter.   The big

fear Who had us deeply in his fist is
no longer,can you imagine it . . .

For all the closeness he was feeling for Elaine and Nancy, Cummings still lived apart from them. He did not care much for Elaine's "imbecilic" friends, "the Rue de Rivoli crowd," made up mostly of American and British socialites, while she did not warm as readily to his new Paris friends. Brown, Dos Passos, Mitchell (when in town), and Seldes were always welcome at her place, but she did not maintain a salon as she had in New York to entertain her lover's Paris cohorts. This meant (not unhappily for either of them, it seems) that they often spent evenings with their own groups.

Indeed, the contrast between their lives was great. Elaine lived in luxury, with both a personal maid and a nanny and spent freely. Cummings, on the other hand, lived in one room at the rather shabby Hôtel Le Havane (that doubled, as he found out, as a bordello). His expenses ran about eighty-five dollars a month for food, lodging, and entertainment. Elaine could spend that much in a day. And while he was not adverse to her picking up the check for drinks or dinner, he did not allow her to support him beyond that. Nor, as he noted in his journal, did he often stay at her place: "I never insisted on staying the night with Elaine. It was her apartment."

Cummings seemed equally in love with Paris and his life there as with Elaine. In Paris, where art and artists mattered, he felt himself an individual, whole, an "IS:"

> . . .someone was morethanalive
> with love;with love;with love—love of whom?
> love:paris;la france,une fille and at least
>
> (while every night was a day and a day was dimanche)
> seven or-not to exaggerate—certainly five
>
> selves beyond every human imagining my;
> whereas,in this epoch of mindandsoul,to feel
> you're not two billion other unselves.

It was not just with his compatriots in the American colony that Cummings socialized. By the summer of 1922, he had become friends with poet and fiction writer Louis Aragon, a leader of the Dadaists in Paris, and editor, with Philippe Soupault and André Breton, of the French literary magazine *Littérature*. It is not clear how Cummings met Aragon. It was probably through their mutual friend Malcolm Cowley, but it could have been through Thayer, who had already published Aragon in the *Dial*. Thayer, in fact, on Pound's recommendation, had asked Cummings in 1920 to translate a short story by Aragon. Though Cummings turned down the request, Aragon's work had impressed him. And Cummings was known to Aragon in advance of their first meeting, through his contributions to the *Dial*.

The two had quite a lot in common. Though Aragon, at twenty-six, was two years younger than Cummings, he had served in the war and shared his American friend's views on the conflict as a sordid, dehumanizing affair for all involved. Like Cummings, he was also a leftist, but what bound them most together was their total commitment to the revolution of the word. For Cummings, this revolution had begun in his graduate year at Harvard when he began to experiment with language. For Aragon, Dada had led him to a new poetics of verbal spontaneity. In 1922, Dada, as a movement, was fairly moribund in Paris. Because of personal conflicts within the ranks of the Paris Dadaists—chiefly squabbles between Tristan Tzara, Francis Picabia, and André Breton, who all vied for leadership—Aragon had followed his closest friend, Breton, in deserting the group. But Dada, whose aim was disruption of the status quo, even of art, still resonated with Aragon. Cummings, who was in opposition to what he perceived as staidness in art, found himself very much drawn to this Frenchman and his views.

Aragon, according to Mark Polizzotti, the biographer of André Breton, was possessed of a "seductive charm that was aided by his verbal brilliance, both in conversation and in the amazing facility with which he wrote." French writer Philippe Soupault described Aragon as a "stunning, tireless 'talker,' detecting something unusual on every street corner." In these descriptions, Aragon seems very much like the young Cummings who was also charming, a brilliant conversationalist, and a keen observer of street corner miracles. Both men, in fact, reveled in walking in the streets; and from these walks came inspiration for art. Cummings's poems as well as his sketches were often directly inspired by scenes on the street. Among Aragon's most important books is *Le Paysan de Paris*, a record of strolls through the streets of Paris.

Since Cummings was already writing radically, Aragon's impact on his verse was minimal. A few poems, though, with lines such as these, "the dress was a suspicious madder,importing the cruelty of roses" do reveal Cummings's appropriation of the French new spirit in poetry in which images gain an intense originality through radical juxtaposition. Or for a more sustained example:

> **my Nose puts on sharp robes of uncouth odour,for an onion!for**
> **one—onion for.   putrescence is Cubical   sliced-nicelybits**
> **Of,   shivers ofcrin Ging stink.dull, globular glows and**
> **flatchatte ringaroom**

Aragon was also responsible for introducing him to the works of a number of French poets, including Breton, Soupault, Lautréamont, and most likely, Guillaume Apollinaire. Apollinaire was probably already known to Cummings—he had written the program notes for the production of *Parade* that Cummings had seen on his first trip to Paris—but Aragon certainly prompted his friend to take a closer look at Apollinaire. While Cummings was always quick to say that it was Pound who had introduced him to the impact of the visual arrangements of words and lines on poetry, Cummings far more resembles Apollinaire in his experimental work of the early 1920s than Pound.

Like Cummings, Apollinaire wrote lyrics of great beauty and tenderness that often, as in Cummings, teetered on the edge of sentimentality. But a far more important resemblance can be found in the quest for freshness not just through highly original and evocative imagery but through the way lines are punctuated (or unpunctuated) and laid out on a page. Apollinaire's last book, *Calligrammes*, issued in 1918, less than a year before his death in 1918 from influenza, carried visual arrangement to an extreme. Indeed, Apollinaire referred to the "calligrammes" as picture-poems, for the shape of the words mirrors the meaning. A poem about the Eiffel tower, for instance, is written in the shape of the tower.

Cummings only occasionally attempted such an obvious visual arrangement; nonetheless, Apollinaire's sense that a poem also communicates through its design most certainly resonated with Cummings, perhaps pushed his own experiments further along. When Cummings did attempt visual typographical arrangements that reflected a poem's meaning, his representations were far more subtle than Apollinaire's. Critic

George Wickes observed that Cummings, in contrast to Apollinaire, "has a power beyond mere description to convey being and motion so that they can be heard, seen and felt."

Cummings did not need Apollinaire as a model, for as Wickes noted, "Cummings would have been an original poet if Apollinaire had never existed. But the similarities between them are inescapable and extend far beyond technique.... His poetry seems a continuation of Apollinaire's, though none the less original for all that." The comment is apt. Cummings was, in many respects, the true heir—knowingly or unknowingly—to Apollinaire's experiments with form. By 1913, Apollinaire had dropped all internal punctuation from his poems and began to break his lines in a deliberately nontraditional manner. He also delighted in stretching grammar and syntax, though not in such an extreme a manner as Cummings. And, of course, the visual arrangement of words on a page was important for both poets.

There are other parallels, as well. Both, for instance, were enthralled with street life and used their observations of humanity of all classes as subjects of their poems; both loved the circus and animals (Apollinaire even wrote a modern bestiary); both were heavily influenced by painting; both wrote love poems of great intensity, with highly erotic overtones; and for all the seriousness with which they crafted their work, they were never afraid to employ humor or slang.

Just as Cummings did not need Apollinaire as a model, he did not need him for validation of his own experiments, either. But he must have taken to heart that his French counterpart was held in such high esteem by Aragon, and other French poets such as Cocteau and Morand, who Cummings admired.

Cummings and Aragon did not spend all of their time in cafés engaged in conversations about "audacious" writers such as Apollinaire, or with their own attempts to revolutionize words. Indeed, forays into outrageousness were not confined merely to verse. Malcolm Cowley recalled an evening he spent with Cummings, Aragon, and Dos Passos. After a dinner with numerous bottles of wine, the trio went back to Cowley's apartment. At some point the conversation turned to the topic of books. Cowley offered the opinion that he was feeling overrun by books, yet at the same time, "felt an unreasoning and almost Chinese respect for the printed word." He added, "We all had that weakness," but all agreed that they should endeavor to overcome it.

> I went over to the shelves and pulled down an assortment of bad review books and French university texts that I wouldn't need again. After tearing some of them apart I piled them all on the asbestos mat in front of the stove; then I put a match to the pile. It was a gesture in the Dada manner, but not a successful one, for the books merely smoldered. We talked about bad writers while the smoke grew thicker; then Cummings proved that he was a better Dadaist—at least in someone else's studio—by walking over and urinating on the fire.

Samuel Putnam, an editor for the *Paris Tribune* records a similar incident in his memoir of Paris during those years, but in his account (as related to him by Aragon), Cummings, Cowley, Matthew Josephson, and Aragon set on fire, then urinated on a deluxe edition of the seventeenth-century French writer Racine. It is likely Aragon was describing the same event to Putnam, though with considerably more color. On the other hand, this certainly could have been an antic that Cummings, Aragon, and Cowley felt was worth repeating.

In June, Cummings, Elaine, and Nancy, along with Elaine's maid and Nancy's nanny, set off for Pornic, a town in the south of France. The goal of the trip for Elaine was a vacation; for Cummings, who toted canvases, brushes, and watercolors, it was an opportunity to paint in Cézanne country. Since Harvard, Cummings had counted Cézanne among his favorite artists. With the exception of a few landscapes he had painted in New Hampshire, he had not imitated his style. Instead, he focused his painting energy largely on abstracts. During the spring of 1922, however, he began to use a palette similar to that of Cézanne but "employing it in watercolors" rather than in oils. Once in Pornic he not only appropriated Cézanne's palette, but also his vision of light and shape.

The results—executed in watercolors—are among the best landscapes Cummings ever created. Cézanne's notions of color theory and "modulations" are in full evidence; at the same time, Cummings was humble enough not to try to directly imitate his hero. The Pornic paintings are impressionistic in color, representative in detail, delicate owing to the medium of watercolor, yet solid by virtue of the concentration of shapes. In short, like all of Cummings's work, they are uniquely his own.

Although Cummings stayed less than three weeks in Pornic, he produced at least ten finished watercolors. He would undoubtedly have preferred to stay with Elaine and Nancy and keep painting, but he had to return to Paris by mid-July as his parents arrived for a visit. His folks did not linger too long in Paris, as Edward was on his way to Venice to attend another World Peace Foundation conference and had persuaded his son to accompany him and Rebecca on a leisurely trip to Italy. While Cummings seemed to have gotten along fairly well with his parents—even enjoyed himself—he also wrote to Brown that he was consuming Chianti at the rate of a half-liter twice a day, perhaps a sign that he was not all that comfortable. At least part of his unease had to do with Italy itself. Mussolini had come to power, and with him a vast change. "We found ourselves getting shoved off all the sidewalks of *Roma* by enthusiastic cohorts of Black Shirts.... We sought refuge in a stationery shop. Before our eyes reposed a series of coloured post cards celebrating the recent cataclysm. The first card at which we glanced depicted Mussolini, in the role of Christ, raising *Italia*, in the role of *Lazarus*, from the dead."

By late August 1922, he was back in Paris after a "tour of the world in toytea [thirty] days." He was glad to be "back home" and off his feet. Or as he reported to Brown, "I am in no condition to do more than sell Bluejay Corn and Bunion Plasters among the poor whites."

Over the summer, Cummings's poems had again appeared in *Broom*, and in Gorham Munson's magazine *Secession* that was published in Berlin. Through John Peale Bishop, a former *Vanity Fair* editor who was then living in Paris, he had also gotten work accepted by the little magazine *S4N*. Mitchell, and probably Bishop as well, had persuaded *Vanity Fair* to take a total of eleven poems for the magazine.

Cummings truly felt he was on his way as a poet. Thayer did, too. In August he wrote to Watson from Vienna suggesting that Cummings be given the *Dial* Award of two thousand dollars for 1922. Watson balked, feeling that it should go to T. S. Eliot, who wanted Eliot's new poem, *The Waste Land*, for the journal and felt the best way to secure it was to offer Eliot the prize. Since March, Thayer and Watson had been negotiating with Eliot—mainly through Pound—for the rights to publish the poem.

The issue was the price. Thayer was willing to pay $150; however, Eliot wanted more, having learned that other contributors were paid at higher rates. He proposed to Thayer the sum of £856. Thayer was outraged and told Eliot so. To complicate matters, Horace Liveright had also accepted the poem for publication, offering an advance of $150. If the *Dial* wanted to publish the poem first, they would not only have to pay more, but negotiate with Liveright to delay the book publication until after *The Waste Land* had appeared in the *Dial*. By August, Thayer was incensed over the whole business despite Pound's continual attempts to convince him that the poem was worth fighting for. Or as he told Thayer, "[Eliot's] poem is as good in its way as Ulysses in its way—and there is so DAMN little genius, so DAMN little work that one can take hold of and say 'this at any rate stands', and makes a definite part of literature." Watson largely shared Pound's view, hence his idea of sweetening the offer by coupling publication with the award.

But even if Thayer would not agree to offer Eliot the award, Watson still did not feel Cummings was the right choice. In August, in response to Thayer's repeated suggestion that Cummings be given the award, Watson wrote Thayer that he preferred Pound for the award "if Eliot doesn't get it. That is it would be a much more advantageous thing to give it to him than to Cummings. While his (EEC's) drawings are good, I don't think his poems will make as good a showing as usual in the Jan. number. And Pound will be popular with a few, but Cummings with nobody."

By September, Watson and Seldes had worked out an arrangement with Eliot to which Thayer gave his assent. The *Dial* would pay Eliot $150 for the poem, give him the two thousand dollar award, and buy 350 copies of the book from Liveright. Liveright would, as a result, delay publication until December 1922. On October 15 the *Dial* made publishing history by printing *The Waste Land* in its October issue.

It is unclear whether Cummings was aware of Thayer's efforts to give him the award, but his response to Eliot's poem was not positive. Cowley remembered that Cummings wanted to know "why Eliot couldn't write his own lines instead of borrowing from dead poets." Cummings's reaction in his journal was even less polite: "i'll ask you for a peace that passeth understanding to bed! to bed! i seek a peace which passeth understanding." It is probably just as well that Watson assigned the review of *The Waste Land* to Edmund Wilson instead of to Cummings, as Pound had suggested.

In January 1923, Cummings accompanied Elaine, Nancy, and Elaine's entourage on a long trip to the French and Italian Riviera, then on to Rome and Venice. Cummings was even more appalled by the rise of fascism in Italy on this visit than he had been the previous summer. In a letter to his mother he described the streets as swarming with "scrawny hollow-chested,knock-need sneering lopsided betassled youths crying 'For God for country and for Yale' every few minutes.... Whatever part of them is visible to the naked eye is covered with pimples.... When there are enough of them they hold up traffic and call themselves the Fascist army.... I wish...that some of the castor oil which these knight errants forced down the throats of the communists had found its way to Fascist bowels." His aversion to these "fascist louts" was so intense, that Cummings could not even find much to like in the country:

> Concerning the innumerable catacombs, cathedrals, museums, ruins, etc. which recall an illustrious past and which have inspired so much bad and good poetry, philosophy and criticism, we beg to opine (1) that the ceiling of the Sistine Chapel is worth all the rest of *Italia* dead and undead (2) that we love Venice much but that we love Coney Island more (3) that one small church of Santo Tomé (Spain) which contains El Greco's *The Burial of Count Orgáz*, houses more aesthetic intensity than does the whole *Galleria degli Uffizi*.

Cummings did manage to get one very good poem out of Italy, "(ponder,darling,these busted statues," a modernist mix of Marvell's "To his Coy Mistress" and Shelley's "Ozymandias." After the opening, that comments Shelley-like on the fallen grandeur of a once great civilization, he proceeds, like Marvell, to urge his lover to seize the day for love:

when the your- and my-
idle vertical worthless
self unite in a peculiarly
momentary

partnership(to instigate
constructive
Horizontal
business. . . .even so,let us make haste
—consider well this ruined aqueduct

lady,
which used to lead something into somewhere)

By mid February, Cummings had had enough of Italy. Elaine, who found the country far more enchanting, wanted to remain in Florence. Cummings did not argue with her, but he did not return to Paris either. Instead, he went to Vienna to visit Thayer. He could not have made a worse choice. He wrote his mother on the fifth of March, a couple of weeks after his arrival, that "Vienna is the most utterly desolating small town or hamlet which (I now believe) exists, with the possible exception of that part of Brighton [Massachusetts] occupied by the abbatoir." Again, he was immensely disturbed by the oppressive political atmosphere: "The fascisti of Vienna…spend their time hunting Jews—I saw the police charge on horseback the other day to stop a fight:made me feel weakly in my liver or lights,or both. Woman screaming."

Thayer gave Elaine his own report of Cummings: "Mr. Cummings walks about with folded arms, a Daniel come to judgment. He is very dissatisfied with Vienna and its inhabitants of both sexes." In an attempt to show Cummings that Vienna was not as awful as he felt it was, Thayer wined and dined him, and tried to acquaint him with artists and writers. Even this did not bring Cummings fully around, as Thayer told Elaine, "I have ameliorated the unrenumerativeness of Cummings's stay in Vienna by introducing him to [Franz] Werfel whom he found most objectionable, and to Dr. [Arthur] Schnitzler, against whom he had nothing definite. He was good enough to be enthusiastic over a play by [Frank] Wedekind and a dwarf and a tattooed lady."

Paris was a welcome sight to Cummings when he returned in early April. The welcome was made even sweeter when he learned that Thomas Seltzer had accepted *Tulips & Chimneys* for publication. It was all due to Dos Passos, who had taken the manuscript back to the United States the year before and had begun peddling it to publishers. Or as Cummings told his sister, "He [Dos Passos] of his perfectly own volition,dragged said Selzer [*sic*] over the coals,rubbed his nose in merde,and otherwise frighteningly buldozed him to the extent of signing a contract to print myself."

Thomas Seltzer, the uncle of Charles and Albert Boni, had been involved early on with Boni & Liveright. He owned a one-third share of the firm and was listed as vice president. But his primary contribution to the house was as an editor of the Modern Library, for which he also provided several translations. Among the more important translations he did for Boni & Liveright were books by Trotsky, French novelist Henri Barbusse, and the Hungarian writer Andreas Latzko. All were politically oriented, as was Seltzer, who had served as an editor at the communist magazine the *Masses*. None of these volumes sold terribly well, which led to an ongoing dispute between Boni and Seltzer on one side and Liveright on the other.

Despite poor sales, Boni and Seltzer wanted to continue publishing foreign authors, while Liveright wanted to nurture young, home-grown talent. By July of 1918, the differences had become so great that Boni and Liveright decided to flip a coin to determine who would take over the press. Liveright won the toss and became majority owner. Boni left the firm, as did Seltzer. By 1919, he established himself as Thomas Seltzer, Inc. When he acquired *Tulips & Chimneys*, he was beginning to make a reputation for himself by publishing books by D. H. Lawrence, Arthur Schnitzler, and Marcel Proust.

The twenty-eight-year-old Cummings was delighted that Seltzer wanted to publish the book, but also worried about changes being made. While willing to concede that certain poems, because of their overt eroticism, might have to be eliminated from the printed book, he did not want the arrangement altered. Nor was he willing to accept "improvements, however happily conceived by however brilliant minds." He also felt the ampersand in *Tulips & Chimneys* was sacred: "On this I am portland cement and carrara."

As thrilled as he was by the acceptance of his manuscript, Cummings still felt he was as much a painter as a writer. His parents, however, were urging him to devote himself more to the literary arts. But he would have none of it. Shortly after his return to Paris in April, he informed his parents that he was "working harder than anyone expected Paris to make an inhabitant work-at,as I think I told you, painting. Am often encouraged, strange as this may appear." To his sister he wrote that "I started,some years ago,against the continual advice of my elders,to paint as I saw fit."

Dos Passos recalled that during this period "though Cummings preferred to describe himself as *artiste-peintre* he was never bashful about his role as a poet." That he was productive as a painter is indicated by his shipping to Brown fifty-nine watercolors that year. In addition, hundreds of sketches in crayon, pencil, and ink survive from this period, as well as several small oils.

In June, Dos Passos was again in Europe and stopped off to visit Cummings. Gilbert Seldes was also in Paris on *Dial* business. The three met up for a night out on the town. They began on the right bank at the Café de la Paix. In the early hours of the morning, as Dos Passos remembered, "full of wine and François Villon and Cummings's imagery we embarked in a cab for the *rive gauche* in search of a little *boîte* Cummings had discovered there. In a particularly dark little alley Cummings decided to alight for the purpose of taking a leak. Immediately he was seized by a pair of *agents de police* in cloak and kepi who appeared from nowhere. 'Un pisseur' they cried and marched him off to the police station."

Both Dos Passos and Seldes attempted to intervene, but the gendarmes were resolute. Dos Passos, apparently more vocal than Seldes, even tried to persuade the police to release Cummings by informing them "in noisy French that the gentleman was America's greatest poet." When that tactic failed, Dos Passos tried to evoke memories of the war in which all three of the Americans had served on the side of France. But even that strategy proved unsuccessful in getting Cummings released. At the police station, both Dos Passos and Seldes were pushed out the door when they tried to accompany their friend inside. Dos Passos was not to be deterred and tried to enter a second time. This time, he remembered, "they threw me out bodily."

When Cummings finally emerged, his friends were waiting for him on the sidewalk. Dos Passos recalled that Cummings appeared "somewhat shaken, because he remembered La Ferté all too well. In his hand he had a summons to appear in court next day." By the next morning Seldes had gotten in touch with French writer Paul Morand, who worked for the government. Morand immediately responded, and was able to squelch the charges against Cummings. Dos Passos noted that "the success of Gilbert's call on Morand made an impression on all of us. It proved there was something in the notion of a republic of letters."

Cummings was apparently not terribly contrite. Within a week, he and Dos Passos "subsequently threw a shindig chez Cowley at Giverny." The occasion was apparently a farewell party for Cowley who was returning to the United States. Though no one left a detailed record of the event, Cummings did remark in a letter to Brown that he was "glad to have heard…that the Giverny fracas left [Cowley] uninjured."

Thayer was also in Paris early that summer of 1923. His visit somewhat disturbed Cummings who remarked to Brown that he saw "a different kind of Thayer from what left America. (It was less agreeable,by far,than what had been my host last winter in Wien.)" Indeed, despite two years of psychoanalysis by Freud (the reason for his residency in Vienna), Thayer seemed more erratic than ever. While Cummings had long been aware of a "neurotic streak" in Thayer, he now found him increasingly paranoid. During Thayer's visit, Cummings was subjected to more than one of his friend's long diatribes about most everybody.

Among those on Thayer's hit list were Pound, "the Idaho barker," whom he wanted to fire as Paris editor. He also was sure that Samuel Craig, the secretary-treasurer of the *Dial* was not properly managing the money (the *Dial*, in fact, was hemorrhaging cash); he was even beginning to doubt the abilities of his managing editor, Gilbert Seldes. With Watson, he was also often at odds. Watson's support for Pound particularly irritated him; he also resented Watson's concern that the magazine was publishing "too many German things." The German and Austrian material, of course, had all been acquired by Thayer. Given that Thayer had managed to get work from Thomas Mann (*Death in Venice*), Oscar Kokoschka, Arthur Schnitzler, Freud, and other luminaries, his struggles with Watson over the German language contributions were justified. His other complaints, however, as Cummings quickly realized, were largely without substance.

By July 1923, Cummings again found himself following Elaine and her entourage to the coast of France. They traveled separately. Elaine, Nancy, the nanny, and the maid had journeyed by boat to Biarritz; Cummings took the train. They also stayed in separate places. Elaine and company put up at the fashionable Hotel Carlton in Biarritz while Cummings found cheaper accommodations, first in Saint-Jean de Luz, then after a few days in the village of Guéthary. He did not particularly care for the atmosphere (or prices) in Saint-Jean, but found nearby Guéthary more to his liking. Or as he wrote to Brown, "I struggle to occasional achievement if it suns(instead of pouring)will be content. The air smells of clover."

One plus for Cummings was the Basques, whom he found quite pleasant. The Basque language, "approximating Esquimaux," fascinated him and he admired the people with their "Kat-like Kuriosity" who "don't seem to care whether it hails snows or merely piddles. Nothing can persuade me that these folks are inhibited."

Cummings remained in Guéthary until the end of August, having finally found accommodations that suited him: a tiny maid's room on the fourth floor of the Hôtel Juzau for two dollars and fifty cents a day, including meals. He spent a fair amount of time by himself, drawing, writing, and hiking. A few times a week he would take the train to Biarritz to be with Elaine and Nancy, but he so disliked the prices and pretentiousness of the resort town that he limited his visits. Occasionally Elaine and Nancy, or Elaine alone, would visit him in Guéthary, but for the most part Cummings made the trek to see them. His relationship with Elaine by this point had settled into a familiar pattern. Although attached to one another, they led fairly separate lives. One of his notes described the contrast between them like this: "I am essentially an Artist, secondarily a Man(aesthetics, ideas,Beauty) but SHE [Elaine] is primarily a Woman(living (life) things,FUCKING)." As Cummings saw it, these different values were responsible for the differences in their lifestyles. For Elaine, "living meant having things,people,money." For Cummings, life was about making art. Consequently, Elaine could not really enter his "Bohemian" world; and he certainly did not feel comfortable in her realm of luxury. Although occasionally these contradictory perspectives resulted in conflict, more often it was an arrangement that suited Cummings for, as he noted in his journal, he was not really interested in "being a husband to Elaine. I want her [Elaine] only as a mistress."

Nancy, now three and a half, seems to have become increasingly important to him, but again his role was much more that of a doting grandfather or uncle than that of a father. He took her to the circus, carried her on his shoulders as his father had carried him, and invented games to play with her. "Mopsy is always just slightly more amazing," he wrote his mother. "Elaine and I shall search the city one day for a fine seat,foldupable,which Mopsy can use when tired of strolling at grande velocita." While he had apparently still not informed his parents that Nancy was his own daughter, his letters home contain frequent, always glowing, often rhapsodic reports of her. Given how sensitive Rebecca was to her son, it is hard to imagine that she was not somewhat suspicious of the true nature of Cummings's involvement with Mopsy. Yet true Yankee reserve operated on both sides; neither Cummings nor his parents broached the subject of Nancy's actual identity. Another six months would go by before Cummings finally told the truth about Nancy to his parents.

By early September, Cummings, Elaine, and Nancy were all back in Paris. Their time together was rather bittersweet as Elaine was returning to New York at the end of the month. "Elaine and Mopsy and myself have tea,now and then,at Notre Dame;and the waiter gives Mopsy sugared cake of strange variety...also I have been known to sit with Elaine upon straw chairs in the district called les grands boulevards of an evening. Last night we dined at place du Tertre."

Elaine had just left for New York when Cummings learned that his grandmother, Nana Cummings, had died. On receiving the news, he wrote his mother a letter filled with his remembrances of Nana. Among his memories was that she had first taught him piano: "Of all the piano teachers I have ever had,she is the only one whom I really liked and did not partially or wholly detest." But what had moved Cummings the most was that "she alone(of the entire family)agreed with myself During the War(in fact,during my incarceration at Devens)that it was nothing to die about. 'I hate War,' she said. I think this is the pleasantest thing I ever heard her say." Although he told his mother that he "felt no surprise" on hearing his grandmother had died, he was rather shocked that she had left him one thousand dollars in her will: "The thought of Nana's death involving money had never entered my brain."

Over the summer, Seltzer had edited *Tulips & Chimneys*. The final version was far different from the manuscript. More than half of the original compilation had been cut, and while the general arrangement remained the same, the order of poems within the sections was often altered. The excisions were partly the result of Seltzer's taste—he found the more radical experiments just too radical. But the major reason he eliminated so many poems was that he feared that their overtly sexual content would result in the book being banned, or even worse, that they would cause his press to be shut down.

Among the poems he rejected were "twentyseven bums give a prostitute the once / -over," whose lines such as "eyes say the breasts look very good: / firmlysquirmy with a slight jounce, // thirteen pants have a hunch" seemed a little too risqué to publish safely. A similar fate met "her careful distinct sex whose sharp lips comb," and "a blue woman with sticking out breasts hanging." Of course, there was no question of printing a poem as graphic as "i like my body when it is with your / body," with its graphic lines: "i like,slowly stroking the,shocking fuzz / of your electric fur,and what-is-it comes / over parting flesh."

Seltzer's fears were justified. Just the year before, in 1922, the New York Society for the Suppression of Vice, led by John Sumner, had seized three of Seltzer's titles: D. H. Lawrence's *Women in Love*, Arthur Schnitzler's *Casanova's Homecoming*, and the anonymous *A Young Girl's Diary*, which carried an introduction by Freud. Though Seltzer won the case that fall, the controversy over *Women in Love* would not die.

John Ford, a New York supreme court justice, scandalized that his sixteen-year-old daughter had managed to acquire a copy of the book from a lending library, aligned himself with Sumner. Together, they took their case against "obscene books and the publishers who publish them" to the New York legislature. The draconian Clean Books Bill, crafted largely by Sumner and Ford and introduced by sympathetic members of the House and Senate, cleared the state assembly with ease. Sanity, however, prevailed in the state senate, and the Clean Books Bill was defeated in May of 1923. Despite his victory, Seltzer well knew that a sizable array of official and unofficial forces were aligned against him, waiting to pounce. He simply did not want to instigate another round of litigation, particularly for a book of poems that would probably sell few copies.

While Cummings could understand that Seltzer needed to be wary, and accepted the excisions as preferable to bowdlerizing his poems, he could not comprehend why Seltzer chose, apparently at the last minute, to eliminate the sacrosanct ampersand from the title. By the time he learned of the change, *Tulips and Chimneys* was already at the printer. Advance copies of the book reached Cummings toward the end of October. The lack of the ampersand in the title greatly bothered him, as he felt that the publisher had taken undo liberties with his style. But, in general, he was pleased with the job Seltzer had done. Cummings's design of his poems had been respected, and unlike in the first edition of *The Enormous Room*, there were only a few minor typos.

Even before the publication of *Tulips and Chimneys*, Cummings's work was attracting attention through his magazine appearances and through a network of friends. In October, Brown's friend Louis Kantor, who had praised in print *The Enormous Room*, had come to Paris. Together they went to visit Pound who was helping Ford Madox Ford with the launch of a new Paris-based magazine, to be called the *transatlantic review*. The visit was not entirely for social purposes: both Pound and Ford wanted some poems from Cummings for the first issue, scheduled for January, 1924. Cummings dutifully handed over five poems. Pound, reading them on the spot, took four of them. He would have taken them all, he told his mother, except that Pound judged the fifth as "being too rough for the Hinglish Sensor." He summed up the meeting by telling his mother that "I have for some years been an admirer of Pound's poetry:personally,he sometimes gives me a FatherComplex."

Pound was not his only admirer. Ford, too, was quite taken with Cummings's work: "Mr. Cummings with the bravery and logic of relative youth attempts cadences and surprises the we who are old, old and not brave long since abandoned and in so far as he succeeds he deserves the well wishes of all humanity who use the pen for even so little a matter as a note to go by post." Such was his enthusiasm for Cummings that when the magazine's designer could not fit the title on the cover in uppercase letters, Ford opted for setting it all in lowercase. It reminded him, he said, of Cummings's "typographical modernity."

Thayer, too, was still at work promoting Cummings. On November 26, 1923 he wrote to Cummings "I got through your agents, Dos Passos & Co, those poems which Seltzer had providentially withdrawn from 'Tulips and Chimneys.' I selected from among these four, which we are running in the January number." He enclosed a check for one hundred dollars in payment for the work. Edward Cummings, too, was delighted with the book that Seltzer sent directly to him. As usual, he translated his support for his son's endeavors into cash, adding one thousand dollars to Cummings's letter of credit. By the end of November, Cummings was twenty-one hundred dollars richer than he had been a month before (one thousand dollars from his grandmother's estate, one thousand dollars from his father, and one hundred dollars from Thayer). This, he thought, would allow him to remain another year in Paris. But sometime in early December, Cummings received a letter from Elaine pleading with him to return to the United States. Within a few weeks, Cummings had boarded a ship bound for New York.

His two and a half years in Europe had been eventful, productive, and rich in inspiration. When he sailed for Portugal with Dos Passos in 1921, he was known (if known at all) as the author of a few eccentric poems published in the *Dial* and the painter of a few canvases that had been hung in large group exhibitions. He was returning home at the age of twenty-nine as the author of two major books, with scores of magazine publications, and a trunk full of drawings and paintings. If not exactly a conquering hero returning from abroad, he could at least hold his head high: he was a "someone" not an "anyone." It was a far different voyage home from the one he had taken at the end of 1917 when he had been ejected from France. And this time Elaine and Mopsy met him at the docks.

thirteen

Tulips and Chimneys

By the time Cummings moved into his West Village studio at 50 ½ Barrow Street in early January, of 1924, the first reviews of *Tulips and Chimneys* had already begun to appear. Poet Robert L. Wolf wrote the first assessment, in the *New York World* on November 8, 1923. While admitting that when he first read Cummings in magazines he had been inspired with "rage and scorn," he now had to acknowledge that *Tulips and Chimneys* had won him over: "It is a very disconcerting thing to admit, reluctantly, that it is good, that it is extraordinarily good, that it contains, in its own individual and unprecedented style, as beautiful poems as have been written by any present-day-poet in the English language."

Cummings's friend, Matthew Josephson, reviewed the work for the *New York Tribune*. Noting that the poems in *Tulips and Chimneys* were "selected by his publishers with one troubled eye on the Vice Society," he went on to say that "Cummings is a fertile and irreverent fellow; out of great insolence and enthusiasm he is prone to try 'stunts' in public, nay, in holy places." Though the *New York Times* had objected to the "Bolshevist" *Enormous Room*, the paper praised Cummings's debut as a poet: "He does write poetry, and often reaches a high and concentrated pitch of emotion that even his mannerisms cannot hide," declared Herbert Gorman in a joint review of *Birds, Beasts and Flowers* by D. H. Lawrence and *After Disillusion* by Robert L. Wolf (who had reviewed Cummings).

Early in 1924, Harriet Monroe, the editor of *Poetry* weighed in, as did Edmund Wilson in the *New Republic*. While both found much to like in

Cummings, they were both baffled, even annoyed by his style. Monroe was so bothered by Cummings's "eccentric system of typography" that in quoting Cummings she supplied "the usual quantity of periods, commas, capital letters, and other generally accepted conventions of the printer's art." She concluded her review by saying that "altogether a meticulous high-spirited poet salutes us in this volume. But beware his imitators!" Wilson, who reviewed *Tulips and Chimneys* in tandem with Wallace Stevens's *Harmonium*, liked Stevens better than Cummings. After declaring that Stevens was a master, he noted that "a master is precisely, as yet, what Cummings is not. Cummings's style is an eternal adolescent, as fresh and often as winning but as half-baked as boyhood. A poet with a real gift for language, for a melting music a little like Shelley's, which rhapsodizes and sighs in soft vowels disembarrased by their baggage of consonants, he strikes often on ethereal measures of a singular purity."

Only Brown, reviewing the work for *Broom*, of which he was now the United States editor, and Watson, writing under his *Dial* pseudonym W. C. Blum (an amalgam of William Carlos Williams and the hero of *Ulysses*, Leopold Bloom) lauded unreservedly Cummings's "stylistic innovations." Brown shrewdly noted the connection of Cummings's poetry to his painting, while also commenting that speed was an organizing principle in Cummings's work "in which each verbal unit functions at its highest velocity." By way of further explanation he wrote: "Cummings seldom attempts to achieve momentum through the utilization of mass, the violent and often painful impact of his poems is the active manifestation of speed; their formal beauty has the quality common to racing cars, aeroplanes, and to those birds surviving because of their swift wings." Watson's review in the January 1924 *Dial* also appreciated Cummings's "ability to convey a sense of speed," as well as the poet's "rapid unfailing lyrical invention" that is grounded in his "feeling for American speech."

Though furious that Monroe had felt the need to "standardize" his style, Cummings was generally pleased with the reviews of *Tulips and Chimneys*. He should have been, for even when reviewers were critical of his style, they were still generally positive about his work as a whole. In contrast to many of the reviews of *The Enormous Room*, no one, in fact, had bashed him. At the same time, he was unhappy that Seltzer had omitted more than half of the poems he had originally selected for the manuscript. As published, he felt the volume was not as reflective as it should have been of his bolder experiments with both form and subject.

Even in its greatly abbreviated form, however, *Tulips and Chimneys* deserved the praise it received. The first forty-nine poems, gathered under the general heading "TULIPS" contained a fair amount of work Cummings had written at Harvard and in the period following his graduation. "Epithalamion" begins the volume that now numbered sixty-six poems, followed by "Of Nicolette." There is also "in Just- / spring," "Tumbling-hair / picker of buttercups,“ "when god lets my body be" and "your little voice / Over the wires came leaping," all poems written around 1915 and/or 1916. Only two of the poems (out of five) that are grouped under the subhead "LA GUERRE" were preserved in Seltzer's edition, but the two that did make the cut, "O sweet spontaneous" and "the bigness of cannon," represent Cummings at his anti-war best: "the bigness of cannon / is skilful, / but i have seen / death's clever enormous voice…at Roupy / i have seen / between barrages, // the night utter ripe unspeaking girls."

In the section entitled "PORTRAITS" is his masterful "Buffalo Bill 's / defunct," along with "spring omnipotent goddess thou dost." All of these poems were written before 1920.

The much smaller second section of the book, numbering just seventeen poems, and grouped under the general heading "CHIMNEYS," contains poems more recently written; but, even most of these verses date from before 1922. All are called sonnets, though not all conform to the conventional form in their rhythm or rhyme scheme. Under the subheading "SONNETS—REALITIES" are such gems as "the Cambridge ladies who live in furnished souls / are unbeautiful and have comfortable minds," and "'kitty'. sixteen,5'1",white,prostitute. // ducking always the touch of must and shall, / whose slippery body is Death's littlest pal." The next section "SONNETS—UNREALITIES" contains six poems, among them the vivid sonnet "a wind has blown the rain away and blown" and the meditative "a connotation of infinity," written on shipboard on his first voyage to France. The volume concludes with "SONNETS—ACTUALITIES," a group of five sonnets including the love poems "yours is the music for no instrument" and "notice the convulsed orange inch of moon."

Like most first books of poems, *Tulips and Chimneys* is somewhat uneven. Along with such stunning poems as "the Cambridge ladies who live in furnished souls" or "Buffalo Bill 's / defunct" are less accomplished lyrics like "when citied day with sonorous homes," or "ladies and gentlemen this little girl." But even when Cummings falters, he is still interesting, worth reading, and always has something to say. But perhaps, most important, his voice is always his own: genuine, unique, and resonant. Indeed, no poem in this first collection is entirely without merit.

As a document charting his growth as a poet, *Tulips and Chimneys* is fascinating. The apprentice poet of "Epithalamion," or "Of Nicolette," or "All in green went my love riding" is still quite concerned with form. Rhyme and meter, conventional spacing, and capitalization are the norm; the language even tends toward archaisms and nineteenth-century floweriness.

Other poems, such as "i spoke to thee" or "unto thee i," probably written in 1916, are transitional in that they employ the lower-case capital "i" but maintain the diction of the nineteenth century. The mix of the modern with the language of a past century does not work all that well:

> i spoke to thee
> with a smile and thou didst not
> answer
> thy mouth is as
> a chord of crimson music
>   Come hither
> O thou,is life not a smile?...

The breakout poem in *Tulips and Chimneys* is "in Just- / spring," also originally written in 1916. It seems almost to be by a different author. And in some ways it was, for the experiments with form and language he began attempting around this time so delighted Cummings that he never really looked back. The language of "in Just- / spring" is contemporary and totally unaffected. Though Cummings is not yet taking too many liberties with syntax, the spacing (lengthened between words to slow the reader down, or word clustering to speed up the movement) reflects his developing concern with the shape of a poem.

Other devices that will ultimately become hallmarks of the Cummings style, also make their first appearances in *Tulips and Chimneys*. Among them: parentheses, the splitting of words by line breaks, the lack of punctuation, the paradoxical pairing of words, the use of "un" as a prefix, and the famous lowercase "i" all are in evidence. No one in American poetry at that time was altering in such a major way how words were presented on a page. No one, with the possible exception of Gertrude

Stein, was so concerned with phonemic values, or with mimicking, in every small detail, what language actually sounded like to an attuned ear. Nor were any of his poet peers as attentive to the visual integrity of a poem as it was printed on a page.

This is not to say that other poets were not also making breakthroughs. Wallace Stevens and T. S. Eliot, American heirs of the French Symbolist tradition, were crafting exquisite, mysterious poems, musical in their lines, evocative in their associations. For them, the associations between words and what they evoked were more important than, as it was for Cummings, the association *between* words. Marianne Moore, similar to Cummings in her insistence on using line and stanza breaks to emphasize the significance of words or phrases for both the eye and ear, was dissimilar from Cummings in that her poems are not so much expressions of what is, but what could be. William Carlos Williams, while also concerned with meter and rhythm, was far more involved in saying what needed to be said directly, without elaboration, and without calling attention to itself as an expression. Pound, by this point involved with writing his monumental *Cantos*, had as his aim to incorporate all he knew, read, experienced, and speculated upon into verse that would stand, as Homer and Virgil and Dante had stood, as records of the human intellectual experience.

Each of these poets, of course, was working to transform what a poem could be, even what language could be. Cummings, far less of a theoretician than Pound, Stevens, or even Williams, was not attempting to set out principles for anyone else to follow. He simply was writing poems that said what had to be said in a way that he felt it should be said. His poetic practices were not seen by him as idiosyncrasies, but as a way to focus the reader's attention on how language is constructed, and to create emphasis on the expression of expression. Or as William Carlos Williams noted, "With cummings [*sic*] every syllable has a conscience and a specific impact."

For Cummings, speech was not static or regular. It rose and fell, contracted and expanded in accordance with the importance a speaker placed on certain words, phrases, or even syllables. His poems were meant to reflect these modulative nuances. It was a favorite theme of Pound's, who was insisting as early as 1915 that "energy or emotion expresses itself in form."

While Cummings was certainly aware of Pound's pronouncements, a source closer to home was an even more important model: "Sam Ward, a

New Hampshire farmer and dear friend of mine, used to write to me. I remember once he wrote: 'we had a Big snow.' He'd write 'i' not 'I'—because 'I' wasn't important to him. I got letters and letters from him. It is the most natural way. Sam Ward's way is the only way. Instead of it being artificial and affected, it is the conventional way that is artificial and affected. I am not a scholar but I believe only in English is the "I" capitalized."

While a good many of the poems in *Tulips and Chimneys* do contain lowercase "i"'s and many other devices meant to emphasize, in poet Louis Zukofsky's words, "the American language as she is spoke," the experiments with form and style are quite limited because of the large number of poems eliminated from the collection. Occasionally their use seems almost incidental, even gratuitous. For example, in "it is at moments after i have dreamed," from the "SONNETS—UNREALITIES" section of the book, the parentheses, while arguably placed in a traditional manner, are not used to great effect:

it is at moments after i have dreamed
of the rare entertainment of your eyes,
when(being fool to fancy)i have deemed

with your peculiar mouth my heart made wise;. . .

The piling up of paradoxes in "my love is building a building" similarly do not have the power he gets out of the contrasting pairings in other poems (including many excised from the volume). Nor again, do his parentheses function as powerfully as in more accomplished poems. The use of these devices here owe more to cleverness than craft:

my love is building a building
around you,a frail slippery
house,a strong fragile house
(beginning at the singular beginning

of your smile)a skilful uncouth
prison,a precise clumsy

prison(building thatandthis into Thus,
Around the reckless magic of your mouth)...

But then there are the poems—and there are a great many of them—where the experiments are fully realized. In "i was considering how," the spacing, line breaks, parentheses, and unique language all have definite reasons for existing, make this simple observation into a vivid experience for the reader:

i was considering how
within night's loose
sack a star's
nibbling in-

fin
-i-
tes-
i
-mal-
ly devours

darkness the
hungry star
which
will e

-ven
tu-
al
-ly jiggle
the bait of
dawn and be jerked

into

eternity.   when over my head a
shooting
star

Bur s

(t
into a stale shriek
like an alarm-clock)

There is nothing arbitrary here: the style, with its fractured syntax and spacing, is in concert with the content. Each word is necessary, each phrase sharpened and fresh. Even the ending turns the predictable into the unpredictable by the striking image of a "stale shriek / like an alarm-clock."

This poem is more representative of the collection as a whole than those previously cited verses that are less successful. Edmund Wilson was right to say that the twenty-nine-year-old Cummings was not yet a master. But he was on his way.

fourteen

Marriage and UnMarriage

More than poetry was on Cummings's mind as he settled into life in New York after two and a half years abroad. He had returned, he told his father, because he was "following the suggestion of a friend with whose daughter I am anxious to exchange greetings." The exchange of greetings with both the daughter and her mother developed quickly into more than that, for by early March, Cummings was preparing to do what had been heretofore unthinkable for him: marry. Nothing in Cummings's voluminous private jottings indicates how he came to be persuaded to marry Elaine. One cryptic note implies that Thayer, now also in New York, had some hand in it: "Freud tells Thayer I should marry E[laine]." Clearly his desire to acknowledge Nancy as his daughter had something to do with it. Even so, it was Elaine who proposed marriage to Cummings. While Cummings may have had misgivings, he set aside his concerns and accepted her offer.

On March 14, he wrote to his mother that he and Elaine wanted to be married immediately: "The least complicated way is for me to apply for a license in New York & be married on the same day. Naturally,I should prefer that father marry us at 104 Irving Street—without gifts,fuss,or festivities,and with only yourself,Elizabeth and Aunt Jennie present."

If this were not enough of a shock to his parents, his next words most certainly were:

> But I don't know whether father will like to officiate when he understands that our idea of marrying is principally this: once married,I can adopt Mopsy,becoming legally the father of my

> own child—a procedure which,for variously incredibly intricate reasons,was not feasible before. Incidentally,you may be sure that,so far as Thayer is concerned,there was never the slightest deceit involved,& that we three(Elaine,Thayer & myself) are now & always have been the best of friends.

Although he was distressed at his son's "sin," Edward put aside his actual feelings, and wired back upon receipt of the letter that he would be proud to marry them. On March 19, 1924, at 12:30 PM in the living room at 104 Irving Street, Reverend Cummings pronounced his son and Elaine husband and wife. Present as witnesses were Rebecca, Elizabeth, and Cummings's aunt Jane. Mopsy, then four, did not attend, having been left in the care of her nurse in New York.

There was no honeymoon, but the couple did spend the first night of their married life at the luxurious Fairmont Copley Plaza Hotel in Boston. As his notes reveal, Cummings, although twenty-nine and sexually experienced, felt awkward, unsure of himself and of marriage:

> My embarrassment at travelling with Elaine—in train
> in Hotel Copley Plaza
> ...I as husband "that is awfully funny—that I should be anybody's husband!" I said aloud.
> To think of little self dressed up as a monkey
> I am afraid TO FACE PEOPLE, TO BE
> SEEN WITH ELAINE
> ....
> "Let's be interesting till midnight." E[laine] wanted to wait, midnight, till bedtime (We didn't)
> ....
> I cannot get erection a 2nd time
> lack of pash-ness
> I stay all night.... Before I never insisted on staying all night!!!

The next day they left Boston on the 1:30 PM train and were back in New York early that evening.

Marriage did not significantly alter Cummings's life. Though he did move into Elaine's apartment on Washington Square, he initially kept his studio at 50 ½ Barrow Street as a place to work, and spent a great deal of his time there. As before, Elaine's place became a gathering spot for Cummings's friends; the only difference now was that Cummings himself was also partly in residence. Dos Passos recalled that "at that time I probably felt nearest to being at home with Cummings and Elaine. Elaine's apartment, when I dropped in for tea, was made particularly delightful by the presence of little Nancy.... Cummings was at his most charming in the company of a small child."

Nancy, in fact, was becoming more important for Cummings. After his return from France, he even began to occasionally set aside time to be with her. He read to her, invented stories to tell her, took her on outings to the zoo, and at FAO Schwarz's toy store he bought her a bird in a cage. He instructed her to call him Estlin rather than Mr. Cummings. He did not feel he could impose on her to call him "father," as he thought this would only confuse her. Legally, of course, he was not her father. But this was a matter he and Elaine hoped to resolve by having Cummings adopt her. Cummings approached Thayer a few weeks after the marriage to discuss the matter with the legal father of his child. Thayer not only thought it a splendid idea, he even agreed to pay for the adoption. Within days he had consulted his lawyers who drew up the papers. On April 25, 1924, Nancy legally became Cummings's child, though she did not take his name, nor was she informed of the event. Among Thayer's papers is an invoice from the New York law firm of Evarts, Choate, Sherman, and Leon, dated May 1, 1924, for $909.62. The amount was to be paid for "legal fees incurred on behalf of Scofield Thayer for the adoption by Edward Estlin Cummings of Nancy Thayer."

The late winter and spring of 1924 was a good one for Cummings. He had both his independence and the love of a woman and child. Or as he wrote, "i am nearest happiness—i feel that i possess E[laine] & M[opsy] i do no work for them,i am free,i assume no responsibilities—yet i have them to love:to praise:to be proud of."

If not callow, the self-assessment of his situation was considerably egocentric. It was also true; for Cummings, freedom to create his own work outstripped in importance his relationship with others, even with those whom he loved and wanted to love him. He was perfectly content as long as the relationship did not impinge upon his independence, did not require involvement beyond being a convivial, lively presence who paid attention to Elaine and Nancy when it was convenient for him. Only to his art was he truly and irrevocably dedicated.

Art, for Cummings, was still very much both poetry and painting. In February he had spent nine days toiling on a "40"x50" 'ABSTRACT' canvas," in order to make the deadline for the new Independent Artists' Show. The painting was number twelve in his *Noise* series. According to critic Milton Cohen, *Noise Number 12* "appears to grow out of a Cubist-influenced drawing of a black saxophone player. Both works feature a horn as their central motif. The painting, however, develops into a visual metaphor for jazz itself: flowing, twisting, and jaggedly syncopated rhythmic lines, silhouetted hints of faces and hands making music."

Whether the critic for the *New York Sun and Globe* noticed the figurativeness hidden in the abstraction is unclear, but he was aware of who had painted the picture. In the first paragraph of his review of the show he comments positively on the painting, noting that it was done by "E. E. Cummings, better known as a poet and novelist."

Cummings, despite his devotion to painting and his numerous appearances as an artist in the *Dial*, had already begun to establish a far greater reputation for himself as a writer than as a painter. Indeed, his verbal art was translating itself into something of an actual career. Though dependent on Elaine (and from time to time his father) for his day-to-day support, he was beginning to earn a little spending money through magazine publication. Between the fall of 1923 and the spring of 1924, he published twenty-five poems in magazines ranging from those with wide circulation such as *Vanity Fair* and the *Dial* to the smaller, but highly literary *Broom* and the *transatlantic review*. But he was still chafing over Seltzer's omission of so many of the poems from his original manuscript of *Tulips and Chimneys*. Consequently, he let it be known to Thayer, Dos Passos, Watson, Brown, and anyone else sympathetic to his plight, that he was seeking publication of the poems eliminated from that book.

Thayer, who had long been an enthusiast of Cummings's more daring work (in every sense) shared his friend's desire to see these poems in book form. Accordingly, he passed on the group of "withdrawn poems" to Lincoln MacVeagh who was in the process of starting up the Dial Press. MacVeagh, whom Thayer had known at Harvard, had been an editor at Henry Holt before joining the *Dial* as secretary-treasurer at the end of 1923. He had ostensibly replaced Samuel Craig, who had increasingly drawn Thayer's fire the previous year over his perceived financial mismanagement. Despite holding the same position as Craig, MacVeagh had little to do with the magazine; instead his duties were primarily confined to running Dial Press.

In April, MacVeagh looked over the manuscript and made a selection of forty-one poems. But like Seltzer, he too was wary of possible censorship, and selected only those poems that in his estimation would not incur the wrath of the New York Society for the Suppression of Vice. Cummings was pleased that more of his work would be printed in book form but was still frustrated that MacVeagh resisted publishing the entire manuscript of poems that remained after Seltzer's selection. Or as he wrote to his mother on May 24, 1924, "the entire Tulips & Chimneys may possibly have made an appearance per 71 different selective passages conducted by 407 publishers."

Samuel Jacobs was the printer responsible for Seltzer's edition of *Tulips and Chimneys*. While unhappy about the selection, Cummings was delighted with the care Jacobs had taken with the typesetting. As a result, not long after MacVeagh had made his cuts, he approached Jacobs at his shop on Eighth Street, with the idea of bringing out a private edition of the poems remaining from the manuscript, along with thirty-four additional poems. The supplementary material was not, for the most part, new verse; rather, they were poems Cummings himself had eliminated from the final manuscript he had prepared in 1922 to give to Dos Passos. (Even Cummings realized that a number of these poems would put off potential publishers.) He included them now, however, because a privately printed book was not subject to censorship.

In a letter to Jacobs, in which he enclosed the new manuscript, he wrote that "on rereading, I was ever so pleased to discover that my most personal work had been carefully omitted by both Thomas&Lincoln. I hope that you will publish this under your own coatofarms. Nobody else in the world can set what I like best of my own poems." Jacobs readily accepted the job. The book not only restored the bolder, more sexually explicit and "personal" poems, but also the ampersand. In fact, the volume that Jacobs would issue the following year would be called *&*.

During the period of this flurry of activity with publisher and printer, Elaine, then just twenty-eight, was attempting to cope with the death of her younger sister, Constance, who had died of the flu compounded by double pneumonia only two weeks after Elaine's marriage to Cummings. Although Cummings did accompany Elaine to Constance's funeral in Troy, New York, he does not seem to have been terribly supportive of Elaine or even of little practical help. Instead, he carried on as usual, painting, writing, and socializing with his friends. Because the estate was rather complicated, Elaine needed to confer with her sister Alexis, who was then living in England but traveling somewhere on the continent.

On April 4, 1924, Cummings wrote to his mother of the events and Elaine's plans: "Probably—since there are any number of important papers to be signed without delay—Elaine will leave for Paris in May,with Mopsy,and Eva and Mopsy's nurse Winifred,and spend the summer months abroad,returning next autumn to New York.... Elaine is naturally tremendously tired;but I hope that in a few days she will have recovered from the strain of last week's happenings." He gave no indication that he had any desire to accompany his family or even regrets about the need for their imminent departure; instead, he devoted the remaining part of the letter to informing his mother about his doings.

By early May, Elaine, Nancy, and their retinue were in France. Cummings, who had now moved out of Barrow Street, set up his easel in the now empty nursery at the Washington Square apartment he shared with Elaine and Nancy. Although he mentioned in one letter home that he missed his wife and daughter, for the most part he seems to have immersed himself in his own life. He rose late, often ambled to Khoury's Middle Eastern Restaurant for breakfast, occasionally dropped by the offices of the *Dial* or *Vanity Fair* in the afternoon, and after supper, if not too drunk, worked late into the night. Socializing was as an important activity for Cummings at that time, as was his work. He regularly met up with Dos Passos, Nagle, Lachaise, Brown, and Brown's girlfriend, Sue Jenkins, who worked as an editor at a pulp magazine called *Telling Tales*. There was also a new friend, a twenty-four-year-old poet from Cleveland named Hart Crane, whom Cummings found delightful, intense, and a wild and willing drinking companion. On more than one occasion,

Cummings and Crane careened through the streets of Manhattan, the one supporting the other, as they made their way from one speakeasy to another.

Crane had admired Cummings's poetry since first reading it in magazines, and found *The Enormous Room* "a stimulating article" and "a real inspiration in language and humanity." Cummings, too, had been impressed with Crane's work that he had also seen in the little magazines. But because Cummings was in Europe and Crane in New York, they had not had an opportunity to meet, despite having several friends—Munson, Josephson, and Cowley—in common. Then, in late April of 1923, a rather down-and-out Crane met Brown who put him up in his apartment for several weeks. He and Brown shared a common interest in the arts, and after Brown introduced him to burlesque, with that "art" form, as well. After Cummings's return, Brown made the introductions. By May, Crane was writing his friend, writer Waldo Frank, that he counted Cummings as one of the best people to talk to in New York. Cummings described Crane as a "buff, healthy, pink woodchuck" who "played Scriabin and Ravel." Although he was well aware that Crane was gay, his sexual orientation was not an issue. In fact, Cummings noted in his journal that he could appreciate Crane's "homosexual appeal."

Malcolm Cowley had met Crane the year before. Like Cummings, he too was drawn to him, and even got him a job as a copywriter with his own employer, Sweet's Catalogue Service. Cowley remembered Crane as "a solidly framed and apple-cheeked young man." "I regarded [his homosexuality] as an item of personal gossip, as if I had been told that he had a birthmark on his back or suffered—as he did—from constipation. He did not look or talk like a homosexual; he looked like a country boy masquerading in a business suit, and his speech was northern Ohio except for a few big words and a larding of waterfront obscenities."

In mid-June of 1924, Cummings's carefree life was shattered by a letter he received from Elaine. The message was blunt: on the ship going over to France in early May she had fallen in love with another man and wanted a divorce. She also informed him that she intended to remain in Europe until at least the fall. Cummings was devastated, outraged, confused, and, at least initially, unbelieving. He comforted himself temporarily by deciding that her shipboard romance would not last, that she would "come around in her senses" and return to him. In his despair he consulted friends and family. Watson advised caution, but told him "not to give up Elaine or Nancy."

His father was furious: "He would beat the man UP!" Cummings wrote in his notes. Then quoting Edward, added, "'Any man who would come fooling around with my wife would get what was coming to him.'" Cummings wanted to fight, but was paralyzed and inactive. He spent his days waiting for some outside event—Elaine's disaffection with her new lover, perhaps—to decide matters.

Then, in late June, Elaine and Nancy appeared unexpectedly at the apartment. Cummings did not record particulars of her return, but his notes indicate that she came back not to be with him, but to "wage war." Indeed, the intervening months since her departure had only strengthened her sense that she was through with Cummings. She insisted on a divorce as quickly as possible. "There is no way out," a despairing Cummings wrote to himself.

Had Cummings not been so self-involved, he might have been able to see how truly dissatisfied Elaine was with the marriage. Her flirtation with rebellion against her upbringing had come to an end once she had actually married Cummings. She no longer desired to play the role of mistress, of which he was so fond; she wanted a husband who would live with her, take care of her (at least emotionally), and be a true father to his daughter. In the one letter from Elaine to Cummings that has survived from this period, she chided him for wanting to "be like a child." In contrast, she noted that she had matured: "Within the last few years I have continued to gain strength of character. I am no longer a passive person to the point of misery. I know where I stand. And I know what I want. And most difficult of all, I know when I have made a mistake."

But Cummings could not see that he had made a mistake. Indeed, he expressed the notion that he was the happiest he had ever been in the months following their legal union. Marriage, however, for him, was not at all the same as it was for Elaine. For Cummings, it amounted only to recognition that he and Elaine had agreed to formalize their off-and-on relationship of six years, and not that this would mean their way of being with each other needed to change. For Elaine, it meant a partnership with intimate involvement in one another's lives.

While Elaine presumably had expectations that once they were married Cummings would finally assume the responsibilities of a husband and father, he felt absolutely no compunction to do so. In the two months they spent together as a married couple, Cummings steadfastly refused to alter his mode of being or living. While he did nominally reside with Elaine and Nancy at Elaine's apartment, he spent more time in his studio, even sleeping there on occasion. His work and his own social life continued to hold far more importance for him than did his marriage. As before, in both New York and Paris, he consciously avoided becoming part of his wife's life, eschewing contact with her circle of friends whom he felt to be too uppercrust, boring, and pretentious. He could not even make minimal concessions. Because she wanted him to "look nice" when they went out for an evening on the town, she bought him a suit. He would not even try it on.

In short, he saw no reason to change anything about the way he conducted himself. This clearly confounded Elaine: "You who live as an advanced poet and reactionary [rebel] at other moments fall back into an inability to adjust yourself to a change in your private life." Elaine's accusation was right on the mark. For all of his love of revolt, he was quite self-content with the way he lived and saw no reason to rebel against his decidedly adolescent behavior. He bought himself off by deciding that he was being true to his bohemian ethic that snubbed its nose at conventionality in any form. Elaine saw it as simply a refusal "to accept things as a man would."

Most important, she was keenly disappointed that she and Nancy were still continually in the background to be enjoyed only on his schedule. And when she pleaded for more attention, he charged her with being controlling. To which she responded, "You are pretending to yourself that I rule you in order to prove to yourself how effectually you have hidden your ego." Had Constance not died, Elaine might have been able to overlook her husband's self-absorption for a little longer. But Cummings demonstrated to her that despite her need for him, he could not (or would not) involve himself too deeply in her life, or even her tragedy.

At the same time, it does not appear as if she went to Europe to escape the marriage. But certainly she was predisposed toward a change. That change happened serendipitously in the form of an Irishman named Frank MacDermot. According to Nancy Thayer, "at this time Frank was slim, dark-haired with light blue eyes, and very good looking.... Frank had left Oxford a classicist and historian with a magnificent eighteenth-century legal mind." When Elaine met him he was working as a merchant banker in the American office of the English firm of Huth & Company. Unlike

Cummings, he had money, moved in the same set as she did, and fully accepted his status as an adult member of society. While in Paris, Elaine had spent as much time as possible with him, returning with him to New York.

Cummings continued to try to persuade Elaine that he was the man she was destined to be with, but Elaine could not see it. She continued to see MacDermot regularly, and would not relent in her demand for a divorce. Though Cummings and Elaine had frequently bickered, the skirmishes between them were now far more intense. Ugly scene followed ugly scene, with accusations hurled back and forth. She reproached Cummings for his egocentrism, of never being interested in her life or in Nancy, but only in his own. He countered by saying the same could be true of her, yet realized there was more than a hint of truth in what she was saying. His notes are filled with statements such as these:

> i tried to interest her in my life—my wants & likes dislikes. (i never was interested in her life) i raved against it: under name of 'the R de R' [Rue de Rivoli crowd—his name for her rich Paris friends]. really,i wanted the R de R. really i wanted the same thing she did. I wanted her(people)to give them to me—I didn't want to earn,win,them for myself. my raving was a way of covering my feeling of inferiority.

In other notes he confessed his feeling of "shame" about hurting her, yet even then still attempted to justify his words or actions. "I don't enjoy hurting her but she does enjoy hurting me.... She acts as if she is suffering—I try to project myself into her. I say: 'she is hurt I am hurting her' and I STOP instead of KNOWING THAT SHE LIKES TO SUFFER,that suffering is an expression of her PLEASURE in love."

In mid-July, Cummings decided to leave New York for a time in order to "breathe different air." He went to Cambridge to visit his parents, then to Gloucester, Massachusetts, to consult with his old friend Stewart Mitchell. From there he went up to Georgetown, Maine, to spend some time with Nagle and Lachaise at their summer house. After his return to Cambridge, he met up with Watson who drove him to their place in the Adirondacks. The pell-mell trip mirrored Cummings's own frantic self. But when he returned to New York in late July of 1924 with the Watsons, he felt his whirlwind sojourn had done him some good; he was particularly grateful to the Watsons who had been tremendously supportive of him.

His buoyed spirits did not last long; within days his mood had again turned black. His father had strongly advised him again to stand up to MacDermot, but Cummings found it difficult to do so, as his notes reveal:

> I really do value her life more than mine
> —because she is so beautiful
> —because she is so much to:Mopsy
> ....NOW IF THIS WERE THE MOTIVATION of my losing Elaine and Mopsy, ALL RIGHT
> i.e.
> i love her more than anything alive
> she does not love me
> i will help her—although it's the last thing i desire to do,i will give her up.
> BUT!!
> If the motivation really is:
> I REALLY DON'T WANT Elaine & Mopsy,<u>ENOUGH TO FIGHT for them both</u>;
> I am giving them up BECAUSE I AM A COWARD
> then———
> i had better DIE.
> ....question—IS to want to give her up
> =
> to be afraid to fight other man?

One night he and Watson went to New Jersey where Cummings bought a .38 Remington automatic pistol, but he was ambivalent as to how he would use the revolver. Perhaps he would kill his rival with it; perhaps he would use it on himself. He wrote several suicide notes—all addressed to Elaine—just in case that seemed ultimately the course of action he would take. One of them reads:

> I am awfully sorry to die,to go away,to not be anyone anywhere anymore. You can't imagine how sorry I am,because if you could imagine. But never mind. I don't really think I'm connected with trees,really,or really stars,or you,or my

> father and mother,or the fingers which hold this pen,or with any part of the earth or with thought. I may be a wish. Perhaps there is a wish land out of which(a part of me which you cannot kill and I cannot kill)came once.... What's that? I can kill us and give us dreams. Come on and look at this toy,it's a gun:you(or I)pull this which is called a trigger. So. And what happens? A lot of blood and the inside of my head,called brains,all over everything. But me? Where's this me? Where's this little me going to be? Little,littler,gone,not:nonexisting. There:you see nobody can imagine one thing, nobody can feel non-existing. How circumscribed we are. Like a circle talking about its circumference.

With perhaps this note or another like it in his pocket, a distraught Cummings showed up at the Washington Square apartment with the gun fully loaded, intending to kill himself in front of Elaine. He recorded the scene in his notes:

> She pleads not to handle it [the pistol] people are always getting hurt accidentally.
> I:please let me do this:it may HELP ME, to have you see me do it
> E gets up,turns back,stands at door.
> I recite:I musn't,because you are finer and because of Mopsy.
> Then tensely,pulling bullets out. Cartridge snapped on to carpet)

On another occasion, Cummings waited with his pistol outside the apartment when Elaine and MacDermot were out together. This time he apparently thought he might shoot MacDermot: "I waited till they drove up,inyellow taxi: i rushed to door—BUT AT THE DOOR,I WAS AFRAID—let her hold me back until too late,& he had driven away." The scene haunted him, mainly because of his "lack of fight," not because he had come close to attempting murder.

Rage, grief, and bewilderment were the emotions vying for control of Cummings during late July and early August. If his notes are a reliable assessment of his thinking—and given his prolixity in analyzing the situation, they seem to be—what is remarkably absent in these jottings is any real attempt to understand why Elaine might have wanted to leave him. While he did concede from time to time that he was self-centered or "less than responsible," these insights never seemed to gain the upper hand. He did note that he and Elaine were always somewhat mismatched—she had wealth and he did not; she was beautiful and he was not; she was in love with material things, he with art. It rarely occurred to him that his own desire for personal freedom, which often translated into blatant disregard of Elaine and Nancy, had anything to do with her seeking a divorce. He could not see how his own desire for separateness from her in order to pursue his work or social life had much bearing on the issue. He failed to perceive how over the years of their relationship he had always consciously and visibly held himself apart from both Elaine and Nancy, never fully entering into their lives.

For Cummings, knowing that he loved Elaine and that he expressed his love for her in countless poems was all that he felt necessary to indicate to her how esteemed she was in his view. As an artist he felt it his duty to make art, to place it above all else. But that did not mean, in his mind, that he was not being responsible to Elaine or even that he was not sharing his work with her. Indeed, Cummings saw Elaine as his muse, and in making art that she inspired, he considered that he was generously giving back to the muse the fruits of that inspiration.

A conversation he recorded in his notes shows how Elaine did not see the equation in this way:

> "...I do appreciate your work,I think: really, I don't talk about it because I haven't any words to explain."
> "O—But the thing I feel you don't understand is—that it's based on you. That even if you're not the model,it's the fact of you in my life which matters everything."
> "No I don't think so. I feel outside of it (your work)."

As a follow up to this exchange, Cummings drafted a letter to Elaine, that he probably never sent.

> I could not understand why my poems,etc. meant nothing to you,or seemed to mean nothing,when it came to a show-down;or why you could not understand by then how much i felt you,really,&how terribly hard i was trying by then to create something in me which should be perfectly worthy of your love—something which should be almost as proud & as capable of beauty as yourself.

Cummings was clearly shattered by Elaine's inability to see that her true function in his life was as his muse. Rather than realize that this very notion was ego-based, for him it was proof that what he most valued she did not. Her failure to comprehend her importance for him as an artist only served to amplify his bitterness, causing the rift between them to grow even larger. While it is fairly evident—even by his own admission—that Cummings wrote or painted chiefly for himself, he really seemed to have believed that her presence—at least in his consciousness—was a catalyst for creation. His "success" was due in part to her "being there." She countered this argument by saying that *The Enormous Room* was written largely before Cummings even knew her. He shot back that he thought his "poems were better," a point with which she agreed, but did not feel she could take any credit for them.

While Cummings could not understand why she wanted a divorce, it was becoming clear to him that she was steadfast in her determination to make her life separate from his. None of his stratagems, ranging from aggressive hostility to rather abject pleading, had changed her mind. Because he could not see any way to win her back, he began to concede defeat—at least to himself. In late July he decided he would accept a divorce.

His father, however, still cast a giant shadow over his son; and since Edward was vehemently opposed to his son capitulating, Cummings also had his father's approval to consider. On July 26, 1924, he wrote Edward that he and Elaine both felt it best to get a quick divorce, either in Nevada or Paris, and inquired as to which place he thought would be more expedient. In explaining why he had decided to succumb to Elaine's demands, he noted that "I have the right to act as seems to me necessary.... I am consulting you here as a token of my appreciation for your efforts for me,and for no other reason. Only I can & do realize what I have lost,& what I am losing." Edward advised Paris.

Cummings duly informed Elaine of his decision by telegram and letter. Her response was a mix of warmth and resolve: "I am glad in your letter to see you did realize that to take refuge in another person wasn't getting you anywhere. And after all that's the point you're going to be happy & you never will be till you live, yourself."

But now, unsure about what he had done, he decided to seek out Thayer—the one person who knew Elaine as well as he did. He had not consulted with Thayer before, not because he had not wanted to, but because Thayer, who had been growing increasingly mentally unstable, had in June collapsed from nervous exhaustion, compounded by eye problems, and had spent some time in a Manhattan sanitarium. After his release, Thayer had gone to Edgartown, where Cummings visited him in early August.

Thayer was sympathetic but not helpful. He espoused his doctrine of free love along with a large dose of Freudian analysis. A fair amount of the visit was also taken up with Cummings attempting to calm down Thayer who was becoming increasingly irrational, sure that others were "out to get him." Cummings came away from the visit even more distraught. Though he recognized that Thayer was so distracted by his own demons, he also still believed that Thayer had some insights on his dilemma. Already feeling that perhaps Elaine felt him inadequate as a lover, Cummings seized on a remark along these lines by Thayer, and began to berate himself anew. He devoted numerous pages in his notes to reviewing his sexual experiences with Elaine, and decided that his inability to give Elaine an orgasm was proof that he was a failure as her lover: "IF I HAD DONE MY JOB AS HUSBAND PROPERLY&ALL THIS WOULDN'T HAVE OCCURRED. it was my fault.... All she wanted was TO GO OFF.... This was worst thing a Man could know about his life—this failure." He ultimately decided that he had made the right decision to grant her a divorce.

When Cummings returned to New York, he moved out of the Washington Square apartment and into the Hotel Lafayette. Though still wild with anguish, he kept his emotions under better control. On two occasions, he even met his rival. His notes record one of the meetings:

> I've decided I'm not worthy of the lady in question,& so I'm going to do everything to help her get the divorce. What happens then is,of course,her own affair. I turn to him. He is standing,taller than I. Grave.
> I:Do you consider that honourable?
> he:why—if you ask me—yes.

On August 12, Cummings wrote his parents a letter in which he expressed his new "realizations:"

> Only now,as incredible as it may seem,do I realize that I never attempted to understand the person for whom I thought i cared most in my life.& who understands me better than anyone alive. Once to understand this person is,for me,at last to understand myself:I owe her everything fine in my life—I have hurt her more than anyone but myself,perhaps,can ever know—there remains only 1 course:one way to show her how deeply I comprehend my own selfishness & how I recognize her own fineness—to help her,so far as I can help her,in the divorce.

At about this time he seems also to have given up on the notion of suicide. His self-pity quotient was still strong, but he had discovered a reason to live:

> I decided definitely that to kill myself would be merely to avoid facing the most important issue in my life. At the same moment that I overcame the selfish desire to commit suicide,and not until that moment,did the true issue emerge. So long as I had been thinking merely of me against a rival,I was merely overcome with a feeling of inferiority in my own behalf. The true issue is simply this: Nancy.

On August 25, Cummings, then twenty-nine, and Elaine, twenty-eight, dined for the last time alone. Although Cummings and Elaine had been "together" for three years, and off and on for six, the actual marriage had lasted only two months.

The next morning he said his good-byes to her and Mopsy, but did not go down to the docks to see them off on the *Aquitania* for France where Elaine had decided to resettle.

fifteen

The Life and Times of Edward Seul

On September 8, 1924, two weeks after the departure of Elaine and Mopsy, Cummings moved from his temporary lodgings at the Hotel Lafayette into a small third-floor room at 4 Patchin Place, in the West Village. Patchin Place, then as now, was not a street but a series of brick row houses overlooking a central courtyard filled with shade trees. The entrance, off 10th Street, had an unimposing iron gate, more for decoration than security. The room itself had no bath, and was furnished with only a combination wood and coal stove, but it had good light. The leaseholder at the time Cummings moved in was Dr. J. Sibley Watson. He had rented the room a few months before, not for his own use, but so that his friend who lived in the adjacent third-floor room could work undisturbed by the noise of neighbors. Watson's friend was John Cowper Powys, the English writer and *Dial* contributor. Now that another friend was also in need, Watson graciously responded with the offer of the room.

Powys was not the only writer who had made Patchin Place home. Among the more illustrious previous inhabitants were the poet Hilda Doolittle (H. D.); the radical writer John Reed, whose lecture Cummings had attended while at Harvard; novelist Theodore Dreiser; and Irish man of letters, Padraic Colum.

The move into Patchin Place was far more significant than Cummings could have realized at the time. First, 4 Patchin Place would be, in one combination of rooms or another, Cummings's home for the rest of his life. Second, it marked a turn in benefactors; up until this point Thayer had been Cummings's major supporter among his friends. Watson and his wife, Hildegarde, would from now on replace Thayer as Cummings's guardian angels. They had been close before (Cummings was even the nominal godparent of their son Michael), but they had not provided their friend with the degree of help—financial, artistic, and emotional—that Thayer had. But with their assistance to Cummings during his breakup with Elaine, and now with this gesture, the Watsons and Cummings entered into a much tighter friendship.

Cummings was still reeling from the breakup with Elaine when he set up his easel and typewriter at Patchin Place. The relative calm he displayed—at least outwardly—after consenting to the divorce was now collapsing regularly. He churned the matter over and over, deciding one minute that he was right in his decision, then abruptly reversing his thinking. He signed up for boxing lessons at a local gym on 14th Street with the hope they might make him more aggressive. He also kept his pistol at bedside and the thought of suicide still reared itself from time to time in his thoughts.

But he was not able to devote all of his time to self-torture, for in early September he began writing a series of satirical pieces for *Vanity Fair*, the magazine that had rejected him as a staff member in 1916. Despite the torment in his personal life, the image Cummings projected to the general public in these sketches was far from that of a soul in anguish. His first humorous bit, "The Soul Story of Gladys Vanderdecker," published under the byline of "the Society Editor of Vanity Fair," is a rather silly tale of a New York heiress, Gladys Vanderdecker, who throws away her money and place in society to marry a low-life chauffeur. Though perhaps he saw it as a private burlesque of the situation between him and Elaine, the parallels are far too tenuous to construe any real autobiographical analogies.

Regardless of his intentions, the editor, Frank Crowninshield—who was already an admirer of Cummings's verse—"liked it greatly," and signed him up for another piece, this one on moviemaking. On September 27, 1924, he wrote to his mother that "I have been very busy doing absolutely nothing at Astoria,across the river,where the Famous Players—Lasky Corporation hang out. Mr. Frank Crowninshield,editor of Vanity Fair,got me the chance to visit the studio during 4 weeks on salary compatible with the environment(Richard Dix,Jaqueline

Logan,Beebbee Daniels,Gloria Swanson,etc.) The latter makes 7000$ a week,work or loaf."

Cummings got two pieces out of his time in Astoria. The first was "Vanity Fair's Prize Movie Scenario," a parody of the commercial film industry. Cummings's "film script," supposedly authored by a hot embosser from Pennsylvania named C. E. Niltse (Estlin E[dward]. C[ummings]., spelled backwards), parodies the films in vogue in the 1920s, complete with melodramatic scenes set in preposterous foreign locations. Cummings was at his most sophomoric in this piece; indeed, it is more reminiscent of the satirical humor he indulged himself in at Harvard than the more absurdly extreme and biting Dada writing he had appreciated in Paris.

The second article, "A Modern Gulliver Explores the Movies," which carried the byline Sir Arthur Catchpole, is more directly linked to his visit to the movie studio, but it could hardly be construed as reportage. More than half of the article is taken up with his train trip to Astoria; the other half is a satirical sketch of life on the set. Though somewhat less adolescent than the "Movie Scenario," it is hardly Cummings at his best.

Crowninshield did not see Cummings's humor as sophomoric. He wrote Cummings, "I can't get enough of you, because you have exactly the touch we need." Indeed, Crowninshield was so charmed that he continued to commission Cummings to write additional sketches for the magazine: "I also need a lot of what we call 'turns.' That is, down the back material. I could pay $40 for these, and could use a good many. They run to about 1100 words. They should be rather light; perhaps a little dialogue, short plays or satires, or nonsensical verse." Cummings complied. It was easy money. Over the next few years he would publish thirty pieces in *Vanity Fair*, most of them in a satirical vein.

Though his work on the movies met the approval of *Vanity Fair*'s editor, its silliness might have dashed any possibility of Cummings being asked to write a real screenplay, a desire that he expressed at the time. In fact, he was hoping that the association he had made while in Astoria with the director Paul Sloane might lead to "an opportunity to write a story from material furnished by...Sloane." But no project ever materialized.

Whatever relief Cummings gained from writing humor for *Vanity Fair* dissipated abruptly in October when he received a telegram from Elaine that read simply: "ARRIVED SAFELY BE IN PARIS NOVEMBER FIRST." While not stated, he knew what the message meant: Elaine had secured a court date for the divorce. He drafted several angry replies in response, one of which read: "I assume that my sotospeak carcass is to be transmitted to a foreign clime with more rapidity than you had originally seen fit to lead me to expect,to put it softly." Another read "Thank you very much for 'Arrived Safely'. The rest including the signature,succeeds perfectly in giving me the impression that you consider myself as so much dirt." He sent none of the outraged drafts in reply; instead, he simply wrote curtly that he would be there. She sent him a check for his boat fare and expenses.

On the morning of November 1, true to his word, he checked in to the Hôtel Le Havane in Paris. That afternoon he saw Nancy and her nanny, Winifred, as he was riding in a taxi to the right bank. He left a lengthy account of the meeting:

> Just as am approaching bridge thru citè Isle S. Louis,see Mopsy (tall, pale,high forehead)walking w, Winifred,along the quai.
> i stop taxi—run back,careful to approach from front so as not to scare Nancy invite them to tea (Notre Dame) ask W[Winifred] for E[laine]'s address. reenter taxi—hotel—wash.
> I run to Café ND 15 minutes late—meet Nancy and W coming toward me
> tea
> N happy (our heads,hair,touch)
> she invites me back.
> Am playing with Nancy in E's apartment…when E enters.
> Fear. "Hello Elaine"
> "Hello Estlin"
> Nancy is sent other room. goes, rapidly.
> She says she wrote me, to Hôtel Havane, not to come to her apartment.
> She is still. I,tears in voice,tell her I didn't get her letter:"do you think I'd have come if I'd known you didn't want me?"

> (hurt, indignation am surprised at my own acting)
> She relief, immediately kind but cold.
> I say I've brought my tuxedo,if she'd like to come to Moulin Rouge with me—she:I can't go out in the evenings. I:why? Because Winifred doesn't speak French. I can't leave Nancy.

Despite the ache in his heart, Cummings was not all that displeased to be in Paris, a city he loved. He jotted down his impressions in an unpublished prose work that he titled "Mr. Anyone at the Window:"

> Boulevard Saint Germain,this a little wonderful,the feline laundered slenderness of procession; intelligent darkness in daylight,houses,slowlyness of moving;plumes,strutting: through staring streets in which micelike gestures of the lifting of hats are.

Another sketch reads:

> He came out just at noon: the little Place Saint Michel banged and footed in shallow hard sunlight: from all which upreaching the boulevard hung in a white fog and through a dense fog amputated sprouting trees poked punched here and there by black blunt hobgoblin shapes.

He had also begun work on another prose narrative at about that time, an autobiographical novel whose protagonist Edward Seul agonizes over the loss of the great love of his life, sometimes called Heloise, sometimes Elaine, and their daughter. Though clearly an attempt to exorcise the demons that possessed him, Proust's *Swann's Way*, a gift from Elaine, was a definite literary inspiration. In one scene Proust's novel figures prominently:

> After reading a little,he suddenly discovered an idea:to write, à la Swann's Way,the story of his life from the moment that he received the telegram telling him to come to Paris and divorce Elaine. This idea had arrived to him in Paris,perhaps where—after many struggles—he had read a little in the book which she had given him("it interested me

> enormously" she had written him)or perhaps not until,turning to the last page of the section "Swann in Love" he had read the final sentence,and suddenly known what he had previously merely suspected—that in giving him this book to read she was giving him,in her delicate obscure way,the key to the present situation, the secret of himself.*

Other sections of the "Edward Seul" narrative are Proustian in tone in their meditative descriptive quality, but clearly Freudian in their orientation:

> The elephant had been his child fetish;until he realised that its extraordinary power over him was based on the likeness of the elephant's trunk...to his father's large(and by himself as a little boy much envied) penis.... In Paris,one autumn,he had been unable to enter the door of his hotel without first looking down the rue Saint André-des-Arts and seeing,behind it and above it, the spire of Saint Germaine des Prés and the top of the Tour Eiffel. These two symbols he had analyzed out of his life,realising after a terrible struggle,that their power over him was due to their connection(subconscious,of course)with his father: the spire,or church,gave his father's profession:the top of the tower was a replica,again,of his father's bull-like penis.

Cummings did not spend all of his time walking the streets, meditating on his life, and sketching in both words and images his observations of Paris and his heartbreak over Elaine. He also looked up his friends John Peale Bishop, Lewis Galantière, and Louis Aragon. He paid a visit to Ford Madox Ford, who had taken his poems for the *transatlantic review*, and dined on

* The final sentence of this section, in C. K. Scott Moncrieff's translation, reads: "And with that old, intermittent fatuity, which reappeared in him now that he was no longer unhappy, and lowered at the same time, the average level of his morality, he cried out in his heart: 'To think that I have wasted years of my life, that I have longed for death, that the greatest love that I have ever known has been a woman who did not please me, who was not in my style!'"

occasion with fellow New England poet Archibald MacLeish and his wife Ada. Journalist Burton Rascoe was also in Paris at this time, and recalled an afternoon and evening he and his wife spent with Cummings and Galantière at the MacLeishes' elegant house in St. Cloud, just outside of Paris. According to Rascoe, Cummings held forth from the moment they arrived at chez MacLeish, and kept up a "coruscating cascade" through a dinner they later had at a neighborhood restaurant. Among the pronouncements Rascoe recorded was a monologue on poets and artists:

> Poets and artists, especially in America, make me sick. What right has such a beggar to take on airs? I have no more interest or respect for a man because he can write a poem or paint a picture that can hang in the Louvre than I have for a man because he can fix the plumbing or design a beautiful motor car.... I am a poet, true enough; but what right have I to be proud of my disease? It's such a shabby, idiotic disease. You know what I want? Money, comfort, love, ease, luxury, the price in my pocket for theatre tickets and good wine. What do I do about getting them? I sit up in a shabby room, shivering with the cold, and use my imagination to keep me warm, thinking about the South Sea Islands and the tropical swamps. Your plumber doesn't do that. He has more sense. He would go out and get some coal and wood to make a fire.... I make poems because it is the thing I know how to do best. In fact, it's about the only thing I know how to do. America doesn't want poems badly enough to make it a profitable business to be engaged in.

MacLeish noted that he thoroughly enjoyed Cummings's company and never tired of hearing him expound. "His memory is astounding. I've heard about Swinburne memorizing and declaiming whole Greek tragedies and Hugo knowing the *Iliad* by heart and all that.... But Cummings is different. I have never been so royally entertained in my life. His mood changes. One melts into the other, tenderness into comicality, burlesque into profundity, snatches of Heine alternating with Rimbaud, advertising catch-lines tied up with Catullus and Longfellow." Ada MacLeish remembered his "burning mind," but also his use of profanity, fueled by alcohol: "Words come tumbling out, disarmingly foul-mouthed. Quite a drinker."

On occasion, Cummings also mingled with other members of the Lost Generation. Rascoe recounts that one evening Ford Madox Ford took him and Mrs. Rascoe to the "*bal musette* near the Panthéon." Already assembled were "Nancy Cunard, E.E. Cummings, Robert McAlmon, and a number of other people whose names I did not catch—and…Mrs. Ernest Hemingway. Hemingway was there, but he and Ford were not speaking.… After Ford had asked my wife and me and Mrs. Hemingway to sit at a table with him, Hemingway said to Mrs. Hemingway, 'Pay for your own drinks, do you hear! Don't let him [Ford] buy you anything.'"

The reason for the ill will between Hemingway and Ford was due to Hemingway's attack in the *transatlantic review* on Eliot, for which Ford felt the need to apologize in print. Hemingway's statement had appeared in a eulogy for Joseph Conrad that he wrote for a special Conrad supplement of Ford's magazine. It read: "If I could bring Conrad back to life by grinding Mr. Eliot into a fine dry powder and sprinkling that powder over Conrad's grave in Canterbury, I would leave for London early tomorrow morning with a sausage grinder."

Though Cummings by this stage felt Eliot's work stilted, overly intellectual, and too reliant on literary allusion, he did not (at least publicly) join sides in the controversy. But privately he probably did lend support to Hemingway, whose company, from time to time, he enjoyed. Like Cummings, Hemingway "was a good man with a bottle," and like Cummings, was an able raconteur. But Hemingway's pugilism and backbiting stood in the way of any real friendship. In general, Cummings preferred Ford, whom he described as "an old school gentleman," to Hemingway. Ford, for his part, continued to print Hemingway in the *transatlantic*, despite Hemingway's rejection of him.

Despite these occasional rambles with his fellow expatriates, Cummings was never an integral member of the large group of Americans and British living in Paris at that time. He either spent time by himself, with a few close friends like Galantière and Bishop, or with Aragon. One of the people he most wanted to meet in Paris was Jean Cocteau, but he failed to do so. Ever since seeing Cocteau's production of *Parade* in 1917, he had been drawn to his work. His novels of the early 1920s, *Thomas L'Imposteur* and *Le Grand Ecart*, had only strengthened his admiration. But it was Cocteau's absurdist ballet *Les Mariés de la Tour Eiffel*, which premiered in Paris in 1922 and in New York in 1923, that instilled in Cummings a desire to meet him. Or as he wrote: "Having been more amused by *Les Mariés* than by anything else in Paris—more, even, than by the police—I entertained a wish to meet the author of this excellent satire."

But a meeting was not to be, mainly because Aragon railed against Cocteau: "A militant *superrealist* writer and one of the most charming of people, by name Aragon, described his distinguished contemporary, Jean Cocteau, in terms so vivid as to convince me that, coming after such a portrait, Cocteau himself would be a distinct climax." According to Lewis Galantière, Cocteau's translator, the thrust of Aragon's attack was largely against the homosexual tone of Cocteau's work. Despite their not meeting—obviously because of Cummings's loyalty to Aragon—Cocteau's dramas would nonetheless have a marked influence on Cummings's own play, *Him*. So, too, would Aragon's own Dadaist play, *L'Armoire à glace un beau soir* [*The Mirrored Wardrobe One Fine Evening*] that Cummings saw when it premiered in Paris in 1923.

It is fairly apparent from Cummings's own record of these months in Paris that he socialized as a way of distracting himself from his own predicament. In spite of revels with friends, his mind was very much on the imminent divorce. In mid-November 1924, about two weeks after his arrival in France, he wrote Elaine a long message in which he proposed a new arrangement. It read in part:

> Twice, at 3 Washington Square, you told me that you loved Nancy more than anyone else—more than you love McD.
> HERE IS YOUR CHANCE TO PROVE THAT.
> Nancy's future (as well as your own future) depends—as you recently pointed out—on her being safe from scandal.
> I agree with you entirely,and regret anything which I may have—unintentionally—done or said which might jeopardise her happiness or yours.
> It is perfectly obvious that,since Nancy loves us both,there is only one way to assure her happiness, and that way is:for you and me to love each other and live together.
> If this should be impossible,there is still something which can

> be done to help Nancy—you can remain my wife in name. In this way,Nancy,at least is protected from scandal-mongers.
> It is understood that—whether you care to live with me,or merely to remain my wife in name—I insist on contributing to Nancy's support,beginning with 100$ a month and working up as I am able to give more.
> THE VERY WORST THING <u>which you could do,so far as both Nancy's and your own reputation are concerned is:to divorce me at this time</u>.

Elaine returned the letter to him, refusing even to discuss his proposal.

Perhaps because of her rejection he showed up at her apartment on the Quai de Bourbon, pistol in his pocket, determined to kill his rival. More than twenty years afterwards he reflected on his action:

> I was once standing in front of a door waiting for it to open so I could kill the man who opened it. I knew he was inside. I knew it for my ears heard a voice which my mind told me was his. I can almost remember pushing the button of the bell with my left hand because the other was in my right outside pocket.... I was going to shoot him through my pocket with a thirty-eight Remington automatic pistol. I'd pried back the safety catch. Now my forefinger lived like a tendril around the trigger. Silence. Then steps. Every[thing] my life had before been was about to die in that illimitable silence—when the door opened & in the doorway stood a kindly middleaged lady who was a dear friend of both my girl and me,at that moment perhaps my staunchest friend.

On another occasion, after hours of "walking the Boul Mich" [Boulevard Saint-Michel] he showed up at her place "in great perturbation:"

> We stand together at a window I ask her Do sit down she sits in a chair.... [I] rise,& stand by her(getting warm,erection) upagainst her,brushing I now do what I had challenged doing earlier....
> I PUT MY HAND DOWN INTO HER DRESS (she

limp,unresisting)
AND FONDLE HER BREAST(R) EXCLAIMING,as I FELT NOTHING, "Ah-h—the breast of Elaine"
I got her to this, as follows:
she—I wouldn't feel pash [sexually aroused]. Reason I don't let you is. It makes me feel cheap
I—you would. You're keeping me off,not because you wouldn't feel pash,
but because you want (stooping,speak low) to keep these things for Him."
she repels further advances
some further talk,I looking out the window,feeling that Why don't I do something at last
finally—she calls my bluff:"You don't do it (something) because you don't want to"
I tremble,grit teeth,rise—mechanically—I really don't want to. but after this challenge!
pick her up,throw her on bed (she fighting) BAD BREATH I kiss her,she's
actually ugly,emanates repulsion for me (smell)
eyes white & wide:horror! THE UNEXPECTED,THE UNIMAGINABLE,UNKNOWN—of which I am afraid
I climb her,go off—she grunts rage
Now I relax a little—she says she must get up &
attend to Nancy,get N up

If Cummings had thought that by raping Elaine he could overcome his "lack of aggression," or that such an extreme act would win her over, he was sorely mistaken, as he quickly came to realize. He slunk from the apartment feeling "afraid, insincere, beaten." "Shameful," however, does not appear among his list of adjectives.

On December 4, 1924, Elaine appeared in the same courtroom she had entered just three years earlier when she had divorced Thayer. The charge prepared by her lawyers was also the same as before: desertion. No mention was made of their having a daughter in common. Cummings did not testify on his own behalf, nor contest the charge. The divorce decree was summarily issued.

Cummings left Paris a few days later without seeing either Elaine or Nancy again. But he did write a farewell note to his daughter—which was probably never sent—on the back of an envelope:

> goodbye dear & next time when I feel a little better we'll ride on the donkeys & next time on the pigs maybe or you will a bicycle & i will ride a swan & next time when my heart is all mended again with snow & repainted with bright new paint we'll ride you & I
> & next time
> I'll ride with you in heaven with all the angels & with the stars & a new moon all gold between me & you & we'll ride together good bye dear you and i both of us having yellow hair quietly will always just touching each other's hands ride.

By Christmas, Cummings was in Cambridge. It was a gloomy holiday, made more so by his father's admonishment that he had not put up a real fight for Nancy. Indeed, both Edward and Rebecca were appalled that Cummings had not made any formal arrangements for seeing Nancy, let alone for joint custody. Cummings admitted that he had not brought the matter of Nancy into the divorce in order to avoid complications. But, now, with his parents' backing, he began reconsidering his position. Edward, pleased that his son had finally understood the gravity of his loss, cabled an attorney friend in Paris, J. B. Robinson, of the French firm Coudert Brothers, to look into the agreement to see if an appeal might be possible. Robinson responded affirmatively, advising that the divorce could likely be overturned since no mention had been made of either Nancy or that Elaine had been previously divorced. By the time Cummings returned to Patchin Place at the end of December, Robinson had begun to act vigorously on Cummings's behalf.

Cummings was hopeful, but not any less distraught. In the pages of the "Edward Seul" manuscript is this account, dated January 1, 1925:

> He sat down,and instead of reading Swann's Way began typing. Eventually there came steps. He noiselessly moved

across the room:picked up and began loading the gun. A pause:paper crinkling:a violent,definite,strange knock. The gun loaded,he moved silently toward the door. The loud knock was repeated:a telegram? Then steps rapidly descended. He opened the door:too late. Well, if it were a telegram,the boy would come around again later.

If this description is fictionalized, it is only slightly so for there were, in fact, a great many cables back and forth between Edward and Robinson, Edward and Cummings, Cummings and Robinson. Finally, on January 26, 1925, Cummings received a telegram from Elaine that he had been waiting for:

HAVE RECEIVED YOUR REQUEST THROUGH COUDERT FOR WRITTEN CONTRACT REGARDING NANCY STOP AM WILLING SIGN CONTRACT GIVING YOU UNLIMITED RIGHT OF VISIT AS AGREED BUT NOT LEGAL CUSTODY FOR ANY PART OF YEAR STOP APPEAL TO YOU NOT GO BACK ON WORD.

Without consulting either his father or Robinson, a delighted Cummings cabled Elaine his assent.

On January 28, he received this telegram from Robinson:

CONSIDER YOUR CABLE TO WIFE PREJUDICIAL TO SUCCESSFUL APPEAL STOP WIFE WILLING YOU HAVE UNLIMITED RIGHT VISIT CHILD BUT CONSIDER CHILD SHOULD LIVE WITH HER IN VIEW OF YOUTH AND FACT YOUR CIRCUMSTANCES DO NOT PERMIT FURNISHING REAL HOME STOP CONSIDER SUCCESS APPEAL DOUBTFUL STOP AM RELUCTANT TO TAKE CASE STOP CABLE US RETAINER ONE THOUSAND DOLLARS.

Cummings did share this news with his father, who, after chastising his son, duly cabled Robinson the one thousand dollar retainer.

On January 30, while entertaining Dos Passos and Nagle in his room at Patchin, he received another telegram from Robinson:

FOLLOWING CABLE JUST RECEIVED WIFE AGREES TO YOUR HAVING CHILD THREE MONTHS YEARLY STOP SHALL WE DRAW UP AGREEMENT TO THIS AFFECT

Cummings borrowed five dollars from Nagle to respond affirmatively to Robinson, but noted in a draft: "correcting text of cable so that 'custody' does not appear (fearing lest I block the divorce)."

A few days later, Robinson telegraphed Cummings that Elaine had signed the agreement, even with the term "custody" included. Both Cummings and his parents were overjoyed. Edward and Rebecca immediately began making plans to have Nancy and their son spend the summer with them at Silver Lake.

With the matter of Nancy now seemingly settled, Cummings began to rebound from his loss of Elaine. He read over the proofs of both *&* and *XLI Poems*, making corrections to the layout and typography. In February he completed another abstraction, *Noise Number 13*, for inclusion in the annual Independent Artists' Show. Like *Noise Number 12*, painted the year before, it is quite accomplished. The palette is rich, yet the colors more harmonious than in some other earlier abstractions. Again, as in *Noise Number 12*, the central detail is a large horn, rendered in color swirls, suggesting that perhaps Cummings was still working off of the saxophone motif he had sketched in Paris a few years before. Cummings described it in verse:

the Forwardflung backwardSpinning hoop returns fasterishly
whipped the top leaps bounding upon other tops to caroming
off persist displacing Its own and their Lives who
grow slowly and first into different deaths

Concentric geometries of transparency slightly
joggled sink through algebras of proud

inwardlyness to collide spirally with iron arithmetics

The exhibition directors were so taken with the canvas that they printed a photograph of it in the show's catalog.

Along with work, socializing with friends also occupied a great deal of his time. Nearly every evening he could be found in the company of Dos Passos, Nagle, Lachaise, and/or Crane, who now lived next door to Dos Passos in Brooklyn in the shadow of the bridge he would soon immortalize. He also saw a fair amount of the Watsons, and of Mitchell, but they rarely accompanied Cummings on his late-night rambles through Manhattan. Brown was not much on the scene during that time, as he was about to marry Sue Jenkins and move to Pawling, New York. But Brown did introduce him to a man named Morrie Werner, who had been his classmate at the Columbia School of Journalism. Although he had worked as a reporter in the Far East, and been the obituary editor for the *New York Herald Tribune*, he was now a full-time biographer. His book on P. T. Barnum was just off the press, and a biography of Brigham Young was in the works. Soon, Werner was added to Cummings's circle.

There was also Joseph Ferdinand Gould, whom Cummings had met the year before, but who now became a more frequent part of the group of Cummings's friends and acquaintances. A Harvard graduate, class of 1911, and descendant of a wealthy and important Massachusetts family, Gould had become by the early 1920s a street person. According to writer Charles Norman, "Joe was five feet four, bearded, and...weighed around 100.... Joe used to be a familiar sight in Greenwich Village streets with a battered, bespattered portfolio lugged to his bosom.... Joe slept on park benches, in hallways and subways, and was occasionally picked up for vagrancy." Gould's claim to fame was a "secret" manuscript—which, in reality, does not seem to have existed beyond a few fragments—entitled *An Oral History of Our Time* that he told everyone numbered thousands of pages.

Gould's supposed credentials as an author were not what drew Cummings and others to him; instead, they found his sharp wit and true Bohemian lifestyle charming. Cummings, in fact, likened him to one of the Delectable Mountains of *The Enormous Room*, that is, a vagabond saint. He would become the subject of several Cummings poems, one of which opens like this:

little joe gould has lost his teeth and doesn't know where
to find them(and found a secondhand set which click)little
joe gould used to amputate his appetite with bad brittle
candy but just(nude eel)now little joe lives on air

> **Harvard Brevis Est for Handkerchief read Papernapkin no laundry**
> **bills likes People preferring Negroes Indians Youse**
> **n.b. ye twang of little joe(yankee)gould irketh sundry**
> **who are trying to find their minds(but never had any to lose)...**

Male companionship was not all Cummings was seeking. During the breakup and struggle with Elaine he had remained loyal to her, hoping that somehow his fidelity to her might be useful in winning her back. But now with the divorce, he was ready and eager for a new sexual relationship. Among his notes are various messages such as "Call up Alice Hall and ask her to sleep with me." (If he called Alice, she apparently was not willing, since Cummings never mentioned her name again, nor does she appear on his list of conquests that he carefully kept in his notebook.)

But late that winter Dos Passos introduced Cummings to Muriel Draper, a noted interior designer who had also been involved with the Chicago Opera. Attractive, thin, and fashionable, Draper was known in New York as much for her parties and collection of interesting friends as she was for her design. In 1909 she had married a singer, Paul Draper, and moved with him to Europe, living first in Italy, then in London. By 1914 the marriage had failed; Paul returned to the United States in a futile attempt to restart his career—bogged down by his habitual gambling and alcoholism. Draper and her two young children, Paul Jr. (who later became a dancer) and Raimond, stayed on in London for another year, returning to New York in 1915 where she embarked on her design career.

At the time Cummings and Draper met, she was thirty-seven, he was thirty-one. They apparently hit it off immediately and within a few weeks were seeing each other fairly regularly. They had interests in common, particularly the theater and contemporary music. Draper seems to have been quite good both to and for Cummings. They went to the theater and concerts together, and frequently dined out. In contrast to Elaine, "who used her money...to make people without money feel poor—i.e. myself as writer," Draper did not. She encouraged him as an artist, advised him to focus his energy on his work. In short, she was a cheerleader, never stingy with appreciative remarks about him and his work.

Draper was apparently quite physically attracted to Cummings as well, but though sexually needy, he was not so interested in her in this way. From his notes about the relationship, it is clear he saw her more as a friend, almost as a "mother figure" who generously comforted him. On at least one occasion, however, their liaison veered from the purely platonic: "She [Draper] sucks me(drunk)off & I feel worlds better."

Elaine, Nancy, and MacDermot returned to New York in late March. Elaine had married MacDermot three weeks after the divorce with Cummings became final on February 7, 1925. Nancy, Elaine, and her new husband, who had resumed his employment as a senior partner in the United States subsidiary of the British banking firm Huth & Company, were now ensconced in Tuxedo Park, a suburb of New York City. Cummings seems to have taken her marriage in stride; his focus now was on seeing Nancy.

In this spirit of reconciliation, he sent Elaine a copy of *&* that he had dedicated to her. She wrote him back, thanking him for the book and his dedication, and invited him to come out to Tuxedo Park to visit Nancy. Cummings responded, asking when he should come. To his surprise, Elaine told him that she could not set a specific date since Nancy was too nervous and troubled to allow her a visit from her father. Months of struggle ensued. As the wrangling intensified, Cummings learned that it was MacDermot who was setting up obstacles to his visitation rights.

In late April or early May, after a telephone conversation with MacDermot, Cummings wrote him a lengthy letter in which he laid out his point of view: "Having helped you to obtain what you wished(divorce)I was both surprised and extremely hurt to discover that—instead of using your influence with E[laine] to help me obtain what I wished(3 months custody)you were taking precisely the opposite course in proof of which your statement that,even if E should agree to my having the child for 3 months this year,you would fight it tooth and nail."

After a lunch with MacDermot, probably in June, in which MacDermot refused to alter his position—even threatening, it seems, to take Elaine and Nancy to Ireland if Cummings persisted—Cummings wrote to Watson, asking him if he would see MacDermot: "It is dirt, to suggest to you that you meet him:yet he knows—because I told E[laine]—that you are my best friend. My father,perhaps, would thunder him out of the universe." Watson did arrange to see MacDermot, but the visit was futile.

Cummings wrote his father about the matter, enclosing a copy of the letter he had written to Watson. Edward responded to his son on July 19, 1925, but the predicted thunder was directed as much against Cummings as against Elaine and MacDermot:

> I am not in the least surprised that E & Co. have repudiated the Paris contract and refused to grant you the access to and partial custody of your daughter which was the price of the un-contested court proceedings. They are running true to form. And so are you. First they find you don't mean business in regard to the three month custody. Encouraged by that, they next refuse access. Finally they ask you to call it off and give up your daughter forever, turn her over to the tender mercies of an unspeakable cad, who has every reason to look upon her as a perpetual embarrassment,—and has no scruples of any kind except safety-first.
>
> I am not in the least surprised that nothing came of your serio-comic interview with "Co," and that nothing came of W's [Watson's] friendly intervention. All such procedure is calculated to confirm E & Co in their well grounded conviction that you are not to be taken seriously; that promises, agreements and legal contracts made with you can always be squirmed out of by "diplomacy."

After this blast, Reverend Cummings went on to enumerate the actions he thought his son should follow, including getting a good lawyer and seeking a restraining order against the MacDermots to prevent them from taking Nancy out of the country. He concluded the letter by saying that "as for seeing Co, I am at your service, provided that I have the services of a first class lawyer to draw up some ultimatums as I have indicated."

Cummings, this time, took his father's advice and sought an attorney. Muriel Draper introduced him to Judge Richard Campbell, who assigned an associate, William McCool to review the custody agreement. McCool was not optimistic. On August 22, 1924, Cummings wrote his father that according to the attorney he "would have not one chance in a million of winning." He explained McCool's reasoning: "I am an artist, not wealthy, live by myself,etc." At the same time the lawyer advised Cummings to tell the MacDermots that he had consulted counsel and was going to seek "an immediate showdown."

If Cummings did confront the MacDermots, nothing positive resulted—at least quickly. But late in the fall or early in the winter there was a small breakthrough and Cummings was allowed to see Nancy, accompanied by her nanny, on at least three occasions. From Cummings's accounts, recorded as parts of his "Edward Seul" manuscript, the encounters were fraught with emotion (on Cummings's part), but at the same time were conducted rather formally:

> The Watcher (Central park)
>
> There is this hill. There are little people on the end of this hill. One of these little people is you. As I approach,as I come nearer,climbing,I perceive that the other little people are queer kinds of plants,like little cacti in pots for sale in the flower-market on the Cité, where I bought flowers when I was last in Paris.
>
> Second Time
>
> The absolute certainty of presence gave him a curious feeling of health and of solidity,reminding him of a former himself. It was so wonderfully sure,he trembled lest his eyes should somewhere meet her:destroying the actuality of this sureness by a mere reality. Yet when the thing happened,of which the houses had told him,his mind met her so silently that nothing had been quite so sure....
>
> I'd like you to paint me a picture,when you haven't anything better to do,he said,looking at her,A Picture.
>
> "Yes" she said,quickly and with a beautiful smile, "A sunflower...."
>
> "Goodbye"—she moved wholly to him:with a beautiful quickness brushed his head with her hatbrim and the gesture would have been a kiss, if they had been alone and had dared. Then(erect)she dropped him a curtsey,smiling.

Third Time(last, Central Park)

He stood very still for a moment: then,realising that it was She—that She lived and breathed—he pushed all the tears of his love carefully into one corner of his mind and lifted an absurd hat to the huddled nurse who bowed and smiled and said: Nancy,look who is here. On this she turned,not frightened,surprised a little,and interrupted; knew him and smiled. How are you? Seul said,quite recovered,and rather awkwardly he took off his hat with as much decorum as he would use to some lady whose acquaintance he made for the first time. She and he looked at each other,and he had really nothing to say as (having answered "very well thank you" and smiled) she shyly resumed her playing.

It would be more than another year before he saw Nancy again.

sixteen

Anne

The largely unsuccessful battle to win partial custody of Nancy consumed a great deal of Cummings's energy during most of 1925. But not all of his time was taken up with the fight for his daughter. He did manage to keep writing, producing a fair number of pages in the "Edward Seul" manuscript, as well as some new poems. He also wrote, on average, one article a month for *Vanity Fair*, occasionally two. Most were published pseudonymously, but out of sixteen pieces he authored that year for the magazine, several did carry his byline: "When Calvin Coolidge Laughed" (April 1925), "Seven Samples of Dramatic Criticism" (May 1925), "Jean Cocteau as a Graphic Artist" (September 1925), "The Adult, the Artist and the Circus" (October 1925), and "You Aren't Mad, Am I?" (December 1925). He also published three poems in *Vanity Fair* in May, including "next to of course god america i," and one poem in the October *Dial*.

Of the pieces in *Vanity Fair* that he published that year under his own name, two are quite respectable. His review of Jean Cocteau's *Desseins* is particularly interesting. Unlike the fairly silly satires he was accustomed to writing for the magazine, the subject of this piece—the drawings of a writer—was one near and dear to his heart. And yet Cummings shied away from saying anything terribly profound about the relation between writing and drawing, a matter he had much considered. Instead, he produced an accurate and laudatory review of the book as it was, without venturing into commentary on how one art form influences another. He did take note of Cocteau's statement that a poet "unties writing and ties it up again differently," but failed to interpret what this really meant for Cocteau. Nonetheless, the article itself was obviously meant by

Cummings to be a statement that art—and very good art, at that—could very well be produced by one who is known primarily for his words.

If the Cocteau review largely omitted personal observations, Cummings's "The Adult, The Artist and the Circus," illustrated with his own line drawings, was a wholly individual take on what the circus meant to Cummings. Strident, perceptive, even at times shrill, this article was intended to champion the circus—which Cummings had loved since early childhood—as a true art form. He put it, "Let us not forget that every authentic 'work of art' is in and of itself alive and that, however 'the arts' may differ among themselves, their common function is the expression of that supreme 'alive-ness' which is know as 'beauty.'"

Two books by Cummings also appeared in 1925: *&* in February and *XLI Poems* in April. Although he did add new poems to *&*, both books were mostly culled from the original *Tulips & Chimneys* manuscript. At the same time, they were quite distinct volumes. He explained to his mother, *&* "will not be suppressed(for obscenity)only because privately printed," while *XLI Poems* "is harmless." *XLI Poems*, while not exactly "harmless," is not nearly as bold as *&*. Absent from *XLI Poems* are both Cummings's more experimental verse, as well as some of the more sexually explicit poems that are to be found in *&*. But *XLI Poems* does contain its fair share of worthy verse. And although it was the result of being compiled from those poems rejected by Seltzer, MacVeagh made a fairly unified selection in which vivid imagery, analogous to the painting Cummings was doing, is the principle force driving the majority of the poetry.

His poems for painters, or in which painting actively figures, are intriguing in their own right, but also for what they say about Cummings's dual preoccupation with words and images. His poem for Picasso, originally published in the *Dial* in January 1924, is a celebration as much of the artist's technique as it is of his images:

Picasso
you give us Things
which
bulge:grunting lungs pumped full of sharp thick mind

you make us shrill
presents always
shut in the sumptuous screech of
simplicity

(out of the
black unbunged
Something gushes vaguely a squeak of planes
or

between squeals of
Nothing grabbed circular shrieking tightness
solid screams whisper.)...

It also reveals Cummings's own way of seeing art as sound shapes. Indeed, the cacophony he "hears" in Picasso's work is reflective of his own *Noise* and *Sound* paintings.

In other poems, painters and paintings are also conspicuously present. "of my" is an evocative internalized pastiche of modernism:

of my
soul a street is:
prettinesses Pic-
abian tricktrickclickflick-er
garnished
of stark Picasso
throttling trees

hither
my soul
repairs herself with
prisms of sharp mind
and Matisse rhythms
to juggle Kandinsky gold-fish

away from the gripping gigantic
muscles of Cézanne's
logic,

oho.
a street
there is

where strange birds purr

While certainly an homage to his slightly older contemporaries, and to the extraordinary explosion of talent Cummings witnessed first-hand in Paris—Picabia, Picasso, Matisse, Kandinsky—the true hero of the poem is Cézanne, whose gigantic legacy had to be reckoned with by every modern painter.

Many of the poems in *XLI Poems* are not so successful in making significant statements or in truly displaying what Cummings could really do with language. Part of the reason for this is that a fair number—particularly those in the "Sonnets" sequence that ends the volume—date from either his days at Harvard or not long after. Two poems, "this is the garden:colours come and go" and "Thou in whose swordgreat story shine the deeds," were previously published in *Eight Harvard Poets*. While certainly accomplished verse for a poet in his late teens or early twenties, they do not have either the range or felicity of expression that many of the poems he was writing more recently did. His paean to New York, "by god i want above fourteenth," written upon his arrival in Manhattan following his discharge, is an exception. In this poem the language is tight, the explosive rhythmic form a reflection of the street-life frenzy with its screeches, purrs, stops, and starts:

by god i want above fourteenth

fifth's deep purring biceps,the mystic screech
of Broadway,the trivial stink of rich

frail firm asinine life. . . .

The nine poems that make up the "Portraits" section are generally of later composition, and reflect a greater sense of innovation. Three are prose poems in the best French manner. In these verses in prose, the images run riot, but in a fully engaging way. "at the ferocious phenomenon of 5 o'clock i find myself gently decompos-" is a grotesque New York cityscape in which the poet sees himself trapped in the jaws of monster Manhattan. His portrait of Scofield Thayer, "conversation with my friend is particularly," is a cubist collage, but the heaping up of adjectives and extraneous words ultimately mars the effect, as if a painter has daubed too much paint on a canvas. Nonetheless, it is quite interesting, particularly in contrast to the formal "portrait" he sketched of Thayer while at Harvard, "ST." In the later poem Thayer is described as having a "sadistic modesty," while "his mind is seen frequently / fingering the exact beads of a faultless languor." The poem ends with the summation: "an orchid whose velocity is sculptural."

XLI Poems ultimately succeeds because the language is exceedingly rich, the metaphors striking and exact, the images fresh. While maybe "harmless" in comparison to *&*, it is nonetheless a volume of which any poet could have been proud.

Although published two months before *XLI Poems*, the poems in *&* are generally of later composition. It is also a more interesting volume, containing some of Cummings's more challenging work. He warned his mother, "this concatenation of poems,if found in a Cambridge bookstore,or on a table in Cummings,Sr.,home would cause liberal arrests lawsuits mayhems and probable massacres." Both *XLI Poems* and *&* are organized into sections with similar headings to those in his first book, *Tulips and Chimneys*. As might be expected from the sorts of verse in *XLI Poems*, the headings in this book correspond more to the conventional poems found in *Tulips and Chimneys*, whereas the divisions in *&* are more reflective of the more radical work in that volume. In *XLI Poems*, for instance, Cummings grouped poems under the familiar *Tulips and Chimneys* headings of "SONGS," "CHANSONS INNOCENTES," "PORTRAITS," and "LA GUERRE." In *&*, the Cummings sections also present in *Tulips and Chimneys* are "POST IMPRESSIONS," "PORTRAITS," "SONNETS—REALITIES" and "SONNETS—ACTUALITIES." Part of the reason for the same divisions is that the author originally had included many of the poems in the two later books under these headings in the first book. But in neither case was the grouping arbitrary. The verse in "POST IMPRESSIONS," for instance, is made up of painterly poems in the manner of the post-impressionists. "PORTRAITS" contains word portraits, although they are hardly representational sketches in either form or subject.

The range in style and subject in *&* is quite wide, wider than in *XLI Poems*. In the first section, for instance, is one of Cummings's more evocative cityscapes, "Paris;this April sunset completely utters," along with the raucous, even grotesque poem, "i was sitting in mcsorley's." Though on the surface they seem to have little in common, both are, in fact, poems made by a poet who was also a painter. Indeed, the first draft of "Paris;this April sunset completely utters" was scribbled in pencil on the back side of an envelope, which he further embellished with swirls and planes, some with colors noted. It was almost as if he could not decide whether he was writing a poem or sketching a picture—perhaps both.

> Paris;this April sunset completely utters;
> utters serenely silently a cathedral
>
> before whose upward lean magnificent face
> the streets turn young with rain,...

"Paris;this April sunset completely utters" is a poem-painting that describes what the poet saw at twilight in Paris. It is a presentation of what was before the poet's eyes in June, 1922; nothing less, nothing more. "i was sitting in mcsorley's" is also a sketch, but the vision in this poem is an inebriated rendition of what was. Although "outside it was New York and beauti- / fully snowing" the interior is "snug and evil...the slobbering walls filthily push witless / creases of screaming warmth." It is this rank interior that is the subject of the poem:

> and i was sitting in the din thinking drinking the ale,which never
> lets you grow old blinking at the lowceiling my being pleasantly was
> punctuated by the always retchings of a worthless lamp.
>
> when With a minute terrif   iceffort one dirty squeal of soiling light
> yanKing from bushy obscurity a bald greenish foetal head established
> It suddenly upon the huge neck around whose unwashed sonorous muscle
> the filth of a collar hung gently....

These were not the verses that Seltzer or MacVeagh rejected because of fear of prosecution for obscenity. Instead, it was poems such as "between the breasts / of bestial / Marj lie large / men who praise // Marj's cleancornered strokable / body" that caused them to shy away. There were many more of this sort in the collection that explicitly described sexual acts.

Despite Cummings's desire to make sexuality a central theme in *&*, his view of sex was not altogether salubrious. His numerous portraits of prostitutes and their "johns" are almost all rather depressing. For all of his interest in and even enamor of prostitutes, he obviously realized the sordidness of paying for sex. This was not simply a Puritan streak asserting itself; rather, he clearly could see the objectification and subjugation of women for what it truly was. His description, for instance, of an army camp whore as seen through the eyes of one of her clients is not erotic in the least. Instead, the sexual act is rendered with crudity:

> **i had cement for her,**
> **merrily**
> **we became each**
> **other humped to tumbling**
>
> **garble   when**
> **a**
> **minute**
> **pulled the sluice**
>
> **emerging.**
>
> **concrete**

The contrast between poems that sketch relations with prostitutes, and those that describe relations between lovers makes it apparent that Cummings is hardly condemning sex, or that he himself saw the act in the vulgar terms he attributes to the clients of prostitutes. Indeed, his attitude toward sex was quite different once he became involved with Elaine, as reflected in the poems written for her. Given, however, that Cummings often noted in his private writings that he did not always feel sexually successful, these poems can perhaps be read more as idealized versions, driven by feeling and desire, rather than performance. In "i will be" the erotic theme is central but presented far more delicately, more feelingly, and far more creatively than in his poems about whoring and whores:

> i will be
> M o ving in the Street of her
>
> bodyfee l inga ro undMe the traffic of
> lovely;muscles-sinke x p i r i n g S
> uddenl
> Y totouch
> the curvedship of
> Her-
> ...kIss her:hands...

His best poem in this vein, and one of his best known lyrics, is this wonderfully direct and exuberant celebration of lovemaking that he wrote for Elaine:

> i like my body when it is with your
> body. It is so quite new a thing.
> Muscles better and nerves more.
> i like your body. i like what it does,
> i like its hows. i like to feel the spine
> of your body and its bones,and the trembling
> -firm-smooth ness and which i will
> again and again and again
> kiss, i like kissing this and that of you,
> i like,slowly stroking the,shocking fuzz
> of your electric fur,and what-is-it comes
> over parting flesh....And eyes big love-crumbs,
>
> and possibly i like the thrill
>
> of under me you so quite new

XLI Poems was not widely reviewed; *&* received only a single review, and this in tandem with the other volume. The critical silence that greeted *&* was mainly because, being privately printed, it was not widely circulated. The six assessments of *XLI Poems* were generally favorable, though Cummings's "eccentric" poetic form still confounded more than one critic. Mark Van Doren dismissed his experiments as "tricks," while Christopher Morley, writing in *Saturday Review*, suggested that his experiments, though "always interesting," would not endear him to many readers. Of all the reviews, the only substantive one was by the new managing editor of the *Dial*, Marianne Moore, who wrote an essay on both *&* and *XLI Poems*. While Moore cautiously tiptoed around the more explicit poems in *&*, choosing to quote only verses that did not have erotic or sexual themes, she concluded by saying that "Mr. Cummings has in these poems, created from inconvenient emotions, what one is sure is poetry."

Cummings was pleased with *XLI Poems* and especially with *&*, but because of the turmoil in his custody battle for six-year-old Nancy, he could not feel either triumphal or even jubilant. But two events in 1925 did manage to jolt Cummings out of his preoccupation with the loss of his daughter. The first was an announcement he received from his father that he had lost his job, the second was meeting Anne Barton.

What had happened in Boston was that the membership of his father's church, the South Congregational, voted during the summer to merge with the First Church, the more prestigious of the two, and one of the oldest churches in Boston. Since there was a job for only one minister, sixty-four-year-old Edward Cummings was given the title Minister Emeritus and replaced by the younger head of the First Church. Edward was so crushed that Cummings actually went up to Cambridge to see him. After all the assistance his father had given him, Cummings felt it only right that he should now be the one to offer support. He recorded the homily-like talk that on arrival he had with his father. It was a speech very much like the sermons his father was accustomed to delivering, both to parishioners and to his own son. For at least a brief moment, Cummings had become his father:

> He came quietly down the front door steps…moving as if he were full of darkness. Suddenly I decided to try an experiment;& I said:

> "You can only see that you've lost the church,but that isn't so." He looked at me. "In losing the church" I said "you've entered the world. You're a worldly person;why deny it?" We stood face to face. "Only a small part of you could possibly fit in that church." I said almost angrily "—all the rest of you had to remain outside. You're like a child who shut his finger in the door. Now the finger's out of the door & that finger hurts you but it won't hurt you long. And what if it hurts horribly—you're free! Now you can move,love,be & do things;because you are yourself again: now(for the first time in years)you're really you. And I know this really you—he's all sorts of people,can do any number of things & do them beautifully. Believe me, instead of feeling sorry the church let you go,I thank heaven it did. I think getting getting out of the church was the very best thing that could have happened to you. I congratulate you I said to him. "I feel every thing's fine!"
>
> His great shoulders straightened,he began to grow high;his head climbed nobly into the sunlight;& his wonderful voice said slowly, "if you feel that way about me, I'll feel that way." Then he smiled. He drew me tenderly to him.

By mid-summer Edward had rebounded, throwing his energy into the directorship of the World Peace Foundation, a private association of citizens concerned with "breaking swords intc plowshares." He even began making a few repairs to the houses at Silver Lake and at Joy Farm. He kept himself fully engaged with his son's struggles for custody. But from the moment of Cummings's arrival in Cambridge to bolster Edward, father and son had entered into a new relationship. Cummings, in his father's eyes, had finally become a man. They could now talk more as equals, with mutual understanding and affection. Cummings could now "stop fighting [his] father" and Edward could ease up on trying to control his son. It was a profound breakthrough and a necessary one.

If coming to the aid of his father made Cummings look more like a man to Edward, meeting Anne Barton made Cummings *feel* more like a man. It was Cummings's new friend, writer Morrie Werner, who introduced them, and the result was instant combustion.

When the two met, Barton was twenty-six, four and a half years younger than Cummings and recently divorced from cartoonist and illustrator, Ralph Barton. Together they had one daughter, Diana, then four years old, of whom she had custody and for whom she received alimony. Originally from Ossining, New York, home of Sing Sing Prison, Barton was the daughter of a sexually and physically abusive policeman, Leroy Minnerly. She had left her unhappy home to venture to New York City at sixteen, and because she had little education or training, relied on her attractiveness to make her way by working as an artist's model. This is how she had met Ralph Barton, a young artist on the rise, whom she married in 1917 when she was just seventeen. But the marriage was now behind her, Ralph Barton having taken up in 1923 with Carlotta Monterey, the lead actor in Eugene O'Neill's *The Hairy Ape*.

Cummings was not the first man to attract her since she and Barton had parted—she had been in a relationship with the son of an Italian admiral named Palladini, and was involved at the time she met Cummings with a man named Douglas, an older wealthy businessman with whom she exchanged sexual favors for gifts and cash. Cummings was not initially bothered by Barton's other affairs. Indeed, he seems to have been rather pleased that she was "easy," as he was more interested in sex than in having any real or lasting relationship. Cummings wrote in his notes, "1st I thought she was a whore. I didn't care what she did. She was simply somebody to screw—my chief concern was with my wife and child."

Barton, like Elaine, was quite attractive, but in a different way from Cummings's former spouse. Where Elaine was refined, elegant, and somewhat reserved, Barton was, in Cummings's words, "common, even vulgar." But she was also quite witty, lively, assertive, and a talker. She was also a match for Cummings in her fondness for alcohol. Even more enthusiastic than Cummings about partying, she never passed up an opportunity to join in festivities of any sort, hitting the booze from the moment she arrived until she left. At a social gathering Barton could usually be found with a lipstick-smudged cigarette in one hand, a glass filled with liquor in the other. In many ways she was the ultimate 1920s flapper.

Her looks were also a considerable asset. More pert than beautiful, with large twinkling hazel eyes, bobbed light brown hair (occasionally dyed blonde), and a button nose, she resembled a farm girl newly arrived in the city rather than a cosmopolitan sophisticate. Very aware of her appearance, she always dressed in the latest styles, carefully choosing attire that accentuated her slender, but well-proportioned figure. "If Annie came into a room," said Cummings, "every man's prick hit the ceiling."

By early July of 1925, Cummings and Barton were spending a great deal of time together. Almost every afternoon he would head over to her apartment at 55 Charles Street, a short walk from Patchin Place. If he returned home, it was not until the early morning hours. By late summer, Cummings began introducing her to his friends. Worried that perhaps they would reject her out of a loyalty to Elaine, of whom they had all been quite fond, and with whom some, like Dos Passos, still maintained friendly relations, he was pleased that they fully welcomed Barton. Cummings was also pleased that Barton, unlike Elaine, was quite happy to accompany him on his nightly rambles with friends from restaurant to speakeasy to perhaps a friend's apartment for a nightcap (or two or three).

Barton was initially quite good for Cummings. Within weeks of meeting her he became more outgoing and far less morose and prone to self-pity. Although still engaged in his struggle for custody of Nancy, Barton provided a welcome distraction from his troubles. He ceased to keep the pistol by his bedside and gave up any thoughts of suicide. He even began to become reconciled to the idea that his battle over Nancy with Elaine and MacDermot might be a prolonged one. Barton, too, had had a custody fight for her daughter, Diana. As a result of her own difficulties, she was able to provide both insight and consolation for Cummings and free him from his own self-absorption. This feeling, translated into poetry, emerged as:

. . . you give me

courage
so that against myself
the sharp days slobber in vain: . . .

Because sex with Barton was easy and good, he began to let go, as well, of the image of himself as a less than satisfactory lover. Indeed, he later noted that Barton really introduced him to sex. With her it was not fraught, not anxiety-producing the way it had been with Elaine. One difficulty, for instance, he had always had with Elaine was her inability to reach orgasm before he did. With Barton, this was not a problem. Or as Cummings put it rather coarsely but succinctly, "She gloried in fucking."

Cummings did not stop writing poems during the breakup with Elaine. In fact, he chronicled the change in feeling about love and his lover in a series of poems that are hauntingly tender, occasionally bitter, and often beautiful:

i am a beggar always
who begs in your mind

(slightly smiling,patient,unspeaking
with a sign on his
breast
BLIND)yes i

am this person of whom somehow
you are never wholly rid(and who

does not ask for more than
just enough dreams to
live on)...

While "i am a beggar always" teeters on the edge of self-pity, and as a result loses some of its force, "i go to this window" is a far more powerful expression of loss precisely because Cummings heads off the transparent emotions of woe in the middle part of the poem, transforming them at the end into images of wonder:

i go to this window

just as day dissolves
when it is twilight(and
looking up in fear

i see the new moon
thinner than a hair)

making me feel
how myself has been coarse and dull
compared with you,silently who are
and cling
to my mind always

But now she sharpens and becomes crisper
until i smile without knowing
—and all about
herself

the sprouting largest final air

plunges
          inward with hurled
downward thousands of enormous dreams

Although Cummings managed to produce some very fine poems during his period of torment, he was far less productive than usual. To be sure, his pieces for *Vanity Fair* and his work on the "Edward Seul" manuscript did consume some of his creative energy, but it also seems that he was unable to throttle his despair enough to produce much poetic work. But the modicum of happiness that came from his relationship with Barton freed him from his agony sufficiently that the poems began to flow more readily. The work also became lighter in spirit and love could again be a topic no longer only associated with pain. It was during this period that he produced one of his greatest love poems, "since feeling is first:"

since feeling is first
who pays any attention
to the syntax of things
will never wholly kiss you;

wholly to be a fool
while Spring is in the world

my blood approves,
and kisses are a better fate
than wisdom
lady i swear by all flowers.   Don't cry
—the best gesture of my brain is less than
your eyelids' flutter which says

we are for each other:then
laugh,leaning back in my arms
for life's not a paragraph

And death i think is no parenthesis

If Barton was helpful in breaking him out of the doldrums, another boost certainly came in early October 1925 when he received a letter from Watson asking him if he would be willing to accept the *Dial* Award for that year. Although Thayer had proposed Cummings for the award in 1922, Watson had not felt Cummings had produced enough important work to justify him being the recipient that year. Now, however, Watson was more enthusiastic, concurring with Thayer that the award should go to Cummings. Within a day, Cummings had informed Watson of his delight at being selected. He was also quite pleased that Watson had asked Marianne Moore, now acting editor of the *Dial*, to provide a review of his work. The award was prestigious (previous recipients included Sherwood Anderson, T. S. Eliot, and Marianne Moore) as well as of considerable monetary value—it came with a check for two thousand dollars.

When the official announcement of the award was published in the January 1926 *Dial*, Cummings was catapulted into a different league in the public arena of literature. Horace Liveright not only asked him for a new book, but decided also to remarket *The Enormous Room*, hoping to capitalize on his author's new fame. Despite his earlier anger over Liveright's botched first edition of *The Enormous Room*, he agreed to give the publisher a new book of poems, even assenting to Liveright's request that he add an "introduction."

As for *The Enormous Room*, Cummings could say little. Liveright had not officially allowed the book to go out of print, although he had remaindered a number of volumes of the first printing of twenty-two hundred copies. These copies were offered to Cummings at thirty cents each. Cummings did not buy any, but his father did, taking a hundred with the intention of sending them to every senator. (In the end, Cummings persuaded his father to send them only to his friends.) But now that Cummings had won the award, Liveright withdrew any remaindered copies, restored the two dollar price, and began actively selling the book again.

There were also dissenters over the award. Poet Yvor Winters, no fan of Cummings despite Hart Crane's continual attempts to convince him otherwise, wrote a blistering letter to Moore in which he compared her prose about Cummings to a crow who picks over the ash heap and leaves the ashes behind. Poet Maxwell Bodenheim was equally miffed, wondering how Moore could possibly have chosen Cummings as the recipient.

By February 1926, Cummings had put together his new collection for Liveright, and had begun work on making his "Voice Weedable for the Gwate American Publick" in the form of his preface. The task was not easy, as he told his mother, "am supposed to edit my new collection of poems, write a preface,explaining same,and submit to publishers. No sinsh. Particularly as this (coming)volume is entitled:IS FIVE(short for:Twice Two is Five,hasten to add.) But even so how will M. et Mmme. Everyone compwehend?—such is the curse of awithmetic."

By March he submitted the manuscript, including the preface, to Liveright. It was probably not the sort of statement Liveright was looking for. It read in part:

> At least my theory of technique,if I have one,is very far from original;nor is it complicated. I can express it in fifteen words,by quoting The Eternal Question And Immortal Answer of Burlesk,viz. "Would you hit a woman with a child?—No,I'd hit her with a brick." Like the burlesk comedian,I am abnormally fond of that precision which creates movement.
>
> If a poet is anybody,he is somebody to whom things made matter very little—somebody who is obsessed by Making.
>
> ....
>
> Ineluctable preoccupation with The Verb gives a poet one priceless advantage:whereas nonmakers must content themselves with the merely undeniable fact that two times two is four,he rejoices in a purely irresistible truth(to be found,in abbreviated costume,upon the title page of the present volume.

Liveright undoubtedly realized that it was useless to press for further elucidation. When he issued *Is 5* two months later, in June of 1926, it carried as a foreword Cummings's statement exactly as he had written it.

Cummings was not trying to be cute in his quotation of vaudeville comedians, or on his insistence that two times two does not always make four. Discerning readers would have realized that he was actually informing them of how he wrote and how they should read. Precision, surprise, exquisite timing, and making for the sake of making, truly are what Cummings was about.

Is 5 was a mix of older poems, some dating from the early 1920s, and newer poems that he had written as recently as late 1925 or early 1926. Divided into five sections—mirroring the title—the book is remarkable for its unique, and by this point fully recognizable, voice that was Cummings's alone. More mature, masterful, and controlled than his three earlier books of poems, *Is 5* is filled with wit, ingenuity, satire, love, loss, and beauty. Poet Louis Zukofsky called it "sensuously evocative, sometimes fanciful." Malcolm Cowley asserted, years after its publication, that it is "still the liveliest," among all of Cummings's books of poems.

The book begins with five sonnets he had published in *Broom* in 1923. Under the group title "Five Americans," these portraits of prostitutes are more reminiscent of similar poems in his earlier collections. Less sardonic than some of his other verses about prostitutes, however, "Five Americans" more than anything, are attempts to render speech as it was actually spoken. "Gert," for instance, even portrays the poet's struggle to find the right words to describe attributes of his subject. After choosing "joggle," "jounce," and "toddle," he finally has to admit that "there's no sharpest neat / word for thing." By the end of the poem he simply decides to reproduce her voice, "gruesome:a trull / leaps from the lungs'gimme uh swell fite // like up ter yknow,Rektuz,Toysday nite.'"

Following these portraits was "POEM,OR BEAUTY HURTS MR.VINAL," a poem that aroused a fair amount of controversy when it was published in *S4N* in 1922. An attack on Harold Vinal, secretary of the Poetry Society of America, its initial publication resulted in the magazine being flooded with a stream of vindictive responses, causing Matthew Josephson to print a defensive response. The poem is noteworthy less for its swipes against Vinal, than for the method he used to launch his attack: the adroit use of advertising slogans, clichés, and common brand names. Cummings's point is that "certain ideas gestures / rhymes,like Gillette Razor Blades / having been used and reused / to the mystical moment of dullness emphatically are / Not To Be Resharpened." Ultimately, the poem is more clever than profound.

Other protests—against war, injustice, and the mechanization of society—were handled with greater creativity. His well-known "my sweet old etcetera" is a wonderfully satirical but quite pointed commentary on war:

...my

mother hoped that

i would die etcetera
bravely of course my father used
to become hoarse talking about how it was
a privilege and if only he
could meanwhile my

self etcetera lay quietly
in the deep mud et

cetera
(dreaming,
et
   cetera,of
Your smile
eyes knees and of your Etcetera)

Equally effective in its denunciation of a society who rejects the downtrodden is "a man who had fallen among thieves," the poet's updating of the biblical parable of "The Good Samaritan." In Cummings's version, the victim is a bum, passed by "a dozen staunch and leal / citizens." In "it really must," Cummings sketches a portrait not of a derelict, but of a struggling man, looking squarely at the vicissitudes of his life:

it really must
be Nice,never to
have no imagination)or never
never to wonder about guys you used to(and them
slim hot queens with dam next to nothing

on)tangoing
(while a feller tries
to hold down the fifty bucks per
job with one foot and rock a

cradle with the other)...

Humor, as always, is present in *Is 5*. Among his more comic poems is his celebration of natural beauty over "art." For example, "since feeling is first," also in *Is 5*, Cummings, in his artful way, suggests that life is more than art.

mr youse needn't be so spry
concernin questions arty

each has his tastes but as for i
i likes a certain party

gimme the he-man's solid bliss
for youse ideas i'll match youse

a pretty girl who naked is
is worth a million statues

Among the best poems in the collection are those that chronicle the end of his marriage (cited earlier in this chapter). Less strident, rich in imagery, tightly composed with every word counting, they mark a distinct development in expression. Unlike many of Cummings's poems in which someone else's speech or manner is used to express his own feelings, he does not hide behind any mask in these verses. Instead, he allows himself to render his emotions as they were, with directness, verve, and considerable mastery. One of the most moving of these poems, "supposing i dreamed this)" is a meditation on his loss, his hope:

love being such,or such,
the normal corners of your heart
will never guess how much
my wonderful jealousy is dark

if light should flower:
or laughing sparkle from
the shut house(around and around
which a poor wind will roam

Is 5 was the poetry of a poet wailing—against genteel poetry, against war, against the values of a society that values only the mechanized, material world over its individuals, and against the loss of love. But it was not just a book of protest poems; it also celebrated the individual, be he the good Samaritan or the lover who gives himself or herself fully to love. As special beings, they were for Cummings worthy of being praised in the loudest and most unmistakable voice. For all of its range and depth, *Is 5* is remarkably unified. It was truly a stunning volume, a major book of poems.

When *Is 5* was published on June 14, 1926, the reviews were generally laudatory. Genevieve Taggard, writing in the *New Republic*, shrewdly observed that "when reading the poetry of E.E. Cummings it is the eye that first comes awake. The eye opens, then the ear hears—and somewhere between…the imagination gets a little drunk." In *Poetry*, Maurice Lesemann wrote that the book "was full of boisterous energy" and "great gusto." He also noted that "as in the later work of Joyce, there is a strenuous effort to meet all the manifestations of externality without flinching: an effort to say yes to the world."

Cummings's work was also noticed abroad. Poets Robert Graves and Laura Riding devoted a chapter to Cummings in their important 1927 book, *A Survey of Modernist Poetry*: "We are dealing here with a modernist who seems to feel no obligation to the plain reader, and to work solely in the interests of poetry.… Our suggestion is not that poets should imitate Mr. Cummings, but that the appearance of poems like his and the attention they demand should make it harder for poetical exercises to be passed off as poetry."

seventeen

Him

With *Is 5* turned in to Boni & Liveright, regular money in his pocket from his *Vanity Fair* articles, and two thousand dollars from the *Dial* award in the bank, Cummings decided in late March of 1926 to take Barton and her four-year-old daughter Diana abroad. He may also have had an ulterior motive for the trip. Although initially quite tolerant of Barton's affair with Douglas, by that spring he had become jealous of the attention lavished on her by her older lover, apparently in his late 40s, whom Cummings dubbed the "merchant prince." He hoped a long hiatus away from New York might result in Barton ending her affair with Douglas.

The trip lasted three months, the better part of it spent in Paris. They did make a short side trip to Italy, mainly because Barton wanted to, but chiefly stayed in Venice, the one city in Italy Cummings did not find overwhelmingly fascist and oppressive. Paris, despite its rain, still enchanted Cummings, as it did Barton. He visited his old haunts, looked up a few friends like Galantière and Aragon, and happily introduced his new lady and her daughter to cafés, museums, the circus, and the street performers in Montmartre. He and Barton even took in the Folies Bergère where they saw Josephine Baker perform.

Cummings was so struck by Baker that he wrote a piece for *Vanity Fair* on her and her revue: "Herself [Baker] is two perfectly fused things: an entirely beautiful body and a beautiful command of its entirety. Her voice (simultaneously uncouth and exquisite—luminous as only certain voices are luminous) is as distinctly a part of this body as are her gestures, which emanate a spontaneous or personal rigidity only to dissolve it in a premeditation at once liquid and racial."

Paris also inspired him to write another article for the magazine, this one on the city of the French, not the one that tourists usually saw. He sets up the contrast between the two aspects of the city in the first paragraph where he makes the distinction between "Paree," the Paris of tourists, and "Paname," "its most alive aspect, the inner part; the secret of secrets, unpurchasable wither by His Britannic Majesty's pounds or by his Yankee Excellency's dollars." He concludes with a rhapsodic hymn to the delights of "Paname:" "Beneath 'Paree,' beneath the glittering victory of 'civilization,' a careful eye perceives the deep, extraordinary, luminous triumph of Life Itself and of a city founded upon life…a heart which throbs always, a spirit always which cannot die. The winged monsters of the garden of Cluny do not appear to have heard of 'progress.' The cathedral of Notre Dame does not budge an inch for all the idiocies of this world."

Cummings also began working on turning his "Edward Seul" pages into a play. The early drafts, some written in Paris, but most after he returned, are autobiographical, absurd, and highly steeped in Freud, whom he had been reading over the last couple of years at Thayer's suggestion. The turn to playwriting was a result of several factors, not the least of which was a long-standing interest in performance. He was also inspired in part by Dos Passos, whose play, *The Garbage Man*, had been staged in New York just prior to Cummings's departure for Europe. In addition, he had admired Cocteau's work for the theater, as well as that of Aragon. He had reviewed, as well, several New York theater productions in two essays for the *Dial* before leaving for Europe. And finally, Barton was an enthusiast of the theater, which may have further contributed to his desire to write his own play.

In essence, the play Cummings began in Paris was not so terribly different from the "Edward Seul" prose version, though the sections relating to Nancy were entirely omitted. The central plot revolved around a love triangle in which Edward is in love with Anna, who is in love with Jan. From Cummings's notes it is clear he conceived the play as a symbolic working out of Freudian concepts. Edward represented the ego; Anna the superego; Jan (in the first draft the janitor who inhabits the cellar) the unconscious. In one early version of the play, Edward decides to kill his rival, or alternately himself, with a pistol he brandishes from one scene to another. In another version, Anna is in love with Edward but is afraid of becoming pregnant. In this version, Jan is a hunchback—a reference to the unconscious proceeding by hunches, not by thinking. Fortunately, Cummings abandoned the overt acting out of Freud's notions, and in the end wrote a play that is less obviously Freudian, far more entertaining, and a great deal more experimental.

Edward Seul (the play), while not very good theater, is interesting for what it says about Cummings's attempt to work out both his issues with Elaine and with Barton. Ostensibly these problems were the same: betrayal—Elaine with MacDermot, Barton with Douglas. But they were also different, at least at first. He had deeply loved Elaine; however, he was enthralled with Barton as a sexual object. As a result, he did not initially hold her to the same standards as he did Elaine. But by the time he and Barton had traveled together to Europe, Cummings was more than just infatuated with Barton; he was in love. Consequently, the drafts of the play fused his predicaments with both Elaine and Barton in a vague attempt to unravel the situation and perhaps even find a solution to his dilemma—adultery, compounded with jealousy—through psychology. But mostly, these fragmentary scenes were transformations into art of the anguish in his soul.

When Cummings, Barton, and Diana returned to the United States in early July, Cummings went up to Silver Lake to work on his play. Barton and her daughter remained in New York. Contrary to Cummings's hopes, within a few days of her return Barton met up with Douglas who, after lunch, took her on a shopping spree. She did not try to hide the matter from Cummings, writing him about it in detail on July 14, 1926. But she also told him that he should not be worried about it since she loved him and this made her happy. Whatever misgivings Cummings may have had, he shoved them aside, dedicating himself to work on the play.

By the end of summer Cummings had nearly finished his work for the theater, which now bore a new title, *Him*. Far different from the first drafts, *Him* is a play about a playwright (Him) trying to write a play, of which various scenes are staged as plays within the larger drama. Alternating at irregular intervals with these mini productions are scenes between Him and his lover (Me), as well as a series of sequences in which the Weird Sisters, portrayed as three old women knitting as they sit in rocking chairs, make absurd pronouncements on life, death, and the dramatic action enfolding around them.

Him is ultimately a melange of all of Cummings's likes and dislikes, hobby horses, and ideas, as well as a fair amount of autobiographical detail, all stitched together with a tremendous sense of the poetry implicit in the American language. Highly ambitious, the play operates on several levels simultaneously: as the phantasmagoric dream-like unfolding of the twin consciousness of both Him and Me; as barbed social commentary; as a clever and comic homage to burlesque, the circus, Coney Island, and to the Dada and Surrealist theater of Paris; and finally as a play about a play seemingly being written on stage.

As *Him* opens, the audience confronts the Weird Sisters, who function in the manner of the Greek chorus, with nods to Shakespeare and the Fates of Greek mythology. The sisters are seen sitting in their rocking chairs in front of a backdrop that depicts a doctor anesthetizing a woman. The heads of both the doctor and the woman, however, are not painted; rather, holes have been cut out of the fabric through which protrude the heads of the actors playing the doctor and the patient. Cummings, it seems, wanted his audience to be aware that the tableau is to function as a living part of the performance, perhaps even suggesting that the scenes that unfold in front of it are to be taken as an ether dream of the patient, Me, the lover of Him.

From the very first line, uttered by one of the sisters, "We called our hippopotamus It's Toasted," it is evident that this will not be a conventional or realistic drama, but instead a play that pushes the boundaries of sense and nonsense. As the patter continues between the Sisters, non sequitur follows non sequitur, broken only by the appearance of the Doctor, who, having left his position behind the backdrop, enters with Him. Introductions are exchanged: the Doctor tells the Sisters that Him is a distinguished foreign visitor whose "nomb D. ploom" is "Mr. Anybody." Him then confesses to the Sisters that his real name is "Mr. Everyman, Marquis de la Poussière." The Sisters we learn are Miss Stop, Miss Look, and Miss Listen

The next scenes in Act I are generally between Him and Me. In Scene II, the plot of the play is revealed: Him is trying to write a play, but with difficulty. Me is curious about it, but Him prefers chatter to revelation. In an aside, however, Him confesses that his mantra is "'An artist, a man, a failure, I MUST PROCEED.'" Scene III, a reworking of his earlier

Edward Seul drama, continues the conversation between Him and Me, but here the notion of Him's jealousy is introduced. Jan, Edward's rival in the first drafts, has been replaced by The Man in the Mirror. As in the earlier versions, though, Him brandishes a pistol, at one point threatening to shoot himself, at another moment, The Man in the Mirror. Finally, Me diverts Him's attention by asking him again about the play, to which he responds:

> HIM: This play of mine is all about mirrors.
> ME: But who's the hero?
> HIM: (*To her*): The hero of this play of mine? (*Hesitates.*) A man…
> ME: Naturally. What sort of man?
> HIM: The sort of man—who is writing a play about a man who is writing a sort of a play.

Act II is given over to eight scenes from the play Him is writing, each presented for the edification and commentary of Me. These skits are a combination of vaudeville revues, Dadaist theater, and Freudian theory. While imbued with comedy, they were clearly also meant to be seen as satirical swipes at politics, art, and social injustice. In Scene VIII, for instance, Mussolini, in the guise of Napoleon, is portrayed as an imbecilic potentate, surrounded by fawning homosexual underlings, issuing orders for the sake of issuing orders. In Scene IV, Cummings parodies Eugene O'Neill's expressionist drama *The Great God Brown* by having his actors, Will and Bill, exchange identities by donning masks, like Dion and Brown in O'Neill's play. And while in O'Neill the consequences are tragic, in Cummings the murder is performed as farce.

John Sumner, the notorious head of the Society for the Prevention of Vice, is skewered in Scene V, where an African American troupe engaged in performing a bawdy version of the song "Frankie and Johnie" are interrupted by a man from the audience who attempts to prevent the singer from uttering the word "cock." In the end, the female singer rebuffs the "president pro. tem." of the "Society for the Contraception of Vice" by producing a "Something" "which suggests a banana in size and shape and which is carefully wrapped in a bloody napkin." At such a sight the vice preventer runs screaming, while the chorus finishes the song.

Other satires include a sketch of a wealthy businessman blind to poverty, starvation, and social unrest; a soap box orator attempting to get rich by selling a "snake-oil" potion; and a parody of what passes for civilized conversation. Even Freud gets rather humorous treatment in these skits in the form of an Englishman who lugs a trunk onto stage that he tells an inquiring detective is his unconscious.

The last act of the play is a mixture of what had come before, yet with renewed intensity. There is another scene, this one quite tender between Him and Me in which the conversation, written like a series of prose poems, echoes many of Cummings's themes: love, nature, the mystery of life, and the inevitableness of death and loss. In the second scene, the Weird Sisters return and have a wonderfully absurd conversation laced with advertising slogans about guinea pigs, the gist of which is contained in this line: "He doesn't see why guineapigs can't have children if children can have guineapigs."

Scene III, reminiscent of the plays within the play of Act II, is a hilarious restaurant scene in Paris in which Cummings levels his sights on rich American tourists abroad. After another scene with the Weird Sisters, and another between Him and Me, the play reaches its climax in Scene VI. In this scene, Cummings wrote his love of the circus, particularly the sideshows, directly into *Him*. But this is hardly Ringling Brothers. Here, most of the characters from scenes in Act II, as well as the Weird Sisters, intermingle with various sideshow freaks, including the Eighteen Inch Lady, The Tattooed Man, Nine Foot Giant, Missing Link, Queen of Serpents, and various others. The Barker holds center stage, herding everyone across the stage, announcing the marvels and wonders to behold and yet to be beheld.

At the end of the scene, the crowd of onlookers gathers around a shrouded booth. After a long buildup by the Barker of the "cornbeefuncaviare uv duh hole shibang…Princess Anankay duh woil's foist un foremohs exponunt uv…duh Royal Umbilicul Bemgul Cakewalk," the Barker notices Him at the side of the stage. He beckons him over: "Crawl right up un all fives fellur give duh Princess uh fiftyfifty chawnce wid youse kiddo she'll boost your slendiferous bowlegged blueeyed exterior out uv duh peagreen interior uv pink poiple soopurconsciousness." But when the curtain is finally pulled back, the promised Princess is revealed as a woman in white holding a newborn. After a short interval, "the woman's figure proudly and gradually lifts it head: revealing the face of ME. HIM utters a cry of terror."

In the next and final scene of the play, Him and Me are alone in the same room in which they made their debut in the first act. There is no sign of a baby, nor talk of it. Instead, Him and Me converse about the set itself, Me pointing out that it only has three walls. This observation leads Me to notice that there is an audience beyond the invisible wall. Him then asks what the people are doing. "They're pretending that this room and you and I are real," says Me. Him responds that he wishes he could believe this but cannot; Me asks why he doubts. "Because this is true," replies Him. *Him* thus comes to a close.

This "plot" summary hardly conveys the power or poetry of Cummings's remarkable drama that pre-dated by a quarter century the theater of the absurd. Indeed, like the plays of Beckett, Genet, Ionesco, and other "absurdist" playwrights, Cummings's drama is less an attempt to present a story than to convey the essence of the human condition. Like all theater of the absurd, *Him* defies easy interpretation. Cummings, speaking through Him, in fact, instructs his audience not to try to find a specific meaning in the play: "It is about anything you like, about nothing and something and everything, about blood and thunder and love and death." At the same time, Cummings scatters clues throughout the drama about his intentions, as when Him reads to Me from his notebook:

> These solidities and silences which we call "things" are not separate units of experience, but are poses, self-organizing collections. There are no entities, no isolations, no abstractions; but there are departures, voyages, arrivals, contagions.... I do not stroke edges and I do not feel music but only metaphors. Metaphors are what comfort and astonish us.

"Departures, voyages, arrivals, contagions:" these are the elements of *Him*, the keys to the dramatic development that must be nonlinear because "self-organising collections" are not linear. Instead the action is presented as a series of metaphors—all scenes in the play are, in fact, metaphors—that "both comfort and astonish." Cummings's aim, therefore, can be seen as an attempt to express the wholeness of the human experience freed from logic and from the traditional emphasis on the exterior of that experience, rather than on its interior.

Roger Shattuck, one of the first critics to note Cummings's connection to the French theater of the first decades of the twentieth century, defines the type of artistic technique used in *Him* as "Simultanism:" "It found a childlike directness of expression free of any conventional order. It reproduced the compression and condensation of mental processes. It maintained an immediacy of relationship between conscious and subconscious thought. It encompassed surprise, humor, ambiguity, and the unfettered association of dream."

While Cummings was certainly in revolt against conventional theater that he considered "thoroughly dead" and "balderdash," his intent in *Him* was not simply to debunk this more staid notion of what constituted drama. Instead, he was attempting to offer the public a different experience of the theater, one that broke down the boundaries between audience and performers, that offered spectators a performance that was "intensely alive." Such aliveness for Cummings was occasionally present in contemporary performance, most notably in the avant-garde theater of Strindberg, Aragon, and Cocteau in which dreams and the unconscious figure prominently. Indeed, the scene with the mirror is reminiscent of Aragon's Dadaist play, *L'Armoire à glace un beau soir* [The Mirrored Wardrobe One Fine Evening], in which a husband believes his wife has hidden her lover in a mirrored armoire. Strindberg and Cocteau had paved the way for the dramatic exploitation of the non-logic of dreams; however, Cummings's primary models were popular entertainment: burlesque, the circus, and the Coney Island Amusement Park.

In three of Cummings's best pieces for *Vanity Fair*, written between 1925 and 1926, he made an eloquent case for these forms of entertainment as "art which is alive." In his article on burlesque, he argues that "what is frequently referred to as 'abstract,' 'cubistic' and even 'futuristic,' painting is fundamentally similar to such use of the American language as this…: 'so I pulled out my pickaxe and I cut his ear from throat to throat.' Moreover, those of my readers who are already acquainted with the 'neurotic' or 'ultra-modernistic' music of Arnold Schönberg will need no introduction to the agonizing tonality of those 'sets' and 'drops' among which the hero-villains of the burlesk stage shimmy, glide, strut and tumble."

The spectacle of the circus, too, was seen as being on a par with the best of artistic creations:

> The present writer wishes to state (1) that an extremely intimate connection exists between Con Colleanos' forward somersault (from and to a wire in mid-air) and Homer's Odyssey (2) that a sure method of understanding Igor Stravinsky's *Le Sacre du Printemps*, is to study the voluminous precision and fugal delicacy of Mr. Ringling's "Ponderous Pachyderms under the direction of the greatest of all animal trainers" (3) that El Greco, in painting, and "Ernest Clark, in his triple somersaulting and double-twisting and reverse flights through space" give strikingly similar performances, and (4) that the fluent technique of seals and of sea lions comprises certain untranslatable idioms, certain innate flexions, which astonishingly resemble the spiritual essence of poetry.

In essence, Cummings is saying that the circus is as much an art form as literature, music, or painting, and that an astute observer can learn as much about the intricacies of enthralling an audience by studying this popular entertainment. In other words, Homer's suspenseful storytelling is akin to the exquisite sense of timing necessary for an aerialist; Stravinsky's precise manipulation of seemingly chaotic sound patterns is not so different from an animal trainer's mastery over obstreperous elephants. As for the "fluent technique" of barking seals, he is making a case for sound, rhythm, and cadence as essential components of poetry.

But Coney Island, which in Cummings's eyes meshed "the theatre with the circus," was perhaps his biggest inspiration. Not only did his idea for a painted backdrop with holes cut out for heads probably derive from those at the amusement park, but so did his notion, expressed most directly in the last scene of *Him*, that the audience is an integral part of the performance.

The brilliance of Cummings was to see the potential in these popular forms of "theatre" and then fuse them with his own avant-garde tendencies in order to create a drama that ultimately made some very serious statements about the future of performance itself in which the barriers between audience and actors are broken down, as is the barricade that separates the conscious from the unconscious, or dreams from waking life. It is not necessary to produce a masterpiece to make an important contribution to art, and *Him* was not a masterpiece. But it was distinctive, compelling, and unique, a work way ahead of its time.

When Cummings returned to New York from New Hampshire in September 1926, *Him* was nearly completed. By October he had given the play to a typist to prepare for submission to Carol Brandt of the literary agency Brandt & Brandt, to whom he had been introduced by one of the other authors they represented, John Dos Passos.

During Cummings's absence over the summer, Barton had tidied up his room at Patchin Place, even buying a new bed. Cummings was pleased with Barton's decorating touches, a sign, he thought, that she was taking a real interest in his life. The matter of Douglas, however, still lingered. Indeed, her theme song could have been lifted from Cole Porter's lyric "I'm always true to you darling in my fashion." But Cummings decided it was easier to believe Barton's statements that she did not any longer exchange sex with Douglas for money and goods, because he wanted to see it that way. In love, he decided to put his energy into the relationship, perhaps in the process ensuring a future with her. It was apparently not difficult to believe: Barton continually professed her own love to Cummings.

On the evening of November 2, 1926, Cummings and Barton were at a get-together at the apartment of their friend, the writer Morrie Werner, when Cummings's sister, Elizabeth, now living in New York, arrived and asked to speak privately with her brother. The news she brought was terrible: on the way to New Hampshire in a blinding snowstorm, their father and mother had been struck by a train while crossing the railroad tracks; their father was killed instantly, their mother was alive, but barely. Cummings and Elizabeth were on the next train to New Hampshire.

"A day later," Cummings recalled, "my sister and I entered a small darkened room in a country hospital. She [Rebecca] was still alive—why, the head doctor couldn't imagine. She wanted only one thing: to join the person she loved most. He was very near her, but she could not quite reach him. We spoke, and she recognized our voices. Gradually her own voice began to understand what its death would mean to these living children of hers; and very gradually a miracle happened. She decided to live."

Over the next day or so, Cummings and his sister learned more of the details of the accident. On their way to Silver Lake in their new Franklin, Edward and Rebecca were caught in a snowstorm in the Ossipee Mountains. Rebecca was driving, but her visibility was impaired. Edward finally persuaded Rebecca to stop so that he could clear the windshield. He then got back in the car and Rebecca drove on. "Some minutes later," according to Cummings, "a locomotive cut the car in half.... When two brakemen jumped from the halted train, they saw a woman standing—dazed but erect—beside a mangled machine; with blood 'spouting' (as the older said to me) out of her head. One of her hands (the younger added) kept feeling of her dress, as if trying to discover why it was wet. These men took my sixty-six year old mother by the arms and tried to lead her toward a nearby farmhouse; but she threw them off, strode straight to my father's body, and directed a group of scared spectators to cover him. When this had been done (and only then) she let them lead her away."

Within a few days, Rebecca began to improve, but she kept telling her children that there was something wrong with her head. Cummings and his sister began to understand gradually that she did not mean her fractured skull. "As days and nights passed," explained Cummings, "we accidentally discovered that this ghastly wound had been sewn up by candlelight when all the town lights went out at once." Cummings and his sister made a decision to transfer her by ambulance to Peter Bent Brigham Hospital in Boston. According to Cummings, Rebecca actually enjoyed the ambulance ride. "She conversed cheerfully with its chauffeur, and refused to lie down because by doing so she'd miss the scenery en route. We shot through towns and tore through cities. 'I like going fast' she told us; beaming."

Once in Boston she was operated on immediately and insisted that she be able to watch the procedure in a hand mirror. She emerged from the operating room in a wheelchair, "very erect, and waving triumphantly a small bottle in which (at her urgent request) [the surgeon had] placed the dirt and grime and splinters of whose existence his predecessor had been blissfully unaware. 'You see?' she cried to us, smiling 'I was right!'"

With Rebecca on the way to recovery, Cummings finally allowed himself to grieve for his father. He was glad for the rapprochement that had occurred the year before when he had finally been able to offer comfort and consolation to Edward after his discharge from the ministry. He also felt pangs of guilt over some of the harsh rebukes he had directed toward his father, regretted his occasional "asinine behaviour." At the large funeral held in Forest Hills Cemetery in Boston at the end of November 1926, he sobbed as he listened to the eulogies spoken for the "great good man."

He set down his own reflections five or six years later:

how dark and single,where he ends,the earth
(whose texture feels of pride and loneliness
alive like some dream giving more than all
life's busy little dyings may possess)

how sincere large distinct and natural
he comes to his disappearance;as a mind
full without fear might faithfully lie down
to so much sleep they only understand

enormously which fail—look:with what ease
that bright how plural tide measures her guest
(as critics will upon a poet feast)

meanwhile this ghost goes under,his drowned girth
are mountains;and beyond all hurt of praise
the unimaginable night not known

This was not a eulogy, but a meditation. But the eulogy would come:

my father moved through dooms of love
through sames of am through haves of give,
singing each morning out of each night
my father moved through depths of height

this motionless forgetful where
turned at his glance to shining here;

that if(so timid air is firm)
under his eyes would stir and squirm...

"my father moved through dooms of love" would become one of Cummings's best known poems.

Other unsettling news also reached Cummings late in 1926: Thayer, who had been becoming increasingly unstable, had suffered a major nervous breakdown and was hospitalized in his hometown of Worcester. Cummings was not totally surprised. For at least two years he had been aware that Thayer was deteriorating mentally, and had witnessed first-hand his mounting paranoia. At the same time, he had not fully realized how truly disturbed and delusional his friend had become. Indeed, when Watson informed him that he had procured a handgun for Thayer during the summer of 1925, Cummings was nonplussed. After all, Watson had helped him obtain a gun the year before. Even Thayer's letters to Cummings in which he ranted and raved about a rival art collector, Dr. Albert Barnes, who he claimed "was out to get [him]" did not seem to indicate to Cummings the extent of Thayer's personality disorder.

Cummings did express disappointment on learning that Thayer had decided to resign from the *Dial*, but the news was hardly shocking. Even before the official announcement in June 1926, Cummings was well aware that Thayer was devoting himself more and more to collecting art, and that his interest in the day-to-day business of the magazine was flagging. It was no secret to Cummings that for most of 1926 Thayer had largely turned over the handling of editorial and business matters to Watson and Marianne Moore, who upon Thayer's resignation became the journal's editor.

Only one example of Thayer's erratic behavior seemed to have sparked Cummings's attention: when a man showed up at Patchin Place to inquire about a "man named Thayer" whom he claimed had seduced his sixteen-year-old son. In a letter to Elaine he told her of the incident: "He asked if I'd seen any boys at [Thayer's] apartment,etc. My denials are emphatic and distinct.... Obviously his chief interest was in finding out whether my friendship with T. was a homosexual one:at one moment I burst out laughing and said: My dear fellow,if you think I'm homosexual I can tell you I am not.... The rest of the time I assumed the attitude that his suggestions were 'preposterous.'" Although the visit was disturbing and he wanted Elaine to make sure that she did not compromise Thayer in case the man showed up at her door, Thayer's pederastic proclivities were seen by Cummings simply as that, not as any form of madness.

But Thayer's collapse this time was very serious. Dr. Watson went twice to visit him in January and reported that Thayer had been diagnosed as schizophrenic, an assessment with which he seemed to concur. "Meanwhile it does not look as though he were being done harm at the Worcester hospital," wrote Watson in January 1927, "at least he seemed improved the second time I saw him."

Despite Watson's optimism, Thayer never recovered. He spent the next fifty-five years—he died in 1982—either institutionalized or in home care. While many, like Cummings and Watson, initially wrote or visited him, within a year or so of his decline he stopped replying to letters and his attendants turned visitors away. Thayer's business advisor, Hermann Riccius wrote, "I feel that Scofield's mind is, as it were, in a dream from which he is not to be roused by any means we are aware of, and our actions toward him are no doubt presented to his intellect through the phases of a terrible dream."

Cummings's last visit to Thayer was in October of 1930, prompted by a surprise telegram from Thayer inviting him to come see him at his home in Worcester. The visit was brief, and Cummings came away feeling that his friend was a "captive of his nurses and mother," unable either to express himself freely or even or exert any semblance of control over his life.

It was a tragic end to a man who had been a luminary, a true mover and shaker in the world of art, a person, in Cummings's words, of "courage and courtesy, taste and intelligence, prodigious patience and incredible generosity."

Cummings had not seen Nancy, now seven years old, for a year, even though the MacDermots had moved from Tuxedo Park to Manhattan that fall. It is unclear why the long gap in visits came about, but it seems that Cummings, involved with Barton and his work, then absent in Europe for several months, and later preoccupied over his mother's accident and his father's death, had largely given up on visitation. But Elaine had hardly been cooperative even before any of these events had transpired, giving Cummings more than ample reason to feel the case was hopeless. She—and never Nancy—had curtly acknowledged the receipt of gifts from Cummings or his family. In addition, Elaine had suffered two (probably psychosomatic) paralyses of her hips that left her immobile for months at a time. In February 1927, however, the matter resurfaced when Cummings received a cable from Elaine asking him to legally cancel his adoption of Nancy. An infuriated Cummings responded that he would do no such thing and urged his mother to "hold on tight to any adoption papers or other documents."

Rebecca, now fully recuperated, was equally disturbed at this turn of events. On February 23, 1927, she wrote a courteous but frank letter to Elaine: "As you know I have been, and still am, ready and eager to have N[ancy] at any time and to pay her expenses while she is with me—You have always refused to let her come, even for a visit, and E[stlin] has been repeatedly denied, even his right to see her. You will pardon me if I cannot see that to be E[stlin]'s daughter will be 'injurious' to N and I personally think 'skeletons' are better not 'shut up in closets.' In any case, let me assure you that he and I stand ready to accept our responsibilities for Nancy and to do our best for her."

Elaine backed down in her demand. It seems the flurry of communication resulted in Cummings being able to have a visit again with Nancy. On March 4, 1927, he wrote his mother excitedly:

> I've seen Nancy! She looked pale,and Elaine said she was underweight and small for her age—you may imagine my reaction—but Nancy and I had a wonderful time walking up and down the room,joking,imitating each other,and making fun of things in general. Then we drew pictures for each other—eight of hers are on the mantlepiece here.

Elaine was present throughout the visit and later MacDermot showed up as well. Fortunately, Cummings's longtime friend, Stewart Mitchell, who had continued to maintain relations with Elaine, also arrived. "He immediately sensed his part," wrote Cummings, "and took care of the MacDermots conversationally,so that Nancy and I could play together."

Though Cummings did not know it at the time, this would be the last time he would see Nancy until she was an adult. Within a month the MacDermot's moved to Ireland. The custody battle was over—decisively lost by Cummings. Nancy Thayer would grow to adulthood thinking that Thayer was her father.

Although Cummings had given *Him* to his new literary agents in November of 1926, they were not able to find either a producer or publisher for the play. Cummings had sent a copy to Marianne Moore in October who was quite taken with its ingenuity. In a letter on November 5, 1926, she asked Watson whether he would consider publishing excerpts from it in the magazine, noting that she thought the play "good, and, perhaps foolishly, told [Cummings] so." Watson, agreed to Moore's suggestion, asking Cummings to have Brandt & Brandt send it on to the *Dial*. Moore made an initial selection; Watson, by now equally enthusiastic, selected additional scenes to add for publication. By the time the excerpts were published—in August 1927—*Him* had found a publisher. It was again Liveright who took a chance on the play, issuing it in October 1927. It was dedicated to Anne Barton.

Though grateful to Liveright for being willing to publish the play in book form, Cummings, as usual, wrangled with Liveright over word cuts the editor felt had to be made because of their obscenity. The most serious argument was over the ribald version of "Frankie and Johnie" (supplied by Edmund Wilson) in which Cummings had the lines "and there she saw her Johnie / just a finger fucking Fanny Fry." Liveright suggested alternatives. In the end the line was published with dashes rather than "finger fucking." Cummings could not bring himself to offer a euphemism.

The play was also beginning to attract the attention of theater companies. Lawrence Langer, a director at the Theatre Guild, who had been given a copy of the play by Muriel Draper, was quite enthusiastic; but, because of the obscenities in the play could not get the Guild to take it on. Meanwhile Henry Alsberg, a director at the Provincetown Playhouse, the company that had brought Eugene O'Neill to fame, had read the play over the summer while in Europe. When he returned to New York, he told his fellow board members—Eugene O'Neill, James Light, and M. Eleanor Fitzgerald—that "*Him* had to be done." O'Neill's opinion is not recorded; Light apparently liked the play but felt it presented enormous technical difficulties. Fitzgerald, on the other hand, was totally enthusiastic, eventually convincing the others that Alsberg was right. According to Cummings, "*Him* was only produced by the Provincetown Players because Fitzi insisted that it should be." By the end of 1927, *Him* was announced for the 1928 season.

Despite the good news, Cummings could not fully revel in his triumph. The problem was Barton. Over the summer he, Barton, and Diana, now six, had gone up to Silver Lake and had greatly enjoyed themselves. He felt he had drawn closer to Diana, and without the distraction of parties and the attention of Douglas, Barton had seemed a different person, as well. But upon their return to New York at the end of August, the relationship dramatically crumbled. She not only immediately hooked up with Douglas again, she also began seeing a younger man, Peter Finley Dunne. For Anne, the new affair was simply a fling, nothing more. She attempted to assure Cummings that she was only "following her impulses," but that she still loved him. Cummings, on the other hand, could not accept her dismissal of the romance as infatuation. For him, it signaled only crass betrayal.

On September 4, 1927, he wrote to his mother that he was "through with Anne." "Needless to add, I stood as much as I could—then retreated. I think this will(if anything)help her. So,as the French say,'Courage'! That's what I'm trying to think about." Six days later, however, he wrote Rebecca that Barton had gotten a job as a fashion model at $100 a week, and that the situation between them was improving. This letter was followed by another two days afterward in which he informed his mother that he and Barton had "made up."

But less than a week later, the reconciliation was no more: "Anne is, to use her own words,'just rapidly disintegrating'. Threw up her job after a halfhour or so.... The only thing which could possibly keep us together now is her love of Joy Farm." Money was also an issue. She "wants money," Cummings told his mother, "but wants it handed to her in the shape of 'support' by a husband." Cummings, who in his words was "a moneyless beloved," was hardly in a position to support her the way she wanted. As a result, she felt justified in returning to Douglas "who has money,buys her giddy things,pays her rent,promises that he'll give Diana $50,000." Cummings countered that she should "earn her way out of this mess," a proposition that went nowhere: "She lacks ambition to do that;or rather,she thinks she's too good to work for her living again and good enough to get a rich husband."

Toward the end of September they again reconciled briefly; perhaps because Cummings agreed to pay her way to Europe for a brief trip. When she returned on October 22, 1927, eight days after Cummings's thirty-third birthday, he had hopes that perhaps a change of scene had done her some good. But when he arrived at the pier, Douglas was waiting for her. He returned to Patchin Place alone.

He recorded the aftermath in his notes:

> After many pleading notes, the last being double—birthday letter,plea—A[nne] (whose Homeric arrived at 10 AM)came to P[atchin] P[lace] about 4:30.... Only 2 hours sleep since she left(Sept 24),drinking all the time,nothing but champagne,enjoyed herself tremendously,never laughed so much,her laugh rang out "all over the Homeric" & "god knows the H[omeric] needed it," everything "swell" or "grand", shook the dice at social functions with "the pretty girls on the ship" (coming back) men all the way over (Isle de France) Slept with people? I ask "O don't let's go into that.... Not with people,only 1 person...and so handsome.... I'm not sorry;I'm glad I did it. I think it was part of the change.... I needed to do it but that's all over." I thank her for telling me, "O you'd have known anyhow." Shows cable "To my princess whom I love." "O it was all very incestuous—everyone thought we were brother and sister—we looked alike." I ask: Did he look like your brother? "O no. Like me."

As difficult as this situation obviously was for Cummings, he did not break with Barton. He had already decided during her absence that she should undergo psychoanalysis and had even asked Watson for a referral Now, even more, he thought a psychiatrist might help her moderate what he felt were frequent manifestations of manic-depressive behavior. He had also come to believe that her promiscuity was linked to the sexual abuse she had experienced as a child.

The psychiatrist he chose to help Barton was Dr. A. A. Brill, "supposed to be one of America's foremost, translated Freud's Traumdetung,etc." But Brill was expensive. As a result, he wrote his mother asking her for one thousand dollars from his share of the estate left to him by his father. "I love Anne," he explained to Rebecca, "and I should like her to be happy in herself—I've done my best;all I can do now is to let a better mind than mine—an impartial mind—do its best. She deserves her freedom,if that's to be her fate,or I deserve her love,if that's to be my fate."

Rebecca had already given Cummings one thousand dollars not long after his father died, but he had used this mainly to commission a bust of himself from Lachaise and to send Barton to Paris. His mother immediately sent him the money.

He recorded the results of the sessions with Brill in his notes:

> Women need luxury.
>
> I have no right to interfere with her promiscuity, since I have not enough money to compete with Douglas—albeit my objections are normal.
>
> All women who have had sexual relations with their father are promiscuous always.
>
> For a large sum he could analyze her & perhaps remove her father complex but this would be useless unless she had money, so let her come back to him [Brill] after she's married money!
>
> She is neurotic,but has no neurosis. "A victim of circumstances—" "unhappy childhood."

To his mother he reported a more succinct version of her sessions with Brill: "He sized her [Barton] up as a golddigger. This did not please A[nne], as you may guess." In the same letter he also explained the complications facing Barton: "Her merchant prince has promised her $75,000 for Diana when he dies & gives A the income while he lives. But A is convinced that if she married someone else,the mp [merchant prince] would withdraw Diana's inheritance(as well as her own income). I cannot support A(in the luxury to which she is accustomed—i.e. $7,500 a year)."

Barton apparently did not return to Brill for further sessions; Cummings, though, did seek out a psychiatrist for himself, but did not go for more than a few consultations. Unable or unwilling to change her behavior, Barton, at twenty-nine, four years younger than Cummings, continued to cause her lover grief. But he could not give her up. Despite himself, he was in love with her, and continued to feel (although it is hard to see why) that eventually she would be able to cease her shenanigans and make a life with him. During the short periods in which she seemed devoted to him, and him alone, he was totally enthralled with her. She was fun, witty, engaging, sexy, and demonstratively adoring of him. Indeed, between the moments of darkness and despair there were interludes of drinking and partying, in which both Cummings and Barton played the couple.

Hart Crane recalled a particularly wild night in November 1927: "After a riotous competition with Cummings and Anne in which (I don't *know* but I'm sure) I won the cocktail competition I found myself in Clark St. station along about 3 o'clock playing with somebody's lost airedale. The cop who rushed at me, asking me what I was doing is reported to have been answered by 'why the hell do you want to know?!!!'" Duly arrested, Crane spent the night in jail. But the next day he was back at Cummings's apartment. "Beer with Cummings in the afternoon which was almost better than evening before, as C's hyperbole is even more amusing than one's conduct, especially when he undertakes a description of what you don't remember. Anyhow I never had so much fun jounced into 24 hours before, and if I had my way would take both C'gs and Anne along with me to heaven when I go."

But by the end of the year, Cummings was once again in the doldrums. On December 30 Barton returned from a holiday visit to her mother in upstate New York, and dropped by to see Cummings. The visit was disturbing: "Anne was a completely different person—scarcely able to sit still because she's been drunk for so long—venomous when she wasn't malicious—telling of one mean deed after another with relish—in short, more destructive,more unhappy,than I've ever seen her in my life(and I've seen her quite both). The mania is certainly at its height(or rather depth). I actually feel that the only thing for me is to pray,and I do."

What Cummings prayed for is uncertain, but the day after writing this letter a temporary exit from the situation presented itself in the form of Emily Davies Vanderbilt, whom he met at a New Year's Eve party hosted by Muriel Draper. At the time Cummings met Vanderbilt, she was in the process of divorcing William Vanderbilt, great-grandson of the railroad tycoon, Cornelius Vanderbilt. Blonde, statuesque, charming, and gorgeous,

Emily Vanderbilt spent most of the evening talking and drinking with Cummings. Within a few days they were in bed together.

Some years later Emily was described by Thomas Wolfe, who portrayed her as Amy Carelton in *You Can't Go Home Again*, as a woman who "was many things, but no one could call her good." But at the time Cummings knew her, she was far less "notorious" than she would become. Indeed, as Cummings noted, "the lady has played me straight." Their affair was brief, lasting for about two months, but it seemed to have regenerated Cummings.

The fling with Vanderbilt, whether intentional on Cummings's part or not, also resulted in Barton launching a major effort to win back her lover. A wary Cummings was not immediately receptive to Barton's pleas, but gradually she began to win him over. As rehearsals began for *Him* in late February of 1928, Barton and Cummings were seeing each other again, though they were not officially back together. Cummings, in fact, was enjoying his freedom, relishing opportunities to have other women. Besides Vanderbilt, he also had a brief affair with Hazel Webster, a pianist at Sam Schwartz's Black Knight Club, a place he frequented during the rehearsals of the play. The relationship with Webster was purely physical, consisting apparently of only a few nights together.

He found Patty Light, the wife of *Him*'s director, James Light, enormously attractive and charming, as well. At some point that spring, the two of them ended up in bed. In his notes Cummings recorded that "she was good to screw but we only did it once." It is not clear whether James Light immediately knew of the one night stand, but within a couple of months he was certainly aware of it when Patty learned she was pregnant. The three discussed the matter at this point as she believed Cummings was the father. Cummings breathed a major sigh of relief when "Jimmy persuaded her to have an abortion." Neither man was ready for a child, and given the uncertainty of paternity, Patty was apparently not too keen on having a baby either. The friendship between the three of them continued amicably.

This brush with potential fatherhood did not seem to damper Cummings's desire for further sexual exploits. William Carlos Williams reported in a letter to Ezra Pound that Cummings "is said to have his door open on Patchin Pl. #4 for any woman who wants to be fucked—and he does it all the time. Gossip perhaps." While hardly a prude, Williams worried that Cummings was giving himself over too much to women and wine: "[He] seems to be drunk most of the time.... God knows what will become of him.... Going to hell. Wish to god I could see more of him. For what? Just the manners of a graceful (drunken) mind—lost in fucking perhaps, I dunno."

Williams need not have fretted about his friend. Despite Cummings's excesses (or at least a desire for them) he was not allowing anything to draw him too far away from his major creative focus that spring: the production of *Him*.

eighteen

Viva Cummings

Him presented the Provincetown Playhouse with a number of production obstacles. How to stage the play was the first and foremost consideration in the mind of James Light, who was chosen to direct. The play had seventy-two roles, which did not include "crowds, beggars, black figures, jazz dancers, shapes," thus raising the cast to somewhere around 105 members. Since there was no way so many actors could be employed (or paid), Light, Cummings, and the set designer Eugene Fitsch created a series of charts in order to determine how the same actors could play a variety of roles. Eventually they succeeded in compressing the cast to thirty.

With this problem solved, they turned to that of the physical set. Since the theater had no wings nor overhead flies, scene shifting—and there were twenty-one scenes—was not easy. "The problem was to rig the stage," remembered Light. "Cummings had a designer's sense; by his direction, the room was turned out—a really magical thing." The magic was actually a technical solution: the stagehands, with help from cast members, lowered scenery through a trap door—really a slot in mid stage—into the cellar. "The actors rehearsed scene changing like a military drill," recalled Henry Alsberg, who had brought the play to the theater company. Eventually they managed to change the set in ten seconds.

The other problem was financing, for which Cummings was no help. *Him* required six thousand dollars to present, three times more than the average production. Watson put up some money, as did Felix Warburg and Mrs. Harry Payne Whitney. Muriel Draper also raised funds from her uptown friends, and put in some of her own money.

Casting the play was not easy, either. Because the acting budget was frozen at eight hundred dollars a week, it was hard to attract established talent. In the end, however, they did manage to cast all the parts, all with relatively unknown actors. William Johnstone, just twenty years old, who had previously only played small parts in other plays, was given the role of Him. Erin O'Brien-Moore, a former model with little acting experience, was cast as Me. Lawrence Bolton played The Doctor (and a good many other roles).

As written, the play was four hours long. It was obvious that *Him* had to be cut, but Light, Alsberg, and Cummings made the decision to rehearse the play in its entirety so that Cummings could best hear and see where cuts were needed. Light remembered that "after the second week of rehearsal, he began to cut the script to tighten it. He's a dramatist—he could see where he had overproved his point, and cut." The playwright was fascinated with the rehearsals, and actively participated. "When actors wanted a reading of a line, they went to Cummings," recalled Light. "They found out more from him than I could ever give them in direction."

Cummings was also delighted by the performances: "William Johnstone made a marvelously attractive unhero,& lovely Erin O'Brien-Moore proved an absolutely perfect Me; while the vivid versatilities of Lawrence Bolton as The Doctor more than amazed everyone (including perhaps himself)."

Him, or as the program had it, *him* by e.e. cummings—the first appearance of Cummings's name and title all in lowercase—opened on April 18, 1928, to a packed audience. Among those in attendance were William Slater Brown, poet Louis Zukofsky, William Carlos Williams, and Malcolm Cowley. In anticipation of possible difficulties his audience might have with the drama, Cummings wrote a "Warning" that was included in the program. It concluded with these remarks: "Relax and give the PLAY a chance to strut its stuff—relax, don't worry because it's not like something else—relax, stop wondering what its all 'about'—like many strange and familiar things, Life included, this PLAY isn't 'about,' it simply is. Don't try to despise it, let it try to despise you. Don't try to enjoy it, let it try to enjoy you. DON'T TRY TO UNDERSTAND IT, LET IT TRY TO UNDERSTAND YOU."

The spectators apparently took Cummings's words to heart. *Him* played to a packed house for its entire run of twenty-seven performances.

It would have continued running even longer, but the revenue from ticket sales could not outpace the costs of production. One of the more enthusiastic spectators was William Carlos Williams who began proclaiming to anyone who would listen that *Him* was the most original play he had ever seen. After the play closed, he invited Cummings out to his house in Paterson, New Jersey, to tell him so in person. In his autobiography, Williams recalled the visit:

> It was a very quiet day, no one on the streets. I had given him [Cummings] specific instructions how to get here, so that when it got to be nearly one o'clock, knowing his reputation for indifference to conventional order, I went out to look for him.
>
> I shall not forget the impression I got of a lone person meandering up a deserted Park Avenue stopping at every store window to look intently in at the shoes, ladies wear, now and then a bank window perhaps, or at an Easter card, or a brace and bit in Dow's hardware store.
>
> Mother had fixed up a chicken. Afterward we talked, if one could talk during such a visitation. Mother was interested because his father had been a Unitarian minister—not that she wasn't alert to his general aspects. We had a batch of Persian kittens in the kitchen at that time. We played with them on the dining room table. He thought they resembled birds in the nest.

The majority of critics, however, were far from enthusiastic. The negative response did not surprise Cummings, for the play had already been bashed when it was issued as a book in November of 1927. Edmund Wilson, writing in the *New Republic* shortly after *Him*'s publication, did understand what Cummings was attempting to achieve. "*Him*, for all its stretches of balderdash and its admixture of puerilities, [is] a book which should be read by all persons who prefer the real thing in literature, no matter how drunk and disorderly, to the well-intentioned imitation, no matter how carefully dressed. It may be that in the wit, the fantasy and the lyric beauty of *Him* we find the germ of an important dramatic poet."

Poet Louis Zukofsky, in a review of the play for Ezra Pound's short-lived magazine *Exile*, was even more enthused: "Mr. Cummings is not merely the perfect acrobat or the genius carefully, yet easily and very skillfully inhabiting everything which we really are and everything which we never quite live. His intention is not to be serious, but to be very serious and get away with it."

But the insights of Wilson and Zukofsky were not shared by most reviewers of either the book or its performance. Indeed, only one drama critic, John Anderson of the *New York Journal*, found any merit in the play at all. He first noted "the quivering intensity of its writing...lyrically lovely, with a felicity of phrasing that is often superb," and concluded by saying that "*him* is provocative theatre." But Anderson was a lone voice. The dozen other reviewers of the production despised it. Comments like these from George Jean Nathan were typical: "incoherent, illiterate, preposterous balderdash, as completely and unremittingly idiotic as the human mind, when partly sober, can imagine." Or these of Alexander Wolcott: "fatiguing, pretentious and empty." Brooks Atkinson's bash of the play in the *New York Times* elicited a response from John Dos Passos who noted that in tandem with "modernism in painting and with the psychology of Freud...[*Him*] attempts to generate feelings and ideas rather than put them immediately up to the understanding, and...aims to express sensations rather than tell about them." He concluded by admonishing Cummings's critics: "It won't do you any good to curse at it for not being like 'Broadway.'"

Just as Dos Passos had taken up cudgels on behalf of his friend, so too did the playhouse itself. During the second week of its run, they issued a sixteen-page pamphlet entitled *him AND the CRITICS* in which they printed alternative assessments of the play. Contributors defending the play included critics such as Edmund Wilson, Stark Young, and Foster Damon, as well as fellow poets Conrad Aiken, William Rose Benét, and Genevieve Taggard. Gilbert Seldes wrote the introduction.

The battle lines over *Him* were interesting. On one hand were intellectuals and artists along with the general theater-going public who fully supported the play; on the other were the drama critics of the New York papers, who, accustomed to the tamer fare of Broadway, simply could not see nor accept that *Him* was not only breaking new ground in the theater, but that it was doing so rather magnificently. The victory ultimately went to Cummings whose startlingly original drama would pave the way for the theater of the absurd a quarter-century later.

Noise Number 13 *(1925), the last of* Cummings*'s major abstract oils, which he described as a "Forwardflung backwardSpinning hoop."*

A Cummings self-portrait, circa 1930.

The mercurial and promiscuous Anne Barton, Cummings's second wife, decked out in fashionable mid-1920s flapper garb.

Cummings's sexual fantasies often found their way into erotic sketches, such as this one of a young, nude woman posing.

Anne Barton and her daughter by a first marriage, Diana, pose on the shore of Silver Lake in the summer of 1928.

Sketch of Anne Barton from the mid-1920s. Despite her rather cruel treatment of him, Cummings found her charms hard to resist.

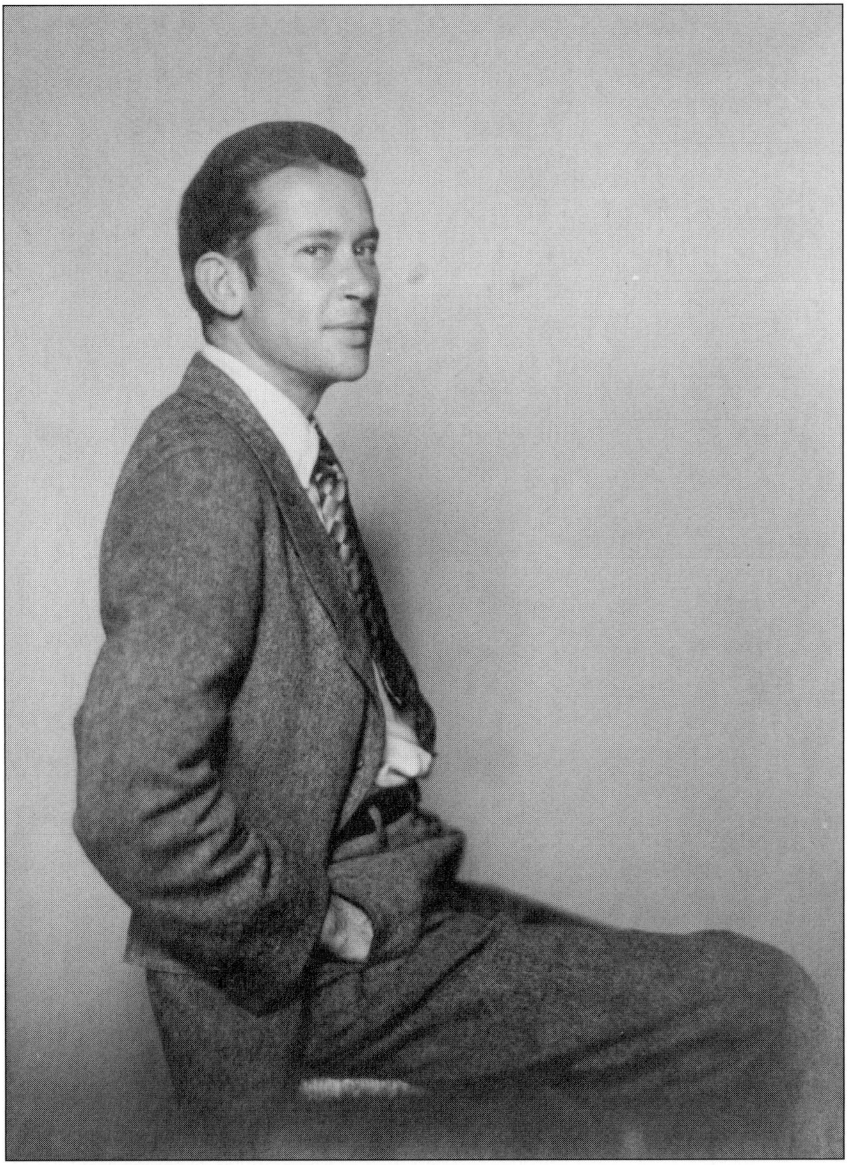

Cummings in a photo from the 1930s by his friend and patron James Sibley Watson, taken at Cummings's long time Patchin Place residence.

*Reverend Edward Cummings and Rebecca Cummings,
the poet's parents, in a photo from the mid-1920s.*

Marion Morehouse, whom Cummings met in 1933, in a fashion shot from the early 1930s.

Drawing of Marion Morehouse from around 1940.
Marion, a photographer and model, loved to pose for Cummings.

Ezra Pound, one of Cummings's closest friends and allies in making literature new, at about the time of his release from St. Elizabeth's hospital in 1957. Note the photo of Cummings in the background.

Cummings in a photo taken by Manuel Komroff in 1939 or 1940.

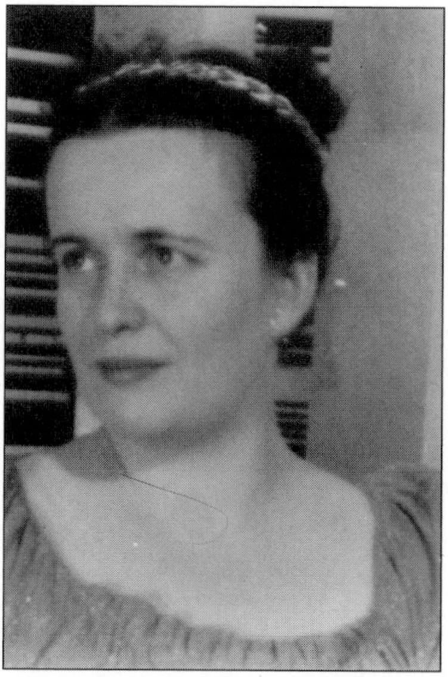

Marion Morehouse in a photo from the mid-1950s. She shared Cummings's life from 1933 to 1962.

Rebecca Cummings at Joy Farm in the 1940s.
Even in her old age Rebecca doted on her only son.

A reflective Cummings, a few years before his death in 1962, poses for an author's photograph on the porch at the summer house at Joy Farm.

The last photo (summer, 1962) of Cummings who stands with Marion in the yard at Joy Farm.

The Provincetown Playhouse did not need further verification of Cummings's achievement. Or as Light said, "I am very proud of doing this play. The Provincetown was the place for poets. We were off Broadway in two senses—it was located at 133 MacDougal Street, and it was 'off' Broadway spiritually. We gave the bird a chance to sing, and when he sang, we asked for his next work." This "next work" was actually announced for the next season, but Cummings, despite the happiness he had discovered in the theater, could not come up with a new play for the following year. If he had intended to produce a play for the year after, he would have had to have found a new venue: the Provincetown Playhouse went out of business in December 1929.

Although Cummings was rarely interested in writing anything anybody else thought he should, why he did not attempt to capitalize quickly on his public success probably had more to do with changes in his life rather than with reluctance to produce a play "on demand."

The main change was the renewal of his relationship with Barton whom he had been seeing off and on during the rehearsals and run of *Him*. By late spring Barton and Cummings were a couple again, making plans to go to Europe for the summer. In early July, along with Barton's daughter, Diana, and Rebecca (who was now living in New York), they traveled to Paris for six weeks. Perhaps the calming and benign presence of Cummings's mother helped to make the trip a pleasant one, for all accounts indicate that the travelers were a picture of domestic harmony. Cummings delighted in showing his mother *his* Paris, something he had not been able to do when she and Edward had previously visited. And Rebecca was more than willing to look after Diana, leaving the lovers plenty of time to explore the city on their own. When they returned that fall to New York, the connection between them was still strong.

It is unclear whether Barton was still involved with Douglas or others during that fall of 1928, but it seems that she was becoming increasingly devoted to Cummings. Perhaps Cummings was simply coming to terms with the situation, in part because around the end of the year he began an extensive round of psychoanalysis with a Viennese follower of Freud, Fritz Wittels. Wittels and Cummings connected from the beginning. Wittels apparently found Cummings interesting as a patient; Cummings declared Wittels "a genius." Between December 1928 and February 1929 Cummings met with Wittels on thirty-five occasions, paying out during this period $975 for the consultations. Cummings felt the money was worth it. Or as he wrote: "He symbolizes for me the merciful(the miraculous)non-necessity for any convention,any rule or rote or repetition—the privilege of one particular individual to(entirely on his own)explore some totally new dimension;he is the poet of Freedom & Opening;his tenderness is fearless." Their relationship, which evolved over the years into a friendship, continued until Wittels's death in 1950.

From Cummings's notes, it is evident that he felt Wittels was quite helpful to him. The "wise doctor" forced his patient to examine not just the situations in which he found himself, but to probe their causes, to see how at times he aided in creating his own misery. He pushed Cummings to examine his life from childhood onward and helped him see the role his father played in his development and attitudes, as why it was necessary for Cummings to rebel. He prodded Cummings to unravel his actual feelings about Elaine, about fatherhood, and about Barton. The upshot was that Cummings began to see that his rebellion against accepting responsibility for his own actions was costing him psychically. Or as he wrote:

> I have never grown up
> assumed the responsibilities of a man
> I prefer to have a mistress because it won't hurt me so much
> when I lose her (as, a wife)
> Self-pity = comfort

Ironically, his father had told him the same thing on more than one occasion, but he could *hear* it from Wittels.

It was apparently his desire to assume "the responsibilities of a man" that prompted this announcement to his mother (who was visiting Cummings's aunt in Cambridge) on March 26, 1929: "I feel like marrying Anne! Please keep it a <u>secret</u>—but please also let me have my divorce papers(aren't they in Cambridge safe deposit vaults?)as she says we must show our proof of asunder(respective)in order to legally unite(collective).

On May 1, 1929, Cummings, then thirty-four, and Barton, thirty, married at All Souls (Unitarian) Church at Fourth Avenue and 20th Street. Dos Passos was best man; his mother and sister were the official "witnesses." Barton, Cummings, and others spent the days leading up to the ceremony in an alcohol haze. Edmund Wilson has left this account of the event:

> Dos [Passos] with his withered bachelor's button—drinking at Hoboken—they had been stewed for days—married in what they called "the church of the Holy Zebra"—Dos had put them through it—Cummings had taken several baths, one after the other; he had felt his arms and legs getting numb, as if they weren't there—Ann [*sic*] went to sleep and slept for days and couldn't wake up—awful moment just before the ceremony (Cummings's mother and sister were there) when, after everything had been most nonchalant and amiable, they all began snapping at one another.
>
> The sad German band—we had them come to the table and play the wedding march. —Cummings looked unusually washed and well and carried things off with an excellent easy distinguished manner.

On May 3, Cummings, Anne, and Diana sailed for Europe for an extended honeymoon trip that would last until the end of July. They had not been in Paris long before they met up with Anne's former husband, Ralph Barton, and his new wife, French composer Germaine Tailleferre, a member of the renowned circle known in France as *Les Six*. It seems the encounter was arranged by Anne in advance, rather than being a serendipitous event. Contrary to Cummings's expectations, he actually liked Ralph Barton: "Anne exaggerated;he's not a villain;she made him one,it was all <u>her</u> fault." Barton apparently took to Cummings, as well. He appreciated his work as a writer, and as a cartoonist himself, admired Cummings's line drawings that had appeared in *Vanity Fair* and the *Dial*.

As Barton and Tailleferre were about to embark on a chauffeured driving trip to Southern France, they invited Cummings, Anne, and Diana to join them. The trip was not a particularly happy one. Barton and Tailleferre were having difficulties and when together bickered incessantly; the quarreling stopped only when during part of the trip Tailleferre went off on her own for several days. Cummings and Anne had their share of disputes, as well, but in comparison to their hosts, seemed almost harmonious. Barton enjoyed his time with Diana, ostentatiously lavishing attention on her.

On their return to Paris in early June, Cummings and Anne placed Diana in a French convent school for a month so that they could actually embark on a honeymoon. Perhaps because Cummings felt Paris too much a part of his past with Elaine and Nancy—"On to New(honeymoon) vs. Back to Old(child money)"—Austria became their destination. The month-long trip was punctuated by rows, some rather serious: "SCENE. TEARING UP WEDDING CERT etc." "It's all a hideous mistake! I'm going back to Douglas."

Diana was also a source of contention. Cummings thought Diana "spoiled," even "piggish." At the same time, he disapproved of the way in which Anne dealt with Diana's tantrums by throwing fits of her own. And while Anne could see, when calm, that her own outbursts were totally ineffective in controlling Diana, in the heat of the moment her responses were as childlike as that of her daughter. Despite their arguments, Cummings and Anne seemingly remained irresistibly attractive to one another. It was this "electricity" between them that nearly always managed to gain the upper hand, rescue each of them from despair.

After their trip to Austria, they stayed briefly in Paris. Diversion from their domestic spats came in the form of Hart Crane who was also in the city that summer. During the day Cummings took Crane around Paris, showing him the sights. In the evening he and Anne greatly enjoyed escorting Crane from bar to bar. One night, however, after Cummings and Anne had gone back to their hotel, Cummings was summoned to the prefecture of police. Crane, drinking at Café Select, had run out of money to pay his bill, and after causing a scene—shouting at waiters and at the proprietress—had been arrested. Cummings himself arrived drunk to bail his friend out, and the police refused to release Crane into his custody. Ultimately, Crane's publisher, poet Harry Crosby, paid Crane's fine, and sprang him from jail.

In mid-July 1929 Cummings, Anne, and Diana returned to the United States and went up to Joy Farm for the remainder of the summer. Anne, Cummings felt, was really a different person when she was at Joy Farm, as was Diana. The tranquility present in the country seemed to rub off on all of them; the time they spent there was as close to a life of domestic bliss as Cummings would ever achieve with Anne.

Since finishing *Him* in late 1926, Cummings had not been writing a great deal, nor publishing much, aside from a few articles in *Vanity Fair*. But in early 1927 he had a falling out with Frank Crowninshield, the magazine's editor, and after May 1927 was no longer contributing to the journal. The disagreement occurred when Crowninshield asked Cummings to rewrite a piece because he felt it would offend French readers. Entitled "Frenzied Finance," the subject was Cummings's assessment that French financiers were manipulating the value of the franc. Cummings naturally refused to rewrite. Crowninshield backed down, but printed the article in the January 1927 issue with a subhead that read: "An unskilled observer diagnoses some results of the fall of the French franc." Cummings did not object to the "disclaimer" since his thesis—that certain "ill-intentioned Frenchmen" were deliberately attempting to reduce the value of the French currency in order to pay off war debts more cheaply—was left intact. Relations, however, between Cummings and the editor had soured.

The end came within a few weeks when Cummings spurned Crowninshield's suggestion to resume writing "turns," and instead turned in an article entitled "Why I Like America." While hardly jingoistic, Cummings did assert that "France has happened more than she is happening, whereas America is happening more than she has happened." Crowninshield printed the article without alterations, but only accepted one more piece from Cummings, a satirical rewriting of "Mary Had a Little Lamb" in three styles of popular fiction.

By mid-1927, Cummings, now dropped as a contributor to *Vanity Fair*, had to seek new venues for publication. He apparently did try to place some pieces in the summer of 1927 with the *Bookman*, but only succeeded in getting one piece, "Mr. X," a send-up of industrial greed, accepted there. Cummings did not take advantage of the *Dial* during these years. Watson and Moore would certainly have taken poems from him, but it seems he did not even submit any work to them. With the closing of the *Dial* in 1929, due to its continued financial losses, even this steady opportunity for publication had vanished. It would not be until 1930 that Cummings would once again have another new work in print, this time in the *American Caravan*, an annual of American writing edited by Alfred Kreymbourg and Paul Rosenfeld, both of whom were quite friendly with Cummings.

This piece, which appeared at the end of 1929, was called "A Book Without a Title." Cummings probably wrote it in the aftermath of his breakup with Elaine, for he noted years later that it was written "during that awful period of wretchedness." Perhaps he intended to have the work serialized in *Vanity Fair* for which he had been writing. In many respects it is a continuation of the "turns" he was producing for the magazine, but it also has a more serious purpose than simply entertainment: Cummings was trying to alter the relationship between text and reader by means of a fractured narrative in which "sense" is stood on its head.

"A Book Without a Title" consists of eight chapters and a prologue, each illustrated by a single, captioned line drawing. The subject is narrative itself, rather than any plot or series of incidents. Cast in the form of absurd tales, in which logic is suspended and linearity obliterated, "A Book Without a Title" defies readers' expectations of what a story should be. The drawings are of little use in deciphering a meaning. Though representative of scenes, they are not directly representative of elements described in the series of stories; as a result, they add an additional element of surprise to the exposition. Cummings's aim was to force his readers into a new recognition of what reading (or seeing) actually is. That is, to create a text out of the subconscious, where the grammar proceeds by logic and the drawings delineate an identifiable something, but where the structure ultimately becomes an open field for associative reflections.

Cummings was well aware of how outrageous his piece was. In the prologue, titled "An Imaginary Dialogue between ALMOST Any Publisher And A *certain* Author," he attempted to introduce his readers to what awaited them. A sampling of the exchanges:

> PUBLISHER :By all that's holy,THIS IS NOT A BOOK!
> AUTHOR :This *is* a book,by all that's not full of holes.
> PUBLISHER :It will RUIN YOUR REPUTATION as an author!
>
> ....
>
> PUBLISHER :Listen—I CAN'T UNDERSTAND this RUBBISH which YOU'VE got the INFERNAL NERVE to ask ME to PALM OFF on the UNSUSPECTING PUBLIC as A BOOK; and I'M SUPPOSED TO BE an INTELLIGENT PERSON!
> AUTHOR :Is that any reason why you should be afraid to laugh heartily?

The confrontation ends with the "author" pronouncing that if the "publisher" does not like the book, he always has "civilization" that the author characterizes as a "very serious disease...invariably characterized by purely infantile delusions." The flummoxed "publisher" demands to know what are the delusions. The author responds:

> AUTHOR :Such as the negatively fantastic delusion that something with a title on the outside and a great many closely printed pages on the inside is a book—and the positively monstrous delusion that a book is what anybody can write and nobody can't publish and somebody won't go to jail for and everybody will understand.
> PUBLISHER :Well, if THAT'S not a BOOK, what IS?
> AUTHOR :A new way of being alive.

Reminiscent of the "Warning" Cummings had published in the program of *Him*, this prologue was not only poking fun at publishing, but was actually an attempt to elucidate the thesis that underpinned "A Book Without a Title." In essence, Cummings wanted his readers to abandon their stodgy notion of what constituted a book—discursive reading for the sake of a single, prefigured meaning must be cast aside in favor of seeing language for its transformative potential. Language, in other words, is an end in itself. Ultimately, Cummings's piece stands alongside Joyce's *Finnegans Wake* and Stein's *The Making of Americans* as an exhilarating experiment in narrative whose goal is to overthrow the very idea of what we think of as a story. It was postmodern a half-century before postmodernism was said to exist.

Although it is unlikely that Cummings expected "A Book Without a Title" would ever have publication outside the *American Caravan*, in early 1930 the small, new publishing house of Covici-Friede decided to issue the book as a volume in its own right. Founded by Pascal Covici and Donald Friede (previously a vice president at Liveright), the firm initially dedicated itself to producing literary work in fine, often limited editions. Cummings was both surprised and delighted. When the book was issued—without a title at all—and in a handsome edition of 491 copies, each individually signed by the author, it received only one brief review, probably because the publishers did not send out copies of the limited edition for critical appraisal. This one review was not particularly positive. In fact, the anonymous critic for the *Saturday Review* managed only to say that he or she found it "a peculiar melange of satirical nonsense." It was probably just as well no other critics got hold of it, for the unorthodox book would undoubtedly have been soundly thumped. The lack of critical attention did not hurt sales, however, [*No Title*], which sold for seven dollars and fifty cents, was snatched up by collectors and bibliophiles.

The success in terms of sales of the limited edition was apparently exactly what Cummings's publishers expected, for that summer they signed up another Cummings book, *CIOPW*. Unlike any other book by Cummings, this one did not contain his words; rather, it consisted entirely of ninety-nine reproductions of Cummings's artwork. The title reflects the contents: CIOPW stands for Charcoal, Ink, Oil, Pencil, and Watercolor. The book, designed as usual by his friend, typesetter Samuel Jacobs, is a finely made, slightly oversized volume (nine by twelve inches). Though the reproductions are all in black and white, the quality is quite good.

The contents are also interesting. With one exception (*Noise Number 13*), the collection exclusively reflected Cummings's figurative styles rather than his long love affair with abstracts. Indeed, the book could have been subtitled "The World of E. E. Cummings" for the work he chose is representative of people and places that had special significance for him: drawings of the circus, complete with acrobats and elephants; the burlesque shows with their dancers and comedians; self-portraits and portraits of friends including Watson, Thayer, Samuel Jacobs, Werner, Joe Gould, Seldes, Anne, and Diana, as well as a number of nameless nudes; landscapes of Joy Farm and Mt. Chocorua, of Paris and Southern France; still lifes; and quick sketches of Coney Island, merry-go-rounds, shop windows, and people in the streets. All in all it is a fine representation of what caught Cummings's eye, and what moved him to reproduce the world around him.

That abstractions are largely absent from the volume was due in large part to Cummings's fairly recent turn in painting. After finishing *Noise Number 13* in 1925, he abruptly ceased painting entirely abstract canvases. Instead, he focused solely on works with a definite link to a recognizable reality. Although in the late 1920s he was still mixing abstract elements into his figurative canvases, by 1930 he had largely abandoned even that technique. This is not to say that his work was "realistic." His portraits, for instance, have a definite "Fauvish" quality to them, with bold colors that outline a sense of planes, while his landscapes are very much in the tradition of Cézanne's late work. But as *CIOPW* reveals, Cummings was really a master at the quick sketch, the caricature, the line drawing of a body in motion, all of course, figurative in origin.

In many ways the shift was logical. Cummings had never confined himself to abstraction. Landscapes, in both oil and water color, had also always been part of his art, as had portraits and nudes. His fascination with the human form certainly got a boost when he took up with Anne, who, unlike Elaine, loved to pose for him. At the same time it is not entirely clear what caused him to leave abstraction behind, as he had enjoyed a certain success with his *Noise* and *Sound* series. But it seems likely that Cummings simply felt he had exhausted the possibilities of abstraction. Or as he put it, "it leads nowhere." Years later, he tried to puzzle out what caused him to cease painting abstracts, but could not come up with a satisfactory explanation. "Why did I stop painting 'abstractly'...? A[rthur] W[ilson] encouraged me...and S[cofield] T[hayer] himself encouraged me...yet I returned to Nature, to the Mother!"

CIOPW was issued in January of 1931 in an edition of 391 copies with a sale price of twenty dollars. Each book was individually signed by Cummings who chose to use a brush to append his signature. As in the case of [*No Title*] it escaped the notice of critics, but unlike that earlier volume did not manage to sell copies to bibliophiles, or even, it seems, to Cummings's fans. The twenty dollar price was obviously a factor, but what the public wanted from Cummings (when they wanted it at all) were words.

While neither [*No Title*] nor *CIOPW* made much of a splash, the British publication of *The Enormous Room* did. It had taken a while for the book to find a publisher, despite the efforts of T. E. Lawrence (Lawrence of Arabia) to place it with a British publishing house. Although Lawrence and Cummings had never met, Lawrence was so moved by the book when he read the American edition in the early 1920s that he had even given it to his literary agent to market. The agent, however, could not drum up any interest. Lawrence, however, did not give up. He prevailed upon his friend, Robert Graves, for help in getting the book before the British public. To Graves, Lawrence wrote: "I went through *The Enormous Room* again…while yet fresh to living in such enormous rooms, and from it knew, more keenly than from my own senses, the tang of herded men and their smell. The reading is as sharp as being in prison.… I've remembered the book for years, and other people who've read it have been similarly impressed. So I don't think you will regret pushing it vigorously. To produce it in England will be an honourable adventure."

Graves, who was already enthusiastic about Cummings's verse—and had already said so twice in print—now took up the cudgels for Cummings's prose. Finally in 1928 he persuaded John Lane, who had previously rejected it, to publish the book in London. It carried a highly laudatory introduction by Graves, who noted that "it *is* a good book, an unusual book, an exciting book." He also reproduced Lawrence's assessment in full. While these endorsements certainly helped see the work into print, the British reading public probably did not need either Lawrence or Graves to tell them it was a remarkable accomplishment. The book was reprinted twice in two years, its sales far outstripping that of the American publication, and came out in yet another edition in England in 1930.

Among those who bought the English edition of *The Enormous Room* to add to his collection of Cummings's "firsts" was poet Harry Crosby, a rich, fast-living Bostonian, who along with his wife, Caresse, had started the Black Sun Press after moving to Paris in the mid-1920s. Although Crosby had long admired Cummings's work, he had not managed to meet Cummings until December of 1928, when Crosby was in New York on a visit. The meeting was arranged at a hotel. "There were two hundred businessmen [in the lobby]," wrote Crosby, "but we found him huddled up in the corner of a sofa his coat turned up about his ears his hat pulled over his eyes. So does a poet stand apart from the flock a hawk among pigeons." The reason for the meeting was not entirely social; Crosby was apparently interested in acquiring a manuscript for publication from Cummings. It is unlikely that Cummings turned Crosby down, but nothing came of the project.

A year later, in December 1929, Cummings saw Crosby again. The occasion was a party thrown for Harry and Caresse by Hart Crane to thank them for being willing to bring out his second volume of verse, *The Bridge*. Along with Cummings and Anne, the many celebrants included William Carlos Williams, Malcolm and Peggy Cowley, and Walker Evans, whose photographs of the Brooklyn Bridge accompanied Crane's verses in the Black Sun edition. Although the party was to honor the Crosbys, Cummings was equally courted by the guests. Crane and Williams found themselves vying for Cummings's attention with many others, including Harry Crosby, who considered Cummings the "prince among poets."

Malcolm Cowley perhaps best portrayed the way Cummings could become the center of attention at gatherings such as these. Quoting an unnamed poet, Cowley wrote: "'He starts talking to one person in a low confidential voice and the person starts laughing. Then another person drifts up, glass in hand, and bends forward to hear what is being said. Cummings talks lower, faster and funnier, without cracking a smile, and a third person appears. Pretty soon the whole room is grouped around Cummings, everybody laughing, everybody with eyes on him so as not to miss a word.'"

Three days later Crane was to have dinner with the Crosbys and Harry's mother, Henrietta. He brought along a friend, Margaret Robson. When he arrived at the Caviar Restaurant, Harry had not shown up. Dinner was eaten without him. Afterward, the group went to the Lyceum Theatre. Crane providentially left his seat number with the box office. During the first act he was summoned by an usher who informed him he had an urgent phone call. It was not Harry on the line, but Crosby's friend Stanley Mortimer. Harry Crosby, Crane was told, was dead in Mortimer's studio, along with Crosby's latest lover, Josephine Bigelow, a married Boston socialite. It appeared a ritual suicide as both were shot to death with Crosby's automatic that was clutched in Crosby's hand. The door was locked from inside. Crane returned to inform Caresse and Harry's mother. The shock sent Crane to bed for a week.

The tabloids were in a frenzy over the event, splashing sensational headlines across their front pages even days after the event. The literary community also responded. *transition*, the Paris-based literary review, consecrated a memorial issue to Crosby. Hart Crane wrote an elegy for his friend, "To the Cloud Juggler." Archibald MacLeish memorialized Crosby in "Cinema of a Man." Cummings also wrote a poem about the double suicide. But unlike the majority of the tributes, Cummings's poem, while highly artful, mocked the event rather cruelly. The poem ends:

2 boston
Dolls;found
with
Holes in each other

's lullaby and
other lulla wise by UnBroken
LULLAlullabyBY
the She-in-him with
the He-in-her(&

both all hopped
up)prettily
then which did
lie
Down,honestly

now who go(BANG(BANG

In June of 1930, Cummings, Anne, and Diana made what was becoming their annual retreat to Joy Farm, a place all three of them loved. Joy Farm also belonged to them now, as Rebecca had given her son the property. When Cummings went to record the deed he paid tribute to Anne's affections for the farm by recording both of their names as joint owners. That summer was a busy one. Anne threw herself into redecorating and refurbishing the downstairs. Cummings bought a gasoline-powered electric generator so that they could have lights at night. Anne bought two dogs, a hen, and a dozen chicks. Cummings built a large playhouse for Diana, and a study in the woods for himself. Perhaps as a consequence of this nesting, Cummings and Anne got along much more harmoniously than ever before.

The happy couple also hosted a string of visitors that summer. Among them: John Dos Passos and his new wife Katy; the friend who had introduced them, biographer Morrie Werner; and critic Gilbert Seldes and his wife Amanda. Hart Crane and his friend Lorna Dietz came too. Unlike the others, though, Crane and Dietz amused themselves not by walking in the woods or trekking up mountainsides, but by drinking and playing the wind-up Victrola. Crane was not the easiest house guest, either. At some point during their stay, a drunken Crane charged into Dietz's bedroom, screaming that he was sure Cummings did not like him anymore. Dietz tried to shut him up, but Crane's outburst could not be quelled. Cummings and Anne, in the next room, were finally awakened. Since the walls were thin, and Crane's inebriated words loud, Cummings was finally moved to shout back "enough guarantees of affection" to get Crane back to bed.

In August, Cummings and Anne went to Provincetown to visit Edmund Wilson who was living with his new wife Margaret Canby in Eugene O'Neill's house, Peaked Hill. The summer before, Wilson had visited Cummings and Anne at Joy Farm. On that visit, Wilson and Cummings spent hours discussing the new book Wilson was working on, *Axel's Castle*. But the visit to Provincetown was marked more by parties and beach-going than by any serious discussions of literature.

Rather than return to New York from Provincetown, as had been customary, Anne and Cummings went back up to Joy Farm. Neither, it seems, was terribly interested in returning to Manhattan, nor saw any real reason to do so. Europe, though, still beckoned, and by November of 1930 Cummings, Anne, and Diana were in Paris. But within a month they set off on a whirlwind trip across the continent: Lausanne, Munich, Vienna, Budapest, Prague, and Berlin. Cummings delighted in the variety of experience each place offered, and found the continual confusion caused by language difficulties an endless source of amusement. He wrote to Edmund Wilson, "And don't let anybody tell you there aint magic in Mitl Uropa:why I asked a ober in Wien for two vermouths please & instead received a cigar!… Prague,too,contributes her thrills—not to mention trying to explain to a head-czech on a hill that I'd lost the cocher and finally resorting to Ich kam mit ein(?)Mann(?)mit ein(?)Pferd(?)Wo ist er bitte? 'The church' he responded laughingly 'will open at 2'. And so it proved." Christmas was spent in Berlin, where Anne fashioned a Christmas tree out of parsley.

By New Year's Eve they were back in Paris, but set off a couple of days later for Rouen. "The short Rouen trip," he wrote to his mother, "…made me wonder again at France;which certainly has more in it than the rest of creation multiplied by itself. Do you, perhaps, know and recall the crazy houses and lacey gothics of Jeanne d'arc's martyr village?…. Never were stones so punctiliously petticoated. Never was weight so presdidigatorily negated."

On their return from Rouen, they moved into lodgings at 32bis, rue du Contentin that consisted of "one sitting room,a bathroom(WITH toilet),kitchen,& a hall." Though small, Cummings noted that it was far preferable to a hotel room and that they at least had "continuous hot water,a comfortable couch,three kitchen chairs(and such homelike symbols as a coffee grinder."

Since the living quarters were tight, Cummings needed to find a place to work. As usual, he was rescued, this time by Edward Titus, an editor of the Paris-based *This Quarter*, who not only offered Cummings his own studio but also accepted a number of poems for publication in the magazine over four issues. The work that preoccupied Cummings that winter was assembling another volume of poems for Liveright, who had already issued Cummings a contract. The title of the new book was *W*, an abbreviation common in Europe at the time for *Vive* or *Viva*. Walls in Italy or France were, in fact, frequently adorned with graffiti reading *W Mussolini!* or *W PCF!* [Parti Communiste Français].

Five years had elapsed since Cummings had published a book of poems but *W*, or *ViVa*, as the book was also known, was a fine demonstration that Cummings could still be counted on to produce poetry of importance. *ViVa* was, indeed, a remarkable book, a volume in which Cummings ably proved that his poetic craft had grown, that the poet was still leading the charge of radical experimentation, while never abandoning lyric beauty or substance.

All of Cummings's books display a carefully worked out architecture, but *ViVa* is perhaps the most intricately structured. In previous books he had grouped poems into sections, but in this volume, consisting of seventy poems, the verses are simply numbered in Roman numerals consecutively from beginning to end. Nonetheless, the divisions are still present: every seventh poem up to LXIII is a sonnet, while the last group of seven poems are all sonnets. There are fourteen sonnets in all, reflecting the fourteen-line form of the sonnet. Additionally, the poems in the first half are generally portraits (with an abundant number of satires) of individuals in urban society, while in the second half the themes are more varied: painterly impressions of nature; relationships; meditations on life and living; celebrations of love.

ViVa is not an easy book and Cummings made no attempt to ease his readers into its difficulty. The very first poem presents major linguistic challenges, with its words fragmented and dislocated, and yet the theme is a familiar one: a skewering of the "und / ead" (Cummings's favorite term for those not alive to life). Experiments with language continue, as in "XXI," a poem in which the form portrays the tipsy denizens of the speakeasies: "helves surling out of eakspeasies per(reel)hapsingly / proregress heandshe-ingly people." And then there are sound poems, such as "XXIV," where the acoustic possibilities of words or syllables take precedence over syntactical meaning: "bingbongwhom chewchoo / laugh dingle nails personally." Attention to living speech was, as always, a major source of poetic inspiration for Cummings, and *ViVa* contains many poems from and for the ear. "II," for instance, is a poem about card players written completely in drunken tough-guy dialect: "oil tel duh woil doi sez / dooyuh unnurs tanmih..." [I'll tell the world I says / do you understand me]. "XXIII" reprises this type of speech, this time in the mouths of a "buncha hardboil guys" who boast of their prowess as street fighters and who long for "duh good ole days we / spent in '18 kickin duh guts outa dem / doity frogeaters and humpin duh / swell janes on / duh boollevares..." But Cummings also included poems for the eye. "XLV," an emblem poem in the shape of a diamond is a stunning achievement in which the form—that of a diamond-shaped window—mirrors the content: a meditation on death and dying. In "XXXVIII" he fractures words and uses capital letters here and there to present a violent thunderstorm:

n(o)w

        the

how

      dis(appeared cleverly)world

iS Slapped:with;liGhtninG

!

 at

which(shal)lpounceupcrackw(ill)jumps

of

   THuNdeRB

                  loSSo!M...

Not all of *ViVa* was so experimental. The volume also contained the powerful anti-war poem "i sing of Olaf glad and big / whose warmest heart recoiled at war" that memorialized the unflagging pacifist spirit of Cummings's fellow compatriot at Camp Devens. One of Cummings's best-loved poems, "if there are any heavens my mother will(all by herself)have / one," is the sixty-third poem in the volume.

Poems about love and lovers quite naturally are in abundance. Among them is his well-known verse ("LVII") that begins "somewhere i have never travelled,gladly beyond / any experience,your eyes have their silence." There are other gems as well, such as "LX," which concludes

rushing gently swiftly creeping
through my dreams last
night,all of your
body with its spirit floated
(clothed only in

the tide's acute weaving murmur

There are darker verses, as well, reflecting Cummings's travails with both Elaine and Anne. "LXVI," for example, records the poet's sense of loss:

nothing is more exactly terrible than
to be alone in the house,with somebody and
with something)
                                        You are gone.   there is laughter

and despair impersonates a street...

Memories of his suicidal phase over Elaine are given voice in the haunting "in a middle of a room / stands a suicide / sniffing a Paper rose / smiling to a self," and whose last stanza is this powerful image:

(a moon swims out of a cloud
a clock strikes midnight
a finger pulls a trigger
a bird flies into a mirror)

But joy in love ultimately has the last word. The final poem in the volume is an exuberant celebration of love as a force more powerful than any other. The poem ends this way:

> —but if yourself consider wonderful
> that your(how luminous)life toward twilight will
> dissolve reintegrate beckon through me,
> i think it is less wonderful than this
>
> only by you my heart always moves

ViVa is a remarkable achievement. Not only did Cummings amply and ably demonstrate that he was still in the forefront of modernists with his radical experiments with language and poetic form, he also proved that he was a masterful lyric poet, and, quite simply, the master of the love poem. While Cummings's preoccupations with language and his themes of love and the importance of the individual against "the mob" had long been part of his art, in *ViVa* his craft had deepened, his control over subject and form exacting and exact, his expression refined.

nineteen

Worlds of Was (and Is)

On Cummings's previous European trips with Anne, Paris had been more of a stopover than a destination. Now, however, ensconced in their apartment, and with Diana in a Catholic boarding school in Switzerland, Cummings had the opportunity to introduce his wife to the Paris he ardently loved. They strolled in the streets, dined in small restaurants throughout the city, and caroused with French friends and some of the expatriates associated with *This Quarter*. In New York Cummings was largely anonymous, but in Paris he was a personality, a renowned writer, sought out by both the French and Anglo-American communities. As he told his mother, rather modestly, "I may have a touch of recognition here."

Among those who sought Cummings out was Ezra Pound, who was in Paris on a visit. It was the first time the two had met since 1923 or 1924, seven or eight years before. They had exchanged a few letters over the intervening years, and Cummings was frequently discussed in letters between Pound and Williams. Although initially Cummings had been in awe of Pound, his personal contacts with him had not been so satisfactory. "[Pound] sometimes gives me a FatherComplex," Cummings had reported to his mother in 1923. Williams, aware of this, had taken it upon himself to "reintroduce" Cummings to Pound and Pound to Cummings.

Neither was resistant. As Williams told Pound, Cummings remarked "that he only had the most distinguished regard for you but that (being a sensitive person) you had always picked a fight with him when he had seen you." Pound replied to Williams: "If you see Cummings again, assure him that I never picked a quarrel with him. Am curious of god's handiwork, and ask questions of my minors in order to find out what they think, mean, desire, etc."

Apparently Williams's attempt to patch over any rough spots between his two friends was successful, for by the early 1930s Pound and Cummings were amicably (though irregularly) corresponding. And so when Cummings received Pound's note inviting him to join him and his wife, Dorothy, in Paris, he was delighted and arranged a rendezvous at the Café de la Régence. Over drinks, and finally a meal, they talked for hours, sharing literary gossip and enthusiasms. By the time they parted, they had solidified a friendship that would ultimately become a lifetime bond.

Occasionally some forms of recognition did not leave him terribly pleased. Sometime in March he encountered Elaine and MacDermot. About the incident, engineered by his friend John Peale Bishop, he wrote to his mother that "a cordial but unsatisfactory(as usual)time was had,for five minutes." He did learn that Elaine and MacDermot had "recently produced a boy" but did not receive news about Nancy. Why he did not ask is not clear.

In another encounter, at a gathering of expatriates, Cummings offended writer and publisher Nancy Cunard by making what she took to be a disparaging remark about black people in general, and, in particular, her black lover, American jazz pianist, Henry Crowder. What Cummings actually said has not been recorded, but most likely his comment was made not out of malice, or even any conscious prejudice. Cummings was not a racist; indeed, he had consistently abhorred the treatment of blacks by whites, and had often championed, in both private and public statements, equality for blacks both in France and in the United States. But Cummings was at times loose with his tongue and felt free to make idle remarks about people of all stripes. He was also a great mimic, and delighted in affecting the speech of everyone from Boston Brahmins to African Americans. It could very well have been such a routine that Cunard found insulting.

The perceived attack could have also been more personal. Cummings's friend, Louis Aragon, had been cast aside by Cunard in favor of Crowder a couple of years before, and a distraught, even suicidal Aragon had no doubt confided to his friend his antipathy toward his former lover, Cunard. Cummings, out of some distorted sense of loyalty to Aragon, could likely have been prompted to make an uncouth remark. Whatever happened, the incident was ugly; it ended with Cunard apparently threatening Cummings if he did not shut up. Cummings did cease his speech. But it caused a permanent rift between Cummings and Cunard, one that even thirty years later would not be forgotten by either of them.

With Aragon, however, his friendship continued. Aragon by now had a new woman in his life, "goodlooking" Russian-born novelist Elsa Triolet. Although born in Moscow, Triolet had lived in France since the early 1920s. Unlike many Russians in Paris at that time, she was not in exile. Rather, she was an ardent supporter of the Russian revolution. Aragon was already a Communist when he met her, but became even more doctrinaire as his relationship with her continued. In the fall of 1930, he and Triolet journeyed to the Ukraine to attend a conference of international revolutionary writers. By the time they returned to Paris, he had, in the words of Mark Polizzotti, "definitely shed his surrealist skin."

It was the Communist Aragon, rather than the Dada-Surrealist Aragon, who greeted Cummings when they got together that spring. Cummings, of course, had long had sympathy for the Russian revolution, and considered himself left-leaning. But because of his ferocious belief in the individual, he was hardly accepting of any dogma, particularly one that championed the collective over the individual. Nonetheless, he still enjoyed seeing Aragon and was intrigued by Triolet.

Their talks that winter often focused on the Soviet Union. Aragon and Triolet, firm believers in Stalin's vision for radical transformation of his country, urged Cummings to see for himself the wonders of the new Communist state. Cummings had already heard a lot about the Soviet Union from John Dos Passos who had journeyed there in 1928, and from his friend Morrie Werner who had made an excursion in the spring of 1930. Werner, in fact, had wanted Cummings to join him on the trip, but Cummings declined citing the lack of funds as a reason.

But in Paris, he found it less easy to resist making his own trip as he seemed to be continually coming in contact with writers, artists, and intellectuals who spoke glowingly of the new Soviet Union. Among them was a new acquaintance, Russian novelist Ilya Ehrenburg, whom he had met through Aragon. From previous sojourns in Paris he had gotten to know the Russian painter Mikhail Larionov, also the designer for Les Ballets Russes, and his wife Natalya Gontcharova. When Gontcharova learned of Cummings's interest in visiting her homeland, she told him, with tears in her eyes, "Spring is nowhere else." Fired up by all this talk, he cabled his mother in late March asking if he still had a thousand dollars left in his bank account. When she replied that he did, he quickly prepared for his visit, a trip he had decided, it seems from the beginning, to make alone.

On April 9, 1931, he wrote to his mother that he had applied for a Russian visa, which "if am the lil lawd fongleroi they wish—should arrive in 2 weeks:intend to reach Moscow onor before May day(international celebrations):receive Russian lessons daily(except Sunday)at Berlitz (if open;if shut,chez remarkable woman of 45-65 who lives in one room with samovar,a stove,3 dogs(whippets)& one cat.... I find the language just a shy wink harder than Greek."

Cummings's Paris friends were pleased with his decision, and soon the planned trip was the talk of the town. Even the *Paris Tribune*, on April 17, 1931, reported that Cummings "is studying Russian while waiting in Paris for the Soviets to okay his visa." By late April he was still waiting. Finally he got in touch with Dos Passos—then in Mexico—to see if he could help him speed up the process. Dos Passos promptly cabled the Soviet Embassy. By the beginning of May, Cummings had his "Visa without-Party Affiliation."

On May 10 he boarded the second-class compartment of a train for Moscow via Berlin, Warsaw, and Negoreloe, Poland. Along with his personal items, he carried with him a typewriter and gifts—magazines, a toothbrush, neckties, perfume, lanolin—for Triolet's older sister, Lili Brik, who had formerly been the long-time lover of the great Russian poet Vladimir Mayakovsky. He also had with him the manuscript of a long Aragon poem, "Front Rouge," that he had agreed to translate from the French for *Literature of the World Revolution*, an international journal issued in English, of whose editorial board Aragon was a member.

On the eleventh of May, he crossed the "borderofborders." On the Russian side the train was halted and lengthy searches made of all the passengers' belongings. Cummings got through without incident, but as he was heading to the train he was suddenly aware of the enormous change in atmosphere:

> So,in dream moving,preceded by trifles,through very gate of
>
> inexorably has a magic wand been waved;miraculously did reality disintegrate:where am I?
>
> in a world of Was—everything shoddy;everywhere dirt and cracked fingernails—guarded by 1 helplessly handsome implausibly immaculate soldier. Look! A rickety train,centuries BC.

The following day, May 12, he was in Moscow. Before Cummings's departure, Ehrenburg had sent a telegram to his friend in Moscow, the playwright Vladimir Lidin, asking him to meet the famous American writer on his arrival. But once in the Moscow station Cummings quickly realized that neither he nor Lidin had any idea what the other looked like. For some time he searched the station for someone who appeared to be a writerly type, even embarrassing himself by inquiring of a few suspects whether they were Lidin. In the end he had to surrender himself into the hands of Intourist, who directed him to the Hotel Metropole. He was aghast: "Never,in America,has this comrade stopped at a really 'first class' robbing house. Studiously,in Europe,did he avoid the triplestar of Herr Baedeker.... O plutocracy,O socialism—gird we up our loins:forward,into paradox."

As it turned out, getting put into the expensive (five dollars a day, with breakfast) Metropole was somewhat providential, for shortly after his arrival he was introduced by the hotel desk to another American staying at the hotel, Henry Wadsworth Longfellow Dana. Cummings did not actually need an introduction to Dana, a Harvard professor in Moscow to study Russian theater, for he and Dana had known each other in Cambridge. Dana immediately took Cummings under his wing, quickly becoming, in Cummings's phrase, his Virgil. Over the next week Dana was by Cummings's side a great deal of the time, serving as guide and interpreter, taking him to several theater productions.

He also introduced him to a young American couple, David Sinclair (son of proletarian writer Upton Sinclair) and his wife. Because Cummings was distressed over squandering his rubles at the Metropole, and had let Dana know immediately that he would like more economical accommodations, Dana thought the Sinclairs, who were vacating their studio, might be able to lend it to Cummings. They were quite agreeable, but their room, to Cummings's dismay, was atrocious: no running water, a foul-smelling communal toilet, and bedbugs.

Cummings was not impressed either by the two overtly propagandistic dramas that Dana dragged him to on the first two night of his stay. On the second evening with Dana, after the performance of *The West Is Nervous*, they went to a "pseudonightclub" where Cummings launched into a tirade. It was not just the drama, but the cumulative repression he had witnessed in just two days that caused Cummings's anti-authoritarian self begin to feel as confined in the "World of Was" as he had been in "the enormous room." "Comrade" Dana, an apologist for the Soviets, attempted to counter his "10,000 copiously embroidered oathprayers times circa 50,000,000 stumbling pocketthunderbolts" but to no avail. "Long live Is!" Cummings shouted out at one point, then continued raging against the "joyless experiment in force and fear." During the middle of his outburst Cummings noticed that a man had moved from across the room to listen more closely to his fiery speech. He and his host immediately realized that the man was an agent of the GPU, the Stalinist secret police. Cummings soon ended his blasts.

Despite Cummings's outburst, Dana continued to play the host. He took him to the Writer's Club, dragged him to another propaganda play, *Roar China*, and later introduced him to its director, Vsevolod Meyerhold. He also finally met Lidin, who stated that, as Cummings suspected, he had simply not recognized him at the train station.

His visit to Lili Brik, Elsa Triolet's sister, was a highlight of his first week in Moscow. He found Brik, who was fluent in French, charming, welcoming, and delighted with the "capitalist gifts" her Communist sister had sent. He also enjoyed the best meal he had had so far in Russia, complete with fine wine and cognac. At Chez Brik he also met his first "Hero of Work," who wasted no time attempting to indoctrinate a quite resistant, but this time courteous, Cummings.

Salvation from the Hotel Metropole (and Dana's wide-eyed belief in the Soviet experiment) finally came during his second week in Moscow in the form of Charles Malamuth and his wife Joan London Malamuth who invited Cummings to share their apartment in a crumbling mansion. Charles Malamuth had been a professor of Slavic languages at the University of California, but was now working as a correspondent in Moscow. London was the daughter of novelist Jack

London. Dana introduced them, but unlike Dana, neither was as enthralled with Stalin's USSR. As a result, Cummings was able to talk freely, and get straight answers to his numerous questions.

Stalin's policies had severely constrained the revolutionary fervor of Malamuth and London; but, because of the popularity of London's father as a great proletarian writer, they were well connected to the movers and shakers in the literary and theatrical world of Moscow. In fact, Cummings even had the misfortune to witness a dramatization of one of Jack London's stories, which he described as an "unforgivably dramaless preposterosity as improbably would have been assembled by the Lindbergh baby." He also observed on the occasion of this performance how Joan London was doted on, though "she(if politely) unlikes these tributes , notorieties , ghostly attentions."

In between visits to the theater, and lunches and dinners with the literati—including the president of the Writer's Club, Nicolay Efros who warmly welcomed the American comrade—Cummings also managed to tour a "model" prison, take in Lenin's tomb, and even go to a highly disappointing circus that the Soviets had managed to transform into propaganda. Somehow, amid the frenzy of activity, he also managed to translate Aragon's poem, "Front Rouge." Now that Cummings's sympathies had abruptly changed, he found the poem, that he now dubbed "A's hymn of hate," far less appealing than he had earlier. Nonetheless, he delivered the translation to the Revolutionary Literature Bureau for publication in their review.

Although Cummings had been writing regularly to Anne since arriving in Russia, he had not received a single letter from her (or anyone) since his arrival. Finally on May 28, almost three weeks after he had left Paris, he did get a letter from Anne. The news was not good. Her ex-husband, Ralph Barton, had killed himself on May 21. Although Anne did not provide details of his suicide, she did tell Cummings that because Barton had left no will, she had to return to the United States to claim Diana's insurance and settle his estate. According to Edmund Wilson, Barton went to see Diana in her convent school, "egged his daughter on to be a nun, telling her he was going into a monastery himself…just before he killed himself."

Anne had another reason for returning to New York. She was pregnant and had not been able to find an abortionist in Paris. As it turned out, Douglas turned up in Paris at just this time, and accompanied her back to New York. It is unclear whether the announcement of an abortion (or even the pregnancy) was known to Cummings before he left for the Soviet Union. The first mention of it is in a letter from her on May 31; the tone suggests that she had informed him earlier. But since the mail was so erratic, she could have told him about it in a letter he never received, or he could even have known about it earlier. In the very careful diary he kept throughout his Russian trip, curiously there is no mention at all of Anne's condition. In *Eimi*, however, he does reveal "a sketch for a telegram" that he sent on June 3. It reads:

> Don't
> Operate e for someone's name t for two and two for tea a for a name r for reality I suppose e for someone's name p for probably preposterous perhaps perfection possibly pain O for O civilization
> Unless
> that next god damned word?
> Reason

Though cryptically Cummings (with its unattached letters that spell "operate" in reverse order) the sense does come through, clearly indicating that he was not enthusiastic about an operation, presumably an abortion, "unless" she felt there was a legitimate "reason." Either Anne did not heed (or perhaps understand) Cummings's message, or it came after the fact, for she did have an abortion in New York. This may not have been the first time Anne had become pregnant with Cummings's child. A Cummings note states that "Annie would conceive at the drop of a hat." Nothing else in the notes or diaries indicates, however, that she had other abortions while with Cummings. But then Cummings was very much of the opinion that pregnancy was a woman's issue.

Cummings does not state directly in either his diaries or *Eimi* whether it was Anne's letter, or simply his growing distaste for the World of Was that prompted him to make a hasty exit from Moscow. But on May 31, 1931, the same day he received Anne's news, he boarded a train for Kiev. The trip was eventful because he saw first hand the secret police in action: "search here every compartment—I in aisle not approached…then (pp [passport] being Am[erican] apologies—but of a woman…Why she's carrying man's clothes—'You're not a man.)" He only spent a day in Kiev, then went on to Odessa. On the train, he was again accosted by the GPU, but as before, had no difficulties. The journey, however, was far from unpleasant. His Russian traveling companions amused themselves and comrade Cummings by peppering him with questions.

Of all the cities he had seen in the Soviet Union, Odessa pleased him the most, mainly because he felt the young people were still alive to life. Nonetheless, he was eager to leave. After numerous hassles and delays, he was finally able to book passage on a steamer to Istanbul. He was scheduled to depart on June 8, but sailing was delayed for another day. Finally, on June 11, he arrived in Istanbul. After a day in Turkey he was on board the Orient Express for Paris.

The trip to the Soviet Union permanently altered Cummings's views of Socialism: "I feel that whatever's been hitherto told or sung in song or story concerning Russia's revolution equals bunk.… And what has been miscalled the Russian revolution surely is more foolish than the supposable world's attempt upon natural and upon immanent and upon perfect and upon knighthood: an attempt motivated by baseness and by jealousy and by hate and a slave's wish to substitute for the royal incognito of humility the ignoble affectation of equality." At the same time, Cummings did not embrace right wing ideology. Or as he told a Russian painter, "no artist is ever a capitalist."

Cummings's quick return to Paris made the June 14, 1931, *Paris Tribune*: "E.E. Cummings has already left Russia. Cummings went to the land of the Soviets about a month ago, with the announced intention of staying there for many weeks, months or even years.… Why, then, did he leave so soon? Is the supply of inspiration smaller than he foresaw?" On June 20, a front page interview with Cummings in the *Paris Tribune* allowed the traveler to answer the question posed a week earlier. "People talk about the strain and tension of life in the United States," Cummings informed the reporter. "It is nothing to that in Moscow. If you said 'boo' to some of those people they might drop dead. If they are supposed to work 24 hours a day, they try to work 25. If it's 36 they try to make it 37. They are in a peculiarly nervous condition."

By the end of the month, Cummings was back in New York. By mid-July, he, Anne, and Diana were back at Joy Farm where they spent the summer. Cummings worked some on transforming his travel diary into a book, but spent most of his time socializing, relaxing, walking in the mountains, and painting. His art work was a focus again, perhaps in part because he was to have his first major show at the Kokoon Club in Cleveland in August, as well as a smaller exhibition at the Painters and Sculptors Gallery in New York in December.

The Cleveland show had come about as a result of his art book, *CIOPW*, and of the 162 works Cummings exhibited there, most were the originals that had been reproduced in that volume. As pleased as Cummings was to have finally achieved a major one-man show, he turned the matter over to his friend and printer, Samuel Jacobs, who was storing all of the artwork selected for inclusion in *CIOPW*.

Others came to his aid as well. Gilbert Seldes wrote a glowing piece on Cummings for a Cleveland publication, the *Bystander*, and the organizer of the exhibition, collector Philip Kaplan paid for shipping and advertising. Despite these efforts, not one picture was sold. Cummings fared somewhat better in December with his show of twenty-nine works at the New York gallery, even selling a few works on paper, and attracting the attention of the *New York Times* who hailed "Cummings the painter, like Cummings the poet, is first of all an intelligent experimenter."

If Cummings the painter was being lauded, Cummings the poet was not. In early 1931, *Hound & Horn*, a literary journal edited by Lincoln Kirstein, had published a long essay by critic R. P. Blackmur on Cummings's work. Blackmur attacked Cummings for writing poetry that he deemed anti-intellectual, egotistical, and even unintelligible. Cummings himself dismissed Blackmur's essay as "an elaborate model of a W.C.," but others did not. Unfortunately for Cummings, it set the tone for many critics for a good many years to follow, becoming a kind of "party line" in regard to the poet's experiments with language. Even criticism of Cummings written in the last decades of the last century still felt the need to affirm or refute Blackmur's 1931 essay. Had the fashion in criticism followed the lead of Pound, or of Robert Graves and Laura Riding, who consistently championed Cummings, the critical reception might have been quite different.

The Blackmur view was echoed in some of the reviews of *ViVa* that appeared in October 1931. Horace Gregory, who would later become one of Cummings's supporters, led off the round of criticism by calling Cummings "an adolescent songster." Even Cummings's acquaintance, poet and critic Allen Tate, writing in *Poetry*, was ambivalent about *ViVa*, repeatedly citing Blackmur as an authority. He did conclude, however, that "in Cummings's work there is much to amuse and entertain, and much that one admires." William Carlos Williams did take up the cudgel, defending the book in a new leftist journal, *Contempo*, but even Williams was not terribly enthusiastic. Although he noted that the book did have some stunning poems, he also said that *ViVa* "seems definitely an aftermath; not quite in the sense of scholarship but of desire satisfied—not quite real any longer."

In the midst of this barrage of negative criticism, there was good news at the end of the year. Cummings, along with poet Walter Lowenfels, had been chosen to receive the Richard Aldington Poetry Prize for 1931 for the best poems to appear that year in the Paris-based magazine *This Quarter*. The review's editor, Edward Titus, had selected Cummings alone to receive the award, but because Aldington's choice was Lowenfels, the prize of ten thousand French francs (about four hundred dollars) was split between the two American poets. The magazine's editor explained how the decision had been made. First, he printed a statement from Aldington, in which the poet stated that while Titus's choice was "unimpeachable," and that he was well aware that "Cummings is among the best poets now writing in the English language," he also made his case for Lowenfels, whose work, he felt, had been overlooked and needed a boost. Following Aldington's remarks, Titus presented his own position: "Rather than have our 'unimpeachable' award entirely defeated, we agreed, under duress, to a division."

The honor was welcome, the cash even more. America was in depression. Twelve million were out of work; American industry as a whole was operating at less than half its 1929 volume; companies were going bankrupt at such a precipitous rate that the total amount of money paid out in wages was sixty percent less than what it had been just two years before.

Cummings had largely ignored the economic disaster, but by the summer and fall of 1931, even he was beginning to feel the effects. The publishing business was in tumult, with sales declining. While Cummings had never made much money from his books, he began to fear that even the opportunity to publish might vanish if presses went under. The Provincetown Playhouse had already closed, leaving him without a venue for further play productions. But the reality of the worsening conditions really hit home when he observed friends struggling to survive. Jimmy Light, he reported to his mother, "sleeps on a Dr's operating table—Patty somewhere else since they are broke and homeless." Edmund Wilson, Cummings noted, was "Broke but cheerful—expects a revolution." Only Cummings's friend, the perpetually homeless Joe Gould, did not seem to be affected by the economic situation. To keep his own personal ship afloat, Cummings asked his mother for an allowance of one hundred dollars a month, to which she readily agreed.

Although Cummings and Anne had got on well, as usual, when they were together at Joy Farm, by the time Cummings returned to New York late that fall their relationship again became rocky. Anne nagged him for money (perhaps the reason he had asked his mother for the allowance) but that was the least of their problems. Anne, once again, began to pursue other men. On at least one occasion Cummings, as well, ended up in bed with an acquaintance, Renée Oakman. But his motivation was revenge: Anne was apparently having an affair with the woman's husband.

Their quarrels and Anne's humiliation of Cummings was hardly a secret. Brown remembered that Anne "frequently made jokes about what she considered the inadequate proportions of his virile development." Lincoln Kirstein described her as a "bloody horror." Cowley recalled that at a party at his house "Anne was a perfect bitch.... She embarrassed Estlin in such a painful way that I didn't feel comfortable with him afterwards." According to Wilson, at an elegant uptown party Anne flew into a rage, and "seized the fancy guest towels, such as no one would ever think of using, soiled them in the toilet, and threw them across the room." Cummings did not fight back in public, but in private he anguished. He began feeling more and more "cramped." "Where is my breeding, culture, scholar, gentleman, uppercrust?" he asked himself. But unlike when he had been ditched by Elaine, he did not succumb to self-loathing or self-pity. He even cut off sexual relations with Anne as her treatment of him had caused him to feel she was "Unbeautiful."

At the same time, he was reluctant to divorce her. Cummings's hesitation had less to do with his fear of being single again than with his worry that he would lose Joy Farm, which he and Anne now owned in common. Anne was unabashed in letting it be known that she was co-owner of the farm. Werner recalled that one evening when he was dining with Cummings and Anne, she "kept picking on him [Cummings] and I said to her bluntly. 'If you feel that way why don't you get out?' 'I want that property,' she said brutally."

By January 1932 Anne had a new lover, a surgeon named Joseph Girdansky. Girdansky was a large, aggressive, and muscular man who, unlike the gentle Cummings, was inclined to assert himself physically over Anne. A February 1932 doctor's bill to treat Anne for injuries—for which Cummings exchanged a painting and a signed copy of his next book for the medical attention—suggests that Girdansky was not even above beating her.

Werner reported that during this time Anne would show up at parties wearing sunglasses to hide her black eyes. According to Brown, Girdansky was a sadist. Poet Robert Creeley reported that Brown had gone to Girdansky for treatment of a problem with his finger. Girdansky lanced it, "slicing, just so, the tendon, 1st finger, right hand, so it shriveled."

By March the marriage had dissolved. By June, Anne had obtained a Mexican divorce. On her return, she pressed Cummings for her share of Joy Farm. Werner's brother, a Manhattan lawyer, agreed to help Cummings fight her claim. His first step was to file a brief disputing the validity of the Mexican decree. This caused Anne to put forth a compromise: she would relinquish her claim and the farm and allow Cummings to have an American divorce if he gave her all the furnishings she had purchased for Joy Farm, as well as thirty-five hundred dollars. Cummings was apparently willing to accept the deal, but his lawyer advised against it. Anne, as Cummings knew, was now pregnant with Girdansky's child, and desperately wanted to marry her lover so that the baby would not be illegitimate. On August 24, 1932, he wrote to his mother that "everybody is to lie low,put nothing in writing where Anne is concerned,and let her eventually come to me asking for divorce on my terms, namely:Yes, she can have whatever furniture she put into the farm;No,she can't have I(one)cent,let alone any dollars. And willynilly,she must deed her half of the farm back to you."

The actions of Cummings's lawyer continued when it was learned that Anne had married Girdansky in October 1932. Cummings's lawyer now threatened to press to void the marriage unless Anne agreed to the terms he had stipulated for Cummings. For a time the matter was stalled, but by April 1933, Anne signed over her half of the Joy Farm property to Rebecca, in exchange for Cummings withdrawing his suit against her to nullify the Mexican divorce. The era of Anne was now, at long last, over.

At just about the time Anne left Cummings for Girdansky, Cummings became embroiled in another struggle. Called in France, *L'Affaire Aragon*, this tumult in his life was political. In October of 1931, Aragon published "Front Rouge" in a new collection of poems. Because of the overt call to revolution, the book was seized by the authorities, as was all copies in France of *Literature of the World Revolution*, in which the poem had first appeared in Cummings's translation. On January 16, 1932, Aragon was indicted for "inciting soldiers to disobey orders and incitement to murder for purposes of anarchist propaganda." A conviction carried five years behind bars.

The Surrealist group, as well as other intellectuals, were quick to respond. Petitions were circulated on behalf of Aragon, one of which Cummings signed. Aragon's former comrade-in-arms, André Breton, despite his falling out with Aragon a year or so earlier, hastily put together a pamphlet entitled *The Poverty of Poetry*, which sought to defend the poem and its author. But Cummings was nervous. As translator of the inflammatory poem, he worried that if Aragon were actually convicted, he might be refused a French visa in the future. In May, however, the matter was resolved when a new French president pardoned Aragon. In New York, Cummings breathed a little easier.

But bad news of a far more consequential kind had reached Cummings in early May of 1932. His friend Hart Crane was dead. An apparent suicide, Crane had jumped overboard from a ship in the waters off Cuba after a long sojourn in Mexico. Cummings reflected philosophically on his friend's death: "Take Hart Crane's Cuban hurricane—there was Evil with a capital E : while he fought it. When he stopped opposing it & became it,there was Eternity: or whatever is entirely or inconceivably more intense than the most vivid conflict. For conflict,however vitally imagined, is partial—whereas God is whole."

Despite the personal upheavals in his life, Cummings managed to work energetically on his main work at that time—turning his travel diary into a book. By the early spring of 1932 he was nearing completion of a final draft. The book had not been contracted for in advance and while Cummings was working on it, he despaired at times that it would ever see publication. Or as he wrote Watson, "am even now trying to trick a few buffaloes out of some socalled publisher : trouble is,this book may please 12 17/16 less people than the(incredibly)possibly 6 7/8 which was the last." But as Cummings knew, the odds were somewhat against him. *ViVa* had, in fact, not sold well; its publisher, Liveright, was in financial difficulties, and with the depression roaring, other publishers were in similar circumstances. But Covici-Friede, publishers of [*No Title*] and of his art book, *CIOPW*, were staying afloat.

At a lunch in the late spring of 1932, Pascal Covici asked Cummings for "any sort of book." Cummings informed him that he had "A Russian Diary," but warned Covici that the book was "against Russia." The publisher responded that if the author was Cummings, he wanted the book. Covici was true to his word. When Brandt & Brandt, Cummings's agents, delivered *Eimi* to Covici-Friede in the summer of 1932, Covici enthusiastically accepted the book despite its obvious stylistic difficulties, less than straightforward narrative, and its contrarian critical appraisal of the worker's paradise. He even sent the author a welcome advance of five hundred dollars.

At 432 pages, *Eimi* is Cummings's longest book and his most challenging work of prose. While *The Enormous Room* is stylistically different, at times even difficult, *Eimi* is a tour-de-force, unique not only in its assessments, but in the way Cummings assessed. The title is a transliteration of the Greek ειμι meaning "am." As he later commented on the book and its title in relation to his first prose book, "eimi is the individual again;a more complex individual,a more enormous room."

In *The Enormous Room* Cummings turned to Bunyan and allegory; in *Eimi* he used Dante's *Divine Comedy* as a structural device on which to pin the narrative of his trip. But just as Bunyan was dispensable, so is Dante; there is no one-to-one correspondence in *Eimi*, although the parallels are more closely matched than in his first prose work. Henry Dana, his first guide in Moscow, is generally called Virgil; Joan London Malamuth becomes Beatrice; the viewing of Lenin in his tomb is likened to Dante's glimpse of Satan. The overall structure, too, is modeled on *The Divine Comedy*. When entering the Soviet Union, he enters the "Unworld" that quickly becomes his version of the Inferno; Turkey is seen as Purgatory; Paris, naturally, is identified with Paradise. But just as Dante's book is richer when it sketches the Inferno, that of Cummings is too, so much so that the vast majority of the narrative is centered on his experiences in the un(der)world of the Soviet Union.

While allusions to Dante's masterpiece are the most obvious and numerous, Cummings also was perhaps inspired by Aragon's 1922 novel, *Les Aventures de Télémaque* (*The Adventures of Telemachus*), a playful contemporizing of the seventeenth-century French epic by François Fénelon. Just as Cummings used Dante as scaffolding but little else, Aragon did the same with Fénelon, creating a Dadaist text whose aim was to parade language as a force capable of both destruction (of classical literature) as well as creation (of a new narrative style). Derision, satire, buffoonery, linguistic puns, and a sprung narrative are the hallmarks of Aragon's anti-novel, all traits found in Cummings. This is not to suggest that Cummings needed Aragon as a model; Aragon's book served, at best, as a kind of permission to dismantle traditional forms of narration, then reconstruct them in a radically new fashion.

The narrator of *Eimi* is, of course, Cummings, but in the guise of comrade Kem-min-kz, as the Russians called him, often abbreviated to comrade K, alias C or K. The comrade's alter ego—or inner person who freely comments on the actions of comrade Kem-min-kz is the first-person I or me myself. He also refers to this self as Poietes, a transliteration of ειμι (Greek for maker or poet); and at times he is even peesahtel and hoodoznik (Russian for writer and painter). The use of all of these aliases is not just for obfuscation; they truly represent the fragmentation of being that Cummings felt when in the Soviet Union. Only when on board the train to Odessa, and finally on the verge of leaving the Soviet Union, do the selves finally become unified:

> everybody's eating now ; as for comrades Kem-min-kz and Cummings , together with comrades peesahtel and hoodozhnik and also comrade me-myself , that oaf, why we're all 5 aplunging and awhirling into our ambrosia like nothing even a Russian ever saw or heard.

Cummings went to the Soviet Union with his eyes open and without an agenda. But his experiences there, in which he witnessed first-hand the privation and sadness of the Stalinist state, certainly helped him develop an agenda. At the same time, *Eimi* is not propaganda, except perhaps when it came to championing the importance of the individual over the masses. He was too wise (and too much of an artist) to write a tract denouncing the excesses of Communism. Instead, he preferred to allow his portrayal of incident and individuals to make the point much more adequately. Throughout the book, in fact, he allows the "comrades" to satirize themselves, as in this conversation with an ardent Communist:

> Most(I lead)of the autos hereabouts are Fords.
> Yes(trumping)Ford sends us the, what is it...—parts : and we have plant to assemble them...
> Do many individuals own Fords?(mildly.)
> Nono.
> ....
> the difficult thing(tireless unhe thugishly continues)is to understand , first , a mass ; and next , a mass's dictatorship—in other words , to realize that Stalin is expressing , not himself , but the mass.
> You mean , I presume , that comrade Stalin is not imposing his power on others , but is expressing their power.
> (Delighted) : Exactly!

Despite his caustic appraisal of the Soviet Union, Cummings was not so enamored of the West that he was willing to hold it up as a model of liberty and fairness. Indeed, the United States is at times even a vehicle for his satiric barbs.

Although Cummings's actual travel diary numbered only about fifty typed pages, while *Eimi* is over four hundred printed pages, the finished book follows the general outline of the diary. As he noted, "Eimi's source equals on the spot scribbled hieroglyphics." And as in the journal, *Eimi* is structured as a day-by-day account of his five-week trip. But where the diary is cryptic, with actual feelings often suppressed (probably out of fear it might be confiscated by the authorities), the book is brash in both its judgments and observations. Of course, a great many incidents and observations were added and expanded when Cummings actually wrote the book. The resemblance between diary and book is that of a skeleton to a fully fleshed being.

And how fully fleshed *Eimi* is. Little passed by Cummings's eyes without him seeing it, feeling it, hearing it, and ultimately transforming it into a distinctive vision that often surpasses mere description. As in all great traveler's tales—and this most certainly is one—there are alterations of mood and sensibility. Great comic passages sit astride pages in which Cummings expresses anger, frustration, and even fear. Indeed, his satire is practiced in a way that has rarely been seen so artfully in English since the eighteenth century. But so careful a craftsman was Cummings that the turns in his prose reflect the circumstances being described. His descent into Lenin's tomb, for instance, is rendered poetically, the movement of the lines mirroring the pace of the jostling crowd, reflecting the scene playing out before his eyes:

facefacefaceface
facefaceface
faceface
Face
        :all(of whom-which move-do-not-move numberlessly) Toward
the
    Tomb
            Crypt
                    Shrine
Grave.
The grave.

Toward the (grave.
All toward the grave)of himself of herself(all toward the grave of themselves)all toward the grave of Self.
Move(with dirt's dirt dirty)unmoving move un(some from nowhere) moving move unmoving(eachotherish)
:face
Our-not-their
faceface ;
Our-not-her
, facefaceface
Our-not-his
—toward
Vladimir our life!Ulianov our sweetness!Lenin our hope!
all—
(hand-
fin-
claw

foot-
hoof
tovarich)
es : to number of numberlessness ; un
-smiling

It is obvious from the passage just quoted that *Eimi's* style is decidedly idiosyncratic. And yet, it is stylistically idiosyncratic for a reason: Cummings is telling his own story in his own way, pulling out all the stops to create a narrative that is powerful, accurate, vivid, and uniquely his. Because he saw and conceived things in the way he did, he felt he could only render them that way. In defense of his technique, he quoted Cézanne: "Pour l'artiste, voir c'est concevoir, et concevoir, c'est composer." [For the artist, to see is to conceive, and to conceive is to compose.]

Eimi has all the hallmarks of Cummings's love affair with language: puns; syntactical leaps, including extending and running together words and phrases; liberal use (and often witty distortion) of common slogans; the mixing of languages; the use of punctuation and capitalization to achieve particular emphases; negation with his favorite prefix, "un;" and a narrative that hops, skips, and jumps from incident to incident, then often scampers back to recapture another detail. The ultimate effect is that the reader not only is able to witness second-hand thousands of marvelous sights and sounds, but is also given the first-hand opportunity to observe Cummings's poetic intelligence—so alive, vibrant, and imaginative. Consequently, there is not a dull page in the book. Even when Cummings is describing rather mundane matters—such as boarding the tram or attempting to pick up his mail—the rendering of these episodes, because of the sheer power of his prose, is consistently interesting, and anything but soporific.

In essence, *Eimi* is a series of sketches reminiscent of vaudeville, in which one absurd act follows another, with unification provided only by the constant presence of an MC—in the case of the book, Cummings in his various guises. And Cummings is a delightful MC, a fabulous unguide to the raw unworld of the Stalinist Soviet Union.

But *Eimi* is far from an objective account of a tour. Cummings was not a reporter attempting to portray a neutral version of events. As a man of feeling, how he responded to what he saw, heard, and felt in the USSR all serve to enlighten his readers as much about the traveler as his travels. The result is that a reader comes away from the book as informed about Cummings as about his experiences. The portrait that emerges is that of a man frequently baffled by events, but who nonetheless continues to welcome the new and unexpected, never shying away from any opportunity to bear witness. Intrepid, witty, alive to absurdity (since beauty has nearly vanished), Cummings doggedly plunges forward with his eyes and ears wide open. And precisely because he is so attuned to others and to life itself, he cannot be fooled into thinking something other than what he is actually feeling.

He is also a man whose beliefs are directly under siege. While Cummings had long articulated in poems, plays, and in prose his firm conviction that the individual was always far more important than the "mob," he had never been shy at expressing sympathy with the Russian Revolution or Socialism. But in *Eimi*, we see Cummings becoming converted to the cause of individual liberty in opposition to the state. No single incident is responsible; rather, it is the culmination of numerous episodes in which the government asserts its authority over individual expression that makes him fully realize that authoritarian socialism is totally incompatible with the individual.

Among the factors that contributed to this conviction was the suppression of religion. Although Cummings always had a spiritual side, his recoil from the attempted elimination of faith is in some ways curious, for he frequently vented his dislike of religion. But as a staunch individualist, he also thought that one should have the power to choose "unbelief," not be forced to accept that view. He is bothered from the beginning that the cathedral of St. Basil has been turned into a revolutionary (and anti-religious) museum. After initially being deterred by Virgil (Dana), he finally returns to pay a visit. Inside he spies a sanctuary housing a portrait of a Madonna with child, but to his surprise he cannot enter. A crude placard announces "No Admittance." "So ; this little picture is sacred ; noone positively must go near it," muses Cummings.

> I(miraculously nyet grayheaded prodigiously nyet businessman)actually happening to be myself am therefore he to whom nothing either is blessed and cursed ; gradually toward now the picture , the big baby , the wide hands , who strolling
> halts. —Goosefleshed from head to foot
> :touched
> yes!because(but more lightly than by a whisper ; more fatally than by a sword)touched

While not exactly a religious conversion, it is a powerful moment. As he concludes, "I(& myself) are touched ; hitherto , threatened with words , thoughts , carefully who kept , guardedly , our heart."

Cummings is "touched" again when in Kiev, where he is so moved by the "realm of churches" that he enters one. He does not comment much on the actual service, but he does posit some thoughts about the link between churches and the heavens (both literally and metaphorically) and a greater scheme of things than either politics or "humanity:"

> The churches are drowning with stars , everywhere stars blossom , frank and gold and keen. Among these starry miracles time stops , lives a silence which thought cannot capture. Now(touched by a resonance of sexually celestial forms)the little murdered adventure called Humanity becomes a selfless symbol(the doomed assertion of impermanence recoils ; falters

> the loud insignificant intrusion)whereas these stars eternally and all their cathedrals march to some harmony beyond themselves(here the lone star of socialism dies ; defeated by all the stars.

Finally, in Istanbul, in the magnificent church of St. Sophia, the image of silence "which thought cannot capture" once again is evoked:

> voice is made of silence and when his voice pauses the silence is made of voice.
> (Silently
>   as now to
>   whom my,pray-
>   ing my
> self ; bows)

Cummings is not specifically endorsing organized religion, but he is paying far more than lip service to something greater than himself, greater even than words. The last sentences in *Eimi* give final testimony to these growing feelings:

> finally
> (and what
> stars)descendingly assuming
> only shutting gradually this
> perfection(and I am)becoming
>
> silently
>   made
>   of
>   silent.
>   &
>
> silence is made of
> (behind perfectly or
> final rising
> humbly
> more dark

most luminously proudly
whereless fragrant whenlessly erect
a sudden the!entirely blossoming)
Voice
    (Who :
    Loves ;
    Creates ,
    Imagines)
    OPENS

Transcendence is at work here, for Cummings is not only commenting on his return to the "World of Is" from the "World of Was," but also evoking, somewhere beyond clock time and linear space, his own spiritual awakening into life, love, and creativity. It is not unlike Dante's ascendance from Purgatorio, in which he finds himself "remade like new trees // renewed with new foliage // pure and ready to climb to the stars." More than a literary echo, however, this final passage in *Eimi* is, as well, a personal evocation of Cummings's own return to the world of light, voice, fecundity, and imaginative possibility. The self—fragmented into various beings during his Soviet trip—is now quite simply the unified eimi of the title: "I am."

twenty

Carefully into Growing and into Being and into Loving

At just about the same time Cummings completed *Eimi*, he met the woman with whom he would share the rest of his life: Marion Morehouse. Morehouse, a model and occasional actor was about twenty-six, twelve years or so younger than Cummings. Morehouse's early life is sketchy. Although she claimed to have been born in South Bend, Indiana, in 1906, there are no birth records confirming this "fact." She did apparently grow up mostly in Hartford, Connecticut, but one of the Catholic schools she said she had attended—St. Anne's Academy—never existed. St. Anne's School had no records of her having ever been enrolled, nor did the long-established St. Joseph's Academy. What is known is that she arrived in New York, probably from Hartford, in the early 1920s. Drawn by the bright lights of Broadway, she decided to bank on her considerable beauty and break into theater, even before finishing high school.

Her decision proved to be prudent but—at least for the first few years—difficult. She did find work as bit player in various dramas, and as a dancer in some musical reviews, including the Ziegfeld Follies. But despite her dedication to theater, she apparently did not have the talent to become a leading actor on the stage. Consequently, she turned to modeling, a career that perfectly suited her lean, long-legged, nearly six foot frame. By 1925, Edward Steichen was photographing her for *Vogue*.

The photos reveal an absolutely stunning young woman, with large brown eyes, long dark hair, perfect full lips, and a Roman nose. By the early 1930s, her career as a fashion model was well established and she was in high demand. Steichen considered her "the greatest fashion model" he had ever shot. "When she put on the clothes that were to be photographed, she transformed herself into a woman who would really wear that gown or that riding habit or whatever the outfit."

But she was still drawn to the stage and it was the actress, in fact, that Cummings first met on June 23, 1932. Cummings had gone to a play, in which Morehouse had a supporting role, with the director of *Him*, James Light, and his wife Patti. Already acquainted with Morehouse, the Lights had agreed to meet up with her for dinner after the show. Since Cummings was in tow, he naturally was invited along. Whether by chance or design, James and Patti Light changed the lives of both of their friends.

"She's too tall for me," were Cummings's first thoughts on catching a glimpse of the statuesque Morehouse, who, in fact, was only three or four inches taller than Cummings's five feet, eight inches. But over a late-night dinner at Felix's, he apparently changed his opinion and did his best to charm the young actress. By the end of the night, Morehouse was so won over by Cummings that she went home with him.

Over the early part of summer, they saw one another quite often. Cummings remembered that at that time Morehouse "stressed her relationship to the theatre." This pleased him "not only because a loveaffair with an actress seemed glamorous,but for the much deeper reason that...the woman for [him] was someone with a career of her own...someone who didn't lean on [him]."

By July, their relationship had evolved to where Cummings decided to remain in Manhattan rather than go up to Silver Lake. Since Morehouse shared a house on Long Island with others in the theater, Cummings would turn his treks to see her into picnics in the country and at the shore. These visits almost always occasioned a flurry of love letters, often accompanied by drawings (mostly of his "totem," an elephant). One letter reads:

> Let us move our minds out of smallness,out of ideas,out of cities;let us pack all our minds carefully(without breaking anything)and carry them carefully among hills and rivers: come with me among mountains and oceans,let's change our minds,let's go away from not and from must and from if carefully into growing and into being and into loving.

Morehouse, too, was effusive: "You're such a wonderfully marvelous Comrade, Kem-minkz, and I'm so much in love with you I don't know what to do."

Morehouse was primarily attracted to Cummings's irrepressible charm, spontaneity, quick wit, and his accomplishments. Cummings was also handsome. At thirty-seven, he still possessed a kind of boyish face that contrasted with his strong masculine bearing. His dark blonde hair was thinning, but the short cut he sported suited him. His wide-set hazel eyes were soulful and fastened intensely on his interlocutors. When he smiled, as he often did, it was not just with his lips but with his whole face: the high cheekbones lifted, the eyes danced. But even more important for Morehouse than his looks was that unlike other men she had dated, he seemed free of poses, sure of who he was and what he wanted. And what he wanted most at that time was her, a fact he adamantly demonstrated.

He avidly courted her, sent her flowers, and flooded her mailbox with letters in which he continually expressed his adoring feelings. He did not even object to her dislike of his intellectualizing. In a journal entry from the late 1940s, written curiously in the third person, he remembered that "during one of your early meals with her in a little wop speakeasy which she knew of,you were soaring along in your natural way—& she looked at you imploringly;as if to say 'please!don't be intellectual with me;I'm just a woman!' where upon you came down to earth."

In August 1932 Morehouse moved to 8th Street in Manhattan, just a few blocks from Cummings. Now that she was nearby, Cummings made sure she he was on his arm as much as possible, eagerly introducing her to his friends. Edmund Wilson met her that summer and left an account in his journal of his impressions:

> The shape, somewhat exaggerated, of Elaine, way of talking of Ann [*sic*]—did he have this effect on both of making them talk this way?—subdued, low-voiced slightly self-conscious, poking in some modestly, femininely humorous remark. She is pretty, a model, and just like the girls in advertizements [*sic*]: very long tapering arms and legs, pretty hands, Victorian bang over forehead; a lot of facial expression, which Ann [*sic*]

> didn't have—prettily changing, especially when watched, in response to what was being said, but seemed like the variations of the expression of a model in different suits and hats, not spontaneous, not as attractive as it would have been if it had been spontaneous.

Rebecca, to Cummings's delight, approved of her son's "new girl," hoping that perhaps, at last, he had found himself the right mate. Although his mother had been generous and gracious to both Elaine and Anne, she felt genuine affection for Morehouse. Marion, in turn, reciprocated.

Unlike either Anne or Elaine, Marion (as Cummings was pleased to note) had a career and was proud of it. During the fall and winter of 1932–33 she modeled again for Steichen and for the designer Francis Clyne. In March, she did a stint as a runway model for an uptown designer. In a letter to his mother, Cummings expressed his own delight at Marion's success: "her boss(a couturìere of note)—NOTE THE feminine gender—likes her greatly and tells her several times a day that she's the most beautiful girl in N.Y."

Eimi was published on March 28, 1933, in an edition of 1381 copies (the exact number of advance orders). He signed each copy individually, leading him to tell his mother that he "expected to write his name 13 hundred times in a day or so." He then added, "I hope there is someone there to blot." Despite his complaints about getting writer's cramp, Cummings was delighted that he actually had a book to sign. The actual printing of *Eimi* had run into difficulties because the socialist printers had objected to Cummings's indictment of the Soviet Union. Fearing a long delay, or at the least a botched job, Cummings had persuaded Covici to turn the typesetting over to his "personal printer," Samuel A. Jacobs. According to Cummings, Jacobs set the entire 432 page book in seventy-two hours, sustaining himself on a diet of coffee.

The negative reviews began to come in even before *Eimi* was published. George Jean Nathan, editor at *American Statesman*, dubbed it "The Worst

Book of the Month" in the April issue (which hit the newsstands in March). Lewis Gannett, reviewing the book for the *New York Herald Tribune*, was so baffled by the style, that his only wish was that "Cummings would condescend to let his readers read him." The reviewer for the *Boston Transcript* was equally perplexed: "It is difficult for any normal mind to understand what the book is all about." The *Nation*, though left-leaning, did not overtly bash the book's politics, but did take issue with how Cummings chose to transmit his vision: "The reader's powers of instantaneous response become exhausted before he gets through very many of the 432 pages of this particular 'book.'"

An attack from the left did fill the pages of the *New Republic*, however. Nathan Ash, their reviewer, objected that Cummings had never allowed himself to come into contact with the real Russia: "[He] did not speak to—not even meet—a single worker or peasant, nor visit a single factory, nor dam, nor workers' quarters, nor workers' clubs, nor a prophylactic station." (Ash must have failed to read Cummings's account of his train ride to Odessa, or a good number of other passages in which Cummings describes, in detail, conversations with "workers.")

Praise did come from some friends, but by no means from all. Edmund Wilson and Malcolm Cowley, for instance, were disturbed by what they perceived as Cummings's right-wing turn. As a result, their friendship with him remarkably cooled. Muriel Draper, an ardent leftist, broke altogether with Cummings. Others, too, rebuffed him. In his notes, Cummings wrote that two unnamed friends crossed the street in order not to have to share a sidewalk with him. Ironically, many of those who turned against him had been quite taken with his translation of Aragon's Communist anthem, *Front Rouge*, that Contempo Publishers had issued as a pamphlet just six days before *Eimi* saw the light of print.

Although they did not manage to salvage any of Cummings's lost friendships, positive and more balanced reviews did finally begin to appear. In July of 1933, a thoughtful essay on Cummings's two prose works (*The Enormous Room* and *Eimi*) written by Cummings's longtime acquaintance and former *Dial* staffer, Paul Rosenfeld, appeared in the literary magazine *Contempo*. An astute critic, Rosenfeld was the first to note in print *Eimi's* "recapitulation of the great tradition of American letters" as embodied by Thoreau, Emerson, and Whitman, "and other classics of finite selfhood." He also noted that despite the charge of negative critics, *Eimi* is a "self-organizing," even groundbreaking, narrative—what

Rosenfeld ably termed "a new literary genre." Cummings's achievement, for Rosenfeld, was that the author wrote "true stories not only as strange as fiction but full of the fantastic color of the old romances." He then added that "these book are the singular thing, the highly informative document, built of high-tensioned. mixed comic and lyric, virtuosic, swift language forms."

Marianne Moore, too, lauded *Eimi* in a review in *Poetry*, but again her review did not appear until August of 1933, four months after publication. A more sophisticated reader than many (or most), she called the book "a large poem" in which style—equated with "translating"—is defined as a "self-demonstrating aptitude for technique, as a seal which has been swimming right-side up turns over and swims on its back for a time."

By far the most favorable comments, though, came from Ezra Pound. In an article for the *New English Weekly*, written more than a year and a half after *Eimi's* appearance, Pound remarked that he could only find comparable work in the books of Stein or Joyce; and even then, he felt Cummings's narrative superior to the best of both artists. For Pound, Cummings succeeded in taking in the Soviet Union "at the pores," and laying it open "pellucidly on the page in all its slavic unfinishedness, in all its Dostoievskian sloberyness."

Although stung by the first reviews of *Eimi*, the bashing in the press was offset by a letter received in mid-March informing him that he had been awarded a Guggenheim Fellowship of fifteen hundred dollars, to commence on April 15, 1933. The only requirement was that he spend his fellowship year abroad, a hardly unwelcome stipulation. Cummings was probably not terribly surprised that he had been given the grant as the Foundation's executive secretary, Henry Moe, a longtime fan of Cummings's work, had urged him to apply. Cummings's cockiness was evident in his proposal. When asked to state his project he simply responded: "a book of poems."

Upon learning the news, Cummings immediately asked Marion to accompany him on his year-long sojourn. She enthusiastically accepted his invitation; not only did she not wish to be separated from Cummings, she had also long wanted to go to Europe. Over the next month, Cummings and Marion hastily made preparations to travel to Paris. Cummings wrote to Pound in Italy to arrange a possible meeting. Pound responded that he would be in Paris in May, and was looking forward to seeing his friend and meeting his new "paramour." He also asked for work for an anthology, eventually titled *Active Anthology*, he was editing for Faber & Faber in England, and indicated that he had already decided on Cummings's translation of Aragon's "Front Rouge." Cummings replied with a list of passages that could be excerpted from *Eimi*, and gave his assent to the Aragon poem.

Pound, no friend of the left, obviously felt he needed to justify to Cummings—also by this time an anti-Communist—why he wanted to publish Aragon's stridently "bolcheviko" poem. His reasons, he informed Cummings, were these: "1. Because I want it.... 2. Because I think it may be the only way to get the Red Front printed in Eng. (tho' that may be an error).... 3. I want to ram a cert. amount of material into that sodden mass of half stewed oatmeal that passer fer the Brit. mind." Elsewhere, Pound simply noted that "Aragon has written probably the best lyric poem in favour of a political movement that has appeared since Burns's 'A Man's a man for a' That.'" As for the selections from *Eimi*, Pound was delighted. Long before he had weighed in publicly on the book, he had written Cummings of his strong enthusiasm for the travel narrative, perhaps best summed up in this remark: "OH well Whell hell itza great woik."

By the second of May 1933, Cummings and Marion were in Paris, where they immediately sublet an apartment for fifteen hundred francs [about seventy-five dollars] per month near Parc Montsouris in the fourteenth arrondissement from Romanian American novelist Peter Neagoe who, according to Cummings, was "apparently in America at present." Poet Walter Lowenfels served as the intermediary between Cummings and Neagoe. Cummings had known Lowenfels in New York and Paris. He had also been the co-recipient, along with Cummings, of the 1932 Aldington Prize from *This Quarter*.

The apartment, at 10 rue de Douanier (now rue Georges Braque) was on a "tiny new street comprising modern architecture inhabited by at least 2 peintres fameux—Braque & Derain." Though not as convenient a location as some of Cummings's earlier haunts, the accommodations were far better than any he had ever had in Paris. He wrote to his mother, "I greet you from a palace—no less—comprising (1) genuine studio with 18-20 foot ceilings and kitchenette (2) flight of stairs (3) (4) 2 bedrooms

(5) dressing room (6) bathroom (with tub & toilet) (7) porch (8) another flight leading to (9) roof garden—from which Paris may be glimpsed at sunset!"

Once settled in their new lodgings, Marion lined up modeling work. Cummings reported to his mother just a few weeks after their arrival, "The 'Vogue' people are doting on her slightest whim.creeping the boulevards on hands and knees to buy her orangejuice(with just the necessary goût of champagne)etc—as for Baron [George Hoyingen-] Huene,photographer de luxe, he wants us to visit him in Africa whenever he can stop snapping 'the most beautiful woman and the most poised in Paris.'"

If Marion pleased *Vogue*, she delighted Cummings: "Marion's my pride and joy.... Coming to a new language or world she immediately took it by storm without losing any proverbial tête." Cummings reveled in guiding her around Paris, showing her his favorite haunts—the Place du Tertre in Montmartre, the Tuileries, the Jardin du Luxembourg, the cafés and side streets of Montparnasse and the Quartier Latin, and the quais along the Seine. What pleased him even more was that she responded to these beloved places with equal enjoyment. In the evenings they took in the opera, the Folies Bergère, and dined atop Montmartre; long afternoons were spent at the circus, seeing shows at the galleries and museums (including a Renoir exhibition, where a late canvas by the painter was worth in Cummings's estimation "50? times all the world's so-called gold"). Cummings's sketchbooks are, as usual, replete with Paris scenes, but there are several sketches, as well, of Marion, who enjoyed posing for him as much as had Anne.

Marion was also willing to play the enchanting hostess to a string of guests that spring including Ezra and Dorothy Pound, surrealist painter Georges Malkine and his wife, the Lowenfelses, and John Peale Bishop and spouse. Another visitor who came through Paris late that spring was Lincoln Kirstein, the young editor of the literary magazine *Hound & Horn*. Although Cummings had been far from happy with the damning essay on his work written by R. P. Blackmur, which Kirstein had published in the journal, the editor had more than made up for "his error in judgment" by publishing selections from *Eimi* and some poems by Cummings.

Kirstein, more than a decade younger than Cummings, was wealthy (the son of the founder of Filene's Department Store in Boston), highly intelligent, and as passionately dedicated to the arts as had been Scofield

Thayer. Kirstein recalled that he first met Cummings when he was nineteen or twenty. "What attracted me to him," noted Kirstein, "was what seemed his absolute authority as an important figure; I had not known a practicing poet before, and here was someone whose presence proclaimed himself, or itself." He was, in fact, so in awe of Cummings that he scribbled poems of Cummings, reflections on his work, and later records of their conversations in his diaries during the late 1920s and early 1930s.

When Kirstein moved to the same Greenwich Village neighborhood as Cummings in 1930, he took with him *Hound & Horn*, which he had first begun to publish while an undergraduate at Harvard. And as they had friends and acquaintances in common, including Muriel Draper; John Brooks Wheelwright, whom Cummings had known from his Harvard days; and Kirstein's housemate at that time, poet Archibald MacLeish, they began to see each other occasionally. By the time Kirstein got to Paris he was beginning to tire of editing the journal (which was also losing money precipitously); his interest shifted to founding a ballet company. Indeed, he had made his European trip largely to meet with the young Russian choreographer George Balanchine in London, whom he hoped to persuade to join his new company as ballet director.

It was as the organizer of the fledgling American dance company that he approached Cummings early that summer. A firm believer in the intertwining of artistic genres, Kirstein proposed that Cummings write a dance scenario for the new ballet troupe. Cummings remembered that he "asked Marion what its subject should be,& she suggested Uncle Tom's Cabin.... When Marion made her suggestion, I'd never taken seriously UT'sC or read it very carefully all through;though well aware that President ALincoln,meeting the authoress therof,observed 'so you're the little lady who made this terrible war'. I now red [*sic*]—and was astonished."

Despite his enthusiasm, and even a small advance from Kirstein, Cummings did not get to work immediately. Instead, he painted and drew and, as always, wrote new poems for what he (and the Guggenheim Committee) hoped would be a new book. But there were distractions too: the new relationship, the allure of Paris, and, once again, Elaine.

Elaine, with MacDermot, was also in Paris, and had learned from John Peale Bishop that Cummings was once more living in the French capital. Less than two weeks after his arrival she sent him a note: "All I want is that you should agree to make a statement in writing to my local parish priest here confirming the fact that when you & I married it was on the understanding we would each agree to divorce if the other wanted." She did not include any information about Nancy, now thirteen; Cummings apparently did not reply, nor did he mention to his chief confidante in this matter—his mother—about having even received a letter from Elaine.

But the MacDermots were not about to be put off. On May 30, MacDermot himself wrote Cummings: "Your marriage to her [Elaine], though valid legally, was not valid canonically from a Roman Catholic point of view, because of the agreement between you beforehand that it could be terminated at the desire of either party." If Cummings replied this time to MacDermot's entreaty, the letter was lost. But it is unlikely he did. When the matter had reared itself shortly before he left New York, he told his old friend, Stewart Mitchell, who was acting as a go-between, that he would "refuse all favors until she [Elaine] changes her attitude."

Indeed, none of this was news to Cummings. Two years earlier, the MacDermots had sought the same thing, and had apparently succeeded in annulling Elaine's first marriage to Thayer. But Cummings, still enraged that they had prevented him from seeing Nancy, had refused to comply with their request. He was also well aware of why they sought to annul his marriage to Elaine: MacDermot had been elected to the Irish Dáil in 1932 as representative from Roscommon, and had been instrumental in forming a new political party in Ireland, the National Centre Party, in which he hoped to rise in the ranks. In order to clear away impediments to greater success in Irish politics, he felt he needed a Catholic marriage—impossible, of course, if Elaine had been divorced. A Church-granted annulment, however, would allow the MacDermots to have a Catholic ceremony, thus eliminating a possible personal obstacle to his quest for ascendancy.

None of this made an impact on Cummings who, distrustful of both politics and the MacDermots, had no interest in abetting them in any way. But in late June, Elaine caught up with Cummings as he was emerging from a bank in the center of Paris. Confronted, he agreed to meet her. A few days later, he and Marion met "the redoutable queen of 'Old Erin'" for lunch. In a letter to his mother he described the event: "Madame wanted me to see a 'bright-eyed priest' who was also 'little' and 'awfully nice,' and all I had to say was that,when we were married,we did so with the understanding that,if either felt so inclined,both would terminate the marriage in a divorce.... With this testimony of mine, Elaine would be able to marry her Frank in the Catholic Church. Without this testimony, her Frank's numerous enemies(political,especially)would undoubtedly dig up a wicked past."

Upon realizing he had the upper hand, he began to press Elaine about Nancy. She told him that she was at a boarding school at Bexhill in England, and "was not big,but was very intelligent and athletic and etc." Following this exchange, Cummings pushed Elaine further, asking her to write a formal letter stating that if at any time he and his fiancée "were in the Frank vicinity,the Franks would be glad to see us." At this, Elaine "dissolved into tears." Cummings, unmoved, told her he could not see her "bright-eyed priest unless the above mentioned invitations were forthcoming." To this, his former wife replied that while she had no objections, she knew MacDermot did. Cummings said he would write directly to Elaine's spouse.

A few days later, after receiving a positive—even warm response—from MacDermot, the two couples had dinner together. Cummings wrote Werner of the dinner: "They (Marion and la MacD) got onn likee 1 piece knittingcircle;that is they so utterly and incomparably despised each other's out-&-inwards that everything was nice—pronounce 'niece'—and polite." The next day, Cummings "gave requisite testimony to churchood regarding the MacDermots and now feel on top of the World!"

Despite having secured the open invitation to visit the MacDermots, which would have meant seeing Nancy, Cummings did not follow up then, or at any time, on what he had stated was his desired goal. Indeed, Nancy was not at all a factor for him at this point, and while he may have wondered about her from time to time, he was unwilling to exert any real effort to make contact with her again. In light of his actions, his demand seems to have been more a matter of getting the MacDermots to squirm and bow, rather than any true longing on his part.

Travel, however, was being planned; not to England or Ireland, but Tunisia where he and Marion had been invited by photographer Baron George Hoyningen-Heune. On September 13, he wrote to his mother from Hammamet:

> The sea lives a few hundred feet away;this palace is built around a court;we wear handkerchiefs-on-head and bathing-suits-to-beach;the beach—uninhabited save for occasionally goats—outdoes any I've seen;the Mediterrané's warmer than to be imagined;about 20 minutes walk away lies Hammamet(meaning "City of Doves," they say)and patter donkeys and lurch camels(the worstputtogether of all creatures?)and howls a trumpetting phonograph and loll ay-rabz galorie(with occasionally a wedding):behind us,a range of mountains borrowed from the Sandwich line,and not excluding a simulacrum of Chocorua;the land here is full of cactus and low shrubbery and Bedouins whose mansions consist of shelters slightly larger than a banana-skin;heat equals somethingtobegotusedto,almost everyone(alias I)sleeps from noon till afternoon(3PM).

The idyll in Tunisia lasted into the fall. From Cummings's accounts it was a highly peaceful interlude. When not nude sunbathing, swimming, napping, or making love, Cummings painted and sketched and worked sporadically on writing, revising, and collecting poems for a new book. The dance scenario resisted him, though, as he wrote friends: "Am having 1 hell of a time trying to inveigle Uncle Tom's Cabin to become a ballet."

Cummings and Marion remained in Tunisia until November. Their extended stay was due in part to lack of funds, and Tunisia, with free accommodations and food—courtesy of the Baron—proved ideal for making their money last until the next quarterly pay-out from the Guggenheim Foundation. But there was another reason, as well: by early autumn, Cummings was becoming more and more immersed in work, making good on his grant proposal to produce a "bookofpoems." Finally, with the book largely completed, and with a payout in Paris due in December from the grant, both Cummings and Marion felt it was time to return to Europe.

As Cummings felt confident money would be awaiting them in Paris, he and Marion splurged on their sojourn back to Paris. They flew from Tunis to Rome—for both of them their first flight ever—then leisurely toured Italy where Cummings again played the guide for Marion, showing her Rome and Venice. By late November they arrived in a drizzly, fog-shrouded Paris.

Since the "palace" on rue de Douanier was no longer available, they moved into a studio at 11 rue de la Bucherie, just down the street from the present Shakespeare and Company bookstore and across the river from Notre Dame. The cost was "800 francs [approximately $80] monthly for 2 rooms,kitchen(tiny gasstove),both(heatable—via catastrophic-gas-nemesis-water;otherwise cold)toilet in hall."

Contrary to his expectations, however, no money awaited them. As their funds were nearly exhausted, Cummings appealed to his mother, and perhaps the Watsons, to send money. His mother dutifully wired some cash; Hildegarde Watson sent a check. By mid-December, when the last installment of $375 from the Guggenheim arrived, Cummings and Marion booked passage for New York on the *Bremen*. They celebrated Christmas at Patchin Place.

Reentry to Manhattan was not easy. Assailed by money worries, Cummings applied for a renewal of his Guggenheim in early January 1934. He submitted a draft of the book he had "constructed" while away as evidence that he had used the grant money as intended. But this time the foundation turned him down.

Rebuffed, he tried to interest publishers in the new volume of poems. But as with the request to the Guggenheim, he was unsuccessful. Liveright, despite having sold *The Enormous Room* to Random House, who issued it under their Modern Library imprint in January 1934, was in financial difficulties. And when they looked at the meager sales of *Is 5* and *ViVa*, they decided against issuing another Cummings volume. Covici-Friede, stung by the failure of both *CIOPW* and *Eimi*, also rejected the new collection. Despite these setbacks, Cummings's agent at Brandt & Brandt, Bernice Baumgarten, continued to try to interest other publishers in the book.

Since no sale of the verse volume appeared likely in the near future, Cummings, late that winter, pressed Lincoln Kirstein, now also back in New York, for money to work on the ballet: "am now ready to work on TOM;shall need $100 a week for 5 weeks;if you want me to do the ballet,please enclose one century by what somebody loosely called return mail." Kirstein responded immediately, sending Cummings a check for one hundred dollars and offering, as well, to pay in advance for poems for *Hound & Horn.* A grateful Cummings set to work on *Tom*, and also sent Kirstein six new poems for the magazine, all of which the editor accepted, enclosing a check with the next payment for the ballet.

Although it took Cummings longer than five weeks to produce the scenario for *Tom*, by late spring or early summer it was completed. Kirstein, hoping to produce it for the 1934 fall season, gave it to George Balanchine, who now was the chief choreographer for the new American Ballet. He also commissioned Roger Sessions to write the music. But Sessions, engaged with other composing work, kept putting Kirstein off. A frustrated Cummings suggested that Watson's friend, composer Louis Siegel, be offered the opportunity, but Kirstein wanted to stick with Sessions, hoping that eventually he would write a score. Apparently, though, he did ask others, including Aaron Copland, Virgil Thomson, Lehman Engel, and Paul Bowles if they would be interested, but all declined.

That so many initially rejected the opportunity to score *Tom* is not entirely surprising. Though Cummings did produce a danceable scenario, like the book on which it was based, Cummings's version is highly melodramatic, and the scenes recreated by Cummings are generally less than imaginative. It is as if his tremendously bold poetic imagination was held hostage to Stowe's text, impairing his ability to transform the source material into exhilarating twentieth-century fare.

The feel of the scenario, in fact, is not far removed from Stowe's nineteenth-century conception of good and evil. But instead of making use of the dramatic possibilities inherent in the tale, Cummings doggedly followed the book episode by episode. In addition, he was so overtaken by the religious aspect of *Uncle Tom's Cabin* that in the end he produced a highly Christian allegory of redemption that would have no doubt delighted his father. But unlike the unique perspective he brought to bear on allegory in *The Enormous Room*, in *Tom* the characters are so stereotypically symbolic (Simon Legree is so obviously the devil; Tom, Christ) that there is little room for any interpretation, let alone art. Which is to say that a choreographer even as able as Balanchine, or composers as skilled as Sessions, Copland, Thomson, or Bowles, would have had to struggle to make *Tom* into an exciting, viable ballet.

The other major problem is that Cummings's true skill was in language, and words cannot be danced. At the heart of a dance is movement, and while Cummings attempted to envision scenes that are charged with potential for dancing, they are fairly hackneyed. The famous dramatic scene, for instance, in which Eliza crosses the ice is described almost comically:

> Eliza rising: totteringly balancing herself: on the squirming brightness, Eliza leapwhirls to another on which: staggering: she sinks; rises: balancingly: and whirleaps to another—zigzagging gradually her way outward, toward the audience, from brightness to brightness
>
> hither-and-thither meanwhile, in the high distant darkness from which Eliza came, spurt brutally luminous dog-faces; framing with intricate frustrations her crude whirl-leaping-reelsinking-staggerrising-leapwhirling progress.

That Cummings did not produce a better scenario is confounding for at least two reasons. First, he fully understood the art of ballet. Indeed, from his initial experiences of seeing Pavlova and Nijinsky dance in Boston, he had been enthralled with ballet and had continually attended performances in both Paris and New York. Second, Cummings had consistently displayed a unique ability, as in both *The Enormous Room* and *Eimi*, to use literature from the past as a grid upon which to place his own contemporary concerns. And yet, in *Tom* he seemed to have been thoroughly content to lean on the historical aspects of Stowe's text rather than use the book's premise as a springboard for his own artistic creation and social commentary.

Outrage at the treatment accorded blacks is evident in his extraordinary and sympathetic portrait of "Delectable Mountain" Jean le Nègre in *The Enormous Room*. But these were not just sentiments from his youth. These feelings of disgust at the injustices heaped on those with darker skin color were still present at the time he was writing the scenario. A journal entry from around that time notes: "it's rare that anyone is born again into the same race(e.g. my feeling for negroes might = that I used to be one." His sympathies were not only private. A powerful satiric passage from an unfinished play he worked on in the early 1930s clearly denounces the inequality accorded American blacks. Couched in pseudo-legalistic phrasing, the satire presents a series of "indictments" against African Americans that culminates in a "legal" verdict that justifies discrimination, subjection, terrorization, and lynching. The "crime" of which the "Benighted States of Hysteria" finds black Americans guilty is this:

> I hereby affirm that to the best of my knowledge and belief you have been conclusively proved, in flagrante delicto, with full benefit of testimony, to have committed a foul degenerate and inhuman offense against your innocent and unsuspecting fellowcitizens...that hereby you were black in color at the time of your hereby birth.

To be sure, this anger does underlie *Tom*, and yet Cummings does little to exploit the current mistreatment of black Americans. Perhaps he felt that an audience would make the parallels themselves, and, because of the Christian emphasis he worked into his scenario, the social commentary could be easily overlooked in favor of the message of redemption and passive resistance to evil. *Tom* was hardly a biting commentary on the current situation plaguing African Americans in the early 1930s.

Ultimately, *Tom* is an interesting footnote in Cummings's career. Had he written a scenario of his own designing, the results would no doubt have been far more original, certainly more provocative, and perhaps even more danceable. *Tom* does contain a fair amount of evocative poetic language, but like much of Cummings's poetry, it plays better on the ear than on the eye.

Now that Marion had become a major part of Cummings's life, he very much wanted her to share in his enthusiasms. He delighted in introducing her to his friends and escorting her to his favorite places. He was thrilled at being able to show her Paris; but now that summer was arriving he was equally interested in taking her to Joy Farm. His mother, however, apparently expressed concern that the proper New Hampshire locals would look askance at her son bringing his lover to the farm. On July 8, 1934, Cummings responded: "The idea that the natives of Madison would highhat Marion is just a trifle idiotic. She will be my wife,introduced thus by me—as she has been in new York Paris Philadelphia Tunis and many other parts of the world. 'Honi Soit' might apply to Cambridge,Mass,but the Wards and Gilmans—believe me—will never give a thought to such matters. They're better than that and they have something else to keep their so-called minds busy." Nine days later he reported to Rebecca that "all the natives seem to be crazy over my wife."

Although it is obvious that Cummings regarded Marion as his wife, he did not take steps to marry her in a legal ceremony. At the time, he likely felt unable to do so, as he doubted that the divorce Anne had obtained in Mexico was actually valid. That he perhaps did intend to marry Marion can be deduced from his sudden interest that spring in instituting divorce proceedings against Anne in New York. Since Anne did not contest the charge of adultery as grounds for the decree, the process went speedily, and on August 31, 1934, the Nassau County Supreme Court granted the divorce.

But even with this obstacle cleared, Cummings and Marion did not apparently marry then—or ever. There is no marriage license in his voluminous papers; the New York State Bureau of Vital Statistics has no record of their marriage ever taking place; and there is no mention in Cummings's correspondence of any legal union, or celebration. Among his papers is a record of an insurance policy Cummings took out in 1950 in which he named Marion as beneficiary, but listed her relation to him as "none." And yet, Cummings and Marion clearly thought of themselves as being married from this point onward. He almost always introduced Marion as his wife; when she was hospitalized in the 1940s she was admitted as "Mrs. E.E. Cummings;" some of their personal stationery has a header "Mr. and Mrs. E.E. Cummings;" and a Cummings will, dated October 1948, leaves all his property to "my wife Marion (Morehouse) Cummings." The most lasting testimony of their bond, however, is her gravestone that reads: "Marion Morehouse Cummings."

Perhaps because Cummings had been stung twice before, he was reluctant to commit to a legal marriage. Certainly the difficulties he had experienced in his previous divorces would have left him more than a bit wary (at least initially) of entering into a formal union. And yet, it is also evident that he and Marion were devoted to one another from the beginning of their relationship. Unlike his previous legal wives, Marion truly wanted to be with Cummings, to share in his everyday existence, and was consistently supportive of him in every way. Their commitment to one another, even within a year of their meeting, was profound. Over the years their relationship would grow stronger, becoming far deeper than that which any marriage license could possibly bestow upon two beings.

twenty-one

Nourish My Failure with Thy Freedom

The summer of 1934 at Joy Farm was a mix of happiness and disappointment. Happiness suffused Cummings because he was in a place he loved with a woman he loved, who adored him in return. The disappointment was the result of learning that his new book of poems continued meeting rejection after rejection. To further compound matters, Kirstein informed him that Balanchine had decided against staging *Tom*. According to Kirstein, Balanchine thought the scenario was "about *words* rather than the possibility of *steps*." But Cummings quickly converted his dejection to anger. "He couldn't bear to speak to me after Balanchine rejected his ballet scenario," remembered Kirstein.

Cummings had sufficient grounds for feeling down. At nearly forty, despite having published twelve books, not counting his poems in *Eight Harvard Poets*, he not only found his new work meeting rejection, but still needed to rely on his mother for financial support. (He had to request funds from her in July just to make ends meet.) His worries affected his ability to write too: he made little progress on a new play he had hoped to complete that summer.

In mid-August, however, he received a telegram that seemed to indicate a way out of his financial dilemma. It was from Maurice Speiser, a lawyer and patron of the arts, who had first met Cummings in the early 1930s. He described the cable in a letter to his mother:

> Mr. Speiser wired me that Paramount would take me out to Hollywood and back(with wife)gratis and would pay me $300 a week for ten weeks with a raise afterwards if I make

> good,and then another,etc.—he asked me what I thought of the offer. I told him I didn't think much of it and I told him I was seriously busy up here,writing a play—no moviejunk—and he wrote back heartily agreeing and said he'd insist on at least $500 a week for ten weeks in future.

Cummings's bravado notwithstanding, the offer to write a screenplay did intrigue him. As he told his mother, "if i could go out there and back with all expenses paid,stay ten weeks,and clear ten thousand $(irrespective,that is,of the ten percent agent's commission)'t'would be pas mal;but 20,000 would be highly more convenient." In the end, nothing happened; Paramount withdrew its offer. This was not because of Cummings's insistence on more money, but because the director, Joseph von Sternberg, for whom Cummings was supposed to produce a script, decided to employ a seasoned screenwriter. That Hollywood would even consider employing Cummings is not as surprising as it might seem, for in the 1930s a number of well-known writers, such as William Faulkner, F. Scott Fitzgerald, and Nathaniel West, were laboring for the studios. At the same time, Cummings had never produced a linear narrative of any sort, and his one play, *Him*, was far from filmable. It was probably this factor that led von Sternberg to choose a proven screenwriter over the inexperienced and experimentally radical Cummings.

When Cummings and Marion returned to New York from New Hampshire in the fall, Cummings was feeling more than a bit disconsolate. By this point, fourteen publishers had rejected his new collection, *Tom* was off, the play he had pinned his new hopes on was stalled, and even the Hollywood prospect had vanished. But the rejection of the poetry manuscript bothered him the most. He felt confident that the collection included some of his best work and was baffled that not a single publisher was at all interested in it.

Cummings was right in his assessment of *70 Poems*, as the manuscript was called at that time. It did contain remarkable poetry, but what he failed to realize was that publishers, suffering keenly from the effects of the Depression, were having a difficult time selling any books, and poetry, then as now, sold poorly even in good times. Cummings failed to take into account that his previous volumes, with the exception of *The Enormous Room*, had practically no sales. Indeed, as of mid-1935 Boni & Liveright had sold just thirteen copies of *Is 5* and two of *ViVa*; Covici-Friede had sold only one copy of *Eimi*.

Cummings's denunciation of the Soviet Union in *Eimi* may have also contributed to reluctance on the part of publishers to accept the new book. The growing socialist and populist movements that had begun in the 1920s had, by the 1930s, gained significant ground. As Elia Kazan points out, "the Thirties in literature were the age of the plebes—of writers from the working class, from Western farms and mills, who...wore a proletarian scowl on their faces as familiar as the cigarette butt pasted in their mouths." And Cummings—while certainly a champion of the individual—was by no means a booster of the "masses." In short, he was the antithesis of the proletarian writer, and did not hide his contempt for what he termed "the herd." And so just as *The Enormous Room* had won him praise from the left, *Eimi* had alienated a great many of these same supporters (and readers).

There was also the matter of Cummings's complexity as a poet. While experimentation was welcomed (at least by some) in the 1920s, by the mid-1930s the swing was back to work that could be easily digested and understood, and that had a discernible theme. Indeed, the majority of books of verse in English published in the mid-1930s were quite conventional (particularly in comparison to what Cummings was doing). Phyllis McGinley's light verse sold well, as did books by Walter de la Mare, Edgar A. Robinson, and Kenneth Fearing. There were exceptions, of course. Marianne Moore's *Selected Poems*, with an introduction by T. S. Eliot, came out in 1935, as did William Carlos Williams's *An Early Martyr and Other Poems*. But neither Moore nor Williams sold anywhere near the number of books as did more traditional poets such as Robinson or de la Mare.

Poets like Pound, Moore, Williams, and Cummings, lauded in the 1920s for their bold departures from the tradition, were now being excoriated for these same tendencies. Cummings refused to comply with anybody's notion, except for his own, of what was, or was not, literature. Consequently, his desire for striving to be the odd man out was having its repercussions.

This is not to say that he was totally without publications. Parker Tyler, the young editor and writer, published six poems in a 1934 anthology, entitled *Modern Things*. A new magazine, *Alcestis*, took nine poems from Cummings in late 1934, and brought them out in their January issue. And despite the lack of success with interesting composers in setting *Tom*, his lyrics did appeal to composers. In 1935, Cos Cob Press issued a compilation of art songs by contemporary composers. Included in the *Cos Cob Song Volume* were two settings of Cummings poems: the first, "Poet's Song," a complex, almost abstract setting of "in spite of everything" (from *Tulips and Chimneys*) was by Aaron Copland; the second was Marc Blitzstein's lively version of "Jimmie's got a goil" (from *Is 5*).

But these "successes" did not translate into publishers being interested in bringing out a book. With seemingly no possibilities for getting the new manuscript into print, Cummings turned to his mother for help. She willingly agreed to put up three hundred dollars for Cummings's long-time printer, Samuel Jacobs, to issue the book under his own imprint, the Golden Eagle Press. With this news, Cummings placed an acknowledgment to his mother on the last page of the book, and changed the title to *No Thanks*. To make sure his readers would understand the title, he dedicated the volume to the fourteen publishers who had rejected the manuscript. When the book was printed in April 1935, the dedication page listed each of the publishing houses, arranged in the form of a funeral urn:

TO
Farrar & Rinehart
Simon & Schuster
Coward-McCann
Limited Editions
Harcourt, Brace
Random House
Equinox Press
Smith & Haas
Viking Press
Knopf
Dutton
Harper's
Scribner's
Covici, Friede

While certainly a swipe at the publishers who had turned down *No Thanks*, the careful arrangement of their names also indicates the pains Cummings took with the design of the book. Always aware that a collection must have a distinct architecture, Cummings labored over the layout of *No Thanks*, creating an intricately devised volume. In his first schema, typed out and annotated by hand, he visually arranged the poems in the shape of a diamond: a "snow" poem began the book, followed by three more free verse poems, then a sonnet, then three more poems in free verse, followed by a sonnet and so on. In the middle, he placed another "snow" poem, then continued with the alternation of free verse followed by sonnets. But before publication, he created a new pattern, this one in the shape of a V, and with a distinct "cosmic" movement. This final arrangement begins with two poems about the moon, followed by a series of earthly and earthbound free verse poems and sonnets, all arranged in the same alternating pattern as before of three free verse poems followed by a sonnet. At the end of the collection, the heavens are scaled again, with the last two poems being about stars.

Cummings's concern for detail and design was matched by Jacobs who produced—in three separate editions—one of the more exquisite books of his illustrious career as a printer. The "holograph issue," of which only nine signed copies were printed for sale at ninety-nine dollars each, was printed on Inomachi vellum and bound in different colors of leather with hand toolings in gold. The forty-fourth poem in the book was a holograph of "the boys i mean are not refined." The "deluxe issue" of ninety numbered and signed copies priced at twelve dollars and fifty cents, was printed on Whitchurch English handmade paper and bound in blue cloth with red lettering. In place of poem forty-four, was a blank page except for a note that read, "in holograph edition only." Finally, "the trade issue" of nine hundred copies, bound in beige with red lettering and with a red sand dust wrapper, did not contain the holograph poem, nor even mention it. But all three issues are printed so that the book opened from the top rather than the side, thus allowing for longer lines, more space, and for a two-page poem to be read (and seen) in its fullness.

Inside the covers, too, were poems rich in imagery, imagination, and experimentation, as well as a fair number of poems that stated Cummings's personal views on philosophy, politics, and the importance of the individual. Indeed, *No Thanks*, more than any of his preceding volumes of verse, was more explicitly imbued with Cummings's personality—which is to say there was tremendous variety and surprises on nearly every page. The poet's familiar concerns—the natural world, love, sex, and the paramount importance of individualism—receive considerable attention, but the treatment of these themes is consistently fresh, often even startling.

The book opens with a poem-image about the "mOOn Over tOwns mOOn," in which the movement from waxing to waning is expressed through capitalization of all the "o"'s in the first two stanzas, and then in the last stanza by capitalizing all letters except for the "o." The second poem, "moon over gai / -té," is less about the moon than it is a moon's eye view of happenings on the streets of Paris, perhaps during a Bastille Day celebration. Again, Cummings exploits the typography and word arrangements to maximize visual effects. The frenzy of the people on the ground, reflected in the rapidly changing images, provides a counterpoint to the constancy of the moon moving across the sky, taking in the scenes. And though the poem ends and begins with images of the moon, the celestial focus is clearly on the affairs of men, preparing the way for the descent to earthly matters, which is Cummings's major concern throughout most of the book.

Mankind is the subject of the next eight poems. The third poem, a loose sonnet, is pivotal, in that while the concern is on humanity, the poet is still presenting a cosmic vision. The subject here is human mortality, but with a transcendental belief in an immortality for the cause itself of living: "and that which we die for lives as wholly as that which we live for dies." By the fourth and fifth poems in the book, the focus has squarely descended to more mundane human activities. The fourth poem in the book is a fine example of how Cummings was able to convey frenetic action—in this case a boxing match—through violent disjunction to words:

Suddenly by thousand

starings rinsed with
thoroughly million yells they
f-oo-l(whom,blinds;blood)pa-nt
stab are

(slopped giver of not)bang
spurting mesh(faith
-ful which -ly try are ing)...

The next few poems continue the glide downward: the fifth poem chronicles a drunk vomiting in a urinal; the sixth poem derides "little / mr Big / notbusy /Busi / ness notman." The next poem is a more clever tirade than the previous one but is no less caustic in its assertions. Its opening, titular line—"sonnet entitled how to run the world)"—is immediately followed by Cummings's prescription, summed up most succinctly in the next line: "A always don't there B being no such thing." In other words, do not try to run the world because you cannot.

The ninth poem in the book employs words as images; the observation here is of the president, as seen on a newsreel, throwing out the first baseball of the season. But it is also an attack on the pomp of government and on President Roosevelt himself, whom Cummings more and more over the years came to loathe for what he considered Roosevelt's Socialist leanings. But the political ideas do not make the poem interesting; rather, it is the way Cummings uses language. The baseball, tossed by the president, represented by the letter "o," can be seen as being "pitched" from stanza to stanza by the simple device of omitting this letter from a majority of words. By the last stanza, which reads simply, "thr[o]wing a baseball" the ball is seen making a downward arc:

...thr
w
i
n
g
a
b
aseball

The play with words is not just in the physical representation of descending motion: "win" and "gab" are also discernible components of the split letters, providing additional linguistic delights for the careful reader.

The tenth poem in the book, "little man," was, for Marianne Moore, a superb example of how form is tied to subject:

little man
(in a hurry
full of an
important worry)
halt stop forget relax

wait...

As Moore pointed out, the poem "has not a comma in it, but by careful ordering of the words there is not an equivocal emphasis." Indeed, the lack of punctuation hurries the "little man" on his way, line after line.

The tour-de-force of inventive typography, however, is in the well-known thirteenth poem in the book:

```
                    r-p-o-p-h-e-s-s-a-g-r
               who
a)s w(e loo)k
upnowgath
          PPEGORHRASS
                              eringint(o-
aThe):l
      eA
        !p:
S                                  a
                    (r
rIvInG               .gRrEaPsPhOs)
                                   to
rea(be)rran(com)gi(e)ngly
,grasshopper;
```

At first glance, the poem seems nearly impossible to decipher, but a little attention to the arrangement of letters begins to make the meaning clearer: Cummings is simply showing his readers how a grasshopper moves. But, of course, it is more than just a clever visual representation of movement. It is also about the need for readers to pay attention to the details, to how language is constructed, how mysteries (whether in nature or on the page) can be solved with a little patience and a little work. A "translation" would read something like this: grasshopper, who as we look up now, gathering into at, he, grasshopper leaps, arriving grasshopper to rearrangingly become grasshopper.

Not all the poems in *No Thanks* are as compelling as "r-p-o-p-h-e-s-s-a-g-r." While poem sixteen, "may i feel said he / (i'll squeal said she," is an exuberant and quite fun expression of two lovers engaged in making love, it is also decidedly adolescent. Poem eighteen, "this little / pair had a little scare / right in the middle of a bed bed," while also rather sophomoric is not nearly so delicious. And then there is the comment on Hemingway, provoked in part by Cummings's reading of Hemingway's celebration of bullfighting, *Death in the Afternoon*:

> what does little Ernest croon
> in his death at afternoon?
> (kow dow r 2 bul retoinis
> wus de woids uf lil Oinis

The poem, while clever, even playful, is really nothing more than a swipe at Hemingway, provoked, at least in part, by Cummings's envy at Hemingway's success—a success that Cummings felt was based less on talent than on a shrewd ability to market his macho postures to the "herd." The third and fourth lines, "translated," read: "cow thou art to bull returnest / was the words of little Ernest," a parody of Longfellow's line in *A Psalm of Life*, "Dust thout art, to dust returnest."

Cummings may have also had Hemingway in mind when he wrote poem twenty-four:

> "let's start a magazine
>
> to hell with literature
> we want something redblooded
>
> lousy with pure
> reeking with stark
> and fearlessly obscene
>
> but really clean...

The poem is likely a comment about *Esquire*, the magazine for men, which, an indignant Cummings told Pound, paid Oinis (Hemingway) $450 for his "monthly crap." Ironically, *Esquire* would begin publishing Cummings at just about the same time as *No Thanks* appeared. And according to Pound, Hemingway was, at least in part, responsible for convincing the editor, Arnold Gingrich, to acquire work by both Pound and Cummings: "I spose Oinis got me in, and so you."

Cummings's shrillness was not exhausted in these poems. Others, such as "kumrads die because they're told) / kumrads die before they're old," continues the attack on the Soviet Union and on homegrown Communism begun in *Eimi*. And then there is poem forty-four, reproduced in Cummings's hand, and only included in the special holograph edition of the book. It begins:

the boys i mean are not refined
they go with girls who buck and bite
they do not give a fuck for luck
they hump them thirteen times a night...

This poem, although clearly satiric, walks a fine line between praise and scorn for misogyny. While in most of the lines Cummings's portrait is hardly flattering: "they cannot chat of that and this / they do not give a fart for art / they kill like you would take a piss." There is also a certain amount of admiration for the boys' behavior, however crude, as the final stanza clearly reveals:

they speak whatever's on their mind
they do whatever's in their pants
the boys i mean are not refined
they shake the mountains when they dance

This poem shows the paradox inherent in Cummings. He could labor over verse as artistically intelligent as the grasshopper poem; could place art on a pedestal of his own making; could celebrate love with language that is tender, graceful, and enchanting; yet also thoroughly delighted in thumbing his nose at convention, prudery, and intellectualism; and consistently proclaimed the importance of nature and naturalness, including sexuality in its basest form, which he viewed as an instinctual expression of man's basic drive.

But along with such explicit lyrics as "the boys i mean are not refined," are poems that trumpet other sides of Cummings's imagination. The by-now familiar panegyrics to the seasons, particularly spring, make their appearance often in the book, as in the poem that directly follows "the boys i mean are not refined."

sometimes

in)Spring a someone will lie(glued
among familiar things newly which are
transferred with dusk)wondering why this star
does not fall into his mind...

Similarly, poem forty-one associates the seasons with love, and expresses the sentiment in delicate, "refined" language:

here's to opening and upward,to leaf and to sap
and to your(in my arms flowering so new)
self whose eyes smell of the sound of rain...

The awareness of fleeting mortality is another major theme in the collection, making an appearance in ten poems (out of seventy-one). Among the more remarkable poems that address this subject is the beautiful sonnet (poem sixty-one) that posits, in the third stanza, the idea that love, while not able to triumph over death, ensures that life is well lived:

...(love may not care
if time totters,light droops,all measures bend
nor marvel if a thought should weigh a star
—dreads dying least;and less, that death should end)

Poem sixty-five presents Cummings's version of the "Great Chain of Being," in which life and death are seen as cycles, akin to the movement of the universe itself. The poem begins with a statement about the natural continuity of day and night: "if night's mostness(and whom did merely day / close) / opens." It concludes with these lines where the poet celebrates the adventure of life amidst the knowledge of death:

so(unlove disappearing)only your
less than guessed more than beauty begins the
most not imagined life adventuring
who would feel if spring's least breathing should cause
a colour
            and i do not know him
                                                (and

while behind death's death whenless voices sing
everywhere your selves himself recognize)

The well known "come(all you mischief- / hatchers" (poem sixty-seven) addresses the theme of the life/death cycle more playfully. Despite all of man's actions, nature will prevail:

  Is will still occur;birds disappear
 becomingly:a thunderbolt compose poems
not because harm symmetry
 earthquakes starfish(but
  because nobody
   can sell the Moon to The)moon

The last poems in the book are among Cummings's best. Here, Cummings comes full circle, returning, after a long interlude that charted earthly experiences and observations, to a celestial vision. The next to last poem in the volume is a little masterpiece:

brIght

bRight s?? big
(soft)

soft near calm
(Bright)
calm st?? holy

(soft briGht deep)
yeS near sta? calm star big yEs
alone
(wHo

Yes
near deep whO big alone soft near
deep calm deep
????Ht ?????T)
Who(holy alone)holy(alone holy)alone

Critic Robert McIlvane noted perceptively that this poem consists of only eleven words, each repeated as many times as the letters forming the word. "Yes," "big," and "who," for instance are repeated three times, "soft," "near," "calm," etc., four times, and so on. Additionally, the capital letters and question marks are developed progressively, as are the number and length of lines and the number of words per line. All these devices contribute to the meaning, which is quite simply the evocation of a star. The substitution of question marks, the capitalization, and the layout of lines seek to represent a star twinkling in the heavens. But clearly, this is not just any star; given the association of "bright," "calm," and "holy" with the Christmas hymn, "Silent Night, Holy Night," the star in question is likely the star of Bethlehem that guided the Magi to the infant Jesus.

That Cummings should choose to celebrate this symbol of Christianity may at first seem somewhat surprising given his anti-religious stance. Cummings never disavowed spirituality, and, in fact, remained enchanted by the metaphysics of the cosmos—in particular, celestial movements that were seen as elements in the mystery of being. The choice is also likely a nod to his father, who held that the true symbol of Christmas was the star of Bethlehem, "the guiding star of love [that] has never ceased to shine above the cradle of the humblest child, from that first Christmas till now."

The last poem in the volume, which Cummings termed a sonnet despite its having fifteen lines instead of fourteen, is an even more abstract expression of reverence to a celestial power. It follows the evocation of the star in the preceding poem in tone, but is more personal in its statement. The "sonnet" is syntactically complex (a reader must wait twelve lines for the main verb), but with a little work the meaning becomes evident: it is a prayerful apostrophe to a star, the "morsel miraculous and meaningless // secret on luminous..." to "honour this loneliness of even him // who fears and eyes lifts lifting hopes and hands / —nourish my failure with thy freedom:star // isful beckoningly fabulous crumb."

It is a fitting poem by which to end a book rejected by so many.

Although *No Thanks* was privately printed and not widely distributed, it did receive a fair number of reviews, a sign that Cummings was still worthy of serious critical attention. But most of the reviews were far from positive. The anonymous reviewer for the *New Yorker* was bothered by the "disruptive" typography, apparently not seeing at all what Cummings was attempting to do with language. But the critic did allow that perhaps the book was "more communicative" than earlier collections. Kenneth Burke, who had known Cummings for more than a decade during his tenure at the *Dial*, and now reviewing for the *New Republic*, gave the book only fair marks. He liked best the poems that focused on "natural description," was obviously befuddled by the more experimental work, and disliked the political verse.

Politics, in fact, swayed the opinions of reviewers on the left. Lionel Abel, writing in the *Nation*, felt that the book was "not up to Cummings's previous standard," concluding that the volume had "more in common with the clown than the cosmic poet." The Communist *New Masses*, predictably, slammed Cummings. The review, by Isidor Schneider, previously a Cummings's partisan who had written glowingly just two years before of *The Enormous Room*, judged *No Thanks* a "literary act of suicide" that reacted to the collapse of capitalism with a "St. Vitus dance of hysterical individualism." But Cummings did still have a champion in Ezra Pound who held *No Thanks* in such high regard that he began working immediately to get it published in England. But as with his attempts to place *Eimi* with an English publisher, he was unsuccessful with *No Thanks*, as well. He did, however, manage to interest Arnold Gingrich, the editor of *Esquire*, in taking some of Cummings's work. "To run *The Noo Yorker* gaga you need Kumrad Kumminks," he wrote Gingrich in his boost of Cummings. "To git the younger pubk there iz nuthin like Kumrad Kumminks. I mean you got Hem's lots. Cummin'sh has the others."

Gingrich's response was to visit Cummings within days of getting Pound's letter. But because all that Cummings had on hand were poems that were about to appear in *No Thanks*, and Gingrich wanted unpublished ones, Cummings held up official publication of *No Thanks* for two weeks (until April 15) so that Gingrich could print five poems from the book in the May 1935 issue of the magazine that hit the news stands in mid-April. Gingrich also took a political rant, or as Cummings termed it a "cranks article," entitled "Exit the Boob," though he told Pound that Gingrich "didn't seem to much care" for the essay. Obviously Gingrich did like it enough to publish it (in the June 1935 issue), and was willing to pay $150 for it, money badly needed by the nearly indigent Cummings.

Other publication news followed: Cummings's agent, Bernice Baumgarten, had interested a small New York press, Arrow Editions, in publishing the "undanceable" *Tom*. Cummings was pleased and became even more delighted upon learning that Walter Charak, its publisher, and a former classmate of Cummings at Cambridge Latin School, wanted to produce a handsome edition of the scenario.

That spring he also received a boost when he was invited to read at Bennington College, in Bennington, Vermont. The invitation had come about through two undergraduates, Helen Stewart and Dorothy (Dot) Case. Stewart had met Cummings at a party in New York in 1934 and, enchanted by him and by his work, persuaded the College to invite him to read. When he arrived in Vermont in April, he had no idea what to expect. He had never given a public reading, at least to a large group, and was understandably nervous. As for the new college, he only knew it was a women's school and "arty." But the twenty-five dollars plus expenses and lodging that Bennington was paying was more than needed at the time.

Whatever visions his imagination had conjured about the reading could not possibly have matched reality. When he entered the packed hall, the women began to recite in unison the poem about Buffalo Bill. Flummoxed, he simply stood in the wings, flanked by Helen Stewart who was supposed to introduce him. Finally, after the third complete recitation of the poem he walked onto the stage, plucked a handkerchief from his breast pocket and waved at the adoring crowd. Though he could not have known it at the time, this would be the first of many readings he would give, almost all to audiences as appreciative as the Bennington women.

Despite the thrill of appreciation he was soundly handed at the college, and despite the appearance of *No Thanks*, the publications in *Esquire*, and the good news that Charak wanted to issue *Tom* in the fall of 1935, Cummings was hardly feeling flush with success. At forty, he was finally having to face the harsh reality that he could not get by on the meager sums he was earning from his work. The freedom that he so cherished to be his own man, to do as he pleased, write as he pleased, was being seriously undermined by his chronic lack of funds. For years he had relied on the generous support from his mother, who doled out a regular allowance from his father's estate, and on several occasions, shelled out her own money as well. As a young man he had come to detest a favorite phrase of his father, who according to Cummings continually reminded him that sooner or later he would have to "face the music." These words were undoubtedly ringing in Cummings's ears that year, but by the late spring of 1935, he could no longer shrug off the admonition.

He and Marion made a decision: they would try their luck in Hollywood. Though the offer sent through Speiser had come to nothing, other friends of theirs, including Eric and Jere Knight, whom they had met through Speiser in the early 1930s, and Marion's former roommate, Aline MacMahon, were more than making it in Hollywood, and urged them to come.

MacMahon, whom Marion knew from her first year in New York, had moved to California a few years before and was working as an actress. In her letters to her old friend, she told Marion that since she was still young, just twenty-nine, she could likely get work in the movies or modeling. The Knights, with whom they had spent some time during the summer of 1934 at their farm in Pennsylvania, were also quite encouraging. Originally English, Knight, best known as the author of *Lassie Come-Home*, had long lived in the United States; his wife was a Philadelphian. They had gone out to Los Angeles in the fall of 1934 because Knight had been offered a screenwriting job with Fox Studios.

Letters from Knight to Cummings during 1934–35 continually exhorted him to come out to California. Cummings did not exactly reject

Knight's urgings, but could not bring himself to make a commitment. But he was more than intrigued by the possibility. In fact, Cummings had been interested in writing a screenplay since 1925 when he produced a mock "movie scenario" for *Vanity Fair*. Now, bolstered by Knight's entreaties, he began to be convinced that he could make a go of it in Hollywood. That spring Cummings finally made the decision to venture West: "I've had my hardest(to date)year in New York," Cummings wrote his Aunt Jane. "Our only chance of $ seemed to be Hollywood."

With the decision made to go to California, the next step was to figure out how to get there. As money was more than tight, Cummings was hoping to get to Los Angeles as cheaply as possible. The answer to the dilemma arrived in the form of the son and daughter-in-law of Edward Titus, the Paris-based publisher of *This Quarter* that had regularly published Cummings. As Cummings explained: "This lad [Titus] had recently married & was leaving New York,with his wife(who appeared pleasant enough),for California,via Mexico.... The conveyance was a Packard 'straight 8'.... Lad and lassy enthusiastically invited Marion and me to share their racer to Mexico City,to be their house-guests while in Mexico,and to drive up in style to California."

The trip began smoothly enough. They made stops along the way, including in Washington, D.C., and in New Orleans, where the travelers were hosted by writer John Peale Bishop and his wife, who were on an extended visit there themselves. But once they crossed the border into Mexico, things went from bad to worse. A landslide blocked the road, forcing them to take the train to Mexico City. By this point, open warfare had broken out between Marion and Mrs. Titus, who could find nothing redeeming in Mexico and did not keep her jingoistic feeling to herself. According to Cummings, "the lassy turned out to be a complete moron of the omnivorously show-off variety. This didn't exactly surprise me;but it hurt Marion. After all,one woman doesn't enjoy seeing another make a fool of herself of her native land and of her husband. The lad(completely under moron's influence)disintegrated with a velocity which both hurt and surprised Marion and myself." By the time they reached Mexico City, they parted company.

The problem now was that Cummings and Marion did not have the funds to continue on. On June 11, after settling in at a "16th rate hotel," Cummings used his last five dollars, found in the watch pocket of the trousers he had changed into "with a view to impressing the aborigines," to send a hasty wire asking for fifty dollars to his mother, who was now living back in Cambridge with Cummings's aunt Jane.

Normally in his communications with his mother he was charming, and even nonchalant about asking for money. But his panic is evident in the telegram he sent his mother: NO MAIL AT WELLS FARGO AND NO MONEY HAVE YOU SENT ANYTHING? By that afternoon his anxiety vanished when he picked up the money (Rebecca had wired one hundred dollars), and along with it discovered a note informing him that his aunt Jane had five hundred dollars for him that she had been expecting to send him later in the year. With that news, Cummings called in that cash, too, and he and Marion set about exploring Mexico City and environs.

They made good use of their two-week stay in Mexico City, going to the bullfight (which Cummings rapidly sketched in his notebook), marveling at the murals of Rivera, Orozco, and Siquieros, traveled up to the colonial town of Taxco and to Cuernavaca and visiting the pre-Columbian ruins of Teotihuacan. But what impressed Cummings most about Mexico were the native people:

> the so-called Indians(Mexican)are the finest people I've met—so of course everybody is trying to bring them up to date. Altruism thy name is Jealousy! They ((Ind[ians])) work only because when or if they enjoy that. Otherwise,no hay. Discovered what an 'uncivilized' person is:a person who won't do something he doesn't want very much to do,especially when offered(as an inducement)everything which he doesn't actually need.

By early July they had arrived in Los Angeles, having "shot up from May He Ko [Mexico] (a city)via(1)Ford trimotor,11 1/2hours(2)Douglas bi-,5 hours." Although Cummings complained that "never have I less enjoyed migration," he was awed when on the second leg of the trip, from El Paso to Los Angeles, the copilot "politely invited us in to behold all the pretty dials,which looked so like NY-by-night that I might have wept."

The Knights met them at the airport, and whisked them off to their house in Santa Monica. Within a week, Cummings and Marion had rented an apartment at Casa Maria, 849 11th Street, for forty-seven dollars a month. On July 9, Cummings wrote his mother that "one needs a car even more than a garden because everything is miles away from everything else.... Luckily we have 2 autos lent us whenever we want them,with chauffeurs—alias our friends Knight and Hertz." Hertz was David Hertz, a screenwriter at Metro-Goldwyn-Mayer, whom Marion had known in New York. Her old roommate, Aline MacMahon, put her limousine at their disposal, as well.

In the same letter, Cummings noted that he was "placidly awaiting a probably nonexistent offer to 'start my stuff';but feel sure they're better off without anyone of the slightest seriousness or integrity or(whisper!)intelligence. Occasionally I daydream of offering to 'build a picture' at the price of 20,000$.... Marion's looking for jobs,&swimming nobly in sometimes violent surf."

The next day Cummings again wrote his mother, but the focus this time was on their lack of finances: "We haven't much left of our gaudy wealth.... How we still have nine dollars is,all things considered,miraculous;to me,at least—but then,have always been an optimist of the most dangerous variety,and nine dollars or no nine dollars we're still thriving." Rebecca responded to the fairly obvious plea for money by sending her son a check.

Though Cummings had "a scenario in mind" that he thought he might be able to sell to "Messers Metro Goldfish and Mayer" he also was aware that the cinema executives were not interested in "poetic properties(let alone spiritual riches)." Hertz, MacMahon, and Knight all tried to help. Hertz attempted to persuade the great German director Joseph von Sternberg that Cummings was just the man he needed to write his next script, but von Sternberg apparently did not share his feelings. MacMahon introduced him to Irving Thalberg, production chief at Metro-Goldwyn-Mayer. Again, nothing came of this. Knight took him to Disney Studios, thinking that Cummings's unique brand of zaniness and ability to draw might suit the cartoon maker; however, the studio bosses expressed no interest.

With the rejections mounting, Cummings confessed to his mother that his prospects were "nil and voodoo;for the obvious reason that No man sees higher than his Head as I believe a philosopher named Herr Neitche or something of the sort painfully pointed out."

He also recorded his response, in poetic form, to the movie industry:

The Mind's(

i never you never
he she or it
never we you and they never
saw so
much heard so much smelled so much

tasted
plus touched quite so And
How much nonexistence
eye sed bea

yew tea mis
eyesuck unyewkuntel finglestein idstings
yewrety oride lesgo eckshun

kemeruh daretoi
nig

)Ah,Soul

The parenthesis are important here, as is the transcription into standard English of the lines rendered phonetically. The comment on Hollywood sits before and after the parenthesis, which can be deciphered as the mind's asshole. Between the parenthesis is a description of a director at work who tell the actress, "I said bea / uty Miss / Issacs and you can tell Finkelstein it stinks / you ready all right let's go action / camera they're tur / ning.

The poem, while clever, is also crude—an indication of how Cummings was reacting to the movies and to the rejections both he and Marion were suffering, for she was faring no better in her search for an acting job. Despite the help of friends who circulated her photos to producers and talent scouts, no one called her. MacMahon personally tried to interest Joseph von Sternberg in her, but he was as uninterested in her as he was in Cummings. A bewildered Cummings wrote to his mother that he could not see why von Sternberg "shouldn't spend the rest of his career photographing her." As with the dismissal of his own talents by the "moguls," Cummings was sure the fault was with the studios, and not with

Marion: "Concerning the unutterable difference between Theatre and 'movies',there's no such thing as acting here."

Despite the lack of employment, Cummings and Marion did manage to divert themselves. Cummings, in fact, rather liked the physical beauty of southern California—the Santa Monica Mountains in varying shades of green, brown, and gray; the profusion of flowers; but most of all, as he told Pound, "1 miraculous ocean!!!" He painted, sketched, and wrote. The inhabitants, however, suited him less well: "It takes any native of California anything from an hour to 200 years to receive an impression of any variety whatsoever. They're about as quickwitted out here as stomach-pumps & twice as useless as burnt matches." As for others, he deemed them "chiefly Iowa farmers,on dit—of unmitigated docility." He also heaped derision on the "cinema-workers,who reek of the proverbial complex de l' inferiorité & are principally kikes."

East Coast snobbishness, alone, cannot excuse the anti-Semitism evident in reported remarks, notes, poems (Finkelstein, in his poem, is clearly representative of Jewish producers), and letters home. Cummings, like many of his generation, thought little of using derisory epithets when speaking of Jews. From his days at Harvard, he had often characterized Jews as "Hebes," "Yids," or occasionally even "kikes." To some extent, this was simply a mannerism. Jewish friends, such as Morrie Werner, Paul Rosenfeld, or his psychiatrist, Fritz Wittels, had learned to look beyond Cummings's crude characterizations and were able to see that his loose talk was merely talk, consistent with his character that tended toward negative categorization of any group of people until an individual emerged. Lincoln Kirstein, who was Jewish and a benefactor, on the other hand, noted that he could not say that Cummings "was more anti-Semitic in his specifics than Ezra Pound; both had their favorite Jews, but cummings [*sic*] was 'naughty'."

In Hollywood, however, his "naughtiness" evolved into a deeper anti-Semitism, a response, in all likelihood, to his rejection by several Jewish producers. Rather than see that these producers undoubtedly were acting as individuals, not as Jews, it was easier for Cummings to lash out at them—not as "moronic" producers, but as members of a certain group. His own politics played a role, as well, since he equated Jews with

Socialist leanings. Marion might also have helped influence his attitudes, for she was decidedly anti-Semitic, and rather outspoken in her prejudice. His chief correspondent at the time, Ezra Pound, whom Cummings held in high esteem, if nothing else, certainly abetted Cummings's views.

Regardless of the reason, Cummings was decidedly drifting toward, and becoming quite cozy with, knee-jerk responses toward groups, Jews especially. As he wrote Watson, "O the juse the juse / they don't amews." And when, in 1935, boxer Max Baer, who displayed a Star of David on his trunks, lost the heavyweight championship to African American Joe Louis, Cummings could not contain his delight: "Something whispers to yours truly that the Big Year for the Kikes is o'er."

Not everyone with whom he associated was derided. He greatly enjoyed the company of the Knights and often sat up late drinking with Eric. A frequent subject of their conversations was the "loss" of children, for Knight, as well, had lost custody of his daughters through a previous divorce. Of his new acquaintances, he liked photographer Edward Weston who asked Cummings to sit for some photos. "Hope he's as good at that [portraiture] as he is at seaweed ploughed-fields sand erosions & cypressroots!" he wrote to his mother. And he had only praise for sculptor and furniture designer Isamu Noguchi, whom he met through Marion.

Noguchi, as it turned out, was responsible for getting the nearly destitute Cummings and Marion out of California. Noguchi was on his way to Mexico and needed someone to drive his car to the Texas-Mexican border, as his driver's license had been revoked for speeding. Cummings jumped at the opportunity to leave "Ever-Ever Land." Since mid-August, as he wrote Pound, he had been trying "to wangle enough jack out of somewhere else to get the Hell out of anywhere pronto." While he still did not have much "jack," he and Marion could at least count on free transportation to Texas.

In early September they were on their way, stopping at the Grand Canyon for a few days to take in the vistas. Cummings was awed by the magnificence of the terrain, filling his sketchbooks with landscapes. Despite the free transportation, Cummings and Marion were down to their last few dollars when they arrived in Texas. Cummings wired

Rebecca, who quickly sent them train fare home. By late September, Cummings and Marion were back in New York.

twenty-two

Never the Soft Adventure of Undoom

After their return from California, Cummings and Marion stayed only a few days in New York before heading to Silver Lake. Cummings was much in need of the tranquility of New Hampshire in the fall. Over the next three weeks, he spent his days taking long walks in the woods, sometimes alone, sometimes with Marion, and often sketching scenes from nature. He also poured over Thomas Mann's *Joseph and His Brothers*, which moved him to jot down quotes, as well as observations inspired by the novel. Most of the observations had to do with the mystery of the spheres, from which he quoted extensively. He was particularly taken with Mann's statement that "Not only do the heavenly and the earthly recognize themselves in each other, but thanks to the revolution of the sphere, the heavenly can turn into the earthly, the earthly into the heavenly, from which it is clear that gods can become men and on the other hand men can become gods again."

Indeed, he was so aroused by the idea that he extended the notion: "My destiny is coalescing w.[ith] a universal one:on which more & more I impress myself & it expresses itself through me." It is hard to know exactly what Cummings is trying to say about himself here, but in the context of Mann, the poet seems to be implying that his ideas about things are in accord with a greater movement in the universe, that he is in the right, validated by the very cosmos. More and more Cummings was beginning to entertain such attitudes, was able to question himself less and less, and was positive that his views—whether on art, politics or people—were the only possible way of seeing things. Coming off of the disastrous trip to California, there is also reason to believe that he was attempting to convince himself that it was those who were inhabiting the universe who were out of whack, and that he himself was in accord with the universe itself. He underlined this part of a sentence from Mann: "what happens in the earthly repeats itself in the heavenly sphere and contrariwise." This one was also underlined: "Bottom is soon top and top bottom." Many of the quotes he recorded from Mann he also sent to Pound, exhorting him to read the book.

A less sinister explanation is also possible. In one of his jottings from the following year, he wrote: "Noone can live spiritually who allows himself to become rigid,noone can die spiritually who keeps himself attune to Nature—I touch the tree."

The New Hampshire idyll came to a an abrupt halt, however, on October 17, 1935, when Cummings learned of the death of his long-time friend, sculptor Gaston Lachaise, a victim of leukemia at the age of fifty-three. Although he and Lachaise had not been as close in the 1930s as in the decade earlier, he was still a significant person for Cummings. A week later, Cummings and Marion were back in New York for the funeral. Henry McBride, who had been the art critic for the *Dial*, and who, in 1918, had written the first article on Lachaise for the *New York American* (Cummings had written the second in 1920), wrote a tribute to his old friend for the *New York Sun:* "The tawdry, ineffective funeral I would not have had otherwise. It was in the tradition. That's the way we buried Melville. That's the way we buried Poe. Greatness would not be greatness if it could be understood generally.... Not but there had been some admirers! There had always been a few. Perhaps the most notable was E. E. Cummings, the poet; himself so slightly acknowledged as to be practically of no use."

Cummings did not make his feelings public at the time; he felt, having written two articles on Lachaise—the first for the *Dial*; another for *Creative Arts Magazine* in 1928—that he had already fervently preached the importance of Lachaise. But years later, he did comment in a preface to a catalog of the sculptor's work held at the Weyhe Gallery in New York that "the achievement of Lachaise remains passionately and serenely itself—a marvel and a mystery : the spontaneous and inevitable expression of one fearlessly unique human being."

Another reason, as well, brought Cummings back to New York at this time: the publication of *Tom* by Walter Charak's Arrow Editions on October 15, 1935. When Charak had signed up the book, he assured Cummings that he would produce a handsome volume. The publisher was true to his word: *Tom*, printed in Santa Fe, New Mexico, by the Rydal Press, was beautifully designed and produced. The somber typography lends a weight to the text, while the color frontispiece—a reproduction of a Ben Shawn painting of Uncle Tom created especially for the book—adds an additional element of beauty.

Cummings was inordinately pleased with the book, as were the majority of reviewers. The *Boston Evening Transcript*, *Stage*, and even the *Nation*, previously quite critical of both *Eimi* and *No Thanks*, lauded Cummings's achievement. The reviewer for *Time* wrote that *Tom* was "an imaginative updating, free from Mr. Cummings' customary savage wit." Horace Gregory, writing in *Poetry*, noted that "Mr. Cummings sees the stage, and on the stage he visualizes action."

Despite the praise heaped on the scenario, no ballet producer rang up Cummings. Rumors began to float around New York, however, that Kirstein, with Muriel Draper's backing, was going to mount a production of *Uncle Tom's Cabin*. At first Cummings thought that perhaps Kirstein was going through with the previously cancelled staging of his *Tom*, but when Charak asked Kirstein about it, the producer reportedly told him that he had written his own scenario and that Russian composer Nicholas Nabokov was writing a score.

An embittered Cummings wrote Hildegarde Watson: "You might be amused to learn that Kumrads Kirstein and Draper, Inc are said to be collectively enceinte re a one-&-only-original & jenyouwine(Avoid All Substitutes)'Uncle Tom's Cabin':the climax whereof is rumored to reveal a white & a black chorus unanimously declaiming 'workers of the world unite.'" It is impossible to know what was actually going on. Kirstein later denied that there had ever been such a production planned.

In January 1936, however, a young composer named David Diamond did come forward to write a score. Although only twenty-one, Diamond had studied at Rochester's Eastman School of Music, and was at that time a student at Dalcroze Institute in New York, studying with Roger Sessions. While in Rochester he had met Hildegarde Watson, who had introduced him to Cummings's work. After moving to Manhattan in the summer of 1935, he became friendly with Aaron Copland. Through the combined efforts of Hildegarde Watson and Copland, who probably was the first composer to set a Cummings poem to music ("Poet's Song," 1927) he was moved to write to Cummings about creating music for the ballet. Cummings responded immediately, sending him a copy of *Tom*.

Unlike others, including Sessions, Copland, and Virgil Thomson, who had all turned down the opportunity to write a score for the ballet, Diamond was enthused: "This is a real ballet script you have given me," he told Cummings. During that winter, they met on several occasions to discuss particulars. Diamond even convinced Cummings to add a song to be sung by slaves during a dance of religious ecstasy. Their meetings continued until late that spring, when Diamond left for Paris with the hope, while there, of interesting Leonide Massine, noted choreographer of the Ballet Russes, in putting on the work.

By August, Diamond had completed the score, but Massine declined to produce the ballet. *Tom*, in fact, was never staged, though finally, in 1985, the music was performed under the title *First Orchestral Suite*, and a recording is now available. While Diamond and Cummings had no success getting *Tom* danced, the happy consequence of their collaboration was a lifetime friendship.

When Cummings and Marion returned to New York from New Hampshire during the fall of 1935, they managed to find an apartment for Marion just two doors down from Cummings, at 8 Patchin Place. The rent was forty-five dollars a month for two rooms. Though they had lived together in Paris, Tunisia, New Hampshire, and Los Angeles, they had always maintained separate residences in New York. And while both wanted to be in close, if not immediate, proximity to one another, Cummings was not keen on sharing his place with anyone. Since 1924, he had lived and worked in the same fourteen by twenty foot room on the third floor of 4 Patchin Place, and was quite adamant about maintaining his own space. But with Marion now living so nearby, her apartment quickly became their shared quarters, where they ate, lounged, and entertained. Most days, Cummings remained in his studio, however, and often slept there, as well. Even after Marion moved into the first floor of number 4 the following year, they maintained the same arrangement, as they would for the rest of Cummings's life.

Financial problems continued to plague Cummings. It was mainly his mother who kept him somewhat solvent, sending him, in addition to his occasional "allowance," extra cash for his birthday, at Christmas, and when special needs arose. Although he does not specify the amount, she must have given him quite a generous check for his forty-first birthday in 1935, for he responded, "'very little cheque' indeed! It looked like the proverbial million $ to me." He then went on to tell her, "my 6 months of royalties from all my works(except Eimi,which is 500 odd $ behind its publisher's advance—in debt,that is)turned out to be 6 dollars and some cents." The continual support allowed him to effect an unrepentant stance, part bravado, part real:

if i

or anybody don't
know where it her his

my next meal's coming from
i say to hell with that...

Cummings did make a little money from publishing in magazines, most notably an article on burlesque for *Stage* (March 6, 1936). The 1936 annual of new writing, *The New American Caravan*, edited by Alfred Kreymbourg, Lewis Mumford, and Paul Rosenfeld published "Speech (from a forthcoming play)." James Laughlin, founder and editor of the new publishing house, New Directions, included poems by Cummings in both his 1936 and 1937 anthologies, *New Directions in Prose and Poetry*.

More significantly, through a chance encounter in Santa Monica with an English publisher, Roger Roughton, he managed to get a small collection of verse in print in England, his first in that country. The book, titled *One over Twenty*, consisted of twenty poems that Cummings selected from all his previous books. Though few in number, the poems were among his finest. Among the inclusions were "Buffalo Bill 's," "Spring is like a perhaps hand," "i sing of Olaf glad and big," and "sonnet entitled how to run the world)." Roughton issued the book in December of 1936 under his imprint Contemporary Poetry and Prose Editions. He even paid Cummings a small advance.

Cummings also earned sums here and there from his paintings. He sold *Portrait of Gardie* to the Watsons in 1936. Also that year he received a commission from the father of Helen Stewart, the young woman who had organized his Bennington reading, for a portrait of Helen. Stewart and her friend Dot Case had moved to the Village in the spring of 1936, and during that period they both became quite friendly with Cummings and Marion. Aside from arranging for the portrait, Stewart also frequently took Cummings and Marion out to eat at restaurants beyond their means, and both young women were far from stingy with gifts, ranging from bouquets of fresh flowers to carved elephants for his collection.

There were other new acquaintances that year, too, most of them, like Stewart, Case, and Diamond, much younger than Cummings. Jane Auer, a young woman just twenty, who was struggling to become a writer; the charming twenty-year-old John Latouche, who was trying to make his way in New York as a song lyricist; and Harry Dunham, 26, filmmaker and writer, and Paul Bowles, 25, an up-and-coming composer, were among Cummings's older admirers. Their visits, according to Bowles, had the flavor of "audiences," with Cummings "holding court."

But Cummings also extended himself to the young people. He took Bowles to his first burlesque show, encouraged Latouche in his lyrics, and clearly delighted in the company of Auer who regaled him with gossip about the Village. Bowles recalled that before he had met Cummings, composer George Antheil had told him that Cummings was a "son-of-a-bitch." "Cummings was not a son-of-a-bitch at all," said Bowles. "He reminded me of members of my own family: eccentric, intolerant, and querulous. The great advantage he had over them, apart from his intelligence and talent, was his capacity for enjoying the act of living."

Perhaps most important for Bowles and Auer, it was through Cummings that they got together as a couple. Although they had met once before, Bowles recalled that Auer "was not communicative." But when they next saw each other at a Cummings party in February 1937, the two of them, along with Dutch painter Kristians Tonny and his wife Marie-Claire Ivanoff, who had come along with Bowles, hatched a plot to go to Mexico together. In 1938 Jane Auer married Paul Bowles. They both went on to become distinguished writers.

The string of bad luck with publishers that the forty-two-year-old Cummings had been enduring was reversed in the spring of 1937 when the poet received word from his agent that a young editor named Charles "Cap" Pearce at Harcourt Brace was interested in publishing a volume of *Collected Poems*. It was *No Thanks* that had apparently engendered the idea in Pearce, who realized not only that Cummings was a major poet, but also that it was near impossible for readers to obtain any of his books. As numerous as his publications were, they had been issued by various publishers, all in fairly small editions, and some, among them *&* and *XLI Poems*, were out of print. It was not an easy sell. Harcourt Brace had turned down *No Thanks* and Pearce's suggestion that the firm now issue a *Collected Poems* "met with somewhat reluctant approval."

A delighted Cummings began securing rights to all his earlier volumes, even buying from Seltzer the rights to *Tulips and Chimneys*, and from the Dial Press, *XLI Poems*. But the volume was, in the end, not to be a true "collected poems." According to Pearce, he did propose a complete book, "but e.e.c. made the decision to limit it." While this may have been Pearce's recollection, their correspondence shows that he played a major role in the ultimate selection of work. At the same time, Cummings did make initial selections. In May he wrote Pearce that "the enclosed list represents what I like,irrespective of whether it's obscene or unsetupable. What I don't like is,naturally,whatever I don't feel to be myself."

The total amounted to 184 poems from published volumes plus twenty new poems, for a total of 206. Cummings chopped the most from the early books, but wanted *ViVa* and *No Thanks* republished in their entirety. But over the next few months the inclusions (and omissions) changed. By mid-summer the count swelled to 315 poems, including twenty-two new poems, mostly verse that Cummings had published in anthologies or periodicals since the appearance of *No Thanks*. The breakdown, by volume of the final selection was as follows: from *Tulips and Chimneys*, forty-seven; *&*, forty-nine; *XLI Poems*, twenty-five; *Is 5*, sixty-eight; *ViVa*, fifty-four; *No Thanks*, fifty. The selection represented 293 poems previously published in books, out of a total of 394 possibilities.

Though Cummings argued for the inclusion of some poems that Pearce suggested be stricken, for the most part he went along with

Pearce's suggestions. In the end, the two not only omitted 101 poems from previous collections, but also rearranged the selections, perhaps feeling that a new architecture was now warranted. The changes in order in the early volumes did not significantly impact the ultimate impression, but the new arrangement in the poems from *No Thanks* do dramatically change the way that volume is represented. Gone is the careful descent from the heavens to the earth, then upward again to celestial concerns; as a consequence, the sequence of poems appears to be far more random, almost a hodge-podge.

The omissions and inclusions do not always reflect the soundest poetic judgment, either. While Cummings may have wanted for personal reasons to eliminate "Epithalamion" and "Puella Mea," from the edition, it is hard to see why he would have opted to keep a poem as slight as "her / flesh," with its rather awful line "i had cement for her," and rejected his vivid portrait of the denizens of a Manhattan bar: "i was sitting in mcsorely's. outside it was New York and beauti- / fully snowing" (both from *&*). It's hard to fathom why he cared to preserve from *No Thanks*

theys sO alive
                    (who is
                                        ?niggers)...

and eliminated, from that same volume, the rather exquisite

we)under)over,the thing of floating Of
;elate
shyly a-live keen parallel specks float-ing create
height,...

But clearly, from the correspondence between Cummings and Pearce, the poet was more interested that his typography be followed exactly, and that the "poem-pictures" were laid out in a manner that would reveal their structure, than in at least some of the contents.

Most of the final assembling of *Collected Poems* was done while Cummings and Marion were once again in Europe. Never one to stay put if he had some money, Cummings decided to use the four hundred dollar advance from Harcourt Brace, along with three hundred dollars Jacobs had received from anthologies for reprint rights to poems from *Tulips and Chimneys*, *&*, and *No Thanks*, for him and Marion to go abroad. The trip, in part, was prompted by an invitation from English zoologist Solly Zuckerman, whom Cummings had met earlier that year in New York, to visit him in London.

In mid-June 1937, they embarked for England. It was hardly the best time for a European visit. The continent, in fact, was on the brink of war. Hitler, in power in Germany since 1933, had already embarked on his genocidal campaign against the Jews. He had also made his designs on neighboring Czechoslovakia and Austria well known, sending tremors throughout Europe. Desire for conquest was not confined to Hitler's Germany. Mussolini, who had ruled Italy since 1922, invaded Ethiopia in 1935, and had formed an alliance with Hitler by 1936. The Spanish Civil War was raging, pitting the Socialist Republican government against the right-wing Falangist insurgents headed by Francisco Franco (and aided by Mussolini and Hitler).

In England, the newly elected prime minister Neville Chamberlain was attempting to assure the British that appeasement of Hitler was the best policy, but a sense of unease gripped the population. The effects of the Great Depression, which had ravaged not just the economy of the United States but of Europe as well, were still being keenly felt. Unemployment was rampant all over the continent, resulting in social unrest, with the result being growing numbers of adherents to the Socialist and Communist parties in France and England.

While Cummings was certainly aware of the events in Europe, he was so preoccupied with his own life that the increasing world tensions remained on the periphery of his existence. He remained a staunch isolationist in regard to American intervention in Europe, and was convinced, given what he regarded as the tragic blunder of the First World War, that the United States had no business getting involved in the affairs of European nations.

Through Zuckerman they found lodgings in a Chelsea rooming house. "Chelsea is sad," Cummings wrote. "I especially inhabit Paultons Sq & generally spend half my time trying to give it an apostrophe." It was not just the grimness of the time that cast a pall over Chelsea. Not long after their arrival, Cummings and Marion had gone to a party at Zuckerman's.

Among the guests was the noted British philosopher A. J. (Freddie) Ayer. Aside from analytic philosophy, Ayer's other passion was women, and that evening he set his sights on Marion. Over the next couple of days he invited Marion to lunch and eventually wooed her into his bed. The day after the tryst a repentant Marion confessed all to Cummings, claiming that she had succumbed to the moment. She also assured Cummings that he was the only man she loved or wanted, and that the sex with Ayer had been a mistake. The air was thick for a day or so, but after a few long head-clearing rambles around London, Cummings recovered from Marion's brief betrayal. He even managed to see Ayer again, whom he actually liked. By the time they left London, a nascent friendship had begun that would flower over the next several years.

Cummings also had other matters on his mind. On June 21, he wrote to Rebecca about his visit to the MacDermots: "Marion & I were given tea at the Carlton Hotel…by the MacDermots;both of which look older. He's retired from Irish politics,he says;also that Nancy is in Vienna 'being finished' & will be 'brought out'(& presented at court)next year—& that she's well."

Cummings expressed no regret that he was unable to see Nancy, now seventeen; indeed, he was quite content just to learn what she was doing and that she was well. The strong feelings he once had about the "loss" of his daughter had greatly dissipated, or at the very least, he had come to accept that she was no longer even a small part of his life. The attitude was a mix of callousness and realism. He had come to realize over the years that while he still may have had feelings for Nancy, she certainly would not have been able to reciprocate. To press now for a reunion, in fact, struck him as slightly absurd. Since Elaine had managed so well to keep her distant, he was not even sure she would have any idea who he was. And he was not willing to find out.

In mid-July, he and Marion were in Paris, again staying in their former residence, the studio at 11 rue de la Bûcherie. Finances were again precarious and Marion sought work as a model, but this time had no success.

Although she had kept her phenomenal looks, her age—she was at least thirty-one—was against her. She found that younger models were in demand by the couturiers and fashion photographers.

Since Marion was unable to find employment, money was becoming a major problem; in fact, Cummings was down to his last twelve dollars. On August 4, he wired his mother: UNLESS CHECK ON WAY PLEASE TELEGRAPH 300 DOLLARS AMERICAN EXP PARIS. Two days later he was able to cable back, "thanks."

In London, Cummings became increasingly aware of the European worries that war might break out soon; in Paris, he found the mood even bleaker. Everywhere he went the threat of war seemed to be a major topic of conversation. The civil war in Spain was also much nearer to the French than to the Americans, several thousand miles away. On Bastille Day, the Communists had planned huge demonstrations in favor of the fragile Spanish Republic. On the streets that day, Cummings, though by no means a friend of the left, was appalled at the French government's response: the streets and squares were filled with riot police, army troops, even tanks.

He recorded the atmosphere in a piece of doggerel:

red-rag and pink-flag
blackshirt and brown
strut-mince and stink-brag
have all come to town...

By mid-August, Cummings and Marion had run through their cash again. He appealed to his mother, and on August 17, he received another check, this time for eighty dollars. But since eighty dollars was not enough to get them home, he cabled his mother again, this time instructing her to borrow $150 from their acquaintances, William and Mildred O'Brien. Apparently, the money came as Cummings and Marion sailed back to New York on August 28.

September, as usual, was spent in New Hampshire where Cummings wrote, at Pearce's suggestion, an introduction to the forthcoming book. By the time he and Marion returned to New York in October, he had completed it. By November the book was being set by Quinn & Boden printers in New Jersey and Cummings, concerned that the typesetters follow his copy exactly, actually went to the press to ensure accuracy. In a letter to Pound, he remarked humorously that one of the printers told him "'owe boi yoo musda bin ona too wiks drung widda wumun wn yoo rode dad.'" [Oh boy, you must have been on a two weeks drunk with a woman when you wrote that.]

He had one other task to complete before publication: to record a few of the poems in the book so that Harcourt Brace could issue a promotional record to entice booksellers to stock the book. Among the poems Cummings recorded were "since feeling is first," "somewhere i have never travelled,gladly beyond," and "Buffalo Bill 's." This was perhaps the first time a publisher had used an audio recording to help boost sales. Unfortunately, the record was distributed only to booksellers and not available to buyers as a supplement to the *Collected Poems*.

Another book was in production, as well. Since Cummings had bought back the rights to *Tulips and Chimneys*, *&*, and *XLI Poems*, he and Jacobs decided to reissue the first volume as Cummings had envisioned it nearly twenty years before. The "archetype edition" as Cummings and Jacobs dubbed it, combined all three early books, with the poems arranged in their original order. The title also carried the original ampersand.

Tulips & Chimneys came off Jacob's Golden Eagle press in October 1937, though the official publication date was December 1937. It was available in two separate editions: a deluxe boxed issue of 148 numbered and signed copies that sold for twelve dollars and fifty cents; and a trade edition of 481 unsigned copies, priced at seven dollars and fifty cents. At long last it was possible to read Cummings's important first book of poems as he had initially conceived it.

And an interesting read it is: with the arrangement of poems restored, the reader gets a real sense of not just a well-worked-out plan, but of how truly extraordinary and unique a poet the young Cummings truly was. The section entitled "Impressions," for instance, is far more resonant and the painter's eye for nuance more strongly revealed than in the truncated version that Seltzer had published. The "Post-Impressions," too, more convincingly show how Cummings was experimenting with language. In the reconstructed edition, the more radical departures from traditional verse of the time that were mostly eliminated from the 1923 book can be seen in the context of the poet striving to record sound and sight as they appeared to him, not as conventionally "poetic" renderings of experience. The nineteen additions to the "Portraits" in the archetype edition provide a far greater sense of Cummings's skill at limning the essence from the surround, as well as demonstrating his range and scope. Though *Tulips & Chimneys* could perhaps be seen as an exercise in ego, it was actually far more than that: it was a necessary volume, a testimony to Cummings's true brilliance as a poet. His original conception had been the right one.

Collected Poems, published on February 24, 1938, was a major book, despite the omissions and somewhat haphazard arrangement of poems. For the first time readers could get a sense of Cummings's achievements, evolutions, and continuity over fifteen years. And just in case the messages of individuality, nonconformity, and delight in living contained in the verse was not clear, the introduction made it explicit: "The poems to come are for you and me and not for mostpeople—it's no use trying to pretend that mostpeople and ourselves are alike. Mostpeople have less in common with ourselves than the squareroot of minusone. You and I are human beings;most people are snobs.... If mostpeople were to be born twice they'd improbably call it dying—."

Part posture, part statement of true-felt, deeply held feelings, the "Introduction" is designed both to create a conspiracy between poet and reader ("You and I are human beings") and to preach his philosophy of poetry and life. In a tone not so far removed from that of a sermon, Cummings expounds on his favorite topics: the triumph of feeling over thinking, the necessity to live fully, and the imperative need for uniqueness. As an illustration of how these principles play out in the work and in the poet, the reader is handed generous helpings of Cummings's sense of his own self: "With you I leave a remembrance of miracles:they are by somebody who can love and who shall be continually reborn,a human being."

Although the introduction can be seen as simply a statement of unbridled egotism, it perfectly fulfills its function of "explaining" the poems and the poet: "never the soft adventure of undoom,greedy anguishes and cringing ecstasies of inexistence;never to rest and never to have;only to grow. Always the beautiful answer who asks a more beautiful question."

As Cummings promised, *Collected Poems* asked more beautiful questions than it gave beautiful answers, revealing a poet who was continually striving—from youth to middle age—to achieve the new. A reader looking for easy statements or "answers" in his most extensive collection of verse to date would not find them. Even in the poems from the first books, there are few definitive closures that sum up how a poem should mean. Indeed, many of Cummings's poems do not end; they simply stop. Consequently, the reader is forced to reencounter the poem again, parse it for meanings, decipher an intent. And more often than not, the "answer" spirals back into a question, since precise statement is not what Cummings is about. Instead, he is intent on expressing his experience of the world in the way that experience expressed itself to him. Every word and even a syllable, parenthesis, or other grammatical marker, releases possibilities of meaning that cannot be facilely measured, even, at times, understood with total certainty.

To read Cummings fully one must, as he implies in his introduction, become a poetic co-conspirator, experience each and every poem on its own terms, and recreate them for one's own self. And when reading becomes something more than a passive exercise of running eyes over words, the reward is significant: the power of his poetics is unleashed, comes tumbling in a whirl out of the intersection where form meets function meets meaning.

While in *Collected Poems* there is certainly a preponderance of verse on similar themes—spring, love, sex, and death; iconoclastic pronouncements about society; and the celebration of nature—the variety of expression and the experiments with the saying, render the verse consistently interesting, fresh, and, to use one of his favorite terms, "alive."

The twenty-two new poems that he chose to include in the collection, though by no means all masterpieces, add to the richness of the book. The second of the new poems is a comment on an enervating lecturer at the YM-YWCA who attempts to reduce the universe to mathematical terms. After a careful reproduction of words, phrases, coughs, and pauses, the poet flees "into the not / merely immeasurable into / the mightily alive the / dear beautiful eternal night."

The eighth of the new poems, "this little bride & groom are," is on the surface simply a description of plastic figurines on top of a wedding cake.

But there is deeper resonance, as well, for Cummings is clearly expressing the notion that the tokens of a marriage do not equate with marriage itself: "...& everything is protected by / cellophane against anything(because / nothing really exists."

Joe Gould, his down and out friend, denizen of the streets of the village, was profiled by name in *No Thanks* (also included in *Collected Poems*). Among the new poems is another that perhaps also pays homage to Gould, or at least one of similar ilk:

my specialty is living said
a man(who could not earn his bread
because he would not sell his head)...

By far the best of the new poems, and justly celebrated, is the last poem in the book, "you shall above all things be glad and young." In keeping with his tradition of always ending his books with a sonnet, this one is too. The sheer beauty of the lines, with their enchanting rhythms and rhymes, teeter on sentimentality, but the force of the poem keeps it in check. Grammatically, too, the poem is a tour de force. The long periodic sentence that begins with the second line and ends with the twelfth, is an elaborate display of the poet's mastery of syntax. An allusion to Shakespeare, not uncustomary in Cummings's poems, particularly sonnets, is also present: his phrase, "that way knowledge lies," is probably a clever echo of Lear's line, "that way madness lies." Finally, though, the poem works not because of its grammar or allusions, simply because it is rather magnificent, with one of the most tremendous closures in modern American poetry:

you shall above all things be glad and young.
For if you're young,whatever life you wear

it will become you;and if you are glad
whatever's living will yourself become.
Girlboys may nothing more than boygirls need:
i can entirely her only love

whose any mystery makes every man's
flesh put space on;and his mind take off time

that you should ever think,may god forbid
and(in his mercy)your true lover spare:
for that way knowledge lies,the foetal grave
called progress,and negation's dead undoom.

I'd rather learn from one bird how to sing
than teach ten thousand stars how not to dance

Reviews began to come in within weeks of *Collected Poems*' publication, and unlike so often before, the majority were positive, if not raves. Paul Rosenfeld, Cummings's long time supporter, led the charge, this time in the *Nation*, that had not looked too favorably on Cummings's recent work. The title of his review, "The Brilliance of E.E. Cummings" sums up the flavor of Rosenfeld's piece. Dudley Fitts, writing in the *Saturday Review of Literature*, noted that Cummings was responsible for "some of the best lyrics of our time." S. I. Hayakawa, the young linguist, in a thoughtful review in *Poetry* remarked that while Cummings's experiments with language may not be poetry, "they succeed eminently in doing what they set out to do." Of the poems that dealt with war, Hayakawa had only praise: "Cummings has written what are certainly our greatest war poems." The critic for the *New York Times Book Review*, Peter M. Jack, also lauded it, placing his poetry in the "tradition of romantic individualism." "The work that Cummings has set himself to do is a poet's work," wrote Peter Jack. "It will never be remembered as current topics versified or political propaganda."

Cummings's longtime friend, John Peale Bishop, used the publication to write a survey of all of Cummings's work. The long essay, published in the *Southern Review*, was an important piece of criticism in that it placed Cummings's work, including *The Enormous Room* and *Eimi*, in the context of his time, and in relation to the modern movement. "At the time when Cummings' manner was formed," wrote Bishop, "it seemed not only possible, but imperative that every element of technique should be recreated.... What could be more natural than that Cummings, who is painter as well as poet, should attempt to emulate in literature the innovations of his contemporaries in painting?" In concluding his remarks on the verse, Bishop noted that "it is only by Cummings' poetry as a whole that we are profoundly impressed. It is not unattached to his personality; but the interest of that personality is in its singular capacity to report the age."

Reviewers for the *New Masses* and the *Daily Worker* did not share the views of Bishop or Jack or Fitts. In the *New Masses*, Rolfe Humphries (who would later anthologize Cummings) only saw Cummings in political terms and took him to task for turning his back on the comrades. The reviewer for the *Daily Worker* remarked that Cummings "sold his poetic birthright for a mess of punctuation marks." The leftist criticism was not only inept but inapt. Cummings had never been a Communist, and while he certainly had Socialist leanings in the 1920s, he had always remained on the outside of any political movement. But because of the large number of societal critiques in his work, both in poetry and in *The Enormous Room*, the left had assumed that Cummings was one of them.

There were other dissenters, as well, who launched their attack not on his politics but on his experimentation with language. Yvor Winters, whose friend Hart Crane had tried unsuccessfully to persuade Winters for years that Cummings was one of America's great poets, came thundering forward in a review for *American Literature*: "The Experimental Movement in American poetry produced beyond any reasonable doubt a handful of remarkable poets. It is my own belief that these poets are misguided in their motivating principles and are consequently limited in their scope; but within certain limits, the best of them are, or have been, genuine artists.... In the work of Cummings, the artistry which gives dignity...is entirely lacking."

A most interesting review, which appeared in *Partisan Review*, was by two writers, Philip Horton and Sherry Mangan. Horton's assessment was negative, Mangan's positive. According to Horton, Cummings's poetry "shows no technical improvement or intellectual development over a period of fifteen years." Mangan countered, "his faults are inseparably the faults of his virtues, and in those virtues—gusto, abundance, magniloquence—he is nearly unique."

Privately, Cummings received innumerable fan letters from the known and unknown. Carl Sandburg wrote that "I must get around to telling this fellow [Cummings] he has much on the ball and I like to watch him pitch in his own chosen world series and he has blue sky and stinking prison flowers and fine lovemaking madrigals and a compassionate identification with conscientious objectors and the dust of very common streets and a capacity for exquisite clowning and inexplicable effrontery and somehow he owns what's under his hat."

Marianne Moore wrote: "The more I study the equivalences here of 'mostpeople's' language, the formidable use of nursery lore, and the further unfortuities,—known to you as technique but never known to lookers-on, the better, live-er, more undimmed and undiminished they seem. Those who are deaf to the sublime, have to be without it; that is their honorarium."

The Pulitzer Prize Committee also took notice of the book, but in the end the poetry prize was awarded to John Gould Fletcher. Originally associated with Pound's Imagists, by the 1930s Fletcher had turned rather uninventively to nature as a source of spiritual inspiration for his work. Winfield Townley Scott, book editor of the *Providence Journal*, wrote a dissent: "I am about to comment on the Pulitzer Poetry Award. My comment is, Nuts.... Those literary editors who did vote in the straw balloting produced a much more intelligent result than the poetry awarders themselves. They voted for unmistakably vital verse.... The real news about the Pulitzer Poetry Prize is who did not get it...E.E. Cummings' 'Collected Poems' did not get it."

With the publication of *Collected Poems*, however, the public became far more aware of Cummings than ever before. It was from this volume—readily available—that anthologists and critics, for years, would begin to select poems. Indeed, in the same year as the book was published, "Buffalo Bill 's" was chosen by Cleanth Brooks and Robert Penn Warren for a critique of form in their important text *Understanding Poetry*. Over the next decade, Cummings would appear in nearly every anthology of American verse. The recognition had been a long time coming, but finally Cummings, despite the difficulty of his work, was beginning to reach much larger audiences and was no longer just a poet for the few, but was becoming a poet for "mostpeople."

twenty-three

Freedom as Breakfastfood

At just about the same time that *Collected Poems* was being published, Cummings was going through a crisis in his domestic life. During the five years he and Marion had been together, they had endured their ups and downs, including her brief fling with Ayer, but "bliss" was the word that usually came to Cummings's mind when he thought of his relationship with Marion. To be sure, he was well aware that Marion reveled in her attractiveness and delighted in the attention she received from men. Cummings, for the most part, tolerated her routine, although, as in the case with Ayer, he quickly asserted himself if he felt that she had crossed the line from flirtation into betrayal. Otherwise, it appears, he took a certain pleasure in watching heads turn when Marion walked into the room.

Sometime in late 1937 or early 1938 Marion strayed again, but this time it was not a mere "roll in the hay," as she had told Cummings about Ayer; it was a prolonged affair. Marion's lover was English director Paul Rotha, then living in New York, who had been introduced to both Cummings and Marion by the Knights. While Rotha was clearly infatuated with Marion, she claimed (at least later) that she was not as in love with him. She certainly enjoyed his attention and the frequent lunches and dinners at posh restaurants like the "21" Club, but did not see their romance as anything more than a casual relationship.

At some point in early 1938, Cummings learned of the affair, probably from Marion herself. Having been down this road too often before, Cummings was angry, hurt, and bewildered. As he was totally devoted to Marion, he had assumed she was as equally devoted to him and could not comprehend how she could be unfaithful. When Cummings confronted Marion, she assured him that he was still the man in her life, and that he should not think otherwise. While she admitted that she enjoyed Rotha's companionship from time to time, his expensive gifts that Cummings could not afford, and the fancy restaurant meals, she was by no means intent on leaving Cummings for the film director. Indeed, she even told Cummings that Rotha had asked her to marry him but she had turned him down. Unlike in the past when Cummings simply internalized his grief and sense of betrayal, this time he demanded that she display this assertion of his importance to her by ending the relationship. In March of 1938, she dutifully complied.

For a time there was a tremendous amount of tension at Patchin Place. Cummings consulted with his psychiatrist, Fritz Wittels, to get a perspective on the situation. Wittels told him to reconcile with Marion, to believe her affirmation of faith in the two of them, and put the affair behind them. Cummings was able to listen to the advice, which was easier to do than before as Marion really had ceased to see Rotha. By the late spring of 1938, he and Marion were once again the happy couple. In the end, the affair was more of a testing of their bond than any serious threat to their union.

Cummings had other worries at that time, though. The critical success of *Collected Poems* did not, unfortunately, translate into a financial boon. By early 1939, Cummings was in dire economic straits, and was reduced to living on fifty-five dollars a month, after rent. This time he did not turn to his mother for additional assistance. Instead he wrote Watson: "as Plato forgot to say to Aristotle I'm trying to borrow money. This would be just simply lousy news in the best of milleniums;and merely much worse if the borrower could offer collateral or whathaven't I." Watson quickly sent him a check. Cummings responded: "Thank you for the 300 and am literally American enough to hope I'll be able to 'make my own way' 'some day' 'soon.'"

1939 would not be the year that Cummings would be able to make his own way; in fact, a good many years would go by before Cummings found himself in that position. Marion, fortunately, did get a few modeling jobs, allowing them to squeak by financially. Despite their rather precarious circumstances, Cummings did not alter his routine: he continued to "wake up circa noon and still fall asleep toward dawn," write, paint, stroll through the village, take in a show now and then, and dine out whenever possible. But the economic insecurity was having an impact: his bitter resentment of the government, institutions, and financially rewarded writers (most of whom he considered unworthy of attention) began to intensify. His letters and notes became shriller and shriller, brimming with denouncements of the "Nude Eel" (New Deal), of Roosevelt, and of any established functionary.

Part of this shift had to do with Marion, who more and more began to exercise prominence in Cummings's life. Her social and political views, while coinciding with those of Cummings, were even more extreme. Despite her own lower-class origins, she did not hold back her disdain for the working classes or of programs designed to help the poor. She regarded herself as an "aristocrat;" or, in her words, "I am a Royalist. There *is* a place in life for Kings and Queens." To further her royal notions, she kept a stack of books on European royalty next to her bed. An isolationist politically, she was vehemently opposed to the United States getting involved in a "European" war, and thought Roosevelt was intent on turning the United States into a Communist country.

Marion, though, was not by any means totally responsible for shaping Cummings's views. By 1939, Cummings shared her political opinions, but for reasons somewhat different from hers. Like many who had endured World War I, he opposed the United States' entry into a war because of direct experience in that previous conflict. As for Roosevelt, he felt that the programs he had enacted, such as those contained in the New Deal, were reminiscent of the social legislation he had seen failing, first hand, in the Soviet Union. For him, these programs threatened individualism and were attempts to turn the poor into "slaves of the state."

It was not a terribly well-worked-out thesis. It seemed not to have occurred to him that he himself relied on the kindness of his mother and the Watsons who certainly doled out "handouts" whenever needed. Indeed, without Rebecca's $150 monthly allowance that paid the rent and a little more besides, he would have been in far worse circumstances. Nor did he seem to be aware that not everyone could rely on such munificent benefactors as his mother or the Watsons. Because of the help he received from family and friends, the Depression, which had left literally millions destitute, had not really touched Cummings directly. As a consequence, he was allowed the luxury of believing that

Roosevelt's plans were not driven by need but by greed for power over the masses.

Cummings did not share Marion's "royalism," however. He still maintained genuine affection for people of all kinds, as long as they were "alive." Most, of course, he judged as being "undead," in other words, being neither alive nor dead. But if a person were able to prove him- or herself as being a "humanbeing" then regardless of views, they were fully accepted by Cummings. Cummings, for instance, was intensely loyal to down-and-out Joe Gould, even passing on fifty cents to his friend whenever he encountered him. He also held writer Max Eastman in high esteem, despite Eastman being a committed Socialist (though anti-Stalinist), translator of Trotsky, and an outspoken defender of Roosevelt's policies.

Archibald MacLeish, however, who was appointed by Roosevelt as Librarian of Congress, and also served as a speechwriter for the president, only earned his wrath. Cummings quickly tagged him as "macarchibald maclapdog macleash." MacLeish, on the other hand, continued to support Cummings, even nominating him repeatedly for membership in the National Institute of Arts and Letters. Cummings was even critical of his old friend Dos Passos who asserted at an international conference in London that because of the turmoil in Europe, "Writers should not be writing now." In other words, this was no time for apolitical, belletristic work.

As cranky as Cummings was, a visit from Pound in the spring of 1939, at least temporarily, put matters into perspective. In a letter to Watson he described his impressions of his fellow poet:

> We don't know if he's a spy or simply schizo,but we do feel he's incredibly lonesome. Gargling anti-Semitism from morning till morning doesn't(apparently)help a human throat to sing. He continually & really tackles dummies,meanwhile uttering ferocious poopyawps & screechburps,as though he suspect somevastinvisible footballgameaudience were surrounding badguy titan-him. Etc if you don't know money you don't know nothing & if you studied economics in college of course you're ignorant etc

> and all of which pleasureless unbecoming being made of the very impurest timidity.

Max Eastman, who dined with Cummings and Pound one evening, recalled that Pound "is himself one-eighth as clever and all-sidedly alive as Cummings. He seemed to subdue Cummings, though, being burly and assertive beside that slim ascetic saint of poetry."

Whatever revulsion Cummings may have expressed to others over Pound's anti-Semitism or his "tackling of dummies," it is unlikely that he did much to counter him. And it was probably not just because of Pound's forcefulness. A document Cummings wrote sometime in 1939 is as rabid as anything Pound ever spoke. In pencil, at the top of the typed page, Cummings scrawled, perhaps as an addition, perhaps as a preamble, these words: "how well I understand the hater of Jews!"

The diatribe, which attempts to form some sort of rational argument, is not much more than a nasty and bigoted rant:

> The Hebraic they—it permeates everything,like a gas or a smell. It has no pride—any more than a snake has legs. Above all:it is low—this heavy,hateful shut something crushes-by-strangling whatever isn't it...makes any quick bright beautiful beginning impossible—stops inspiration just as the spirit's lungs are opening:for it cannot endure free,loving,gay;its own imprisoning pain perpetually must revenge itself on every soaring winged singful bird!.... The difference between Jews and other people seems to be that what's non-racial or differentiating exists(in Jews)only apparently,only superficially;whereas anyone else's identity goes down through innumerable layers right into his or her soul(and always more intense,not less). Anyone else is,so to speak,vertically an individual. The Jew is merely a horizontal layer or surface of individuality—under this,all depths are UN. Also,whereas the Xian's [Christian's] verticality may extend itself upward(when individuality becomes transparent through ecstasy)until the self is merely a between,with as much height beyond it as there's depth beneath, the Jew's self is not even porous;it's as impermeable as it's thin:his depths can never be heights.

Then as an added comment, perhaps to himself, he wrote: "isn't it interesting that the Xianity you worship is Mediaeval -& those boys loathed Jews?"

Marion did nothing to alter his opinions: "M tells me that in 'the dress business' they [the Jews] scream & yell at each other continually—almost;for she's seen an exhausted Jew,panting,out of the world,lost,exhausted...until he found a new victim with which to incorporate—when out pours new invective."

Another entry, though, dated Easter Sunday 1940, reveals a more reflective Cummings in which he expresses the idea that it is impossible to erase such a genuinely gifted group of people: "Mind. Something too nimble to be trod on. How could Herr H. think he'd down the Jews through brutality? He's mad. To all such which they're infinitely superior:the fact of its being may startle them,shock their mobility by inertness:but never could or shall Heavy defeat what is to Heavy merely light—that force,esprit,whom Brute 'force' considers weakness. Nimble is noble,I feel!"

To further balance the picture is a poem, written at about the same time, that gives a very different view from some of the anti-Semitic ramblings in his journal. As always, Cummings was able to distinguish between an individual and a group. The poem lauds, in strong terms, a Jewish tailor, Goldberger, as

...one fearless
one good yes
completely kind
mindheart one true one generous child-
man
-god one eager
souldoll one
unsellable not buyable alive
one i say human being)one

goldberger

Cummings's attitude toward homosexuals, previously quite open and unbigoted, also began to undergo a change in the 1930s. A poem, never published in his lifetime, but probably written in 1933, records an observation of gay men in Tunisia. While not expressly anti-homosexual, the portrait, a mix of pity, intrigue and revulsion, is hardly flattering either:

> bowed by the gaze of pederasts he queens
> upon his toe and minces at the sand
> the sorrows of young werther in his teens
> and in his pants the urging of the hand
>
> near and more near their draping selves redrape
> lascivious hips against insisting sky
> can there be no asylum no escape?
> (his donkey looks mohammed in the eye

A one-line note from the late 1930s was less subtle: "Kweers Kikes Kumrads—the new KKK." And a journal entry written during his stay at Joy Farm in July 1939 began "A visit by a fag [David Diamond] interrupted what I began to feel would be a new summer of achievement." Another passage gives a fuller picture:

> He's a brave little mucker who,minus his gift...would be an afraid-of-Everything-Natural Spoiled-child-of-lowest-middle-class-parents,a misfit jewboy suckled on cinema. He's willing and generous;he's also unlovely and neurotic. As if in punishment for his genius,he wears a sort of halfwrong,a bitterly disguised helplessness.... He makes sudden growls,at our hummingbirds;& at first I thought he was trying to imitate them—then when they retreated,I realised he was repulsing them,shoving them back to where they came from. His fairyact over a bat(UGH!!!aren't they HOAR-ubble!) is the saddest piece of untheatre I've ever had to behold.

These notes, however, only give half the story, for Cummings was also exceedingly generous to Diamond. He let Diamond stay at Patchin Place that summer, rent free, and had invited him to Silver Lake. He secured financial help for him from Dorothy Case and Helen Stewart. And he defended Diamond to Pound who had rebuffed the composer:

> (a) David Diamond is a Jew of(he tells me)the lowest(according to Jews)breed,& born(moreover)on the wrong side of the tracks(as we say in democratic America)
>
> (b)I happen to know that his wrestlings with the angel of poverty were immeasureably complicated by a steadfast refusal to kiss the reigning arse of(projew)Roosevelt II
>
> (c)if Marion hadn't found him 2 poorlittlerich goygirls who were willing to toss some crusts until our very young(22)friend "made good" (i.e.Gug[genheim Fellowship] he probably wouldn't be almost alive but he certainly could be nearly dead

Apparently Diamond's "gift" or "genius" outweighed, in the end, all other generally abstract considerations. This response, though, was typical of Cummings who could easily hold contradictory notions within himself; the heart, however, was truer than his head, for ultimately he was swayed by his personal responses to an individual rather than by some—often ill-conceived—mental construct. As in the case of his poem-portrait of the Jewish tailor, he could see Diamond, the individual, in a very different light, as well. Despite being a "fag" and a "jewboy," he was finally regarded by Cummings as a "humanbeing," and that quality was far more important for Cummings than his sexual or racial identity. These demonstrations of kindness, sympathy, and even friendship for individuals from groups he could work up a case against does not excuse the often ugly attitudes he could muster; nor does it even really explain them. It simply reveals how the heart could, at least at times, overrule the head, how the heart could see reality, even truth, when the mind was foggy and prone to negative stereotyping.

Cummings was at Joy Farm on September 1, 1939. In his notes, he recorded how he learned the news that Germany had invaded Poland:

> am sitting on the roof,after breakfast,working on an image of highest-far-sunlit mountains(our own Chocorua is emerging

from scarves of mist)when the butcher drives up. I hear his 'good Morning' and Marion's voice...his car vanishes.

-She climbs to tell me war's happened:at 6 o'clock this morning. Hitler moved against Poland,the butcher said. "Good" I answer "so I was wrong!" feeling a jar,a kind of superior indecency,a thicksickly shock—and i add(as if to myself alone)"the end of the world"

on verra

then I climb.

Later that evening, he reflected further: "i have a feeling as if German Siegheil and 'democratic' revenge had just locked foreheads in a first complete death or life crash. The soaring wind,the few big stars(erased as soon as written)the vivid blacks in the air,suggest brute violence. If we were at sea I'd be wondering how long man expects nature to lay off his pompous machineries."

Despite his sense of "the end of the world" that had been triggered by the invasion, Cummings remained opposed to the United States' entry into the war. His diary entries from the time, as well as letters to friends, reveal both despair over the state of the world as well as deep concerns over increasing U.S. involvement.

He felt the fall of France in 1940 as a personal blow, but backed Pétain's Vichy government, feeling (incorrectly, as did another noted writer, Gertrude Stein) that the French were still in control of a part of France. He was similarly upset with the Stalin-Hitler pact, but when that collapsed in June of 1941 and the two countries went to war, he was unwilling to lend his support to the Soviet Union. This is not to imply he was pro-Hitler for he clearly was not; it was simply that his revulsion of the Soviet Union was so great that he could not support Stalin. At the same time, he could write his friend Eric Knight that "Adolph Hoi and Joseph Polloi are sensibly butchering each other by the billions. Perhaps."

Although Cummings was quick to state his views to anyone who would listen, he was not terribly well informed of actual world or national events. He refused, for instance, to own a radio: "I have no and never had any and never shall have until having's obligatory(which God forbid!)radio." He also rarely read the papers. His main source of news was primarily Marion who fed him scraps of information that often only served to further ignite his sense of things. Marion, for instance, adored an isolationist columnist and radio commentator, Boake Carter, and delighted in passing on his assessments to Cummings who, in turn, relayed them to Pound.

Marion, in fact, began to hold more and more sway over Cummings. According to some, she increasingly took control in their relationship, which began to affect even the more generous and gregarious side of Cummings. If she found fault with an individual, Cummings apparently was soon echoing her sentiments. He also began deferring, more often than not, to her judgments about matters ranging from politics to when they should leave a party. And as their years together grew, she even began to screen callers at Patchin Place, turning away any—particularly young women—she did not know.

It was also apparently Marion who dragged Cummings to a neighbor's house to hear Charles Lindbergh speak on the radio against entry into the European war, which, according to the aviator, was the result of a conspiracy between the British, Roosevelt, and the Jews to get the United States involved. In a letter to Pound, Cummings commented that "the man who once became worshipped of one thousand million pibbul...is excoriated for,for the nonce,freedom of speech."

His continuous agitation and concerns about the state of the country under Roosevelt, led him, along with Marion, to become an active supporter of Wendell Wilkie, who was running against Roosevelt for president in 1940. He and Marion even "swam at 'Times Square' on 'election eve'" to hear the results of the poll announced. (Roosevelt, of course, resoundingly won.)

Cummings's increasing political dismay was not only confined to notes in his journal, letters to friends, or comments to others. Ever the artist, he also poured his feelings into poems:

> **hate blows a bubble of despair into**
> **hugeness world system universe and bang**
> **—fear buries a tomorrow under woe**
> **and up comes yesterday most green and young...**

and:

as freedom is a breakfastfood
or truth can live with right and wrong
or molehills are from mountains made
—long enough and just so long
will being pay the rent of seem
and genius please the talentgang
and water most encourage flame…

As difficult—in every way—as the years leading up to war were, there were more than a few good moments. During the spring of 1939, Cummings was invited to read at Harvard. The invitation had been extended by poet and literature professor, Theodore Spencer. While Cummings recorded that he "felt wretched before,& nervous during,the ordeal," he thoroughly enjoyed Spencer and his "goddess" girlfriend. "Ted had a great influence on me," wrote Cummings. "Mightily concerned with 'the problem of evil,'he wanted me to write about simple things;& I resented this:'The problem,'I maintained,doesn't exist. But am pretty sure it was after meeting him that I finished a poem to my father:a poem which one line…doomed me to a moral life—the line being 'No liar looked him in the head'…but this feeling of doom was vastly more than counterbalanced by a sense of freedom & exhilaration—a feeling that I was developing a newer deeper dimension."

The poem, "my father moved through dooms of love," is one of Cummings's more magnificent lyrics. The poem had been a long time coming, and was the result of years of mulling over the struggles and, ultimately, the importance of his father in shaping his life. In his journal he noted that while he had written a poem to his mother, "if there are any heavens," he had not been able to celebrate his father despite his strong feelings. "Now I felt that I'd done so," wrote Cummings, "& in so doing had shown the world how to move,what direction to take."

As Cummings's drafts and notes about the poem reveal, he toiled to create the testimony. He began by jotting memories—some prosaic, some poetic. Finally, he hit on the word "doom" accompanied by the line, "no liar looked him in the head," and the poem emerged:

my father moved through dooms of love
through sames of am through haves of give,
singing each morning out of each night
my father moved through depths of height

. . . . .

Scorning the pomp of must and shall
my father moved through dooms of feel;
his anger was a right as rain
his pity was as green as grain

. . . . .

his sorrow was as true as bread:
no liar looked him in the head;
if every friend became his foe
he'd laugh and build a world of snow. . . .

With this poem, reconciliation between father and son was complete.

At the same time Cummings was in Cambridge, William Carlos Williams was reading Cummings's work to a small crowd of forty-seven (mainly fellow poets) at a gathering organized by Williams and by Cummings's old friend and supporter, Ford Madox Ford, now in New York. The idea for the series of readings had been Ford's who, wanting to support poets (Williams in particular), had formed a group in late 1938 that he called Les Amis de William Carlos Williams. The list of charter members was impressive. Among them were Sherwood Anderson, Cummings, Archibald MacLeish, Henry Miller, Marianne Moore, Charles Olson, Katherine Anne Porter, Ezra Pound, Alfred Steiglitz, and Louis Zukofsky. Auden and Isherwood joined after the first meeting in January 1939, at which Williams read. It was Williams who proposed Cummings for the fourth rendezvous, in early May of 1939. But since Cummings was to read that same week at Harvard, it fell to Williams to deliver Cummings's work to the audience.

There is no record of how the poems of Cummings went over, but given those who were in attendance, it is likely that they were greeted with gusto and enthusiasm. MacLeish, the young Charles Olson, Moore, Miller, and Zukofsky were all ardent Cummings partisans. But Williams was perhaps the most unabashed in his praise of his fellow poet: "In the use of language Pound and Cummings are beyond doubt the two most distinguished American poets of today. It is the bringing over of the language of the day to the serious purposes of the poet that is the difficult thing. Both these men have evolved that to a high degree."

The verses that Cummings had been working on since the compilation of *Collected Poems* had grown into another book by the beginning of 1940. Again, Charles Pearce, who had been responsible for the *Collected* volume, wanted to publish it. By this point he had formed his own press, Duell, Sloan, & Pearce, so there was no need to convince "higher-ups" of Cummings's worth. In December 1940, *50 Poems* rolled off the presses. Unlike previous books, *50 Poems* contained less free verse, fewer experiments, and more formal poetry with distinct rhymes, meters, and stanzaic patterns; indeed, only three poems out of the fifty are written completely in free verse. Despite the use of conventional forms, the poems remain unconventional in their use of language, word order, and syntax.

The theme of the book is clearly that of the individual against "mostpeople," a result of his increasing frustration at politics, social institutions, and what he saw as a dangerous trend toward "enforced conformity." But *50 Poems* is far more than just bombast or wails against the status quo. Cummings was always better at expressing his ideas in verse than in his own private jottings on the state of the world, for the creativity he needed to marshal for a poem transformed even the crankiest of rants into powerful art. His celebrated and widely anthologized poem, "anyone lived in a pretty how town," for instance, encompasses Cummings's familiar message of the sanctity of the individual, yet the exquisite combination of sprung syntax and unique ordering of words renders this simple statement in a far more intriguing way:

anyone lived in a pretty how town
(with up so floating many bells down)
spring summer autumn winter
he sang his didn't he danced his did....

As the poem progresses, it becomes more and more evident that the hero of the poem is a typical Cummings "nonhero" (perhaps Cummings, himself) who does not and will not fit into the neat society of the "some-ones" and "everyones" who live in the "pretty" town: "Women and men(both little and small) / cared for anyone not at all." And while some of the children realize that "anyone" is a true individual who exists among the conformist "someones," "down they forgot as up they grew." But "any-one" does find a soul mate who "laughed his joy" and "cried his grief." This is in marked contrast to the rest of the town who hid their feelings and locked step with what was expected of them by a society antithetical to real emotion: they "laughed their cryings and did their dance." The death of "anyone" and his love is not of consequence to the townspeople either:

one day anyone died i guess
(and noone stopped to kiss his face)
busy folk buried them side by side
little by little and was by was...

A more direct, and less successful rendering of the same idea is the poem that begins "there are possibly 2 ½ or impossibly 3 / individuals every several fat / thousand years." The statement, quintessentially Cummings, is also an echo of Emerson's statement in *The American Scholar*: "In a century, in a millennium, one or two men; that is to say, one or two approximations to the right state of every man." "as freedom is a breakfastfood" is yet another take on the same theme, but this poem, though no less strident in its condemnation of society, is a more elabo-rated (and elaborate) set of assertions. Cummings, in this poem, also holds out some hope, at least for personal salvation against the tide of illusion and artificiality: "but love is the sky and i am for you."

For Cummings, love and nature continually offer a counterbalance to science, mob society, and "people socalled." It is also that Cummings, a true lyric poet, needed to sing. In love poems, and/or in verse that cel-ebrate the natural world, the harshness of the voice of the satires and societal commentaries turns sweet and melodious:

newlys of silence
(both an only

moon the with star

one moving are twilight
they beyond near)

girlest she slender

is cradling in joy her
flower than now

(softlying wisdoms

enter guess)
childmoon smile to

your breathing doll

And then there is this wonderful "poem-painting" of a falling leaf, in which the form mirrors the content:

!blac
k
agains
t

(whi)

te sky
?t
rees whic
h fr

om droppe

d
,
le
af

a:;go

e
s wh
IrlI
n

·g

The last poem in the volume is, as was customary, a sonnet. It is an inordinately ambitious poem that attempts to unify all of the themes in the volume—love, individuality, art, nature, and the triumph of these essential qualities over a world that does not seem to value them. The first two stanzas set up the dichotomy between Cummings's values and the struggle that they face in a universe that attempts to reverse the natural order of things:

what freedom's not some under's mere above
but breathing yes which fear will never no?
measureless our pure living complete love
whose doom is beauty and its fate to grow

shall hate confound the wise?doubt blind the brave?
does mask wear face?have singings gone to say?
here youngest selves yet younger selves conceive
here's music's music and the day of day...

After this presentation of the conflict between the real and the artificial, between the true nature of beings and values and the pressure exerted against them, Cummings, in the third stanza, becomes more explicit in his assertion of reality against illusion: "any was a glove / but i'm and you are actual either hand." The closing couplet is both beautiful and positive, an expression of victory:

nor a first rose explodes but shall increase
whole truthful infinite immediate us

50 Poems was not Cummings's greatest volume of verse, although it contained some of his better poems, including "my father moved through dooms of love." But it is a very human book, appropriate for the times. The poses are largely dropped here, and Cummings is laying bare what he saw as truth for all to see. Despite being personally plagued by both external and internal events, he proves, once again, that he can still sing, make us laugh, and make us think.

Reviews of *50 Poems*, for the most part, acknowledged Cummings's achievement. Even R. P. Blackmur, who had launched the first major attack against Cummings, had to admit that the book "is sufficiently admirable to allow for any amount of good will and concession and full assent to method, all warranted by the substance we are permitted to reach." Babette Deutsch, on the other hand, was less impressed. In a witty parody of Cummings's style written for the *Nation*, she took Cummings to task:

> :dearmrcummings it is
> late
> r than you th
> ink...
> ....
> ...we are not asking you for
> something new ,simply
> few
> and (er
>)or better
> ?poems

Though quite clever, Deutsch's attempt to mimic Cummings pointed out quite clearly how unique the poet truly was and how his manipulation of language was not nearly as simple (or as trite) as the reviewer made it out to be. Her review actually revealed the opposite of what she intended, for it convincingly demonstrated that Cummings was a master over words, was not arbitrary (as was she) in the way he chose to rearrange traditional word order, or took grammatical and typographical liberties. Indeed, Cummings always knew what he was doing, and always tried through his unorthodox style to thrust new awareness of the English language on his readers. Deutsch could not see this. Unlike Cummings's meaningful manipulation of words, grammar, and punctuation, her rather poor parody simply fragmented words and injected random punctuation.

Cummings, as *50 Poems* continued to show, was still an original, and an impossible act to follow, even imitate. Or as Louis Zukofsky wrote, "Cummings' best work renders 'everything which we really are and never quite live' in the American language as she is spoke."

twenty-four

Allegiance Only to the Imagination

The United States' entry into the war, following the bombing of Pearl Harbor on December 7, 1941, turned many isolationists into committed warriors. Cummings was not among them. "I like my humble definitions of War," he wrote in his notes. "(1)War is the science of inefficiency (2)War is when goys go chewsh when everyone's the chosen ('Gott mit uns');when the angry Jehovah gets back His Own."

Some of his friends, like Eric Knight, were in uniform, causing Cummings to judge him a "damned fool" for signing up. (Perhaps Cummings was right: Knight died in a plane crash in North Africa in 1943.) And when there was talk of a draft for men even of his age, forty-seven, he became apoplectic. "The only nation to whom I owe allegiance is imagination," he wrote in his journal.

Cummings, in fact, had nothing to fear from the draft, for he would never have passed the physical exam. By 1941 his health was becoming a problem: he suffered terrible backaches, had sciatica in his hip, and chronic pain in his left leg. He consulted an osteopath, recommended by Hildegarde Watson, and his regular physician, but neither was able to help him overcome the constant pain, particularly in his back.

Finally, in January of 1942, he went to Boston to see an orthopedist, Dr. Frank Ober. After the initial consultation, Ober recommended a lift to wear in his left shoe, but after examining the x-rays of his spine, discovered that Cummings was suffering from acute osteoarthritis. Within weeks Cummings began wearing a custom-made corset. "It resembles armour," he told his mother, "but I feel like somebody living in a drain-pipe(with his legs and arms & head sticking out)rather than like an ancient Roman,though stoicism comes in mighty handy these days." He quickly dubbed his armor, "The Iron Maiden," but because it did help relieve some of the pain, he wore it faithfully. As for the expenses, Sibley Watson sent a check to cover both physician and corset.

As the war continued, more and more of Cummings's friends, such as Dos Passos, Werner, Eastman, and MacLeish, were rallying around the flag. Cummings, though, remained steadfast in his belief that war—any war—was wrong. And as during the lead up to the war, his feelings found expression in poetry. Churchill and Roosevelt were satirized in:

it was a goodly co
which paid to make man free
(for man is enslaved by a dread dizziz
and the sooner it's over the sooner to biz
don't ask me what it's pliz)

Then there was also his famous epigram:

a politician is an arse upon
which everyone has sat except a man

In a more serious vein, he took up the cause of the Japanese Americans interned in camps by creating a parody of bigoted (probably drunken) speech:

ygUDuh

ydoan
yunnushstan

ydoan o
yunnuhstan dem
yguduh ged

yunnuhstan dem doidee
ygududuh ged riduh
ydoan o nudn
LISN bud LISN

dem
gud
am

lidl yelluh bas
tuds weer goin

duhSIVILEYEzum

A "translation" of Cummings's phonetic dialogue reads: You gotta. You don't? You understand? You don't? Oh you understand. Them you gotta get, you understand, them dirty you gotta get rid of. You don't? Oh nothing. Listen bud Listen. Them goddamn little yellow bastards we're going to civilize them.

During these years, he also wrote one of the greatest anti-war poems ever written:

plato told

him:he couldn't
believe it(jesus

told him;he
wouldn't believe
it)lao

tsze
certainly told
him,and general
(yes

mam)
sherman;

and even
(believe it
or

not)you
told him:i told
him;we told him
(he didn't believe it,no

sir)it took
a nipponized bit of
the old sixth

avenue
el;in the top of his head:to tell

him

Nature, of course, was also a retreat for Cummings—not just in poetry, but in life: "what Freedom—to sit among my hills:yes,they are my! For i love them,and only to the lover does the beloved belong—while a true great day empties itself in very fire into illimitable space,God's Own generosity. And after one sunset has ended,behold!another begins;when gold is over,enters blood! God's gold. God's blood."

Nature and Joy Farm, in particular, became more and more important for Cummings as the war continued to rage in both Europe and the Pacific. There, in the solitude of his hills, he painted and sketched and worked to put together yet another volume of poems. Though somewhat less social than he had been—in part due to the constant pain in his back, in part because his preferred company was Marion—there were some new friends, all younger than Cummings. Lloyd Frankenberg, a young novelist, and his wife, the painter Loren MacIver, lived nearby and visited frequently. Frankenberg had long been a fan of Cummings's work and delighted in listening to Cummings expound on whatever topic came into his head. He also shared Cummings's belief in pacifism and during the war served as a conscientious objector. MacIver also thoroughly enjoyed both Cummings and Marion. She encouraged Marion in her passion—photography—and, in turn, received support from both Cummings and Marion for her painting. She was moved when Cummings prominently displayed her painting "LilacTime," an homage to Cummings, complete with balloon man and organ grinder.

Village neighbors Kenneth Patchen and his wife, Miriam, also became friendly with Cummings and Marion during these years. Although sixteen years younger than Cummings, Patchen had already published more than a half-dozen books of poetry and a remarkable novel, *The Journal of Albion Moonlight.* The bond between Cummings and Patchen extended beyond writing: Patchen, too, was an outspoken pacifist; he suffered from a serious and painful spinal ailment that forced him to rely on a cane; he was, as well, a visual artist. Patchen's work also often exhibited an attention to typographical details, gleaned, perhaps in part, from his attention to Cummings.

Cummings liked Patchen's intensity, his commitment to words, and his gift. In September 1943, he noted in his journal, after receiving a copy of a new Patchen book of poems (probably *Cloth of the Tempest*) that his young friend "had stuff, mean substance. His two motifs,brutality and tenderness,both show it.... P is a mudpie which occasionally holds a super- or sub- human footprint; this is just the opposite of 'academic' dried up downcold deathly-rigid formalities('verse')."

Of a very different temperament and style was the short story writer and novelist wannabe, John Cheever, then in his late twenties, who, like so many young people, looked up to Cummings. They probably met through Malcolm Cowley who had published Cheever's first stories in the *New Republic;* but, as Cheever was also a resident of the Village, he could simply have knocked on Cummings's door at Patchin.

After Cheever was inducted into the army in 1942, he kept up a correspondence with Cummings and Marion. When put on guard duty at his camp in Georgia, "guarding" a group of "Southern boys who run around the yard like a pack of dogs," he told Cummings that he frequently thought about *The Enormous Room*, one of his favorite books. Cummings, at one point in the fall of 1942, sent him five dollars and a red leaf from a New Hampshire tree, figuring that Cheever could use both the money and a reminder of what autumn was like in New England.

There was also the twenty-seven-year-old poet originally from the Philippines, José Garcia Villa, who had been an ardent fan of Cummings since the appearance of *Collected Poems*. In fact, Garcia Villa admitted that he learned to write poetry "by studying principally the work of E. E. Cummings." Finally, in 1941, Garcia Villa, who was then in graduate school at Columbia, wrote a second fan letter to Cummings (the first had not been acknowledged) that managed to interest Cummings enough to invite the young poet to come by Patchin Place for a visit. "The first thing that struck me about Cummings," noted Garcia Villa, "was that he did not look American but more like an Oriental: his eyes were fairly small and with a sort of slant; his cheekbones were prominent too." The visit was pleasant, but fairly uneventful. Garcia Villa did leave some poems, however, and within a week was invited back. Cummings had been impressed. From that time on, the young poet was numbered among Cummings's friends.

Cummings and Marion also had a new neighbor at 5 Patchin Place, directly across the courtyard. Djuna Barnes, author of *Nightwood*, the hallucinatory novel that broke barriers in terms of what fiction could be, moved into the two room apartment in September 1940. Reclusive, alcoholic, cantankerous, Barnes largely kept to herself, though she did, from time to time, stray across the courtyard to have tea with Cummings and Marion. Even more outspoken than Cummings, these gatherings were a mix of gossip about other writers, denunciations of publishers, and exchanges of acerbic wit. But Cummings, who could certainly be vitriolic—particularly about the state of the nation and the world—was far outmatched by Barnes who could muster a rant like few others.

In the late spring of 1943, an opportunity came to Cummings to publish a new book of poems. It happened the way his books used to happen: through friendship. In this case, his young friend Helen Stewart, who was now working at Henry Holt and Company, persuaded William Sloane, head of the trade division, to ask Cummings for a new book of verse. Charles Pearce, his former editor and booster, was not terribly disappointed to lose Cummings as an author. Despite his belief in Cummings's work, *50 Poems* had not sold well at all. In fact, Cummings's royalties, after the five hundred dollar advance had been paid back, amounted to very little: half-year statements from 1941 to 1943 show figures of $14.94, $6.00, $.75, and $9.75. Cummings, naturally, was pleased at the prospect of getting out a new book, and by the late fall of 1943 had delivered his manuscript of fifty-four poems, titled *1 x 1*, to Holt. By March of 1944 it was in bookstores.

1 x 1 is one of Cummings's very best books. Along with the verse quoted earlier in the chapter, the collection contained such gems as "pity this busy monster,manunkind," "all ignorance toboggans into know," "darling!because my blood can sing," and "it's over a(see just / over this)wall." This last marvelous poem, on the surface a charming description of a "thief" stealing Gravenstein apples, is also resonant with the Biblical tale of Adam and Eve. For Marianne Moore—who could at times be a very harsh critic—this poem counted among just a few that had made "an indelible impression" on her. For Moore, it was not just what was said, but how Cummings said it, that was so impressive. She noted the way the simple rhymes in the last stanza—"wall," "fall," "round," "sound," and "ground"—hasten the tempo:

But over a(see just
over this)wall
the red and the round
(they're gravensteins)fall
with kind of a blind
big sound on the ground

As usual, *1 x 1* was a mix of political and social commentary, as well as celebrations of nature and love. But there is something else besides: an increased insistence on order, and even mathematical precision. Indeed, in *1 x 1* Cummings returned to creating an architectural arrangement for the book that was lacking in *50 Poems*.

The book is divided into three sections: "1," "X," and "1." The first sixteen poems begin with experiential observations of the natural world and then move to the "unnatural" world, the world of man, which allows him to introduce the satires on politicians, salesmen, etc. The last two poems in the first division look back at the poems that have come before and at the poems to come that are more meditative in their essential qualities. The contemplative emphasis then extends itself to poems that consider love. Again, the last poem in this section, though it retains the inner, quieter mood, also anticipates what will come in the final segment: exuberant, life-filled poems that sing of spring, flowers, greenly things, and love triumphant.

Although Cummings was quite vocal in his opposition to logic, science, and even math, as is evident from the careful construction of his sections in this and other books, he was not opposed to a tight structural integrity. The poems, too, are by no means devoid of a kind of arithmetic certainty. He was a great counter of syllables and lines, and eschewed titles of poems in favor of numbers. In this book, the tendency toward precision is even more pronounced.

Even the title of the volume suggests mathematics, but for Cummings, of course, the titular "one times one" has multiple connotations. In the last poem of the first section, he writes "one's not half two. It's two are halves of one." And the last poem in the book, a love poem but uncharacteristically not a sonnet, ends with the assertion, "we're wonderful one times one."

In reviewing the book for the *Nation*, Marianne Moore did not mince words: "This is E. E. Cummings's book of masterpieces. It will provoke imitation, but mastery is inimitable." Others agreed. Peter DeVries, writing in *Poetry*, noted that "Cummings's poetry with its celebration of the individual human identity is particularly nourishing and reassuring today when the identity is either destroyed by mass violence or submerged in the mass discipline that shall save it. He remains a pure voice to hear, and he embodies a healing faith."

The public apparently agreed with DeVries. Sales of *1 x 1* were good—at least during its first year—and even led to increased buying of both *Collected Poems* and *50 Poems*. The Poetry Society of America took note as well, awarding it the 1944 Shelley Memorial Prize of $670. Among the judges was Jean Starr Untermeyer, poet and wife of Louis Untermeyer, the anthologist famous for including an ample selection of his own work and that of his wife in his anthologies. Either Jean Starr Untermeyer missed this poem in *1 x 1*, or had a good sense of humor about her husband:

mr u will not be missed
who as an anthologist
sold the many on the few
not excluding mr u

To add a further irony, the award was presented by the president of the Society, Harold Vinal, whom Cummings had pilloried in the 1920s in his well-known "POEM,OR BEAUTY HURTS MR.VINAL."

It was not just in print that Cummings was putting himself before the public again. In March 1944, he had a one-man show of his paintings, his first in a decade, at the American-British Art Center in New York. It was a large show consisting of forty-five oils and fifteen watercolors. The subjects were divided into landscapes (many of Joy Farm and environs) and portraits (including nudes)—the dominant themes in his work since the late 1920s. Although the overt experimentation found in much of the poetry is absent in the paintings, there were correspondences in both subject and motivation. As with the poetry, Cummings's painting builds organically, at times almost mysteriously, rather than by objective formulation. Or as he wrote in his notes in 1940:

> apparently I've found my style in painting
> —it's NOT
> painstakingly washed flat surfaces sans brushstrokes
> fine camel's hair delineation-by-outline
> building up a careful sum out of parts
>
> it's chunking ahead with a big brush held loosely & loaded with paint.
> Out of the crisscrossings,"mistakes",etc a picture Builds itself—chiefly INWARD,thru GREYS.

The process, then, can be seen as subjective and spontaneous; a chance swatch of color in one portion of the canvas leads to the creation of another. In other words, the paint informs the painter and the complimentary feeling within the artist leads him to take further liberties with representative description. In another reflection on his painting, also from 1940, he noted that his "forte" as a painter was "SELFexpression vs. capturing(an Impression of)the object," and "verb vs. noun." This was also his "forte" in poetry.

In the catalogue for the show, Cummings elaborated more fully on this notion. He could have been writing about his poetry as easily as his painting:

> Art is a mystery.
> A mystery is something immeasurable.
> In so far as every child and woman and man may be immeasurable,art is the mystery of every man and woman and child. In so far as a human being is an artist,skies and mountains and oceans and thunderbolts and butterflies are immeasurable;an art is every mystery of nature. Nothing measurable can be alive;nothing which is not alive can be art;nothing which cannot be art is true:and everything untrue doesn't matter a very good God damn.

Cummings was not able to bask in either his exhibition or in the reception of *1 x 1*, for the woman whose several portraits graced the gallery, and to whom the book was dedicated, Marion, then just thirty-eight, was in the hospital. The diagnosis was severe rheumatoid arthritis, a chronic illness. At first, Cummings expected that a week or so in New York Hospital would be all that was needed but by March 1944, after nearly a month of treatments, her condition had not improved. A series of different diets and medications were tried, and even a tonsillectomy, but her condition remained the same. Finally, in April her doctor, Frank Peters, began to give her gold injections. These seemed to have a beneficial effect. By June she began physical therapy, but still could not walk on her own.

Friends, of course, came to the rescue. Marion's room was a hub of activity, with friends coming and going on a regular basis, leaving behind flowers and gifts. The Watsons let Cummings know that their checkbook was available to pay the doctor bills. Cummings's aunt Jane volunteered to pay the hospital expenses. Others, like Loren MacIver and Miriam Patchen, not only visited Marion regularly, but took care of Cummings as well: feeding him, cleaning the apartment, running errands.

Cummings visited Marion almost daily, and when not visiting wrote her letters, always signed with an elephant or penguin sketch. His letters are filled with sentiment and extravagant expressions of praise: "You,looking and being(in spite of all your troubles)so beautiful and so gay,made me myself completely forget there was any such thing as 'war.'"

By August, when it was still apparent that Marion would not be released from New York Hospital any time soon, Cummings agonized over whether he should go up to Joy Farm alone or not; Marion convinced him he should, holding out the possibility that perhaps she could come up with a nurse for a few days. But this was not to be. Lonely, he stayed only three weeks. "I realize,being up here alone,how a pagan must have felt after christianity had marched noisily into his favorite grove and blessed away the protecting spirit whom he had silently worshipped there. You are the Tutelary Genius of Joy Farm;you are its Guardian Angel. Without you,this hilltop and all its inhabitants—its birds and crickets and butterflies and flowers—are lonely."

On his return from Joy Farm he exclaimed, "I can't work without a woman(as an artist,I require to be in love & to be loved)." The lack of a sex life since January, due to Marion's ailment, was affecting more than his work. His notebook pages from the time are filled with sexual fantasies.

> Sober, I'm interested in the imaginary girl per se;who may be a virgin(maid)or a grande dame(queen) or a bitch(harlot). But in my drunk picture,the imaginary girl is always a bitch,we're always eager for each other;& precisely what makes us eager is the presence of the 3rd person,to whom she belongs(her 'husband');who (1)may urge her to fuck me (2)share her with me—three in a bed (3)try to hinder us,but in vain—we triumph over him...le cocu(e.g. he passes out & we screw in the same room,or even bed,with unconscious him.

The fantasies remained fantasies. Cummings himself admitted, "Obviously the fundamental part of me <u>doesn't</u> wish amours.... And Marion,being a Beautiful woman,has(consequently) immense power over me—there's also the puritan in myself:the forbidder,the no-sayer." Another entry further elaborates his viewpoint: "my relationship with Marion is of a complexity(love)which makes all mere sexuality(lust)negligible—so that,to get merely pash about a girl,I have either to work myself into a wholly unnatural lather...or(as in the case with Patty [Light])drink myself into a coma."

By the late fall of 1944, Marion was able to walk on crutches but was still confined to the hospital. On November 22, the day before Thanksgiving, Cummings wrote that "Marion will have been in the hospital 9 months i tell her she ought to be delivered." The "delivery" was not to come, though, until January 1945 when Marion, though needing to use crutches, was finally released. After a brief interlude at a hotel so that they would not have to be bothered by domestic duties, they returned home where the friends who had been so devoted to both of them continued to give their support.

During the time that Marion had been hospitalized, Cummings had been maneuvering to take over more rooms at Patchin Place. With the financial assistance of Hildegarde Watson, who agreed to pay the extra rent, Cummings was able to take over the entire second floor of Patchin. They now had as their residence two rooms on the first floor, two rooms on the second, and Cummings's long-time studio on the third floor. Marion set up a photographic studio in the back room of the second floor, having now decided to dedicate herself to photography. The first floor, and one room on the second, served as their common space, though both of them still considered the first floor as Marion's apartment.

Though the space was quite ample, the furnishings were minimal and decidedly beat up. The couch sagged, chair legs were held together with twine, a throw covered the horsehair protruding from an overstuffed easy chair. It apparently bothered neither of them, or at least it did not bother Cummings. "Money and society are trivial," wrote Cummings in his journal. Another entry, headed "Cummings' law," is defined as, "anyone who has more than a dime in his pocket is a moron." Their physical ailments had also put matters in a different light, revealing the value of life and living: "imagine being the sort of person to whom…miracles don't mean anything whatever! We must deal very simply and kindly with those people:they're not merely 'deaf' and 'dumb' and 'blind',they're so infinitely sick that any 'sickness' we suffer is riproaringlyhealthy by comparison."

Their health, however, was still an issue. Because of the pain in his back that continually plagued him, Cummings was unable to sleep, and began resorting more and more to Nembutal, a sleeping pill. He was also beginning to look older: his hair was thinning and deep creases were forming around his mouth. Marion retained her stunning looks, but she, too, took a battery of pills. Though she was able to hobble around by spring with just a cane for support, Marion nonetheless had days where she could barely get out of bed. Even though Cummings was just fifty and Marion around thirty-nine or forty, their bodies resembled those of people much older. Cummings looked at his mother, now eighty-six, and saw the future: "How pitiful can be old age!" he wrote in his journal. "The mind's stowed. It tend's to repeat itself at small intervals. She is frequently unsteady on her poor cramped feet(whose toes are like a clutching hand;thanks—she says—to toosmall shoes decades ago)—especially when she begins to turn a corner or starts going somewhere after getting up from a chair. Her deafness is a fixture."

Despite their afflictions, Cummings and Marion both managed to work, Marion at photography at which she was becoming more and more deft, Cummings at writing and painting. Cummings was mostly engaged in writing poetry, but in response to a request from Oscar Williams, who was editing a symposium for *Harper's Magazine* titled "War and the Poets," Cummings cranked out a prose piece titled "Is Something Wrong?" The views expressed were in keeping with his pronouncements throughout the war, for he remained staunchly opposed to the conflict. The first paragraph posed the question, "Is something wrong with America's so called creative artists? Why don't our poets and painters and composers and so forth glorify the war effort? Are they Good Americans or are they not?" The essay then went on to give Cummings's answers. Noting that Americans frequently changed sides, depending on who the new perceived enemy was, he concluded that no "human being (such as an artist) is a good American." He next went on to state why artists could not glorify the present conflict: "when you confuse art with propaganda, you confuse an act of God with something which can be turned on and off like the hot water faucet."

No one asked him to comment publicly on the death of President Roosevelt in April 1945. But he did reflect on it in his journal: "Having told Marion that I'm sorry he couldn't live out his war,but that at least he'd died with his boots on,hear—inside my mind—a halfline from Shakespeare 'the dog is dead.'" Not content, however, to confine his opinion to his journal, he let loose on Roosevelt in one of his less brilliant poems. It begins:

F is for foetus(a

punkslapping
mobsucking
gravypissing poppa...

Though he remarked that he "felt vastly relieved when Mr. R. disappeared," his feelings about Truman were, at best, ambivalent. He wrote his mother, "as somebody remarked,'Now we don't have to hear about The Common Man anymore because he's right where he belongs:in the White House.'"

Politics, though certainly a major preoccupation of Cummings during the war, did not totally overtake him. He was still writing poems about love and the transcendence of art. Painting, too, was again in the forefront of his activity. During the spring of 1945, in fact, he was preparing for yet another one-man show, this time at the Memorial Art Gallery in Rochester, New York. This exhibition of forty-three oils, eight watercolors, and two drawings had been arranged by Hildegarde Watson. It went up in May. Much of the work had been previously exhibited at his show in New York in 1944, but there were also a few new paintings, including a self-portrait and several New Hampshire-inspired landscapes.

At Hildegarde Watson's urging he also supplied a "foreword" for the catalogue. Rather than write a straightforward statement on his work, he chose to invent a dialogue between himself and an imaginary interlocutor. Witty, at times facetious, with a plentiful supply on non-sequiturs, the dialogue is also informative:

> Tell me, doesn't your painting interfere with your writing?
> Quite the contrary : they love each other dearly.
> They're very different.
> Very : one is painting and one is writing.
> But your poems are rather hard to understand, whereas your paintings are so easy.
> Easy?
> Of course—you paint flowers and girls and sunsets; things

that everybody understands.
I never met him.
Who?
Everybody.
Did you ever hear of nonrepresentational painting?
I am.
Pardon me?
I am a painter, and painting is nonrepresentational.

These statements reflect both Cummings's sense of what he would later call his "twin obsessions"—poetry and painting—as well as his belief that what others took to be representational art was for him something quite different. He was not interested in simply reproducing what was in front of him; instead, he wanted to impart emotion into the work. His palette, for instance, is not the palette of realist painters, and if one looks closely at even his most "representational" paintings, it quickly becomes evident that the colors are not the colors of the "real world." Or as he put it, "instead of borrowing direct from tubes,to invent." The composition, too, is not altogether "natural." Impossible skies of deep swirls loom over Mt. Chocorua or over Paris rooftops; branches of trees form geometric compositions of their own, exceedingly interesting in their own right. "What i now seek to master," wrote Cummings in the 1940s, "is expressing myself thru a person in the way(Tao)'i feel to do'(as Lachaise,bless him! would say)through nature."

Despite having had two major shows in the space of a year, Cummings's work did not sell. In a note written around that time, he reflected on his lack of success:

> S[cofield] T[hayer] let me know he wasn't going to put me into the Dial Portfolio(of "Living Art")—though a Wyndham Lewis drawing,which I considered totally null,he included—&, en même temps,if I'm not mistaken,averred (semi-playfully)that his starring of me as a poet was quite enough. Have often thought "if I *had* gone into that galèrie I'd be known as a painter,since it was the Dial which "made" me as a poet And even more often marvelled that my paintings didn't attract any museum directors' notice...for even if they weren't anything to write home about(I meditate)

> they'd be a hell of a lot better than most of the paintings by "American" "moderns" in e.g. the Met.

Despite a certain bitterness, Cummings continued to paint, and it was not always such a noble undertaking. In July 1945 he painted from life a young blonde woman named Joan. The event immediately caused a rift between Marion and Cummings, as she suspected, rightly so, that Cummings's interest in his model was not all aesthetic.

> What emerged from J posing is,that M cannot play second fiddle(any more than I could!),& that J is not a bitch. Also—proving my old thesis about the falseness of 2(either,or)i.e. the 3dimensionality of living mystery—that,instead of either my screwing J Or not, comes a 3rd element:I take a kind of noble delight in having J trust me & in not overstepping the bounds of this friendship...in never laying a finger on her,not because I don't want to,or because I'm afraid to,or because I enjoy torturing myself,but because(as I wrote in 'HIM')'the nicest things happen of themselves—ça ou rien.'

Two days later he "severed relations" with Joan, "writing a note with a cheque paying her off." The incident nagged at him, though:

> I made a triple mistake. I thought I could perhaps seduce J & anyhow paint a Venus,while keeping M—I couldn't:M wanted to leave me;& J wasn't interested in me either sexually or aesthetically.
>
> When I assured M that I loved her&actually,there was never any question of love for J;merely a letch—though I dimly felt that out of this letch might come(if I screwed J)love,a child,marriage,a home,etc...all the things I've fought to deny M...just because J was a virgin and I'd never had one)M gallantly told me she didn't care what I did so long as I loved her.

The possibilities of what was not, though, were quite exciting to him. In his papers he wrote both a poetry and prose version of what might have been. The poem—a series of fairly explicit quatrains—is rather silly. The longer prose piece is more developed, particularly in the second draft. In this version, an artist named Harold asks a young woman who shows up at his door if she had ever considered posing. She replies that she had not but was willing. It does not take long for Harold to seduce her. Curiously, the focus is less on the actual sex the two of them have, than on the psychic maneuvering by the artist to get her in bed. The prelude was obviously of far more interest to Cummings than the goal.

The flirtation led to the fantasy, the fantasy to the writing about it, and the writing to a new sense of being grounded in his actual reality: "to desert someone I've lived with happily strikes(& has always struck)me as ignoble;I may fancy myself a Don Juan,but I suspect that—deep down—what i want of a woman is not merely sexuality but love."

In April 1948, though, fantasy turned briefly to reality. After attending a gallery opening, Cummings and Marion went back to Dot Case's apartment for drinks. As the evening wore on, Cummings and Case both became more and more inebriated. Marion finally went home, leaving Cummings and Case alone. According to Cummings, Case had always been attracted to him, often flirting with him playfully. But he always behaved himself like a gentleman. On this evening, however, his better judgment obscured by alcohol, he decided to see if what he had perceived to be Case's interest in him was genuine and began making advances toward her. Soon after, they ended up having sex, but as Cummings recalled, he "did it perfunctorily." After returning home in the early hours of the morning, he realized he had left his corset behind. When he finally roused himself around the middle of the day, a hungover Cummings confessed all to Marion. Though initially angry, she soon got over it, even offering to ring up Case about the forgotten "Iron Maiden."

Case, Cummings, and Marion remained friends. This was also the last time Cummings "strayed." The lingering guilt he felt was far more troublesome than the brief enjoyment he took in the act.

He did continue to fantasize, however, and his notebooks are replete with numerous erotic drawings and poems. So numerous was the verse that he even compiled a manuscript of 271 erotic poems that verged on the pornographic. The manuscript is neatly typed, as if intended for publication. It is hard to imagine who he thought—in the late 1940s or 1950s—might publish such a book, as censorship was still alive and well. Perhaps he thought Jacobs, who had printed other volumes, might take on the job. As for the poems, themselves, they range from silly to crude, as these (rather tamer) examples show:

See how my lifted loveflesh begs
to disappear between your legs

. . .

lapping her nipples at his sweetest leisure
caressing thoroughly her parts of pleasure
and tonguing thoroughly her parts of pleasure

. . .

to bite her lips, her Nipples now to kiss,
then, gliding downward, tongue her clitoris

. . .

prettily blushing beyond any rose
and her chemise pulling her breasts above
she unto him herself all naked shows
making his stiffened penis drip with love

twenty-five

We Know Who We Are

An entry in Cummings's journal for February 1943 reads: "Marion points out the announcement of Nancy's marriage in the paper [*New York Times*]. I stare at the photo, recognize noone,feel nothing. Later have the feeling:good,Now I'm free."

Although the marriage of Nancy to Joseph Willard Roosevelt, grandson of Theodore Roosevelt and a naval officer, was surprising news, Cummings had known for at least two years that his daughter was in the United States. Dos Passos had seen her in New York in 1941, and had told Cummings about their meeting. Cummings wrestled with seeing her himself, but Marion strongly advised against it. She reasoned doing so would only disturb him and interfere with his work. He discussed the matter with his psychiatrist, Fritz Wittels, but he, too, felt that Cummings should not rush in, further telling him that he was certain that at some future point the matter would work itself out in a more natural way. Cummings also apparently confided in his young friend Dorothy Case, for in May of 1941, she offered to take Nancy to lunch and give Cummings her opinion of how she was and what she was like. By this point Cummings had obviously decided to heed the advice of Marion and Wittels, since he declined her offer.

Apparently Cummings did not know that Nancy was still under the impression that she was Scofield Thayer's daughter. On July 28, 1941, in fact, she had contacted Thayer's lawyer, Hermann Riccius, to learn more about her "father" and stated, as well, that if Thayer needed anything she would be willing to help. She also made it a point to ask Riccius not to inform Elaine of the inquiry. Shortly before Nancy had been sent to the

United States, Elaine had urged her not to look up Thayer when she got to New York. Thayer had long ago gone mad, Elaine told her daughter, and was shut off from the world. The news fell hard on Nancy, who had only thought previously that her "parents" had been divorced, and that was the reason for the lack of communication.

Perhaps because Nancy was now old enough to have access to the trust fund Thayer had established for her in 1922, Elaine had herself contacted Riccius in 1940 to learn how much was in the account. In May 1940, she received a reply from the Guaranty Trust in New York that the total estimated value came to $87,668.75.

Nancy, apparently, did not tap into the fund when she arrived in New York in June of 1941, for she quickly took a job as a typist in the office of Your Secretary Incorporated, owned by Mrs. Kermit Roosevelt. It was through her boss that Nancy met Mrs. Roosevelt's son, Willard, who would become her future husband. Though Willard Roosevelt was in the navy, he was stationed nearby and was able to spend many evenings at home. Soon he was courting Nancy. He proposed marriage to her just before he was about to be sent to Europe.

Once engaged, Nancy moved to Virginia, near the Norfolk Naval Base. Because she was fluent in French and German and had a good command of Italian, she obtained work as a translator with the Foreign Broadcast Intelligence Service in Washington, D.C. But after she married Roosevelt in 1943, when he was on leave, she quit her job and settled down as a navy wife at a house near the Norfolk base.

In the summer of 1945, Nancy's mother-in-law rented a summer place in the mountains of New Hampshire, just up the road from Joy Farm. Since Nancy was pregnant and Willard was in the Pacific, Mrs. Roosevelt invited her to spend the summer there, away from oppressive Virginia heat. Cummings's friend from childhood, Billy James, son of William James, lived nearby and over the summer became quite friendly with the new residents. In early August, shortly after the arrival of Cummings and Marion, James invited them over for lunch. Also present was Mrs. Roosevelt. Over the course of the visit, Cummings learned, as he told Hildegarde Watson, that "madame's grandson = Nancy's husband. Apparently Nancy has just left Chocorua for New York to have a baby."

It is unclear exactly what Cummings said to Mrs. Roosevelt upon learning this news, but he clearly did not inform her that he was Nancy's father. He did ask James to let him know when Nancy gave birth. On September 6, 1945, James dutifully informed his friend that he was now grandfather to Simon Roosevelt. There is no record of Cummings's reaction—neither in his journals nor in letters. But given that he had written at the time of her marriage that he now "felt free," it is likely he continued to try to keep this perspective. At the very least, he held his feelings back.

But he did write a short play that summer and fall that is perhaps a comment on the situation with Nancy. *Santa Claus: A Morality* is a didactic and overblown work, although it does contain some beautiful passages. It is ultimately more interesting in the context of his relationship with Nancy than as a serious drama.

The play attempts to meld together (quite loosely) the Faust legend with a tale of a family reunited. As the play opens, Santa Claus and Death are engaged in conversation. Santa Claus confesses that he is "sick at heart" because he has "so much to give; and nobody will take." Death responds by offering his assistance: "We are not living in an age of gifts," says Death. "This is an age of salesmanship." Therefore, according to Death, Santa Claus needs to convert himself into a salesman. And the product he is to sell is "knowledge without understanding." After some more bantering, Santa Claus reluctantly agrees, at which point they exchange masks. Death now assures Santa Claus that with the mask of science on his face, he will be able to sell something that does not exist. Santa Claus, however, is still stumped. Death then tells him to sell a "wheelmine," "that doesn't exist and never will."

In the second scene, we see Santa Claus, masked as Death, in front of a crowd hawking "preferred stock in a giltedged wheelmine." Although initially successful, the scheme quickly goes awry when a rumor spreads of a terrible accident in the wheelmine, in which miners are buried alive. Santa Claus is flummoxed: "how can I prove I'm not to blame for the damage caused by an accident which never happened to people who are non-existent?" The furious mob eventually catches up with him. With no exit in sight, Santa Claus confronts them, and professes his innocence by claiming he has been deceived by an impostor. To prove that he really is not "Science," as the crowd asserts, but Santa Claus, he tells the crowd that a little girl, who has followed the group, should be the judge of who he really is. When the child identifies him as Santa Claus, the mob is quelled.

In the last two scenes, Cummings largely abandons the Faust story in favor of his other theme: reconciliation and reunion. After the mob has been dispersed, the little girl confesses that she is "looking for someone very beautiful." Santa Claus notes that he is, too, and the two set off to find the "woman" for whom the child is pining. In the last scene, we see the "woman," weeping, imploring Death to come. But instead it is Santa Claus who enters, followed by the mob who dangle Death from a pole and shout, "Science is dead!" But as quick as they have entered, they exit. The play ends with the child reappearing, and the woman, child, and Santa Claus uniting.

Part Medieval morality play (as the subtitle suggests), part Grand Guignol, *Santa Claus* is more ambitious in its concept than in its execution. The two major protagonists, Death and Santa Claus, lack depth, and Cummings's proselytizing about the individual over the "Mob," and the perfidy of "science" is so transparent that it becomes quickly tiresome. What is interesting, from a biographical standpoint, is the relationship between the Child, her mother (the Woman), and Santa Claus. In "Scene Four" the dialogue between the Child and Santa Claus is studded with personal significance for the author:

Child. You remember me?
Santa Claus. Of course I do.
Child. You're different, aren't you?
Santa Claus. Yes;
I am.
Child. Much thinner.
Santa Claus. Do you like me this way?
Child. I guess…I like you any way—if you're you.
Santa Claus. I guess that makes me very happy.
Child. But I guess…
Santa Claus. What do you guess?
Child. You could be happier,
couldn't you?
Santa Claus. Perhaps I could.
Child. —Because you're looking
for somebody?
Santa Claus. I am.
Child. And I'm looking for somebody, too.

Santa Claus. Somebody very beautiful?
Child. O, yes;
she's very beautiful. And very sad.
Santa Claus. Very beautiful and very sad.
Tell me : is she sad because she lost you?
Child. Because we lost each other—and somebody else.
(Confused voices, far offstage)
Goodbye—
Santa Claus. Why are you going?
Child. Don't be afraid:
we'll find her.
Santa Claus. I should never be afraid
of anything in the sky and on earth
and anywhere and everywhere and nowhere,
if I were only sure of one thing.
Child. What.
Santa Claus. Who was that somebody else?
Child. That somebody
we lost?
Santa Claus. Yes.
Child. Can't you guess who?
Santa Claus. Can I?
Child. You.

The play's ending makes the theme of wish fulfillment even more explicit:

Woman. I had remembered love—but who am I?
Thanks, Death, for making love remember me.
(Enter dancing Child : sees Woman, and rushes to her arms)
Woman. Joy—yes! My(yes;O, yes)my life my love
my soul myself… —Not yours, Death!
Santa Claus. *(unmasking)* No.
Woman. *(kneeling to Santa Claus)* Ours.

A fantasy ending, to be sure, but it can certainly be read as Cummings's attempt to make happen on paper (or on stage) what never occurred in real life: reconciliation with Elaine, and the reclaiming of his position vis-à-vis Nancy. It seems more than coincidental that after nearly twenty years of being stalled in the writing of a play, Cummings, with the news of Nancy, could finally produce this drama. In his unpublished story, and subsequent dramatic version of "Seul" he first tried to deal with the personal devastation of his relationship with both Elaine and Nancy, but this earlier work was far darker. More in touch with the finality of Elaine taking up with MacDermot and the eventual loss of his daughter, Cummings in the 1920s could not write a happy ending. Life simply would not permit it. But now, in the summer and fall of 1945, he allowed the unfulfillment of his wish to rise to the surface of his consciousness, and rewrite reality to suit him.

Santa Claus was first published in a special "Cummings Issue" of the *Harvard Wake* in the spring of 1946. The play was accompanied by a poem, "love our so right," and a fairy tale, "The Old Man who said 'Why,'" a story he invented to tell Nancy when she was a child. That Cummings made a connection between *Santa Claus* and Nancy seems evident in his pairing of the play with the fairy tale. He did not go so far, however, as to dedicate *Santa Claus* to Nancy; instead, the dedication was to his psychiatrist Fritz Wittels, with whom he had often discussed Nancy, and who had advised him in 1943 that eventually the matter would resolve itself in its own manner. As it turned out, it would take five more years for any resolution to take place.

In May of 1945, Ezra Pound was arrested in Italy, and five months later brought back to the United States. The charge was treason against the United States, a result of his wartime broadcasts over Rome radio. Cummings reflected on the arrest of his old friend in his journal:

> Wish i could disentangle my psyche from E[zra]'s;to the extent of separating the poet(souvent réussi)& the reformer(accablé de douleurs).
>
> Am aware of 1 thing:to pity the poet=confusion. "the poet" <u>was</u>—he whom M[arion] & I met in Paris;to whom

> Scofield Thayer years before that,introduced me—VS an incoherent bore,whose every other word(cf "fuck'n" in the American army)was "Ikey-Kikey"; & from whom,after many efforts to make him human,M & I ran away(leaving NY). To confuse these 2 persons(to try to make 1 or whole out of them)is murderous nonsense.... Pound may or may not be now "insane"—most certainly he isn't his was;nor has he become his was for years! & never did I feel the "cantos"(except for a line here and there)good....
>
> As for the ethics:P[ound] wrote me that he was retiring(from fascist propagandizing)when the USA entered this war;& would work at translating Confucius. He wrote me that—and he didn't do it.... Instead he raved away frantically at(if not against)America.... Some of his raving was apt;some merely bizarre—anyhow,all was tasteless(frantic).... But America <u>did</u> "win this war":therefore,P(having bet a thousand percent on the completely wrong horse)is in trouble. And now he writes me(in effect) that everybody's mistaken except himself!

To Pound himself, Cummings wrote in September 1945: "I profoundly hope that when we meet again...you'll appear not quite as conscientiously as possible concerned with shallwesay welfare of quote mankind unquote. The younger our nonhero grows,the duller all sciences,including atomic sociology & economic bombery,become."

Publicly, however, Cummings defended Pound. Asked for his opinion on Pound for the magazine *PM*, Cummings thundered, "poetry happens to be an art; and artists happen to be human beings. An artist doesn't live in some geographical abstraction, superimposed on a part of this beautiful earth by the nonimagination of unanimals and dedicated to the proposition that massacre is a social virtue because murder is an individual vice.... Every artist's strictly illimitable country is himself.... An artist who plays that country false has committed suicide;and even a good lawyer cannot kill the dead."

The charges against Pound "as a radio propagandist" were serious and numerous. He was accused of "knowingly, intentionally, willfully, unlawfully, feloniously, traitorously, and treasonably" adhering to the enemies of the United States—Italy and its allies. In addition, he was charged with giving "aid and comfort to the enemy during time of war." The accusations were not without merit. Between January 1941 and July 1943 Pound took to the Rome Radio airwaves on average twice weekly to assert his views, speaking at least 122 times. While many of these broadcasts were hardly treasonous—he discussed literature as much as politics, including Cummings's *Eimi*—a sufficient number were direct attacks on the government of the United States and on Roosevelt's policies that the charges could be seen as warranted. Whether they were pro-Mussolini, as the government asserted, is still a subject of debate.

On November 29, 1945, Pound's lawyer, Julien Cornell, called on Cummings at Patchin, to discuss Pound's upcoming trial on charges of treason, which could carry the death penalty. Cummings listened attentively as Cornell described that he was going to enter an insanity plea for Pound but that expenses for Pound's medical treatment were mounting and Pound's funds were frozen. Just as Cornell was about to leave, Cummings produced from a pile of papers on his desk a check for one thousand dollars he had recently received for the sale of a painting of Mt. Chocorua (exhibited in the Rochester show) to the Watsons. "Please take it and use it for Ezra," Cummings told Cornell. It was an extremely generous act. Cummings could ill afford to give away one thousand dollars. But friendship was friendship, and Cummings was staunchly loyal to his friends, always valuing them far more than money.

Cummings was not alone in coming to Pound's defense. William Carlos Williams, Ernest Hemingway, Archibald MacLeish, Louis Zukofsky, and others rallied around Pound. But Cummings was perhaps his most ardent American supporter. While a few writers, as notable as they were, pleaded for Pound, the general attitude among Americans (and in the press) was not so supportive. Given the huge toll from the war of dead and wounded, the public had little use for anyone who was perceived as being unpatriotic. Pound's partisans knew they had an uphill fight. They nonetheless persisted. In December, Eliot, who had earlier gone on record in support of his old friend, wrote to Cummings from England asking him to see Pound at St. Elizabeths Hospital in Washington where he was confined, and to give him a personal appraisal of Pound's mental stability. He also asked Cummings to inform him immediately when Pound was sentenced so that he could coordinate support in England. Cummings responded that he would do so as soon as it was possible.

On February 13, 1946, Pound went on trial. The four psychiatrists who had examined Pound had come to the unanimous conclusion that he was insane and duly presented their testimony. That same day, the case went to a jury who returned a verdict in three minutes: Pound, they concluded, was clearly of "unsound mind," and therefore unable to stand trial. This did nothing to erase the charges; should he regain his sanity, the trial could proceed. In the indefinite interim he would remain incarcerated at St. Elizabeths Mental Hospital in Washington, D.C.

Cummings and Marion did visit Pound at St. Elizabeths in March of 1946, and were among the very first (aside from his wife, lawyers, and psychiatrists) to be able to see the troubled poet since he had been returned to the United States. Relieved that Pound was not to be executed any time soon, they brought flowers and good cheer. Marion (against hospital regulations) photographed Pound reclining in a government chair, a carnation in his button hole, half a smile on his lined face.

The visit to Pound happened on the return of Cummings and Marion from a six-week stay in Tucson, Arizona. This trip had come about, in a way, through Pound. In 1939 a young Yale undergraduate, James Angleton (who later became the first CIA director), had written to Cummings at Pound's behest, asking him if he would contribute a poem or two to the first issue of a new literary magazine, *Furioso*, of which he was co-editor. Cummings, in part out of friendship to Pound, sent Angleton a satire of Auden and Spender, "flotsam and jetsam / are gentlemen poeds." In the early 1940s, Cummings contributed a few more poems to *Furioso*, and in the process got to know Angleton and his fiancée, Cecily d'Autremont. After Angleton went into the OSS in the early 1940s, Cummings and Marion continued to see Cecily, who had by then married Angleton. In 1945, knowing of the arthritis that afflicted both Cummings and Marion, she arranged for them to go to Tucson to stay in the warm climate for the winter on her parents' compound.

Cummings and Marion arrived in Arizona a week or so before Christmas. Cecily was on hand to greet them, as were her parents, Hubert and Helen d'Autremont. Although Cummings was not sure he would like Hubert, since he was a banker and politician (president of the Arizona Senate), any prejudices quickly faded when he actually met the lively and affable d'Autremont. As for Helen, "this lady looks like Renoir's Madame Charpentier," and is a "shy incredibly generous perfectly sincere doer of good."

Cummings also found the relatives, friends, and neighbors of the d'Autremonts quite fascinating. He particularly took a liking to an Arizona Papago Indian, Juan Xavier, and his wife, a Cambridge, Massachusetts, anthropologist, Gwyneth Harrington. Together they spent long hours in conversation, Cummings eager to learn more of Native American life and philosophy.

During the first month of their stay, Cummings and Marion thoroughly enjoyed themselves. Because the weather was warm, they were able to swim daily in the d'Autremont's pool and take walks in the desert. But by mid-January 1946, the weather grew so cold that the pipes in the house froze, then burst, and Cummings returned to grousing about Arizona. By the end of January, he had reverted to his cranky New England self. "Liveliness,nil. Culture,none." Even the desert that he sketched felt too barren, and he began referring to it as "the country of death." By February they were on a train back to New York, with a layover in Washington so that they could visit Pound.

In May of 1946, Allen Tate, Cummings's friend from the 1920s onward, who had taken a job as poetry editor at Holt, asked Cummings for a new book. Cummings responded with *Santa Claus*, which Tate immediately accepted. On June 6, 1946, Cummings, at Tate's request, sent him a sketch to use as a frontispiece for the little book. "It's a simple line drawing in lead pencil," wrote Cummings, "nothing complicated & gaudy—because "Santa Claus" is neither gaudy nor complicated. It illustrates the play's almost final moment—Santa Claus revealing himself to Woman—because that's the play's climax. And it symbolizes the whole aim of "Santa Claus"—which is to make man remove his deathmask,thereby becoming what he truly is:a human being."

The book was issued just before Christmas in 1946, an attempt by the publisher to create the notion that somehow the play would sit alongside Dickens's *A Christmas Carol* as a perennial yuletide favorite. Holt's hopes were not realized. Even after several years the book had still not sold out its first print run of fifteen hundred copies, and Cummings never earned out his four hundred dollar advance.

As pleased as Cummings was that Holt was going to publish *Santa Claus*, he was even more delighted with the accolades he received in the special Cummings issue of the *Harvard Wake* that came out in early March of 1946. Among the many who chose to comment on the poet's work were William Carlos Williams, Paul Rosenfeld, Harry Levin, Marianne Moore, José Garcia Villa, Allen Tate, John Dos Passos, Lionel Trilling, Jacques Barzan, Lloyd Frankenberg, Karl Shapiro, Theodore Spencer, and Fairfield Porter, who wrote about Cummings's paintings. In a letter to Pound, Cummings commented on the publication: "glad you enjoyed 'Wake'—for which a Philippine-American poet named José Garcia Villa was entirely responsible:he announced(one afternoon)that I should be 'honoured';& all protests proved unavailing. Am myself still dazed by the generosity of nearly everyone concerned—should hate to be called on for an equivalent job[.]"

Another of Cummings's publications that spring (also from Holt) was an introduction he wrote for a collection of the *Krazy Kat* comic strips created by George Herriman. Cummings had been a long-time fan of the strip, that featured a cat, Krazy; a policeman-dog, Offisa Pup; and a mouse, Ignatz Mouse, in a series of madcap adventures. Cummings waxed in his introduction about the virtues of *Krazy Kat*: "What concerns me fundamentally is a meteoric burlesk melodrama, born of the immemorial adage love will find a way. This frank frenzy (encouraged by a strictly irrational landscape in perpetual metamorphosis) generates three protagonists and a plot." He also used the opportunity to sound off on one of his favorite themes: "If only the devilish game of democracy were exclusively concerned with mindful matters as ignorance and knowledge, crime and punishment, cruelty and kindness, collectivists would really have something on the ball. But it so happens that democracy involves the spiritual values of wisdom, love, and joy."

The late summer and early fall of 1946 was spent, as usual, at Joy Farm. Perhaps because he realized that Nancy was also in residence just up the road, he decided to ask his friend Billy James to bring his daughter and her husband, Willard Roosevelt, now back from commanding a ship in the Pacific, to Joy Farm for tea. Nancy immediately accepted the invitation, eager to meet not only a poet she admired, but one who had even been married, though briefly, to her mother. When they arrived, Marion kept Roosevelt and the Jameses outside so that Nancy and Cummings could enter the house alone. "His voice seemed extraordinary, like a bell, like something from afar, almost echoing," recalled Nancy. When the others joined them, Nancy was left "with no place to put this feeling," as the afternoon was consumed in chit-chat and pleasantries.

There were probably a couple of other visits after that one, for when the following August Nancy gave birth to a daughter, Elizabeth, she felt friendly enough with Cummings to write him the news. By then she had moved into an apartment in Long Island City. Late in 1947 she called on Cummings at Patchin, and he asked her if she would be willing to sit for a portrait. Because, with two babies, it was hard for her to get away alone, she was unable to take Cummings up on his offer until May of 1948. Even then, her visits were few, and though she enjoyed talking with Cummings, she found him very reluctant to talk much about Elaine or Thayer, whom she still presumed to be her father. She usually stayed for tea, but because Marion was always present, there was no possibility of real discussion of matters important to her.

Sometime in the fall of 1948, Nancy made a decision to cease sitting for portraits. (By now Cummings was at work on a second, larger canvas). Her reason was that she found herself falling in love with the fifty-four-year-old painter, and felt that if she continued to sit, she would succumb to his charm. Her marriage, as it was, was shaky, and she felt that she did not need any extra push from her infatuation with Cummings. She resolved, however, to finish the sessions, as there was just one more needed.

On that day, probably in the late fall of 1948, the conversation, as usual, was light. But when Marion was called away, she took the opportunity to ask directly about his marriage to Elaine. This time, Cummings was more forthcoming. According to one version of the events, he talked about Elaine and Elaine's sisters, confessing to Nancy that he always suspected that her aunt Alexis was in love with him. Finally, Nancy asked about Thayer, whom she referred to as her father. The conversation came to an abrupt halt. After a long pause, Cummings looked at her directly, and asked, "Did anyone ever tell you I was your father?"

"You cannot mean it," she replied.

"You don't have to choose between us," said Cummings.

Just at that moment Marion returned. Sensing the stillness and the tension in the air, she asked what was happening. "We know who we are," answered Cummings.

There is also another version of what happened that day. According to a close friend of Nancy's, who told him repeatedly about the event, in the course of the session, after Marion had been called away, she confessed to Cummings that she was in love with him. Cummings responded, "But didn't anyone ever tell you that *I* was your father?"

Regardless of how the revelation came about, Nancy was bewildered to the point of being devastated. Throughout her life she had always assumed that the mysterious Scofield Thayer was her father. But Elaine refused to speak at all about her past. For years, she had not even revealed to her daughter that she had once been married to Cummings. Nancy learned this only when as a teenager Elaine carelessly let drop in conversation the phrase, "when I was married to Cummings." Nancy, who by then had read *The Enormous Room* and some of the poetry, pressed her mother for details, but Elaine would only say that the marriage was brief and a long time ago.

Now, at twenty-seven, she had finally learned the truth, and it did not set her free.

On that fateful day, Nancy did not linger at Patchin Place. But at Cummings's invitation she returned. At first, she still refused to believe that Cummings was telling the truth, but she came to realize that she bore a fairly striking resemblance to her father. As a baby, in fact, she looked so much like Cummings that Stewart Mitchell remarked, "I looked in the carriage and saw Cummings looking up at me."

Once she was able to accept the reality, on subsequent visits she learned more and more about how she had come into the world, about Cummings's profound despair over the breakup of the marriage and the loss of his daughter, about the pleasant times he had spent with her as a baby and young child. Curiously, she remembered nothing consciously of her visits with him and pressed him for details in an attempt to jog her memory. But the memory would not be jogged, and she had to be content with making new memories from what Cummings told her. And while Cummings was forthcoming about events, he dissuaded her from calling him "father," telling her that his name was Estlin. Too many years had gone by for him to feel that it was a proper address.

Before long, however, Marion began to run interference. Her jealousy had become more and more ascendant, and she resented there being anyone else in Cummings's life except her. She refused to allow Nancy simply to drop by the apartment, forcing her to make appointments. When she called on the phone, Marion refused to allow her to speak to her father, always using the excuse that he was working and could not be disturbed. When she was able to see Cummings, Marion was rather cold, letting it be known that she would prefer she not visit.

Cummings apparently did not try to overcome Marion's sentiments. A journal entry from around that time reveals his own feelings: "am aware that my child's loveliness is like a summer, a season or surface;that while a part of me forever is her tragic & immediate father,wholly I(shall be &)am(& have been always)somebody whose fate is never of this world…so that while part of me is her tragic & immediate father,I am wholly & permanently someone else."

Over the next year or so, the visits became less frequent, but Marion also altered her attitude some and began to accept Nancy. By 1950, father and daughter were maintaining a cordial, but still fairly distant relationship. Amazingly, Nancy had not informed her husband of the momentous news, nor informed her mother that she was now fully aware that Cummings was her father.

"An extraordinary human being,someone gifted with strictly indomitable courage,died some days ago." So begins a letter dated January 22, 1947, from Cummings to Hildegarde Watson, informing her of the death of his mother. "She was eightseven,very deaf and partially paralyzed:young of heart and whole of spirit. In her will,she asked that her eyes(which had never failed her)be given to any blind person who through them might see." Cummings and Marion went up to Cambridge for the funeral at Forest Hills cemetery. Rebecca was interred next to her husband. Cummings's aunt Jane, herself old and feeble, continued to reside at 104 Irving Street in Cambridge.

Although Rebecca had maintained a cheery outlook on life to the very end of her days, she had felt a lingering sadness that she had never had an opportunity to know her granddaughter. She had seen her as a baby, but apparently had not glimpsed her since. Early on, Cummings (at the urging of both his father and mother) had used access to Nancy's grandparents as a point in his battle for partial custody, but Elaine could not be persuaded on even this score. And while Cummings was able to swallow his loss, neither Edward nor Rebecca were fully able to accept that they would never see their granddaughter again. And now, with both of them dead, it would never be.

Cummings, on the other hand, was still seeing his daughter from time to time. In August of 1949, Nancy wrote to her father asking if she and her family could come to Joy Farm. After apparently some deliberation, he replied that she was welcome to "'spend a night or two';why not 3?" As it turned out, the visit did not take place until July of 1950, but Nancy came alone.

On the second evening of her visit, in response to further inquiries from her about the past, Cummings hauled out letters from Thayer, Dos Passos, Elaine, and others that he had long stored in his old Harvard footlocker.

> N's eager to see the letters,& I give her the whole group,explaining that I don't know what's in it. Later she confronts me with a card from S[cofield] T[hayer],reading:'For value received.' I suggest it's something he wrote when he was crazy, 'But it isn't' N states almost vehemently 'look at the date!' I look,sans enlightenment. 'Do you know when that was?' she asks intensely. 'No,' 'The day after i was born.' Well(I tell her)I still don't understand the message:unless 'it's a grim attempt at humour'. Half contemptuously,wholly disgruntled,saying something like 'well I don't want it!(with a laugh of horror)and I feel how distinctly her opinion of ST has fallen
> did I do right or wrong?

One more day passed before Nancy boarded a train back to New York. Cummings tried to help her with her luggage, but as the train was about to depart he simply dumped the bag on the first available seat and made an exit. "I turned to glimpse a gentle pitying look on my child's face;her indulgent but a little sad smile as picked the big thing up to move it elsewhere. My failure(at the climactic moment)upset me so fearfully that I almost didn't stand & wait for her car to pass—almost but not quite."

The feeling of failure did not subside:

The day after N's going,have a severe depression.

it seems to me that she is real,& that my life here(with M[arion])isn't. What are all my salutings of Chocorua & worshippings of birds & smellings of flowers & fillings of hummingbirdcups etcetc? They're sorry substitutes for human intercourse generally & particularly for spiritual give-&-take with a child or a child-woman whom I adore—someone vital& young—&gay!

twenty-six

Xaipe and Controversy

The mixture of tumultuous emotions occasioned by the reunion with Nancy did seem to have some effect on Cummings's work. Though he continued to write and publish poems occasionally in magazines such as *Poetry*, *Quarterly Review of Literature*, *Horizon*, and the *Hudson Review*, it was not until 1949 that he managed to put together another collection of verse. He was successful in getting a 1947 British publication of *1 x 1* by Horizon, under the direction of his admirer Cyril Connolly. *Him* was also revived in 1948, in a production by the also revived Provincetown Playhouse in New York. A few of his poems were also appearing in French and German translation, and a few critical articles on his work were also published.

Cummings himself also undertook a small translation in 1948, as a result of a commission by the Juilliard Opera Center for a production of the opera-oratorio by Stravinsky and Cocteau, *Oedipus Rex*. His task was to translate Cocteau's two-page "Speaker's Text," an imaginative chorus-like commentary on the play. His translation is accurate, but lacks the flair of the original, reflecting, perhaps, that Cummings took on the project for money rather than because he was terribly inspired by the text.

Money, in fact, was again a concern. Though he had inherited seventy-three hundred dollars from his mother's estate, by early 1949 it was exhausted. In an economic crisis, he asked his old friend Stewart Mitchell for money. Mitchell promptly sent a check for one thousand dollars. Apparently he went through this money, too, for January 30, he wrote Watson to ask for an "allowance." He spelled out his needs in detail:

> I cannot see how to go on unless am sure of 5000$ a year. While my mother lived i had a very small but regular income;& after she died,my father's sister used to give me as much as 2 or 3 hundred$ from time to time—but the aunt's money is now tied up. I "earn" anyhow 1000$ a year in "royalties" & "permissions"—that I can depend on;with a dollar worth 30 cents. Marion's photographing helps out,& sometimes we sell a watercolour,rarely an oil. With herself cooking-in,our bills here(including 125$for rent,all our food,laundry,occasionally even a cleaning-woman,electricity & telephone,& about 50$ for medicines:but not including the doctor or the dentist)come to 350$ a month. The taxes on Joy Farm [previously paid by his mother] were 306$ last year;& the upkeep of the place is something,though very little. I owe 800$.somebody owes me 75$,& have 30$ on hand.

Watson's reply is not in the archive of the Watson-Cummings correspondence at the New York Public Library, but it is likely that Watson did respond with a check for some amount. Hildegarde Watson, meanwhile, offered to rent the one vacant apartment on the third floor of Patchin so that Cummings could work undisturbed by a neighbor. She also arranged a reading for Cummings at the University of Rochester that spring.

But apparently Watson did not come through as munificently as Cummings had hoped, for he also prevailed upon his ninety-seven-year-old aunt Jane to provide him (in advance) with money that he knew was intended for him in her will. Jane Cummings, in fact, was fairly wealthy. Her companion, Philip Davis, who had lived at 104 Irving Street since 1918 (when his nearby house burned down) had left her fifty thousand dollars when he died in the 1940s. And as the last of the older generation, and now the sole proprietor of 104 Irving Street, she had control of the majority of assets of both her brother and sister-in-law. But Jane could not be moved to dispose of any of her money before its time, even for her beloved nephew.

Following his aunt's refusal to part with her money, he applied for another Guggenheim fellowship, stating as his project "a prose account of myself(which would probably be called 'a novel')as unlike Eimi as it is unlike The Enormous Room." The committee rejected the application.

Despite his need for money, Cummings was not willing to compromise. "I can't(& should never pretend to)teach," he wrote Watson. He also refused to cut back where he could. In May of 1949, for instance, he and Marion journeyed to Washington to see Pound at St. Elizabeths, even though they could not afford the trip. In June of 1950, some financial relief did come in the form of the five-hundred-dollar Harriet Monroe Prize from *Poetry* magazine for a suite of seven poems published in the magazine in 1949. But Cummings really was not writing all that much; in fact, visual art was far more a preoccupation. Since he did occasionally sell a painting, perhaps he was gambling that he could generate income from his art work more readily than from his literary efforts. More likely, however, he was simply pursuing the dictates of his inner passion.

The culmination of his recent activity as a painter was another show, again at the American British Art Center in New York from May 12–28, 1949. Cummings exhibited thirty-eight oils, eleven watercolors, and two drawings. In a review of the show for the *New York Sun*, Henry McBride wrote that even though Cummings was best known as a literary "personage," "the paintings he does in his off moments and now shows could be less than they are and yet take considerable rank for their association interest." He then added that "E. E. Cummings the painter could have had a career of note independently of E. E. Cummings the writer."

Cummings could not escape the "Sunday painter" label, although he spent more time engaged in painting than in writing. But his success, even fame, had come not from painting but from words, and in the minds of both critics and the public, his literary output was far better known and of greater consequence. But Cummings himself also paired his creative work. In a note on his work for *Art News*, he wrote: "Possibly a few may enjoy my pictures. Possibly a few may enjoy my poems. And if yes, what could be better?" Cummings's comment was accompanied by a brief review of the show and the reproduction of a self portrait and "Portrait in Shadow." While Cummings was a more than competent painter, he was a far better writer. His paintings chiefly are of interest because of his more lasting contribution to American letters.

Indeed it was the poet, E. E. Cummings, who was most interesting both to the public and to fellow writers—and not just American writers. The

French poet Alexis Léger, better known by his pen name, Saint-John Perse, was an ardent admirer of Cummings's work: "What can I say about your work, to a poet of your pedigree and rank, that won't make you shrink away in horror?" wrote Perse. From the late 1940s until Cummings's death, they kept up a lively correspondence and occasionally saw one another as Léger was then serving the French government in Washington. Cummings, too, was moved by Léger's work, even dedicating a poem to him that evokes with delicate nuances not so much Léger, the man, but Saint-John Perse, the poet. Here's the first stanza:

> **being to timelessness as it's to time,**
> **love did no more begin than love will end;**
> **where nothing is to breathe to stroll to swim**
> **love is the air the ocean and the land...**

An even greater mutual admiration society sprang up between English poet Dylan Thomas and Cummings. They first met in February 1950 when Thomas came to the United States for a reading tour. Although Cummings rarely went to public readings, he and Marion braved the crowd to hear Thomas read to a standing-room-only audience at the YM-YWHA. After the reading, Cummings dispatched Marion back to Patchin in a taxi so that he could "walk the streets alone for hours." The next day, when his host, John Malcolm Brinnin, director of the poetry series at the YM-YWHA, asked Thomas whom he would like to visit in New York, Thomas only mentioned Cummings. Brinnin phoned Cummings, who extended an enthusiastic invitation. Within minutes, Thomas and Brinnin were at Patchin Place. Brinnin recorded that first meeting:

> Once they had overcome a brief, exploratory and mutual shyness, Dylan and Cummings seemed happily at ease and intimately sympathetic as they came upon ways to express the curiously double-edged iconoclasm that marks the work and character of each of them. As our teatime conversation ranged lightly over literary terrain, it seemed to me that some of their judgments showed the acerb, profound and confident insights of artists who in their work have defined a world within the world, and that some showed merely the

> conspiratorial naughtiness of gleefully clever schoolboys. Cummings poetry, both Dylan and I knew, had for years met with determined and outraged resistance in England; often with but a puzzled and tentative interest.... Cummings was touched, I felt, to have been paid the first respect of a British poet whose work he regarded so highly.

This first meeting would lead to a great many more, often in taverns in the Village. By the end of these evenings, the two poets could barely navigate the streets back to their mutual residences. Reflecting on Thomas a few years later, Cummings wrote, "At our first meeting I recognized his kinship with a former friend of mine—a true poet,generous & brave,gifted with immense vitality & complete honesty:who(in his unimaginably perverse way)was going at deadly speed to a doom from which noone could save him. I.e. Hart Crane & Dylan Thomas struck me as two perfectly authentic variations on the Poète Maudit theme: Crane being far-&-away the more vivid phenomenon."

Contrary to what Brinnin reported, there were other British poets who were quite taken with Cummings. Robert Graves, who had early and often written on Cummings and who had been responsible for getting *The Enormous Room* into print in England, had gone on record since the 1920s as saying that Cummings was among the best poets writing in America. Around 1945 his opinion had not changed. He told his biographer Martin Seymour-Smith that apart from Laura Riding he only admired two poets in the United States: Cummings and John Crowe Ransom.

Auden, too, despite having been lampooned by Cummings, regarded him in the first rank of his generation of American poets, placing him alongside Eliot, Pound, Moore, Williams, and Stevens as representative of groundbreaking achievements.

Not everybody, though, was so convinced. The young poet Charles Olson, who had been enthralled with Cummings in the late 1930s and 1940s, even noting in his 1950 statement on poetics, "Projective Verse," that "it is time to pick the fruits of the experiments of Cummings," changed his opinion later that year. In a letter to Robert Creeley, he reacted vehemently to Cummings's reading of *Santa Claus*:

> went out last night to hear cummings read his verse, and think you might be interested to know what a shocker it

> was, what a turkey is his play Santa Claus, what a dirty little man, dirty old man, deathmuggin man. this man who was so long a poet to me, is
> never wld have
> believed, like they say, never
> good god,what a Liar,what a Lie, he is

Creeley, on the other hand, who as an undergraduate had been an editor on the staff of the *Harvard Wake* that had published the tribute volume to Cummings in 1946, never doubted Cummings's genius. As Creeley later recalled, *The Enormous Room* had initially drawn him to Cummings: "I was fascinated by the intriguing rhetoric of that prose, really far more than I was by Joyce's, finally.... I was caught by what it was doing, not by what it wasn't. Its humor, its invention, its exceptionally apt way of locating persons and their relationships, its registrations of time and the fact of a place so confined—were all to me delights."

Cummings's verse also made a huge impact on Creeley. Because of Cummings's breaking down of the barriers of what poetic form was supposed to be, Creeley noted that "I didn't have to worry at all in writing as to whether or not the first letter of the first word of each line of each poem had to be capitalized." Such freedom seemed so natural to Creeley that it was not until years after he had been writing that he realized, only when Louis Zukofsky pointed it out, "what an extraordinary battle it had been to have that convention dropped. And Cummings was probably the most heroic participant in that battle." Any reader of Creeley's work will also note the indirect but very real presence of Cummings in Creeley's line, or in Creeley's words, Cummings's "statement of like order."

Cummings's readers, though, were not getting much nourishment from the poet in the late 1940s. Six years, in fact, had elapsed between the publication of *1 x 1* and his next book of poems, *Xaipe*, or in its transliterated form, "kaierey," the imperative form of *xaípo*, which Liddel and Scott's *Greek-English Lexicon* translates as "*rejoice at, take pleasure in a thing.*" It also notes that the imperative form was used, as well, as "a form of greeting."

While Cummings may have thought that he was both rejoicing and sending greetings, many of his readers did not. Indeed, not long after the book was published in March of 1950, it provoked a great deal of controversy verging on outright disgust. It was a single poem in the volume that repulsed many readers (and critics):

a kike is the most dangerous
machine as yet invented
by even yankee ingenu
ity(out of a jew a few
dead dollars and some twisted laws)
it comes both prigged and canted

The poem had, in fact, been published twice before. It first appeared in the spring 1946 issue of *Quarterly Review of Literature*, but because of the small circulation of the review, few seemed to have seen it. Theodore Weiss, its editor, had apparently objected only to Cummings's original last line, "it comes both pricked and cunted." Cummings made the change to "prigged and canted," and the poem was accepted. His friend, and at that time editor Allen Tate, however, did apparently confront Cummings over the poem in the magazine. Cummings replied that "anyone who resents [the poem]...on the unground that it's 'antiJewish' must either be méchant or eed-yoh—since my Good American point = that the kike isn't(hélas) a Jew." Its next publication was in a 1947 collection published in England, titled *Focus Four: The Novelist as Thinker*. No ruckus was raised from any quarter.

Though Cummings got away with it in 1946, he did not in 1950, despite forewarnings. Besides Tate, Lloyd Frankenberg, who received a copy of the manuscript prior to publication, in fact, objected to two poems. The first was the poem that begins, "one day a nigger / caught in his hand / a little star no bigger / than not to understand;" the second, the nasty epigram quoted above. "Two misgivings," Frankenberg wrote Cummings, "in poem 24 and 46 the words nigger and kike. The first is used affectionately; the second, if I read it right refers to an abstraction. But I have fears that both will be mistaken for unkindness." Cummings didn't get it: "it is more than kind of thee,monsieur,to warn me of le public's reaction to 2 Wild Words(see how they run). And yet the(however painful)fact that America is not a free country doesn't,I feel,justify anyone's behaving like a slave or three."

Others, too, attempted to dissuade Cummings from publishing the poem. Philip Vaudrin, his editor at Oxford University Press, who had eagerly signed up the book, pleaded with him to remove it, but Cummings held firm. Paul Rosenfeld, too, despite his longtime support and admiration for Cummings, was personally affronted. Cummings "personally & patiently explained its 'meaning'" and apparently Rosenfeld was mollified. A friend of the Watsons, a young artist named Evelyn Buff Segal, had also been horrified when she saw the poem in galleys. In a letter to Hildegarde Watson, Cummings wrote of Segal's reaction:

> She [Segal] lifted out of all my 71 poems the one and only poem in any way related to her race,& immediately objected to it;began telling me what I should & shouldn't Write,etc. Oddly enough,the little poem states(in effect)that a "kike" is what becomes of a jew—not every jew & not any—thanks to the machineworld of corrupted American materialism:i.e that America(which turns Hungarian into "hunky" & Irishman into "mick" and Norwegian into "squarehead")is to blame for the "kike."

In part, Cummings felt compelled to explain the poem to Hildegarde Watson because the book was dedicated to her. Perhaps because he sensed that even his most devoted ally might object to the poem, he offered to withdraw the dedication, but not the poem, itself: "it suddenly occurs to me that perhaps the presence of this poem in a book dedicated to yourself might cause you embarrassment. So I'm enclosing a copy of the poem;& if you'd rather not have your name in the book just telephone:am sure the printer can still make changes." Hildegarde Watson maintained her position that she was honored to have a Cummings book dedicated to her, and the dedication of *Xaipe* remained, as did the poem.

Although it was David Daiches who, in an otherwise positive review of *Xaipe*, first lamented Cummings's inclusion of the poem in the book, the fire storm did not really begin until the announcement in late 1950 that Cummings had been selected by the Academy of American Poets to receive its award of five thousand dollars. Although there was grousing from several quarters that a poet so untraditional as Cummings should be awarded the prize, Virginia Kent Cummins, editor of the formalist magazine, the *Lyric*, leveled the charge of anti-Semitism. By August 1951, enough denunciations and pronouncements had been made that writer Alex Jackinson asked noted writers and critics to offer their responses to the perception that Cummings was anti-Semitic. The results appeared in the August 20, 1951, issue of *Congress Weekly*.

Jackinson, himself, excused Cummings, noting, "to him nothing is sacred. This may still not excuse his poking fun at Jews, but when viewed (as it should be viewed) as a part of Cummings's larger mural of paeans and prejudices, it is his collective good taste more than his anti-Semitism which becomes suspect." Stanton Coblentz, a long-time Cummings hater, however, stated emphatically that "Cummings as a writer is socially as vicious as he is poetically base." Critic Leslie Fiedler wrote, "Cummings is like everyone else (somewhat) evil, and like few others, a remarkable artist.... Certainly, when the attackers of Cummings (or Eliot or Ezra Pound or Céline) are revealed as men motivated not so much by a love for Jews as by a hatred for art, I know where to take my stand." William Carlos Williams had the last word: "We give the artist freedom requiring only that he use it to say *Whatever He Chooses to Say*. We do not suppress him when he happens to say something which we dislike or to which we are for various reasons officially or individually opposed. If as a congregation of committed communicants in the religion of that democracy which has drawn us all together we intend to survive—we must respect that duty of the artist."

Although not necessarily chastened, Cummings was quite upset that so many could not see that his poem was satiric. But finally he did come to understand (a consultation with Dr. Wittels, himself Jewish, seems to have helped) that his words were perceived as vicious. Cummings parodied himself in the following poem:

tate told

him:he couldn't
believe it(frankenberg
told him;he wouldn't believe
it) paul

rosenfeld
certainly told him, and
his editor & evelyn
(yes

buff)
segal:
(he didn't believe it,no

sir)it took
a symposium and
an examination
by old fritz
wittels
of the inside of his head:to tell

him

Cummings had a point, however, in asserting that the poem could be construed as a comment on anti-Semitism. A careful reading of the epigram shows that Cummings is saying that it is Yankees, i.e., WASPs, who have invented the notion of the "kike." And though ambiguous, the lines "(out of a jew a few / dead dollars and some twisted laws)" can also be directed toward certain anti-Semitic Christian preachers, active in the 1930s and 1940s, such as Reverend Winrod who raised money to try to enact anti-Jewish immigration legislation.

The poem aside, Cummings's letters and jottings in his journal during the 1930s and 1940s do indicate quite strongly that he was not above being anti-Semitic. It was maybe an inherited condition from his New England upbringing, but nonetheless inexcusable in a man of his intellect, imagination, and refinement. He, of course, bought himself off by the old "some of my best friends are Jewish" line, and this was true. But just as with his easy contempt for the "Mob" or "mostpeople," he was too easily swayed by his righteous sense of his own uniqueness and his belief in the individual. For Cummings, most Jews were "kikes," unless proven otherwise.

Though he never withdrew the poem from subsequent publication, he never read it in his public readings either. Nor did he ever write (or at least publish) another like it. Perhaps he had finally learned that such words—whether intended satirically or not—were not just offensive and unbecoming, but vicious.

The controversy over "a kike is the most dangerous" obscured for some the genuine quality and importance of many of the other poems in *Xaipe*. In many ways, the book is a remarkable volume, worthy of the award; a "brilliant choice," William Carlos Williams said.

Xaipe opens and closes with poems about the end of day. The sixty-nine poems in between range from quiet observations of nature and the seasons to reflections on death and dying to social comments to elegies for three dead friends to poems that reflect the title in their exuberant depictions of life and living. The care Cummings took with words, grammar and syntax, and line and stanza breaks, his exquisite sense of verbal timing, his still highly acute ear attuned to the nuances of vernacular speech, and the link between form and substance are evident in nearly every poem in the book.

The sixth poem in the collection, for instance, is a meditation on what it means both to live and die, conveyed by an artful use of syntax and surprise:

dying is fine)but Death

?o
baby
i

wouldn't like

Death if Death
were
good:for

when(instead of stopping to think)you

begin to feel of it,dying
's miraculous
why?be

cause dying is

perfectly natural;perfectly
putting
it mildly lively(but

Death

is strictly
scientific
& artificial &

evil and legal)

we thank thee
god
almighty for dying

(forgive us,o life!the sin of Death

The point is fairly simple: Death (with a capital "D") is final and "scientific" and "artificial;" but, dying, with a lower case "d," is "perfectly natural," even "mildly lively." The expression of the idea is more complex, relying on a host of grammatical and syntactical devices to convey the meaning. The closed parenthesis in the first stanza, for example, suggests a cycle, initiated by the open parenthesis in the last line of the poem. Within this cycle Death, a noun, is contrasted with dying, a verb tense, reflecting Cummings's long-held notion of the supremacy of nouns over verbs. The lowercase "dying" is also linked to the individual—depicted as "i" and "thee"—a way for the poet to demonstrate the intimacy the individual has with the process of dying. This is in marked contrast to Death, a concept, rather than an active verb-filled progression on the part of humankind.

The next three poems in the book fittingly follow this poem as they are all elegies on the deaths of friends: Peter Munro Jack, a critic and friend who lauded Cummings's work; his longtime friend Paul Rosenfeld; and writer Ford Madox Ford, who had championed Cummings since the early 1920s. The elegies are tender and heartfelt, and in keeping with the sentiments expressed in "dying is fine)but Death" celebrate life rather than death. In the elegy for Ford, for instance, he writes:

a(vastly and particularly)live
that undeluded notselfpitying

lover of all things excellently rare
obsolete almost that phenomenon
(too gay for malice and too wise for fear)
of shadowy virtue and of sunful sin

The fourteenth poem in the collection is likely a poetic rendering of his feelings about his reunion with Nancy and of the progression between accidental finding, to deliberate seeking, to the culmination in which feeling floats "in silence."

out of a more find than seeks

thinking,swim(opening)grow
are(me wander and nows to the

power of blueness)whos(explore my unreal in

-credible true each new

self)smile.   Eyes.   & we
remember:yes;we played with a piece of when

till it rolled behind forever, we touched a shy
animal called where and she disappeared.

Out of more(fingeryhands

me and whying)seek than finds
feeling(seize)floats(only by

only)a silence only made of,bird

Among the more famous poems in the book is the wonderful sonnet "when serpents bargain for the right to squirm," Cummings's comment on the triumph of nature over that "unanimal mankind." Though certainly an attack on what Cummings perceived as the ills of leftist ideologies, the voice is lyrical rather than shrill, celebratory of the power of the natural order of the planet. The first stanza conveys his sense of things:

when serpents bargain for the right to squirm
and the sun strikes to gain a living wage—
when thorns regard their roses with alarm
and rainbows are insured against old age...

The closing couplet, which concludes the long sentence that has formed each of the three preceding stanzas, answers the question of what we will believe when nature begins imitating institutions:

then we'll believe in that incredible
unanimal mankind(and not until)

The twenty-eighth poem is another elegy, this one for his mother who "was and will always remain:who i am." The poem walks a fine line between sentiment and sentimentality, but never succumbs to bathos. The last lines are particularly moving:

"and poets grow;and(there—see?)children" nor
might any earth's first morning have concealed
so imaginably young a star

Although World War II had been over for five years when *Xaipe* appeared, a good many of the poems had been written either during the war or immediately following its aftermath. Poem forty records a GI's one-sided conversation, in which the speaker, talking probably to his wife or lover, attempts to explain away possible indiscretions. But as the poem goes on, he finds himself frustrated, "i can't make / it clearer war just isn't what / we imagine." The last lines carry an all-too familiar message:

...but you
must understand
why because
i am
dead

When atomic bombs were dropped on Hiroshima and Nagasaki, Cummings was horrified by the destruction, deaths, and sheer power of man's sinister invention. The forty-first poem in the collection is his reaction in the form of description. To emphasize the horror, he focuses on two individuals, victims of the blasts:

whose are these(wraith a clinging with a wraith)

ghosts drowning in supreme thunder?ours
(over you reels and me a moon;beneath,

bombed the by ocean earth bigly shudders)

never was death so alive:chaos so(hark
—that screech of space)absolute(my soul
tastes If as some world of a spark

's gulped by illimitable hell)

and never have breathed such miracle murdered we
whom cannot kill more mostful to arrive
each(futuring snowily which sprints for the
crumb of our Now)twiceuponatime wave—

put out your eyes,and touch the black skin
of an angel named imagination

There were not as many radical experiments with language in *Xaipe* as in preceding books, but one of the more successful of them is Cummings's description of a cat in poem fifty-seven, "(im)c-a-t(mo)." In a 1954 note to his Japanese translator, he commented on how the poem can be read:

> I am looking at a relaxed "c-a-t";a creature motionlessly alive—"(im)(mo)b,i;l:e"
>
> suddenly,for no apparent reason,the animal executes a series of crazily acrobatic antics—"Fall(-)leAps!flOat(-)tumblIsh>-drIft(-)whirlF(Ul)(lY) &&&"
>
> after which,he wanders away looking exactly as if nothing had ever happened...whereas,for me,the whole universe has turned upside-down in a few moments

Here is the poem:

(im)c-a-t(mo)
b,i;l:e

FallleA
ps!fl
OattumblI

sh?dr
IftwhirlF
(Ul)(lY)
&&&

away wanders:exact
ly;as if
not
hing had,ever happ
ene

D

Perhaps the best known poem in *Xaipe* is "i thank You God for most this amazing," a sonnet that truly reflects the titular meaning of "rejoice." This exuberant celebration of being alive amidst "the leaping greenly spirits of trees / and a blue true dream of sky" also reflects Cummings's deepening religious sense: "how should...human merely being / doubt unimaginable You?" This is not the only poem in the volume that touches on Christian subjects. Poem fifty, for instance, describes the poet's encounter with Jesus: "my heart / flopped over / and lay still / while he passed." But his ultimate view is not necessarily that of Christian mystics. When he glimpses Jesus up close, he has to remark that he is "made of nothing / except loneliness."

Cummings always had a spiritual bent, but as he got older spirituality became of more importance. His religious side, however, was, as he admitted, closer to a belief that God resides in all living things than that of the more conventional religion of his father. Or as he told British philosopher A. J. Ayer, who accused him of being "almost an animist:" "'Almost'? 'I AM an animist'."

Indeed, for Cummings, the exceptional design of the planet, if not the universe, in which everything had its place, in which nature is a force alive, even godly, is the subject of countless poems. Organized religion, in fact, is dealt with rather harshly in poem forty-nine: "this is a deaf dumb church and blind / with an if in its soul / and a hole in its life." The transcendental philosophy of Thoreau was much more to his liking than even the broadly inclusive religion of Edward. For his father, Christ was central; for Cummings, salvation was to be found in embracing the natural world where the miracle of life (of both the vegetable and animal worlds) was indubitable and always visible.

In February 1951, Cummings's aunt Jane, whom the year before he had tried to persuade to part with money from her will in advance, died. She left him $17,423.64. Cummings and Marion went up for the funeral, then, as 104 Irving Street was to be sold, Cummings and Marion explored the old house "from attic to cellar," retrieving items of importance to him. Between this money and the five thousand dollars received the year before from the Academy of American Poets, Cummings was finally able to support himself comfortably. Then, in March, to further aid the poet who no longer needed to be aided financially, came news that Henry Allen Moe, director of the Guggenheim Foundation, had "all-on-his-own resubmitted...last year's downturned application." And this time, the committee looked favorably on his request. "This should make plausible a glimpse,after 13 winters!de l'Europe," he wrote to Dos Passos in early April, "et aujourd'hui même the pilgrims applied passports."

On May 7, Cummings and Marion sailed on the Queen Mary. Their first stop was Paris, but Cummings was distressed by the changes the war had wrought on his favorite city. After just a few days, they departed for Rome, from where he wrote his impressions to Hildegarde Watson: "On the surface only did feel Paris was Paris;and that's a very sad feeling for me since(as you know)I love Her.... The people haven't recovered their spirits(the last war obviously hurt them far more than it hurt the Italians)and whose streets were only half-lit & whose prices were fantastic—not that Rome isn't expensive." Despite his sense of the enormous change the war had wrought on Paris, he told Watson that he and Marion planned to return for July and August, after spending time in Italy and Greece.

Italy, with Mussolini gone, pleased Cummings far more than it had in the 1930s, and Marion, who was making her first visit to Italy, was enchanted by both Rome and Venice. Greece, however, was more disappointing for Cummings. It was hot, dusty, and climbing up and down the precipitous streets, paved in cobblestones, turned his back into a "sea of pain." Cummings was now fifty-six, Marion forty-four, and while neither was hardly old, their bodily afflictions were those of people generally much older than themselves. In addition to joint problems, after just a few days in Athens, both he and Marion fell ill with stomach complaints. But what was perhaps most bothersome for Cummings was that despite his excellent knowledge of ancient Greek, he could neither speak nor understand the modern language and felt at a keen disadvantage. By early June, he and Marion were back in Paris.

The city appealed more to Cummings on his return, and after a few days, he once again found himself enjoying the City of Light. The long lines of Parisians waiting outside of shops to buy rationed provisions bothered him, though, as did the general atmosphere of defeat. Nonetheless he enjoyed strolling the familiar streets, sketchbook in hand, and dining in some of his favorite restaurants that had survived the war and German occupation. The rise of Socialism and Communism in France worried him, but he was glad to see that for the most part the city had not been "socialized,communized or otherized." By July, however, he was ready to head home and, over Marion's objections, changed their return passage from the twelfth of August to the twelfth of July. Now that summer was upon them, he wanted to be at Joy Farm, "the one dearest thing to me in this world."

twenty-seven

Ordeals by Audience

The ostensible reason for Cummings's trip abroad in the spring and summer of 1951 was to work on the prose account of himself, but there is little evidence that he did much work on the project. That summer at Joy Farm, however, he did begin writing some autobiographical narratives—mostly memory snatches—but without any definitive structure or outline. Since the work is so fragmented, it is hard to know exactly what Cummings had in mind. However, these mnemonic excursions would turn out to form a blueprint for the next opportunity that came his way.

The boon was announced in a letter from Harvard's provost, Paul H. Buck: "On behalf of Harvard University, I have the honor to extend to you a cordial invitation to accept a one-year appointment as Charles Eliot Norton Professor of Poetry for the academic year 1952–53 with a salary of 15,000." Although Buck did not state it in his letter, it was Archibald MacLeish, then Boylston Professor of Rhetoric at Harvard, who had proposed Cummings's candidature.

Cummings was flummoxed by the invitation. He had spent the last thirty-five years railing against intellectuals and professors and fulminating over the provincial attitudes in Cambridge. Now he was asked to spend a school year in Cambridge, and join the ranks of those he had skewered both publicly and privately. A day later another letter arrived, this one from John Finley, Professor of Classics and Chairman of the Faculty Committee on the Norton Professorship. Finley began his letter by saying that he could not imagine anyone "whose presence at Harvard would rouse more widespread interest or who would be welcomed more eagerly." He also spelled out in great detail, what Cummings's "duties" would be:

> The terms of the professorship require a series of not less than six lectures.... These have commonly been divided between the two college terms, and have tended to fall in November and December and again in March and April. Incumbents of the professorship are always asked by one or another department to give added instruction, formal or informal, for graduates or undergraduates, during one of the two college terms.... On the other hand, there exists in terms of the professorship no obligation, express or implied, that a man assume such an added task. The sole stipulation beyond the giving and the publishing of the lectures is that of residence in Cambridge and of some association with faculty and students throughout the year.

As pleased as he was by the invitation and the handsome salary that went along with "six-hours of holdingforth," he was not eager to be in Cambridge. He also wanted to be at Joy Farm "when the trees turned red," an event rarely missed, and so he wrote to Buck asking if he could "postpone his appearance until October 15th." He further requested specific information about what was required in terms of content. Buck quickly consented to Cummings's request and Finley responded, "as for your freedom in choosing and treating your subject, it is clearly limited only by federal and state laws." On March 11, 1952, Cummings wrote to Buck: "I've decided to accept the appointment. Thank you for giving me so much time."

Cummings worked on and off on his "lectures" that spring but was increasingly filled with self-doubt as to whether anything he had written was of any use. He was now fifty-seven, and felt that he had been so long out of the classroom that he had no idea even what constituted a lecture. In May, he and Marion visited Pound at St. Elizabeths, and judging from the letters between them during that period, the "Snortin" Lectures were a prime topic of conversation. In fact, Cummings was convinced that Pound should be the one delivering the talks. Pound was, in his customary way, encouraging Cummings to seize the opportunity. To aid him, he threw ideas at Cummings in letter after letter. He suggested that Cummings should emphasize that prosody is "the articulation of the total sound of a poEM." Cummings, of course, was not going to speak about anything resembling how poems should be written, but did write to Pound, "shall do my best,anyhow,to not possumize." "Possumize" was a reference to T. S. Eliot, who had delivered the Norton Lectures several years before.

During the summer of 1952, Cummings and Marion retreated to Joy Farm where Cummings finally got down to working on the lectures in earnest. By the early fall he had decided, as he wrote to Hildegarde Watson, "to divide each of my 6 'lectures' into 35 & 15 minute periods;chattering about myself during the 1st [period],& devoting the second to a reading(sans comment)of poems which I like by poets whom I respect." But even with this plan, the writing was not easy: "I used to wake up re-re-writing resignations to that très gentil professor Finley," Cummings remarked. By September, he had completed three of them.

At the end of September 1952, Cummings and Marion left Joy Farm (well before the trees turned) to go to New York to bid adieu to Nancy and her children who were relocating to Austria for a year. Her marriage to Roosevelt was over and she desperately needed to have a change of scenery. Cummings's willingness to leave Joy Farm much earlier than usual was somewhat surprising. During the last couple of years, Cummings had not seen Nancy often, and only once alone. But Cummings was so withdrawn on that one occasion—a dinner at a Chinese restaurant—that Nancy decided the effort to get to know her father better had failed. She was also somewhat hurt that Cummings was not particularly drawn to his grandchildren, Simon, then seven, and Elizabeth, five. He did send handmade cards and drawings (usually of elephants) for birthdays and at Christmas, and they responded in kind, but the connection was minimal.

Nancy still felt love for the man who did not want her to call him "father," but was also disturbed that there could be no real development. "What are you doing at the other end of fathership?" she wrote to him in September 1952. "And how in my naked presumption did I manage <u>my</u> end? I hope never to forget the force of rejection, (at the moment of discovery) of what was too much dreamed about to be real—so that the force was the measure of the dream."

When Nancy and her family sailed on October 3, there must have been relief all around. There could now be a physical reason for distance.

On October 15, Cummings and Marion moved into a small house at 6 Wyman Road in Cambridge, far enough away from campus to afford them privacy. On October 25, 1952, he delivered his first lecture in Saunders Theatre, where thirty-seven years before he had delivered his talk on "The New Art." The crowd was overflowing and a good many had to be turned away. Students clung to fire escapes and rapped on the windows with coins, in an attempt to wrangle their way into the theater. Professor Finley introduced Cummings as an Odysseus returning to Ithaca, whereupon the bad boy of poetry strode onto the stage, took his seat, and began slowly to read his first lecture. It began on a cautionary note: "Let me cordially warn you, at the opening of these socalled lectures, that I haven't the remotest intention of posing as a lecturer. Lecturing is presumably a form of teaching; and presumably a teacher is somebody who knows. I never did, and still don't, know. What has always fascinated me is not teaching, but learning."

The recordings made of the event reveal Cummings in fine form as he talked about his mother and father and the legacy they left him. Along the way he reminded the audience that "the socalled poet" was not going to lecture on poetry, but that he would read some of his favorite lines. Which he did: "if there are any heavens my mother will(all by herself)have" and a passage from Wordsworth's *Intimations of Immortality*. The thunderous applause that greeted the end of the first lecture should have reassured him that he was on the right track. And he was. He had a standing-room-only crowd for each of the six "nonlectures."

The last lecture for the fall was delivered on November 25. This time, in fact, a near melée erupted when more than fifty students were turned away and the door to the theater had to be locked to prevent them from pushing in. For the first twenty minutes of the reading, the late arrivals "pounded and fumed outside Saunders Theatre." Inside, Cummings was talking about his "self-discovery" as a young man, in Cambridge and especially at Harvard, a continuation of the second lecture that focused on his childhood in Cambridge. Harvard, he made clear, was less associated in his mind with learning than with the friends he made there: Stewart Mitchell, John Dos Passos, Foster Damon, Theodore Miller, Sibley Watson, and Scofield Thayer.

But at Harvard, this time, it was different. He was not making many new friends, nor was he particularly interested in doing so. He largely shunned students and faculty, retreating to Wyman Road as often as he could. He did see some of Archibald MacLeish and William and Alice James, both old friends. Ted Spencer, a poet and professor of English, of whom he was quite fond, had died from a heart attack in 1949, leaving him without any genuine connection on the Harvard faculty.

He did hit it off with Professor John Finley, who, as he told Pound, "has already preserved me from well nigh not numerable 'social' phenomena." He came to like Jack Sweeney, librarian of the Lamont Poetry Room, more and more. Before he left Harvard, he even made recordings for Sweeney of the poems of Lewis Carroll and Edward Lear. But as he wrote to Hildegarde Watson, "have yet to encounter anybody in any manner connected with Harvard who isn't primevally pink. But that's nothing;beyond a merely gruesome unworldliness. What's truly something is,that even the more developed of my shallwesay colleagues have—& this strikes me as really incredible—no interest in Beauty!"

Part of the problem with Cummings's appreciation of what Harvard had to offer was that Marion decidedly disliked just about every aspect of Cambridge. Things had gotten off to a bad start when, following his first lecture, William and Alice James had thrown a reception for Cummings. Since Cummings was the star and the center of attention, all of the focus was on him, so much so that Marion felt snubbed. Alice James, she said, had not even bothered to introduce her to the other guests. As the months wore on, she became increasingly less interested in the "provincials," and spent a fair amount of her time moping and complaining about missing New York. Both Cummings and Marion were exceedingly glad to return to Patchin Place in December, where they remained until February.

The last three lectures still had to be written and Cummings started working on them right after Christmas. The first three had been autobiographical in nature, but he decided that the last three would shed light on himself, not in formation, but as a formed writer. At the same time, he was worried that he might let down his audience, who had been so appreciative of the first three. He was apprehensive because he was aware that he intended to tackle rather controversial subjects: Ezra Pound, who remained a highly controversial figure; and politics, as revealed in both *The Enormous Room* and *Eimi*.

By the time he and Marion returned to Wyman Road he had drafted all three, but he continued to work on them, particularly the second two, up to the night before they were to be delivered. Wracked by back pain and sleeplessness, he would swallow a few Nembutal each night before going to bed, but even then would frequently awaken. He also worried about Marion, who, he described in a letter to Hildegarde Watson, "becomes a hostage—something not precisely endurable." He further added that, "Marion…deserves a true vacation if anybody ever did." As for his own state, he noted that "later or sooner I always glimpse a miserably exhausted me—tortured in my 'Iron Maid'—awaiting & awaiting & awaiting for some plane or train or boat or maybe hotelroom which doesn't materialize."

Despite his misgivings, he continued to capture audiences. In his fourth lecture, he held forth on the value of the individual over the mob, and read excerpts from *The Enormous Room*, *Eimi*, and various other works that reflected his philosophy of the artist as a human being. Or as he noted in his introductory remarks, "Writing, I feel, is an art; and artists, I feel are human beings. As a human being stands, so a human being is." The lecture concluded with a long testimony for Ezra Pound, "this selfstyled world's greatest and most generous literary figure." There were no boos at the mention of Pound's name; in fact, hearty—not just polite—applause rang out at the end of the fifty minute lecture.

The fifth lecture was slighter than the fourth in terms of commentary, consisting chiefly of Cummings reading from *Him*, as well as ten sonnets of his own. In one of the comments on the play, however, Cummings reveals a great deal about his own regard for the "success" he had now attained. Though couched as an explanation of *Him*, these words clearly reflected Cummings's own sense of himself: "With success, as any world or unworld comprehends it, he has essentially nothing to do. If it should come, well and good.… One thing, however, does always concern this individual: fidelity to himself, No simple (if abstruse) system of measurable soi-disant facts, which anybody can think and believe and know…has power over a complex truth which he, and he alone, can feel."

The last lecture, delivered on March 16, was devoted largely to reading from *Eimi* and *Santa Claus*, Cummings's attempt to convey more of his philosophy of the individual. It was also the riskiest in the sense that, as Cummings correctly perceived, Harvard and Cambridge were fairly left leaning. But his audience took it all in stride. Perhaps they sensed that Cummings's message may have been politically opposite theirs, but ultimately the nonlecturer was so charming that it did not matter. He left his audience with the values that were truly dear to him:

> I am someone who proudly and humbly affirms that love is the mystery-of mysteries and that nothing measurable matters "a very good God damn": that "an artist, a man, a failure" [a quote from *Him*] is no mere whenfully accreting mechanism, but a giving eternal complexity—neither some soulless and heartless ultrapredatory infra-animal nor any un-understanding knowing and believing and thinking automaton, but a naturally and miraculously whole human being—a feeling illimitable individual; whose only happiness is to transcend himself, whose every agony is to grow.

The second term at Harvard was easier than the first, as more old friends were around to cheer him on. His long-time friend Stewart Mitchell came down from Gloucester, along with his old roommate, Tex Wilson, now calling himself Winslow Wilson, who had become a landscape painter in Rockport, Massachusetts. Hildegarde Watson, who had also been present for the first round, came again from Rochester to hear Cummings, and from New York, Lloyd Frankenberg and Loren MacIver. Others from the distant past also showed up. His childhood neighbors, Betty Thaxter and Esther Lanman, still living in Cambridge, renewed their acquaintance. Lanman even organized a cocktail party for Cummings, inviting every member of "the old gang" she could round up, including Cummings's first crush, Amy de Gozzaldi. Her hair, once jet black, was now gray, and Cummings, now fifty-eight, had finally gone bald. They looked at each other self-consciously, then grinned.

He even came to feel that a few on the faculty were worth knowing. Cummings wrote to Hildegarde Watson that Werner Jaeger, author of *Paideia*, the important work on Greek thought and culture, "is amazing—gentle,modest,sensitive, quiet,&(unbelievably since he's an 'intellectual' par excellence)intelligent." He also came to appreciate the Renaissance scholar, Douglas Bush, and while he thought Americanist

Perry Miller was "violent," he nonetheless enjoyed both him and his "lively wife Betty."

But neither he nor Marion could wait until the end of the term. On May 1, 1953, they quit Wyman road and returned to the Village, which, upon his return he told John Finley, "seems marvelously sweet." The prospect of going up to Joy Farm, though, was even more beckoning: "can scarcely wait to smell New Hampshire." It took him a while, though, to decompress from the Cambridge adventure. Only in June 1953, nearly three months after he had delivered his last talk, was he able to write to Hildegarde Watson that "am(j'espère)becoming slightly less hysterical re my 6 Ordeals by Audience."

By mid-June he and Marion were again at Joy Farm where Cummings slowly began to recover from the lectures. In August he was in such good spirits that he even invited Nancy and her children, now back from Europe, along with her new fiancé, Kevin Andrews, to visit. Cummings liked Andrews, a Harvard classicist who had studied under Finley and who had spent several years in Greece, the result of which was his just-published book about medieval forts, *Castles of the Morea.* The visit was brief, pleasant, and unruffled by trauma. Or at least, any discomfort was confined to their respective inner selves. Cummings, in fact, was quite able to put on a good front, be affable, cordial, and funny even when seething on the inside.

A curious document that he wrote around this time reveals in detail what he saw as his two selves. The aim of this account of himself was to attempt to "distinguish clearly two Is,& decide which I'll be."

> one = my before breakfast self
>
> he's short,hateful,& dogmatic—especially re women. Women are either bitches or morons. They have no soul. They are always taking from you—never giving to you;for congenitally they can't give. They're base creatures which a man has got to treat as such. It's a pity we men can't do without women entirely. Anyhow (says this I or self) the true-essence of me is beyond woman;is infinitely superior & equally lonely. ...In fact,this I isn't superior merely to

women,but to everyone. Nobody can understand him,because he's so superior in kind...what a pity he had to be born into this lousy world at all! [ellipses, Cummings]

the other = I

he's warm,cheerful & adventurous,with a quick sense of humor—the world is a perpetual amazement to him—he never knows what he'll run into & is always eager for new experience. If he makes a blunder he's the first to laugh over it. If someone meets his affection with love,he's loyal to the death. He realises the mysterious or essential rightness of Montaigne's statement that "fortune does us neither good nor evil",for(being sensitive)he's aware of millions upon millions of individuals inside him—& according to who he becomes,so will fate prove hostile or benevolent. It's up to him. Wholeheartedly he accepts this responsibility;and recognizes it as the supreme one. Of all others he's innately suspicious—neither fearing nor welcoming them,he relegates them to a subsidiary plane:they are valid or amusing only in so far as they express himSelf—as,through them, he is MORE HE. Not more any established type—a husband,a man,a martyr,a power—someone unique & hitherto unknown or unknowable,whom he alone is wonderfully put in this world only to incarnate. By picking this or this of the million selves,by playing the world-instrument via all its registers,he may(with Luck!)begin to begin an actual a true a sublime I—a whole of which the beforementioned types are mere overdevelopments of certain infintesimal aspects.

This other self is naturally forgiving:the only sternness in him is his work,but that's total.

He has no time to judge people,he's too busy being He

Cummings's reflection on his "two I's" sheds a great deal of light on his personality: ego is manifest in both selves, as is a penchant for control (over himself and others). It is also interesting that neither self is really willing to engage deeply in much else but the work "He" has to do. Furthermore, his attitude toward women—although more misogynistic in his "before breakfast self—" remains neutral, at best, "after breakfast."

This divided nature and its differing projections also, perhaps, accounts for the contrasting views of him at that time. For those who knew and loved him, he was the humorous adventurer of the "other I." But to others, including some of the graduate students who tried to seek him out at Harvard, and occasionally Nancy as well, he projected the crankier, misanthropic "before breakfast self."

William Carlos Williams shrewdly observed that Cummings in his fifties had turned himself into a "fugitive from the people about him who he irritates by telling them they are human beings subject to certain beauties and distempers they will not acknowledge.... It would be all right if e.e. were himself more gregarious, more, what shall we say, promiscuous—at least less averse to the pack—even to very nice packs certified by the very best teachers in the very best schools here and abroad. But he isn't. He feels that among those curious things called americans there isn't one, in this inarticulate jungle, to whom he can say more than—How do you do?... Now he lives in a second Enormous Room, this time of the imagination—so real it is."

Williams's remarks are quite on the mark, for by the time Cummings gave the nonlectures, he had increasingly withdrawn into himself, and become far more critical of the "morons," to use his words, "that make up the masses." Also, as Williams noted, and which was borne out by his lack of involvement with the Harvard students, he was becoming quite resistant, unlike in the decade before, to learn from young people. For instance, to a student who apparently sent him some work, he replied: "why not learn to write English? It's one of the more beautiful languages. And(like any language)it has a grammar,syntax,etc:which can be learned. Nobody can teach you to write poetry,but only you can learn the language through which you hope to become a poet....there must be someone at your college who teaches English Composition."

And yet Cummings was also adept at saying "How do you do?" to the general public. Indeed, he was quite good at putting on a friendly face, which, perhaps, explains why in Cambridge, Cummings was not perceived by others as quite the introverted extremist he was. He seems to have largely projected, to return to the "two selves" analogy, the "other I" on social occasions, even being fairly careful about refraining from expressing his more extreme political views.

Cummings was well aware that his political leanings were not shared by the majority at Harvard. The same year that Cummings gave his nonlectures, several Harvard professors and alumni were under investigation by both the House Un-American Activities Committee (HUAC) and by Senator Joseph McCarthy's Senate Internal Security Subcommittee (SISS) for being Communists or Communist sympathizers.

The hunt for Communists had already claimed one life on campus: noted Professor of Literature, Francis O. Matthiessen, had committed suicide following accusation before a Massachusetts legislative committee that he was a Communist.

And while Harvard did launch an investigation into its own past to determine whether faculty had encouraged students to join the Communist Party in the 1930s, both the president of the university and many faculty at Harvard had denounced the congressional investigations. Indeed, in 1953, the Harvard campus was nearly unified in opposition to what they regarded as a witch hunt. Even a majority of Americans (not just Harvard intellectuals) were becoming increasingly concerned about the congressional investigations. Cummings could clearly see his views were not welcome. As a result, he largely kept them to himself, rationalizing that there was no point in trying to convince "morons" that they were wrong.

Cummings was, however, if not pro-McCarthy, at least sympathetic:

> As a possibly not quite nonintelligent human being,I'm aware that socalled McCarthyism didn't drop unmotivated from the sky—that(on the contrary)it came as a direct result of exactly what it decries:namely,procommunist- &-how-activities throughout the USA,sponsored by Mrs FD Roosevelt & her messianicallyminded partner plus a conglomeration of worthy pals:furthermore,having kept my ears & eyes open,I am unaware that 'tis thanks to the indoctrinary efforts of this gruesome gang of dogooders that Russia is a worldpower & the Korean War murders God knows how many innocent Koreans—not to say guilty Americans—daily.

It was not this hard-line, quarrelsome conservative that audiences were flocking to hear in the mid-1950s, however, when Cummings took on a new career: reading his work to the public. It was the "after breakfast self" whom crowds saw rise, with even apparent delight, to the demands of putting on a show. One woman, an undergraduate at Radcliffe at the time Cummings spoke at Harvard, recalled the excitement she and her friends felt at seeing Cummings. "It was a major event. He was irreverent, funny, handsome, brilliant. His appearance at Harvard was absolutely thrilling to a good many of us who had read his books. To catch even a glimpse of the great man was extraordinary."

Since the 1930s Cummings had been giving occasional readings, but with the success of the Norton Lectures that had now been published by Harvard University Press, he became something of a celebrity, in demand at college campuses and art centers throughout the country. In the year following the lectures, his fee was generally one hundred dollars. But in 1955, he began to get bookings through an agency, Claymore Associates. It was founded by Betty Kray, who had first met Cummings in 1953 when she was assistant director, under John Malcolm Brinnin, at the YM-YWHA Poetry Center. After she signed Cummings to the agency, his fee rose to four hundred dollars, transportation not included, then a year or so later to six hundred dollars.

During the fall of 1955, she arranged so many readings for Cummings that venue blurred into venue. In October, for instance, he read at Northwestern University, the University of Chicago, and the Chicago Art Center. In November, he made another appearance at Harvard, then went on to Dartmouth, and from there back to New York to the Metropolitan Museum of Art. But within a few days he was on the road again: to Queens College in North Carolina, Duke University, and the Institute for Contemporary Art in Washington, where he took the opportunity to visit Pound. In December, he stayed home, but gave readings at the YM-YWHA and at Barnard College. Everywhere he went, the audiences were large and enthusiastic. The only other poet in that era who commanded such audiences and attention was Cummings's friend Dylan Thomas. But by November 1953, Thomas was dead, a victim of alcoholism.

The readings, though, were not just salubrious for Cummings. As Robert Creeley remarked, "Cummings was one of the few poets…whose art moved out of the enclosure of validated 'literature' to the common world of readers and writers and speakers of every kind." It was not exactly a bringing of poetry to the masses, but a reading by Cummings was an event. It brought in not just those avid about poetry, but a great many more who ordinarily did not attend readings regularly. By the mid- to late

1950s, Cummings was among the most popular poets in America, no longer just famous among the famous, but famous among "mostpeople."

Which is not to say that discerning listeners were not still among the audience. William Carlos Williams, amazed by the crowd that turned out to hear Cummings at a reading in New York, noted: "It is an experience to listen for the cadence and not, even in the sonnets, to walk over the open grid of an iambic pentameter—with hot air coming up and the subway rumbling under."

Because of the swarm of folks who showed up at his readings, and to protect himself from the mob, Cummings decided on "rules of engagement" with the audience. In advance of every reading, Betty Kray repeated to the organizers that Cummings demanded that, "There will be no provision for autographing books, attending dinners, receptions and other social functions…and there will be no commentary with the reading." It was not always easy to avoid the fawning public. At a reading at the YM-YWHA, "a bevy of officials whisk[ed] (for I'd stipulated NO Autographs)our ex-speaker out & downthrough a secretbackentrance."

From his many public appearances he was easily recognizable, and particularly on the streets of the Village he was often approached by fans. He usually rebuffed—courteously but firmly—their desire for conversation, but occasionally was happily surprised: "a pretty young girl handed me daffodils,saying 'you don't know who I am but I just wanted to give you these.'"

One admirer of his verse he never met, but would likely have enjoyed meeting, was Marilyn Monroe. Playwright Arthur Miller, Monroe's husband in the late 1940s and early 1950s, remembered Monroe's discovery in a bookstore of Cummings's verse:

> It was odd to watch her reading Cummings to herself, moving her lips—what would she make of poetry that was so simple yet so sophisticated?… There was apprehension in her eyes when she began to read, the look of a student afraid to be caught out, but suddenly she laughed in a thoroughly unaffected way at the small surprising turn in the poem about the lame balloon man—"and it's spring!" The naive wonder in her face that she could so easily respond to a stylized work sent a filament of connection out between us. "And it's spring!" she kept repeating on our way out to the car, laughing again as

> though she had been handed an unexpected gift. How pleased with her fresh reaction Cummings would have been.

Coinciding with Cummings's renown as a reader was book sales. *Xaipe* was enjoying new success in a new printing from its original publisher. Then, in October 1954, the *Collected Poems* of 1938 was replaced with a hefty edition (468 pages) of what was truly an inclusive volume: *Poems 1923–1954*. Issued by Harcourt Brace, they also reissued earlier that same year *1 x 1* (originally published by Holt). Banking on Cummings's celebrity, his new editor, Robert Giroux, who had proposed the volume, decided on a print run of ten thousand copies for *Poems 1923–1954*, an unusually high number for a poetry book. The gamble paid off. Within a year the book had been reprinted twice. It was also selected by a book club, the Reader's Subscription.

The book did not get into print without obstacles, however. These did not come from the press, but from Cummings, who felt the title should read *Poems 1923–1950*, as it did not include poems written after *Xaipe*'s 1950 publication. Cummings was therefore horrified when he saw the galleys. Not only were they filled with printer's errors, Giroux's title was left intact. He and Marion did their best to correct the vast number of typographical errors, and when they returned the proofs, Cummings again asked that the title be changed to reflect accuracy. Nonetheless, more than seventy-five typos still managed to slip through, all of which were corrected in the second and third printings. But despite his efforts, and apparently also those of his agent, Bernice Baumgarten, the book came off the presses with 1954 as the end date of the collection.

No one but Cummings seemed bothered by the inaccuracy of the title. *Poems 1923–1954* was even nominated for the National Book Award. Its major competition was Wallace Stevens's *Collected Poems*. The two books could not have been more different. Stevens was a master of chiseled, intellectual, even abstract verse; Cummings, of course, gave voice to feeling, joy, love, nature, and radical language experiments (not to mention political diatribes). The jury, apparently, was deadlocked for some time, then ultimately decided to compromise: Stevens, then seventy-three, was given the prize; Cummings a special citation.

The result displeased Cummings, who, though slightly acquainted with Stevens, did not like either him or his poetry. Indeed, on the few occasions they had been together, Cummings often turned to taunting Stevens for being a businessman, which Stevens apparently shrugged off. Stevens, on the other hand, though not an admirer of Cummings's verse, had felt Cummings's opposition to war noble. Or as he told Samuel French Morse, "Cummings had behaved better than anyone else during the war." Nonetheless, there was not much love between them.

That same year, Cummings was being considered for the Bollingen Prize, and Wallace Stevens, along with Cummings's friend Allen Tate, was on the committee. According to Tate, "Stevens very much didn't want Cummings to have it." And Stevens got his way.

Cummings, the painter, was also before the public in those years. In 1954 he had another one-man show at the Rochester Memorial Art Gallery of thirty-eight oils, eleven watercolors, and two drawings. Such was his importance for the public by this time that *Art Digest* asked William Carlos Williams, who had previously said in print that he did not like his painting, for an article on Cummings. Williams wrote Cummings about it: "What the hell do I do about this? The *Art Digest* wrote me asking if I would do a review of your paintings and verse for them. I said I would provided I could see the materials...but I can't go to Rochester for the view. Are there any reproductions? I did see your show years ago in N.Y., but although I remember a box of strawberries from it, that is not enough to write a detailed review upon."

Cummings sent Williams some photographs, apparently enough for Williams to write his piece. In his review he commented favorably on Cummings's work, remarking that one painting of a nude reclining on a bed makes one "want to go to bed with her. Even Rubens' women do not give that feeling. It is not a painting of a nude by Mary Cassatt." He also waxed eloquently about the painting of strawberries that he claimed was now owned by poet Marianne Moore: "It is a box of strawberries, pure and simple, painted with realistic but poetic insight, the very scent and taste of the berries, even the feel of them in the mouth when crushed by the tongue against the inside of the cheek is there."

Williams's glowing words about the strawberries, however, were pure invention. Cummings had never painted a picture of strawberries; Moore, though, who was said by Williams to own the painting, did write a marvelous poem about strawberries, and it was probably this poem to which Williams was paying homage. It begins:

> you've seen a strawberry
> that's had a struggle; yet
> was where the fragments, met,
>
> a hedgehog or a star-
> fish…

Cummings did not bother to correct Williams, or let him know that it was a painting of roses that he had given to Moore. A tribute was a tribute, and Cummings was glad for it.

Cummings did supply his own commentary on the exhibition that was also published in tandem with Williams's article in *Art Digest*. Entitled "Videlicet," Cummings asserted that "for more than half a hundred years, the oversigned's twin obsessions have been painting and writing." He concluded by remarking that "one human being considers himself immeasurably lucky to enjoy, both as painter and as writer, the affectionate respect of a few human beings."

The exhibitions continued. In 1955, in conjunction with a reading, the sixty-year-old painter had another one-man show at the Chicago Art Center. And in 1957 he was given another exhibition at the University of Rochester. With his renown as a poet, he even managed to sell several paintings and watercolors at all of these exhibitions.

Another of Cummings's pleasures—travel—had been sorely compromised by the amount of touring he had had to undertake for readings. But Cummings did occasionally still travel for pleasure. He and Marion made a brief European trip in the early summer of 1954, but he had no sooner arrived than he wrote to Hildegarde Watson that he was "crazy for Joy Farm." Within a few weeks, he and Marion were back in New Hampshire. In March of 1956, he and Marion once again decided to go to Europe and planned a twelve-week tour. Their first stop was Spain, which though "icy," was made worthwhile by Goya's paintings in the Museo del Prado. Italy, however, where they next ventured, was even colder than Spain. In addition, as he wrote to Pound, "Venice,city of silence,of poetry,is murdered by motorboats." Florence teemed "from morning to midnight...by every not imaginable species of motorbicycle.... As for poor old Roma,she long ago ceased to exist.... But,O my friend!Italia somehow is still Herself;&always miraculous[.]"

After six weeks, they returned home, cutting their planned trip in half. But even the voyage back was not without incident. Marion fell on a wet deck and injured both her knees; she had to use a wheelchair to disembark.

Physical deterioration, by the mid-1950s had become a fact of life for both Cummings, now 61, and Marion, 51. As he wrote to Hildegarde Watson, he was suffering from "extreme irritability defective vision partial amnesia including shallwesay vocal deterioration." To sleep he had to take Nembutal; and for the chronic pain in his back he used painkillers of various sorts. In the mid-1950s, his hands became masses of "drooling(weeping)sore spots." Neither balms nor x-ray treatments helped. Of a more serious nature were occasional heart fibrillations, but Dr. Ober, in Cambridge, gave him Quinidine that controlled what he diagnosed as "paroxysmal cardiac arrhythmia." He was also experiencing increased gastrointestinal difficulties.

In addition to these physical ailments, he was also bothered by noise. One of the reasons he gave Hildegarde Watson for wanting to take over all of 4 Patchin Place was that he was afflicted by the radio addict in the adjacent room. Marion was even forbidden to have a radio until the late 1950s, but could never have it tuned on when Cummings was downstairs. Depression, too, often claimed him for days at a time.

In the spring of 1955, Sibley Watson arranged to have Cummings examined by his colleague, Dr. Harry Segal, at Strong Memorial Hospital in Rochester. Segal found that though Cummings was "thin" and "high-strung," he did not appear ill, though he did note that he had "bloating, lower abdominal discomfort, diarrhea." Cummings returned to Manhattan feeling relieved that he did not have cancer as he had suspected, and was ready to brace himself (literally and figuratively) for another circuit of readings.

Despite his arthritis and various aches and pains in other parts of his body, Cummings managed, in February 1954, to perform an almost acrobatic feat when he "rescued" his neighbor, Djuna Barnes. She had fallen in her apartment across the courtyard from Cummings and broken her leg. According to writer and editor Charles Henri-Ford, who knew them both, Barnes "reached the telephone and telephoned to Cummings.... Cummings came over but couldn't get in the door—Djuna had locked it and couldn't get to it to unlock it. Cummings went back down the steps and succeeded by various means (trees and the fire escape) in getting through Djuna's window and so coming to her aid. Cummings' later comment: 'I'll never answer the telephone again.'" For years afterward, Cummings would from time to time raise his window and shout across the courtyard, "Are you still alive, Djuna?"

That Cummings actually happened to be home when Barnes was in distress was somewhat unusual, for in that period he was frequently on the road reading to an adoring public. The readings, however, were not all that easy for Cummings. As he wrote to his sister, Elizabeth, "What I generally experience before a reading is a conglomeration of anxieties involving bellyache,hearttrouble,arthritis,diarrhea,& (temporary)blindness." Plane travel was torture because of his back. To Hildegarde Watson he mused that "travel has taught our nonhero that he's approximately 90million years old." But the approbation ultimately made it worthwhile. Despite the complaints, he genuinely enjoyed what he regarded as performances.

Occasionally there were rewards, such as the time Cummings read at the Masters School, a girls prep school in Dobbs Ferry, New York, just south of Scarborough, and his old friend from the 1940s, novelist John Cheever came to hear him. Cheever's daughter, then a student at the school, recalled the event: "My father and I appeared, unannounced, at the stiff little gathering in the headmaster's office before the show, and the two men embraced. The force and openness of their affection for one another seemed to shake that airless, heavily draped room. Cummings was so glad to see a loving face among those furnished souls that he could have wept, although he threw back his head and laughed instead. At the reading, his musical voice held the audience of girls spellbound, and he was called back for encores until he appeared for the last one in his muffler and coat."

The public, in fact, could not get enough of Cummings. From time to time he did turn down invitations, but more often than not instructed Kray to book him. One invitation he was not keen to accept came in early 1957 from the Boston Arts Festival, a month-long free summer event that, in addition to one evening of poetry, featured concerts, plays, and an art exhibition. Archibald MacLeish, Cummings's tireless champion, had proposed him as Festival Poet. He would be paid five hundred dollars plus expenses, and have the pleasure of reading to several thousand people seated outdoors. The only proviso was that the Festival Poet write a poem especially for the occasion. It was this requirement that made Cummings balk. He wrote to David McCord, chairman of the Poetry Committee, that he realized that a "festival poem" would be "something quite foreign to my own feeling."

McCord, however, persisted, as did MacLeish, assuring him that whatever Cummings decided to write would be acceptable. Cummings took them at their word and sent them, that spring, his new poem "THANKSGIVING (1956)," Cummings's angry satirical comment on the Soviet suppression of the anti-Communist Hungarian uprising in 1956. McCord was less than pleased at the overtly political poem, feeling that it was really not in keeping with the spirit of the festival. The business manager, Peter Temple, could not see how they could give Cummings's polemic to the newspapers, as was the custom, to print on the day of the reading. McCord tried to convince Cummings to submit another poem. This, of course, only provoked his ire, and he refused to send another.

A telephone call from the business manager followed who, according to Cummings, told him that "while nobody would dare to refuse to accept Thanksgiving(1956) as the 'festival poem' neither would anybody dare to give it the slightest publicity." But Temple also made it clear that Cummings was still free to read the poem. "Well aware that another 24 hours of said muck could more than easily spoil my holy summer, I stopped fighting at once."

It was exceedingly hot on the evening of June 23, 1957, when Cummings, seated on stage before seven thousand listeners (probably the largest crowd he has ever read to), was introduced by Archibald MacLeish as "the original anti-Communist." MacLeish then presented Cummings with the medal of the festival and told both the crowd and Cummings that he hoped he would read his poem about Hungary. A smile crossed Cummings's face. Archie, as always, had come through, even using a Cummingsism, "unState Department," when mentioning the poem and the situation that occasioned it.

A few minutes into the reading, Cummings read his festival poem, whose first stanzas "caused gasps among the audience."

a monstering horror swallows
this unworld me by you
as the god of our fathers' fathers bows
to a which that walks like a who

but the voice-with-a smile of democracy
announces night & day
"all poor little peoples that want to be free
just trust in the u s a"

suddenly uprose hungary
and she gave a terrible cry
"no slave's unlife shall murder me
for i will freely die"...

The poem's last stanzas brought even more gasps:

uncle sam shrugs his pretty
pink shoulders you know how
and he twitches a liberal titty
and lisps "i'm busy right now"

so rah-rah-rah democracy
let's all be as thankful as hell
and bury the statue of liberty
(because it begins to smell)

Gasps turned to claps. By the end of the reading, the audience, the largest on record for a reading at the festival, was on its feet, demanding an encore. A delighted Cummings happily complied.

From Boston, Cummings went straight to Joy Farm. He had new "non-lectures" to write, this time for UCLA, where he had been invited to deliver two Ewing Lectures in November of 1957. That summer he struggled to put down more autobiographical reminiscences, as well as comments on America "pre-fall" (before Roosevelt) and "post-fall" (after Roosevelt had claimed the presidency and instituted the New Deal). But by September, he still did not have more than scattered notes. Betty Kray, meanwhile, was preparing a series of seven readings for Cummings to give in the west and Midwest before, between, and after the lectures.

But in October, Cummings notified Kray to cancel both the lectures and tour. He was simply not well enough to make the trip. Meanwhile, Hildegarde Watson arrived at Joy Farm, and realized that Cummings was in a serious state, suffering from severe abdominal pain. By early October she got Cummings to Rochester, where on October 10, 1957, he underwent surgery for the removal of his appendix, as well as a benign polyp in the lower colon. He was in a hospital bed on his sixty-third birthday. Cards and flowers (including a bouquet from poet Theodore Roethke) flooded his room at Strong Memorial where he remained for eight days after the operation. Upon discharge, he stayed for another ten days at the Watsons'. By early November, he was back at Patchin, where he convalesced under Marion's care for the next three to four months.

twenty-eight

When Such Marvels Vanish

The year 1958 began with a bang: the Bollingen Committee announced in January that Cummings had been awarded the prize of one thousand dollars in recognition of his lifetime of work. He had been a candidate several times before, but finally the committee saw their way clear to give the Bollingen Prize to Cummings.

In April other good news came, too: Ezra Pound had been released from St. Elizabeths Hospital after twelve years, eleven months, and two weeks of forced confinement. For years, a number of prominent American poets had worked to free him, and eventually the government was persuaded to drop its indictment against him for treason. While he was still judged "incurably insane," the psychiatrists concluded that he was no longer a threat to the government, particularly since he had agreed to return to Italy.

Though Cummings did not contribute directly to the efforts to obtain Pound's release, his continual public statements in support of Pound, now in wide circulation due to the availability of *i six nonlectures*, certainly leant ammunition to the struggle, largely spearheaded by MacLeish and Robert Frost. Now that Pound was free, a jubilant Cummings and Marion rushed to see him before he departed for his home in Italy. They joked, took Pound and his wife Dorothy to dinner, swapped tales, and since both of them were still unreconstructed in their antigovernment views, fumed about the state of the United States. They did manage, however, to agree that Archibald MacLeish had proven to be a "damn good friend" to both of them.

Cummings had been working on another book, his first new publication since *Xaipe* in 1950. It would be called simply 95 *Poems*. In explaining the collection, Cummings wrote, "95 Poems is,ofcourse,an obvious example of the seasonal metaphor—1,a falling leaf;41,snow;73,nature(wholeness innocence eachness beauty the transcending of time&space)awakened. 'Metaphor' of what? Perhaps of whatever one frequently meets via my old friend S.Foster Damon's William Blake/His Philosophy and Symbols;eg(p 225'They' the angels 'descend on the material side…and ascend on the spiritual;this is…a representation of the greatest Christian mystery,a statement of the secret which every mystic tries to tell[.]'" There is indeed a great deal of mystery addressed in the volume, mystery in the Transcendental sense of Thoreau, in which the progressions of the seasons and the ever-changing spectacle of nature reflect (through close observation) the complexity of the cycle of life itself. It is also an affirmation of this cycle, of things that die only to be reborn.

The first poem, for instance, is a meditation on a leaf falling, a metaphor both for autumn and for the poet's sense of quiet awareness of the change in seasons. It is also an example of what he described as a poem "to be seen & not heard" as the visual arrangement on the page is integral to conveying meaning:

l(a

le
af
fa

ll

s)
one
l

iness

As almost always with Cummings's poetry, there is far more complexity than that which initially meets the eye, and, as nearly always, it is punctuation that points toward the greater meaning. The initial letter "l," situated outside the parenthesis, gets reconnected after the image "a leaf falls" to his comment, "oneliness," thereby creating "loneliness." The reason for the division is intended to convey that within "loneliness" exists "oneliness." Yet, the leaf itself, as the parentheses also indicate, is not intrinsically oneley or lonely. It is the observer who feels these twin states of being that the parenthetical falling leaf has triggered. There is one(li)ness with the natural order of things, yet also a sense of loneliness and isolation. Cummings more and more came to dread the return to Manhattan in the fall—after the leaves had fallen in New Hampshire—and it is this sense that likely is imparted. The one(li)ness he could feel at Joy Farm was also a harbinger of the loneliness he associated with the lack of natural beauty in New York. But within the poem, the feeling is inexplicable, and remains a profound mystery.

The second poem in 95 *Poems* can be read as a commentary on the poem just discussed. Here, however, Cummings takes greater pains to describe the sensation witnessed in "l(a." The subject again is stillness and the "enormous" natural world, but the dreamer, despite a desire to do so, cannot taste the "imaginable mysteries," "beyond death and life."

to stand(alone)in some

autumnal afternoon:
breathing a fatal
stillness;while

enormous this how

patient creature(who's
never by never robbed of
day)puts always on by always

dream,is to

taste
not(beyond
death and

life)imaginable mysteries

The mystery that is identity is the focus of the tenth poem in the book in which four girls (Maggie, Milly, Molly, and May) are described as who they are by what they find at the beach. The sing-song of the rhyme belies the deeper intent, which is that who we are determines what we seek out in life. What the girls find, in some sense, is predetermined by our own natures, for the objects retrieved are neutral. It is what we see in them that create their value. Or as the last couplet concludes, "For whatever you lose(like a you or a me) / it's always ourselves we find in the sea."

Poem sixteen, which begins "in time of daffodils(who know / the goal of living is to grow)" is also another statement on the interrelationship between "humanbeings" and the natural world; but in this poem, widely anthologized, the meaning is that flowers—daffodils, lilacs, and roses—can all teach us about both living and dying:

and in a mystery to be
(when time from time shall set us free)
forgetting me,remember me

The nineteenth poem is again a poem in which parentheses convey meaning. As in "l(a" it allows the poet to present two images simultaneously, that of a bee in the only rose, the other an unmoving sleeping figure:

un(bee)mo

vi
n(in)g
are(th
e)you(o
nly)

asl(rose)eep

Parentheses are used more conventionally in poem forty-one, which unlike "un(bee)mo," contains only one observation: snow falling. It is a painterly poem in that its vertical extension depicts the snow descending:

Beautiful

is the
unmea
ning
of(sil

ently)fal

ling(e
ver
yw
here)s

Now

Not all the poems in the volume are concerned with nature, though nearly all convey some sense of the mystery of life (and death). There are portraits, among them that of an organ grinder who carries a cockatoo; of the "icecoalwoodman" Dominic, who has rescued a doll from an ash barrel and now displays it over the radiator grill on his delivery truck; of a drunken pencil seller and of another drunk who has collapsed on the street; and of a platinum floozy. Satire is still present, as in "THANKSGIVING (1956)" and more subtly in poems such as "ADHUC SUB JUDICE LIS" (the title, a quote from Horace translates as "thus far before the courts") in which he describes the testimony of four brawlers. He also makes use of other personages and living things in his poems to deliver his barbs. A "crazy jay blue" stands in for the poet, who like Cummings, has a "hatred of timid / & loathing for…unworlds." Joe Gould, who died the year before the volume was published, makes a reappearance as a social commentator who claims that "the only reason every wo / man // should / go to college" is so that she will not ever be able to say "if i / 'd / OH / n / lygawntueco // llege."

No Cummings collection, of course, would be complete without love poems, and 95 *Poems* contains several. Poem forty-five is a simple declaration: "i love you much(most beautiful darling)," as is poem ninety-two, "i carry your heart with me(i carry it in / my heart)." Poem fifty-two is a more mature reflection on aging and love in which the poet wonders whether his lady's fingers that "fly" while sewing are "afraid that life is / running away from them." But, as he tells us in the poem's conclusion:

> isn't she a
> ware that life(who
> never grows old)
> is always beau
>
> tiful and
> that nobod
> y beauti
>
> ful ev
> er hur
>
> ries

If Cummings is saying in this poem that life is going fast enough without hurrying, he was well aware that time was fleeting. Death, in fact, is much on the sixty-four-year-old poet's mind in this book. Poem after poem raises the specter of death. In poem twenty-three, he meditates on an "albutnotquitemost / lost" graveyard, but morbidity is swallowed by the deep blue of sky. In poem forty-eight, the reality of death cannot fade because the poet cannot ignore the feeling of "a world crylaughingly float away / leaving just this strolling ghostly doll / of an almost vanished me." The sixty-ninth poem, in its affirmation of life, also contains an awareness of death:

> . . . And(darling)never fear:
>
> love,when such marvels vanish,will include
> —there by arriving magically here—

and everywhere which you've and i've agreed
and we've(with one last more than kiss)to call

most the amazing miracle of all

In a more humorous vein is his reflection on growing older, which begins:

old age sticks
up Keep
Off
signs)&

youth yanks them
down...

In keeping with the cyclical theme, birth is also celebrated. Poem forty-two, "from spiralling ecstatically this" celebrates the blossoming of "a newborn babe" over which "time space doom dream...floats the whole // perhapsless mystery of paradise." Poem sixty-seven also celebrates birth, presumably that of his fourth grandchild, Ionna, since Cummings sent a copy of the poem to Nancy on learning the news.

The religious side of Cummings is also present in 95 *Poems*. Poem seventy-seven, "i am a little church(no great cathedral)" is both a portrait of an actual church (Saint-Germain de Charonne in Paris), as well as a reflection on the poet's obedience to a higher authority. Although Cummings worked and reworked the poem (there are eighty extent drafts), the result was more sentimental than brilliant; clichéd images ("around me surges a miracle of unceasing / birth and glory and death and resurrection") turn the poem into a cloying triteness. The uncharacteristic lack of enjambment (almost all the lines are end-stopped) also gives it a clunky, predictable feel. Far better evocations of his spiritual self are found in other poems, such as poem eighty-nine, which begins "now what were motionless move(exists no // miracle mightier than this:to feel)," or poem eighty-four that conjures the sun.

Cummings was risking repeating himself in *95 Poems* with the by now familiar employment of his favorite images: spring, flowers, birds, drunks, moons, love, etc. But for the most part, he pulls it off with freshness underscored by his exquisite craft. At the same time, he was not venturing much beyond where he had been eight or even twenty years earlier: the price, perhaps, of being so masterful so early on. There is, of course, greater maturity, less offhandedness, and far less cuteness than in many of the earlier volumes. And each poem bears his unique stamp of Cummingsness: the use of grammar, syntax, and punctuation to convey meaning; a sense of how a poem appears visually on the page; and a concern with honest expression. No one else wrote like Cummings, and Cummings wrote like no one else.

By 1958, his poems of affirmation and joy, and his celebrations of nature, transcendence, and love were beginning to run against the grain of what was becoming contemporary American poetry. New voices, such as those of the Beats (Allen Ginsberg's groundbreaking *Howl* was published in 1956), were blaring about the best minds of their generation "destroyed by madness, starving hysterical naked, / dragging themselves through the negro streets at dawn / looking for an angry fix." Other poets, such as Robert Lowell, John Berryman, and W. D. Snodgrass were writing confessionally about themselves and their dark nights of the soul. Elizabeth Bishop, spinning off from Marianne Moore, was welding direct observation of the real world with private reflection on what the outer could mean for the inner. The New York Poets, such as John Ashbery, Kenneth Koch, Barbara Guest, and Frank O'Hara were experimenting with language, but in a more abstract way than Cummings. Charles Olson, admittedly Pound's disciple, was toiling away at the *Maximus* poems, that like the Cantos, were "poems including history." Robert Creeley, Robert Duncan, Paul Blackburn, and Denise Levertov, under the tutelage of Olson, but with an eye on Williams, Zukofsky, and Pound, were attempting to say complex things in simple ways.

In a sense, though, they all owed Cummings a debt. He, too, had paved the way for poetry as social criticism that found favor with poets like Alan Ginsberg, Lawrence Ferlinghetti, and Gregory Corso. Cummings had not shied away from writing poems that gave vent to personal emotion and feeling, such as those of Lowell or Berryman. Experimentation with language, though different in Ashbery, Guest,

O'Hara, or James Schuyler, was certainly made more acceptable by the attention that Cummings devoted to words. In addition, their attention to painting echoed that of Cummings who created poem-pictures. Cummings's legacy even trickles down to Olson, Levertov, Creeley, Duncan, and others. Olson's sense of line and his social commentary, while Poundian, also calls Cummings to mind. Cummings's legacy is far more pronounced in Creeley, particularly in the love poems that are not afraid to make ardent, even simple, declarations within complex forms. Duncan wrote more than a few poems that are paeans to the natural world, and, like Cummings, often did so in rhyme and strict meters.

Reviews of 95 *Poems* were mixed. Robert Graves, then in America where he finally met Cummings for the first and only time, gave the book a rave in the *New York Times Book Review*. Winfield Townley Scott, picking up on both the numerous poems to nature and the religious tone, wrote in *Saturday Review* that the book "is the latest important expression of the New England Transcendental tradition." But John Berryman, reviewing the book in the *American Scholar*, did not feel that any poem in the book was "up to the standard of his finest work." Edward Hood, writing in *Shenandoah*, was even more scathing: "Cummings cannot play upon and extend convention; he must smash it, escape society and the public tradition, and be individual to the point of anarchy. Thus his language tends to isolation and privacy. Its only vital content is his own mind, which remains, for us, permanently unknowable." On the other hand, Harold Schonberg, in an article on Cummings for the *New York Times Magazine*, took delight in the fact that "our rebel poet, still rebels."

William Carlos Williams also came through in a review for *Evergreen Review*: "The feeling of a primitive language pervades the book, a country atmosphere of New England…but the world of the poem is, in fact, one of Cummings' own creation."

Williams's piece, to some extent, was written to make amends for a comment he had made on a television program, "Nitebeat," in 1957. In response to a question by Mike Wallace, as to whether he regarded Cummings's poem "(im)c-a-t(mo) / b,i;l:e" as a poem, Williams said he had to "reject that effort as a poem." As a result of Williams's "rejection," relations between he and Cummings had cooled. But after his review, letters were again exchanged. According to Paul Mariani, Williams's biographer, the letter of reconciliation that Cummings sent Williams resulted in Williams's own poem, "Poem:" "I was much moved / to hear / from him if / as yet he does not / concede the point / nor is he / indeed conscious of it / no matter." He sent a copy of it to Cummings.

It was probably about this time that Cummings and Williams met in New York. Cummings, in his journals, left a record of the visit: "he almost died(coronary;stroke)but is all-over-the-place as usual;& regrets only that he 'didn't go to bed with' more women in the past, being now almost unable....'now I wake up with a hearton & say to myself:O hell! if I wake up Flos,she'll have to go and take a piss;& by that time it'll be gone."

Cummings could definitely sympathize with his infirm friend. A note dated January 1959 entitled "Myself & Me(A Dialogue)" gives Cummings's assessment of his own state:

> What's wrong with you?
> I'm unhappy
> Why are you unhappy?
> Because I feel Un.
> "Meaning which" as Joe Gould used to say.
> Old & impotent
> Impotent sexually?
> Yes.
> Toward whom?
> M[arion].
> Why don't you try somebody else?
> That's the trouble—I guess I-don't-want-to enough.

Intermittent impotency, in fact, had been plaguing Cummings for several years. He had, since around the time of the Norton Lectures, gone "months with no sex." Reflecting on this in 1959 he wrote, "my chief trouble is that I exhaust myself in imagined exploits...with entirely desirable & immeasurably passionate bedfellows;often virginal & always young. Unfortunately, the bolder I am in my daydreams,the more timidly I avoid any possible liaison with flesh&blood girls,clinging to(e.g.)Marion for protection."

This "timidity" accompanying desire was very much present when he was in Cambridge. On one of the rare occasions that Cummings mingled with students—at an afternoon tea at his house on Wyman Road—a young Radcliffe undergraduate, Ann Grant, a pretty blonde, gave him "a look." "[F]eel shock:as if by lightning," wrote Cummings. "realise this is love's arrow—am really wounded!" For the next few years he obsessed about "la blonde" or "la bl" turning over and over in his head what might have been. Another woman, identified in his notes only as Duplessis, also caused his heart to palpitate. He became so obsessed, in fact, that he consulted his doctor who, perhaps in jest, suggested that Cummings "lay the girl." But Cummings was content to dwell on the fantasy.

Another woman also caused him more than a moment of desire. This time, he recorded the arousal (and fantasy) in verse:

just when i'd decided that my youth
of sixty years was almost over, ruth
showed me such titties,in another moment
gave me a look
deprived her of her raiment

Below the poem is a prose version, apparently of what actually happened: "Of what could I be thinking? She was so young,so fresh,so innocent;whereas I—was myself;and 60. Nevertheless my arms went around her waist. Suddenly an amazing thing happened:her whole body drew itself to me,quite as if I had hugged her—yet I'd scarcely dared to touch her. And now,without any conscious volition on my part,my hand wandered upward. As it moulded itself upon her young breast,her head sank on my shoulder." The possibility that this might actually lead somewhere, however, caused Cummings to withdraw his affections abruptly. At this point in his life he was far more interested in the "imagined exploit."

Marion was truly central for him, and while he could occasionally "damn this woman who has such power," he very much welcomed her continued love, affection, understanding, and affirmation. By 1959, in fact, their bond was deeper than it had ever been. He relied on her for almost everything—from keeping unwanted visitors from the door to making his meals, to sharing his ups and downs, both physically and mentally. In turn, he supported her in her photography—at which she was becoming quite skilled—and continually let her know that no one was dearer to him than she.

Cummings very much had a double standard when it came to women. Marion, or older women friends such as Hildegarde Watson or Marianne Moore, were elevated to the status of queens, worthy of courtly worship. In their presence he played the gallant gentleman. He regularly sent Watson and Moore flowers, remembered their birthdays with original cards and drawings, and was always quick to praise their accomplishments. But like many men of his time, he regarded the opposite sex, in general, as objects of either lust or scorn. His roving eye appraised the looks of any woman he encountered, and his private writings contain a number of entries in which he recorded the physical attributes of women he encountered on the street, at the market, or at a party. He also was quick to sketch any "lovely creature" who entered his orbit.

Female objects of desire were also thought of as both "whores" and "bitches." If a woman seemed to him overly flirtatious, she was immediately assumed by Cummings to be a whore. And while "whores" were certainly enticing, they were also usually, to his way of thinking, "bitches," ready to rebuke a man for even the slightest indiscretion. Strong older women, with the exception of his close female friends, were almost automatically assumed to be "bitches."

None of these attitudes deterred him from seeking out women, and delighting—at least until they transformed themselves into bitches—in their company. And women liked Cummings, too. When he put on the charm, as he often did in conversation, they became enthralled. At readings, it was often women who responded most enthusiastically and demonstratively to his performances.

Now that Cummings did not need money, money kept coming. His readings and book sales brought in more than decent sums. Prizes, such as the 1958 Bollingen and the Harriet Monroe Prize from *Poetry* magazine, which he won again in 1962, brought even more. Marion's friend Mina Curtiss, sister of Lincoln Kirstein, also arranged for Cummings to receive regular money through a foundation she had created to assist older writers financially.

Cummings wrote to Hildegarde Watson in June of 1958, "Something called The Chapelbrook Foundation has been paying me 333.33 a month—at last Marion discovered that this is the way…Mina…helps 'writers over 50' whom she likes." And then, in the early spring of 1959, Cummings was awarded yet another grant: this time fifteen thousand dollars from the Ford Foundation to be spread out over two years. The announcement of the award, for which he had neither applied nor even known about, came in person. A representative of the foundation simply showed up at Patchin Place one afternoon and offered him the grant.

Other distinctions also came his way. Charles Norman, who had first met Cummings in the mid-1920s and who throughout the 1950s had struggled with writing a biography of Cummings, finally managed to finish the book and get it in print in the fall of 1958. Norman had not had it easy. Cummings insisted that he have final approval over the manuscript before it went to the publisher. Norman agreed, but when he sent the manuscript of *The Magic Maker* to Cummings, the poet cut large sections, and even rewrote some to suit him. The result was more hagiographic than even the worshipping Norman had intended. Despite Norman's efforts, Cummings wrote to Pound (about whom Norman planned to write another biography), "while we wish the poor little cuss well,we cannot(vide supra)consider him a friend." He also told Pound that he "had absolutely nothing to do with his writing a book about [him]."

Cummings's work was also appearing in translation, an awesome task for even the most distinguished translator. The majority of Cummings's poems, however, could be rendered into other languages with the meaning, if not exact flavor of the original. Words in phonetic dialect, for instance, could be translated into an equivalent phonetic spelling in the target language. The splitting of words, as well, was not so formidable: the translators (at least in the European languages) could make similar divisions. Some poems, however, that depended almost entirely on the turns of English syntax and grammar were either side stepped or had to be reinvented anew by his foreign translators. Cummings, unlike a number of his contemporaries, was fortunate in having translators who were willing to grapple with the peculiarities of his style. The Italian poet Salvatore Quasimodo, who won the Nobel Prize for Literature in 1959, brought out a selection of Cummings's verse, *Poesie Scelte*, in 1958. Pound's daughter, Mary de Rachelwitz, translated his work into Italian, too. Her first selection of thirty poems came out in 1961; a far more substantial selection was issued in 1963. Eva Hesse made versions of a number of Cummings's works in German, including poems and *i six nonlectures* from the mid-1950s onward. *The Enormous Room* also made it into German, courtesy of

Elisabeth Kaiser-Braem and Helmuth Braem in 1955. D. Jon Grossman was responsible for Cummings appearing in French from the early 1950s onward. And Yasuo Fujitomi translated two books into Japanese, the first in 1958, the second in 1962. There were also, in those years, translations into Spanish and Portuguese. Cummings was by now international in his reputation.

George Firmage, initially described by Cummings as "a pathetic specimen of the latest Lost Generation," in actuality was a recent NYU graduate turned banker with a deep interest in literature who began working on a bibliography of Cummings in 1958. But soon, as Cummings told Hildegarde Watson, "what he termed his 'bibliography' grew to be a 'project' involving the publication of all my 'uncollected prose.'" The result of Firmage's efforts was *A Miscellany*, which collected a variety of Cummings pieces, including his Harvard commencement speech and the articles written in the 1920s and 1930s for the *Dial*, *Vanity Fair*, and other magazines. It was issued by the Argophile Press in 1958. Despite Cummings's dismissive tone in his letter to Watson, he was actually quite pleased with the book, noting in the introduction that he was "enlightened via the realization that,whereas times can merely change,an individual may grow." Firmage's bibliography came out in 1960. Even after Cummings's death, he continued to labor on Cummings's behalf, meticulously editing the "typescript" editions of *The Enormous Room* and many individual volumes of his poetry. These valuable editions presented Cummings's work in exactly the form he had wanted it (instead of how printers had chosen to compose his texts).

At the end of 1957, when Cummings completed *95 Poems*, he instructed his agent that he wanted her to place the book with "anybody who dared republish EIMI." But, as he wrote to Hildegarde Watson, "Heroical BB [Bernice Baumgarten] promptly tackled my regular publishers(miscalled Harcourt,Brace)only to hear they were 'crazy about the poems' but etcetera ad infin." Baumgarten was successful, however, in interesting Barney Rossett, the maverick avant-garde publisher of Grove Press into reissuing *Eimi* in both hard and soft covers.

Cummings was delighted to have this book back in print. He even provided a new schematic preface for this new edition that sketched a day-by-day outline of the contents. So grateful, in fact, was Cummings to Rossett for having the courage to reprint *Eimi*, that he agreed to allow Grove to issue the first-ever selection of Cummings's verse in the United States. In November 1959, *100 Selected Poems*, chosen by Cummings, rolled off the presses. This paperback, which sold for just one dollar and forty-five cents, could, within months, be found on bookshelves in countless apartments and in dorms across the country. Five thousand copies were sold in just the first year and the book has continued to sell since then—Grove (now Grove/Atlantic) still has it in print.

In 1960, there was also the first substantial English edition of his work, *Selected Poems 1923–1958*, published by Faber & Faber. "How do you suppose my ms ever got past Doubtless Thomas [T. S. Eliot, editor at Faber & Faber]?" he quipped to Hildegarde Watson.

The first full-length critical book on Cummings, Norman Friedman's *E. E. Cummings: The Art of His Poetry*, also appeared in 1960. That and subsequent books by Friedman remain, even now, among the best and most incisive contributions to Cummings scholarship ever published.

Cummings's poems, due to their inherent musicality, had been set to music as far back as the early 1930s by composers such as Aaron Copland, Marc Blitzstein, and Lehman Engel. David Diamond, aside from the score for *Tom*, had also written a number of pieces in the 1940s and 1950s, as had Vincent Persichetti and Paul Nordoff. In the 1950s and 1960s, though, composers seemingly flocked to Cummings's poems for inspiration. Among them were John Cage, Morton Feldman, Peter Schickele, and Peter Dickinson, who, each in his own way, expanded Cummings into another dimension.

Cummings himself had considered writing a libretto for a musical comedy based on *Uncle Tom's Cabin* in the early 1950s, but seems to have never gotten beyond making a list of song titles, occasionally accompanied by a few lines. More dear to him were his numerous attempts to create another play: "my gift is(I pray)to create a form as greatly deep as tragic drama—as Sophocles' Oedipus or Shakespeare's Anthony and Cleopatra;& in no wise imitative of them." But inspiration would not come. A scene or two could get written, but never a whole play. Poems, though, still "wrote themselves" on occasion. But more and more

Cummings had to labor over his first inspiration, sometimes writing upward of a hundred drafts of a single poem.

Now that there was no lack of money, Cummings and Marion once again decided to make a European trip. Jack Sweeney, the Lamont Poetry Room librarian, whom Cummings and Marion had gotten to know and like when they were in Cambridge, along with his wife Máire, hosted them at their house in Ireland in mid-May of 1959. Cummings, a bit to his surprise, since he associated Ireland with MacDermot, liked the country. Marion initially enjoyed the visit, too, but came down with a respiratory infection and spent most of the visit in bed. In late May, they went to Paris for two weeks, but Marion, still not well, was unable to delight in a city that, like Cummings, she also had come to adore. Cummings had to conclude that "my most recent glimpse of Whatwas onceEurope taught me…not to travel."

By September 1960, however, he and Marion overcame their reservations about further travel and embarked on yet another European sojourn, this one to Italy and Greece. The primary reason Cummings wanted to visit Greece was to see Nancy and his new grandchildren, Ionna, born in 1955, and Alexis, born in the summer of 1960. Nancy, in fact, had not been well and had even been hospitalized in London not long after her new baby's birth. Cummings, suddenly concerned about her health, had telephoned her when she was in the hospital in England and apparently made the decision then to visit that fall after she had returned to Athens.

To make their trip more comfortable, he and Marion sailed first class on the *Valencia* to Palermo. After a week in Sicily, they went to Southern Italy—Naples, Sorrento, and Rome—but Cummings found none of these cities to his liking. In addition, he was in considerable pain because of his back and quaffing a variety of pills—including the tranquilizer Equanil, several Nembutals to help him sleep, and Probanthine for his intestinal problems. After a few days in Rome, he wanted to return to the United States but decided to push on to Athens.

By the end of October they were in Athens, staying at the Hotel Grande Bretagne, that, in its remodeled state, reminded Cummings more of a hospital than a luxury hotel. He thought, in fact, he might need a hospital. The voyage to Athens had greatly aggravated his back and, to make matters worse, his heating pad that he relied on to soothe the pain did not fit the Greek electrical outlet. They could not easily get in touch with Nancy either since she did not have a phone. Finally, Marion wrote her a terse note asking her to come to the hotel. As soon as she heard from them, Nancy and Andrews promptly arrived, but by this point Marion was in a stew. She had complaints about everything, including the Greek electrical system. Andrews promptly fetched a Greek heating pad and took it to the room; but, Marion, now in high dudgeon, opened the door only wide enough to admit the heating pad, and then slammed it in his face. Since she had not bothered to listen to Andrews's instructions as to how to use it, it blew a fuse when she plugged it in.

Nancy, having still not seen her father, left him a note: "We are as Kevin tried to say, at your disposal at all times but, not wishing to intrude & being perhaps rather too much aware of this possibility it seems best to leave the modus up to you—even at the risk of seeming, Estlin, less loving toward yourself than I feel; this has always seemed the lesser / or better / risk & very possibly I have always been wrong; I have very little to go on."

Cummings responded with a note of his own, saying that he would very much like to see her and her family. The next day Marion and Cummings were invited to Nancy's small house halfway up Mount Lycabettus, which looked directly on the Acropolis. Though everyone else seemed to have recovered, Marion, unhappy that her control over Cummings and their lives, in general, had been usurped by Nancy and her family, continued to be truculent. She fumed about "being invited to a mere family lunch with grandchildren present, implying that Cummings was too important a man to be asked to join the children at the family table."

Cummings did have one enjoyable day when he, Andrews, Marion, and Ionna ascended Mount Hymettus to take in a Byzantine monastery. Only once was he alone with Nancy and the conversation was slight, even strained. But she did learn that the reason for his trip to Athens was to see her. The reality, however, was that he had no sense of what it meant to be a father or grandfather in the flesh. He was better in letters.

By mid-November Cummings and Marion had flown to Paris where they stayed at the Hotel Continental, the hotel where Thayer once stayed. No longer did Cummings need to seek out inexpensive accommodations.

And yet, the luxuriousness of the hotel could not compensate for his failing health. In late November 1960, he and Marion jetted home.

twenty-nine

Steering for Dream

Cummings was happy to be back at Patchin, where he could resume his regular routine of rising late, eating a large breakfast, and afterward retreating to his studio upstairs to write or paint. In the evening, he would sometimes see friends, mostly those he had known for years. He was not exactly shutting down, but he was not letting much new (including people) come in, either. But he delighted in those he had known for half a century or more. In a letter to Hildegarde Watson he described a visit from Marianne Moore: "what a marvellous person! I had the feeling that if a dozen unworlds collapsed while she was talking with us we'd scarcely notice the difference."

But even his home was not as sacred as it had been. The owner of Patchin Place, Hugh Keenan, was frustrated with the low rent he was receiving and decided "to chop 4 [Patchin Place] into 6 oneroom 'apartments' 'with all modern conveniences.'" Marion appealed to the city to prevent the action from taking place, but the court found in favor of Keenan. A frustrated Cummings wrote to Robert Frost (though it is unclear whether he actually sent the letter) to ask him to intervene on his behalf: "am threatened with eviction from 4 PP after living here 30some years. And here's the only urban spot I can work.... The fact that am threatened(And How)plus the fact that I can(& do)work,is all I want you to know. It goes without adding that if President K lifted his finger on my behalf I still wouldn't dream of playing ball with him."

Though President Kennedy did not come to the rescue, the *Village Voice* took up the cause, blaring the news that Cummings was to be evicted. Meanwhile, others were putting pressure on Mayor Robert Wagner to intercede. Finally, in February 1962, Wagner did exactly that and the city denied Keenan a building permit. Invited to celebrate the event, he and Marion appeared at City Hall, where they were "copiously snapshotted with-&-without Mayor Wagner."

As he was "unspeakably thankful" to Wagner, he did not feel compromised in appearing with him at City Hall. Cummings was quick to turn down an invitation to dine at the White House, with President and Mrs. Kennedy and "70some crooks punks and preknowbellists." He also rejected an invitation to appear in a symposium honoring Thoreau that the Interior Department had planned. Again, his objection had to do with it being a government-sponsored event, for Thoreau was certainly near and dear to his heart.

A new project was occupying his time and attention in 1962—writing "captions for a book of 50 photographs by Marion(they're superb!)." The book, published in 1962, was called *Adventures in Value*. The photographs—portraits, landscapes, cityscapes, and close-ups of flowers—are each "commented" on by Cummings. These "captions" are not meant to be descriptive of what Marion photographed, rather they are Cummings's personal reactions. At times, this meant that a photograph conjured a quote form literature, Blake for instance. At other times, there was a brief personal notation. There are also two poems that are both in response to portraits: one of Marianne Moore, the other of David Diamond. The poem for Diamond begins:

he isn't looking at anything
he isn't looking for something
he isn't looking
he is seeing

The poem for Moore, while not a genuine acrostic, does use the device of beginning each line with a letter of her name:

M in a vicious world—to love virtue
A in a craven world—to have courage

R in a treacherous world—to prove loyal
I in a wavering world—to stand firm...

There were also other poems that Cummings intended for another book. Most were quiet, meditative reflections. The natural world (observed up close) was still a source of wonder and inspiration:

one

t
hi
s

snowflake

(a
li
ght
in
g)

is upon a gra

v
es
t

one

But in much of the verse from the last two years of his life, death was the overwhelming presence, often coupled with dream:

now is a ship

which captain am
sails out of sleep

steering for dream

And:

while a once world slips from
few of sun fingers numb)

with anguished each their me
brains of that this and tree
illimitably try
to seize the doom of sky

(silently all then known
thing or dreamed become un-

In the final stanza of "now does our world descend," recognition of what was to come did not equal resignation:

but from this endless end
of briefer each our bliss—
where seeing eyes go blind
(where lips forget to kiss)
where everything's nothing
—arise,my soul;and sing

Not all of the poems he was writing in 1961–62 were so grave. He could still be his irreverent self when moved to do so. When he learned of the death of Anne (Barton) Girdansky, he penned these lines:

annie died the other day

never was there such a lay—
whom,among her dollies,dad
first("don't tell your mother")had;
making annie slightly mad
but very wonderful in bed
—saints and satyrs,go your way

youth and maidens:let us pray

Death, though, as Cummings knew, was fast approaching. He curtailed his readings and retreated more and more into himself. But when he did venture forth before an audience, his frailty was more than evident. Poet Edward Foster attended one of Cummings's last readings in New York and recalled that he was rather shocked at Cummings's appearance. The poet sat stiffly on stage in a straight-backed chair, his voice, previously so resonant, was now weak, with a decided tremble. He did not interact with the audience.

The summer of 1962, was spent, as usual, at Joy Farm. He could still take delight in the chipmunks that came up on the porch to receive the peanuts he left for them in a cookie jar. The hummingbirds, too, were a source of joy. Charles Norman recalled that Cummings told him that at summer's end they "'bow good-by'" before heading south. As if on cue, two hummingbirds appeared outside the screen on the porch: "Like tiniest helicopters the hummingbirds rose straight up to the top of the screen, then descended, five or six times, turned and were gone."

Neither the hummingbirds nor Cummings was aware that when they bowed to him on the morning of September 2, 1962, it would be the last time that either Cummings would witness them, or they him. That afternoon, after chopping wood, he came into the house, ascended the stairs to the second floor, and collapsed—the victim of a cerebral hemorrhage.

n
OthI
n

g can

s
urPas
s

the m

y
SteR
y

of

ss
tilLnes
s

Epilogue

On September 6, 1962, three days after he had died, Cummings was buried in the family plot, just off Tulip Avenue, at the vast Forest Hills Cemetery in Boston. In stark contrast to the attention his death had received around the world, the funeral itself was exceedingly private. There was no cortege of friends and admirers, no fanfare, no publicity at all. Indeed, only a few were present at the brief service: Marion; Nancy's two teenage children, Simon and Elizabeth; and Marion's friend Mina Curtiss.

Curtiss had driven down the day before from her country house in Western Massachusetts to meet Marion at the Fairmont Copley Plaza Hotel in Boston. She, it seems, had made the burial arrangements as Marion was too overwhelmed to do much of anything but grieve. Marion had apparently managed to inform Nancy, still in Europe, who, in turn, let her two oldest children, then in the United States, know of the death of the grandfather whom they hardly knew. Old friends, with the possible exception of the Watsons, were not informed of the service. But Sibley Watson was unable to get down from Rochester, New York, and Hildegarde was in Athens. The simple service, however, was as Marion wanted it. Cummings's gravestone is as he wanted it: a slab of New Hampshire granite with only his full name and dates engraved upon it.

In the years following her partner's death, Marion stayed on alone at Patchin Place and summered in New Hampshire. According to her friend,

Maryette Charlton, Marion "was valiant, lonely, heartsick, but continued to work on many Cummings projects." Among these projects was the assembling of Cummings's last book, *73 Poems*, that came out in 1963. In this task she was assisted by George J. Firmage, Cummings's bibliographer.

She continued taking photographs, but her major passion was still Cummings. She oversaw republications of his work; sold his voluminous papers and correspondence to Harvard's Houghton Library; and donated more than two hundred of his paintings, sketches, and drawings to Luethi-Peterson Camps in Rhode Island. Nancy's children had attended the camp and, in response to a request for a donation, Marion gave them the artwork to sell for fundraising. The camp, however, simply stuck the art in a barn. In 2001 the collection was acquired by bookseller Ken Lopez, who is now briskly selling off the individual works.

Marion died of throat cancer in 1969, less than seven years after Cummings. She is buried alongside her partner. Her headstone reads: Marion Morehouse Cummings, 1906–1969.

Nancy, now in her eighties, has lived for years in London.

Over forty years have passed since Cummings last physically inhabited the earth he so loved. Yet he is still very much with us. His work—both poetry and prose—continues to resonate in the hearts and minds of readers around the world. Most of his books are in print, including the authoritative eleven-hundred-page *Complete Poems, 1904–1962* that was issued in 1994, one hundred years after his birth.

Cummings did not single-handedly change the map of American poetry, but he had a great deal to do with it. Along with a few others, he forever altered what a poem could be. He called attention to the sound and shape of verse, demolished the sanctity of the left margin, used every device of grammar to showcase the importance of words—even at the phonemic level. Never, however, were his poems divorced from feeling, from humanity, from life itself. Intelligent but not intellectual, his verse remains alive, a constant gift that continues to amuse, infuriate, engage, and even occasionally overwhelm his diverse readers. He remains vital. Or as William Carlos Williams wrote: "cummings is the living presence of the drive to make all our convictions evident by penetrating through their costumes to the living flesh."

In the last months of his life, perhaps in anticipation of the inevitable, Cummings wrote these lines:

> Gently
> (very whiteness:absolute peace,
> never imaginable mystery)
> descend

Notes

ABBREVIATIONS

Books and Publications

CP E. E. Cummings, *Complete Poems: 1904-1962* (New York, NY, Liveright Publishing, 1994).

E E. E. Cummings, *Eimi* (New York, NY: Grove Press, 1958).

ER *The Enormous Room*, George Firmage, ed. (New York, NY: Liveright Publishing, 1978).

MR E. E. Cummings, *A Miscellany Revised*, George J. Firmage, ed. (New York, NY: October House, 1965).

P/C Pound/Cummings: *The Correspondence of Ezra Pound and E. E. Cummings*, Barry Ahearn, ed. (Ann Arbor, MI: University of Michigan Press, 1996).

Six E. E. Cummings, *i: six nonlectures* (Cambridge, MA: Harvard University Press, 1953).

SL *Selected Letters of E. E. Cummings*, F.W. Dupee and George Stade, ed. (New York, NY: Harcourt, Brace and World, 1969).

Other Resources

BE Beinecke Library, Yale University

EC Edward Cummings (EEC's father)

EEC Edward Estlin Cummings

HL Houghton Library, Harvard University (call numbers are given for items in the Cummings Manuscript Collection)

HRC Harry Ransom Humanities Research Center, University of Texas (Cummings Papers)

NYPL New York Public Library, Berg Collection (the *Dial* Papers of Dr. J. Sibley Watson)

RHC Rebecca Haswell Cummings (EEC's mother)

NOTE ON CAPITALIZATION

ix ...following his convention: For further information on the capitalization of Cummings's name, see Norman Friedman, "Not e.e. cummings": *Spring*, January 1992.

NOTES TO PREFACE

xi "beauty all alone": bMS Am 1892.7 (132).

xi "Poet Stood for Stylistic Liberty": *New York Times* (September 4, 1962): 1.

xii "Whitman's one living descendant": Quoted in *AnOther E.E. Cummings*, ed Richard Kostelanetz. (New York: Liveright Publishing, 1998), viii.

xiii "verse from an unwritten volume": John Dos Passos, *The Best Times* (New York: New American Library), 83.

xiii "a human being": *CP*, 461–62.

xvi Linking the words he wrote with the life he led: See also J. V. Cunningham, "Epigram No. 11" in *Collected Poems & Epigrams* (Chicago: Swallow, 1971), 111.

xvi "concentrate of titanic significances": Marianne Moore, *The Complete Prose*, ed. Patricia C. Willis (New York: Penguin Books, 1987), 643.

NOTES TO CHAPTER 1: THEIR SON

1 "not more than 8 stitches—no ether": HL: bMS Am 1892.10 (21).

1 "christened the boy at 5:00": Ibid.

3 "the masses of mankind": *Harvard College Bulletin* (1898), 152.

4 "installed all his own waterworks": *Six*, 8.

1–4 Information on Edward Cummings is derived primarily from the following: *Boston Transcript*, August 21, 1900; Harvard University Archives; Boston Public Library Reserve Collection (South Congregational Church archive); The Massachusetts Historical Society; E. E. Cummings's miscellaneous notes; and Richard S. Kennedy, *Dreams in the Mirror: A Biography of E.E. Cummings* (New York: Liveright Publishing, 1979).

4 "obliterated his name from the family archives": *Six*, 11.

5 "her father had been hanged": Ibid.

5 "as she smiled": *Six*, 12.

5 "humanly and unaffectedly generous": *Six*, 11.

5 "joyous fate and my supreme fortune": Ibid.

5 "love was the axis of my being": HL: bMS Am 1892.7 (131).

4–6 Information on Rebecca Haswell Clarke Cummings is derived primarily from The Massachusetts Historical Society; E. E. Cummings's miscellaneous notes; Louise Diman, *Leaves from a Family Tree*. Providence: Roger Williams Press, 1941; and Richard S. Kennedy, *Dreams in the Mirror: A Biography of E. E. Cummings* (New York: Liveright Publishing, 1979).

6 "dimple in his right cheek": Rebecca's notes on EEC's infancy: HL: bMS Am 1892.10 (21).

6 "Estlin has known all his letters": Ibid.

6 "go to college with Fader": Ibid.

6 "saw wood in mitre saw": Ibid.

7 "and he made his Moder harder": Ibid.

7 "Holy Bible, and The Arabian Nights": *Six*, 27.

7 "two pieces of toast one orange": bMS Am 1892.10 (21).

7 "baby monkeys climbing a tree": Ibid.

7 "I was in bed": Ibid.

8 "Beaming in his look": Ibid.

8 "whenever aloneness palled": *Six*, 26.

8 "a garden of magnificent roses": *Six*, 25.

9 "Lanman…the celebrated Sanskrit scholar": *Six*, 25.

9 "beyond imagining imagination": *Six*, 32.

9 "something moves in a rackpool": HL: bMS Am 1892.7 (131).

9 "as the tide came in" [ellipsis, EEC]: Ibid.

10 "I'll see you there, Sir!"): Ibid.

10 "'100 acres more or less,' November 15th, 1898": HL: bMS Am 1823.9 (16).

11 …more simply called Jack: Ibid.

11 "Read to Estlin": Ibid.

12 "less fortunate than themselves": Boston Public Library Reserve Collection.

12 "That They May Have Life More Abundantly": Ibid.

13 "my mother—out of her body"): HL: bMS Am 1892.7 (146).

13 "brought her feet and she cried lustily": HL: bMS Am 1892.10 (21).

NOTES TO CHAPTER 2: IN JUST- SPRING

15–16 Information on Cummings's family home: HL: bMS Am 1892.7.

16 "but I loved to help my father and brother": HL: Elizabeth Cummings Qualey, *When I Was a Little Girl* (manuscript memoir) bMS Am 1823.9.

16 "let me help him turn the windlass": Ibid.

16 "we were forbidden to scream unless we were hurt": Ibid.

17 "and sometimes spent the night there": Ibid.

17 "and had a few peanuts then we popped corn": Quoted in Richard S. Kennedy, *Dreams in the Mirror*, 24.

17 "We dress(hurriedly.)": HL: bMS Am 1892.7 (131).

17 "that I Lied saying No, I don't think so": Ibid.

17 "(steam running down) chuttling, pumpingheartlike": Ibid.

18 "notion must strike you as fantastic": *Six*, 23.

18 "place where he could thrive": *Six*, 26.

18 "called for his Farmers and Cowboys": HL: bMS Am 1892.8.

18 …his "totem": *MR*, 111.

18 … forest-bred African Lions: HL: bMS Am 1892.8.

19 "32 elephants little and big": Ibid.

19 "Ticket will be taken up and not renewed": Ibid.

19 "NOTA BeNE runs,controls him": HL: bMS Am 1892.7 (201).

19 "I was always afraid of my father": Ibid.

20 "the good,the true,the beautiful": Ibid.

20 "SLIM ARMS AND UNDERSIZEDNESS": Ibid.

20 "three feet, four inches tall)": HL: bMS Am 1823.9 (16).

20 "a lesser triad: healthy & honest & brave": HL: bMS Am 1892.7 (121).
20 "he was always my playfellow": *Six*, 26–7.
21 "CRIED Every Single Day": HL: bMS Am 1892.7 (201).
21 "a whiz at arithmetic": Ibid.
21 …belief in his father's authority on religious subjects: Ibid.
21 …face of adversity: Richard S. Kennedy, *Dreams in the Mirror*, 22.
22 …congregation were invited home for Sunday dinner: Ibid.
22 "the truest power is gentleness": *Six*, 30.
22 "equal in attainment of the seventh grade pupils": HL: bMS Am 1892.10 (11).
23 …who along the way meet Robin Hood: HL: bMS Am 1892.7; HL: bMS Am 1892.4; HRC.
23 "Lorna Doone…and Treasure Island": *Six*, 27–28.
23 …accurate in detail and names of characters: HL: bMS Am 1892.8.
23 "The separating curtain,—it is death": *CP*, 1054.
24 "They told stories about us, our animals, and all sorts of things": HL: Elizabeth Cummings Qualey, *When I Was a Little Girl*, bMS Am 1823.9.
24 "easycoming strokable creatures?": HL: bMS Am 1892.7 (211).
25 "threw snowballs containing small rocks": *Six*, 31.
25 "because I was afraid of being beaten": HL: bMS Am 1892.7 (211).
25 "…balloons of all colors tugging at their strings": HL: Elizabeth Cummings Qualey, *When I Was a Little Girl*, bMS Am 1823.9.
25 "far / and / wee": *CP*, 27.

NOTES TO CHAPTER 3: POET OF SIMPLICITY

27 "Free Trade and Protective Tariff": HL: bMS Am 1892.6.
28 "O symbol of liberty,waving anew!": *CP*, 1055.
28 "to daylight and night to morning": *CP*, 1057.
28 "Building of the Ship": HRC (commencement program).
28 "and lived in terror of being found out": HL: bMS Am 1892.7 (201).
29 "reading *L'Homme Qui Rit* of Victor Hugo": Ibid.
29 …frequently prayed for God to forgive his transgression: Ibid.
29 …masturbation assumed an overpowering importance: Ibid.
29 "and first thing they know it's happened": Ibid.
30 "I'll give him a box on the ear": Ibid.
30 "(Mary's sorry she hurt you.)": Ibid.
30 "never take any more of my F[ather]'s hypocrisy [?]": Ibid.
30 …leafs rolled into "cigars" in his tree house: Ibid.
30 …sport amusing and thrilling: Ibid.
30 …causing him to double up in pain: Ibid.
31 "while really hating her": Ibid.
31–33 Information on Cambridge Latin derived primarily from *Annual Report of the Superintendent of Schools*, Cambridge, MA (1907, 09, 10); HL: Cambridge Rindge and Latin School, Official Records; bMS Am 1892.7; Cambridge Public Library (miscellaneous documents).

31 “god forgive our SHORT comings”: HL: bMS Am 1892.10.
32 “rightful inhabitants of my wronged native land”: *Six*, 27.
32 “downstairs my father built himself a desk”: HL: Elizabeth Cummings Qualey, *When I Was a Little Girl*, bMS Am 1823.9.
32 “and cubbyholes for books and things”: Ibid.
33 “sentimental stories”: HL: bMS Am 1892.10.
33 “a weird lamp post on a road of dreams”: *CP*, 1054.
34 “the blood-stained mercy-seat”: HL: bMS Am 1892.
34 “dangerous fireworks on the fourth of July”: *Six*, 29.
34 “that gladness is next to goodliness”: *Six*, 30.
35 “or I may not or may put to it”: *Six*, 29.
35 “fits you best,—our faithful friend”: HL: bMS Am 1892.11.
36 …ultimately triumph over athletics: Ibid.
36 “Never any more, My God”: HL: bMS Am 1892.7 (201).
36 “With sex I associate, also, GUILTINESS”: Ibid.
36 “Face the music”: Ibid.
36 “How I hate that phrase”: Ibid.
37 “against Edward’s “long black snake”: Ibid.
37 “not daring to ask for something”: Ibid.
37 …thoroughly humiliated and miserable: Ibid.
37 “would like to KILL HIM”: Ibid.
38 “never caught him napping”: George Santayana, *Character and Opinion in the United States* (New York: Norton, 1967), 97–98.
39 “Fearfully,never”: *CP*, 1069.
39 “The Story of a Man and a Pack of Cards”: HRC.
40 …decided to major in Greek in college: HL: bMS Am 1892.10.
40 …Robert Cowley and Edward Estlin Cummings: Richard S. Kennedy, *Dreams in the Mirror*, 39.
41–42 The near-drowning incident is described in Elizabeth Cummings Qualey, *When I Was a Little Girl*, HL: bMS Am 1823.9.
42 “We two, know lies not here at rest”: HRC.
42 “things seem to be bad”: HL: Elizabeth Cummings Qualey, *When I Was a Little Girl*, bMS Am 1823.9.

NOTES TO CHAPTER 4: A SMATTERING OF LANGUAGES, A FIRST TASTE OF INDEPENDENCE, AND THE TRUEST FRIENDS

43 …fifty dollars more than the tuition: *Harvard College Bulletin* (1911) 331.
43 …horrors of venereal disease: HL: bMS Am 1892.7.
44 “entirely unknown among them”: George Santayana, *Character and Opinion in the United States*, 49–50.
44 …but the work’s eroticism: Quoted in Charles Norman, *E. E. Cummings: The Magic Maker*, rev. ed. (Boston: Little, Brown & Co., 1972), 30.

45 "from portals unsurpassed": HL: bMS Am 1892.5.
45 "Impressions Which Various Vowels Give the Ear": HRC.
46 "in the gold had'st shot!": *CP*, 912.
46 "all its broken, yellow teeth": *CP*, 907.
46 ...dive into an onstage pool: HL: bMS Am 1892; letters: Dory Miller to EEC; bMS Am 1892.4; notes for *six nonlectures*: bMS Am 1823.4 (104).
47 "an exclamatory / tooth-pick": *CP*, 84.
47 "losses are restored and sorrows end": HL: 69C-257.
47 "glory equally with the deeds": HRC.
48 ...never overtly suggestive (Dory Miller to EEC): HL: bMS Am 1892.4.
48 ...explorations of classical, medieval, and romantic literature: HL: Class Notes, bMS Am 1892.7.
49 "Ringed with the rhythmical fair": *CP*, 1073.
49 ...Kuno Francke, founder of Harvard's Germanic museum: HL: bMS Am 1892.7.
50 "strange with rare birds after rain": *CP*, 855.
51 "I've been writing sonnets ever since": *Six*, 29–30.
51 "beneath their sheltering wings": *CP*, 916.
52 ...last of the Cs (Cummings): Norman, *E. E. Cummings: The Magic Maker*, 35.
52 "modern music and poetry and painting": *Six*, 50.
53 "socialists, pacifists or worse": Malcolm Cowley, "E.E. Cummings" in *New England Writers and Writing*, ed. Donald Farber (Hanover, NH: University Press of New England, 1966), 182–83.
53 "descriptive of much that is published": Quoted in Norman, *The Magic Maker*, 33.
54 "the truest friends any man will ever enjoy": *Six*, 47.
54–56 On Cummings's fellow editors: Cowley, "E.E. Cummings" in *New England Writers*, 182–83; Norman, *The Magic Maker;* Kennedy, *Dreams in the Mirror;* HL: bMS Am 1892.7.
55 "flying / Rimbaud / at the moon": John Dos Passos, *USA Trilogy* (New York: The Modern Library, 1937), 303.
56 "taking his money all the time": HL: bMS Am 1892.7 (201).
56 ...vomiting into the river: Ibid.
57 "toured the booths, half-piffed": Ibid.
57 ...to ask her out: Ibid.
58 "rose breathed in the gloom": *CP*, 863.
58 "first time a girl ever had": HL: bMS Am 1892.7 (212).
58 "feeling her up": Ibid.
58 "or go the whole hog": Ibid.
59–60 On Cummings's course of study (1913–15): HL: class notes: bMS Am 1892.7.
60 "Stands. Smoking": Ibid.
60 "trembles the tremendous soul": *CP*, 911.
61 "cruel bugle sang before": *CP*, 15.
61 "of putting things": John Dos Passos, "P.S. to Dean Briggs": in Brooks Atkinson, ed., *College in a Yard* (Harvard University Press), 57.
61 "lack a man's strength": HL: bMS Am 1892.7 (212).

61 “persuasiveness of treatment”: Ibid.
62 “Boston had her points”: *Six*, 47–8.
62 “aristocracy since Ming”: *Six*, 48.
62 “knocked twice before entering”: *Six*, 48.
62 “shy and private in the Cambridge fashion”: Cowley, “E. E. Cummings” in *New England Writers*, 183.
62 “very unobservant or very wise”: Quoted in Norman, *The Magic Maker*, 33.
63 “The New Art”: Commencement Bulletin, Harvard University Archives.
63 ...achieve this distinction: *Harvard College Bulletin* (1916), 309.
63 “painting, sculpture, music and literature”: *MR*, 6.
63 ...Donald Evans, and Gertrude Stein. Ibid., 11.
64 “probably why Boston laughed”: Ibid., 7.
64 “ordinary to the abnormal”: Ibid., 8.
64 “absolutely unperturbed”: S. Foster Damon, *Amy Lowell: A Chronicle with Extracts from Her Correspondence* (Hamden, CT: Archon Books, 1966), 312.
64 “brought down the house”: Ibid., 212.
65 “with regular / feel faces. *MR*, 10.
65 “will discover for himself”: Ibid., 10.
65 “any man will ever enjoy”: *Six*, 47.

NOTES TO CHAPTER 5: THE GRADUATE STUDENT AS POET

67 ...also Doris: HL: bMS Am 1823.7 (23).
68 “the yellow lover”: *CP*, 43.
68 “besides physical attraction”: HL: bMS Am 1892.7.
69 “I had given birth to a god”: HL: bMS Am 1892.7 (211).
70 “high and pure of his son”: Ibid.
70 “sour grape scorn in silence”: Quoted in Norman, *The Magic Maker*, 33.
72 “well written as good prose”: Ezra Pound, “Affirmations” in *Selected Prose, 1909–1965*, ed. William Cookson (London: Faber & Faber, 1973), 345.
72 “cannot be worked into dados”: Ibid, 345.
72 “rudiments) of my writing style”: HL: bMS Am 1892.7.
73 “pallid the leash-men”: Ezra Pound, “The Return” in *Personae (New York: New Directions, 1971), 74.*
73 “not for ears but eye—moved me”: HRC.
75 “made a run for the stairs”: S. Foster Damon, *Amy Lowell: A Chronicle with Extracts from Her Correspondence* Damon, 214. For a poetic version of the event, see John Wheelwright’s poem “Dinner Call” in *Collected Poems* (New York: New Directions, 1971), 284.
77 “buckets over Rupert Brooke!”: HL: bMS Am 1892.5.
77 “nuzzle of the sea”: HL: bMS Am 1892.5 (reworked in *Tulips & Chimneys* in *CP*, 19).
77 “bold rather than happy”: HL: bMS Am 1892.5.
78 “but don’t do it again”: Ibid.

79 …only with a C: Ibid.

79 …dress party in his elegant lodgings: Background information on Scofield Thayer drawn from the Beinecke Library, Yale University, Scofield Thayer Collection; Nicholas Joost, *Scofield Thayer and the Dial* (Carbondale, IL: Southern Illinois University Press, 1964); Hildegarde Lasell Watson, *The Edge of the Woods: A Memoir* (Lunenburg VT: Stinehour Press, 1979); and EEC's notes and journals.

80 "Hotel 'Richmond'": HL: bMS Am 1892.7 (222).

80 "make [him] go off": Ibid.

80 …Worcester, Massachusetts: Watson, *The Edge of the Woods*, 89–90.

80 "turn all heads in their direction": Ibid., 90.

80 "vermilion heels of the period'": Ibid., 88.

80 "wherever Scofield was present": Ibid., 89.

81 "great heart shall hide?": *CP*, 87.

81 "Anonymous," "monosyllabic," "mysterious": HL: bMS Am 1892.7.

81 "he's so natural": Moore quoted in Watson, *The Edge of the Woods*, 84.

82 "such a handsome person": Ibid., 81–82.

82 "to bed next day": HL: bMS Am 1892.7 (222).

83 "discredited our country": Theodore Roosevelt, in *First Flowering: The Best of the Harvard Advocate*, ed. Richard M. Smoley (Reading, MA: Addison-Wesley, 1977), 181.

83 "Year of the Peacemaker": Boston Public Library Reserve Collection.

83 "eyes shut / tight": *CP*, 933.

84 "children comfort thee": *CP*, 876.

84 "it is only War": HL: bMS Am 1892.5.

85 …Dos Passos and Cummings were in attendance: HL: bMS Am 1892.7.

85–86 Background information on Elaine Orr: HL: bMS Am 1892.7 (198); and Kennedy, *Dreams in the Mirror*.

86 "no association with money)": HL: bMS Am 1892.7 (198).

86 "prettier than Elaine": Watson, *The Edge of the Woods*, 83.

86 "the lily maid of Astolot": Dos Passos, *The Best Times*, 82.

86 "was so beautiful": Stewart Mitchell quoted in "Newport Meeting with Charles Norman & Merilyn Lafferty": *Spring*, November 1984.

87 "audible great rose!": *CP*, 5.

87 "paraphrase of death)": Ibid., 6.

88 "his wandering word": Ibid., 7.

88 "rather my idea of him": HL: bMS Am 1892.7 (198).

89 "some excellent advice": Quoted in Damon, *Amy Lowell: A Chronicle with Extracts from Her Correspondence*, 363.

89 "a while longer": EEC / RHC (June 22, 1916) HL: bMS Am 1823.10 (156).

89 "considered the money 'unearned'": HL: bMS Am 1892.7 (198).

NOTES TO CHAPTER 6: POETIC EXCURSIONS

91 "when I should/not": EEC / S. Thayer (October 25, 1916) BE.

92 "to the quivering string)": Quoted in Watson, *The Edge of the Woods*, 87–88.

92 "hauntingly and slow": *CP*, 144.
93 "commas and silly colons": EEC / S. Thayer (October 25, 1916) BE.
93 "shgiht ym llit": HL: bMS Am 1823.5 (146).
94 "the silver of the moon": *CP*, 68.
94 "organizations of colour and line": EEC / RHC (June 18, 1918) HL: bMS Am 1823.1 (156).
94 "single moving ThingInItself": EEC / RHC (November 25, 1919) HL: bMS Am 1823.1 (156).
95 "fullest incipient power": William Slater Brown, *Broom* #6 (1924).
95 "vertical progression": HL: bMS Am 1823.7 (23).
96 "drink / dear": HL: bMS Am 1823.7 (23).
97 "consciousness of the experience": HL: bMS Am 1823.7 (23).
97 "blubber boobied": HL: bMS Am 1823.7 (22).
97 "sumptuously arranged wedding": Watson, *The Edge of the Woods*, 83.
98 …for a speech!): HL: bMS Am 1892.7 (23).
98 "experience would eradicate": Quoted in Norman, *The Magic Maker*, 52.
99 "he is only fair": Ibid., 52.
99 "overused poetic material": Ibid., 52.
98–100 Charles Norman provides a fine and detailed account of the pre-publication history of *Eight Harvard Poets* in *E.E. Cummings: The Magic Maker.*
100 "an enormous room, twenty by twenty": EEC / RHC (January 2, 1917) HL: bMS Am 1892.7 (181).
101 "immemorial races and nations": *Six*, 5.
101 "of diverging nationalities": EEC / RHC (January 2, 1917) HL: bMS Am 1892.7 (181).
101 "some prefer to name it": EEC / RHC (January 20, 1917) Ibid.
102 "blue eyed boy": Drafts of "Buffalo Bill 's" HL: bMS Am 1823.7 (21).
102 "Mister Death" *CP*, 90.
103 "career in the publishing business": EEC / FJ Reynolds (February 25, 1917) HL: bMS Am 1892.1.
103 "owed him my independence": HL: bMS Am 1892.7.
103 "soon as it is done": EEC / RHC (April 2, 1917) HL: bMS Am 1823.7.
103 "alarm clock's servant)": EEC / RHC (March 31, 1917) HL: bMS Am 1823.7.
103 "get a nickel cigar": EEC / RHC (March 18, 1917) HL: bMS Am 1823.1 (156).
104 …for service in France: EEC / Richard Norton (April 7, 1917) HL: H 795.148.25 F, Bx 18.
104 "fit of laughter": EEC / RHC (April 7, 1917) HL: bMS Am 1823.1 (156).
104 "is automatically conscripted": EEC / RHC (April 7, 1917) Ibid.
104 "toward France my eyes": EEC / S. Thayer (April 23, 1917) BE.
105 "before I get there": EEC / RHC (April 18, 1917) HL: bMS Am 1823.1 (156).
105 "unchanging scene": EEC / EC (April 17, 1917) HL: bMS Am 1823.7 (22).
105 "little lost woodchuck": EEC / RHC (April 23, 1917) HL: bMS Am 1823.1 (156).
105 …seventy-five cars and 120 men: *New York Times* (March 29, 1917), 3.
105 "your unutterable keeping": EEC / S. Thayer (April 23, 1917) BE.

106 "I want to kiss them!!!": EEC / RHC (April 27, 1917) HL: bMS Am 1823.1 (156).
106 "From Betsy, Mother, Jane, Nana and Dad": EC / EEC (April 28, 1917) HL: bMS Am 1823 (296).
106 "heavenless heaven": HL: bMS Am 1823.7 (18).
106 "lift ing in / curviness": Ibid.

NOTES TO CHAPTER 7: LA GUERRE

107 "grinning from the mast-head": EEC / RHC (May 4, 1917) HL: bMS Am 1823.1 (152).
107 "'neath Talcott Williams at Columbia, incidentally": EEC / Dillwyn Parrish (May 4, 1917) HRC.
108 "to the Hôtel du Palais": EEC / RHC (May 11, 1917) HL: bMS Am 1823.1 (152).
108–111 Details of the Paris interlude drawn from: HL: bMS Am 1823.7 (7) to (20) and EEC's sketchbooks, bMS Am 1892.7 (122) to (147).
108 "and sometimes again at supper": Ibid.
109 "a few fists were raised": Roger Shattuck, *The Banquet Years* (New York: Vintage, 1968), 153.
110 "with blatant exceptions" EEC / Dillwyn Parrrish (n.d. May 1917) HRC.
110 "How we flee them!": Ibid.
110 "this fresh earth": EEC / RHC / EC (June 4, 1917) HL: bMS Am 1823.1 (156).
110 "many deaths about them": Quoted in Kennedy, *Dreams in the Mirror*, 141.
111 The French phrases in the poem, in English: Mimi of / the fragile voice / who excites the [Boulevard] Des / Italiens / the whore with the ivory throat / Marie Louise Lallemand / Aren't I pretty / dear? all the English love me, / the Americans / too.... "good backside, good Paris ass?" (Marie [Mary] / Virgin / Pray / For / Us): *CP*, 56.
112 "Death that Love is so and so": *CP*, 117.
112 "bosch guns without results": EEC / RHC (July 2, 1917) HL: bMS Am 1823.1 (156).
113 "and go 'home'": EEC / RHC (July 2, 1917) Ibid.
113 "sans taste, imagination, etc.": EEC / RHC (July 2, 1917) Ibid.
113 "et particulièrement de moi": EEC / RHC (August 9, 1917) Ibid.
114 ...to join the army: Ibid.
114 "action or anything else": EEC / RHC (August 2, 1917) Ibid.
114 "La guerre—non, non": EEC / RHC (August 9, 1917) Ibid.
115 "sensescent institution": William Slater Brown quoted in Norman, *E.E. Cummings: The Magic Maker*, 87.
115 "opportunity for fraternization": *ER*, 3.
116 "the French authorities": Brown quoted in Norman, *E.E. Cummings: The Magic Maker*, 87.
116 ...dropping bombs on Germans, he replied that he would not: *ER* , 13.
116 ...aviation service in good faith: EEC / RHC (October 14, 1917) HL: bMS Am 1823.1 (156).

116 "quiet French uniform": *ER*, 4.
116 "of frightening proportions": Ibid., 4.
116 "prison you mean": Ibid., 5.
117 "I started to sing": Ibid., 8.
117 "suspicious character": Ibid., 13.
118 "had irrevocably failed": Ibid., p14-15.
118 "some shit I will not eat": *CP*, 340.
119 "and strange customs": *ER*, 35.
119 "to inhabit this desolation": Ibid., 39.
119 "a sweet unpleasant odour": Ibid., 42.
119 "finest place on earth'": Ibid., 46.
119 "laughed for sheer joy": Ibid., 47.
120 "not guilty of treason": Ibid., 83.
121 "the time of my life": EEC / RHC (October 1, 1917) HL: bMS Am 1823.1 (152).
121 "WHAT CAN BE DONE": HL: bMS Am 1823.10 (38).
122 "have plenty of both": EC / EEC (October 17, 1917) HL: bMS Am 1823.10 (12).
122 "best keep butted out!!!!": EEC / RHC (October 24(?), 1917) HL: bMS Am 1823.1 (152).
123 "slowly but well": HL: bMS Am 1823.10 (38).
123 "over the terrified trio": EEC / RHC (October 24(?), 1917) HL: bMS Am 1823.1 (152).
123 "MORE VIGOROUS ACTION": HL: bMS Am 1823.10 (38).
123 "asking help from Washington": Ibid.
124 "cabled as soon as received": Ibid.
124 "HIS OWN MASTER": Ibid.
124 "AMONG THOSE LOST END QUOTE": Ibid.
125 "these two days of anxiety": RHC / EEC (November 23, 1917) HL: bMS 1892 (196).
125 "greatest of all sciences—Art": EEC / EC (December 10, 1917) Quoted in Richard Vernier, "A Lost Cummings Letter": *Journal of Modern Literature* April (1979): 109.
126 "in the reddishness of / Day": *CP*, 948.
126 "believe you were safe": EC / EEC (November 29, 1917) HL: bMS Am 1892 (193).
126 "to particularly straighten myself": *ER*, 229–30.
127 "gone to prison with my friend": Ibid., 231.
127 "see from these windows": Ibid., 233.
127 "uncondemned and admittedly innocent!": Ibid., xxiii.
128 "Cable reply promptly": HL: bMS Am 1823.10 (38).
128 "Foreign Office and Ministry of Interior": William Sharp / Robert Lansing (December 20, 1917) Quoted in Norman, *E. E. Cummings: The Magic Maker*, 88–89.
128 "I almost shouted in agony": *ER*, 237.
128 "look like thirty cents or even less": Ibid., 230.

129 "army de suite or depart": EEC / J Sibley Watson (n.d.) NYPL.
129 "I consented to a severance": Ibid.
129 "alive;alive:alive": *ER*, 241.
129 "acceptes ces baisers!": HL: bMS Am 1892.7 (124).
130 "all pleasant things": *CP*, 950.
130 "A suddenly nakedness—": *CP*, 950.
130–131 "tongue's cold wad knocks": *CP*, 949.

NOTES TO CHAPTER 8: SINGING OF OLAF AND ELAINE

133 …events in the Cummings family: Watson, *The Edge of the Woods*, 87.
133 …had been classified 4F: EEC / RHC (April 9, 1918) HL: bMS Am 1823.1 (156).
134 "ginks born in silk shirts": EEC / Charles Anderson (December 31, 1918) HL: 1823.1 (56).
135 "living and cooking; small and cozy": EEC / RHC (March 12, 1918) HL: bMS Am 1823.1 (156).
135 "neck upward,at least downward": EEC / EC (July 1, 1918) HL: bMS Am 1823 (296).
135 …four cubist works at $150 each: EEC / EC (January 13, 1919) Ibid.
135 "a large electric station": EEC / EC (June 26, 1918) Ibid.
136 "seeing a fitness of form-to-color": EEC / EC (July 4, 1918) Ibid.
136 "more often machinerish elements": EEC / RHC (June 18, 1918) HL: bMS Am 1823.1 (156).
137 "Purity for the first time": HL: bMS Am 1823.7 (21).
137 "—Didn't have the seven!": Ibid.
137–138 "taspend / six / Dollars": Ibid.
138 …marriage was "full of unrest": Watson, *The Edge of the Woods*, 83.
139 "danced with Elaine": EEC / RHC (June 27, 1918) HL: bMS Am 1823.1 (156).
139 "raised cain till all hours": Elaine Thayer / EEC (November 9, 1924) HL: bMS Am 1892 (545).
139 "you have expended upon Elaine": Scofield Thayer / EEC (May 21, 1918) HL: bMS Am 1892 (861).
139 "someone wronged—suffering, rudely treated—abused": HL: bMS Am 1892.7 (198).
139 "somebody's wife…my friend's": Ibid.
139 "IDEE FIXE OF RIGHT & WRONG": Ibid.
139 "an angel, a superhuman person": Ibid.
140 "Thayer's vulgarity or roughness": Ibid.
140 "I was purely passive": Ibid.
140 "I go off TOO SOON": Ibid.
140 "turning away from Elaine but it was not conscious": Ibid.
141 "absolute and individual success in existence": EEC / EC (June 1, 1918) HL: bMS Am 1823 (296).
141 "an artist in the army.'" EEC / RHC (July 29, 1918) HL: bMS Am 1823.1 (156).

141 "whatever,as I expected": EEC / RHC (August 14, 1918) Ibid.
141 "high psychological examination": EEC / RHC (August 14, 1918) Ibid.
141 "this weevil dodger": EEC / RHC (August 31, 1918) Ibid.
142 "pair of human beings": HL: bMS Am 1823.4 (104).
142 "all I hold to be life": EEC / RHC (September 11, 1918) HL: bMS Am 1823.1 (156).
142 "we can use 'em for <u>fertilizer</u>": EEC / RHC (August 14, 1918) Ibid.
142 "<u>So we stick 'em</u>": EEC / RHC (September 25, 1918) Ibid.
143 "I have no sister": HL: bMS Am 1892.7 (90).
143 "They do that on principle down there": EEC / EC (December 14, 1918) HL: bMS Am 1823 (296).
143–144 "more blond than you": *CP*, 341.
144 "dined together magnificently'": Quoted in Watson, *The Edge of the Woods*, 87.
144 "young albeit 'Private' poet": Ibid., 87.
144–145 "I may not see Sco till hours and hours": Elaine Thayer / EEC (n.d., fall, 1918) HL: bMS Am 1892 (545).
145 "She can (on occasion) be faithful": Scofield Thayer / EEC (September 11, 1918) HL: bMS Am 1892 (861).
145 "sex was sinful": HL: bMS Am 1892.7 (198).
145 "manure-shaped head": *CP*, 207.
145 "hinging thighs": *CP*, 206.
146 "my seeing blood": *CP*, 205.
146 "riant belly's fooling bore": *CP*, 203.
146 "amiable putrescence": *CP*, 209.
146 "huge passion like a business": *CP*, 205.
146–147 "slender and bright was": *CP*, 960.
147 "the lips of death": *CP*, 209.
147 "exactly perishing sexual": *CP*, 204.
147 "lovingly to and fro": *CP*, 959.
147 "my deathly body's deadly lady": *CP*, 946.
147 "coarse but INTELLIGENT": HL: bMS Am 1892.7 (198).
148 "new position as KP": EEC / RHC (January 2, 1919) HL: bMS Am 1823.1 (156).
148 ...had his name on it: EEC / EC (January 13, 1919) HL: bMS Am 1823 (296).
148 "and most un-at-home": EEC / EC (January 13, 1919) Ibid.
148 "with only 3 completed": EEC / EC (January 13, 1919) Ibid.

NOTES TO CHAPTER 9: POET, PAINTER, AND PAPA IN NEW YORK

149 "an open fire,2 closets": EEC / RHC (February 19, 1919) HL: bMS Am 1823.1 (156), 192–93. Information on post World War I New York drawn from Frederick Lewis Allen, *Only Yesterday* (New York: Harper & Bros, 1931), 19–20.
150 "I'm to pieces pleased": EEC / Hildegarde Watson (February 24, 1922) NYPL.
151 ...added James Joyce (Ulysses): (April 28, 1917) HL: bMS Am 1823 (296).

151 …*Noise* as "more swimmingish": EEC / RHC (March 18, 1919) HL: bMS Am 1823.1 (156).
152 "of the abstract in art": *New York Sun*, March 30, 1919, 14.
152 "an ace of selling 'Sound')": EEC / RHC (April 24, 1919) HL: bMS Am 1823.1 (156).
152 "Sensation of the Independent?": Ibid.
152 "the regular exhibition price": EC / EEC (April 26, 1919) HL: bMS Am 1823.10 (12).
152 "buy either of my things": EEC / Scofield Thayer (n.d.) BE.
153 …which side of the painting was up: EEC / RHC (April 7, 1919) HL: bMS Am 1823.1 (156).
153 "or: this cubic pulp SELFS": HL: bMS Am 1892.7 (69).
153 "other nouns are kept": Ibid.
154 "A Verb;an IS." *ER*, 168.
154 …oneself and with others: Compare Buckminster Fuller's well-known pronouncement: "I know I am not a category. I am not a thing—a noun. I seem to be a verb, an evolutionary process—an integral function of the universe": in Fuller, *I Seem To Be A Verb* (New York: Bantam Books, 1970).
154 "summer may be beautiful)": *CP*, 961.
155 "with an operation": HL: bMS Am 1892.7 (197).
155 "but in my work": HL: bMS Am 1892.7 (198).
155 "imagines that it isn't wrong": Ibid.
155 "in MoreThanYou": Ibid.
156 …bring out a book of his poems: EEC / Scofield Thayer (n.d.—July 1917) BE.
156 …house separate from the Thayers.): EEC / RHC (July 21, 1919) HL: bMS Am 1823.1 (156).
156 …instead he felt only detachment: HL: bMS Am 1892.7 (198).
156 "play tennis occasionally": EEC / RHC (July 21, 1919) HL: bMS Am 1823.1 (156).
156 "with love to deliciae meae puellae": EEC / Scofield Thayer (August 16, 1919) BE.
157 "neurotic turning away from Elaine": HL: bMS Am 1892.7 (198).
157 "it is called PUELLA MEA": EEC / Scofield Thayer (September 19, 1919) BE.
157 "mine is a little lovelier": *CP*, 21.
157 "body filled with May)": *CP*, 20.
158 "spontaneous meadow of her mind)": *CP*, 22.
158 "keep your dead beautiful ladies": *CP*, 20.
158 "Eater of all things lovely—Time!": *CP*, 26.
158 "upon frailness)": *CP*, 26.
159 "Tulips = Two Lips Chimneys = Penises": HL: bMS Am 1892.7 (198).
159–160 For information in the founding of the *Dial*: Nicholas Joost, *Years of Transition: The Dial 1912–20* (Barre, MA: Barre Publishers, 1967) and Joost, *Scofield Thayer and the Dial* (Carbondale, IL: Southern Illinois University Press, 1964), 12–20.
160 "take on literary characteristics": EEC / RHC (November 25, 1919) HL: bMS Am 1823.1 (156).
160 "lucky to have such friends": Ibid.

160 "four-full-pages of drawings by me": EEC / RHC (December 19, 1920) HL: bMS Am 1823.1 (156).
160 "small letter should follow a period": EEC / ST (n.d.—1920) BE.
161 "any of the regular periodicals": *The Dial*, January 1920.
161 "Thayer takes care of her—hospital": HL: bMS Am 1892.8 (61).
161 "refer to the girl as Thayer's": Brown quoted in Kennedy, *Dreams in the Mirror*, 200.
162 "Elaine angry,or merely dead?": EEC / Scofield Thayer (September 2, 1918) BE.
162 "I refuse to admit it": HL: bMS Am 1892.7 (198).
162–163 "(idealization:strongest at same time)": Ibid.
163 "Thayer here shines": Ibid.
163 "i:passive": Ibid.
163 "nothing, only my art": Ibid.
163 "my little circle,art": Ibid.
163 "result is extremely becoming": EEC / Elizabeth Cummings (February 3, 1920) HL: bMS Am 1823.1 (510).
163 "decided not to baptize 'little Elaine'": EEC / RHC (May 22, 1920) HL: bMS Am 1823.1 (156).
164 "new and fundamental": *MR*, 15.
164 "under conventional art": Ibid., 17.
164 "a few hours at best": Ibid., 18.
164 "by thinking, of thinking": Ibid., 18.
164 "crisp organic squirm—the IS": Ibid., 19.
164 "wanted three in particular": EEC / RHC (January 19, 1920) HL: bMS Am 1823.1 (156).
164 "say the same at home": Ibid.
165 "For Christ's sake. amen": EEC / Scofield Thayer (January 10, 1919) BE.
165 "two numbers of the Dial that I have seen": T. S. Eliot, *The Letters of T.S. Eliot, Volume I: 1898-1922*, edited by Valerie Eliot (New York: Harcourt Brace Jovanovich, 1988), 376.
165 "collection of instupidities": *MR*, 27.
165 "Wyndham and the Lewis": Ibid., 27.
165 "tempos by oral rhythms": Ibid., 28.
166 "comment is disgusting": Ibid, 29.
166 "resides in said Wyndham": Ezra Pound / Scofield Thayer (August 4, 1920) BE.
167 "(of solongs and,ashes)": *CP*, 108.
168 "sound has its own peculiar silence!": HL: bMS Am 1892.6 (29).
168 "implies its own punctuation": HL: bMS Am 1823.7 (19).
168 "the hands of these unique gentlemen": EEC / EC (May 22, 1920) HL: bMS Am 1823 (296).
169 "spectator and sympathizer": EEC / EC (May 6, 1919) Ibid.
169 "painting,poetry,etc.": EEC / RHC (January 20, 1920) HL: bMS Am 1823.1 (156).
169 "Everlasting Rhythm is somethingelse": EEC / RHC (November 25, 1919) Ibid.

169 "paintings by E.E. Cummings should be included": EEC / RHC (May 9, 1920) Ibid.
170 "a striking bit of post-impressionism": *New York World*, (March 12, 1920) 8.
170 "they are bound to be admired": *New York Evening Post* (March 12, 1920) 11.
170 "I dare say or go under": EEC / RHC (March 2, 1922) HL: bMS Am 1823.1 (156).
170 "the irregularity of noise": HL: bMS Am 1892.6 (29).
171 "flannel shirt and my ideas": EEC / EC (June 22, 1920) HL: bMS Am 1823 (296).
171 "summer working on his manuscript": EC / EEC (June 26, 1920) HL: bMS Am 1823 (296).

NOTES TO CHAPTER 10: THE ENORMOUS ROOM

173 "hence need for solitariness": EEC / EC (June 17, 1920) HL: bMS Am 1823 (296).
173 "say a two hour conversation": EEC / EC (May 8, 1918) Ibid.
174 "Meet Me...": *ER*, 96.
174 "single moving ThingInItself": EEC / RHC (November 25, 1919) HL: bMS Am 1823.1 (156).
174 "should like to see [Elaine's] kid": *SL*, 73.
174 "haven't done nawthing else": Ibid., 74.
175 "you are a great writer": EEC / EC (October 2, 1920) HL: bMS Am 1823 (296).
175 "corduroy trousers—!": *SL*, 74.
175 "confidence outside of...friends": Ibid., 74.
175 "happen here and there": EEC / EC (October 18, 1920) HL: bMS Am 1823 (296).
175 "about through with your French Notes": EC / EEC (November 18, 1920) HL: bMS Am 1823 (296).
177 "Which minute bit is art": *ER*, 166.
178 "do justice to timelessness": *ER*, 83.
178 "'finest place in the world' said B's voice": *ER*, 80.
179 "laughing,bumped with the last darkness)": *ER*, 214.
179 "firmly into immortal sunlight" [ellipsis, EEC]: *ER*, 242.
179 "boosted me into a condition of mysterious happiness": *ER*, 37.
180 "the ponderous ferocity of silence": *ER*, 55.
180 "toothless and viscious titter": *ER*, 55.
180 ...committed to memory while at Harvard: EEC / Scofield Thayer (August 2, 1915) BE.
181 ...the *Dial* under Johnson had turned down: EEC / Scofield Thayer (November 12, 1918) BE.
181 "fat kind of joke on nobody": *ER*, 241.
181 "but also with its individuality": Getrude Stein, *The Autobiography of Alice B. Toklas*. (New York: Random House, 1934), 213.
181 "it is one of the great books": Ernest Hemingway quoted in Carlos Baker, *Hemingway: A Life Story* (New York: Scribners, 1969), 548.

NOTES TO CHAPTER 11: ABROAD

184 "for the sound of words": Dos Passos, *The Best Times*, 83.

184 "calls it a noise and numbers it": *New York Evening Post* (February 28, 1921) 7.

185 "we managed to get work done": Dos Passos, *The Best Times*, 85.

185 "Italian speakeasy…for supper": Ibid., 83.

185 "a word from her would heal all sores": Ibid., 83.

185 "seizures described in the Greek lyrics": Ibid., 83–84.

185 "young people drink too much": Ibid., 83.

185 "hell-bent for Persia": Ibid., 85.

186 "Walt Whitman-narodnik optimism about people": Ibid., 87.

186 "looked to him like plainclothes Jesuits": Ibid., 88.

186 "extraordinary experience": EEC / RHC (March 2, 1921) HL: bMS Am 1823.1 (156).

186 "extremely valuable capacity": EEC / RHC (April 22, 1921) Ibid.

186 …El Greco's *Burial of Count Orgaz*: EEC / RHC (May 26, 1921) Ibid.

187 "Paris toward night,inMai": *CP*, 904.

187 "with a view of publishing it": Quoted in Norman, *The Magic Maker*, 104.

187 "much more than Scribners": EEC / RHC (June 2, 1921) HL: bMS Am 1823.1 (156).

187 "old men,wrists and laughter": *CP*, 994.

187–188 "wisely a decayed yellowish width of beard": *CP*, 995.

188 "microscopic birds sing fiercely": *CP*, 996.

188 "beautiful wild swans flying overhead": Edmund Wilson, *The Twenties*, ed. Leon Edel (New York: Farrar, Strauss, Giroux, 1975), 207.

189 "a certain paranoid trend": Scofield Thayer / Elaine Orr Thayer (June 3, 1921) BE.

189 …dissatisfied with the attorney she'd chosen: Scofield Thayer / Elaine Orr Thayer (June 3, 1921) BE.

189–191 Information about the Cummings/Elaine relationship drawn mainly from Cummings's notes: HL: bMS Am 1892.7 (198).

191 "dined(whisper)at Voisin,etc.": EEC / RHC (July 23, 1921) HL: bMS Am 1823.1 (156).

191 "somebody,and intricate": Ibid.

192 "Cummings is stupid to sneer at W.L. [Wyndham Lewis]": Ezra Pound / Sibley Watson (August 4, 1920) BE: Dial/Scofield Thayer Collection.

192 …Cummings as a translator for poems by…Paul Morand and for a story by…Aragon: BE: Ezra Pound / Scofield Thayer (June 28, 1920) and Ezra Pound / Scofield Thayer (July 12, 1920).

192 "abandonnant sa femme et son enfant": (July 28, 1921) BE: Scofield Thayer Collection.

192 …recorded value was one hundred thousand dollars: (November 1, 1921) Ibid.

192 …not Elaine who proposed the large sum; it was Thayer: Scofield Thayer / Elaine Orr Thayer (May 10, 1921) BE.

193 …responsible for driving Elaine into Cummings's arms: HL: bMS Am 1892.7 (198).

193 "is the boss—controls things": Ibid.
193 "feel poor—i.e., myself as writer": Ibid.
193 "trying to buy him": Ibid.
194 "should like to understand her": EEC / Scofield Thayer (October 26, 1922) BE.
194 "am headed not to Vienna,therefore": *SL*, 81.
194 ...arriving August 15: EEC / RHC (August 15, 1921) HL: bMS Am 1823.1 (156).
194 "Or Eleven Nights Without a Bar-Room": EEC / EC & RHC (July 23, 1921) Ibid.
195 "E.E. Cummings...not Edward Estlin)": EEC / RHC (n.d.—November 1921) Ibid.
195 "'chuck it,' said etc.": EEC / RHC (n.d.—November 1921) Ibid.
195 "use the sketches your son did": Quoted in Norman, *The Magic Maker*, 104.
196 "Caught in the French Net," and "The Enormous Room": EC / EEC (November 15, 1921) HL: bMS Am 1823 (296).
196 "Title of book The Enormous Room": EEC / EC (November 25, 1921) HL: bMS Am 1823 (296).
196–197 "with my voice / are / playing": *CP*, 1002.
197 "and the gendarmes": EEC / RHC (n.d.—Fall 1921) HL: bMS Am 1823.1 (156).
197 "spires curl with darkness": *CP*, 1003.
198 "myself that I didn't want E": HL: bMS Am 1892.7 (198).
198 "whispering like a drunken man": *CP*, 305.
199 "hold more dear and fragile than death": *CP*, 999.
199 ...Cummings was remorseful: HL: bMS Am 1892.7 (198).
199 "all the time he loved [Elaine] he was attracted to whores": Ibid.
199 "'Mopsy appears to me'": EEC / RHC (Januray 13, 1922) HL: bMS Am 1823.1 (156).
200 "borrowed 800 fr. from me to get home with": EEC / RHC (February 26, 1922) Ibid.
200 "publishers to Hell in my behalf anent some poems": Ibid.
200 "the commerce of art": HL: bMS Am 1892.7 (162).
201 ...Loeb...had taken them: EEC / RHC (Februrary 26, 1922) HL: bMS Am 1823.1 (156).
201 "Chez-eux des braves": Ibid.
202 "I shall give the book to noone I like": EEC/ RHC (May 13, 1922) Ibid.
202 "money,or any-thing-damned-else": *SL*, 87.
202 "not merely an eye-sore but an insult": Ibid., 88.
203 "which could have been chosen": EC / EEC (June 6, 1922) HL: bMS Am 1823 (296).

NOTES TO CHAPTER 12: AN AMERICAN IN PARIS

205 "none the less precious metal": Robert Littell, "Garbage and Gold," *The New Republic*, May 10, 1922.
205 "mined without a patient pickaxe": Louis Kantor, "The Enormous Room," *New York Herald Tribune*, May 14, 1922.

206 "the book is quite worthwhile": Thomas L. Masson, "A Pilgrim's Progress in France," *New York Times*, May 28, 1922.
206 "small part, of the truth": Editorial, *New York Times*, May 29, 1922.
206 "part of his honest convictions": Katherine Fullerton Gerould quoted in Allen, *Only Yesterday*, 62.
206 "the incredible animal Man": Ben Ray Redman, "Man the Animal," *The Nation*, June 7, 1922.
207 "anything else under heaven": John Dos Passos, "Off the Shoals": *The Dial*, July 1922.
207 "seemed of "first importance": Gilbert Seldes, "Accuracy and Beauty," *The Double Dealer*, August 1, 1922.
207 …"the supreme test" for art: John Peale Bishop, "Incorrect English: Experiments in Style Calculated to Make the Purist Turn Over in His Grave," *Vanity Fair*, July 1920.
207 "pen that makes literature": Gorham Munson, "Syrinx," *Secession*, July 1923.
208 "30 (triente) Enormous Rooms": EC / EEC (June 19, 1922) HL: 6/19/22, bMS Am 1823 (296).
208 "stuck on himself": EC / EEC (April 2, 1922) Ibid.
208 "ever,from anyone,anywhere": EEC / Elizabeth Cummings (May 3, 1922) HL: bMS Am 1823.1 (510).
210 "nervous system of the American literary colony": Malcolm Cowley, *A Second Flowering* (New York: Viking, 1973), 57.
210 "most vierge et l'enfant": *CP*, 997.
210 "Mopsie enjoys the heat": EEC / RHC (May 31, 1922) HL: bMS Am 1823.1 (156).
210 "green tables under the trees": EEC / RHC (May 31, 1922) Ibid.
210–211 "no longer,can you imagine it": *CP*, 1004.
211 …his new Paris friends: HL: bMS Am 1892.7 (198).
211 "It was her apartment": Ibid.
211 "two billion other unselves": *CP*, 997.
212 "facility with which he wrote": Mark Pollizotti, *Revolution of the Mind: A Life of Andre Breton* (New York: Farrar, Straus, Giroux, 1995), 68.
212 "something unusual on every street corner": Ibid.
213 "suspicious madder,importing the cruelty of roses": *CP*, 74.
213 "flatchatte ringaroom": *CP*, 184.
214 "can be heard, seen and felt": George Wickes, *Americans in Paris* (New York: Doubleday & Co., 1969), 115.
214 "the less original for all that": Ibid., 118.
215 "urinating on the fire": Malcolm Cowley, *Exile's Return* (New York: Viking, 1951), 159.
215 …French writer Racine: Samuel Putnam, *Paris Was Our Mistress* (New York: Viking, 1947), 184.
215 "employing it in watercolors": EEC / RHC (March 2, 1922) HL: bMS Am 1823.1 (156).
216 …consuming chianti at the rate of a half-liter: *SL*, 90.

216 "*Lazarus*, from the dead": *MR*, "How I Do Not Love Italy," 164.
216 "in toytea [thirty] days": *SL*, 90.
216 "among the poor whites": Ibid.
217 "definite part of literature": Ezra Pound / Scofield Thayer, (March 9, 1922 and October 22, 1922) BE.
217 "but Cummings with nobody": Sibley Watson / Scofield Thayer (August 16, 1922) BE.
217 "borrowing from dead poets": Cowley, *Exile's Return*, 134.
218 "peace which passeth understanding": HL: BMS Am 1892.7 (204).
218 "its way to Fascist bowels": EEC / RHC (n.d.—1923) HL: bMS Am 1823.1 (156).
218 "whole *Galleria degli Uffizi*": *MR*, "How I Do Not Love Italy," 167.
219 "lead something into somewhere)": *CP*, 997.
219 "occupied by the abbatoir": EEC / RHC (March 5, 1923) HL: bMS Am 1823.1 (156).
219 "Woman screaming": Ibid.
219 "its inhabitants of both sexes": Scofield Thayer / Elaine Orr Thayer (March 12, 1923) BE.
219 "dwarf and a tattooed lady": Ibid.
220 "signing a contract to print myself": EEC / Elizabeth Cummings (July 28, 1923) HL: bMS Am 1823.1 (510).
220 For the information on Seltzer: Walker Gilmore, *Horace Liveright: Publisher of the Twenties* (New York: D. Lewis, 1970), 19–20.
220 "portland cement and carrara": EEC / John Peale Bishop quoted in Norman Freidman, *E.E.Cummings: The Growth of a Writer* (Carbondale, IL: Southern Illinois University Press, 1964), 37.
221 "strange as this may appear": EEC / RHC (April 23, 1923) HL: bMS Am 1823.1 (156).
221 "paint as I saw fit": EEC / Elizabeth Cummings (May 2, 1922) HL: bMS Am 1823.1 (510).
221 "never bashful about his role as a poet": Dos Passos, *The Best Times*, 133.
221 "marched him off to the police station": Ibid., 133.
221 "America's greatest poet": Ibid., 133.
221 "they threw me out bodily": Ibid., 133.
222 "summons to appear in court next day": Ibid., 133.
222 "notion of a republic of letters": Ibid., 133.
222 "Giverny fracas left [Cowley] uninjured": *SL*, 101.
222 "my host last winter in Wien.)": Ibid., 101.
222 "too many German things": Scofield Thayer / Sibley Watson (March 27, 1923) BE.
223 "air smells of clover": *SL*, 96.
223 "these folks are inhibited": Ibid., 96.
223 "(life) things,FUCKING)": HL: bMS Am 1892.7 (198).
223 "things,people,money": Ibid.
224 "I want her [Elaine] only as a mistress": Ibid.
224 "strolling at grande velocita": EEC / RHC (May 17, 1923) HL: bMS Am 1823.1 (156).

224 "dined at place du Tertre": EEC / RHC (September 15, 1923) Ibid.
224 "partially or wholly detest": EEC / RHC (October 4, 1923) Ibid.
224 "I ever heard her say": EEC / RHC (October 4, 1923) Ibid.
225 "money had never entered my brain": EEC / RHC (October 4, 1923) Ibid.
225–226 On Sumner, Ford, and censorship: Gilmore, *Horace Liveright*, 60–72.
226 "rough for the Hinglish Sensor": EEC / RHC (October 24, 1923) HL: bMS Am 1823.1 (156).
226 "sometimes gives me a FatherComplex": EEC / RHC (October 24, 1923) Ibid.
226 "as a note to go by post": Ford Madox Ford quoted in Max Saunders, *Ford Madox Ford: A Dual Life*, vol. II (New York: Oxford University Press, 1999), 152.
227 "typographical modernity": Ibid., 137.
227 "we are runing in the January number": Scofield Thayer / EEC (November 26, 1923) BE.

NOTES TO CHAPTER 13: TULIPS AND CHIMNEYS

229 "present-day-poet in the English language": Robert L. Wolf, "E. E. Cummings' Poetry," *New York World*, November 18, 1923.
229 "in holy places": Matthew Josephson, "A New Poet," *New York Tribune*, November 25, 1923.
229 "even his mannerisms cannot hide": Herbert Gorman, "Goliath Beats His Poetic Breast While Critics Gape," *New York Times*, December 9, 1923.
230 "But beware his imitators!": Harriet Monroe, "Flare and Blare," *Poetry*, January 1924.
230 "ethereal measures of a singular purity": Edmund Wilson, "Wallace Stevens and E. E. Cummings," *The New Republic*, March 19, 1924.
230 "surviving because of their swift wings": William Slater Brown, "Tulips and Chimneys," *Broom*, January 1924.
230 "feeling for American speech": W. C. Bloom (J. Sibley Watson), "The Perfumed Paraphrases of Death," *The Dial*, Januray 1924.
231 "the night utter ripe unspeaking girls": *CP*, 55.
232 "O thou, is life not a smile?" *CP*, 32.
233 "every syllable has a conscience and a specific impact": William Carlos Williams, "Lower Case Cummings," *Selected Essays* (New York: New Directions, 1954), 263.
233 "energy or emotion expresses itself in form": Ezra Pound, "I gather the Limbs of Osiris," *Selected Prose, 1909–1965*, ed. William Cookson (London: Faber and Faber, 1973), 34.
234 "only in English is the 'I' capitalized": Quoted in Harvey Breit, "E.E. Cummings," *The Writer Observed* (World: Cleveland & New York, 1956), 63.
234 "your peculiar mouth my heart made wise": *CP*, 145.
234–235 "reckless magic of your mouth)": *CP*, 165.
235–236 "into a stale shriek / like an alarm-clock)": *CP*, 65.

NOTES TO CHAPTER 14: MARRIAGE AND UNMARRIAGE

237 "to exchange greetings": EEC / EC (December 5, 1923) HL: bMS Am 1823 (296).
237 "should marry E[laine]": HL: bMS Am 1892.7 (198).
237 "Aunt Jennie present": EEC / RHC (March 14, 1924) bMS Am 1823.1 (156).
237–238 "best of friends": Ibid.
238 "on staying all night!!!": HL: bMS Am 1892.7 (198).
239 "of a small child": Dos Passos, *The Best Times*, 132.
239 "rather than Mr. Cummings": HL: bMS Am 1892.7 (90).
239 ...informed of the event: Dial / Thayer Collection (n.d. (1924)) BE.
239 "of Nancy Thayer": Ibid.
239 "to be proud of": HL: bMS Am 1892.7 (198).
240 "40"x50" 'ABSTRACT' canvas": EEC / RHC (May 13, 1924) HL: bMS Am 1823.1 (156).
240 "hands making music": *MR*, 54.
240 "poet and novelist": *New York Sun and Globe*, March 6, 1924.
241 "conducted by 407 publishers": EEC / RHC (May 24, 1924) HL: bMS Am 1823.1 (156).
241 "best of my own poems": Quoted in Norman, *The Magic Maker*, 162.
242 "last week's happenings": EEC / RHC (April 4, 1924) HL: bMS Am 1823.1 (156).
243 "language and humanity": Hart Crane, *The Letters of Hart Crane*, ed. Brom Weber (Berkeley, CA: University of California Press, 1952), 141.
243 ...talk to in New York: Ibid., 182.
243 "Scriabin and Ravel": HL: bMS Am 1892.7 (212).
243 "homosexual appeal": Ibid.
243 "waterfront obscenities": Malcolm Cowley, *A Second Flowering: Works and Days of the Lost Generation* (New York, NY: Viking, 1973), 196.
244 "'was coming to him'": HL: bMS Am 1892.7 (198).
244 "There is no way out": Ibid.
244 "be like a child": Elaine Orr Thayer / EEC (November 9, 1924) HL: bms1892 (545).
244 "have made a mistake": Ibid.
245 "in your private life": Ibid.
245 "as a man would": Ibid.
245 "hidden your ego": Ibid.
245 "eighteenth-century legal mind": Quoted in Kennedy, *Dreams in the Mirror*, 254.
246 "feeling of inferiority": HL: bMS Am 1892.7 (198).
246 "PLEASURE in love": Ibid.
247 "to fight other man?": Ibid.
247–248 "talking about its circumference": Ibid.
248 "snapped on to carpet)": HL: bMS Am 1892.7 (90).
248 "had driven away": HL: bMS Am 1892.7 (198).
249 "outside of it (your work)": HL: bMS Am 1892.7 (201).
250 "beauty as yourself": Ibid.
250 "poems were better": Ibid.

251 "what I am losing": EEC / EC (July 26, 1924) HL: bMS Am 1823 (296).
251 "you live, yourself": Elaine Orr Thayer / EEC (August 6, 1924) HL: bMS Am 1892 (545).
251 ...in early August: Scofield Thayer / EEC (June 6, 1924) BE; Scofield Thayer / Sibley Watson (August 6, 1924) BE.
251 "out to get him": Scofield Thayer / EEC (August 15, 1924) BE.
251 "his life—this failure": HL: bMS Am 1892.7 (198).
252 "if you ask me—yes": Ibid.
252 "help her,in the divorce": EEC / RHC & EC (August 12, 1924) HL: bMS Am 1823.10 (24).
252 "is simply this: Nancy": HL: bMS Am 1892.7 (198).

NOTES TO CHAPTER 15: THE LIFE AND TIMES OF EDWARD SEUL

255 ...marry a low-life chauffeur: EEC / RHC (September 7, 1924) HL: bMS Am 1823.1 (156).
256 "touch we need": Crowninshield quoted in Kennedy, *Dreams in the Mirror*, 273.
256 "or nonsensical verse": Crowninshield / EEC (September 25, 1924) HL: bMS Am 1823.
256 "material furnished by...Sloane": EEC / RHC (September 27, 1924) HL: bMS Am 1823.1 (156).
258 "so much dirt": HL: bMS Am 1823.10 (25).
259 "can't leave Nancy": HL: bMS Am 1892.7 (198).
259 "hobgoblin shapes": Ibid.
260 "the secret of himself": Ibid.
260 "his father's bull-like penis": Ibid.
261 "business to be engaged in": Cummings quoted in Burton Rascoe, *We Were Interrupted* (Garden City, NY: Random House, 1947), 180.
261 "Quite a drinker": William H. MacLeish, *Up Hill With Archie* (New York, NY: Simon & Schuster, 2001), 62.
262 "buy you anything": Cummings quoted in Rascoe, 185.
262 "a sausage grinder": Hemingway quoted in Baker, *Ernest Hemingway*, 135.
263 "this excellent satire" *MR*, 98.
263 "a distinct climax": Ibid., 98.
263 ...Cocteau's work: Lewis Galantiere quoted in Norman, *The Magic Maker*, 186.
264 "my staunchest friend": HL: bMS Am 1892.7 (198).
264 "in great pertubation": Ibid.
264–265 "get N up": Ibid.
266 "each other's hands ride": HL: bMS Am 1892 (545).
267 "come around again later": HL: bMS Am 1892.7 (198).
267 "GO BACK ON WORD": HL: bMS Am 1892.8 (12).
267–268 "TO THIS AFFECT": HL: bMS Am 1823.10 (41).
268 "(fearing lest I block the divorce)": Ibid.

268 "with iron arithmetics": *CP*, 313.
269 "picked up for vagrancy": Quoted in Norman, *The Magic Maker*, 136.
270 "had any to lose)": *CP*, 410.
271 "I feel worlds better": HL: bMS Am 1892.7 (198).
271 "fight it tooth and nail": EEC / Frank MacDermot (draft) (n.d.) HL: bMS Am 1892.7 (198).
272 "out of the universe": EEC / Sibley Watson (draft) (n.d.), Ibid.
272 "squirmed out of by 'diplomacy'": EC / EEC (July 19, 1925) HL: bMS Am 1892 (193).
272 "as I have indicated": Ibid.
273 "an immediate showdown": EEC / EC (August 22, 1924) HL: bMS Am 1823.10 (24).
274 "resumed her playing": HL: bMS Am 1892.7 (198).

NOTES TO CHAPTER 16: ANNE

276 "is known as 'beauty'": *MR*, 114.
276 …*XLI Poems* "is harmless": EEC / RHC (January 5, 1925) HL: bMS Am 1823.1 (196).
277 "solid screams whisper.)": *CP*, 95.
277–278 "strange birds purr": *CP*, 69.
278 "frail firm asinine life": *CP*, 119.
279 "velocity is sculptural": *CP*, 96.
279 "probable massacres": EEC / RHC (January 5, 1925) HL: bMS Am 1823.1 (156).
280 "turn young with rain": *CP*, 183.
280 "creases of screaming warmth": Ibid., 110.
280 "collar hung gently": Ibid., 110.
281 "emerging. / concrete": *CP*, 99.
282 "her:hands": Ibid., 195.
282 "you so quite new": Ibid., 218.
283 …experiments as "tricks": Mark van Doren, "First Glance," *Nation*, July 8, 1925.
283 …to many readers: Christopher Morley, *Saturday Review of Literature*, September 5, 1925.
283 "is sure is poetry": Marianne Moore, *The Dial*, January 1926.
283–284 "drew me tenderly to him": HL: bMS Am 1892.7 (198).
285 "my wife and child": Ibid.
285 "common, even vulgar": Ibid.
285 "hit the ceiling": Ibid.
286 "slobber in vain": *CP*, 294.
286 "She gloried in fucking": HL: bMS Am 1892.7 (198).
286 "dreams to / live on)": *CP*, 299.
286–287 "thousands of enormous dreams": Ibid., 302.
287–288 "death i think is no parenthesis": Ibid., 291.
288 …a review of his work: Walter Sutton, ed., *Pound, Thayer, Watson and The Dial: A Story in Letters* (Gainesville, FL: University of Florida Press, 1994), 310.

288 ...leaves the ashes behind: Marianne Moore, *The Selected Letters of Marianne Moore*, ed., Bonnie Costello (New York, NY: Knopf, 1997), 223.
289 ...as the recipient: Ibid., 22.
289 ...the form of his preface: EEC / RHC (February 26, 1926) HL: bMS Am 1823.1 (196).
289 "the curse of awithmetic": Ibid.
290 "of the present volume": *CP*, 221.
290 "sometimes fanciful": Louis Zukofsky, "American Poetry 1920-1930," *Prepositions* (Berkeley, CA: University of California Press, 1981), 81.
290 ...books of poems: Malcolm Cowley, *A Second Flowering: Works and Days of the Lost Generation* (New York, NY: Viking, 1973), 97.
291 "Toysday nite": *CP*, 225.
291 "Not To Be Resharpened": Ibid., 228.
291 "of your Etcetera)": Ibid., 275.
292 "cradle with the other)": Ibid., 240.
292 "worth a million statues": Ibid., 245.
293 "a poor wind will roam": Ibid., 293.
293 "a little drunk": Genevieve Taggard, "The Poet of the Instant," *The New Republic*, September 8, 1926.
293–294 "say yes to the world": Maurice Lesseman, "The Poetry of E.E. Cummings," *Poetry* December 1926.
294 "passed off as poetry": Robert Graves and Laura Riding, "Modernist Poetry and The Plain Reader's Rights," Guy Rotella, ed. *Critical Essays on E.E. Cummings* (Boston, MA: Hall, 1984).

NOTES TO CHAPTER 17: HIM

296 "at once liquid and racial": *MR*, 161–2.
296 "his Yankee Excellency's dollars": Ibid., 154.
296 "the idiocies of this world": Ibid., 158.
296 ...Freudian concepts: Drafts and notes of "Edward Seul" (the play) HL: bMS Am 1823.4 (15).
298 "'I MUST PROCEED'": E.E. Cummings, *Him* (New York, NY: Liveright, 1927), 13.
299 "a sort of a play": Ibid., 29–30.
300 "can have guineapigs": Ibid., 99.
300 "poiple soopurconsciousness": Ibid., 143.
300 "cry of terror": Ibid., 144.
301 "Because this is true": Ibid., 145.
301 "love and death": Ibid., 35.
301 "what comfort and astonish us": Ibid., 28–29.
302 "unfettered association of dream": Shattuck, *The Banquet Years*, 349.
302 ...what constituted drama: *MR*, 129–30.
302 "intensely alive": Ibid., 129.

302 "glide, strut and tumble": Ibid., 129.
303 …essence of poetry: Ibid., 114.
305 "She decided to live": *Six*, 12–13.
305 "let them lead her away": Ibid., 12.
305 "the town lights went out at once": Ibid., 13.
305 "she told us; beaming": Ibid., 13.
305 "'I was right!'": Ibid., 13.
306 "the unimaginable night not known": *CP*, 418.
307 "his eyes would stir and squirm": *CP*, 520.
307 …Thayer's personality disorder: Scofield Thayer / EEC (August 15, 1924) BE.
308 "suggestions were 'preposterous'": EEC / Elaine Orr MacDermot (draft) (n.d.) HL: bMS Am 1892.7 (198).
308 "the second time I saw him": Quoted in Sutton, *Pound, Thayer, Watson and the Dial*, 321.
308 "phases of a terrible dream": Ibid., 335.
308 …control over his life: EEC / Sibley Watson (October 19, 1930) NYPL.
308 "incredible generosity": *Six*, 50.
309 "or other documents": EEC / RHC (February 13, 1927) HL: bMS Am 1823.1 (196).
309 "our best for her": RHC / Elaine Orr MacDermot (February 23, 1927) HL: bMS Am 1892.4 (46).
309 "on the mantlepiece here": EEC / RHC (March 4, 1927) HL: bMS Am 1823.1 (156).
309 "could play together": Ibid.
310 …moved to Ireland: EEC / SW (n.d.—February 1927) NYPL.
310 "told [Cummings] so": Marianne Moore / Sibley Watson (November 5, 1926) BE: Dial Collection.
310 …offer a euphemism: HL: bMS Am 1892.7 (198).
310 "*Him* had to be done": Quoted in Norman, *The Magic Maker*, 215.
311 "insisted that it should be": Ibid., 215.
311 "I'm trying to think about": EEC / RHC (September 4, 1927) HL: bMS Am 1823.1 (156).
311 …was improving: EEC / RHC (September 10, 1927) HL: bMS Am 1823.1 (156).
311 …he and Barton had "'made up'": EEC / RHC (September 12, 1927) HL: bMS Am 1823.1 (156).
311 "her love of Joy Farm": EEC / RHC (September 17, 1927) HL: bMS Am 1823.1 (156).
312 "he'll give Diana $50,000": Ibid.
312 "get a rich husband": Ibid.
312 "'Oh no. Like me'": HL: bMS Am 1892.7 (198).
313 "Freud's Traumdetung,etc": EEC / RHC (October 22, 1927) HL: bMS Am 1823.1 (156).
313 "that's to be my fate": Ibid.
313 "'unhappy childhood'": HL: bMS Am 1892.7 (198).
313 "as you may guess": EEC / RHC (November 8, 1927) HL: bMS Am 1823.1 (156).

313 "i.e. $7,500 a year)": Ibid.
314 "to heaven when I go": Hart Crane, *The Letters of Hart Crane*, 310–11.
314 "to pray,and I do": EEC / RHC (December 30, 1927) HL: bMS Am 1823.1 (156).
315 ...than she would become: Thomas Wolfe, *You Can't Go Home Again* (New York, NY: Scribners, reprint, 1978), 246.
315 "has played me straight": EEC / RHC (n.d.—January 2, 1927) HL: bMS Am 1823.1 (196).
315 "we only did it once": HL: bMS Am 1892.7 (198).
315 "to have an abortion": Ibid.
315 "Gossip perhaps": Ezra Pound, *Pound/Williams: The Selected Letters of Ezra Pound and William Carlos Williams*, Hugh Witemeyer, ed. (New York, NY: New Directions, 1997), 87.
316 "I dunno": Ibid., 86–87.

NOTES TO CHAPTER 18: VIVA CUMMINGS

317 "a really magical thing": Quoted in Norman, *The Magic Maker*, 216.
317 ...to the theatre company: Ibid., 216.
318 "overproved his point, and cut": Ibid., 217.
318 "give them in direction": Ibid., 217.
318 "(including perhaps himself)": Ibid., 218.
318 "LET IT TRY TO UNDERSTAND YOU": HL: bMS Am 1823.1 (39).
319 "birds in the nest": William Carlos Williams, *Autobiography* (New York, NY: New Directions, 1951), 258–59.
319 "important dramatic poet": Edmund Wilson, *The Shores of Light* (New York, NY: Farrar, Straus & Young, 1952), 285.
320 "get away with it": Louis Zukofsky, "Him," *Prepositions*, 1981.
320 "provocative theatre": Quoted in Norman, *The Magic Maker*, 226.
320 "can imagine": Ibid., 226.
320 "pretentious and empty": Ibid., 225.
320 "for not being like 'Broadway'": Ibid., 225.
321 "declared Wittels 'a genius'": EEC / RHC (December 28, 1928) HL: bMS Am 1823.1 (156).
322 "his tenderness is fearless": Quoted in Kennedy, *Dreams in the Mirror*, 302.
322 "Self-pity = comfort": HL: bMS Am 1892.7 (198).
322 "legally unite(collective)": EEC / RHC (March 26, 1929) HL: bMS Am 1823.1 (196).
323 "easy distinguished manner": Edmund Wilson, *The Twenties*, Leon Edel, ed. (New York, NY: Farrar, Straus & Giroux, 1975), 429.
323 "it was all <u>her</u> fault": HL: bMS Am 1892.8 (46).
324 "I'm going back to Douglas": Ibid.
324 ...even "piggish": Ibid.
324 ...sprang him from jail: John Unterecker, *Voyager; A Life of Hart Crane* (New York, NY: Farrar, Straus & Giroux, 1969), 597.

325 "the French franc": *MR*, 179.
325 "awful period of wretchedness": HL: bMS Am 1892.7 (198).
326 "afraid to laugh heartily?": *MR*, 215–16.
328 "satirical nonsense": *In Brief Saturday Review of Literature*, November 22, 1929.
329 "it leads nowhere": Quoted in Norman, *The Magic Maker*, 248.
329 "to the Mother!": HL: bMS Am 1892.7 (198).
330 "an honourable adventure": Robert Graves, "Introduction," *The Enormous Room* (New York, NY: Liveright, 1970), vii.
330 "hawk among pigeons": Harry Crosby quoted in Geoffrey Wolff, *Black Sun: The Brief Transit and Violent Eclipse of Harry Crosby* (New York, NY: Random House, 1976), 268.
331 …Harry's mother: Ibid., 287.
331 …to bed for a week: Hart Crane, *The Letters of Hart Crane*, 348.
332 "now who go(BANG(BANG": *CP*, 319.
333 …get Crane back to bed: Quoted in Unterecker, *Voyager: A Life of Hart Crane*, 635.
333 …serious discussions of literature: Wilson, *The Thirties*, Leon Edel, ed. (New York: Farar, Straus & Giroux, 1975), 37.
333 "And so it proved": *SL*, 89.
334 "presdidigatorily negated": EEC / RHC (January 17, 1931) HL: bMS Am 1823.1 (156).
334 "kitchen,& a hall": Ibid.
334 "a coffee grinder": Ibid.
335 "loSSo!M": *CP*, 348.
336 "tide's acute weaving murmur": Ibid., 370.
336 "despair impersonates a street": Ibid., 376.
336 "a bird flies into a mirror": Ibid., 339.
337 "my heart always moves": Ibid., 380.

NOTES TO CHAPTER 19: WORLDS OF WAS (AND IS)

339 "recognition here": EEC / RHC (April 9, 1931) HL: bMS Am 1823.1(156).
339 …to his mother in 1923: EEC / RHC (October 24, 1923) HL: bMS Am 1823.1 (156).
339 "when he had seen you": *Pound/Williams: The Selected Letters of Ezra Pound and William Carlos Williams*, Hugh Witemeyer, ed. (New York, NY: New Directions, 1997), 87.
340 "think, mean, desire, etc": Ibid., 88–89.
340 …did not ask isn't clear: EEC / RHC (April 9, 1931) HL: bMS Am 1823.1 (196).
340 …jazz pianist, Henry Crowder: P/C, 396.
341 …by either of them: Ibid., 395.
341 …novelist Elsa Triolet: *SL*, 226.
341 "his surrealist skin": Polizzotti, *Revolution of the Mind*, 358.
342 "Spring is nowhere else": *E*, 11.

342 "harder than Greek": EEC / RHC (April 9, 1931) HL: bMS Am 1823.1 (156).

342 "to okay his visa": Hugh Ford, ed., *The Left Bank Revisited: Selections from the Paris Tribune 1917-1934* (University Park, PA: Pennsylvania State University Press, 1972), 127.

342 "borderofborders": *E*, 7.

343 "A rickety train,centuries BC": *E*, 8.

343 "forward,into paradox": *E*, 15.

344 "experiment in force and fear": *E*, 48–49.

345 "the Lindbergh baby": *E*, 95.

345 "ghostly attentions": *E*, 95.

345 "just before he killed himself": Edmund Wilson, *The Thirties*, 155.

346 "at the drop of a hat": HL: bMS Am 1892.7 (198).

347 "affectation of equality": *E*, 247.

347 "smaller than he foresaw?": Hugh Ford, *The Left Bank Revisited*, 128.

348 "nervous condition": Ibid., 129.

348 "an intelligent experimenter": KGS, "An Experimentalist's Exhibition," *New York Times*, December 6, 1931.

348 …others did not: EEC / RHC (April 9, 1932) HL: bMS Am 1823.1 (156).

349 "an adolescent songster": Horace Gregory, "An Adolescent Songster," *New York Herald Tribune*, December 13, 1931.

349 "much that one admires": Allen Tate, *Poetry*, September 19, 1932.

349 …two American poets: *This Quarter*, July–September 1931.

349 …needed a boost: Ibid., 5.

349 "to a division": Ibid., 7.

349 …two years before: Frederick Lewis Allen, *The Big Change: America Transforms Itself, 1900-1950* (New York, NY: Harper & Bros., 1952), 147.

350 "expects a revolution": EEC / RHC (October 27, 1931) HL: bMS Am 1892 (295).

350 …the woman's husband: HL: bMS Am 1892.7 (198).

350 "his virile development": Brown quoted in Kennedy, *Dreams in the Mirror*, 325.

350 …a "bloody horror": Lincoln Kirstein, "The Kirstein Exchange," *Spring*, December 1981.

350 "comfortable with him afterwards": Cowley quoted in Kennedy, *Dreams in the Mirror*, 325.

350 "across the room": Edmund Wilson, *The Thirties*, 189–90.

350 …he asked himself: HL: bMS Am 1892.7 (198).

351 "Unbeautiful": Ibid.

351 "she said brutally": Quoted in Kennedy, *Dreams in the Mirror*, 325.

351 …above beating her: Ibid., 325.

351 …hide her black eyes: Ibid., 506.

351 "so it shriveled": Charles Olsen and Robert Creeley, *The Complete Correspondence*, v. IV (Santa Barbara, CA: Black Sparrow Press, 1982), 48.

352 "back to you": EEC / RHC (August 24, 1932) HL: bMS Am 1823.1 (156).

352 …Mexican divorce: EEC / Sibley Watson (April 11, 1932) NYPL.

352 "anarchist propaganda": Polizzotti, *Revolution of the Mind*, 373.
353 "God is whole": HL: bMS Am 1892.7 (198).
353 "which was the last": EEC / Sibley Watson (March 28, 1932) NYPL.
354 "a more enormous room": *Six*, 65.
355 …saw or heard: *E*, 282.
356 "scribbled hieroglyphics": *E*, 122–23; HL: the diary is deposited in bMS Am 1823.4 (100).
356–357 "numberlessness ; un / -smiling": *E*, 241.
357 "c'est composer": quoted in Friedman, *E. E. Cummings*, 123.
359 "than by a sword)touched": *E*, 90.
359 "guardedly , our heart": *E*, 90.
360 "defeated by all the stars": *E*, 265.
360 "my / self ; bows)": *E*, 496.
361 "Creates , / Imagines) / OPENS": *E*, 431–32.

NOTES TO CHAPTER 20: CAREFULLY INTO GROWING AND INTO BEING AND INTO LOVING

364 "whatever the outfit": Edward Steichen, *A Life in Photography* (New York, NY: Doubleday, 1968), 86.
364 …five feet, eight inches: HL: bMS Am 1892.7 (225).
364 "didn't lean on [him]": Ibid.
364 "and into loving": EEC / Marion Morehouse (July 1932) HL: bMS Am 1892.1 (99).
365 "what to do": M. Morehouse / EEC (July 31, 1932) HL: bMS Am 1892.3 (11).
365 "you came down to earth": HL: bMS Am 1892.7 (221).
365–366 …if it had been spontaneous: Wilson, *The Thirties*, 317.
366 "the most beautiful girl in N.Y": EEC / RHC (March 4, 1933) HL: bMS Am 1823.1 (156).
366 "someone there to blot": Ibid.
366 …a diet of coffee: Quoted in Norman, *The Magic Maker*, 264.
367 "The Worst Book of the Month": George G. Nathan, *The American Spectator*, April 1933.
367 "to let his readers read him": Lewis Gannett, *New York Herald Tribune*, April 9, 1933.
367 "what the book is all about": Quoted in Norman, *The Magic Maker*, 274.
367 "this particular 'book'": William Troy, "Cummings' Non-Land of Un," *The Nation*, December 12, 1933.
367 "a prophylactic station": Nathan Asch, "Descent into Russia," *The New Republic*, April 26, 1933.
367 …a sidewalk with him: HL: bMS Am 1892.7 (111).
368 "swift language forms": Paul Rosenfeld, "The Enormous Cummings," in ***ΕΣΤΙ**: E. E. Cummings & the Critics*, SV. Baum, ed. (East Lansing, MI: Michigan State University Press, 1962), 73.

368 "on its back for a time": Marianne Moore, "A Penguin in Moscow," *Complete Prose* (New York: Viking Penguin, 1986), 301.
368 …superior to the best of both artists: Ezra Pound, *Ezra Pound Speaking: Radio Speeches of World War II*, Leonard W. Doob, ed. (Westport, CT: Contributions in American Studies, Greenwood Press, 1978), 142.
368 "Dostoievskian sloberyness": Quoted in Norman, *The Magic Maker*, 279.
368 "a book of poems": Kennedy, *Dreams in the Mirror*, 341.
369 "bolcheviko" poem: *P/C*, 22.
369 "passer fer the Brit. mind": Ibid., 23–24.
369 "'a man for a' That'": Ezra Pound, "Personalia": *New English Weekly*, February 23, 1933.
369 "itza great woik": *P/C*, 25.
369 "in America at present": Ibid., 27.
369 "Braque & Derain": EEC / RHC (May 3, 1933) HL: bMS Am 1823.1 (156).
370 "glimpsed at sunset!": Ibid.
370 "'the most poised in Paris'": EEC / RHC (May 26, 1933) HL: bMS Am 1823.1 (156).
370 "any proverbial tête": Ibid.
371 "himself, or itself": Lincoln Kirstein, *Spring*, December 1981.
371 "and was astonished": Ibid, 6.
372 "if the other wanted": Elaine Orr MacDermot / EEC (May 12, 1933) HL: bMS Am 1892.
372 "desire of either party": Frank MacDermot / EEC (May 30, 1933) HL: bMS Am 1892.
372 "changes her attitude": EEC / Stewart Mitchell (draft on back of envelope of letter from Mitchell dated February 18, 1933) HL: bMS Am 1892.
372 …rise in the ranks: Henry Boylan, ed., *A Dictionary of Irish Biography* (Dublin: Gill & Macmillan, 1998).
373 "dig up a wicked past": EEC / RHC (July 2, 1933) HL: bMS Am 1823.1 (156).
373 "glad to see us": Ibid.
373 "'niece'—and polite": EEC / Morrie Werner quoted in Kennedy, *Dreams in the Mirror*, 347.
373 "on top of the World!" EEC / RHC (July 11, 1933) HL: bMS Am 1823.1 (156).
373 "noon till afternoon(3PM)": EEC / RHC (September 1, 1933) HL: bMS Am 1823.1 (156).
374 "to become a ballet": *SL*, 127.
375 "toilet in hall": EEC / RHC (November 24, 1933) HL: bMS Am 1823.1 (156).
375 …money as intended: EEC / Hildegarde Watson (December 11, 1933) NYPL.
376 "loosely called return mail": EEC / Lincoln Kirstein (n.d.) BE.
376 …but all declined: Kennedy, *Dreams in the Mirror*, 370.
377 "leapwhirling progress": E. E. Cummings, *Tom* (New York, NY: Arrow Editions, 1935), 17.
378 "your hereby birth": *MR*, 298.
379 "their so-called minds busy": EEC / RHC (July 8, 1934) HL: bMS Am 1823.1 (156).

379 "crazy over my wife": EEC / RHC (July 17, 1934) HL: bMS Am 1823.1 (156).
379 "my wife, Marion (Morehouse) Cummings": HL: bMS Am 1892.7 (238).

NOTES TO CHAPTER 21: NOURISH MY FAILURE WITH THY FREEDOM

381 "the possibility of *steps*": Lincoln Kirstein, "The Kirstein Exchange," *Spring*, December 1981.
381 …remembered Kirstein: Ibid, 7.
382 "ten weeks in future" EEC / RHC (August 28, 1934) HL: bMS Am 1823.1 (156).
382 "highly more convenient": Ibid.
382 …a seasoned screenwriter: Ibid.
383 "pasted in their mouths": Elia Kazan, *On Native Grounds: An Interpretation of Modern American Prose Literature* (New York, NY: Doubleday, 1956), 153.
386 "we live for dies": *CP*, 386.
386–387 "try are ing)": *CP*, 387.
387 "B being no such thing": *CP*, 390.
387 "a / b / aseball": *CP*, p. 392.
388 "stop forget relax / wait": *CP*, 393.
388 "not an equivocal emphasis": Marianne Moore, "Humility, Concentration, and Gusto," *Complete Prose*, 421.
388 ",grasshopper;": *CP*, 396.
389 "de woids uf lil Oinis": *CP*, 409.
389 "to the "herd": *P/C*, 63.
389 "but really clean": *CP*, 407.
390 "monthly crap": *P/C*, 63.
390 "and so you": *P/C*, 60.
390 "shake the mountains when they dance": *CP*, 427.
391 "fall into his mind": *CP*, 428.
391 "the sound of rain": *CP*, 424.
391 "that death should end)": *CP*, 446.
392 "selves himself recognize)": *CP*, 449.
392 "Moon to The)moon": *CP*, 452.
392 "(alone holy)alone": *CP*, 455.
393 …number of words per line: Robert McIlvane, "Cummings' 'BrIght,'" *The Explicator*, September 1971.
393 "Christmas till now": Edward Cummings, "Christmas Sermon" (1905) BPL.
394 "beckoning fabulous crumb": *CP*, 456.
394 …earlier collections: "No Thanks," *The New Yorker*, May 11, 1935.
394 …the political verse: Kenneth Burke, "Two Kinds of Against," *The New Republic*, June 26, 1935.
394 "the cosmic poet": Lionel Abel, "Clown or Cosmic Poet," *The Nation*, June 26, 1935.
394 "hysterical individualism": Isidor Schneider, "E. (iou)," *The New Masses*, June 25, 1935.

394 ...*No Thanks*, as well: *P/C*, 57, 60.
394 "Cummin'sh has the others": Ezra Pound, *The Letters of Ezra Pound, 1907–1941*, D. D. Paige, ed. (New York, NY: Harcourt, Brace & World, 1950), 266.
395 ...in mid-April: *P/C*, 58.
397 "seemed to be Hollywood": SL, 142.
397 "in style to California": Ibid.
397 "Marion and myself": Ibid.
398 "YOU SENT ANYTHING?": EEC / RHC (June 11, 1935) HL: bMS Am 1823.1 (156).
398 ...Mexico City and environs: Ibid.
398 "doesn't actually need": *P/C*, 77.
398 "Douglas bi-,5 hours": *P/C*, 77.
398 "enjoyed migration": *P/C*, 77.
398 "I might have wept": EEC / Sibley Watson (February 17, 1939) NYPL.
399 "Knight and Hertz": EEC / RHC (July 9, 1935) HL: bMS Am 1823.1 (156).
399 "sometimes violent surf": Ibid.
399 "we're still thriving": EEC / RHC (July 10, 1935) HL: bMS Am 1823.1 (156).
399 "(let alone spiritual riches)": Ibid.
400 ")Ah,Soul": *CP*, 474.
400 "photographing her": EEC / RHC (July 10, 1935) HL: bMS Am 1823.1 (156).
401 "as acting here": EEC / RHC (August 13, 1935) HL: bMS Am 1823.1 (156).
401 "1 miraculous ocean!!!": *P/C*, 77.
401 "burnt matches": EEC / RHC (July 19, 1935) HL: bMS Am 1823.1 (156).
401 "unmitigated docility": Ibid.
401 "principally kikes": EEC / RHC (July 9, 1935) HL: bMS Am 1823.1 (156).
401 "cummings [sic] was 'naughty'": Lincoln Kirstein, *Spring*, December 1981.
402 "they don't amews": EEC / Sibley Watson (September 30, 1935) NYPL.
402 "Big Year for the Kikes is o'er": EEC / RHC (September 26, 1935) HL: bMS Am 1823.1 (156).
402 ...a previous divorce: Kennedy, *Dreams in the Mirror*, 367.
402 "erosions and cypressroots!": EEC / RHC (August 20, 1935) HL: bMS Am 1823.1 (156).
402 ...met through Marion: EEC / RHC (July 19, 1935) HL: bMS Am 1823.1 (156).
402 "Ever-Ever Land": *P/C*, 466.
402 "out of anywhere pronto": *P/C*, 80.

NOTES TO CHAPTER 22: NEVER THE SOFT ADVENTURE OF UNDOOM

405 "become gods again": HL: bMs Am 1823.7 (45); the quote is from Thomas Mann, *Joseph and His Brothers* (New York, NY: Knopf, 1934), 206.
405 "expresses itself through me": Ibid.
406 "and contrariwise": Ibid.; Mann, 206.
406 "I touch the tree": HL: bMS Am 1823.7 (45).

406 "practically of no use": Henry McBride, *The Sculpture of Gaston Lachaise*, Hilton Kramer ed. (New York, NY: The Eakins Press, 1967), 35.
406 "unique human being": EEC, "Untitled announcement," "Gaston Lachaise," NY: Weyhe Gallery, 12/27/55–1/28/56.
407 "customary savage wit": "Ballet on Ice," *Time*, November 4, 1935.
407 "he visualizes action": Horace Gregory, *Poetry*, July 1935.
407 …writing a score: *P/C*, 93.
407 "'workers of the world unite'": EEC / Hildegarde Watson (December 28, 1935) NYPL.
408 …music for the ballet: Vivian Perlis, ed., *Copland: 1900 through 1942* (New York, NY: St Martin's/Marek, 1984), 136.
408 …he told Cummings: David Diamond / EEC (January 30, 1936) HL: bMs Am 1892 (227).
408 …putting on the work: *P/C*, 92.
408 …for two rooms: *P/C*, 90.
409 "and some cents": EEC / RHC (October 17, 1935) HL: bMS Am 1823.1 (156).
409 "to hell with that": *CP*, 475.
410 "holding court": Author interview with Paul Bowles, July 7, 1985.
410 "the act of living": Paul Bowles, *Without Stopping* (New York, NY: Ecco Press, 1985), 189.
410 "was not communicative": Christopher Sawyer-Lauçanno, *An Invisible Spectator: A Biography of Paul Bowles* (New York, NY: Weidenfeld & Nicholson, 1989), 170.
410 …to Mexico together: Ibid., 171.
411 "reluctant approval": Pearce quoted in Norman, *The Magic Maker*, 287.
411 "decision to limit it": Ibid., 286.
411 "to be myself": Ibid., 286.
412 …some of the contents: Ibid., 284–85.
413 "give it an apostrophe": Ibid, 287.
414 …Marion's brief betrayal: Ben Rogers, *A.J. Ayer: A Life* (New York, NY: Grove Press, 1999), 338–40.
414 "& that she's well": EEC / RHC (June 21, 1937) HL: bMS Am 1823.1 (156).
415 …his last twelve dollars: EEC / RHC (August 3, 1937) HL: bMS Am 1823.1 (156).
415 "AMERICAN EXP PARIS": EEC / RHC (August 4, 1937) HL: bMS Am 1823.1 (156).
415 …to cable back, "thanks": EEC / RHC (August 6, 1937) HL: bMS Am 1823.1 (156).
415 …the forthcoming book: *P/C*, 113.
416 [when you wrote that]: *P/C*, 118.
416 "call it dying—": *CP*, 461.
417 "reborn,a human being": *CP*, 461–62.
418 "a more beautiful question": *CP*, 462.
418 "beautiful eternal night": *CP*, 464.
419 "sell his head)": *CP*, 473.

420 "how not to dance": *CP*, 484.
420 ...Cummings's recent work: Paul Rosenfeld, "The Brilliance of E.E. Cummings," *The Nation*, March 26, 1938.
420 "of our time": Dudley Fitts, "Cummings' Poetry," *Saturday Review of Literature*, March 19, 1938.
420 "they set out to do": S. I. Hayakawa, "Is Indeed Five," *Poetry*, August 1938.
420 "our greatest war poems": Ibid, 292.
420 "or political propaganda": Peter M. Jack, "Private Exercise of Poetry," *New York Times Book Review*, June 26, 1938.
420 "contemporaries in painting?": John Peale Bishop, "The Poems and Prose of E. E. Cummings," *Southern Review*, April 1938.
420 "report the age": Ibid, 177.
421 ...on the comrades: Rolfe Humphries, "Anarchist-Poet-Advertiser," *The New Masses*, April 12, 1938.
421 "punctuation marks": *Daily Worker*, March 10, 1938.
421 "what's under his hat": Carl Sandberg quoted in Norman, *The Magic Maker*, 392.
422 "that is their honorarium": Ibid., 293.
422 "did not get it": Ibid., 295.

NOTES TO CHAPTER 23: FREEDOM AS BREAKFASTFOOD

424 ...she dutifully complied: HL: bMs Am 1823.7 (45); Richard Kennedy, "The Elusive Marion Marion," *Spring*, October 1996.
424 ...threat to their union: Ibid.
424 "whathaven't I": EEC / Sibley Watson (February 14, 1939) NYPL.
424 "'some day' 'soon'": EEC / Sibley Watson (February 17, 1939) NYPL.
425 ...whenever possible: *P/C*, 139.
425 "Kings and Queens": Maryette Charlton, "Memories of Marion": *Spring*, October 1996.
426 "macarchibald maclapdog macleash": *P/C*, 159.
426 ...National Institute of Arts and Letters: *P/C*, 146.
426 "Writers should not be writing now": *P/C*, 159.
426–427 "the very impurest timidity" EEC / Sibley Watson (May 30, 1939) NYPL.
427 "slim ascetic saint of poetry": Max Eastman, "MEMORANDUM ON DINING WITH EZRA POUND AND E.E. CUMMINGS," *P/C*, 138.
427 "his depths can never be heights": HL: bMS Am 1892.7 (201).
428 "& those boys loathed Jews?": Ibid.
428 "when out pours new invective": Ibid.
428 "Nimble is noble,I feel!": Ibid.
428 "goldberger": *CP*, 523–24.
429 "looks mohammed in the eye": *CP*, 1017.
429 "the new KKK": HL: bMS Am 1892.7 (203).
429 "I've ever had to behold": HL: bMS Am 1892.7 (201).
430 "could be nearly dead": *P/C*, 133.

430–431 "then I climb": HL: bMS Am 1892.7 (217).
431 "his pompous machineries": Ibid.
431 "by the billions. Perhaps": EEC / EK (July 12, 1940) quoted in Kennedy, *Dreams in the Mirror*, 389.
432 "freedom of speech": *P/C*, 159–60.
432 "on 'election eve'": HL: bMS Am 1892.7 (121).
432 "most green and young": *CP*, 531.
433 "most encourage flame": *CP*, 511.
433 "newer deeper dimension": HL: bMS Am 1892.7 (117).
433 "what direction to take": HL: bMS Am 1892.7
434 "build a world of snow": *CP*, 520.
434 ...to the audience: Max Saunders, *Ford Madox Ford, vol. II*. (New York: Oxford University Press, 1999), 538.
435 "to a high degree": William Carlos Williams, *Selected Letters of William Carlos Williams* (New York, NY: Random House, 1952), 191.
436 "and was by was": *CP*, 515.
436 "the right state of every man": Ralph Waldo Emerson, "The American Scholar," *The Complete Works of Ralph Waldo Emerson*, Vol. I (Boston, MA: Houghton Miflin, 1903), 106.
436–437 "your breathing doll": *CP*, 518.
437–438 "IrlI / n / .g": *CP*, 486.
438 "infinite intermediate us": *CP*, 538.
439 "we are permitted to reach": R. P. Blackmur, "50 Poems": *Southern Review*, 1941.
439 ")or better / ?poems": Babette Deutsch, "e e cummingsesq," *The Nation*, May 17, 1941.
440 "as she is spoke": Louis Zukofsky, "We Moderns," Gotham Book Mart, 1940.

NOTES TO CHAPTER 24: ALLEGIANCE ONLY TO THE IMAGINATION

441 "gets back His Own": HL: bMS Am 1892.7 (201).
441 "allegiance is imagination": Ibid.
441 ...acute osteoarthritis: EEC / Sibley Watson (February 7, 1942) NYPL.
442 "mighty handy these days": EEC / RHC (February 22, 1942) HL: bMS Am 1823.1 (156).
442 ...physician and corset: EEC / Sibley Watson (February 7, 1942) NYPL.
442 "what it's pliz)": *CP*, 552.
442 "except a man": *CP*, 550.
442–443 "duhSIVILEYEzum": *CP*, 547.
443–444 "to tell // him": *CP*, 553.
444 "God's blood": HL: bMS Am 1892.7 (212).
445 "deathly-rigid formalities('verse')": HL: bMS Am 1892.7 (201).
445 ...one of his favorite books: John Cheever, *The Letters of John Cheever*, Benjamin Cheever, ed. (New York, NY: Simon & Schuster, 1988), 81.

445 …like in New England: Ibid., 82.
446 "E. E. Cummings": Jose Garcia Villa, "EEC," *Spring*, December 1984.
446 "cheekbones were prominent too": Ibid, 15.
446 …$.75, and $9.75: NYPL.
447 "an indelible impression": Marianne Moore, *The Complete Prose*, 563.
447 …was so impressive: Ibid., 400.
447 "sound on the ground": *CP*, 543.
448 "mastery is inimitable": Marianne Moore, *The Complete Prose*, 395.
448 "embodies a healing faith": Peter deVries, *Poetry*, June 1944.
448 "not excluding mr u": *CP*, 551.
449 "INWARD,thru GREYS": HL: bMS Am 1823.7 (55).
449 "verb vs. noun": Ibid.
450 "a very good God damn": *MR*, 314–15.
451 "any such thing as 'war'": EEC / Marion Morehouse (n.d.) HL: bMS Am 1892.1 (99).
451 "butterflies and flowers—are lonely": EEC / Marion Morehouse (August 17, 1944) HL: bMS Am 1892.1 (99).
451 "& to be loved)": HL: bMS Am 1892.7 (228).
451 "with unconscious him": HL: bMS Am 1892.7 (235).
451 "the no-sayer": Ibid.
451 "drink myself into a coma": Ibid.
452 "she ought to be delivered": HL: bMS Am 1892.7 (238).
452 …second floor of Patchin: EEC / Hildegarde Watson (n.d.—1944) NYPL.
452 "is a moron": HL: bMS Am 1892.7 (196).
452 "riproaringlyhealthy by comparison": EEC / Marion Morehouse (March 23, 1944) HL: bMS Am 1892.1 (99).
453 "Her deafness is a fixture": HL: bMS Am 1892.7 (231).
453 "like the hot water faucet": *MR*, 321.
453 "'the dog is dead'" HL: bMS Am 1892.7 (231).
454 "gravypissing poppa": *CP*, 635.
454 …at best, ambivalent: EEC / RHC (May 1, 1945) HL: bMS Am 1823.1 (156).
454 "'in the White House'": Ibid.
454–455 "painting is nonrepresentational": *MR*, 316–17.
455 "from tubes,to invent": HL: bMS Am 1823.7 (55).
455 "through nature": Ibid.
455–456 "in e.g. the Met": HL: bMS Am 1892.7 (219).
456 "'ça ou rien'": HL: bMS Am 1892.7 (235).
456 "paying her off": Ibid.
456 "so long as I loved her": Ibid.
457 "not merely sexuality but love": Ibid.
457 "Iron Maiden": HL: bMS Am 1892.7 (225).
458 "penis drip with love": HL: bMS Am 1892.7 (235).

NOTES TO CHAPTER 25: WE KNOW WHO WE ARE

459 "Now I'm free": HL: bMS Am 1892.7 (203).
459 ...what she was like: Dorothy Case / EEC (May 8, 1941) HL: bMS Am1892 (646).
459 ...inform Elaine of the inquiry: Nancy Thayer / Hermann B. Riccius (July 28, 1941) BE.
460 ...lack of communication: Kennedy, *Dreams in the Mirror*, 415.
460 ...estimated value came to $87,668.75: H. J. Kelley / Elaine Orr MacDermot (June 17, 1940) BE.
460 "to have a baby": EEC / Hildegarde Watson (August 9, 1945) NYPL.
462–463 "You": E. E. Cummings, *Santa Claus: A Morality Play* (New York, NY: Holt, 1946), 15–16.
463 "Ours": Ibid., 18.
464–465 "except himself": HL: bMS Am 1892.7 (222).
465 "economic bombery,become": *P/C*, 166.
465 "...cannot kill the dead": *MR*, 313.
465 ...Italy and its allies: Quoted in Noel Stock, *The Life of Ezra Pound* (New York, NY: Pantheon, 1970), 417.
466 "during time of war": Ibid.
466 ...Cummings told Cornell: Ibid. 418.
466 ...as soon as it was possible: *P/C*, 172.
467 ...in Washington, D.C.: Stock, *The Life of Ezra Pound*, 419.
467 ...half a smile on his lined face: Ibid., 422.
468 "sincere doer of good": EEC / Sibley Watson (January, 23, 1946) NYPL.
468 ...Gwyneth Harrington: *SL*, 137.
468 "Culture,none": EEC / RHC (December 26, 1945) HL: bMS Am 1823.1 (156).
468 "the country of death": Ibid.
468 "truly is:a human being": *SL*, 171.
469 "an equivalent job": *P/C*, 177.
469 "three protagonists and a plot": *MR*, 323.
469 "wisdom, love, and joy": Ibid., 326.
470 "almost echoing": Quoted in Kennedy, *Dreams in the Mirror*, 417.
470 ...succumb to his charm: Author interview with Robert Cabot, January 22, 2001.
470 "Did anyone ever tell you I was your father?": Quoted in Kennedy, *Dreams in the Mirror*, 419.
470 "We know who we are": Ibid.
471 "*I* was your father": Author interview with individual who prefers not to be identified by name.
471 "when I was married to Cummings": Quoted in Kennedy, *Dreams in the Mirror*, 415.
471 "looking up at me": Stewart Mitchell quoted in "Newport Meeting with Charles Norman and Merilyn Lafferty," *Spring*, November 1984.
472 "wholly & permanently someone else": HL: bMS Am 1892.7.
472 "who through them might see": EEC / Sibley Watson (January 22, 1947) NYPL.
473 "'spend a night or two';why not 3?": EEC / Nancy (Roosevelt) Andrews (September 1, 1949) HL: bMS Am 1892 (28).

473 "right or wrong?": HL: bMS Am 1892.7 (217).
473 "but not quite": Ibid.
474 "young—&gay!": Ibid.

NOTES TO CHAPTER 26: XAIPE AND CONTROVERSY

475 ...check for one thousand dollars: EEC / Stewart Mitchell (February 14, 1949) HL: bMS Am 1892.13 (266).
476 "& have 30$ on hand": EEC / Sibley Watson (January 30, 1950) NYPL.
476 ...undisturbed by a neighbor: EEC / Hildegarde Watson (February 2, 1950) NYPL.
476 "unlike The Enormous Room": Quoted in Kennedy, *Dreams in the Mirror*, 437.
477 "pretend to teach": EEC / Sibley Watson (January 30, 1950) NYPL.
477 ...they could not afford the trip: *P/C*, 244–45.
477 "E. E. Cummings the writer": Henry McBride, "Attractions in the Galleries," *New York Sun*, May 20, 1949.
477 "what could be better?": E. E. Cummings, "Words into Pictures," *Art News*, May 1949.
478 "shrink away in horror?": St-John Perse, *Letters*, Arthur J. Knodel, Trans. & ed. (Princeton, NJ: Princeton University Press—Bollingen Series LXXXVII:2, 1979), 324.
478 "ocean and the land": *CP*, 768.
478 "alone for hours": John Malcolm Brinnin, *Dylan Thomas in America* (Boston, MA: Little Brown, 1955), 27.
478–479 ...he regarded so highly: Ibid., 27.
479 "more vivid phenomenon": EEC / Hildegarde Watson (January 25, 1959) NYPL.
479 ...John Crowe Ransom: Martin Seymour-Smith, *Robert Graves: His Life and Work* (New York: Holt, Rinehart, Winston, 1982), 406.
479 ...groundbreaking achievements: W. H. Auden, *The Dyer's Hand and Other Essays* (New York, NY: Vintage, 1968), 366.
479 ...changed his opinion later that year: Charles Olson, "Projective Verse," *Selected Writings*, Robert Creeley, ed. (New York, NY: New Directions, 1966), 22.
479–480 "a Lie, he is": Olsen & Creeley, *The Complete Correspondence*, 41.
480 "were all to me delights": Robert Creeley "Thinking of Cummings," *Spring*, New Series, 1994.
480 "had to be capitalized": Ibid., 8.
480 "participant in that battle": Ibid, 8.
480 "statement of like order": Ibid, 14.
481 "both prigged and canted": *CP*, 644.
481 "the kike isn't(hélas) a Jew": EEC / Allen Tate (July 20, 1945) HL: bMS Am 1892.1 (142).
481 "will be mistaken for unkindness": Quoted in Kennedy, *Dreams in the Mirror*, 423.
481 "behaving like a slave or three": Ibid.
482 "is to blame for the 'kike'": EEC / Hildegarde Watson (December 20, 1949) NYPL.

482 "can still make changes": Ibid.
482 …an otherwise positive review of *Xaipe:* David Daiches, "Some Recent Poetry," *Yale Review*, Winter 1951.
483 …the charge of anti-Semitism: Virginia Kent Cummins, "Letter to *The Lyric*," *The Lyric*, Spring 1951.
483 "which becomes suspect": ***ΕΣΤΙ***: *E.E. Cummings and the Critics*, S.V. Baum, ed. (East Lansing, MI: Michigan State University Press, 1962), 175.
483 "he is poetically base": Ibid., 178.
483 "I know where to take my stand": Ibid., 180.
483 "that duty of the artist": Ibid., 182.
485 "a brilliant choice": Ibid., 181.
485–486 "the sin of Death": *CP*, 604.
487 "sinful sin": *CP*, 607.
487 "only made of,bird": *CP*, 612.
488 "(and not until)": *CP*, 620.
488 "imaginably young a star": *CP*, 626.
488–489 "i am / dead": *CP*, 638.
489 "named imagination": *CP*, 639.
489–490 "in a few moments": *SL*, 216.
490 "happ / ene // D": *CP*, 655.
490–491 "doubt unimaginable You?": *CP*, 663.
491 "nothing / except loneliness": *CP*, 648.
491 "'I AM an animist'": EEC / Hildegarde Watson (January 30, 1960) NYPL.
491 "hole in its life": *CP*, 647.
491 …retrieving items of importance to him: *SL*, 212.
491 "last year's downturned application": Ibid.
492 "the pilgrims applied passports": Ibid.
492 "Rome isn't expensive": EEC / Hildegarde Watson (May 12, 1951) NYPL.
492 "socialized,communized or otherized": HL: bMS Am 1823.7 (64).
493 "thing to me in this world": EEC / Hildegarde Watson (May 16, 1950) NYPL.

NOTES TO CHAPTER 27: ORDEALS BY AUDIENCE

495 "a salary of 15,000": Quoted in Norman, *The Magic Maker*, 340.
496 "throughout the year": Ibid., 342.
496 "in terms of content": Ibid., 343.
496 "federal and state laws": Ibid., 344.
496 "so much time": Ibid., 344.
496 …delivering the talks: *P/C*, 317.
497 "the total sound of a poEM": *P/C*, 319.
497 "to not possumize": *P/C*, 317.
497 "poets whom I respect": EEC / Hildegarde Watson (n.d.—fall 1952) NYPL.
497 "that très gentil professor Finley": Ibid.
498 "the measure of the dream": Quoted in Kennedy, *Dreams in the Mirror*, 441.
498 "not teaching, but learning": *Six*, 3.

498 "outside Saunders Theatre": "Crowd Jams Saunders to Hear Last Norton Talk Till Spring Term," *Harvard Crimson*, November 26, 1952.

499 "not numerable 'social' phenomena": *P/C*, 330.

499 "no interest in Beauty!" EEC / Hildegarde Watson (n.d.—November 1952) NYPL.

500 "not precisely endurable": EEC / Hildegarde Watson (February 15, 1953) NYPL.

500 "which doesn't materialize": Ibid.

500 "so a human being is": *Six*, 63.

500 "most generous literary figure": *Six*, 69.

500 "and he alone, can feel": *Six*, 82.

501 "whose every agony is to grow": *Six*, 10–11.

501 "par excellence)intelligent": EEC / Hildegarde Watson (August 25, 1953) NYPL.

502 "lively wife Betty": Ibid.

502 "seems marvellously sweet": *SL*, 223.

502 "can scarcely wait to smell New Hampshire": Ibid.

502 "my 6 Ordeals by Audience": EEC / Hildegarde Watson (June 12, 1953) NYPL.

503 "busy being HE": HL: bMS Am 1892.7 (217).

504 "so real it is": William Carlos Williams, "lowercase cummmings," *Selected Essays*, 264.

504 "who teaches English Composition": *SL*, 222.

505 "not to say guilty Americans—daily": EEC / Elizabeth (Cummings) Qualey (March 27, 1953) HL: bMS Am 1892.13 (321).

506 "glimpse of the great man was extraordinary": Author interview with Joanne Koch Potee, August 1, 2002.

506 "speakers of every kind": Robert Creeley, "Thinking of Cummings," *Spring*, New Series, No. 3, 1994.

507 "and the subway rumbling under": William Carlos Williams / EEC (October 22, 1949) HL: bMS Am 1892.11(343).

507 "with the reading": EEC / Betty Kray (April 11, 1955) HL: bMS Am 1823 (707).

507 "a secretbackentrance": EEC / Hildegarde Watson (December 8, 1954) NYPL.

507 "'I just wanted to give you these'": EEC / Hildegarde Watson (April 8, 1954) NYPL.

507–508 "Cummings would have been": Arthur Miller, *Timebends* (New York, NY: Grove, 1987), 306.

509 ...which Stevens apparently shrugged off: Peter Brazau, *Parts of a World: Wallace Stevens Remembered* (New York, NY: Random House, 1983), 191.

509 "during the war": Ibid., 154.

509 "didn't want Cummings to have it": Ibid., 178.

509 "to write a detailed review upon": William Carlos Williams, *Selected Letters*, 327.

509 "inside of the cheek is there": William Carlos Williams, "Cummings as Painter," *Art Digest*, December 1, 1954.

510 ...were pure invention: Norman, *The Magic Maker*, 250.

510 "or a star- / fish": Marianne Moore, *The Complete Poems* (New York: Macmillan/Viking, 1967), 125.

510 "respect of a few human beings": *MR*, 333–34.
510 …Goya's paintings in the Museo del Prado: EEC / Hildegarde Watson (April 7, 1956) NYPL.
510 "&always miraculous": *P/C*, 322.
510 "vocal deterioration": EEC / Hildegarde Watson (August 9, 1955) NYPL.
511 "drooling(weeping)sore spots": Ibid.
512 "'I'll never answer the telephone again'": Charles-Henri Ford, *Water from a Bucket: A Diary 1948-57* (New York, NY: Turtlepoint Press, 2001), 179.
512 "Are you still alive, Djuna?": Phillip Herring, *Djuna:The Life & Work of Djuna Barnes* (New York, NY: Viking, 1995), 309.
512 "90million years old": EEC / Hildegarde Watson (November 23, 1955) NYPL.
512 "in his muffler and coat": Susan Cheever, *Home Before Dark* (Boston, MA: Houghton-Miflin 1984), 60.
513 "to my own feeling": EEC / David McCord (February 19, 1957) HL: bMS Am 1823.1 (87).
513 "the slightest publicity": EEC / Elizabeth (Cummings) Qualey (July 9, 1957) HL: bMS Am 1892.13 (321).
513 "I stopped fighting at once": Ibid.
514 …situation that occasioned it: Mr. Harper, "Bard in Boston," *Harpers*, September 1957.
514 "gasps among the audience": Robert Taylor, *Boston Herald*, June 24, 1957.
514 "(because it begins to smell)": *CP*, 711.

NOTES TO CHAPTER 28: WHEN SUCH MARVELS VANISH

517 …return to Italy: Stock, *The Life of Ezra Pound*, 447.
518 "'tries to tell'": *SL*, 261.
518 "one / l // iness": *CP*, 673.
519–520 "imaginable mysteries": *CP*, 674.
520 "find in the sea": *CP*, 682.
520 "forgetting me,remember me": *CP*, 688.
520 "asl(rose)eep": *CP*, 691.
521 "here)s / Now": *CP*, 713.
521 "lygawntueco /llege": *CP*, 700.
522 "er hur / ries": *CP*, 724.
522 "almost vanished me": *CP*, 720.
522–523 "the amazing miracle of all": *CP*, 741.
523 "youth yanks them / down": *CP*, 729.
523 "death and resurrection": *CP*, 749.
523 "this:to feel)": *CP*, 762.
524 "for an angry fix": Allen Ginsberg, *Howl and other Poems* (San Francisco, CA: City Lights, 1956), 9.
524 …things in simple ways: See also Michael Franco, *How to Live as a Single Natural Being: The Dogmatic Nature of Experience* (Boston, MA: Zoland Books, 1998).

525 ...rave in the *New York Times Book Review*: Robert Graves, "Corn Can Sparkle Like a Star," *New York Times Book Review*, October 26, 1958.
525 "New England Transcendental tradition": Winfield Townley Scott, *Saturday Review*, January 3, 1959.
525 "up to the standard of his finest work": John Berryman, *American Scholar*, No. 29, 1959.
525 "permanently unknowable": Edward Hood, *Shenandoah*, No. 13, 1959.
525 "our rebel poet, still rebels": Harold Schonberg, "Our Rebel Poet Still Rebels," *New York Times Magazine*, October 11, 1959.
525 "Cummings' own creation": *Evergreen Review*, Winter 1959.
525 "reject that effort as a poem": Quoted in Paul Mariani, *William Carlos Williams: A New World Naked* (New York, NY: Norton, 1981), 716.
526 "it'll be gone": HL: bMS Am 1892.7 (231).
526 "I-don't-want-to enough": HL: bMS Am 1892.7 (226).
526 "clinging to(e.g.)Marion for protection": Ibid.
527 "am really wounded!": HL: bMS Am 1892.7 (232).
527 "deprived her of her raiment": Ibid.
527 "sank on my shoulder": Ibid.
529 "'writers over 50' whom she likes": EEC / Hildegarde Watson (June 12, 1958) NYPL.
529 "writing a book about [him]": *P/C*, 405.
530 "latest Lost Generation": EEC / Hildegarde Watson (June 25, 1958) NYPL.
530 "individual may grow": *MR*, 3.
530 "dared republish EIMI": EEC / Hildegarde Watson (December 25, 1957) NYPL.
530 "but etcetera ad infin": Ibid.
531 "past Doubtless Thomas": EEC / Hildegarde Watson (July 19, 1960) NYPL.
531 "imitative of them": HL: bMS Am 1823.7 (321).
532 "taught me...not to travel": EEC / Elizabeth (Cummings) Qualey (April 15, 1960) HL: bMS Am 1892.13 (321).
532 ...Probanthine for his intestinal problems: EEC / Hildegarde Watson (August 2, 1957) NYPL.
533 "very little to go on": Quoted in Kennedy, *Dreams in the Mirror*, 474.
533 "at the family table": Ibid., 474.

NOTES TO CHAPTER 29: STEERING FOR DREAM

535 "scarcely notice the difference": EEC / Hildegarde Watson (May 12, 1957) NYPL.
535 "'modern conveniences'": EEC / Hildegarde Watson (December 5, 1961) NYPL.
535 "playing ball with him": EEC / RF (n.d.—draft 1961) HL: bMS Am 1892.7 (203).
535–536 ...Cummings was to be evicted: "Poet E. E. Cummings Faces Eviction," *Village Voice*, December 21, 1961.
536 "without Mayor Wagner": *SL*, 270.
536 ...at City Hall: *SL*, 274.
536 "punks and preknowbellists": *SL*, 275.

536 "photographs by Marion(they're superb!)": *SL*, 274.
536 "he is seeing": *CP*, 904.
536–537 "to stand firm": *CP*, 903.
537 "gra // v / es / t // one": *CP*, 833.
537 "steering for dream": *CP*, 781.
538 "thing or dreamed become un-": *CP*, 822.
538 "—arise,my soul;and sing": *CP*, 834.
538 "youth and maidens:let us pray": *CP*, 794.
539 ...interact with the audience: Author interview with Edward Foster, July 1, 2000.
539 "turned and were gone": Norman, *The Magic Maker*, 12.
539–540 "s / tilLnes / s": *CP*, 814.

NOTES TO EPILOGUE

541 ...Marion's friend Mina Curtiss: Kennedy, *Dreams in the Mirror*, 484.
541 ...Hildegarde was in Athens: Sibley Watson / Hildegarde Watson (telegram) (September 3, 1962) NYPL.
542 "on many Cummings projects": Maryette Charlton, "Memories of Marion," *Spring*, October 1996.
542 "costumes to the living flesh": William Carlos Williams, "lower case cummings," *Selected Essays*, 265.
543 "imaginable mystery) / descend": *CP*, 839.

Credits

Photo credits:

The following photographs by permission of the Houghton Library, Harvard University:

Photos 1,3,5,8,19, 21, 23, 27, 29, 30, 31: bMS Am 1892.11 (92)
Photo 2: bMS Am 1823.7 (5)
Photos 4, 6: bMS Am 1823.8 (46)
Photo 9: bMS Am 1823.7 (16)
Photo 10: bMS Am 1823.4 (4)
Photo 11: bMS Am 1823.7 (18a)
Photo 14: bMS Am 1892 (681)
Photos 16, 17, 22: bMS Am 1892.9 (1)
Photo 18: bMS Am 1892.8 (17)
Photo 20: bMS Am 1823.1 (20)
Photo 24: bMS Am 1823 (642)
Photo 25: bMS Am 1892.11
Photo 26: bMS Am 1892.1
Photo 32: bMS Am 1892.17 (79–109)

Photo 28: Manuel Komroff Papers, Rare Book and Manuscript Library, Columbia University.

Index

INDEX OF POEMS BY FIRST LINE

About the Author

Christopher Sawyer-Lauçanno's books include *The Continual Pilgrimage: American Writers in Paris, 1944–1960* and *An Invisible Spectator: A Biography of Paul Bowles*, which was a *New York Times* Notable Book of the Year. He is also a poet and translator, and the long-time Writer-in-Residence at MIT. For *E. E. Cummings: A Biography*, he had unprecedented access to all of Cummings's papers, many of which had been previously sealed. He lives in Turner Falls, Massachusetts.